Little Lulu®

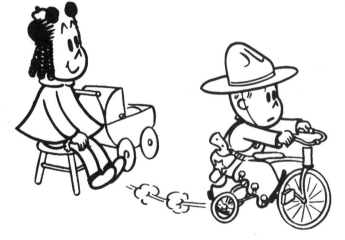

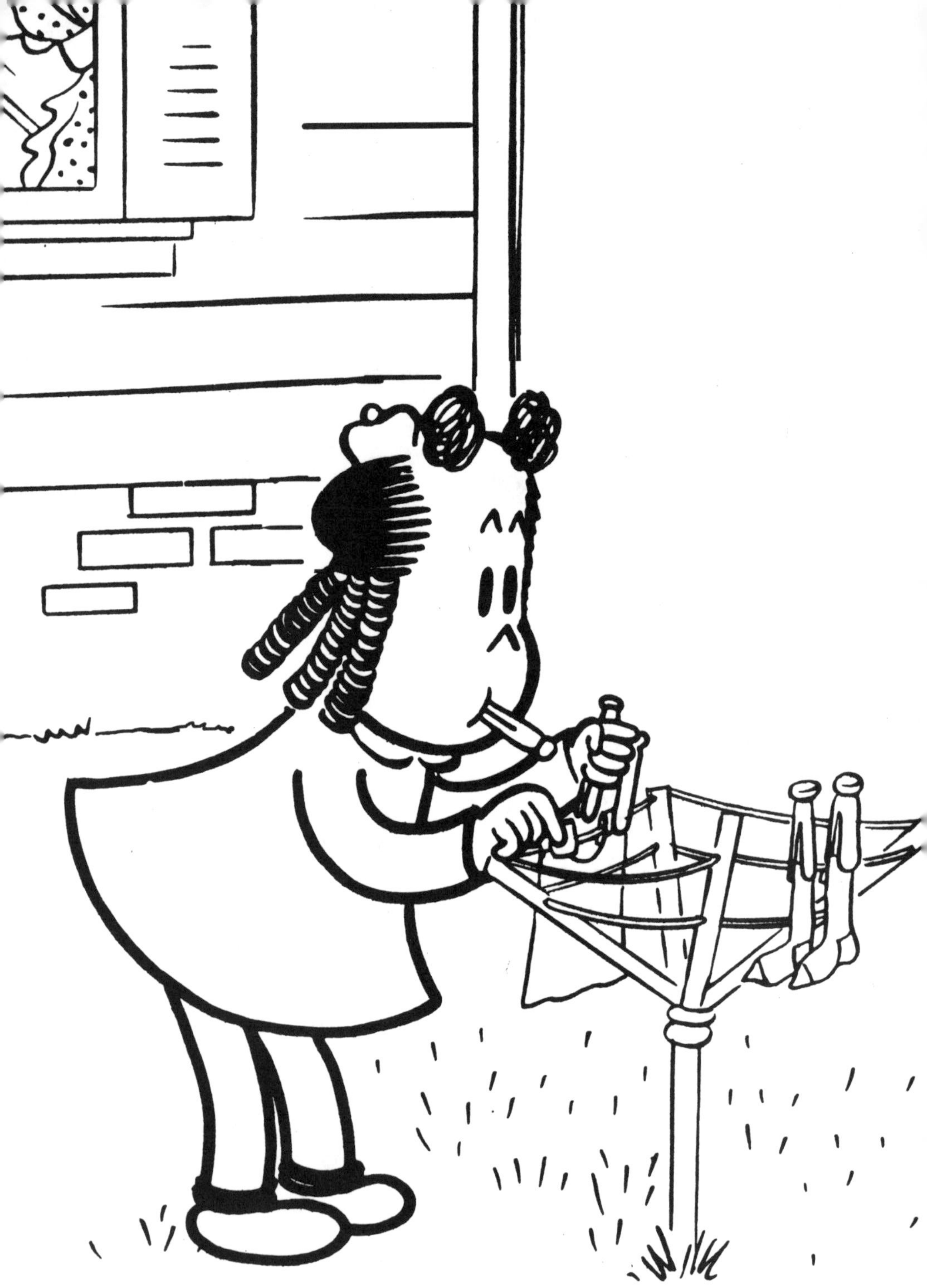

Little Lulu®

Lucky Lulu

Story and Art

John Stanley

and

Irving Tripp

Based on the character

created by

Marge Buell

DARK HORSE BOOKS™

Publisher
Mike Richardson

Editor
Dave Marshall

Collection Designer
Debra Bailey

Art Director
Lia Ribacchi

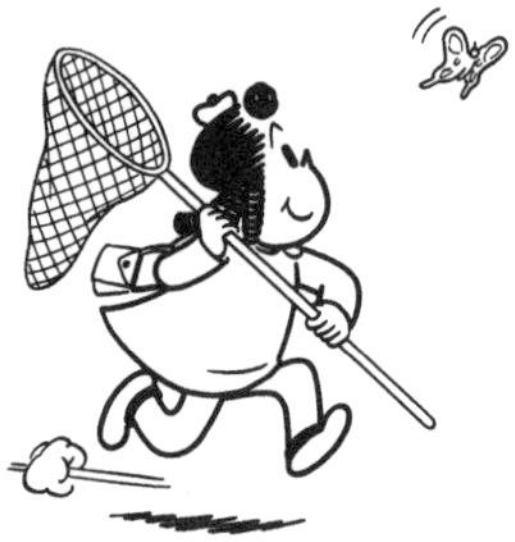

Published by
Dark Horse Books
A division of Dark Horse Comics, Inc.
10956 SE Main Street
Milwaukie, OR 97222

darkhorse.com

Little Lulu ® Vol. 9: Lucky Lulu

The one-page comics on pages 245 to 247
originally appeared in *Dell Comics* issues 110 and 115.

First edition: April 2006
ISBN-10: 1-59307-471-9
ISBN-13: 978-1-59307-471-5

1 3 5 7 9 10 8 6 4 2
Printed in U.S.A.

A note about Lulu

Little Lulu came into the world through the pen of cartoonist Marjorie "Marge" Henderson Buell in 1935. Originally commissioned as a series of single-panel cartoons by *The Saturday Evening Post*, Lulu took the world by storm with her charm, smarts, and sass. Within ten years, she not only was the star of her own cartoon series, but a celebrity spokesgirl for a variety of high-profile commercial products.

Little Lulu truly hit her stride as America's sweetheart in the comic books published by Dell Comics starting in 1945. While Buell was solely responsible for Lulu's original single-panel shenanigans, the comic-book stories were put into the able hands of comics legend John Stanley. Stanley wrote and laid out the comics while artist Irving Tripp provided the finished drawings. After a number of trial appearances in Dell Comics, Lulu's appeal was undeniable, and she was granted her very own comic-book series, called *Marge's Little Lulu*, which was published regularly through 1984.

This volume contains every comic from issues thirty-three through thirty-seven of *Marge's Little Lulu*.

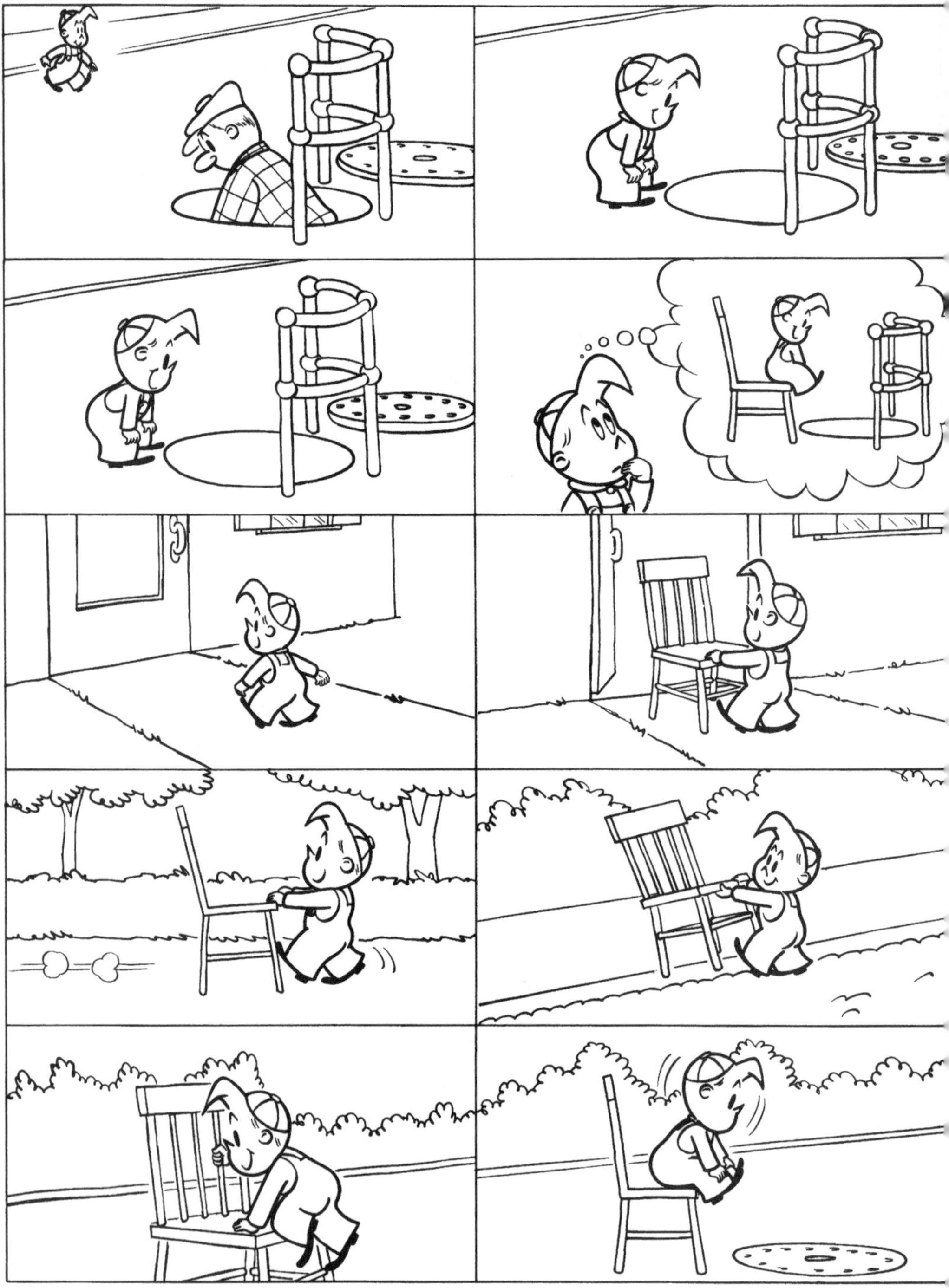

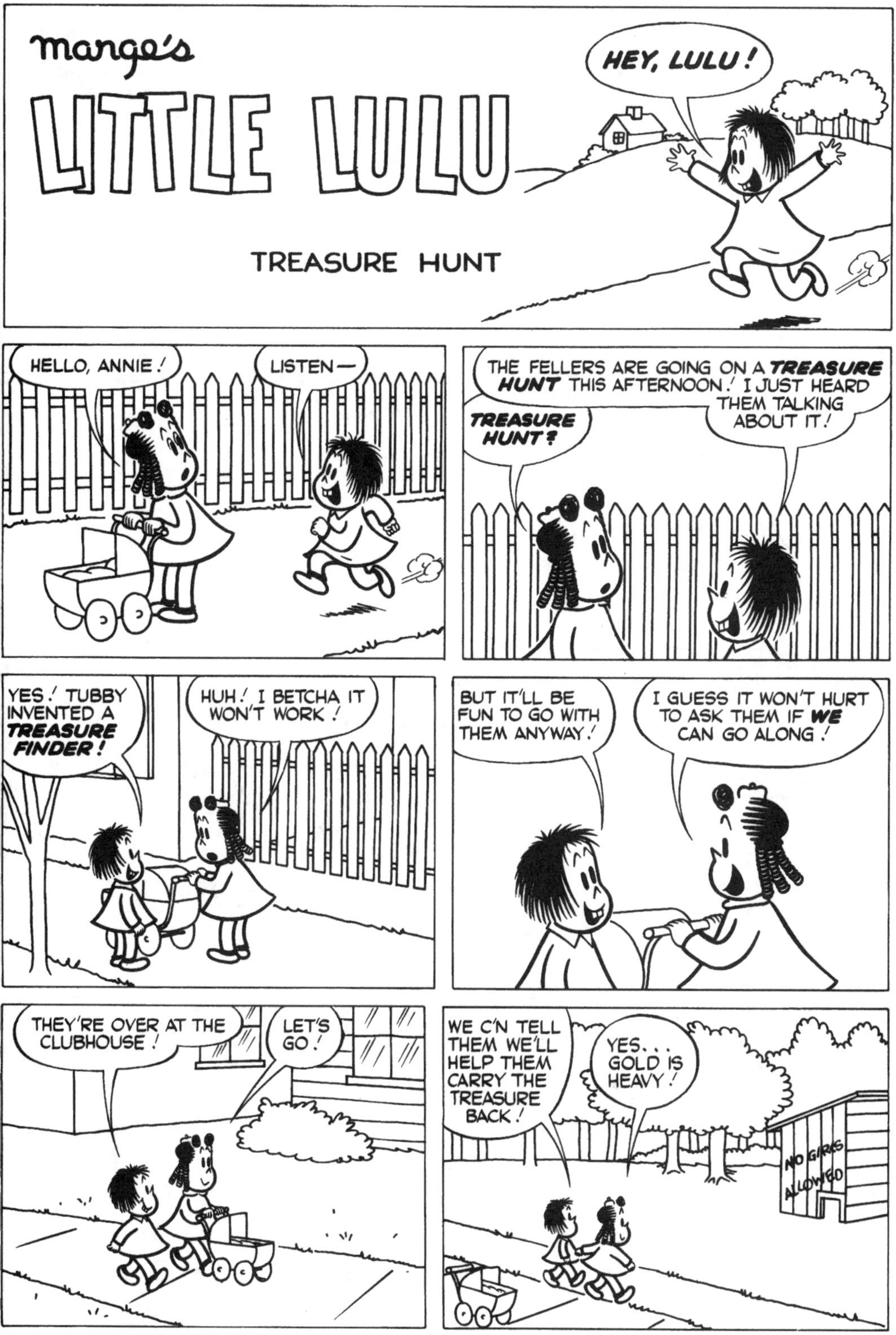
marge's
LITTLE LULU
HEY, LULU!
TREASURE HUNT
HELLO, ANNIE!
LISTEN—
THE FELLERS ARE GOING ON A TREASURE HUNT THIS AFTERNOON! I JUST HEARD THEM TALKING ABOUT IT!
TREASURE HUNT?
YES! TUBBY INVENTED A TREASURE FINDER!
HUH! I BETCHA IT WON'T WORK!
BUT IT'LL BE FUN TO GO WITH THEM ANYWAY!
I GUESS IT WON'T HURT TO ASK THEM IF WE CAN GO ALONG!
THEY'RE OVER AT THE CLUBHOUSE!
LET'S GO!
WE C'N TELL THEM WE'LL HELP THEM CARRY THE TREASURE BACK!
YES... GOLD IS HEAVY!
NO GIRLS ALLOWED

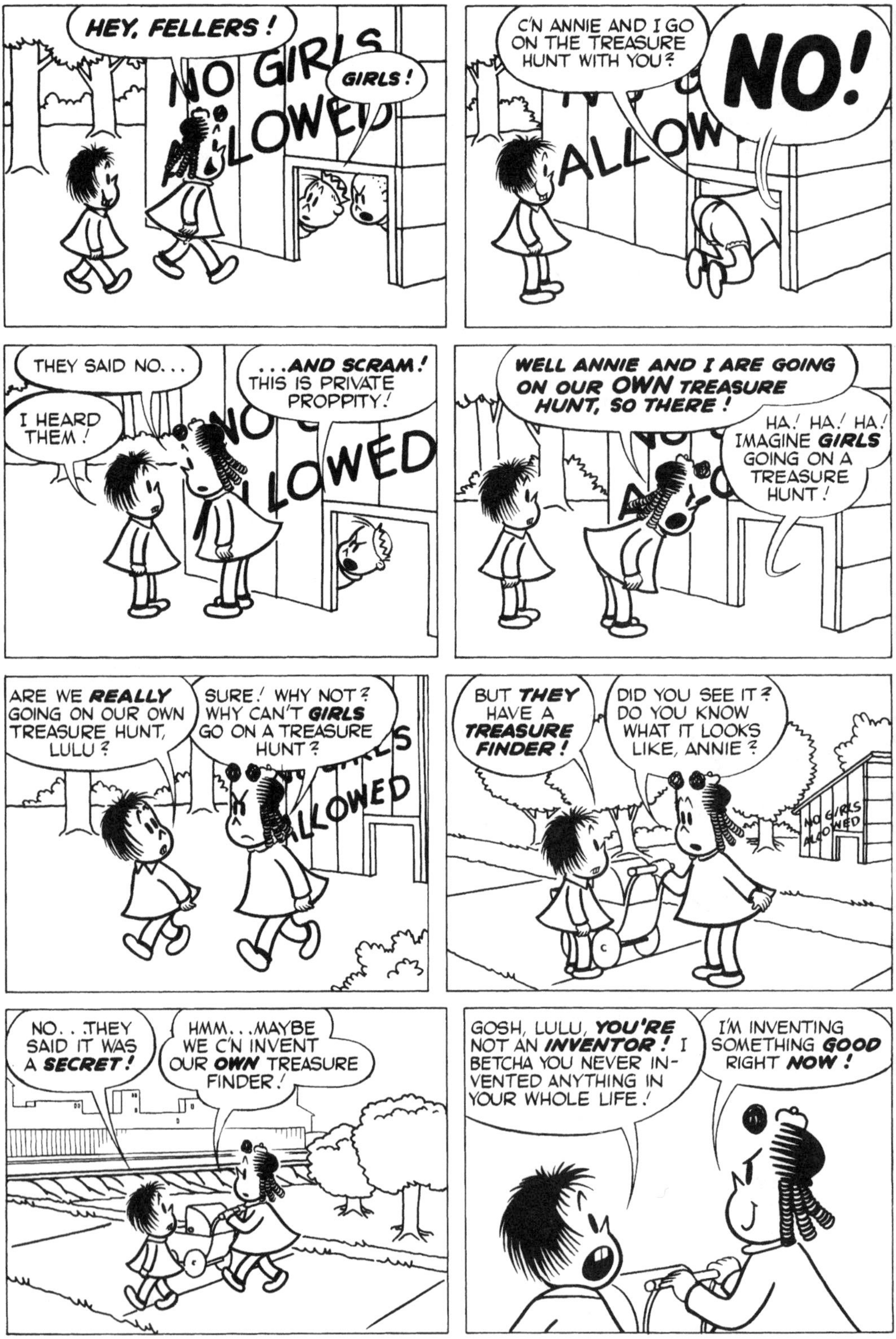
HEY, FELLERS!
NO GIRLS ALLOWED
GIRLS!
C'N ANNIE AND I GO ON THE TREASURE HUNT WITH YOU?
NO!
THEY SAID NO...
I HEARD THEM!
...AND SCRAM! THIS IS PRIVATE PROPPITY!
WELL ANNIE AND I ARE GOING ON OUR OWN TREASURE HUNT, SO THERE!
HA! HA! HA! IMAGINE GIRLS GOING ON A TREASURE HUNT!
ARE WE REALLY GOING ON OUR OWN TREASURE HUNT, LULU?
SURE! WHY NOT? WHY CAN'T GIRLS GO ON A TREASURE HUNT?
BUT THEY HAVE A TREASURE FINDER!
DID YOU SEE IT? DO YOU KNOW WHAT IT LOOKS LIKE, ANNIE?
NO GIRLS ALLOWED
NO...THEY SAID IT WAS A SECRET!
HMM...MAYBE WE C'N INVENT OUR OWN TREASURE FINDER!
GOSH, LULU, YOU'RE NOT AN INVENTOR! I BETCHA YOU NEVER INVENTED ANYTHING IN YOUR WHOLE LIFE!
I'M INVENTING SOMETHING GOOD RIGHT NOW!

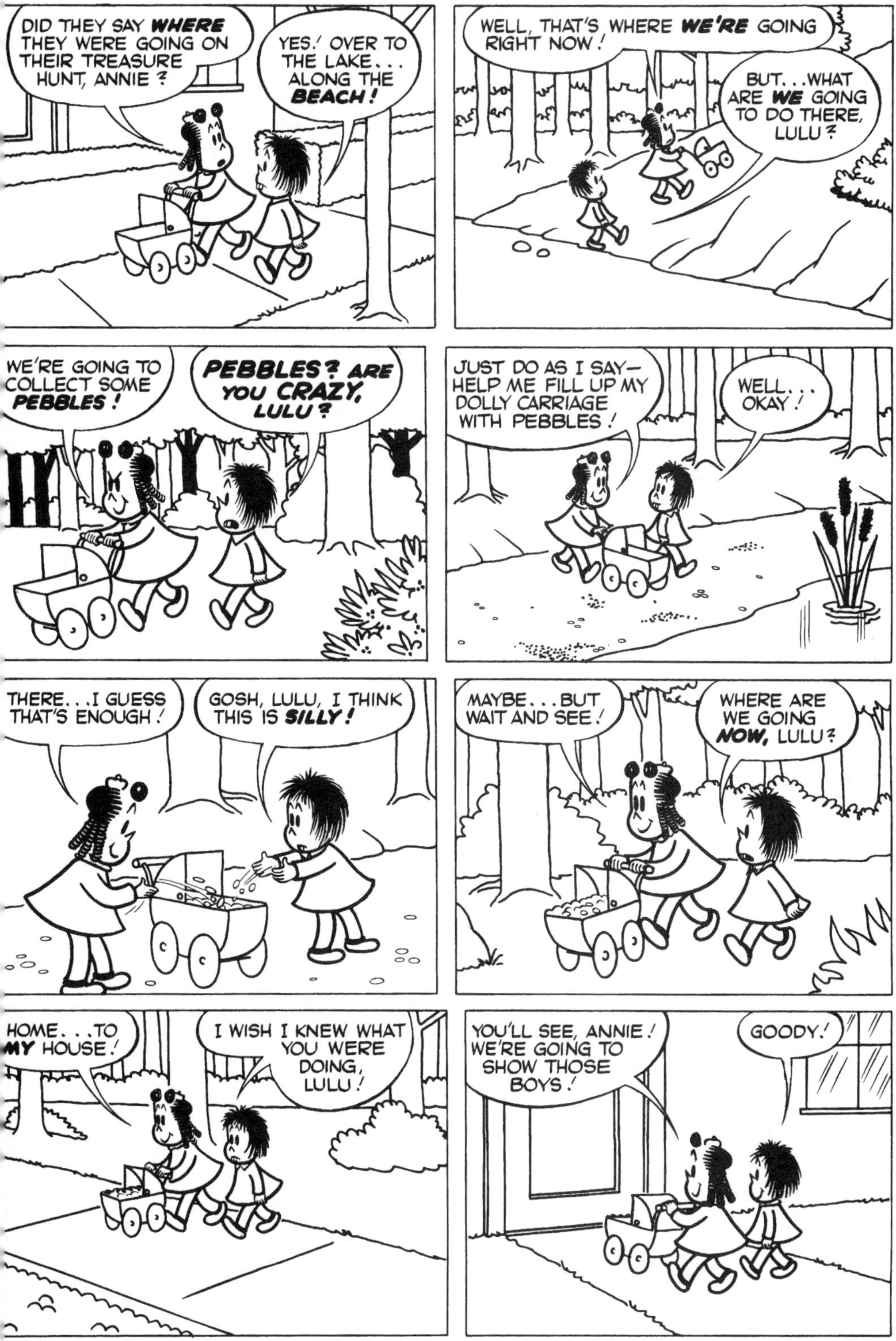
DID THEY SAY WHERE THEY WERE GOING ON THEIR TREASURE HUNT, ANNIE?
YES! OVER TO THE LAKE... ALONG THE BEACH!
WELL, THAT'S WHERE WE'RE GOING RIGHT NOW!
BUT...WHAT ARE WE GOING TO DO THERE, LULU?
WE'RE GOING TO COLLECT SOME PEBBLES!
PEBBLES? ARE YOU CRAZY, LULU?
JUST DO AS I SAY— HELP ME FILL UP MY DOLLY CARRIAGE WITH PEBBLES!
WELL... OKAY!
THERE...I GUESS THAT'S ENOUGH!
GOSH, LULU, I THINK THIS IS SILLY!
MAYBE...BUT WAIT AND SEE!
WHERE ARE WE GOING NOW, LULU?
HOME...TO MY HOUSE!
I WISH I KNEW WHAT YOU WERE DOING, LULU!
YOU'LL SEE, ANNIE! WE'RE GOING TO SHOW THOSE BOYS!
GOODY!

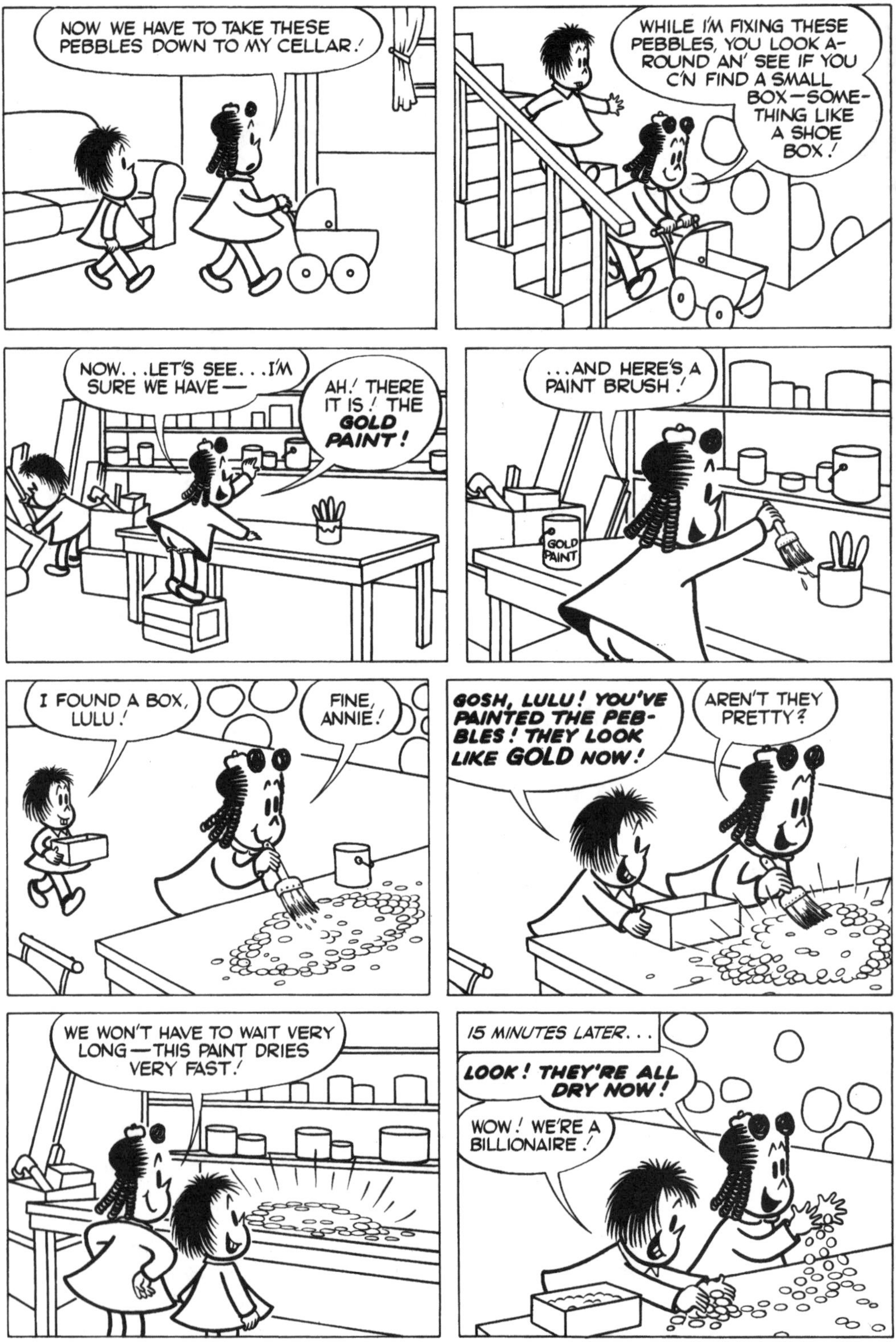

NOW WE HAVE TO TAKE THESE PEBBLES DOWN TO MY CELLAR!
WHILE I'M FIXING THESE PEBBLES, YOU LOOK AROUND AN' SEE IF YOU C'N FIND A SMALL BOX—SOMETHING LIKE A SHOE BOX!
NOW...LET'S SEE...I'M SURE WE HAVE—
AH! THERE IT IS! THE **GOLD PAINT!**
...AND HERE'S A PAINT BRUSH!
GOLD PAINT
I FOUND A BOX, LULU!
FINE, ANNIE!
GOSH, LULU! YOU'VE PAINTED THE PEBBLES! THEY LOOK LIKE GOLD NOW!
AREN'T THEY PRETTY?
WE WON'T HAVE TO WAIT VERY LONG—THIS PAINT DRIES VERY FAST!
15 MINUTES LATER...
LOOK! THEY'RE ALL DRY NOW!
WOW! WE'RE A BILLIONAIRE!

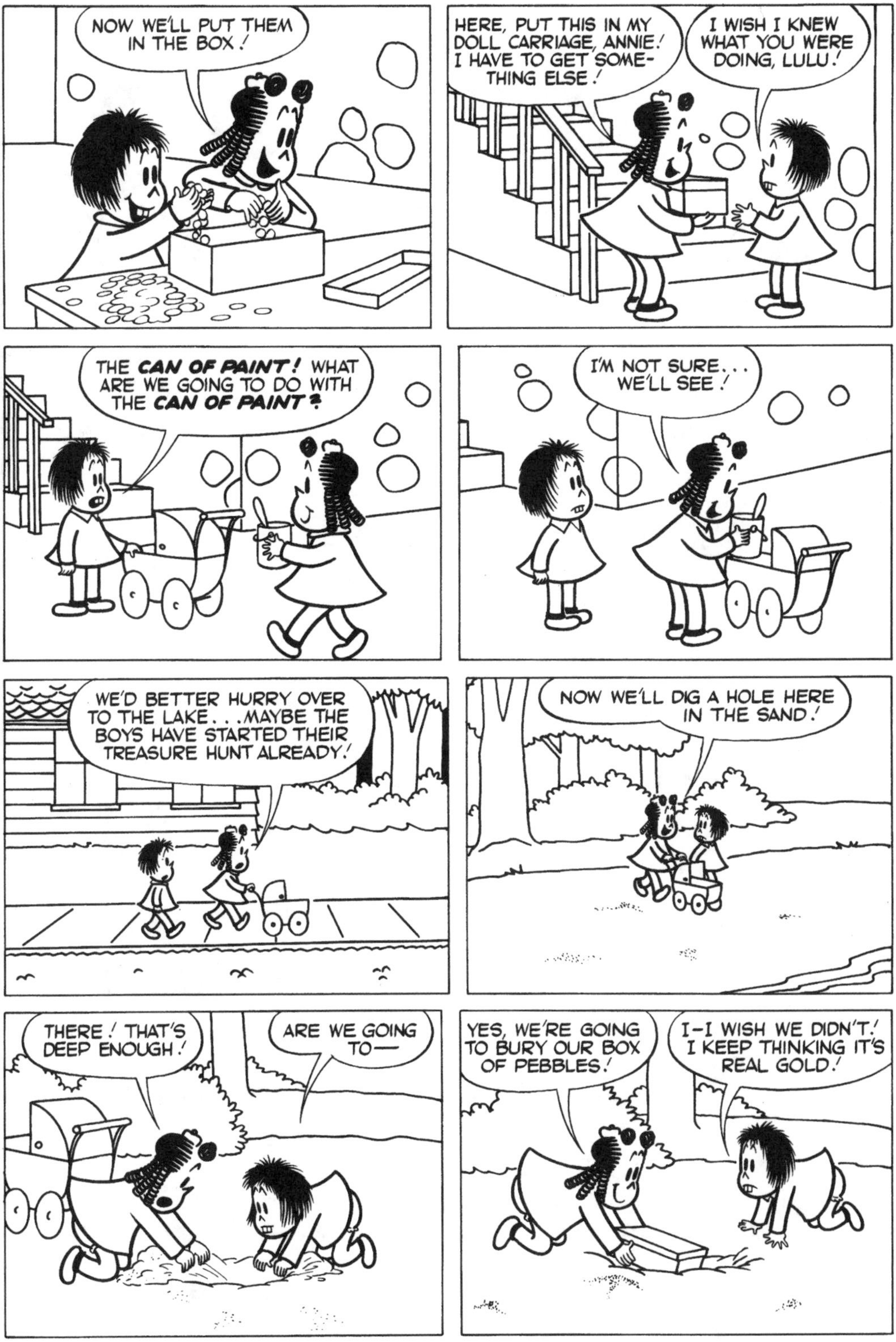
NOW WE'LL PUT THEM IN THE BOX!
HERE, PUT THIS IN MY DOLL CARRIAGE, ANNIE! I HAVE TO GET SOMETHING ELSE!
I WISH I KNEW WHAT YOU WERE DOING, LULU!
THE CAN OF PAINT! WHAT ARE WE GOING TO DO WITH THE CAN OF PAINT?
I'M NOT SURE... WE'LL SEE!
WE'D BETTER HURRY OVER TO THE LAKE...MAYBE THE BOYS HAVE STARTED THEIR TREASURE HUNT ALREADY!
NOW WE'LL DIG A HOLE HERE IN THE SAND!
THERE! THAT'S DEEP ENOUGH!
ARE WE GOING TO—
YES, WE'RE GOING TO BURY OUR BOX OF PEBBLES!
I-I WISH WE DIDN'T! I KEEP THINKING IT'S REAL GOLD!

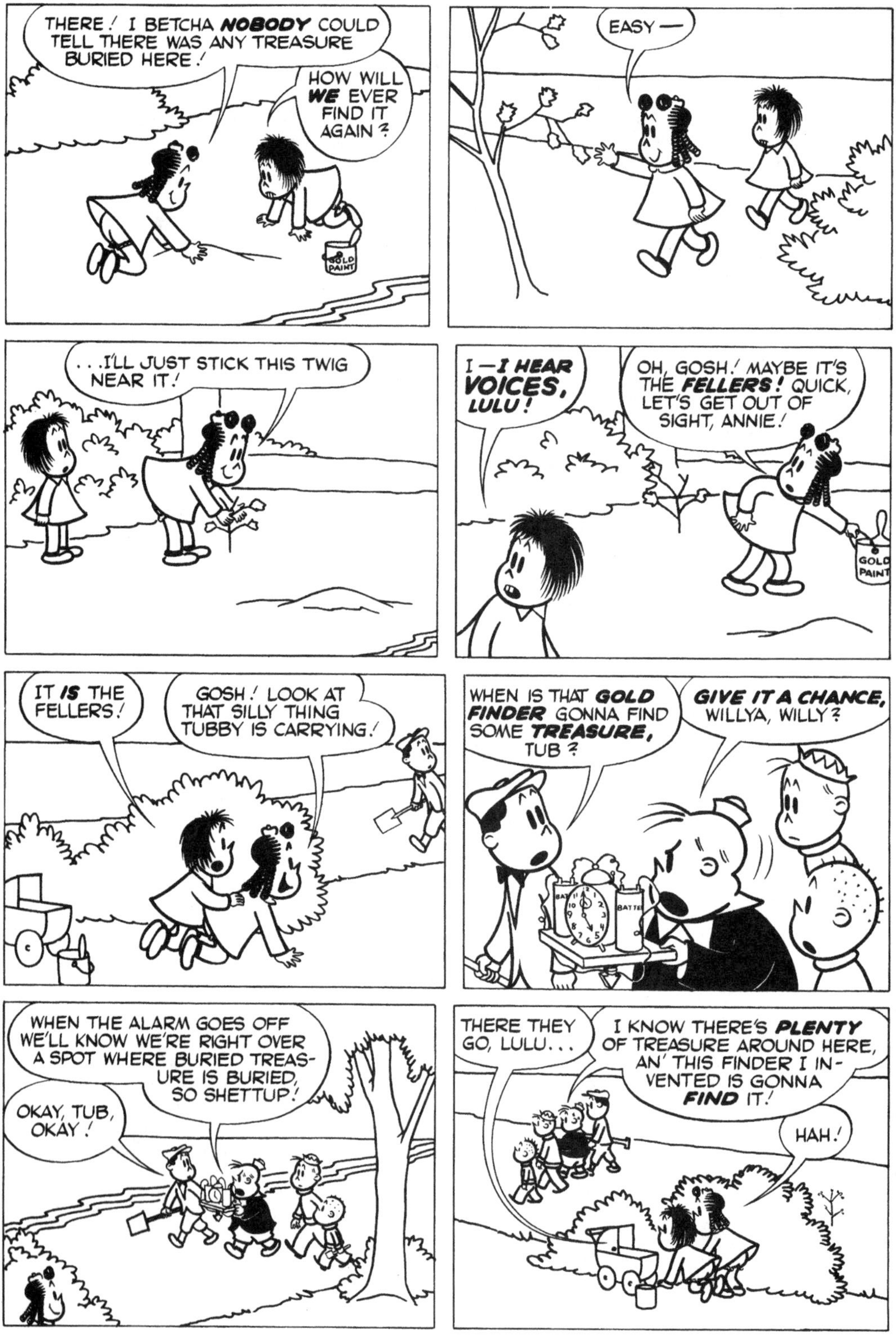
THERE! I BETCHA NOBODY COULD TELL THERE WAS ANY TREASURE BURIED HERE!
HOW WILL WE EVER FIND IT AGAIN?
GOLD PAINT
EASY —
...I'LL JUST STICK THIS TWIG NEAR IT!
I — I HEAR VOICES, LULU!
OH, GOSH! MAYBE IT'S THE FELLERS! QUICK, LET'S GET OUT OF SIGHT, ANNIE!
GOLD PAINT
IT IS THE FELLERS!
GOSH! LOOK AT THAT SILLY THING TUBBY IS CARRYING!
WHEN IS THAT GOLD FINDER GONNA FIND SOME TREASURE, TUB?
GIVE IT A CHANCE, WILLYA, WILLY?
WHEN THE ALARM GOES OFF WE'LL KNOW WE'RE RIGHT OVER A SPOT WHERE BURIED TREASURE IS BURIED, SO SHETTUP!
OKAY, TUB, OKAY!
THERE THEY GO, LULU...
I KNOW THERE'S PLENTY OF TREASURE AROUND HERE, AN' THIS FINDER I INVENTED IS GONNA FIND IT!
HAH!

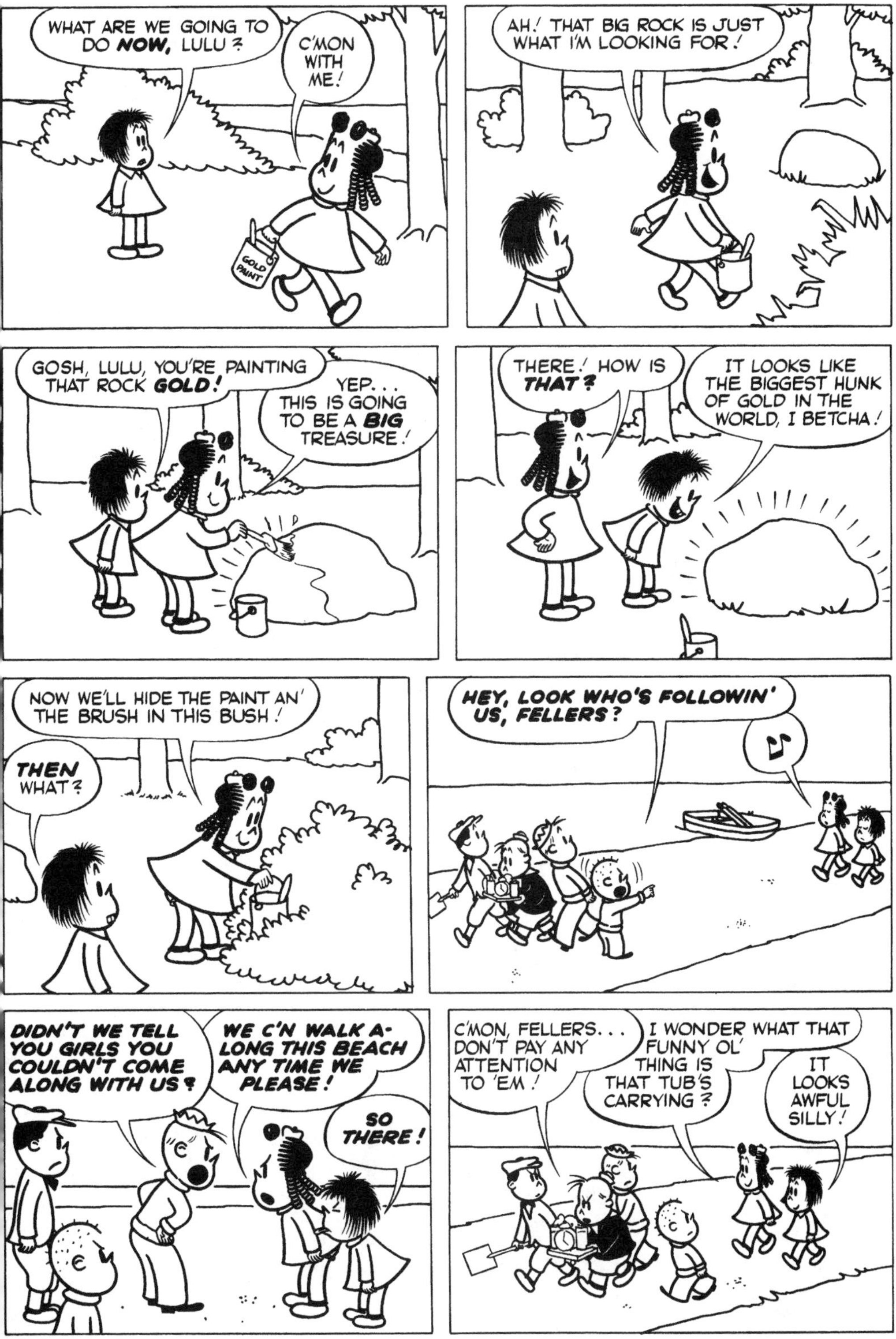
WHAT ARE WE GOING TO DO **NOW,** LULU ?
C'MON WITH ME!
GOLD PAINT
AH! THAT BIG ROCK IS JUST WHAT I'M LOOKING FOR!
GOSH, LULU, YOU'RE PAINTING THAT ROCK **GOLD!**
YEP. . . THIS IS GOING TO BE A **BIG** TREASURE!
THERE! HOW IS **THAT?**
IT LOOKS LIKE THE BIGGEST HUNK OF GOLD IN THE WORLD, I BETCHA!
NOW WE'LL HIDE THE PAINT AN' THE BRUSH IN THIS BUSH!
THEN WHAT?
HEY, LOOK WHO'S FOLLOWIN' US, FELLERS?
DIDN'T WE TELL YOU GIRLS YOU COULDN'T COME ALONG WITH US?
WE C'N WALK A-LONG THIS BEACH ANY TIME WE PLEASE!
SO THERE!
C'MON, FELLERS. . . DON'T PAY ANY ATTENTION TO 'EM!
I WONDER WHAT THAT FUNNY OL' THING IS THAT TUB'S CARRYING?
IT LOOKS AWFUL SILLY!

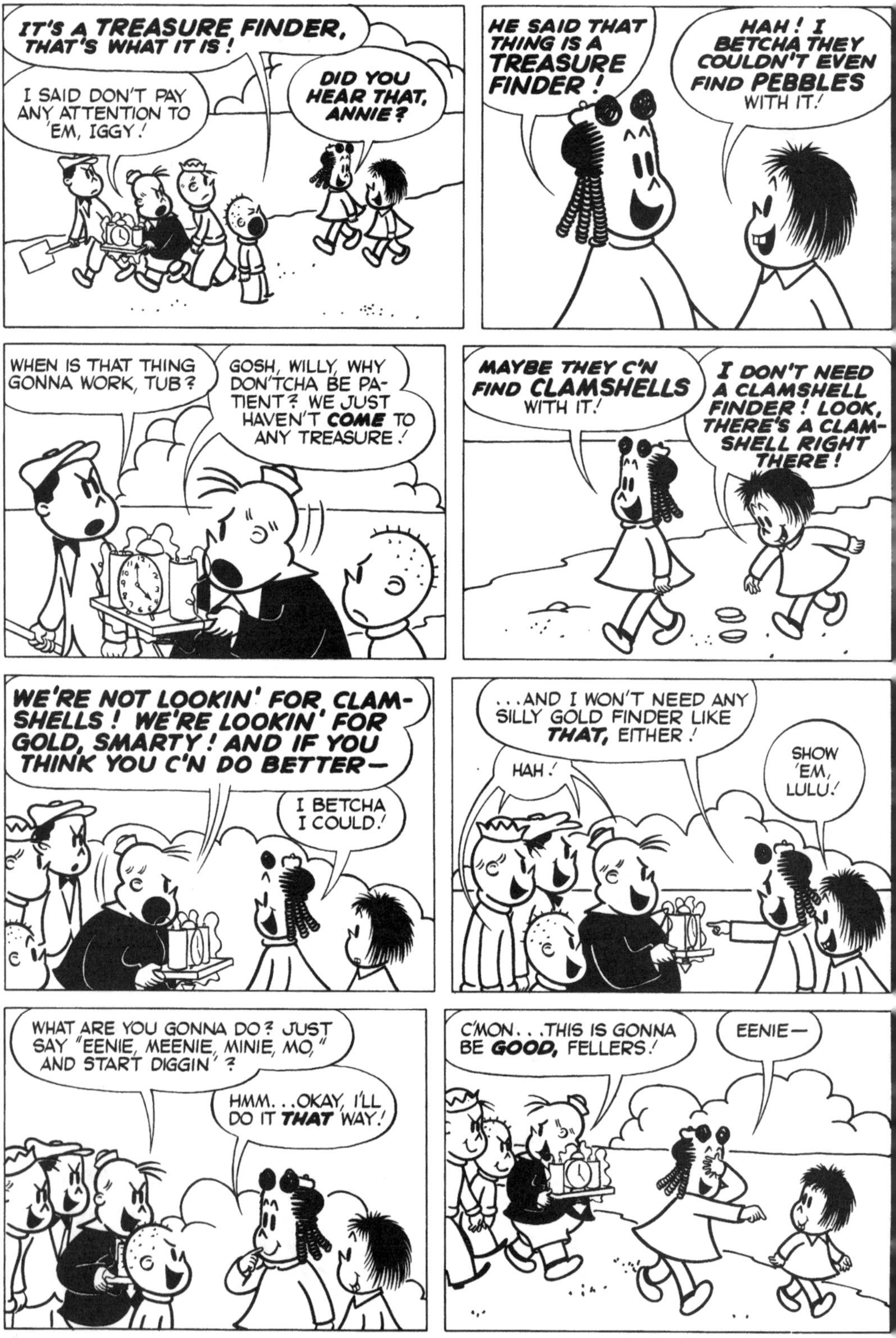
IT'S A TREASURE FINDER, THAT'S WHAT IT IS!
I SAID DON'T PAY ANY ATTENTION TO 'EM, IGGY!
DID YOU HEAR THAT, ANNIE?
HE SAID THAT THING IS A TREASURE FINDER!
HAH! I BETCHA THEY COULDN'T EVEN FIND PEBBLES WITH IT!
WHEN IS THAT THING GONNA WORK, TUB?
GOSH, WILLY, WHY DON'TCHA BE PATIENT? WE JUST HAVEN'T COME TO ANY TREASURE!
MAYBE THEY C'N FIND CLAMSHELLS WITH IT!
I DON'T NEED A CLAMSHELL FINDER! LOOK, THERE'S A CLAMSHELL RIGHT THERE!
WE'RE NOT LOOKIN' FOR CLAMSHELLS! WE'RE LOOKIN' FOR GOLD, SMARTY! AND IF YOU THINK YOU C'N DO BETTER—
I BETCHA I COULD!
...AND I WON'T NEED ANY SILLY GOLD FINDER LIKE THAT, EITHER!
HAH!
SHOW 'EM, LULU!
WHAT ARE YOU GONNA DO? JUST SAY "EENIE, MEENIE, MINIE, MO," AND START DIGGIN'?
HMM...OKAY, I'LL DO IT THAT WAY!
C'MON...THIS IS GONNA BE GOOD, FELLERS!
EENIE—

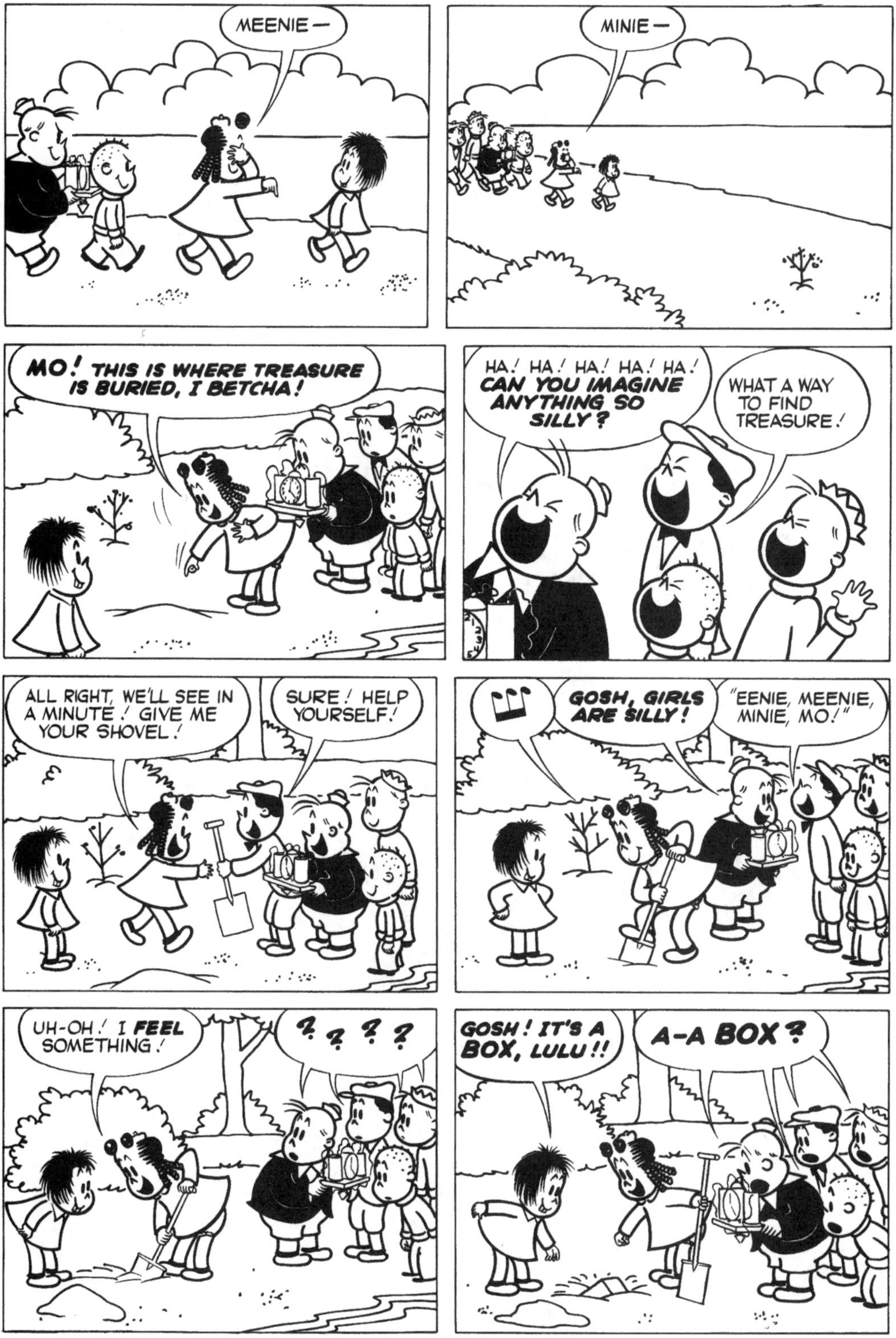
MEENIE—
MINIE—
MO! THIS IS WHERE TREASURE IS BURIED, I BETCHA!
HA! HA! HA! HA! HA! CAN YOU IMAGINE ANYTHING SO SILLY?
WHAT A WAY TO FIND TREASURE!
ALL RIGHT, WE'LL SEE IN A MINUTE! GIVE ME YOUR SHOVEL!
SURE! HELP YOURSELF!
GOSH, GIRLS ARE SILLY!
"EENIE, MEENIE, MINIE, MO!"
UH-OH! I FEEL SOMETHING!
? ? ? ?
GOSH! IT'S A BOX, LULU!!
A-A BOX?

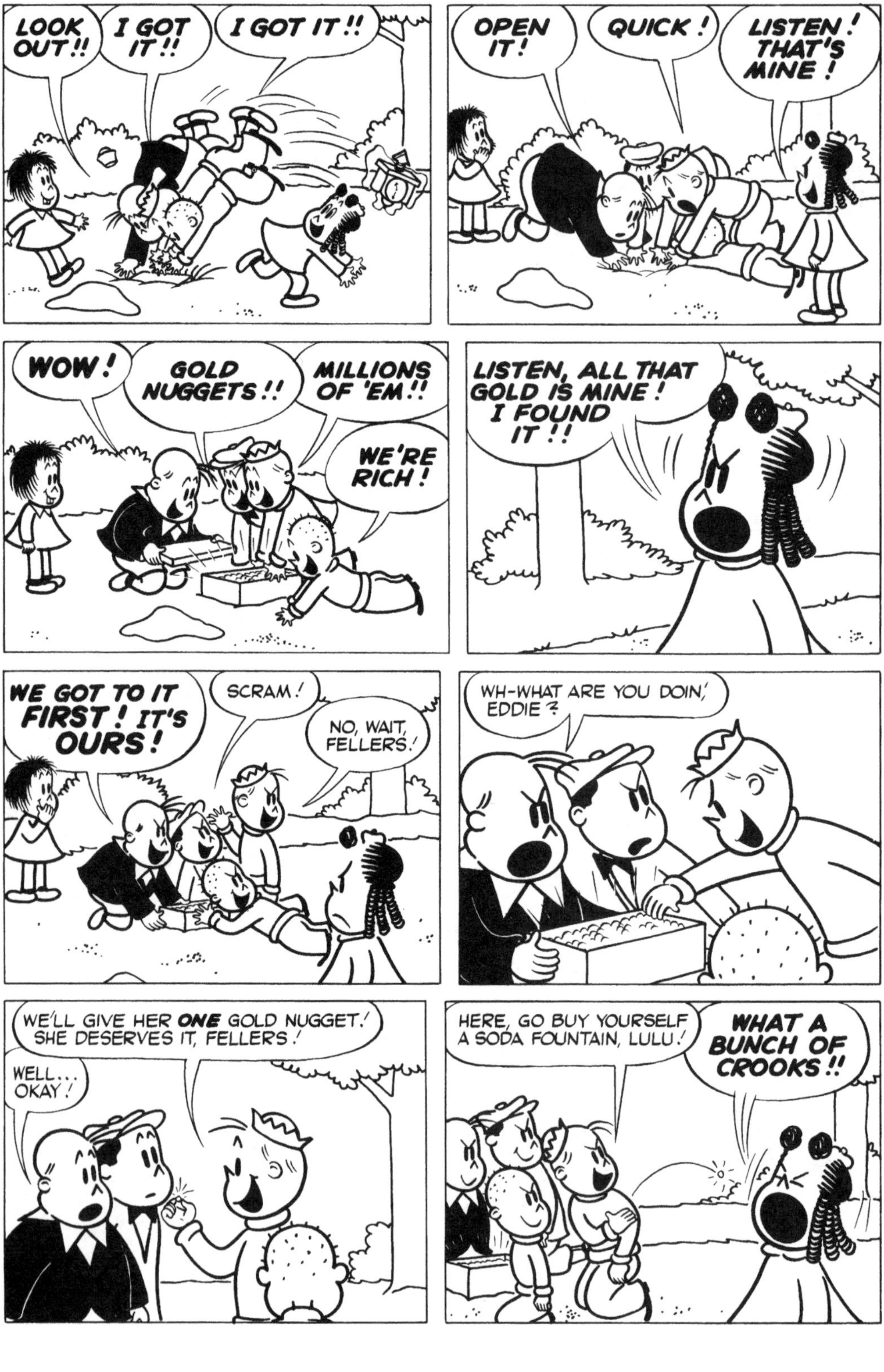
LOOK OUT!!
I GOT IT!!
I GOT IT!!
OPEN IT!
QUICK!
LISTEN! THAT'S MINE!
WOW!
GOLD NUGGETS!!
MILLIONS OF 'EM!!
WE'RE RICH!
LISTEN, ALL THAT GOLD IS MINE! I FOUND IT!!
WE GOT TO IT FIRST! IT'S OURS!
SCRAM!
NO, WAIT, FELLERS!
WH-WHAT ARE YOU DOIN', EDDIE?
WE'LL GIVE HER ONE GOLD NUGGET! SHE DESERVES IT, FELLERS!
WELL... OKAY!
HERE, GO BUY YOURSELF A SODA FOUNTAIN, LULU!
WHAT A BUNCH OF CROOKS!!

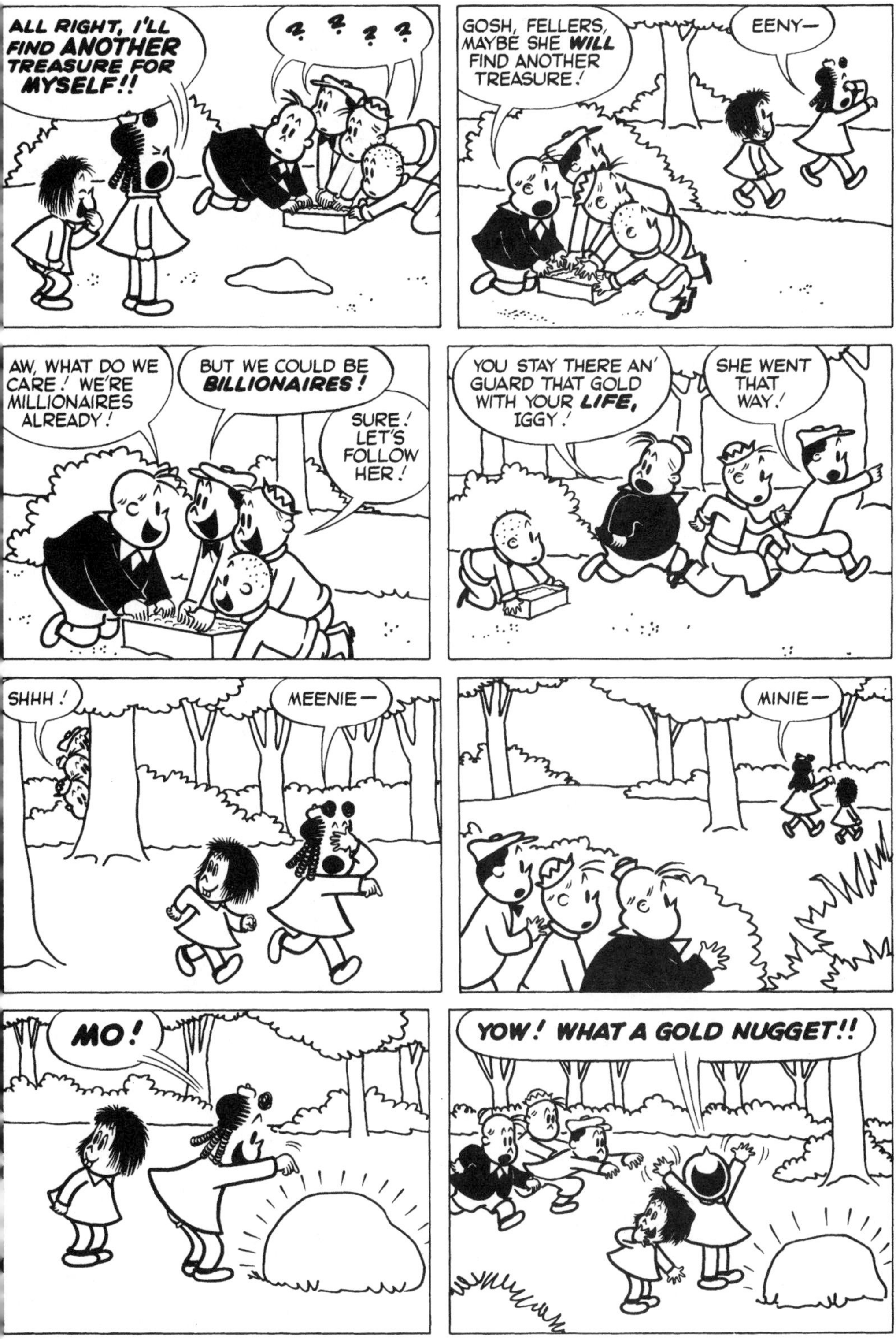
ALL RIGHT, I'LL FIND ANOTHER TREASURE FOR MYSELF!!
? ? ? ?
GOSH, FELLERS, MAYBE SHE WILL FIND ANOTHER TREASURE!
EENY—
AW, WHAT DO WE CARE! WE'RE MILLIONAIRES ALREADY!
BUT WE COULD BE BILLIONAIRES!
SURE! LET'S FOLLOW HER!
YOU STAY THERE AN' GUARD THAT GOLD WITH YOUR LIFE, IGGY!
SHE WENT THAT WAY!
SHHH!
MEENIE—
MINIE—
MO!
YOW! WHAT A GOLD NUGGET!!

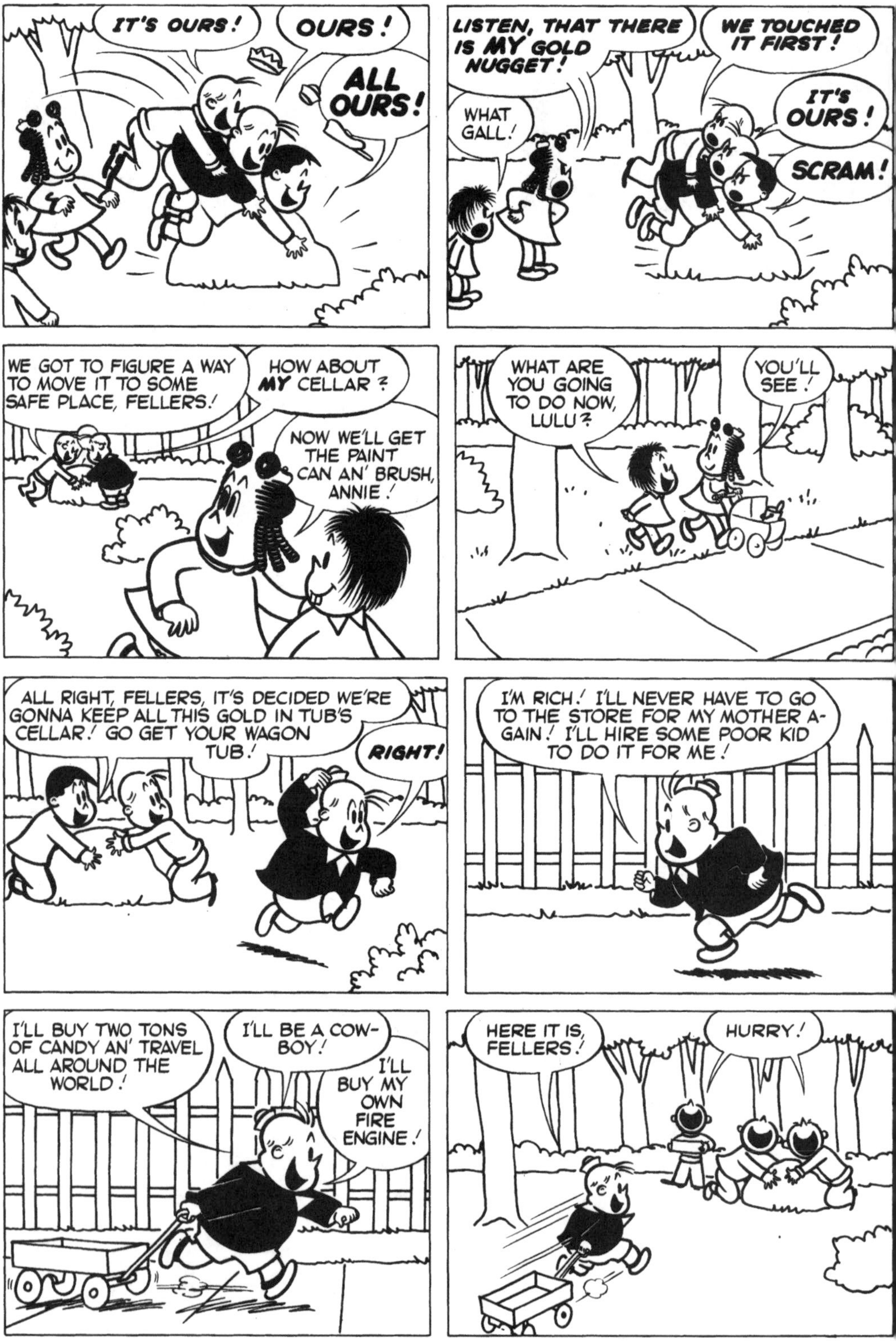
IT'S OURS!
OURS!
ALL OURS!
LISTEN, THAT THERE IS MY GOLD NUGGET!
WE TOUCHED IT FIRST!
WHAT GALL!
IT'S OURS!
SCRAM!
WE GOT TO FIGURE A WAY TO MOVE IT TO SOME SAFE PLACE, FELLERS!
HOW ABOUT MY CELLAR?
NOW WE'LL GET THE PAINT CAN AN' BRUSH, ANNIE!
WHAT ARE YOU GOING TO DO NOW, LULU?
YOU'LL SEE!
ALL RIGHT, FELLERS, IT'S DECIDED WE'RE GONNA KEEP ALL THIS GOLD IN TUB'S CELLAR! GO GET YOUR WAGON TUB!
RIGHT!
I'M RICH! I'LL NEVER HAVE TO GO TO THE STORE FOR MY MOTHER AGAIN! I'LL HIRE SOME POOR KID TO DO IT FOR ME!
I'LL BUY TWO TONS OF CANDY AN' TRAVEL ALL AROUND THE WORLD!
I'LL BE A COW-BOY!
I'LL BUY MY OWN FIRE ENGINE!
HERE IT IS, FELLERS!
HURRY!

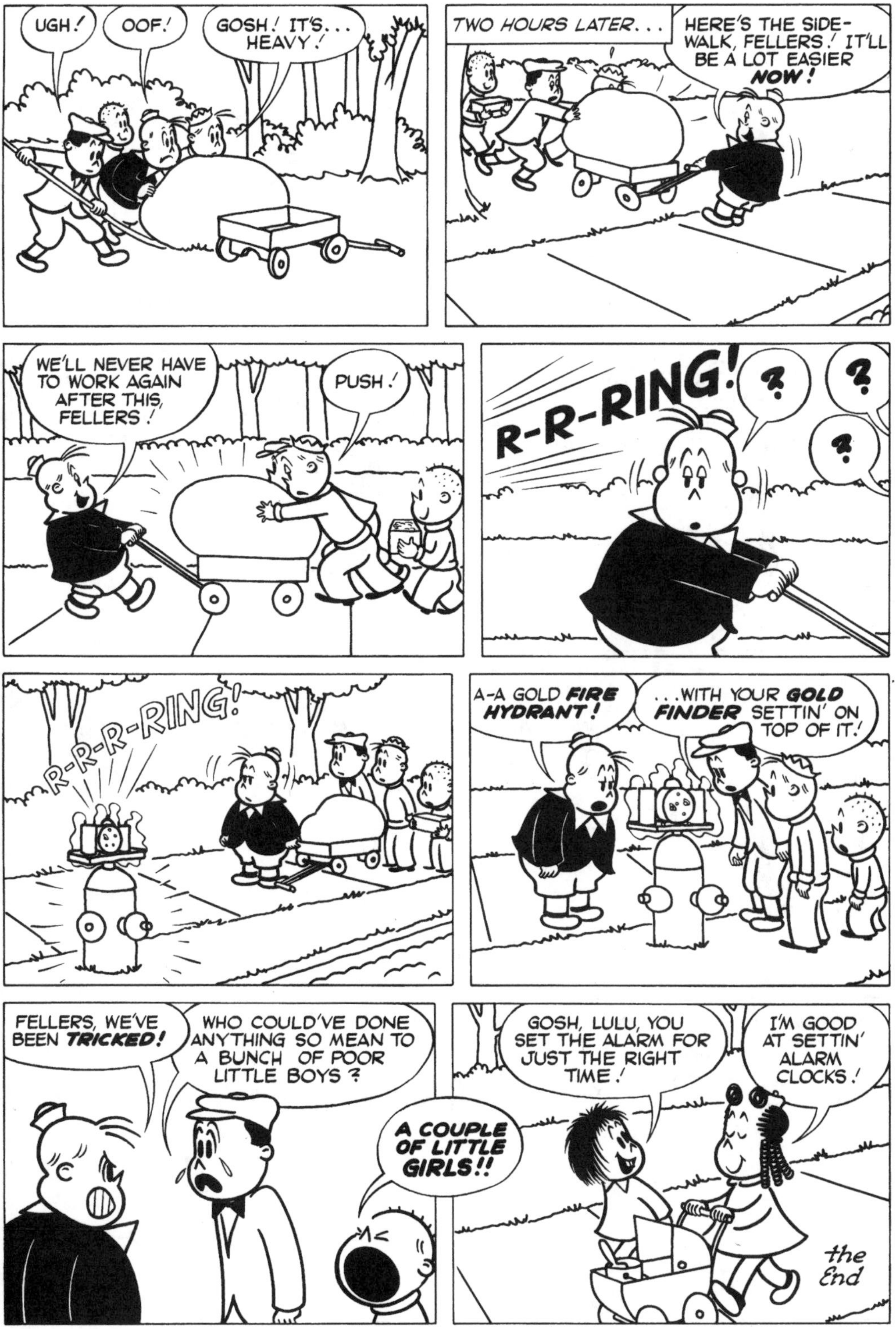
UGH!
OOF!
GOSH! IT'S... HEAVY!
TWO HOURS LATER...
HERE'S THE SIDE-WALK, FELLERS! IT'LL BE A LOT EASIER NOW!
WE'LL NEVER HAVE TO WORK AGAIN AFTER THIS, FELLERS!
PUSH!
R-R-RING!
?
?
?
R-R-R-R-RING!
A-A GOLD FIRE HYDRANT!
...WITH YOUR GOLD FINDER SETTIN' ON TOP OF IT!
FELLERS, WE'VE BEEN TRICKED!
WHO COULD'VE DONE ANYTHING SO MEAN TO A BUNCH OF POOR LITTLE BOYS?
A COUPLE OF LITTLE GIRLS!!
GOSH, LULU, YOU SET THE ALARM FOR JUST THE RIGHT TIME!
I'M GOOD AT SETTIN' ALARM CLOCKS!
the End

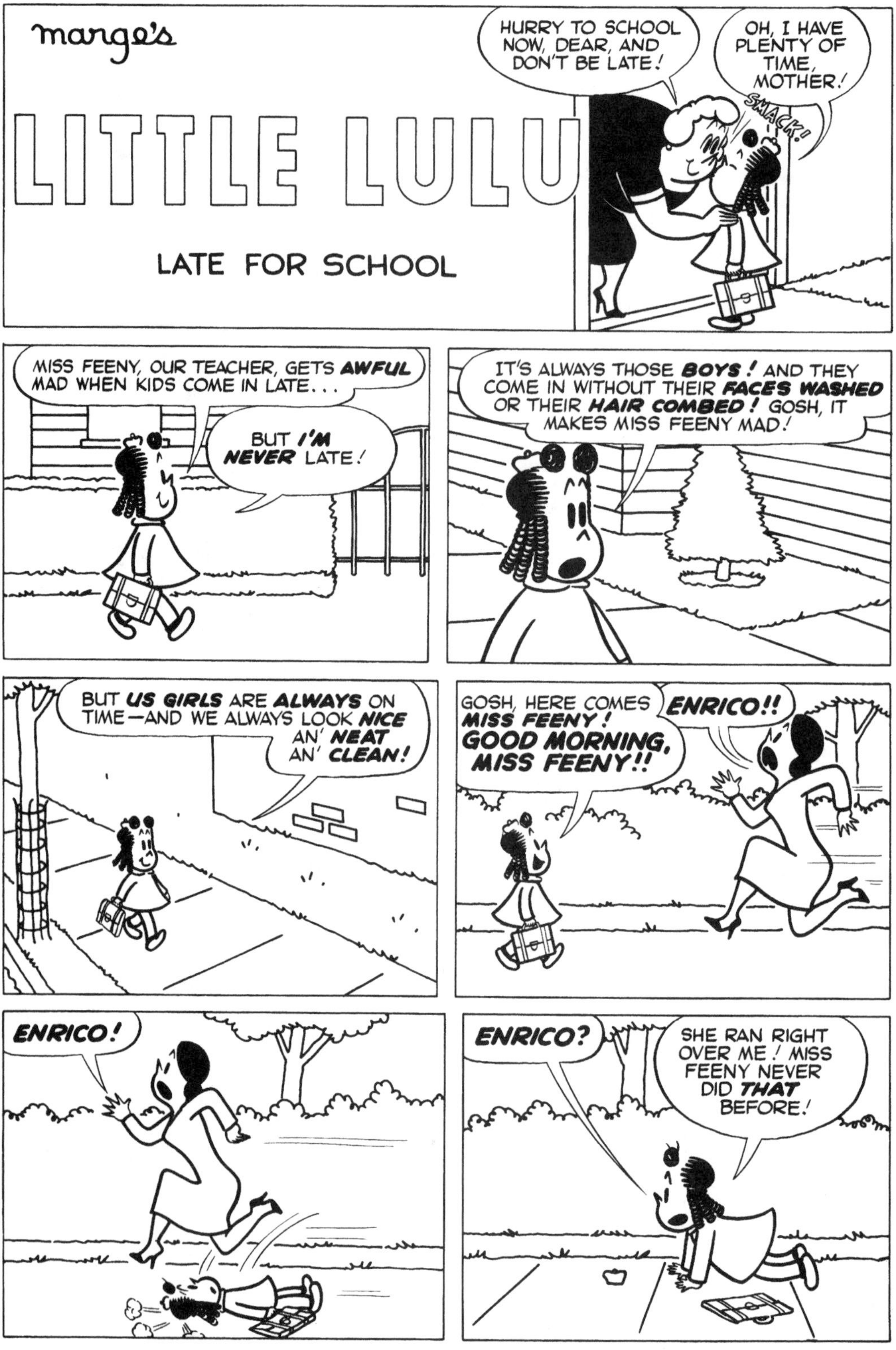
marge's
LITTLE LULU
LATE FOR SCHOOL
HURRY TO SCHOOL NOW, DEAR, AND DON'T BE LATE!
OH, I HAVE PLENTY OF TIME, MOTHER!
SMACK!
MISS FEENY, OUR TEACHER, GETS AWFUL MAD WHEN KIDS COME IN LATE...
BUT I'M NEVER LATE!
IT'S ALWAYS THOSE BOYS! AND THEY COME IN WITHOUT THEIR FACES WASHED OR THEIR HAIR COMBED! GOSH, IT MAKES MISS FEENY MAD!
BUT US GIRLS ARE ALWAYS ON TIME—AND WE ALWAYS LOOK NICE AN' NEAT AN' CLEAN!
GOSH, HERE COMES MISS FEENY! GOOD MORNING, MISS FEENY!!
ENRICO!!
ENRICO!
ENRICO?
SHE RAN RIGHT OVER ME! MISS FEENY NEVER DID THAT BEFORE!

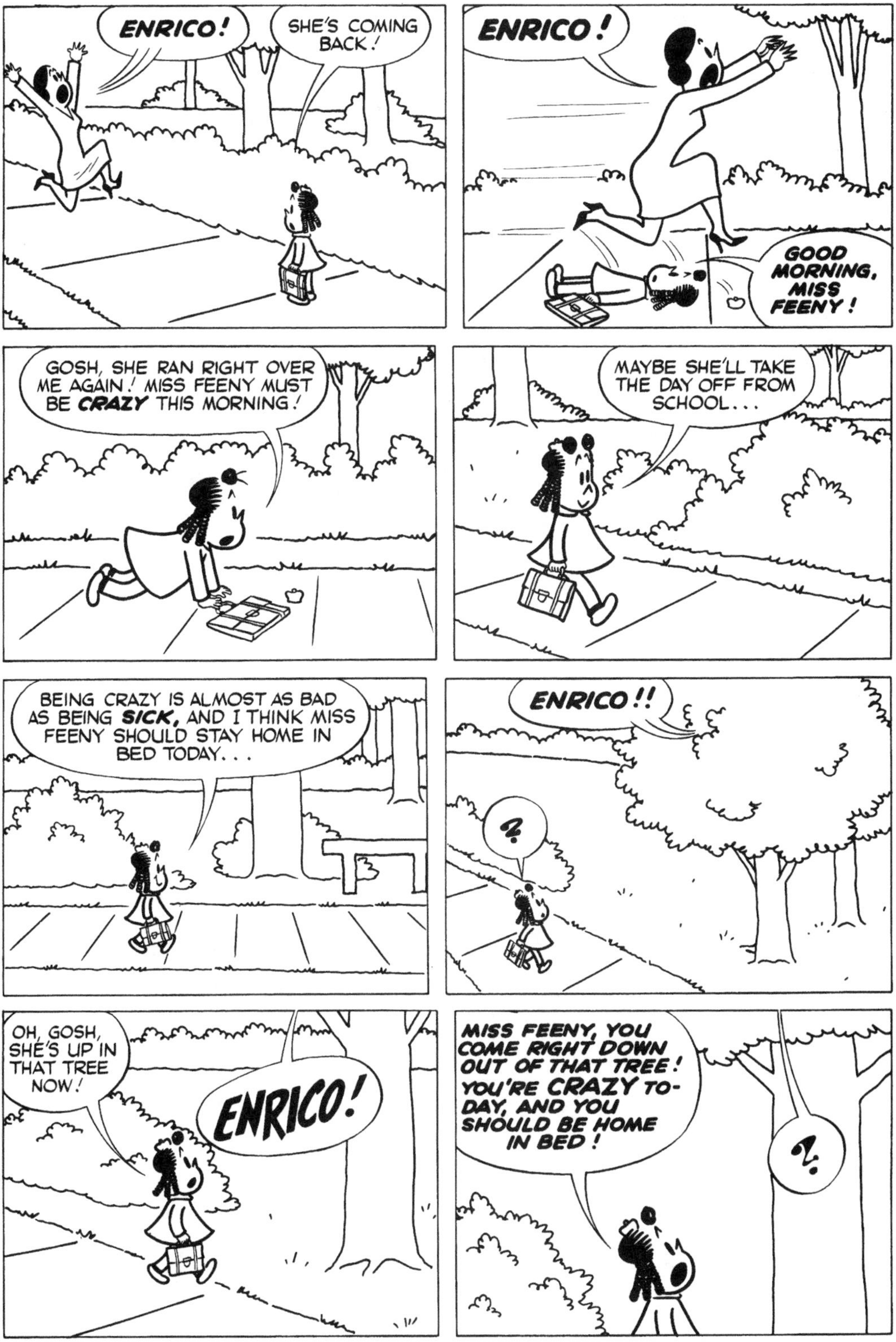
ENRICO!
SHE'S COMING BACK!
ENRICO!
GOOD MORNING, MISS FEENY!
GOSH, SHE RAN RIGHT OVER ME AGAIN! MISS FEENY MUST BE CRAZY THIS MORNING!
MAYBE SHE'LL TAKE THE DAY OFF FROM SCHOOL...
BEING CRAZY IS ALMOST AS BAD AS BEING SICK, AND I THINK MISS FEENY SHOULD STAY HOME IN BED TODAY...
ENRICO!!
?
OH, GOSH, SHE'S UP IN THAT TREE NOW!
ENRICO!
MISS FEENY, YOU COME RIGHT DOWN OUT OF THAT TREE! YOU'RE CRAZY TO-DAY, AND YOU SHOULD BE HOME IN BED!
?

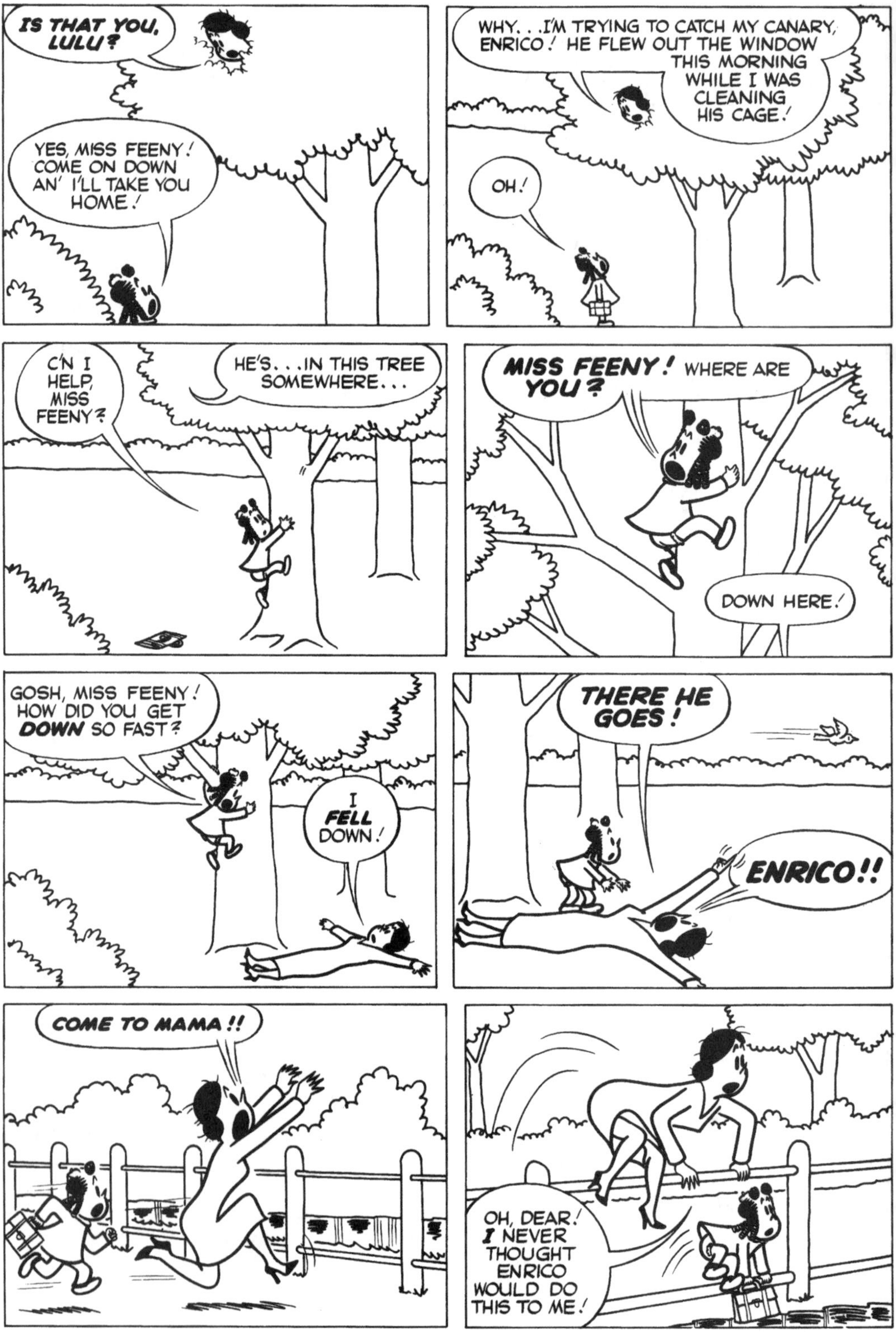
IS THAT YOU, LULU?
YES, MISS FEENY! COME ON DOWN AN' I'LL TAKE YOU HOME!
WHY. . .I'M TRYING TO CATCH MY CANARY, ENRICO! HE FLEW OUT THE WINDOW THIS MORNING WHILE I WAS CLEANING HIS CAGE!
OH!
C'N I HELP, MISS FEENY?
HE'S. . .IN THIS TREE SOMEWHERE. . .
MISS FEENY! WHERE ARE YOU?
DOWN HERE!
GOSH, MISS FEENY! HOW DID YOU GET DOWN SO FAST?
I FELL DOWN!
THERE HE GOES!
ENRICO!!
COME TO MAMA!!
OH, DEAR! I NEVER THOUGHT ENRICO WOULD DO THIS TO ME!

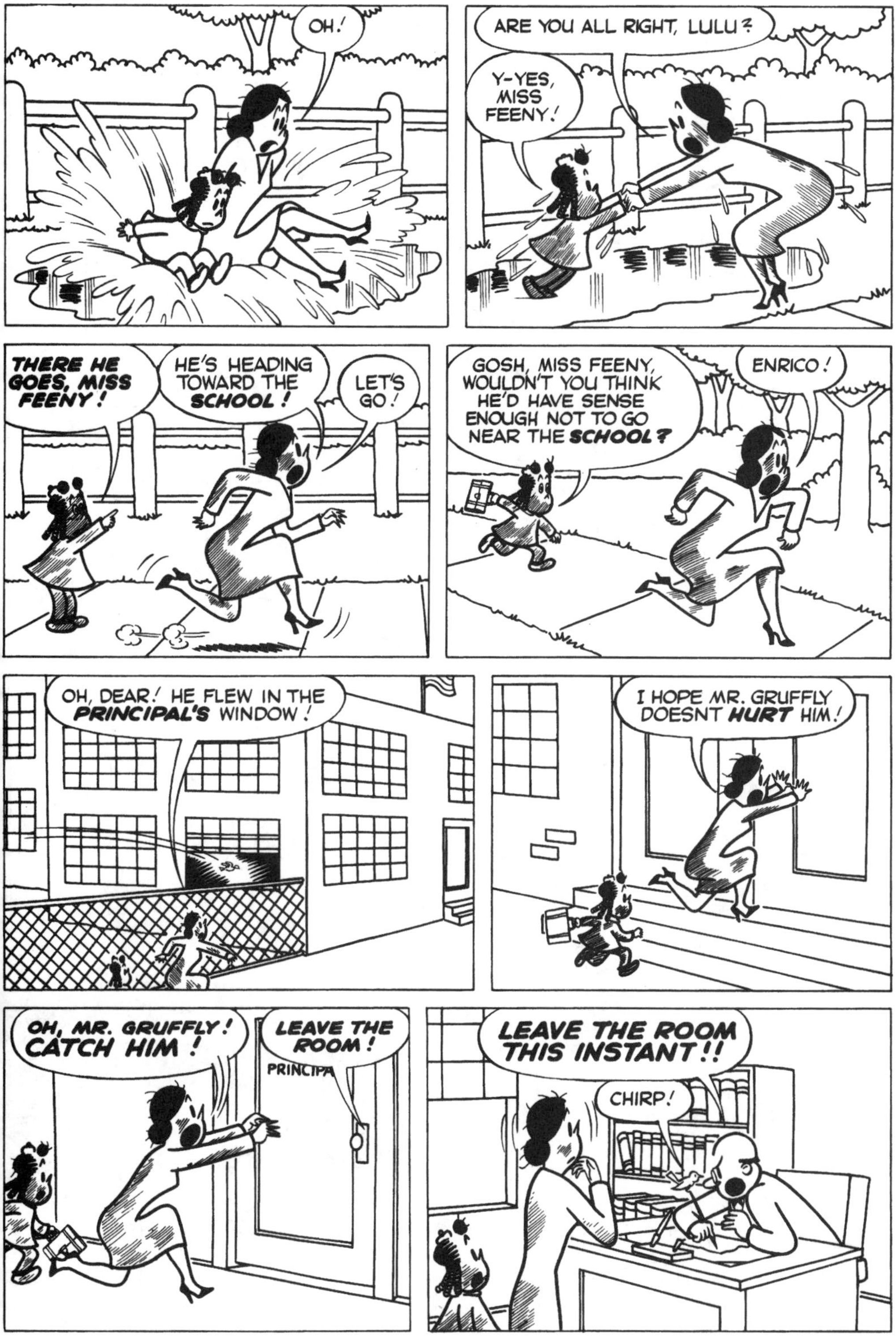

OH!
ARE YOU ALL RIGHT, LULU?
Y-YES, MISS FEENY!
THERE HE GOES, MISS FEENY!
HE'S HEADING TOWARD THE SCHOOL!
LET'S GO!
GOSH, MISS FEENY, WOULDN'T YOU THINK HE'D HAVE SENSE ENOUGH NOT TO GO NEAR THE SCHOOL?
ENRICO!
OH, DEAR! HE FLEW IN THE PRINCIPAL'S WINDOW!
I HOPE MR. GRUFFLY DOESNT HURT HIM!
OH, MR. GRUFFLY! CATCH HIM!
LEAVE THE ROOM!
PRINCIPA
LEAVE THE ROOM THIS INSTANT!!
CHIRP!

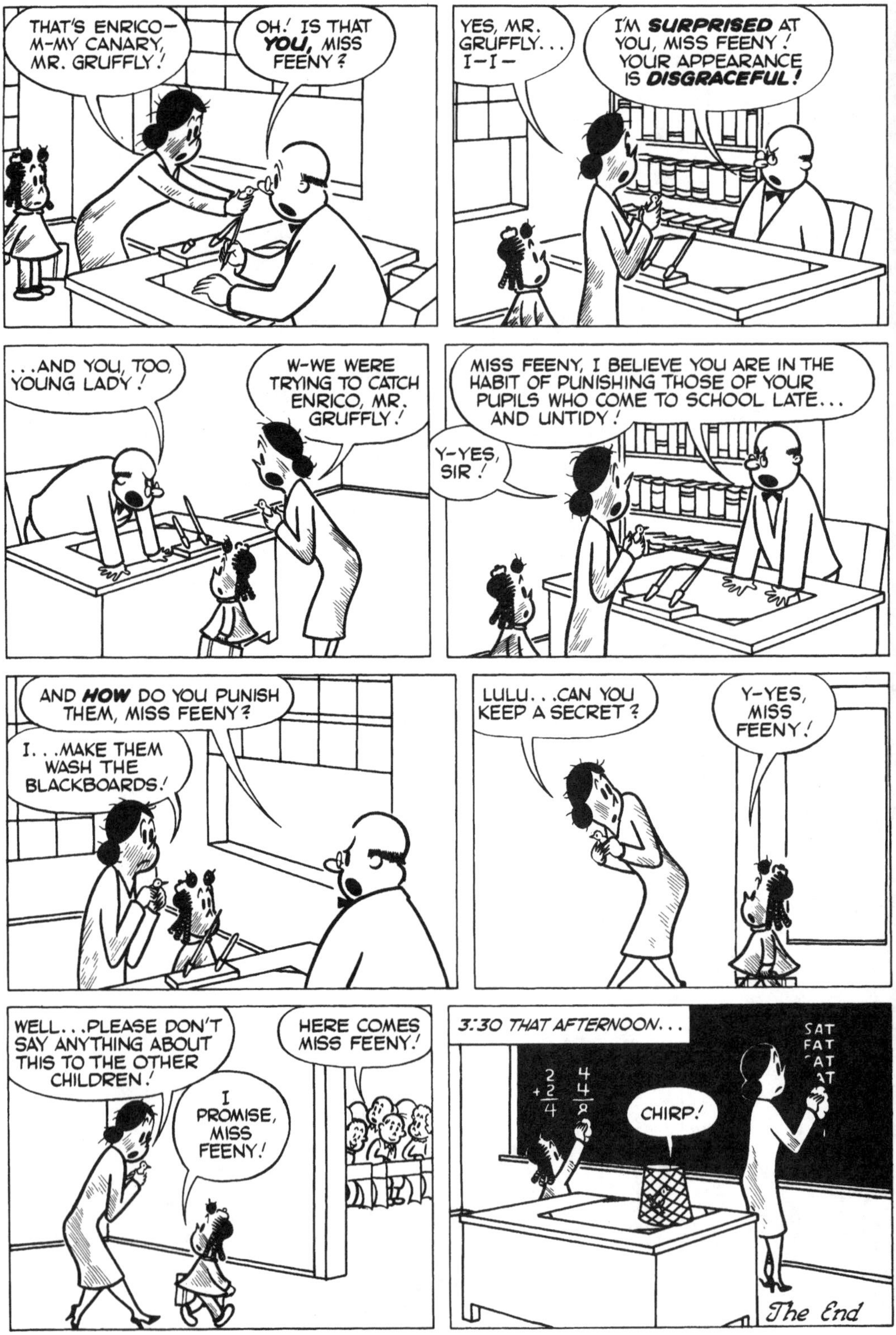
THAT'S ENRICO—M-MY CANARY, MR. GRUFFLY!
OH! IS THAT YOU, MISS FEENY?
YES, MR. GRUFFLY. . . I—I—
I'M SURPRISED AT YOU, MISS FEENY! YOUR APPEARANCE IS DISGRACEFUL!
. . .AND YOU, TOO, YOUNG LADY!
W-WE WERE TRYING TO CATCH ENRICO, MR. GRUFFLY!
MISS FEENY, I BELIEVE YOU ARE IN THE HABIT OF PUNISHING THOSE OF YOUR PUPILS WHO COME TO SCHOOL LATE... AND UNTIDY!
Y-YES, SIR!
AND HOW DO YOU PUNISH THEM, MISS FEENY?
I. . .MAKE THEM WASH THE BLACKBOARDS!
LULU. . .CAN YOU KEEP A SECRET?
Y-YES, MISS FEENY!
WELL. . .PLEASE DON'T SAY ANYTHING ABOUT THIS TO THE OTHER CHILDREN!
I PROMISE, MISS FEENY!
HERE COMES MISS FEENY!
3:30 THAT AFTERNOON. . .
SAT
FAT
CHIRP!
The End

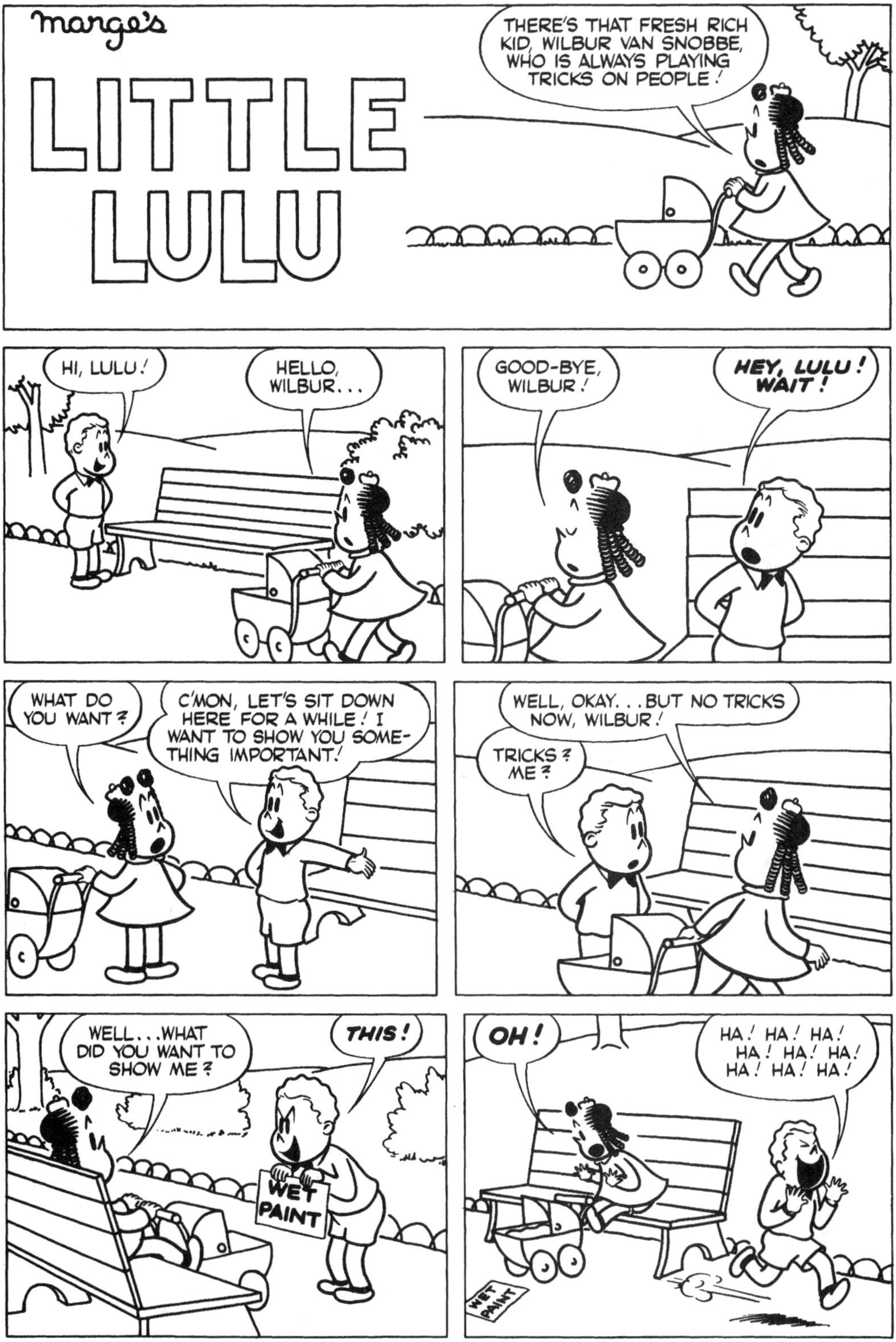
marge's
LITTLE LULU
THERE'S THAT FRESH RICH KID, WILBUR VAN SNOBBE, WHO IS ALWAYS PLAYING TRICKS ON PEOPLE!
HI, LULU!
HELLO, WILBUR...
GOOD-BYE, WILBUR!
HEY, LULU! WAIT!
WHAT DO YOU WANT?
C'MON, LET'S SIT DOWN HERE FOR A WHILE! I WANT TO SHOW YOU SOME-THING IMPORTANT!
WELL, OKAY...BUT NO TRICKS NOW, WILBUR!
TRICKS? ME?
WELL...WHAT DID YOU WANT TO SHOW ME?
THIS!
WET PAINT
OH!
HA! HA! HA! HA! HA! HA! HA! HA! HA!
WET PAINT

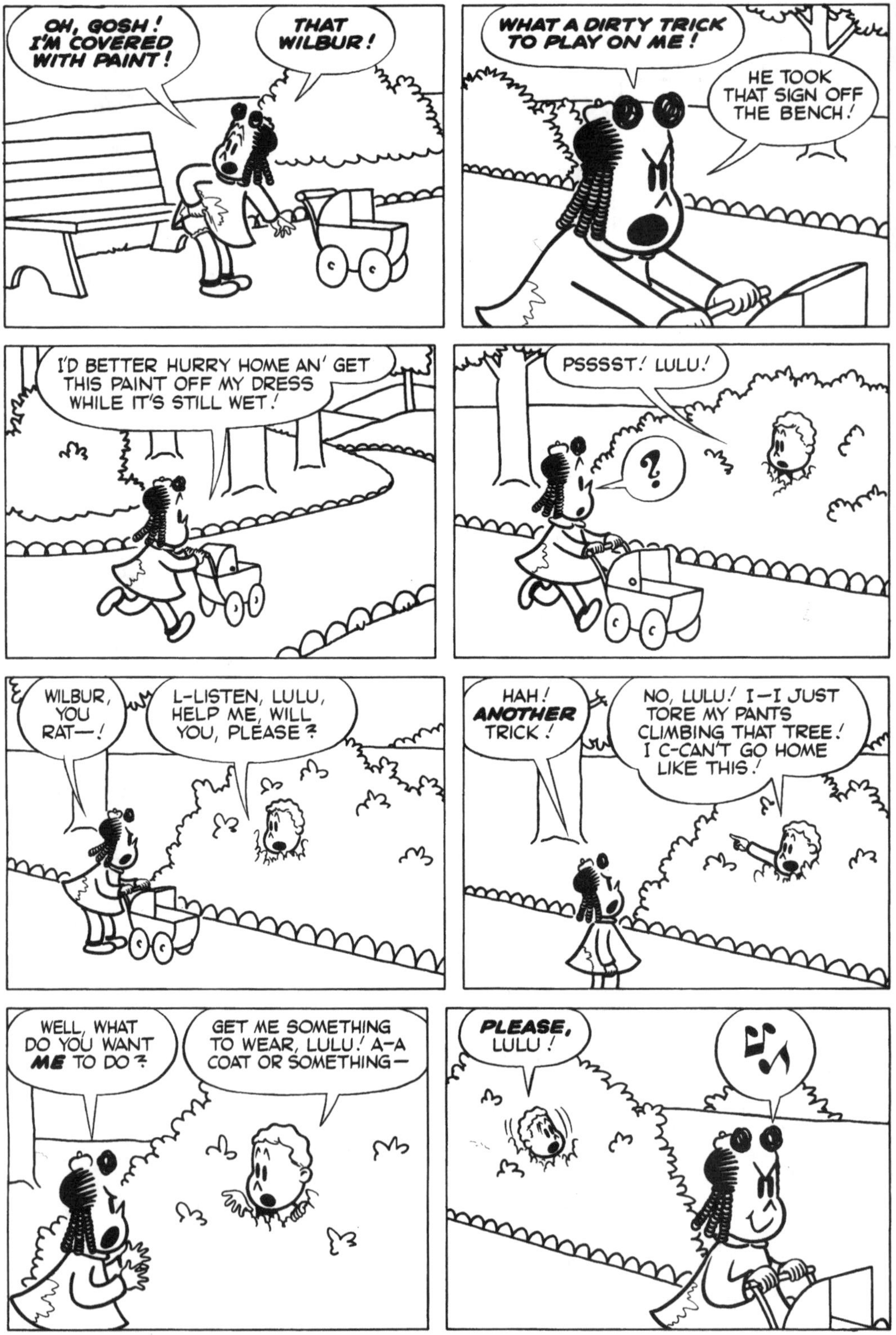
OH, GOSH! I'M COVERED WITH PAINT!
THAT WILBUR!
WHAT A DIRTY TRICK TO PLAY ON ME!
HE TOOK THAT SIGN OFF THE BENCH!
I'D BETTER HURRY HOME AN' GET THIS PAINT OFF MY DRESS WHILE IT'S STILL WET!
PSSSST! LULU!
?
WILBUR, YOU RAT—!
L-LISTEN, LULU, HELP ME, WILL YOU, PLEASE?
HAH! ANOTHER TRICK!
NO, LULU! I—I JUST TORE MY PANTS CLIMBING THAT TREE! I C-CAN'T GO HOME LIKE THIS!
WELL, WHAT DO YOU WANT ME TO DO?
GET ME SOMETHING TO WEAR, LULU! A-A COAT OR SOMETHING—
PLEASE, LULU!

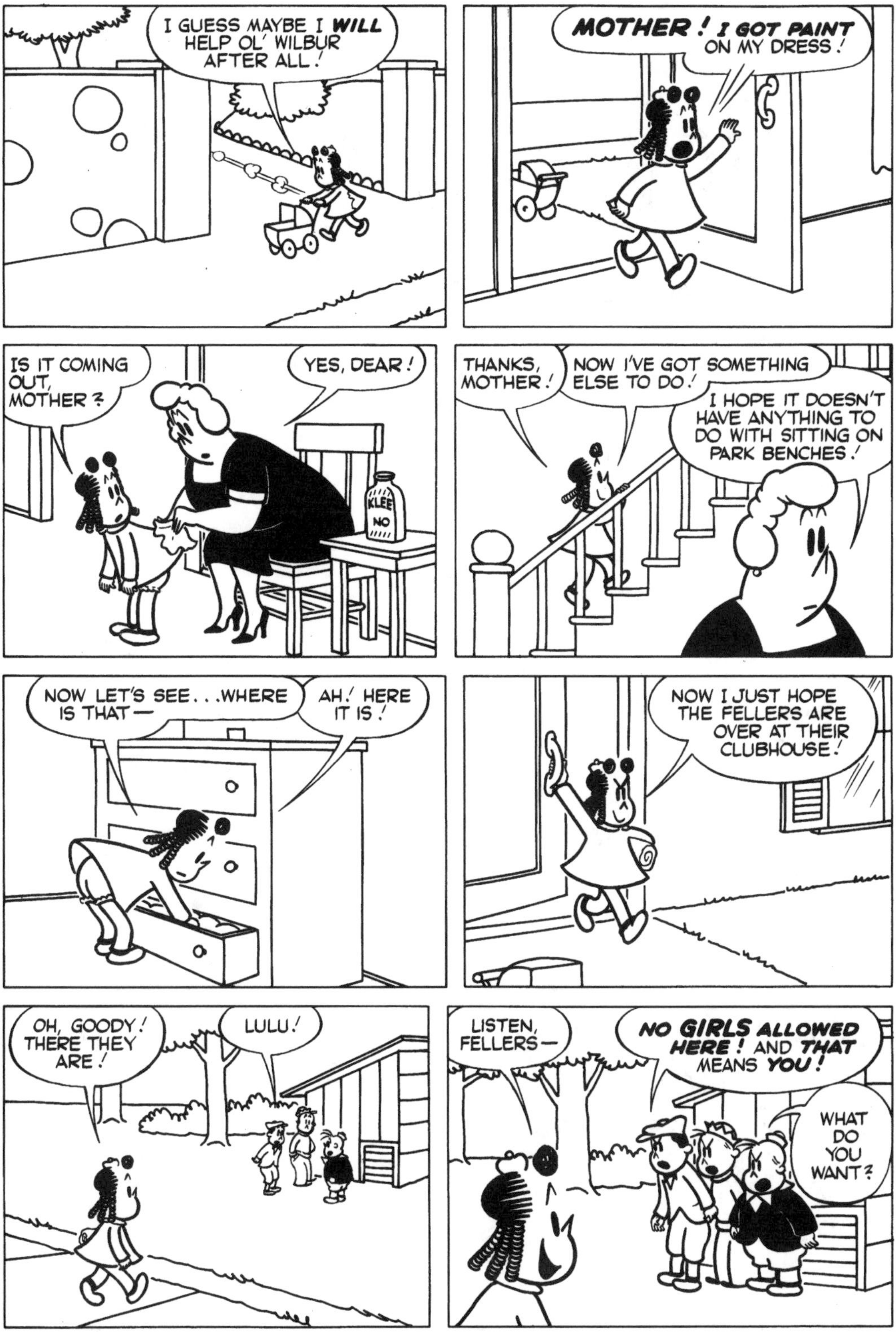
I GUESS MAYBE I **WILL** HELP OL' WILBUR AFTER ALL!
MOTHER! I GOT PAINT ON MY DRESS!
IS IT COMING OUT, MOTHER?
YES, DEAR!
THANKS, MOTHER!
NOW I'VE GOT SOMETHING ELSE TO DO!
I HOPE IT DOESN'T HAVE ANYTHING TO DO WITH SITTING ON PARK BENCHES!
KLEE NO
NOW LET'S SEE...WHERE IS THAT—
AH! HERE IT IS!
NOW I JUST HOPE THE FELLERS ARE OVER AT THEIR CLUBHOUSE!
OH, GOODY! THERE THEY ARE!
LULU!
LISTEN, FELLERS—
NO GIRLS ALLOWED HERE! AND **THAT** MEANS **YOU!**
WHAT DO YOU WANT?

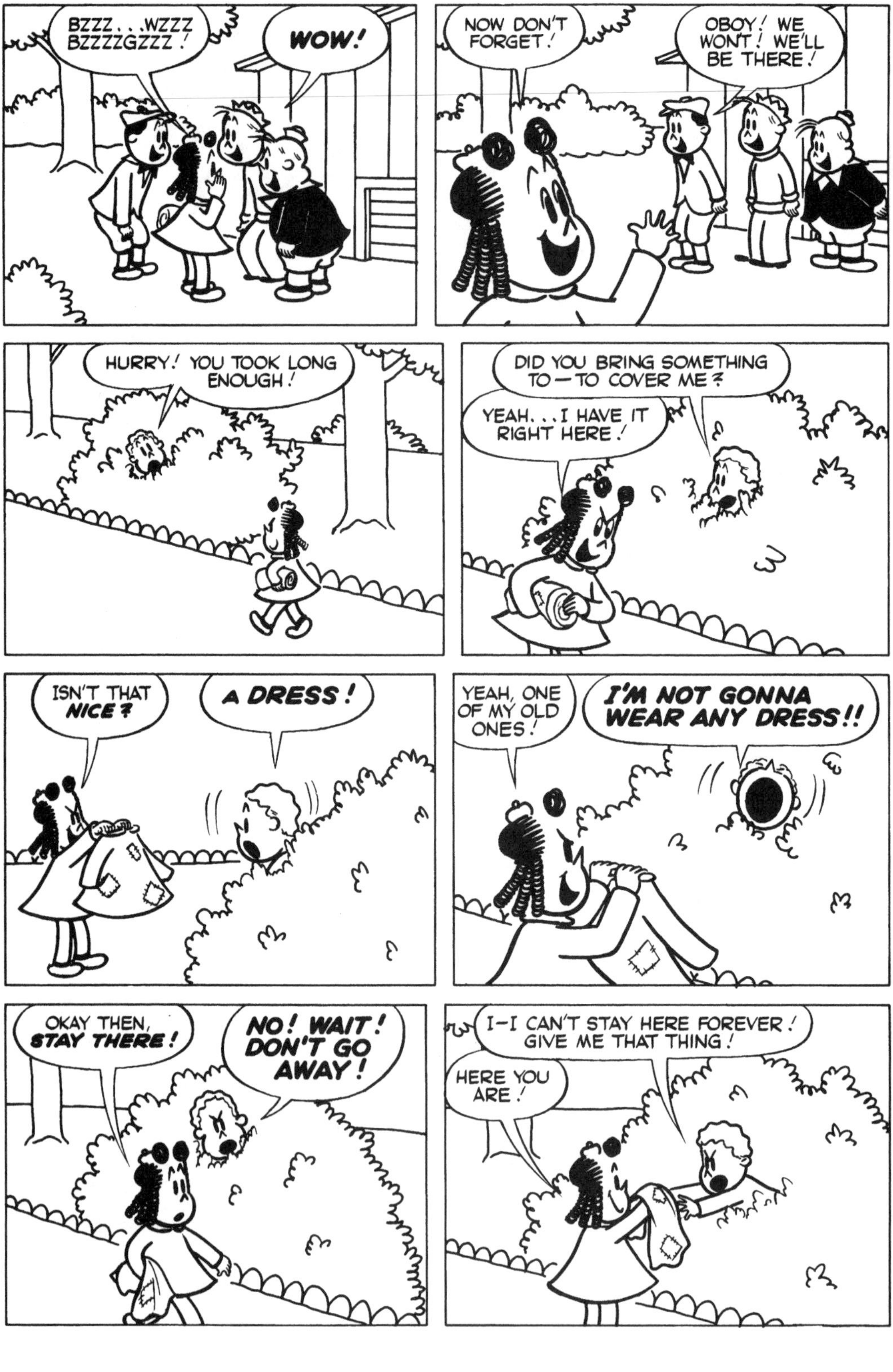

BZZZ...WZZZ BZZZZGZZZ!
WOW!
NOW DON'T FORGET!
OBOY! WE WON'T! WE'LL BE THERE!
HURRY! YOU TOOK LONG ENOUGH!
DID YOU BRING SOMETHING TO—TO COVER ME?
YEAH...I HAVE IT RIGHT HERE!
ISN'T THAT NICE?
A DRESS!
YEAH, ONE OF MY OLD ONES!
I'M NOT GONNA WEAR ANY DRESS!!
OKAY THEN, STAY THERE!
NO! WAIT! DON'T GO AWAY!
I-I CAN'T STAY HERE FOREVER! GIVE ME THAT THING!
HERE YOU ARE!

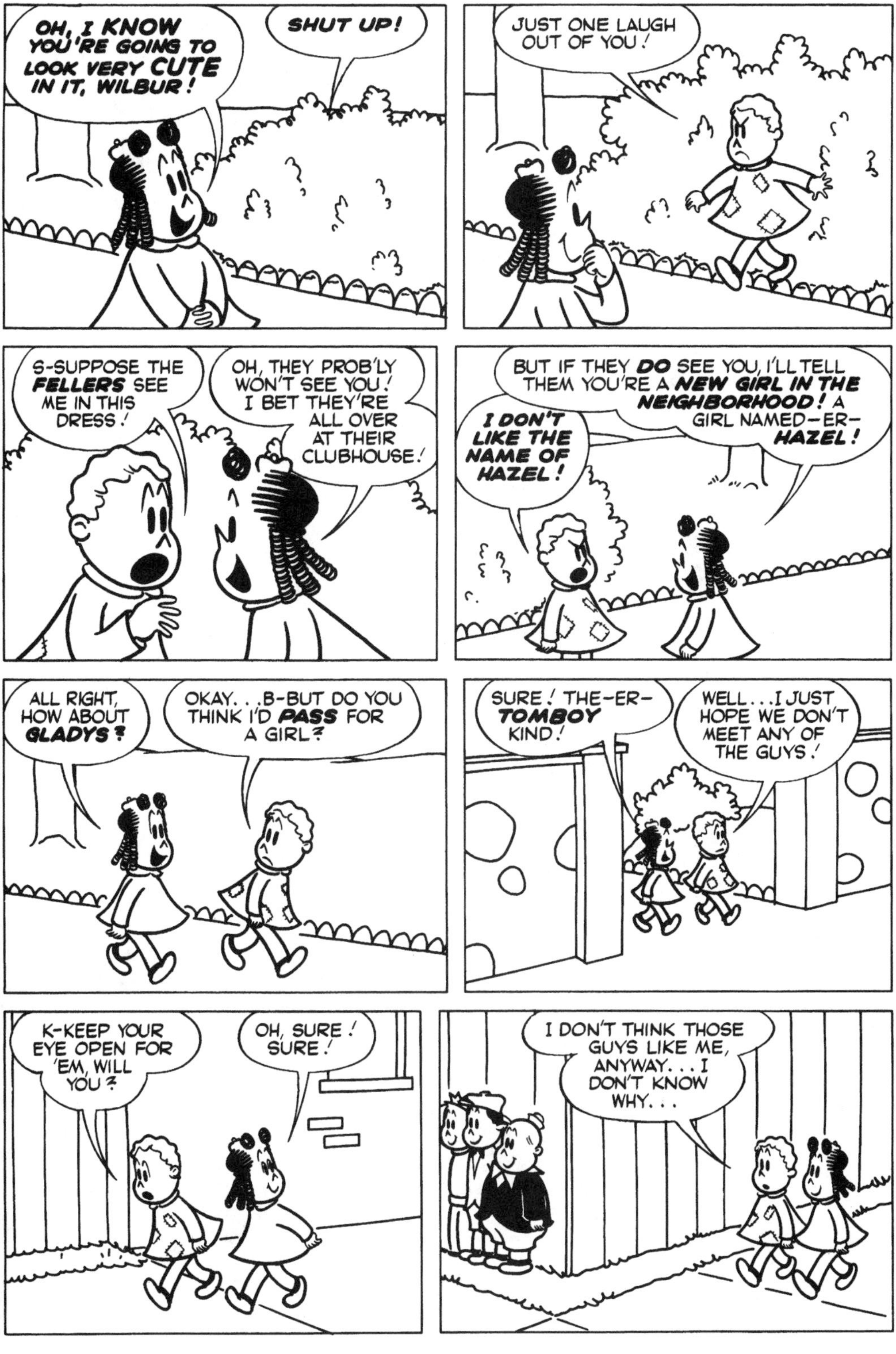
OH, I KNOW YOU'RE GOING TO LOOK VERY CUTE IN IT, WILBUR!
SHUT UP!
JUST ONE LAUGH OUT OF YOU!
S-SUPPOSE THE FELLERS SEE ME IN THIS DRESS!
OH, THEY PROB'LY WON'T SEE YOU! I BET THEY'RE ALL OVER AT THEIR CLUBHOUSE!
BUT IF THEY DO SEE YOU, I'LL TELL THEM YOU'RE A NEW GIRL IN THE NEIGHBORHOOD! A GIRL NAMED—ER—HAZEL!
I DON'T LIKE THE NAME OF HAZEL!
ALL RIGHT, HOW ABOUT GLADYS?
OKAY. . .B-BUT DO YOU THINK I'D PASS FOR A GIRL?
SURE! THE—ER—TOMBOY KIND!
WELL. . .I JUST HOPE WE DON'T MEET ANY OF THE GUYS!
K-KEEP YOUR EYE OPEN FOR 'EM, WILL YOU?
OH, SURE! SURE!
I DON'T THINK THOSE GUYS LIKE ME, ANYWAY. . . I DON'T KNOW WHY. . .

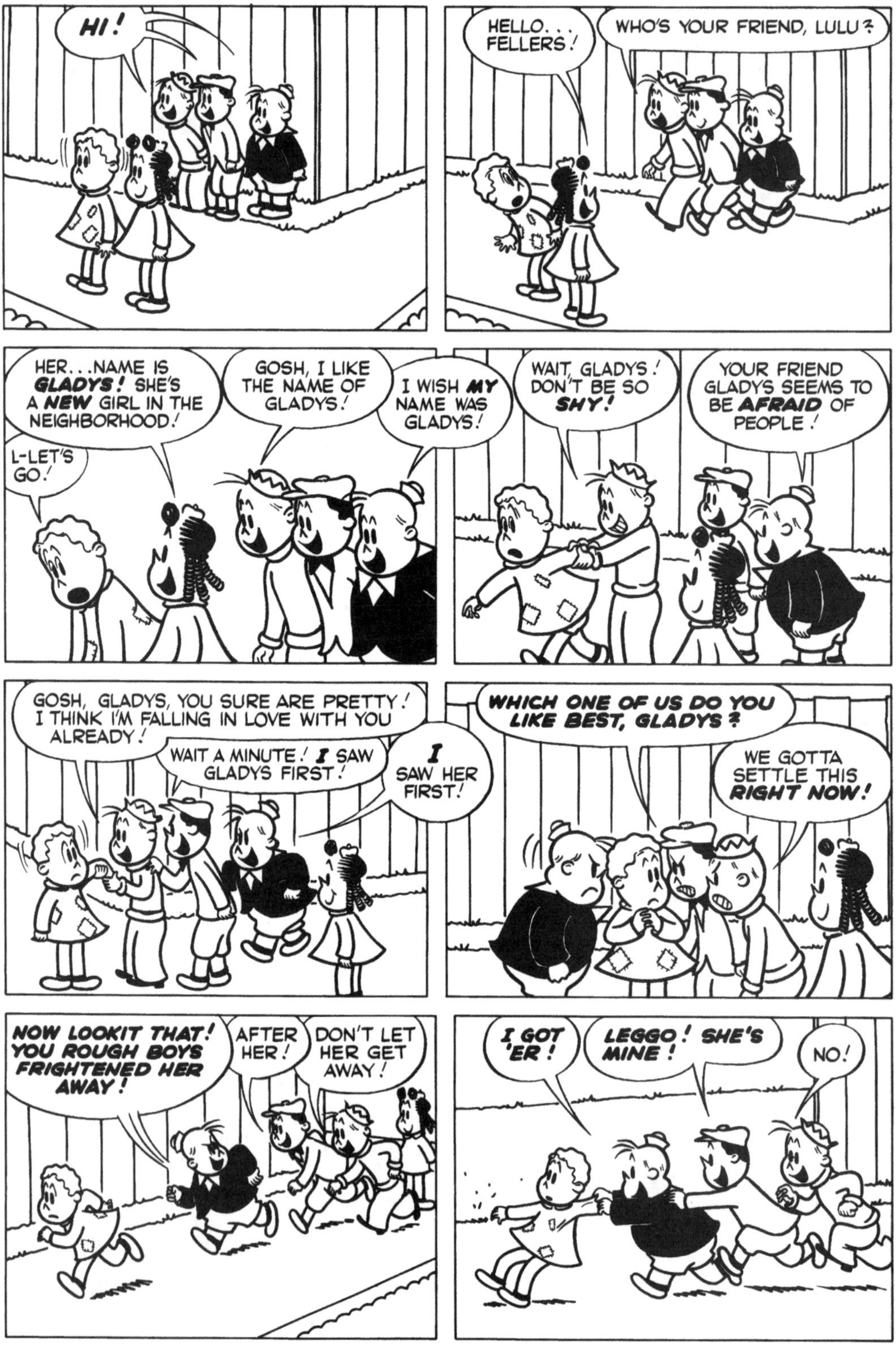
HI!
HELLO... FELLERS!
WHO'S YOUR FRIEND, LULU?
HER...NAME IS GLADYS! SHE'S A NEW GIRL IN THE NEIGHBORHOOD!
L-LET'S GO!
GOSH, I LIKE THE NAME OF GLADYS!
I WISH MY NAME WAS GLADYS!
WAIT, GLADYS! DON'T BE SO SHY!
YOUR FRIEND GLADYS SEEMS TO BE AFRAID OF PEOPLE!
GOSH, GLADYS, YOU SURE ARE PRETTY! I THINK I'M FALLING IN LOVE WITH YOU ALREADY!
WAIT A MINUTE! I SAW GLADYS FIRST!
I SAW HER FIRST!
WHICH ONE OF US DO YOU LIKE BEST, GLADYS?
WE GOTTA SETTLE THIS RIGHT NOW!
NOW LOOKIT THAT! YOU ROUGH BOYS FRIGHTENED HER AWAY!
AFTER HER!
DON'T LET HER GET AWAY!
I GOT 'ER!
LEGGO! SHE'S MINE!
NO!

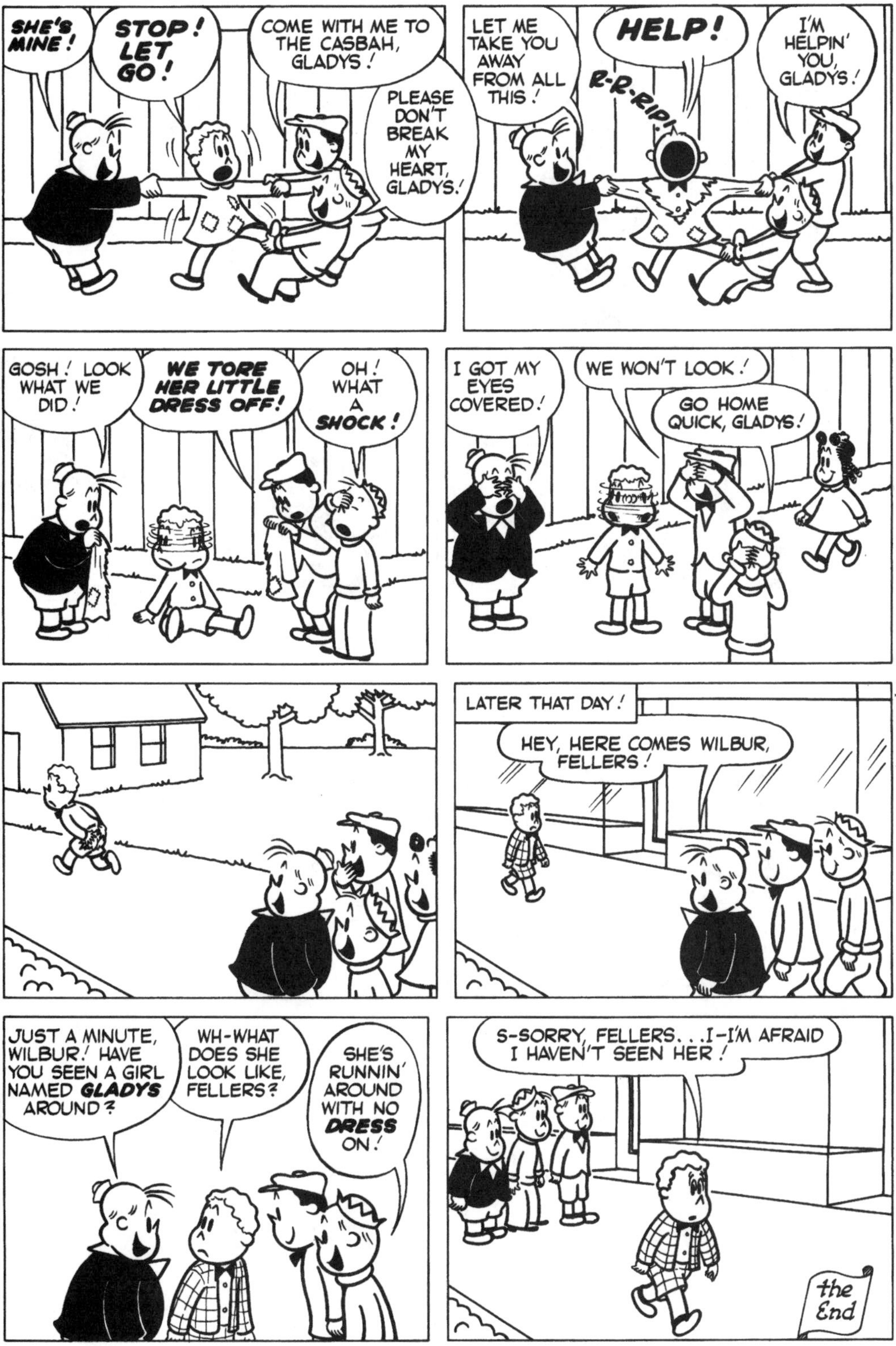
SHE'S MINE!
STOP! LET GO!
COME WITH ME TO THE CASBAH, GLADYS!
PLEASE DON'T BREAK MY HEART, GLADYS!
LET ME TAKE YOU AWAY FROM ALL THIS!
HELP!
R-R-RIP!
I'M HELPIN' YOU, GLADYS!
GOSH! LOOK WHAT WE DID!
WE TORE HER LITTLE DRESS OFF!
OH! WHAT A SHOCK!
I GOT MY EYES COVERED!
WE WON'T LOOK!
GO HOME QUICK, GLADYS!
LATER THAT DAY!
HEY, HERE COMES WILBUR, FELLERS!
JUST A MINUTE, WILBUR! HAVE YOU SEEN A GIRL NAMED GLADYS AROUND?
WH-WHAT DOES SHE LOOK LIKE, FELLERS?
SHE'S RUNNIN' AROUND WITH NO DRESS ON!
S-SORRY, FELLERS...I-I'M AFRAID I HAVEN'T SEEN HER!
the End

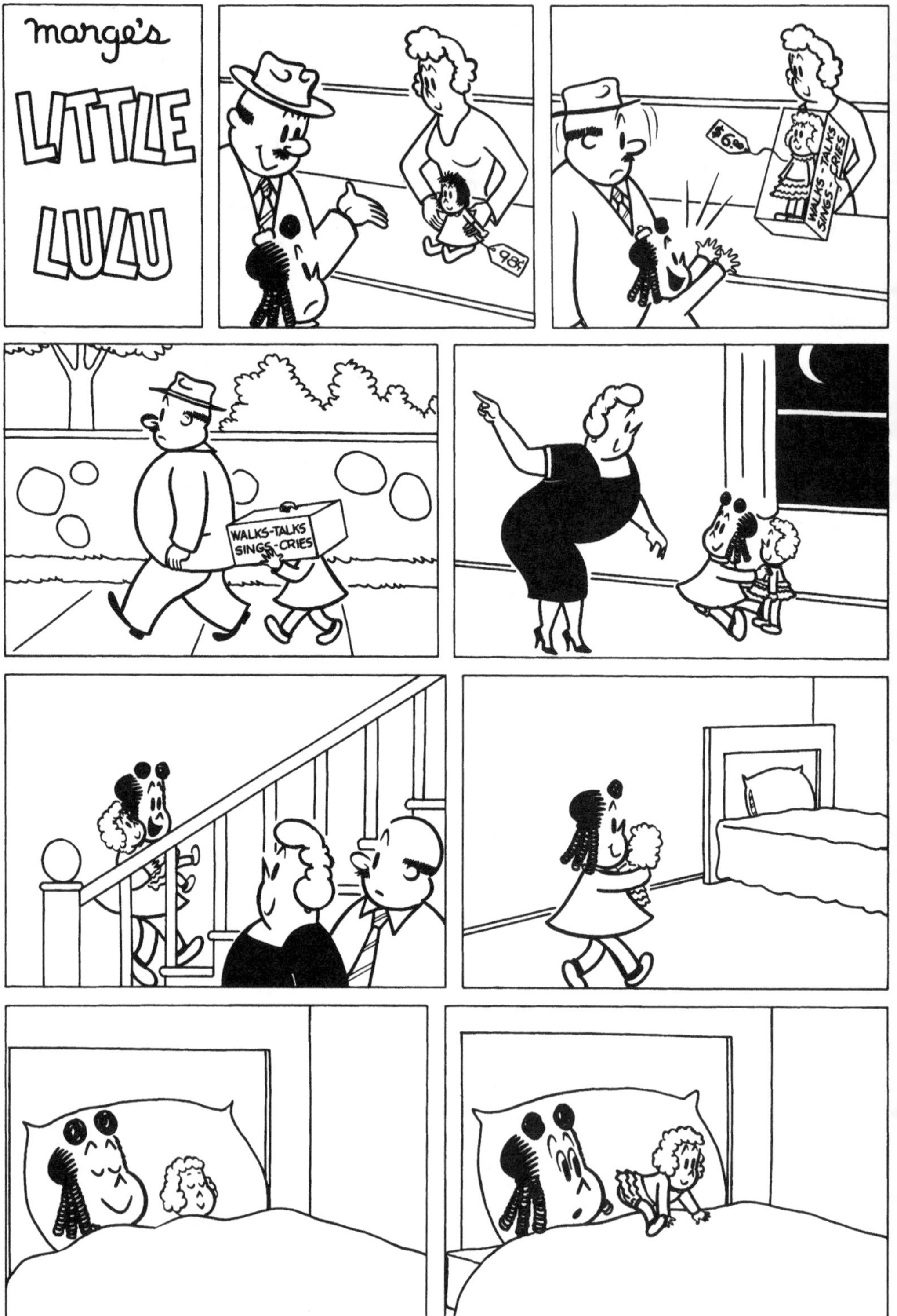
marge's
LITTLE
LULU
98¢
$6.00
WALKS - TALKS
SINGS - CRIES
WALKS-TALKS
SINGS-CRIES

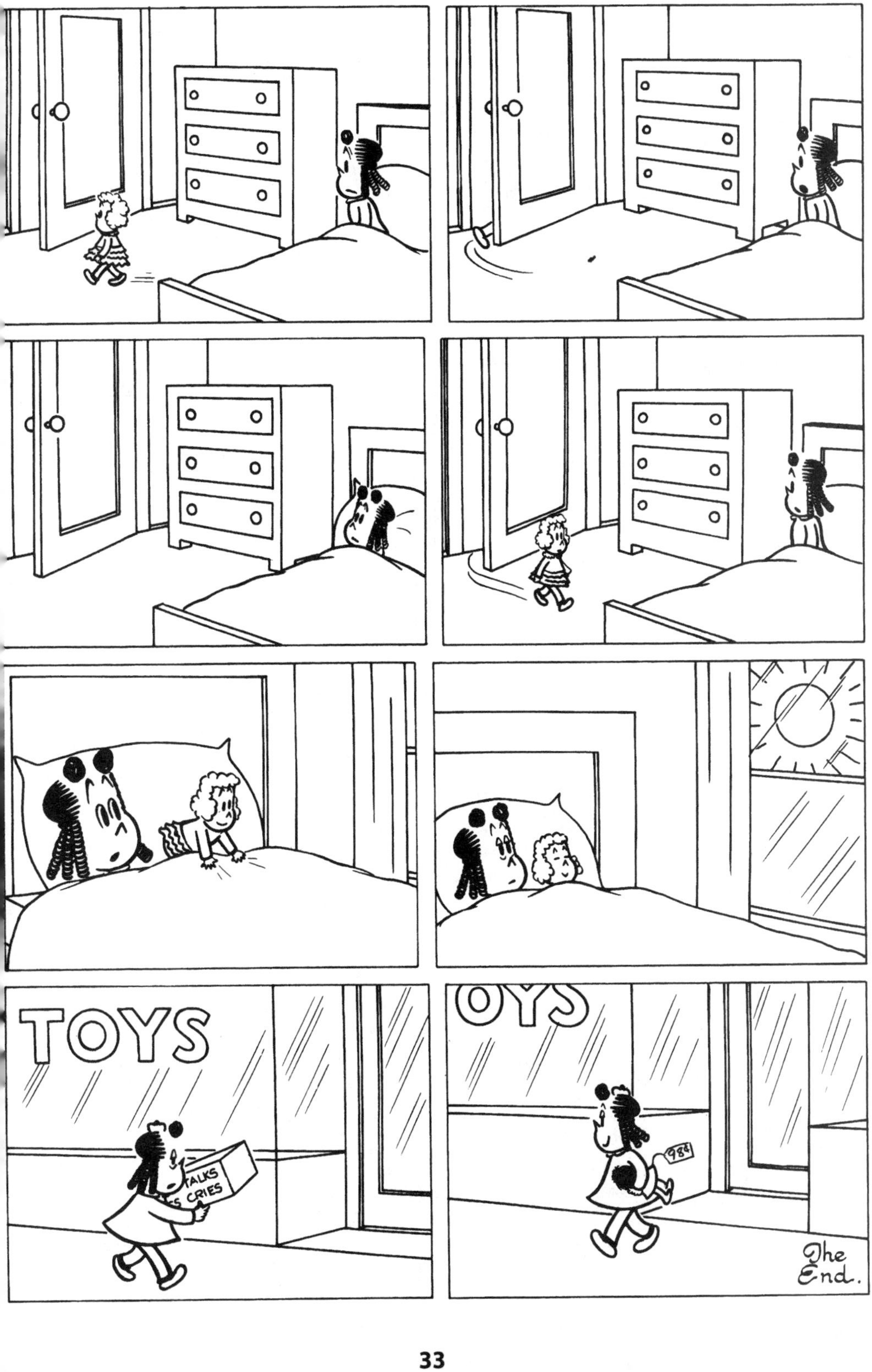
TOYS
TALKS
CRIES
OYS
98¢
The End.

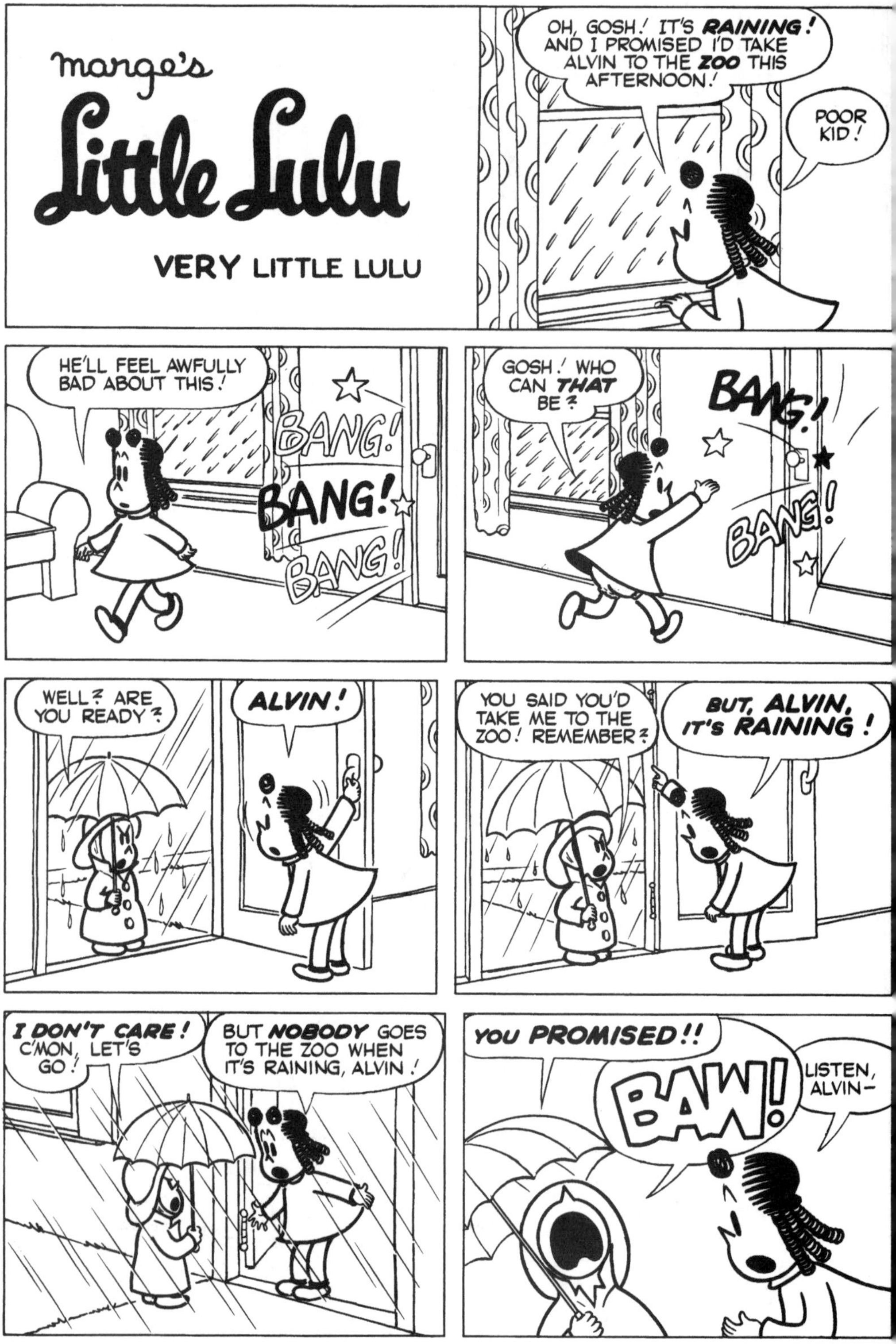
marge's
Little Lulu
VERY LITTLE LULU
OH, GOSH! IT'S RAINING! AND I PROMISED I'D TAKE ALVIN TO THE ZOO THIS AFTERNOON!
POOR KID!
HE'LL FEEL AWFULLY BAD ABOUT THIS!
BANG!
BANG!
BANG!
GOSH! WHO CAN THAT BE?
BANG!
BANG!
WELL? ARE YOU READY?
ALVIN!
YOU SAID YOU'D TAKE ME TO THE ZOO! REMEMBER?
BUT, ALVIN, IT'S RAINING!
I DON'T CARE! C'MON, LET'S GO!
BUT NOBODY GOES TO THE ZOO WHEN IT'S RAINING, ALVIN!
YOU PROMISED!!
BAW!
LISTEN, ALVIN—

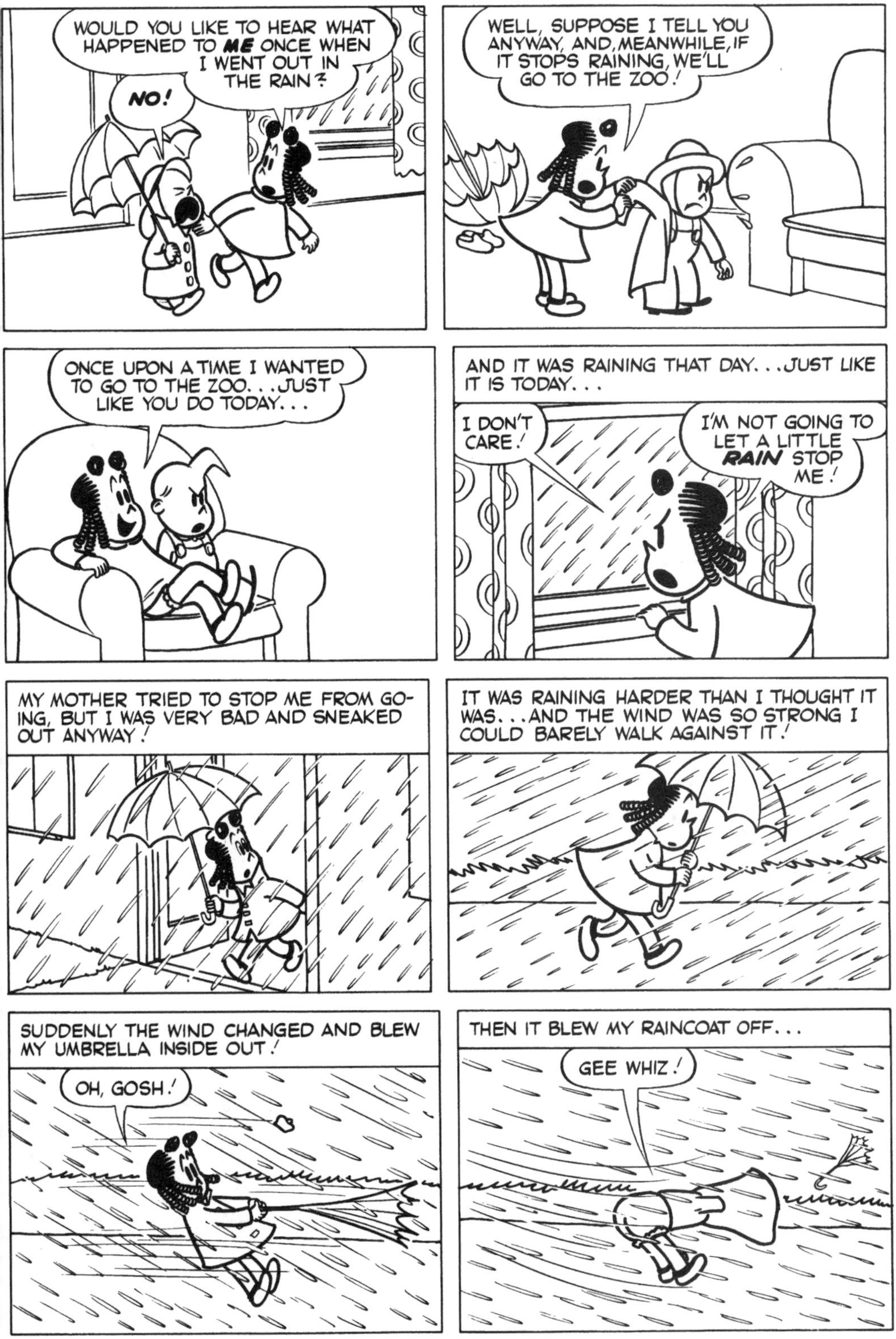
WOULD YOU LIKE TO HEAR WHAT HAPPENED TO ME ONCE WHEN I WENT OUT IN THE RAIN?
NO!
WELL, SUPPOSE I TELL YOU ANYWAY, AND, MEANWHILE, IF IT STOPS RAINING, WE'LL GO TO THE ZOO!
ONCE UPON A TIME I WANTED TO GO TO THE ZOO...JUST LIKE YOU DO TODAY...
AND IT WAS RAINING THAT DAY...JUST LIKE IT IS TODAY...
I DON'T CARE!
I'M NOT GOING TO LET A LITTLE RAIN STOP ME!
MY MOTHER TRIED TO STOP ME FROM GOING, BUT I WAS VERY BAD AND SNEAKED OUT ANYWAY!
IT WAS RAINING HARDER THAN I THOUGHT IT WAS...AND THE WIND WAS SO STRONG I COULD BARELY WALK AGAINST IT!
SUDDENLY THE WIND CHANGED AND BLEW MY UMBRELLA INSIDE OUT!
OH, GOSH!
THEN IT BLEW MY RAINCOAT OFF...
GEE WHIZ!

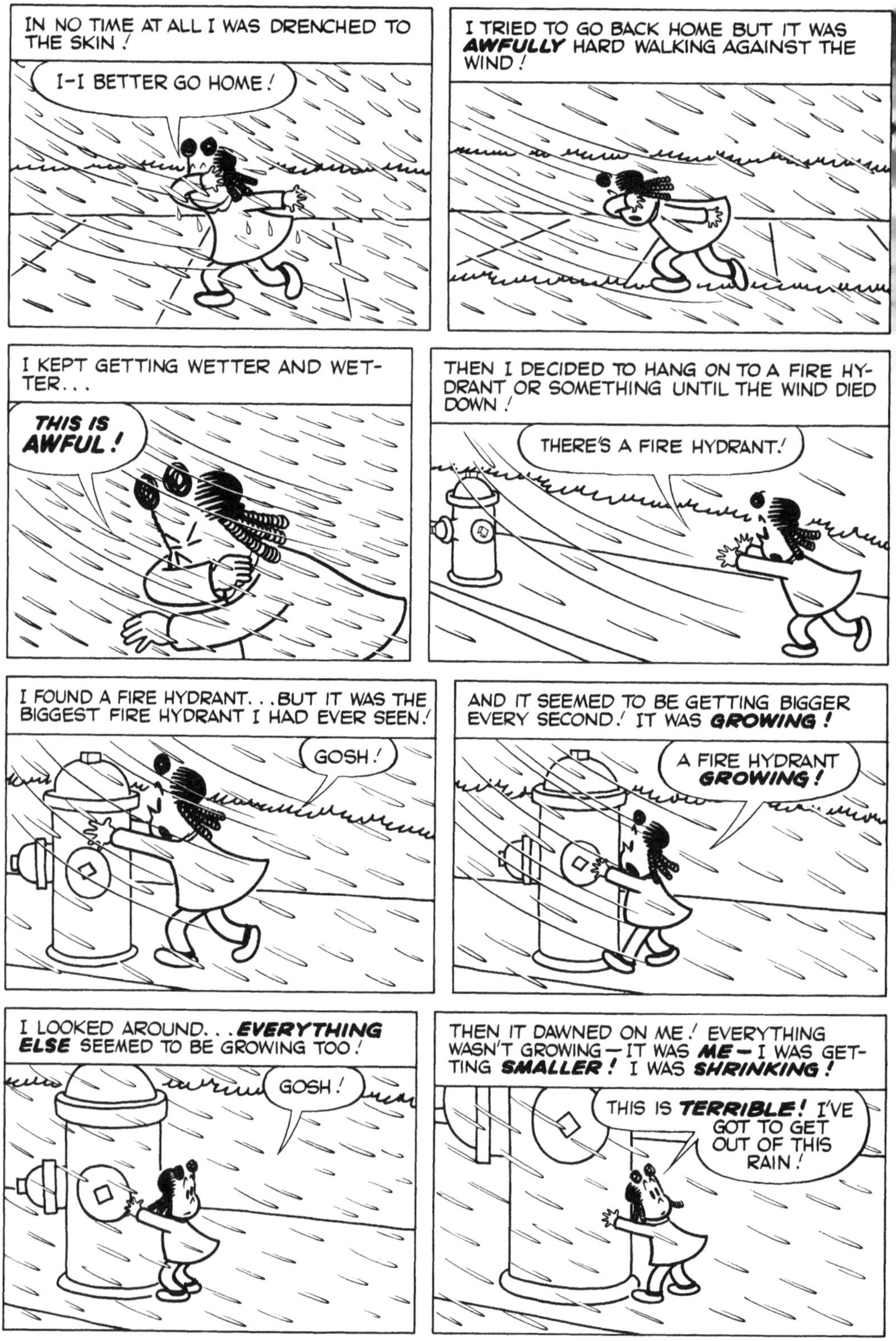
IN NO TIME AT ALL I WAS DRENCHED TO THE SKIN!
I-I BETTER GO HOME!
I TRIED TO GO BACK HOME BUT IT WAS AWFULLY HARD WALKING AGAINST THE WIND!
I KEPT GETTING WETTER AND WETTER...
THIS IS AWFUL!
THEN I DECIDED TO HANG ON TO A FIRE HYDRANT OR SOMETHING UNTIL THE WIND DIED DOWN!
THERE'S A FIRE HYDRANT!
I FOUND A FIRE HYDRANT...BUT IT WAS THE BIGGEST FIRE HYDRANT I HAD EVER SEEN!
GOSH!
AND IT SEEMED TO BE GETTING BIGGER EVERY SECOND! IT WAS GROWING!
A FIRE HYDRANT GROWING!
I LOOKED AROUND...EVERYTHING ELSE SEEMED TO BE GROWING TOO!
GOSH!
THEN IT DAWNED ON ME! EVERYTHING WASN'T GROWING—IT WAS ME—I WAS GETTING SMALLER! I WAS SHRINKING!
THIS IS TERRIBLE! I'VE GOT TO GET OUT OF THIS RAIN!

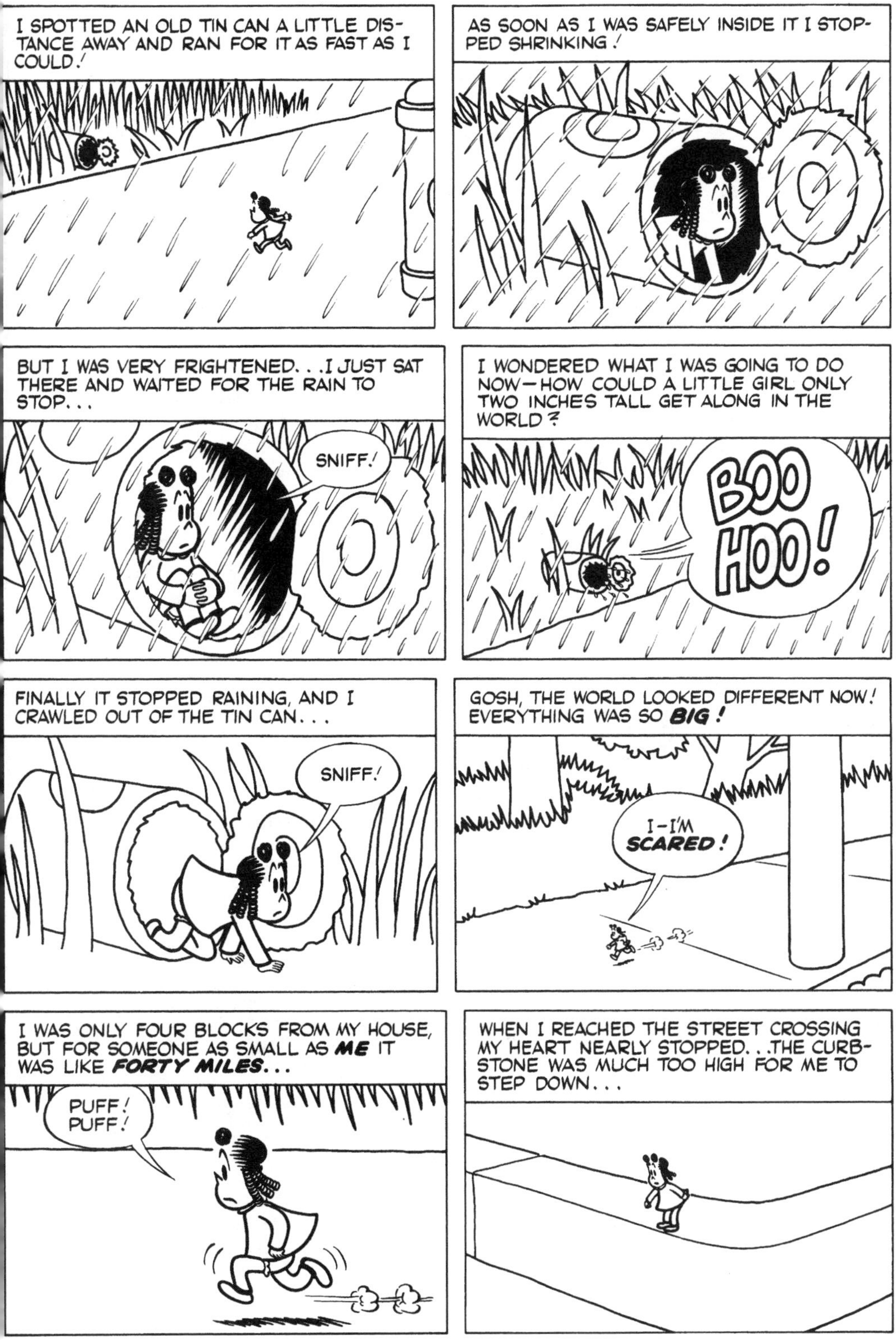
I SPOTTED AN OLD TIN CAN A LITTLE DISTANCE AWAY AND RAN FOR IT AS FAST AS I COULD!
AS SOON AS I WAS SAFELY INSIDE IT I STOPPED SHRINKING!
BUT I WAS VERY FRIGHTENED. . .I JUST SAT THERE AND WAITED FOR THE RAIN TO STOP. . .
SNIFF!
I WONDERED WHAT I WAS GOING TO DO NOW—HOW COULD A LITTLE GIRL ONLY TWO INCHES TALL GET ALONG IN THE WORLD?
BOO HOO!
FINALLY IT STOPPED RAINING, AND I CRAWLED OUT OF THE TIN CAN. . .
SNIFF!
GOSH, THE WORLD LOOKED DIFFERENT NOW! EVERYTHING WAS SO **BIG**!
I-I'M **SCARED**!
I WAS ONLY FOUR BLOCKS FROM MY HOUSE, BUT FOR SOMEONE AS SMALL AS **ME** IT WAS LIKE **FORTY MILES**. . .
PUFF! PUFF!
WHEN I REACHED THE STREET CROSSING MY HEART NEARLY STOPPED. . .THE CURBSTONE WAS MUCH TOO HIGH FOR ME TO STEP DOWN. . .

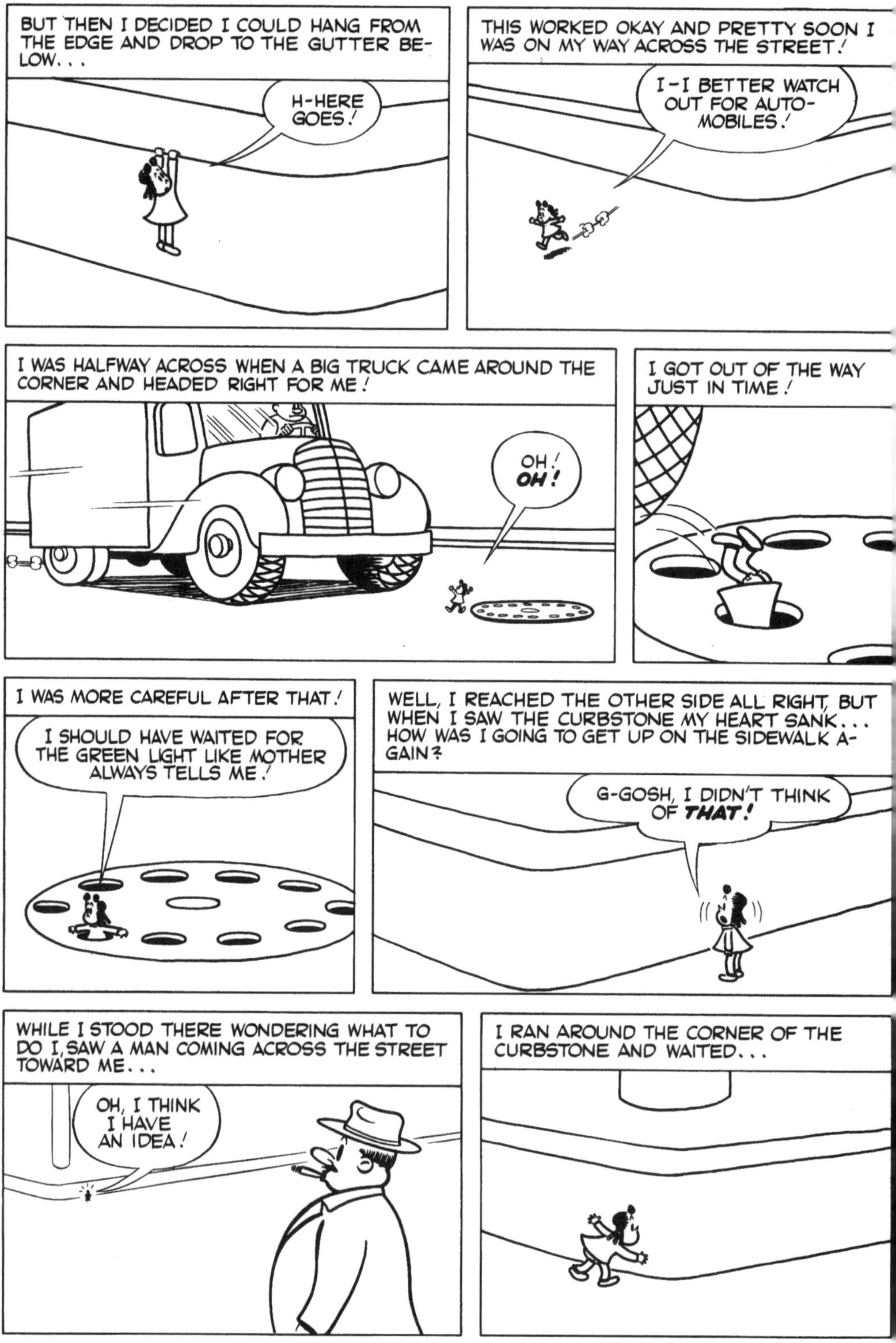
BUT THEN I DECIDED I COULD HANG FROM THE EDGE AND DROP TO THE GUTTER BE-LOW. . .
H-HERE GOES!
THIS WORKED OKAY AND PRETTY SOON I WAS ON MY WAY ACROSS THE STREET!
I-I BETTER WATCH OUT FOR AUTO-MOBILES!
I WAS HALFWAY ACROSS WHEN A BIG TRUCK CAME AROUND THE CORNER AND HEADED RIGHT FOR ME!
OH! OH!
I GOT OUT OF THE WAY JUST IN TIME!
I WAS MORE CAREFUL AFTER THAT!
I SHOULD HAVE WAITED FOR THE GREEN LIGHT LIKE MOTHER ALWAYS TELLS ME!
WELL, I REACHED THE OTHER SIDE ALL RIGHT, BUT WHEN I SAW THE CURBSTONE MY HEART SANK . . . HOW WAS I GOING TO GET UP ON THE SIDEWALK A-GAIN?
G-GOSH, I DIDN'T THINK OF THAT!
WHILE I STOOD THERE WONDERING WHAT TO DO I, SAW A MAN COMING ACROSS THE STREET TOWARD ME . . .
OH, I THINK I HAVE AN IDEA!
I RAN AROUND THE CORNER OF THE CURBSTONE AND WAITED . . .

JUST AS THE MAN WAS ABOUT TO STEP UP ON THE SIDEWALK, I RAN OVER AND JUMPED INTO THE CUFF OF HIS PANTS!

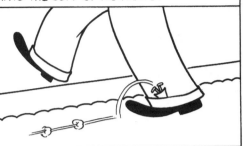

I WAS GOING TO JUMP OUT AGAIN WHEN HE WAS UP ON THE SIDEWALK, BUT I DECIDED I'D RIDE ALONG LIKE THAT FOR A WHILE...

...AS LONG AS HE'S GOING IN MY DIRECTION!

AT THE NEXT CORNER HE TURNED OFF AND WALKED IN ANOTHER DIRECTION...

UH-OH! HERE'S WHERE I GET OFF!

I WAS STILL MORE THAN THREE BLOCKS FROM HOME AND IT WAS BEGINNING TO GET DARK...

GOSH, I'LL NEVER MAKE IT BEFORE *NIGHTFALL!*

I WALKED AND WALKED AND IT GOT DARKER AND DARKER!

MEOWR!

THEN I HEARD SOMETHING THAT SCARED ME AWFULLY BAD—A *CAT!*

G-GOSH!

I'D ALWAYS LIKED CATS, BUT THAT WAS WHEN I WAS *BIG*...NOW THAT I WASN'T ANY BIGGER THAN A MOUSE, MAYBE—

HELP!

WELL, I WAS SO SCARED I DECIDED IT WOULD BE SAFER IF I DIDN'T GO ANY FARTHER THAT NIGHT...

I—I'LL FIND SOMEPLACE TO HIDE!

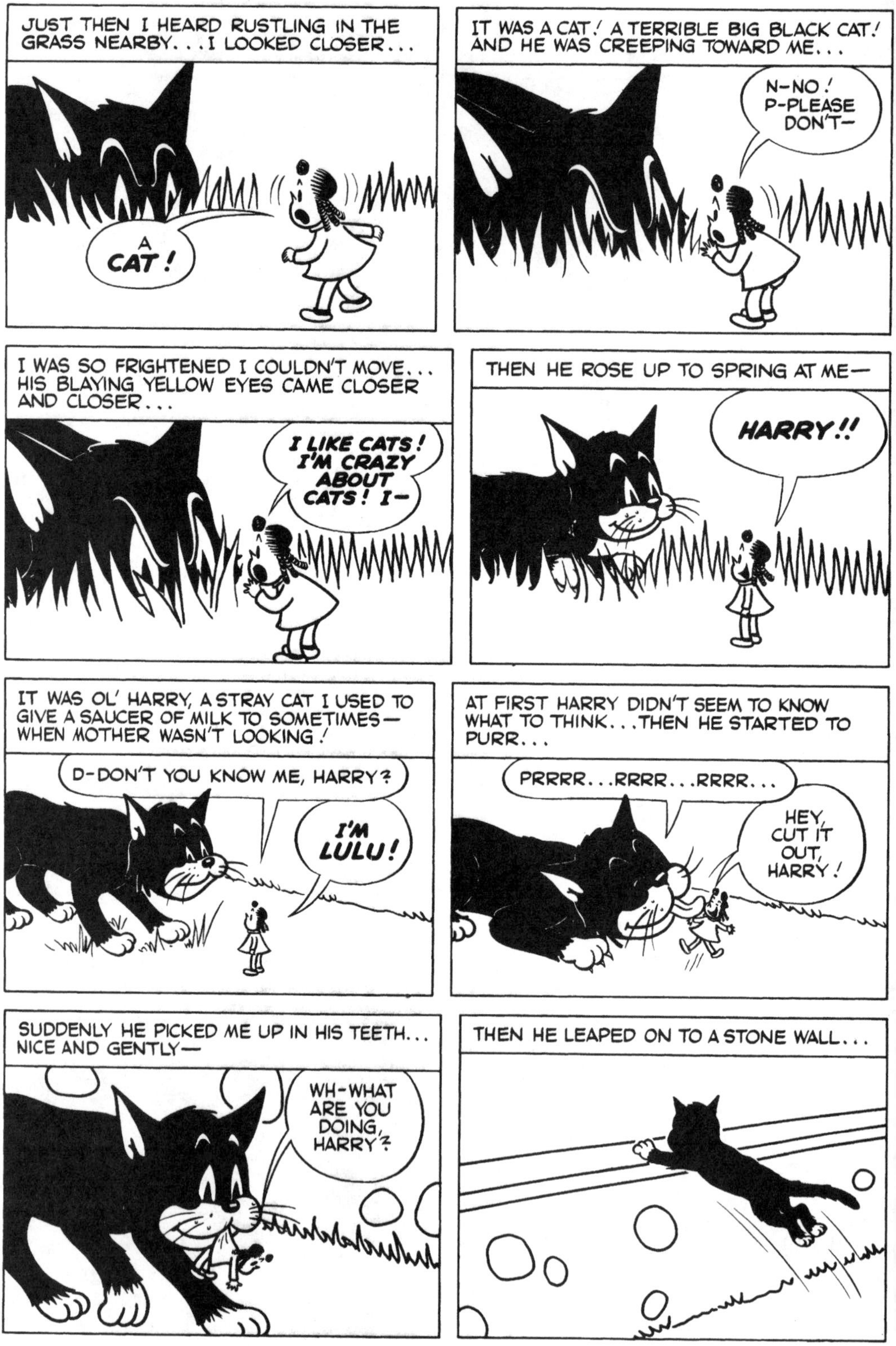
JUST THEN I HEARD RUSTLING IN THE GRASS NEARBY. . . I LOOKED CLOSER. . .
A CAT!
IT WAS A CAT! A TERRIBLE BIG BLACK CAT! AND HE WAS CREEPING TOWARD ME. . .
N-NO! P-PLEASE DON'T—
I WAS SO FRIGHTENED I COULDN'T MOVE. . . HIS BLAYING YELLOW EYES CAME CLOSER AND CLOSER. . .
I LIKE CATS! I'M CRAZY ABOUT CATS! I—
THEN HE ROSE UP TO SPRING AT ME—
HARRY!!
IT WAS OL' HARRY, A STRAY CAT I USED TO GIVE A SAUCER OF MILK TO SOMETIMES—WHEN MOTHER WASN'T LOOKING!
D-DON'T YOU KNOW ME, HARRY?
I'M LULU!
AT FIRST HARRY DIDN'T SEEM TO KNOW WHAT TO THINK. . .THEN HE STARTED TO PURR. . .
PRRRR. . .RRRR. . .RRRR. . .
HEY, CUT IT OUT, HARRY!
SUDDENLY HE PICKED ME UP IN HIS TEETH. . . NICE AND GENTLY—
WH-WHAT ARE YOU DOING, HARRY?
THEN HE LEAPED ON TO A STONE WALL. . .

AFTER THAT I DON'T REMEMBER VERY MUCH, BECAUSE I KEPT MY EYES SHUT TIGHTLY...

I OPENED THEM AGAIN WHEN HARRY DROPPED ME ON THE GROUND!

THERE I WAS RIGHT IN FRONT OF MY *OWN DOOR*! GOSH, I WAS HAPPY!

I SQUEEZED THROUGH THE LITTLE SPACE UNDER THE DOOR AND SHOUTED FOR MOTHER...

MOTHER! MOTHER!

BUT IT WAS LATE, AND MOTHER WAS UP-STAIRS IN BED...

MOTHER! HERE I AM!

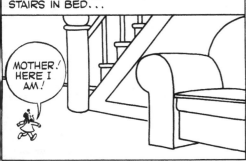

OF COURSE I COULDN'T CLIMB THE STAIRS... I JUST STOOD AT THE FOOT AND HOLLERED UNTIL I WAS HOARSE...

MOTHER! MOTHER!

MOTHER!

BUT MY VOICE WAS JUST AS TINY AS I WAS, AND MOTHER COULDN'T HEAR ME...

MOTHER!

I FELT SO TIRED AND SO LONELY AND SO LITTLE...I FINALLY SAT DOWN AND CRIED...

BAW!

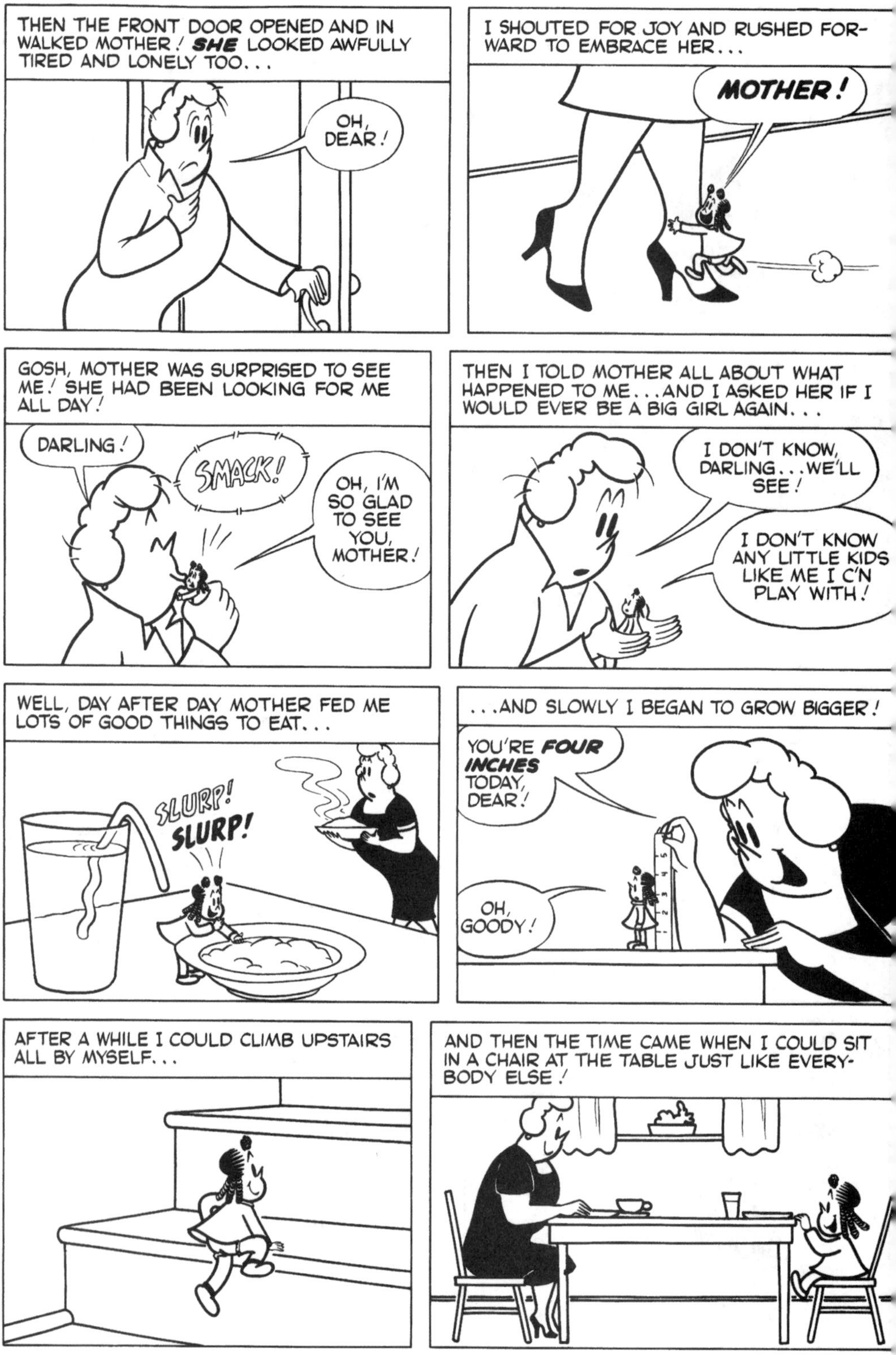
THEN THE FRONT DOOR OPENED AND IN WALKED MOTHER! SHE LOOKED AWFULLY TIRED AND LONELY TOO...
OH, DEAR!
I SHOUTED FOR JOY AND RUSHED FORWARD TO EMBRACE HER...
MOTHER!
GOSH, MOTHER WAS SURPRISED TO SEE ME! SHE HAD BEEN LOOKING FOR ME ALL DAY!
DARLING!
SMACK!
OH, I'M SO GLAD TO SEE YOU, MOTHER!
THEN I TOLD MOTHER ALL ABOUT WHAT HAPPENED TO ME...AND I ASKED HER IF I WOULD EVER BE A BIG GIRL AGAIN...
I DON'T KNOW, DARLING...WE'LL SEE!
I DON'T KNOW ANY LITTLE KIDS LIKE ME I C'N PLAY WITH!
WELL, DAY AFTER DAY MOTHER FED ME LOTS OF GOOD THINGS TO EAT...
SLURP! SLURP!
...AND SLOWLY I BEGAN TO GROW BIGGER!
YOU'RE FOUR INCHES TODAY, DEAR!
OH, GOODY!
AFTER A WHILE I COULD CLIMB UPSTAIRS ALL BY MYSELF...
AND THEN THE TIME CAME WHEN I COULD SIT IN A CHAIR AT THE TABLE JUST LIKE EVERYBODY ELSE!

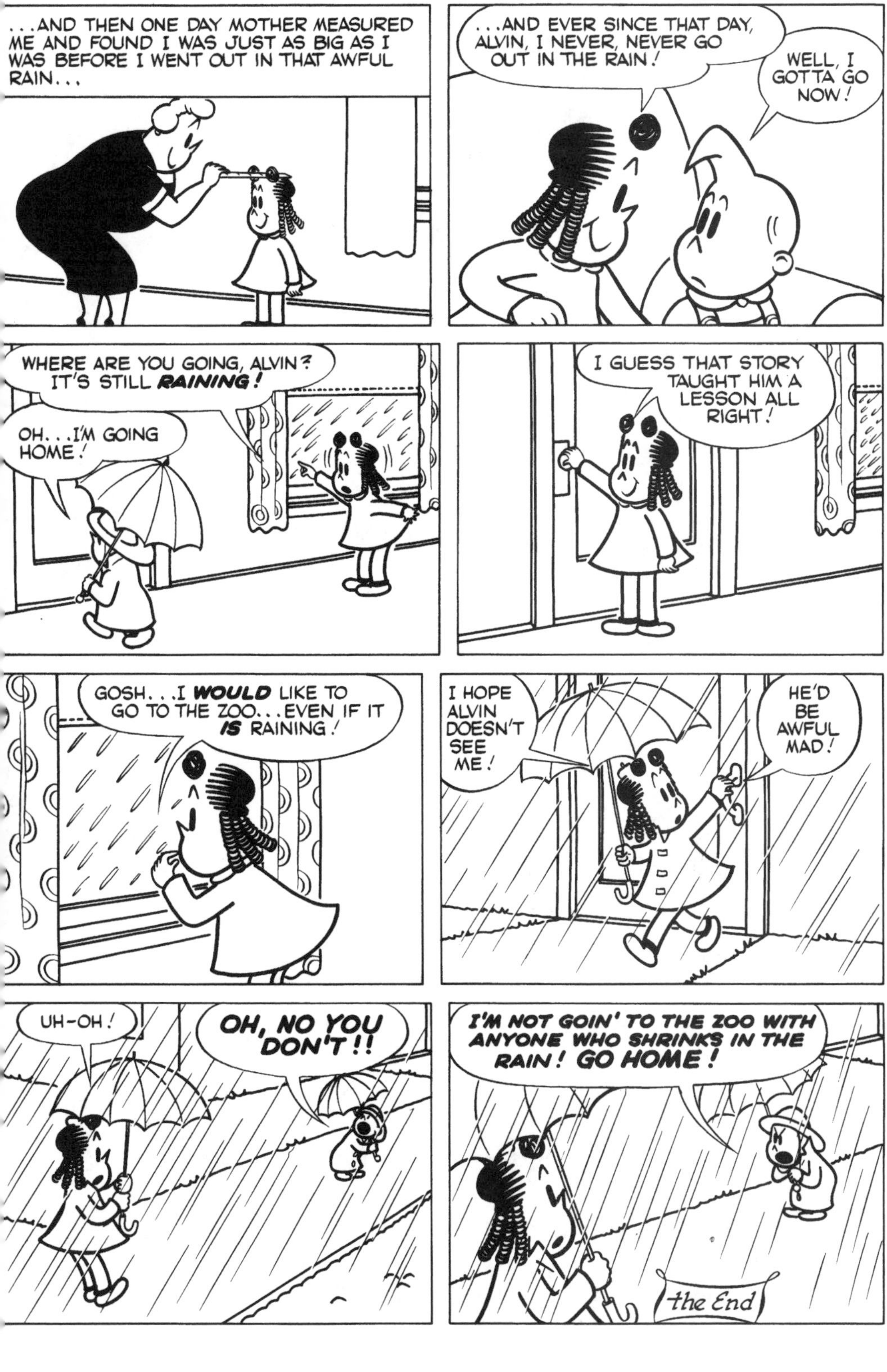
...AND THEN ONE DAY MOTHER MEASURED ME AND FOUND I WAS JUST AS BIG AS I WAS BEFORE I WENT OUT IN THAT AWFUL RAIN...
...AND EVER SINCE THAT DAY, ALVIN, I NEVER, NEVER GO OUT IN THE RAIN!
WELL, I GOTTA GO NOW!
WHERE ARE YOU GOING, ALVIN? IT'S STILL **RAINING!**
OH...I'M GOING HOME!
I GUESS THAT STORY TAUGHT HIM A LESSON ALL RIGHT!
GOSH...I **WOULD** LIKE TO GO TO THE ZOO...EVEN IF IT **IS** RAINING!
I HOPE ALVIN DOESN'T SEE ME!
HE'D BE AWFUL MAD!
UH-OH!
OH, NO YOU DON'T!!
I'M NOT GOIN' TO THE ZOO WITH ANYONE WHO SHRINKS IN THE RAIN! GO HOME!
the End

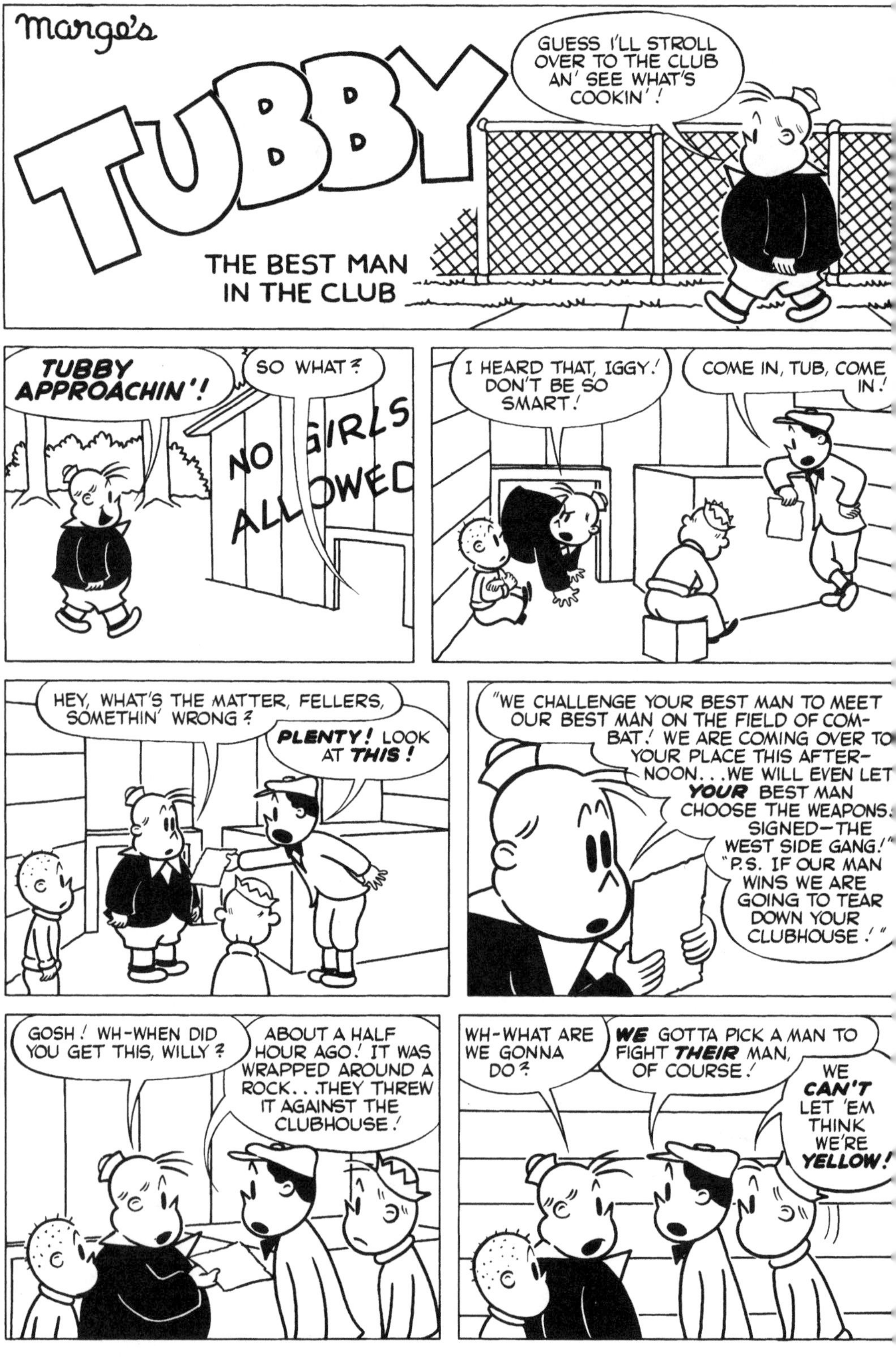
marge's
TUBBY
THE BEST MAN IN THE CLUB
GUESS I'LL STROLL OVER TO THE CLUB AN' SEE WHAT'S COOKIN'!
TUBBY APPROACHIN'!
SO WHAT?
NO GIRLS ALLOWED
I HEARD THAT, IGGY! DON'T BE SO SMART!
COME IN, TUB, COME IN!
HEY, WHAT'S THE MATTER, FELLERS, SOMETHIN' WRONG?
PLENTY! LOOK AT THIS!
"WE CHALLENGE YOUR BEST MAN TO MEET OUR BEST MAN ON THE FIELD OF COMBAT! WE ARE COMING OVER TO YOUR PLACE THIS AFTERNOON...WE WILL EVEN LET YOUR BEST MAN CHOOSE THE WEAPONS. SIGNED—THE WEST SIDE GANG!" "P.S. IF OUR MAN WINS WE ARE GOING TO TEAR DOWN YOUR CLUBHOUSE!"
GOSH! WH-WHEN DID YOU GET THIS, WILLY?
ABOUT A HALF HOUR AGO! IT WAS WRAPPED AROUND A ROCK...THEY THREW IT AGAINST THE CLUBHOUSE!
WH-WHAT ARE WE GONNA DO?
WE GOTTA PICK A MAN TO FIGHT THEIR MAN, OF COURSE!
WE CAN'T LET 'EM THINK WE'RE YELLOW!

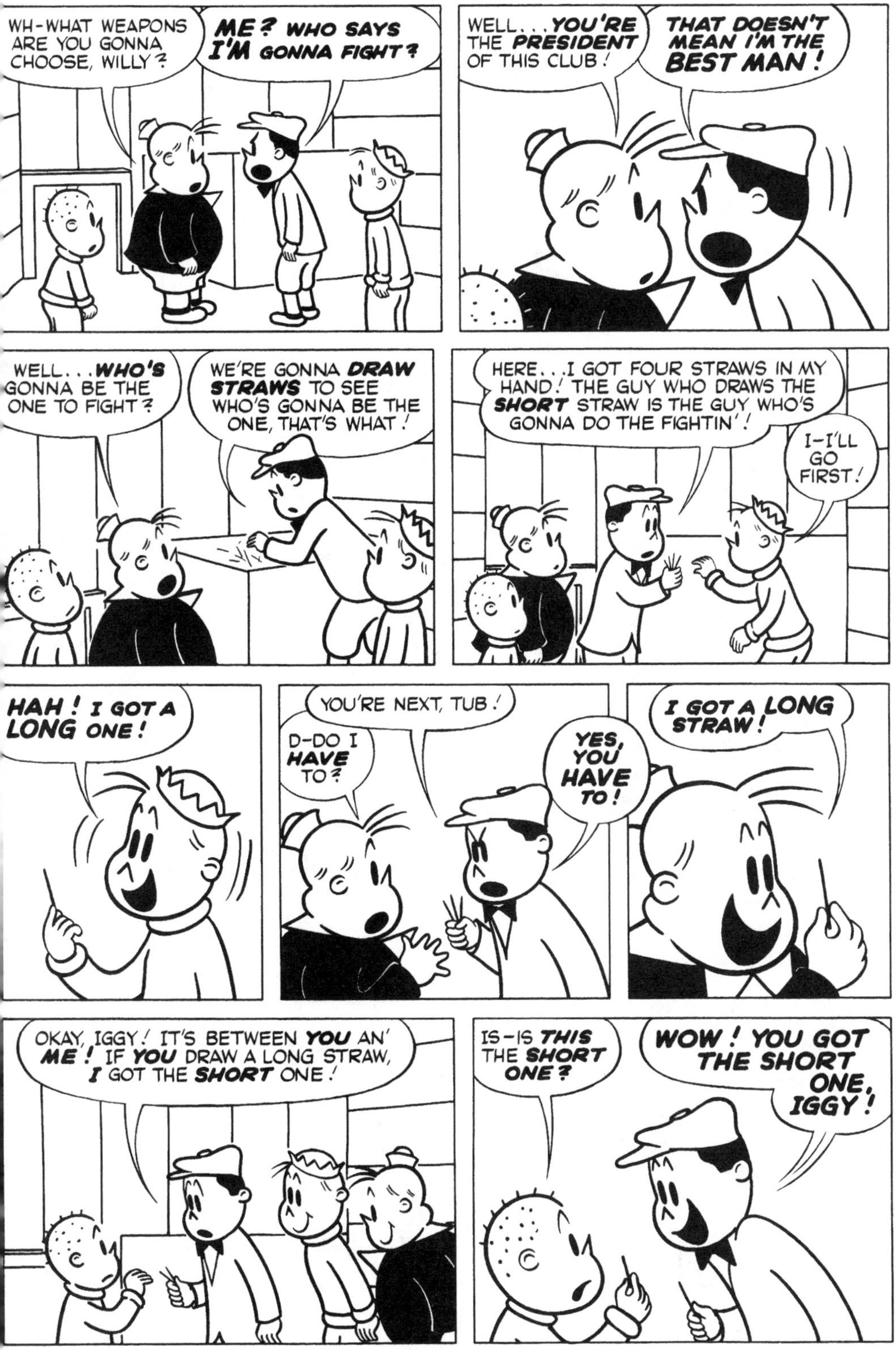
WH-WHAT WEAPONS ARE YOU GONNA CHOOSE, WILLY?
ME? WHO SAYS I'M GONNA FIGHT?
WELL... YOU'RE THE PRESIDENT OF THIS CLUB!
THAT DOESN'T MEAN I'M THE BEST MAN!
WELL... WHO'S GONNA BE THE ONE TO FIGHT?
WE'RE GONNA DRAW STRAWS TO SEE WHO'S GONNA BE THE ONE, THAT'S WHAT!
HERE... I GOT FOUR STRAWS IN MY HAND! THE GUY WHO DRAWS THE SHORT STRAW IS THE GUY WHO'S GONNA DO THE FIGHTIN'!
I-I'LL GO FIRST!
HAH! I GOT A LONG ONE!
YOU'RE NEXT, TUB!
D-DO I HAVE TO?
YES, YOU HAVE TO!
I GOT A LONG STRAW!
OKAY, IGGY! IT'S BETWEEN YOU AN' ME! IF YOU DRAW A LONG STRAW, I GOT THE SHORT ONE!
IS-IS THIS THE SHORT ONE?
WOW! YOU GOT THE SHORT ONE, IGGY!

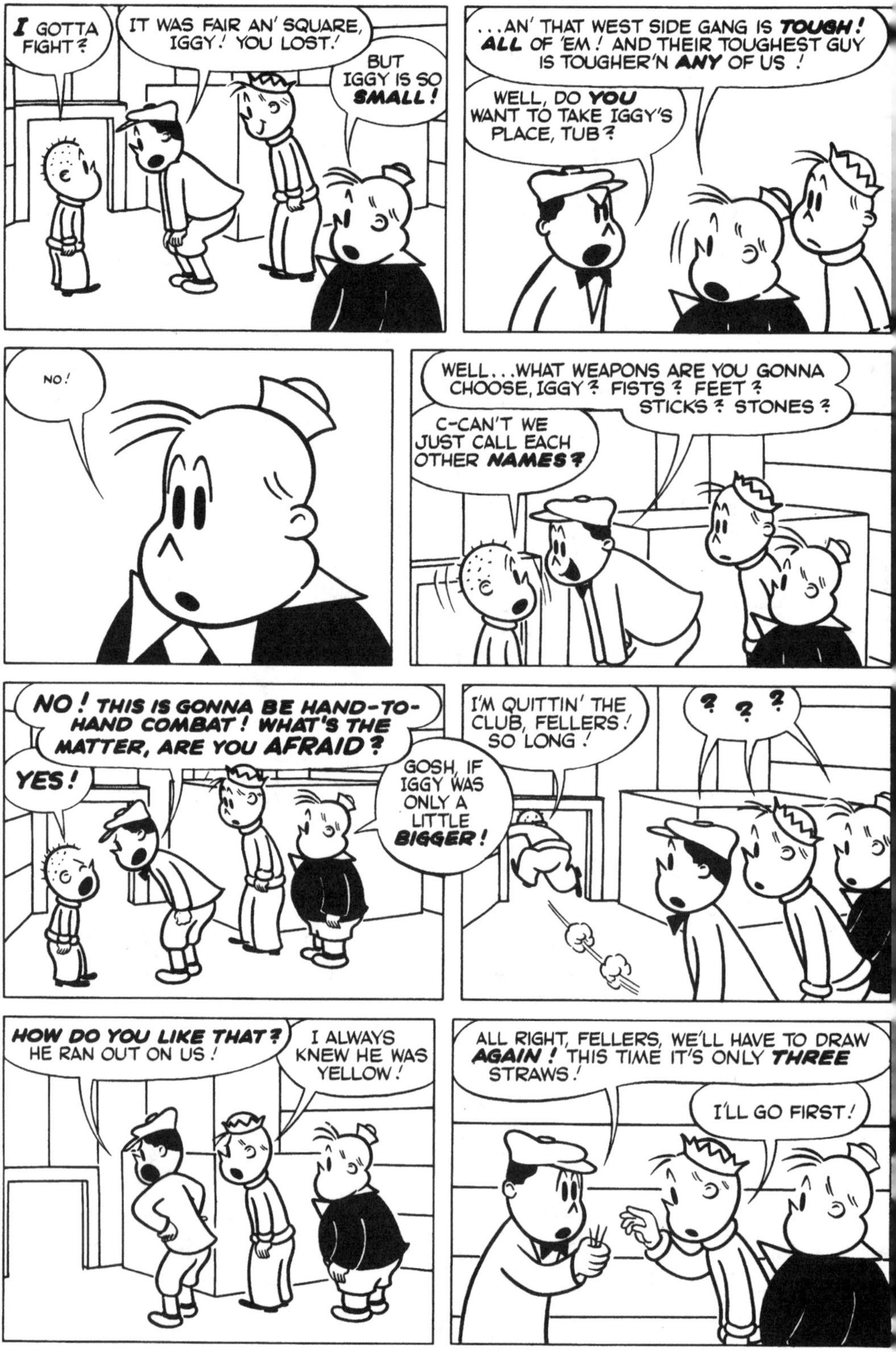
I GOTTA FIGHT?
IT WAS FAIR AN' SQUARE, IGGY! YOU LOST!
BUT IGGY IS SO SMALL!
...AN' THAT WEST SIDE GANG IS TOUGH! ALL OF 'EM! AND THEIR TOUGHEST GUY IS TOUGHER'N ANY OF US!
WELL, DO YOU WANT TO TAKE IGGY'S PLACE, TUB?
NO!
WELL...WHAT WEAPONS ARE YOU GONNA CHOOSE, IGGY? FISTS? FEET? STICKS? STONES?
C-CAN'T WE JUST CALL EACH OTHER NAMES?
NO! THIS IS GONNA BE HAND-TO-HAND COMBAT! WHAT'S THE MATTER, ARE YOU AFRAID?
YES!
GOSH, IF IGGY WAS ONLY A LITTLE BIGGER!
I'M QUITTIN' THE CLUB, FELLERS! SO LONG!
? ? ?
HOW DO YOU LIKE THAT? HE RAN OUT ON US!
I ALWAYS KNEW HE WAS YELLOW!
ALL RIGHT, FELLERS, WE'LL HAVE TO DRAW AGAIN! THIS TIME IT'S ONLY THREE STRAWS!
I'LL GO FIRST!

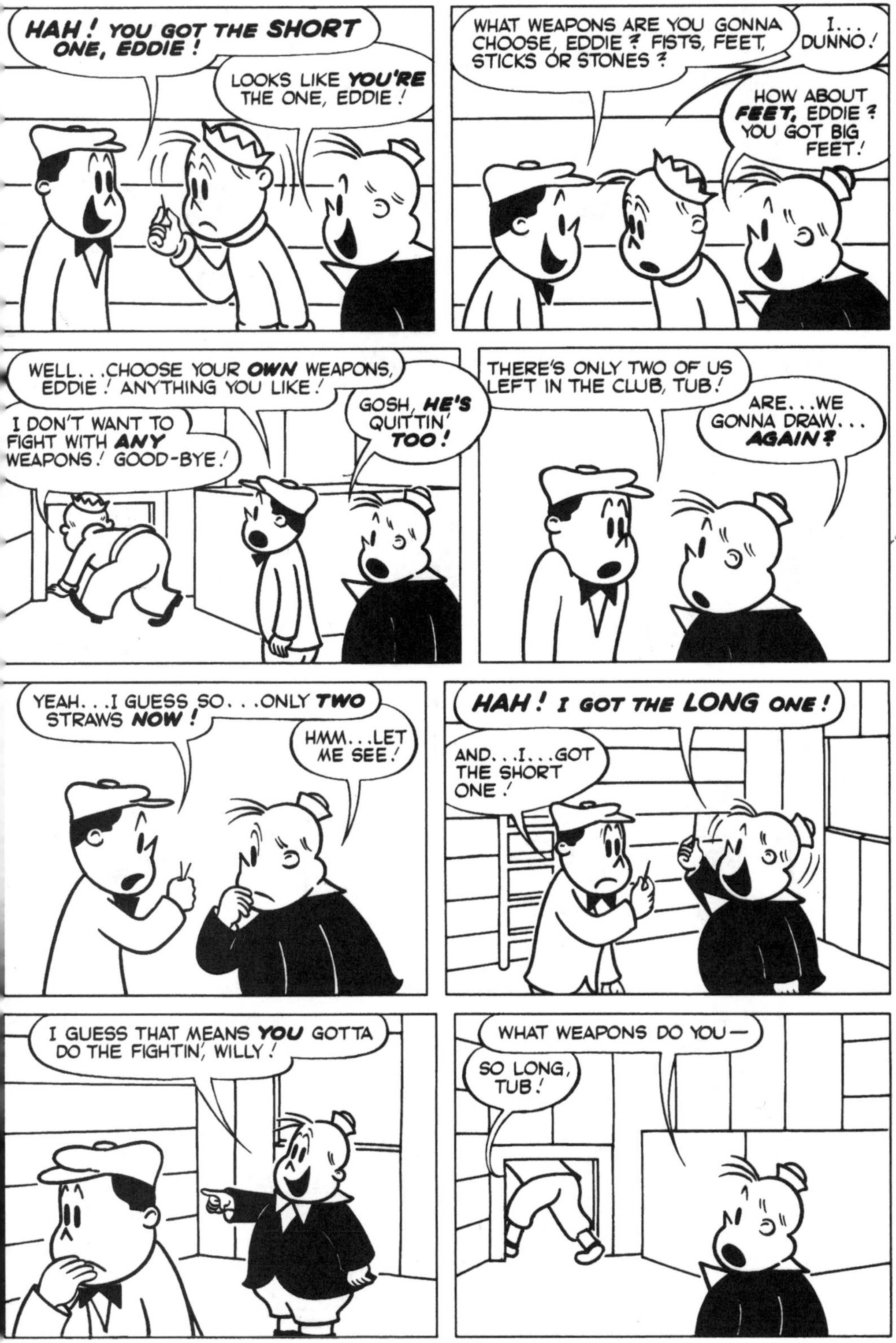
HAH! YOU GOT THE SHORT ONE, EDDIE!
LOOKS LIKE YOU'RE THE ONE, EDDIE!
WHAT WEAPONS ARE YOU GONNA CHOOSE, EDDIE? FISTS, FEET, STICKS OR STONES?
I... DUNNO!
HOW ABOUT FEET, EDDIE? YOU GOT BIG FEET!
WELL...CHOOSE YOUR OWN WEAPONS, EDDIE! ANYTHING YOU LIKE!
I DON'T WANT TO FIGHT WITH ANY WEAPONS! GOOD-BYE!
GOSH, HE'S QUITTIN' TOO!
THERE'S ONLY TWO OF US LEFT IN THE CLUB, TUB!
ARE...WE GONNA DRAW... AGAIN?
YEAH...I GUESS SO...ONLY TWO STRAWS NOW!
HMM...LET ME SEE!
HAH! I GOT THE LONG ONE!
AND...I...GOT THE SHORT ONE!
I GUESS THAT MEANS YOU GOTTA DO THE FIGHTIN', WILLY!
WHAT WEAPONS DO YOU—
SO LONG, TUB!

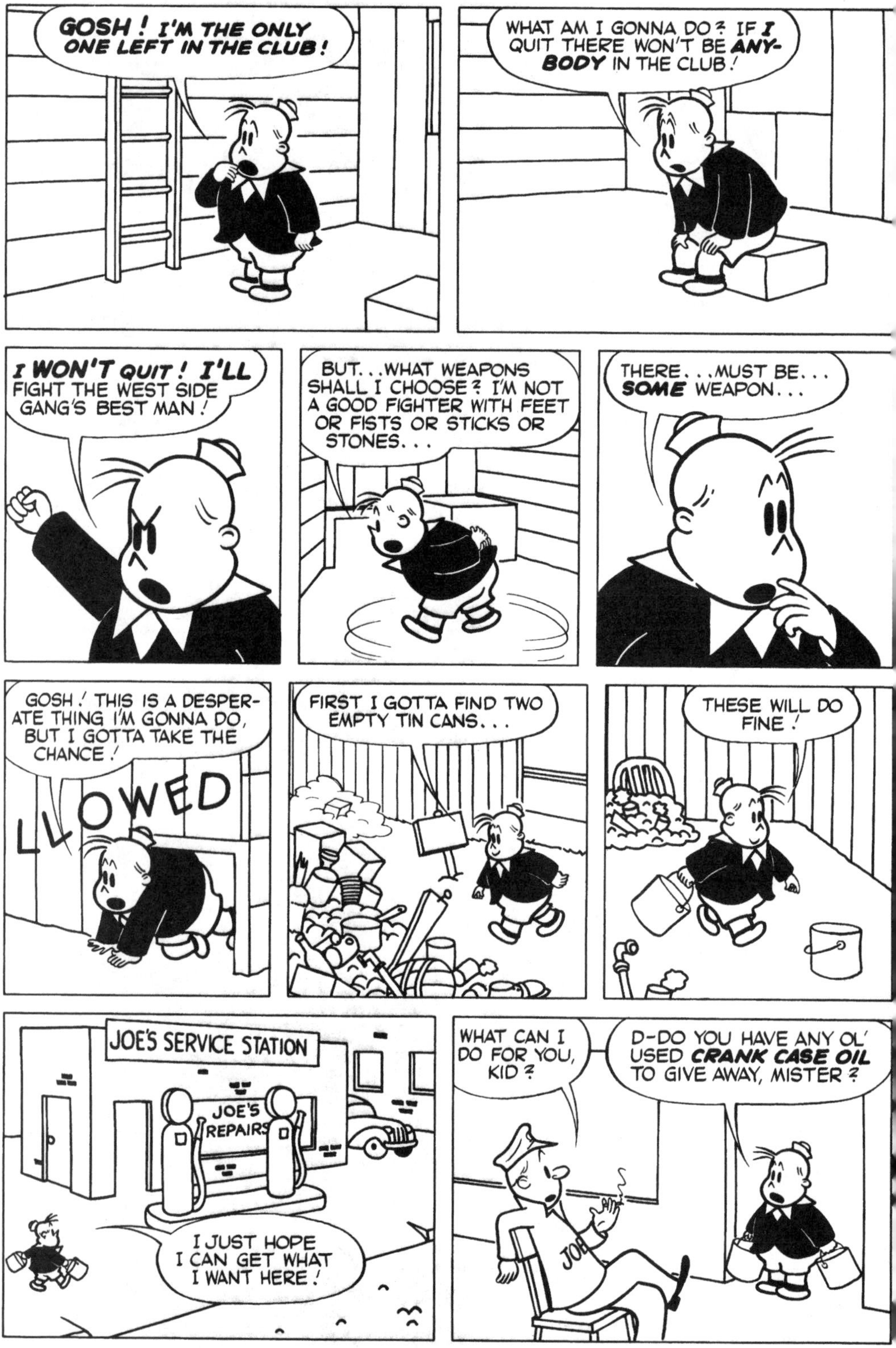
GOSH ! I'M THE ONLY ONE LEFT IN THE CLUB !
WHAT AM I GONNA DO ? IF I QUIT THERE WON'T BE ANYBODY IN THE CLUB !
I WON'T QUIT ! I'LL FIGHT THE WEST SIDE GANG'S BEST MAN !
BUT...WHAT WEAPONS SHALL I CHOOSE ? I'M NOT A GOOD FIGHTER WITH FEET OR FISTS OR STICKS OR STONES...
THERE...MUST BE... SOME WEAPON...
GOSH ! THIS IS A DESPERATE THING I'M GONNA DO, BUT I GOTTA TAKE THE CHANCE !
LLOWED
FIRST I GOTTA FIND TWO EMPTY TIN CANS...
THESE WILL DO FINE !
JOE'S SERVICE STATION
JOE'S REPAIRS
I JUST HOPE I CAN GET WHAT I WANT HERE !
WHAT CAN I DO FOR YOU, KID ?
D-DO YOU HAVE ANY OL' USED CRANK CASE OIL TO GIVE AWAY, MISTER ?
JOE

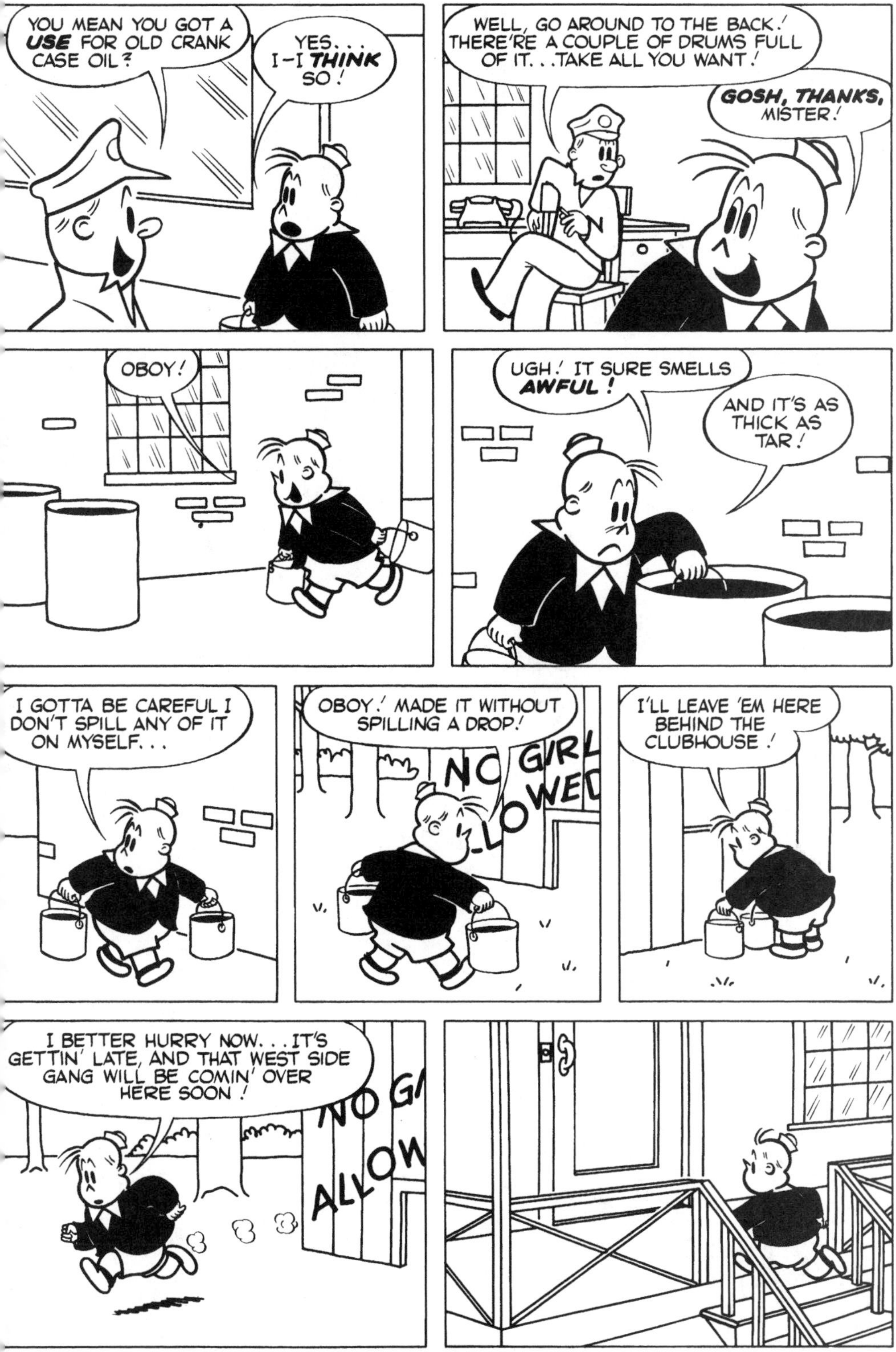
YOU MEAN YOU GOT A USE FOR OLD CRANK CASE OIL?
YES... I-I THINK SO!
WELL, GO AROUND TO THE BACK! THERE'RE A COUPLE OF DRUMS FULL OF IT...TAKE ALL YOU WANT!
GOSH, THANKS, MISTER!
OBOY!
UGH! IT SURE SMELLS AWFUL!
AND IT'S AS THICK AS TAR!
I GOTTA BE CAREFUL I DON'T SPILL ANY OF IT ON MYSELF...
OBOY! MADE IT WITHOUT SPILLING A DROP!
NO GIRL
-LOWED
I'LL LEAVE 'EM HERE BEHIND THE CLUBHOUSE!
I BETTER HURRY NOW...IT'S GETTIN' LATE, AND THAT WEST SIDE GANG WILL BE COMIN' OVER HERE SOON!
NO G
ALLOW

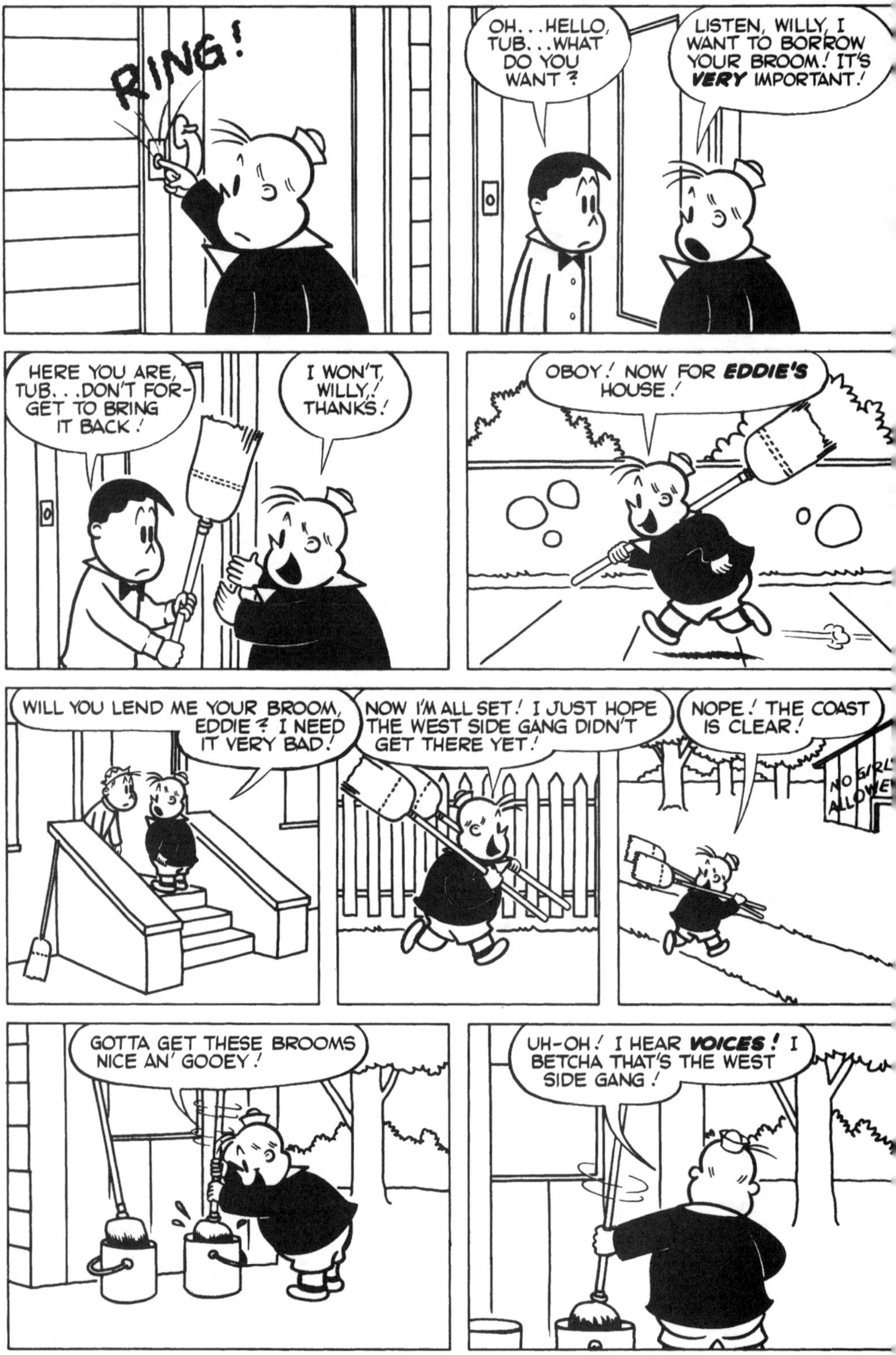
RING!
OH...HELLO, TUB...WHAT DO YOU WANT?
LISTEN, WILLY, I WANT TO BORROW YOUR BROOM! IT'S VERY IMPORTANT!
HERE YOU ARE, TUB...DON'T FORGET TO BRING IT BACK!
I WON'T, WILLY! THANKS!
OBOY! NOW FOR EDDIE'S HOUSE!
WILL YOU LEND ME YOUR BROOM, EDDIE? I NEED IT VERY BAD!
NOW I'M ALL SET! I JUST HOPE THE WEST SIDE GANG DIDN'T GET THERE YET!
NOPE! THE COAST IS CLEAR!
GOTTA GET THESE BROOMS NICE AN' GOOEY!
UH-OH! I HEAR VOICES! I BETCHA THAT'S THE WEST SIDE GANG!

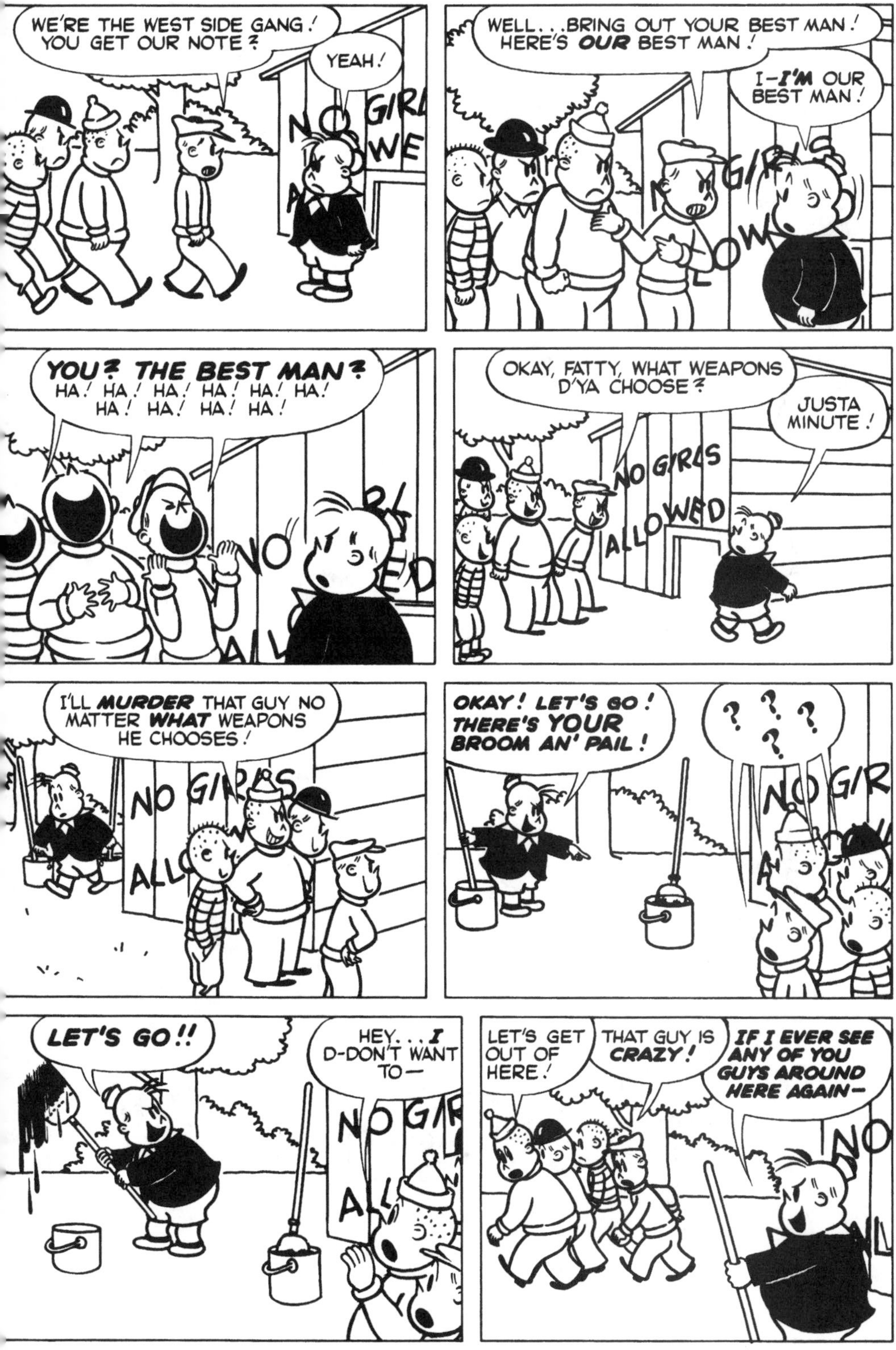
WE'RE THE WEST SIDE GANG! YOU GET OUR NOTE?
YEAH!
WELL...BRING OUT YOUR BEST MAN! HERE'S OUR BEST MAN!
I-I'M OUR BEST MAN!
YOU? THE BEST MAN? HA! HA! HA! HA! HA! HA! HA! HA! HA! HA!
OKAY, FATTY, WHAT WEAPONS D'YA CHOOSE?
JUSTA MINUTE!
NO GIRLS ALLOWED
I'LL MURDER THAT GUY NO MATTER WHAT WEAPONS HE CHOOSES!
OKAY! LET'S GO! THERE'S YOUR BROOM AN' PAIL!
? ? ? ?
LET'S GO!!
HEY...I D-DON'T WANT TO—
LET'S GET OUT OF HERE!
THAT GUY IS CRAZY!
IF I EVER SEE ANY OF YOU GUYS AROUND HERE AGAIN—

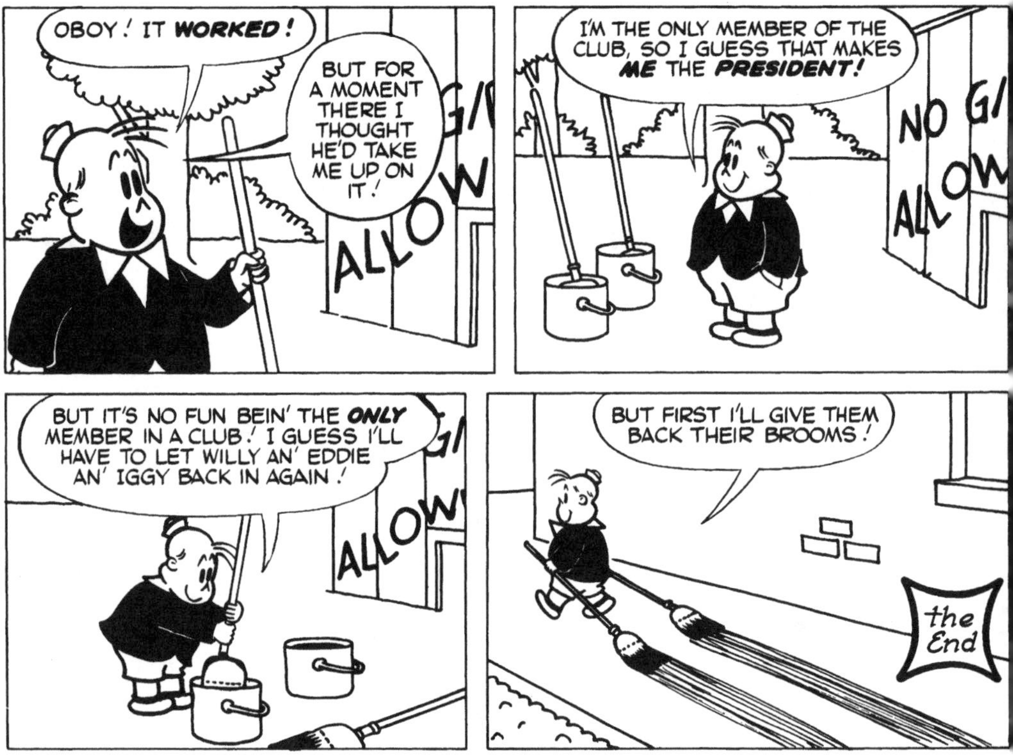
OBOY! IT WORKED!
BUT FOR A MOMENT THERE I THOUGHT HE'D TAKE ME UP ON IT!
I'M THE ONLY MEMBER OF THE CLUB, SO I GUESS THAT MAKES ME THE PRESIDENT!
BUT IT'S NO FUN BEIN' THE ONLY MEMBER IN A CLUB! I GUESS I'LL HAVE TO LET WILLY AN' EDDIE AN' IGGY BACK IN AGAIN!
BUT FIRST I'LL GIVE THEM BACK THEIR BROOMS!
the End

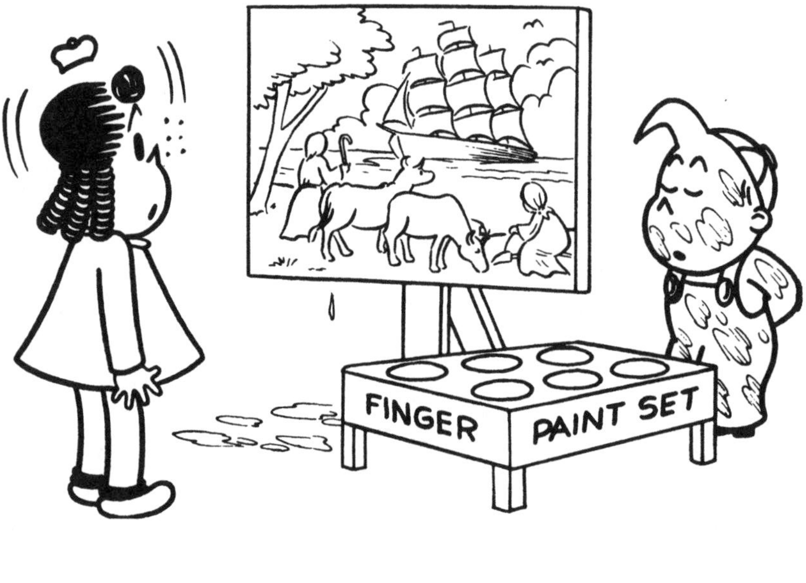
FINGER PAINT SET

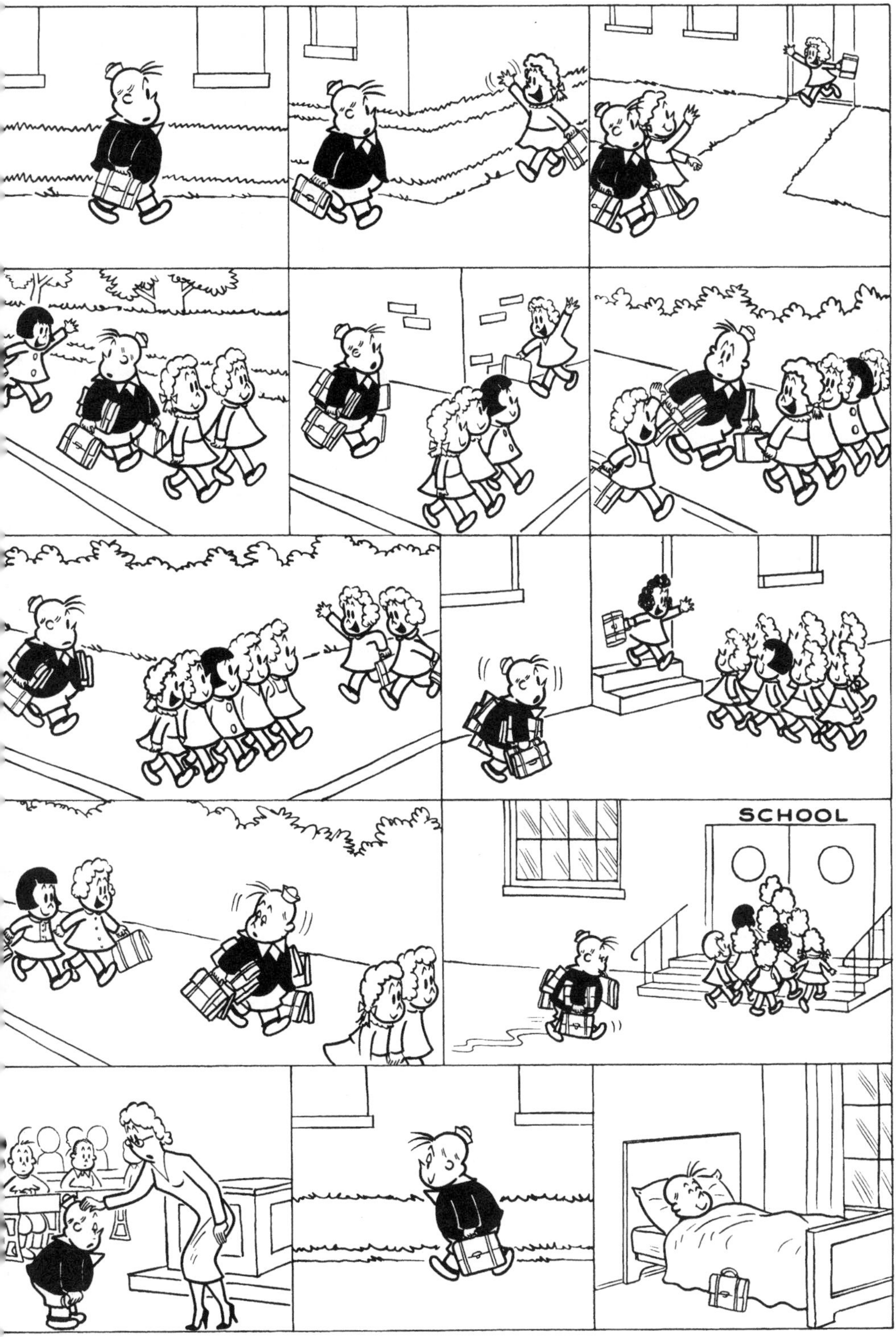
SCHOOL

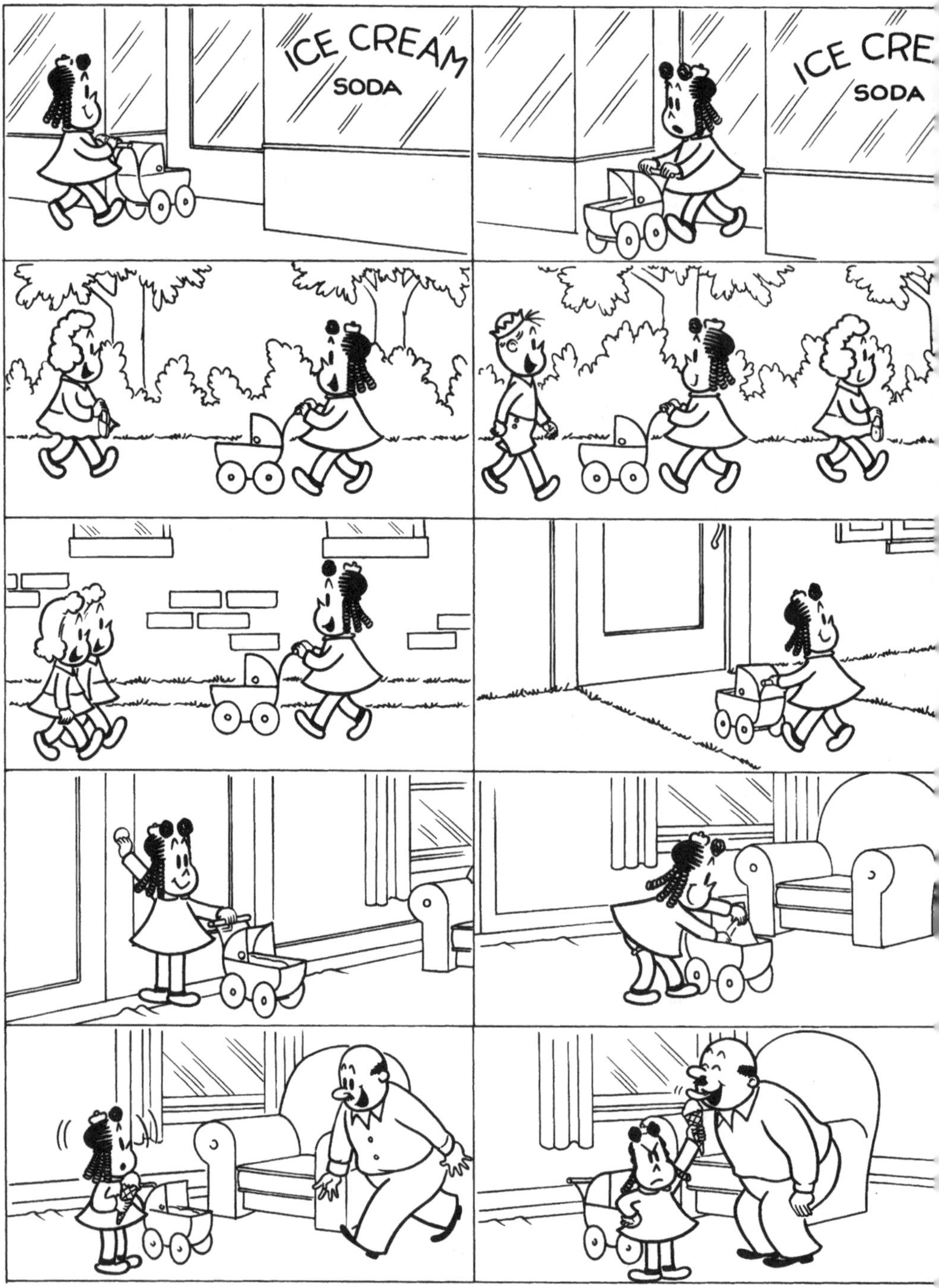
ICE CREAM
SODA
ICE CRE
SODA

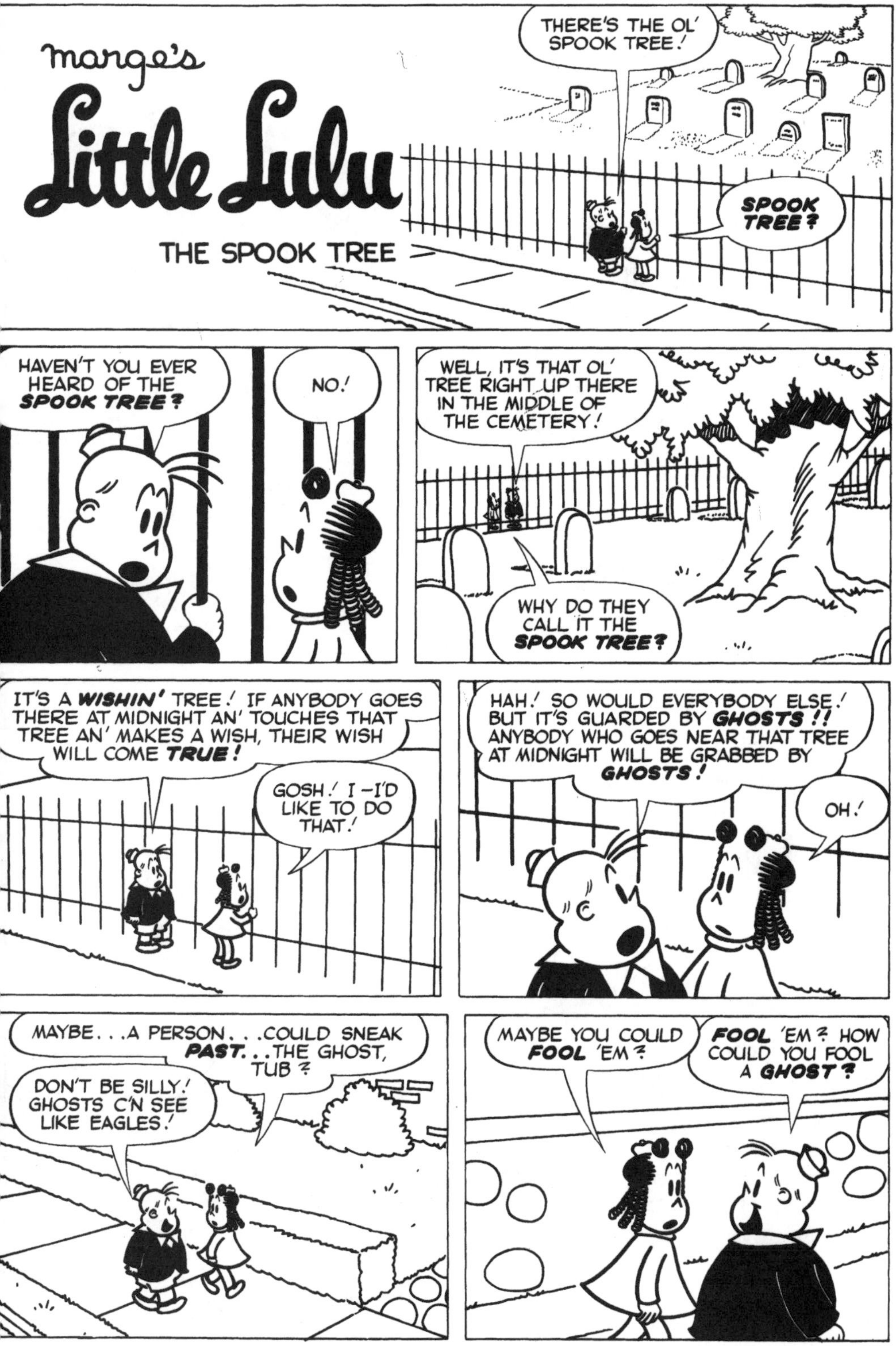
marge's
Little Lulu
THE SPOOK TREE
THERE'S THE OL' SPOOK TREE!
SPOOK TREE?
HAVEN'T YOU EVER HEARD OF THE SPOOK TREE?
NO!
WELL, IT'S THAT OL' TREE RIGHT UP THERE IN THE MIDDLE OF THE CEMETERY!
WHY DO THEY CALL IT THE SPOOK TREE?
IT'S A WISHIN' TREE! IF ANYBODY GOES THERE AT MIDNIGHT AN' TOUCHES THAT TREE AN' MAKES A WISH, THEIR WISH WILL COME TRUE!
GOSH! I-I'D LIKE TO DO THAT!
HAH! SO WOULD EVERYBODY ELSE! BUT IT'S GUARDED BY GHOSTS!! ANYBODY WHO GOES NEAR THAT TREE AT MIDNIGHT WILL BE GRABBED BY GHOSTS!
OH!
MAYBE...A PERSON...COULD SNEAK PAST...THE GHOST, TUB?
DON'T BE SILLY! GHOSTS C'N SEE LIKE EAGLES!
MAYBE YOU COULD FOOL 'EM?
FOOL 'EM? HOW COULD YOU FOOL A GHOST?

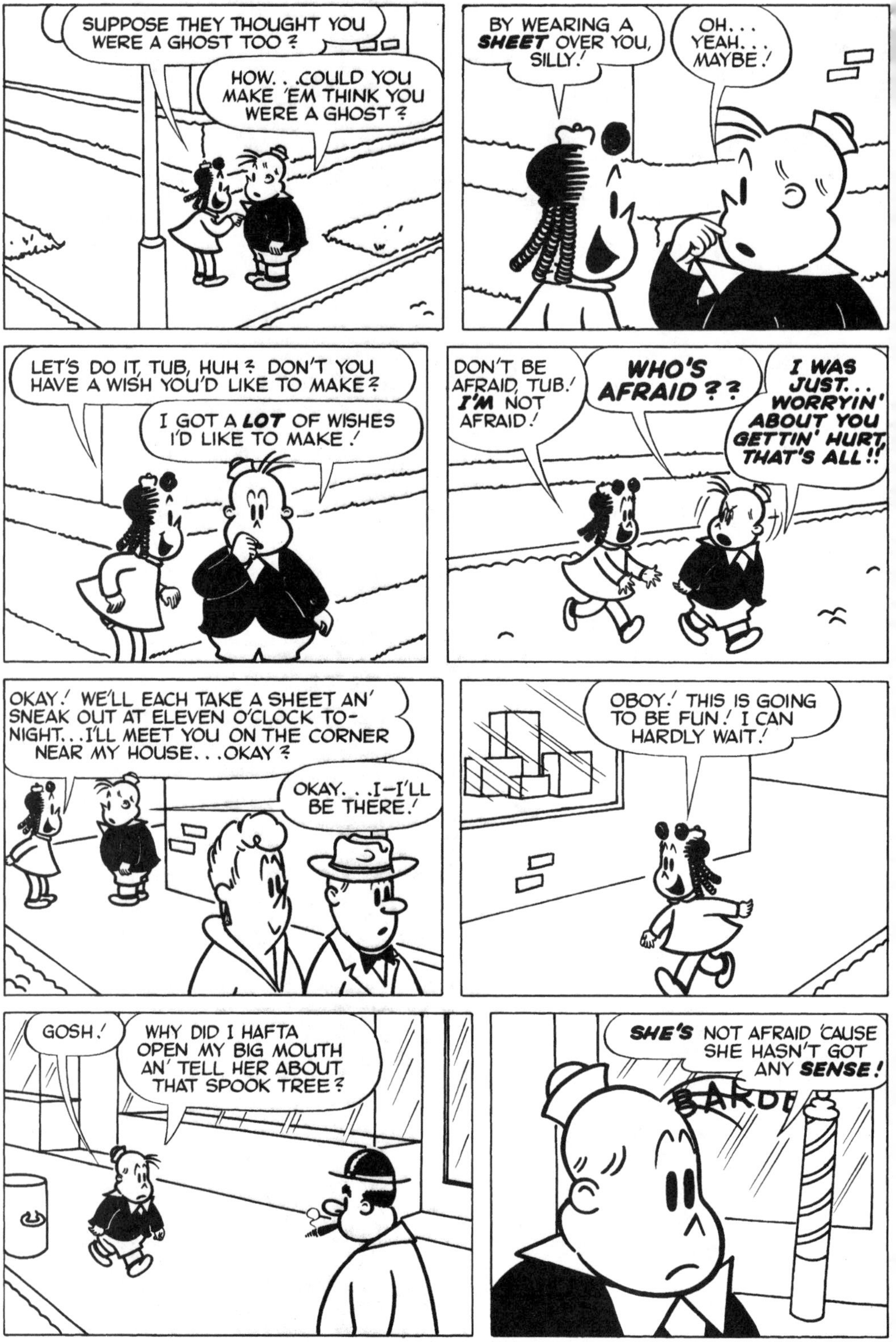
SUPPOSE THEY THOUGHT YOU WERE A GHOST TOO?
HOW. . .COULD YOU MAKE 'EM THINK YOU WERE A GHOST?
BY WEARING A **SHEET** OVER YOU, SILLY!
OH. . . YEAH. . . MAYBE!
LET'S DO IT, TUB, HUH? DON'T YOU HAVE A WISH YOU'D LIKE TO MAKE?
I GOT A **LOT** OF WISHES I'D LIKE TO MAKE!
DON'T BE AFRAID, TUB! **I'M** NOT AFRAID!
WHO'S AFRAID??
I WAS JUST... WORRYIN' ABOUT YOU GETTIN' HURT, THAT'S ALL!!
OKAY! WE'LL EACH TAKE A SHEET AN' SNEAK OUT AT ELEVEN O'CLOCK TO-NIGHT. . .I'LL MEET YOU ON THE CORNER NEAR MY HOUSE. . .OKAY?
OKAY. . .I-I'LL BE THERE!
OBOY! THIS IS GOING TO BE FUN! I CAN HARDLY WAIT!
GOSH!
WHY DID I HAFTA OPEN MY BIG MOUTH AN' TELL HER ABOUT THAT SPOOK TREE?
SHE'S NOT AFRAID 'CAUSE SHE HASN'T GOT ANY **SENSE!**

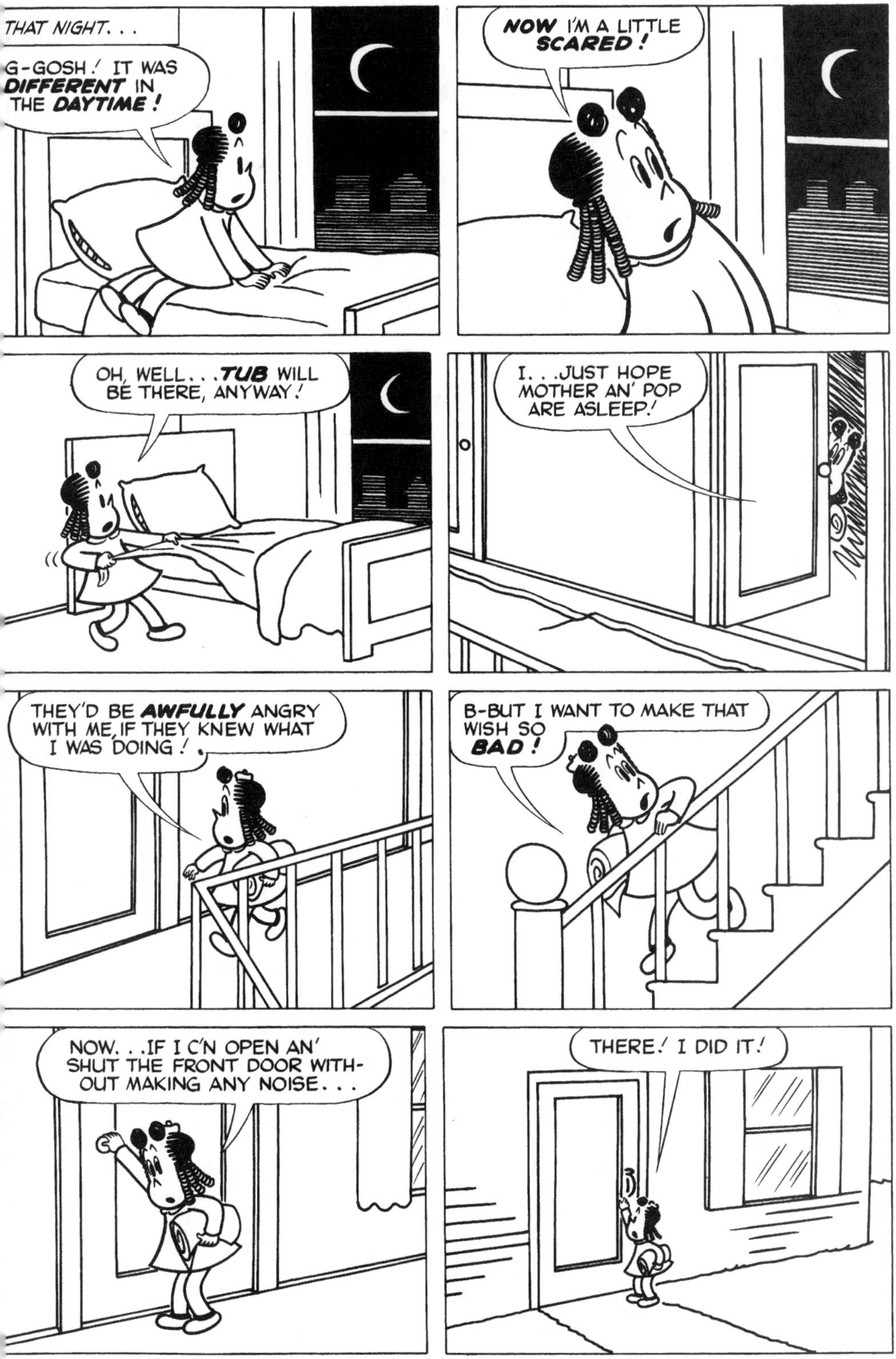

THAT NIGHT. . .
G-GOSH! IT WAS DIFFERENT IN THE DAYTIME!
NOW I'M A LITTLE SCARED!
OH, WELL. . .TUB WILL BE THERE, ANYWAY!
I. . .JUST HOPE MOTHER AN' POP ARE ASLEEP!
THEY'D BE AWFULLY ANGRY WITH ME, IF THEY KNEW WHAT I WAS DOING!
B-BUT I WANT TO MAKE THAT WISH SO BAD!
NOW. . .IF I C'N OPEN AN' SHUT THE FRONT DOOR WITHOUT MAKING ANY NOISE. . .
THERE! I DID IT!

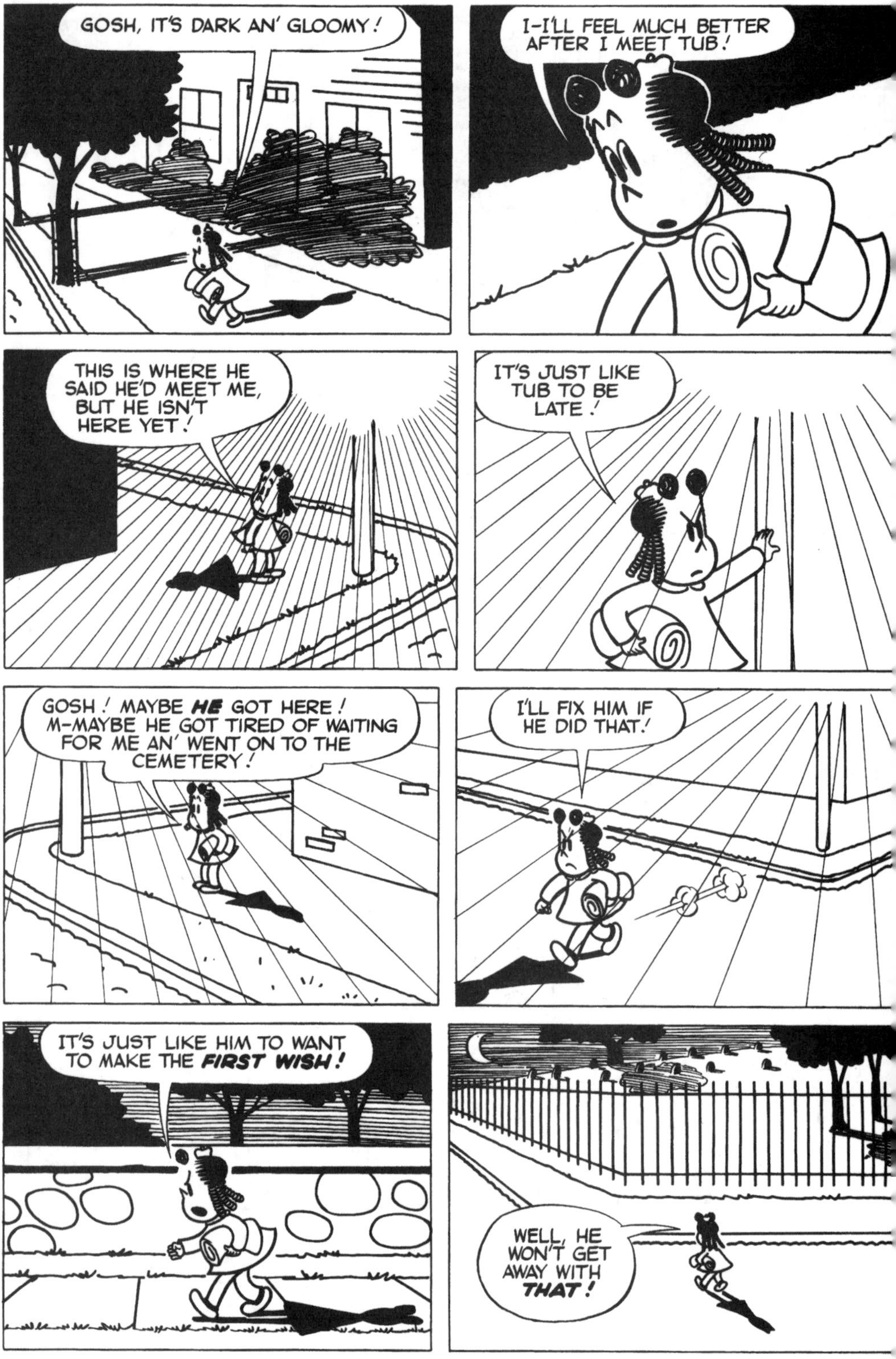

GOSH, IT'S DARK AN' GLOOMY!
I-I'LL FEEL MUCH BETTER AFTER I MEET TUB!
THIS IS WHERE HE SAID HE'D MEET ME, BUT HE ISN'T HERE YET!
IT'S JUST LIKE TUB TO BE LATE!
GOSH! MAYBE **HE** GOT HERE! M-MAYBE HE GOT TIRED OF WAITING FOR ME AN' WENT ON TO THE CEMETERY!
I'LL FIX HIM IF HE DID THAT!
IT'S JUST LIKE HIM TO WANT TO MAKE THE **FIRST WISH**!
WELL, HE WON'T GET AWAY WITH **THAT**!

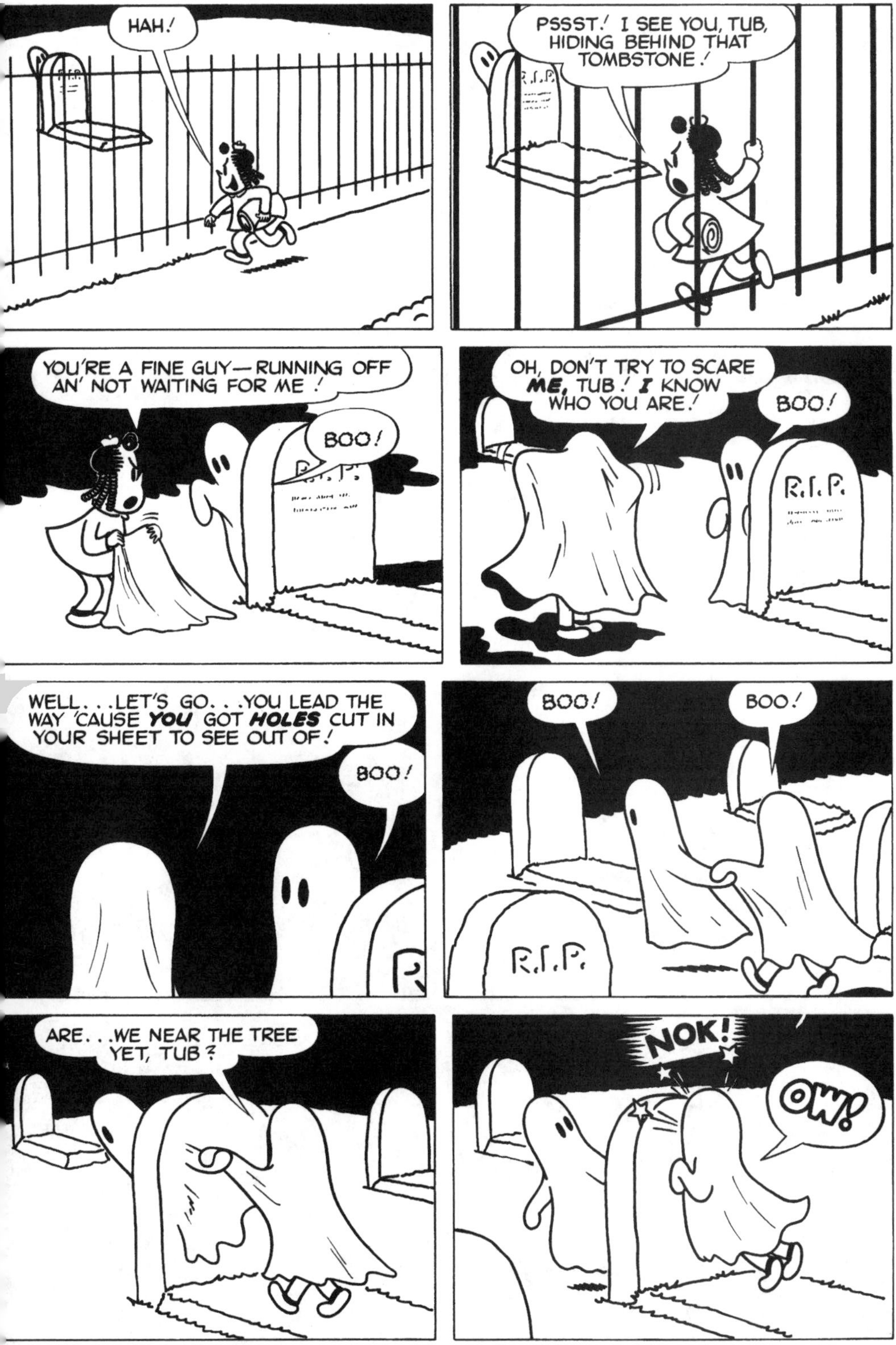
HAH!
PSSST! I SEE YOU, TUB, HIDING BEHIND THAT TOMBSTONE!
R.I.P.
YOU'RE A FINE GUY—RUNNING OFF AN' NOT WAITING FOR ME!
BOO!
OH, DON'T TRY TO SCARE **ME,** TUB! ***I*** KNOW WHO YOU ARE!
BOO!
R.I.P.
WELL...LET'S GO...YOU LEAD THE WAY 'CAUSE ***YOU*** GOT ***HOLES*** CUT IN YOUR SHEET TO SEE OUT OF!
BOO!
BOO!
BOO!
R.I.P.
ARE...WE NEAR THE TREE YET, TUB?
NOK!
OW!

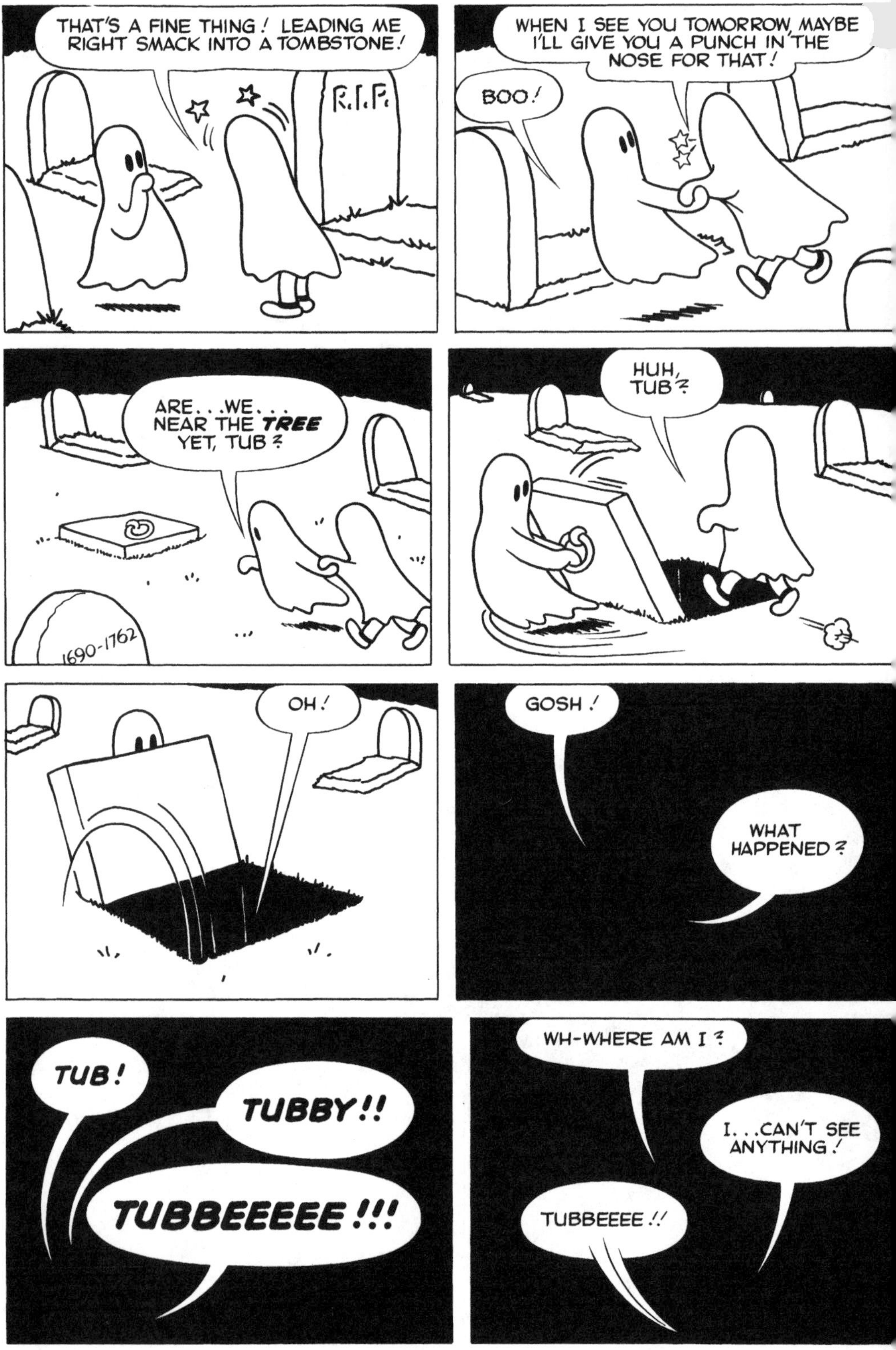
THAT'S A FINE THING! LEADING ME RIGHT SMACK INTO A TOMBSTONE!
R.I.P.
WHEN I SEE YOU TOMORROW, MAYBE I'LL GIVE YOU A PUNCH IN THE NOSE FOR THAT!
BOO!
ARE...WE... NEAR THE **TREE** YET, TUB?
1690-1762
HUH, TUB?
OH!
GOSH!
WHAT HAPPENED?
TUB!
TUBBY!!
TUBBEEEEE!!!
WH-WHERE AM I?
I...CAN'T SEE ANYTHING!
TUBBEEEE!!

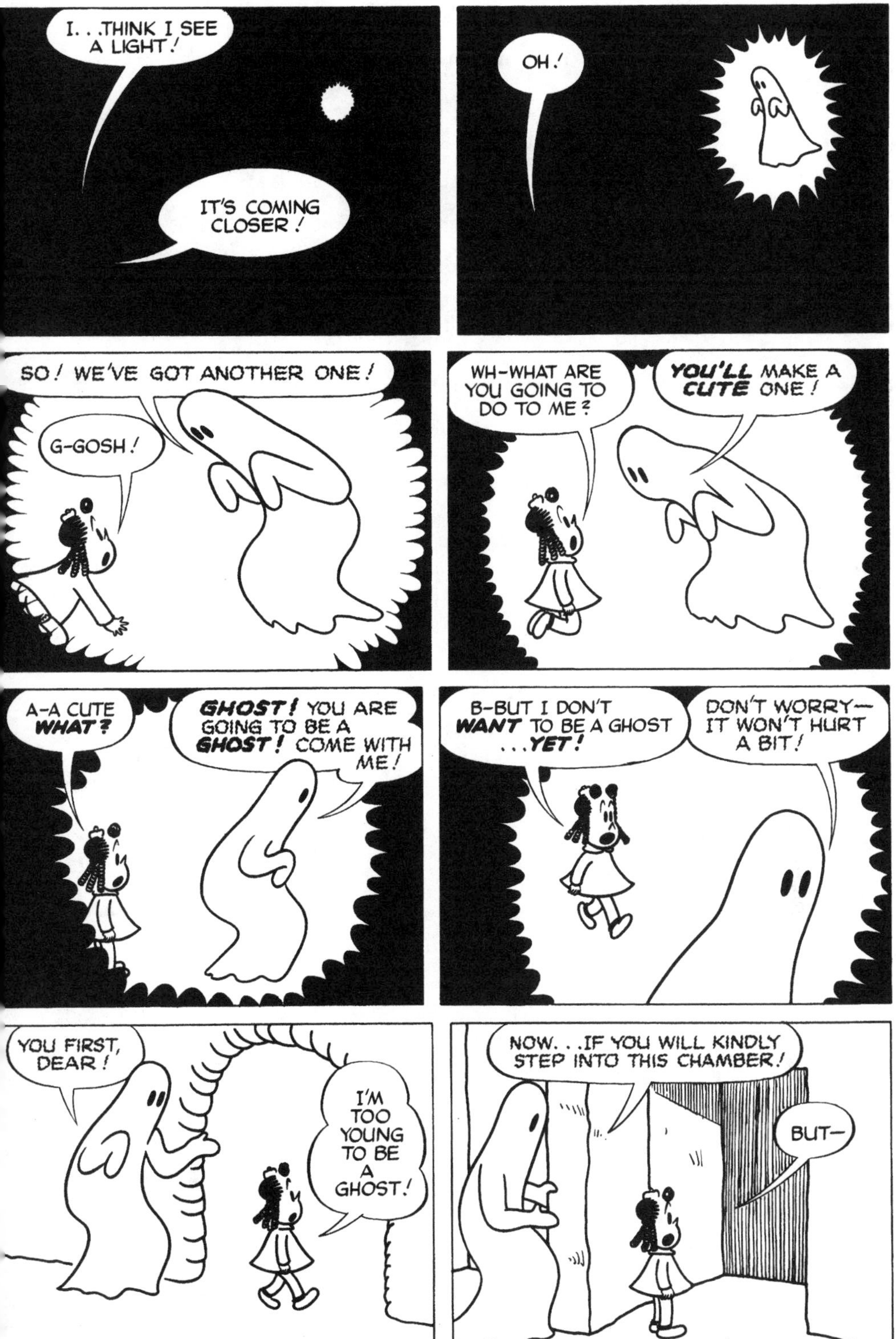
I. . .THINK I SEE A LIGHT!
IT'S COMING CLOSER!
OH!
SO! WE'VE GOT ANOTHER ONE!
G-GOSH!
WH-WHAT ARE YOU GOING TO DO TO ME?
YOU'LL MAKE A CUTE ONE!
A-A CUTE WHAT?
GHOST! YOU ARE GOING TO BE A GHOST! COME WITH ME!
B-BUT I DON'T WANT TO BE A GHOST . . .YET!
DON'T WORRY— IT WON'T HURT A BIT!
YOU FIRST, DEAR!
I'M TOO YOUNG TO BE A GHOST!
NOW. . .IF YOU WILL KINDLY STEP INTO THIS CHAMBER!
BUT—

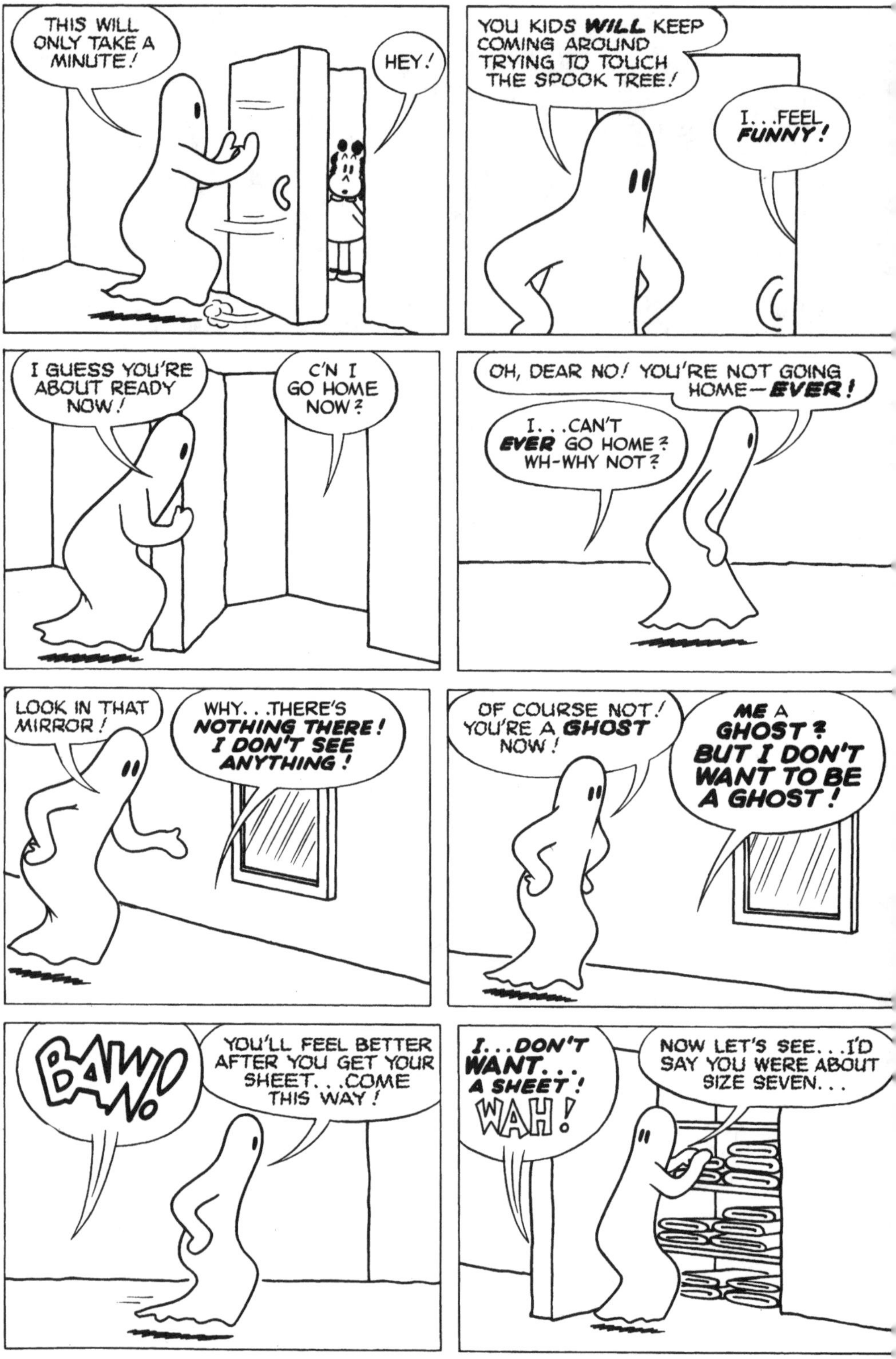
THIS WILL ONLY TAKE A MINUTE!
HEY!
YOU KIDS WILL KEEP COMING AROUND TRYING TO TOUCH THE SPOOK TREE!
I...FEEL FUNNY!
I GUESS YOU'RE ABOUT READY NOW!
C'N I GO HOME NOW?
OH, DEAR NO! YOU'RE NOT GOING HOME—EVER!
I...CAN'T EVER GO HOME? WH-WHY NOT?
LOOK IN THAT MIRROR!
WHY...THERE'S NOTHING THERE! I DON'T SEE ANYTHING!
OF COURSE NOT! YOU'RE A GHOST NOW!
ME A GHOST? BUT I DON'T WANT TO BE A GHOST!
BAWNO!
YOU'LL FEEL BETTER AFTER YOU GET YOUR SHEET...COME THIS WAY!
I...DON'T WANT... A SHEET! WAH!
NOW LET'S SEE...I'D SAY YOU WERE ABOUT SIZE SEVEN...

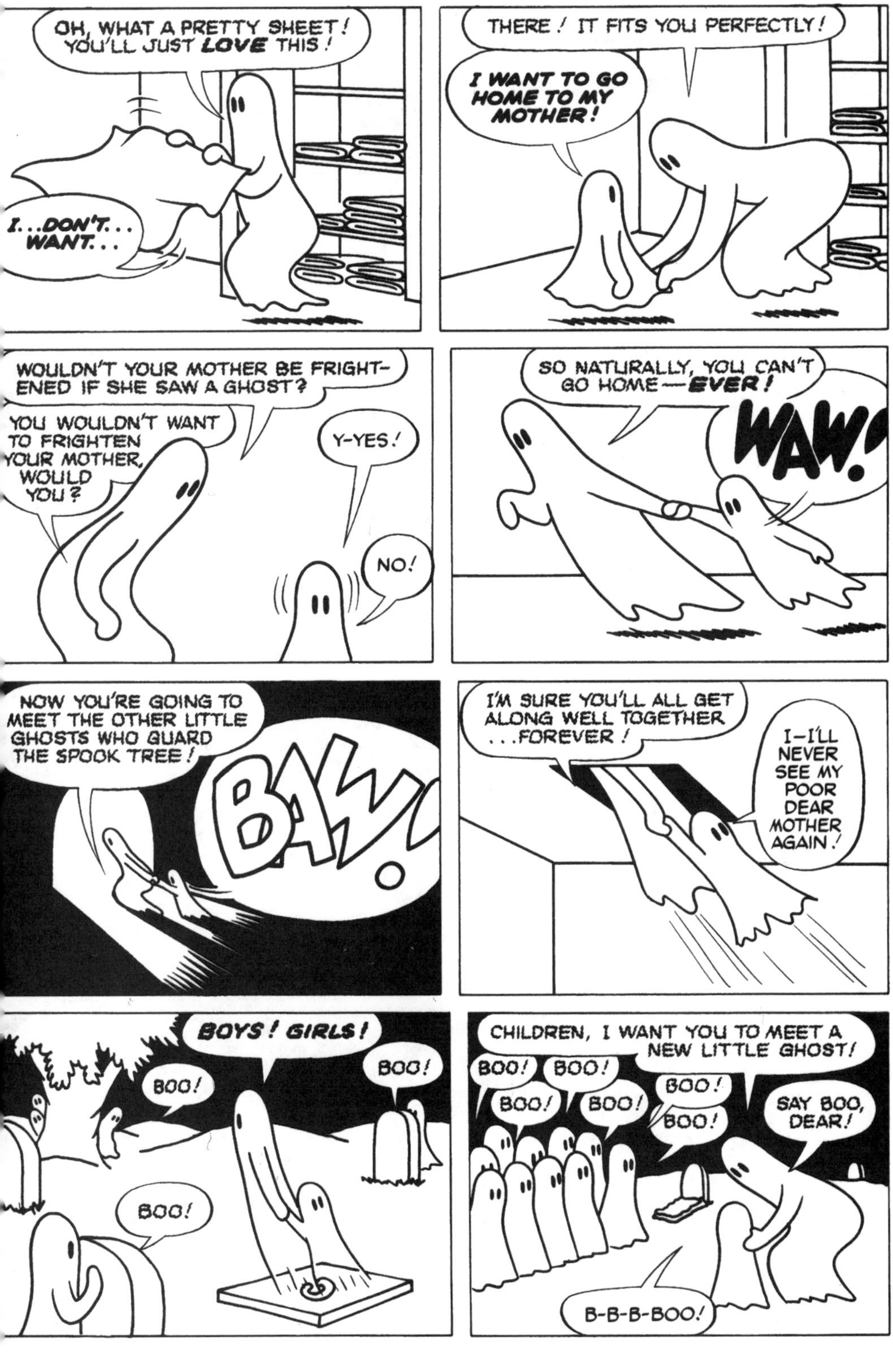
OH, WHAT A PRETTY SHEET! YOU'LL JUST **LOVE** THIS!
I...DON'T... WANT...
THERE! IT FITS YOU PERFECTLY!
I WANT TO GO HOME TO MY MOTHER!
WOULDN'T YOUR MOTHER BE FRIGHT-ENED IF SHE SAW A GHOST?
YOU WOULDN'T WANT TO FRIGHTEN YOUR MOTHER, WOULD YOU?
Y-YES!
NO!
SO NATURALLY, YOU CAN'T GO HOME—**EVER!**
WAW!
NOW YOU'RE GOING TO MEET THE OTHER LITTLE GHOSTS WHO GUARD THE SPOOK TREE!
BAW!
I'M SURE YOU'LL ALL GET ALONG WELL TOGETHER ...FOREVER!
I-I'LL NEVER SEE MY POOR DEAR MOTHER AGAIN!
BOYS! GIRLS!
BOO!
BOO!
BOO!
CHILDREN, I WANT YOU TO MEET A NEW LITTLE GHOST!
BOO!
BOO!
BOO!
BOO!
BOO!
BOO!
SAY BOO, DEAR!
B-B-B-BOO!

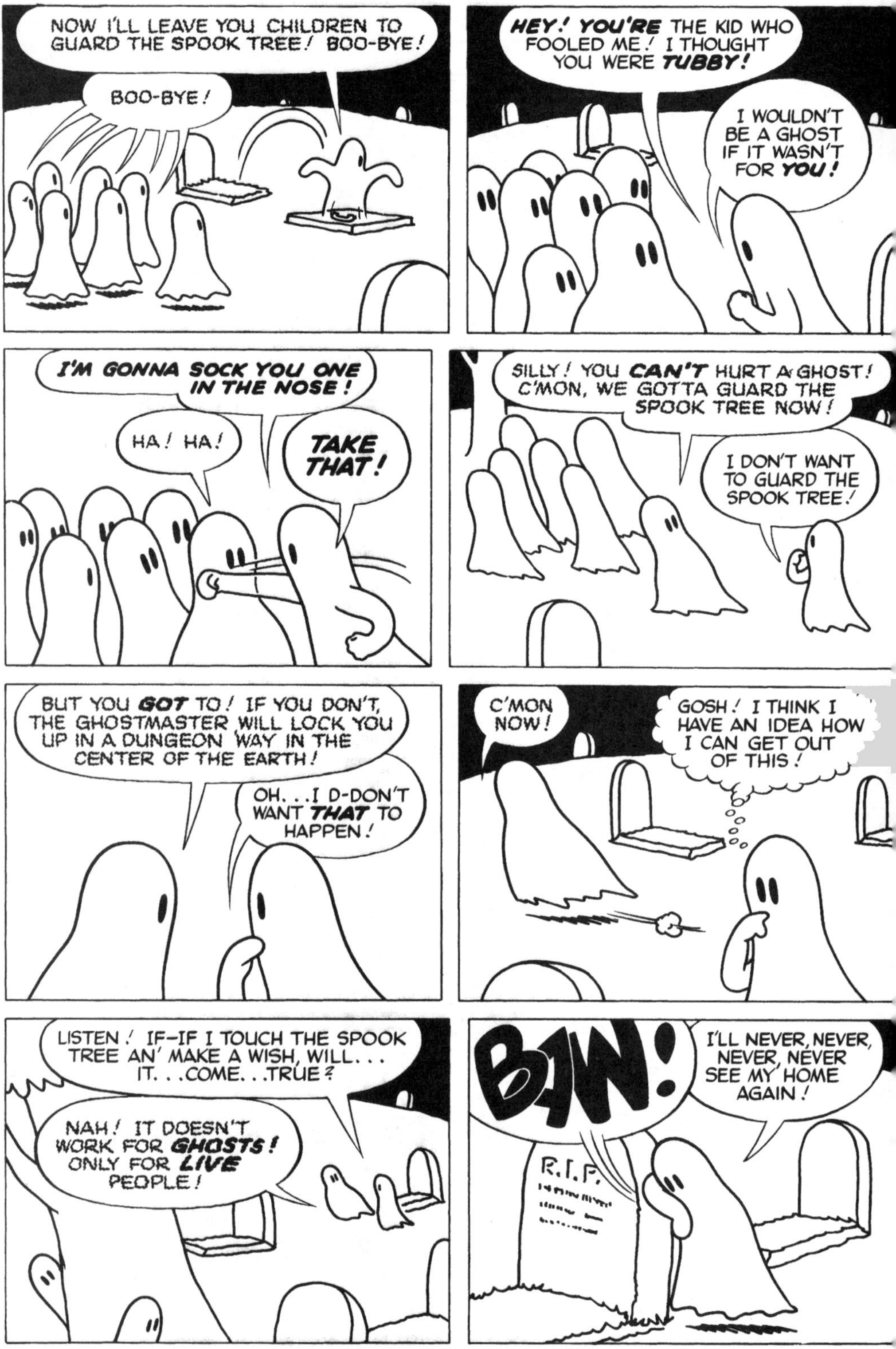
NOW I'LL LEAVE YOU CHILDREN TO GUARD THE SPOOK TREE! BOO-BYE!
BOO-BYE!
HEY! YOU'RE THE KID WHO FOOLED ME! I THOUGHT YOU WERE TUBBY!
I WOULDN'T BE A GHOST IF IT WASN'T FOR YOU!
I'M GONNA SOCK YOU ONE IN THE NOSE!
HA! HA!
TAKE THAT!
SILLY! YOU CAN'T HURT A GHOST! C'MON, WE GOTTA GUARD THE SPOOK TREE NOW!
I DON'T WANT TO GUARD THE SPOOK TREE!
BUT YOU GOT TO! IF YOU DON'T, THE GHOSTMASTER WILL LOCK YOU UP IN A DUNGEON WAY IN THE CENTER OF THE EARTH!
OH. . .I D-DON'T WANT THAT TO HAPPEN!
C'MON NOW!
GOSH! I THINK I HAVE AN IDEA HOW I CAN GET OUT OF THIS!
LISTEN! IF-IF I TOUCH THE SPOOK TREE AN' MAKE A WISH, WILL. . . IT. . .COME. . .TRUE?
NAH! IT DOESN'T WORK FOR GHOSTS! ONLY FOR LIVE PEOPLE!
BAM!
I'LL NEVER, NEVER, NEVER, NEVER SEE MY HOME AGAIN!
R.I.P.

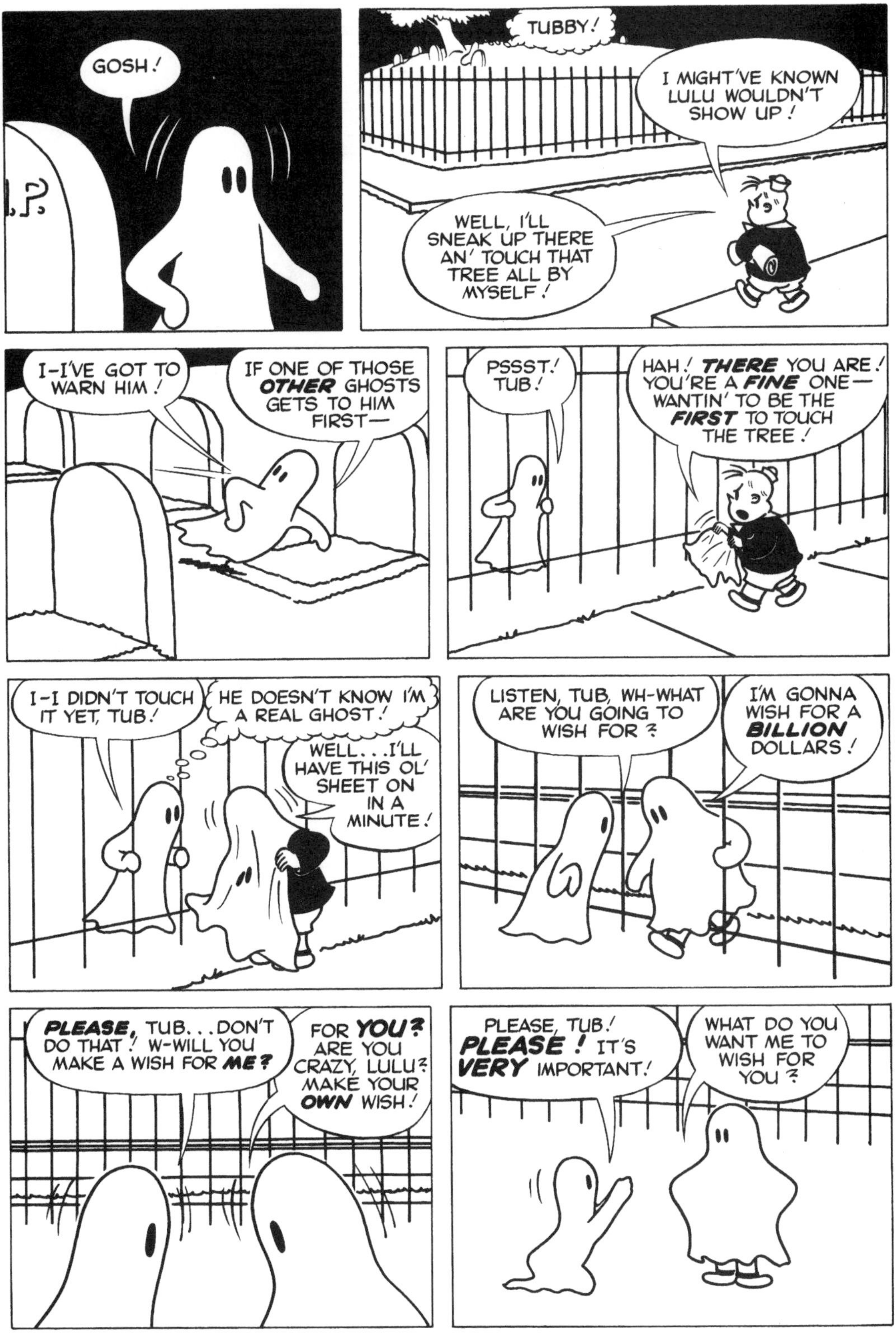
GOSH!
TUBBY!
I MIGHT'VE KNOWN LULU WOULDN'T SHOW UP!
WELL, I'LL SNEAK UP THERE AN' TOUCH THAT TREE ALL BY MYSELF!
I-I'VE GOT TO WARN HIM!
IF ONE OF THOSE **OTHER** GHOSTS GETS TO HIM FIRST—
PSSST! TUB!
HAH! **THERE** YOU ARE! YOU'RE A **FINE** ONE— WANTIN' TO BE THE **FIRST** TO TOUCH THE TREE!
I-I DIDN'T TOUCH IT YET, TUB!
HE DOESN'T KNOW I'M A REAL GHOST!
WELL...I'LL HAVE THIS OL' SHEET ON IN A MINUTE!
LISTEN, TUB, WH-WHAT ARE YOU GOING TO WISH FOR?
I'M GONNA WISH FOR A **BILLION** DOLLARS!
PLEASE, TUB...DON'T DO THAT! W-WILL YOU MAKE A WISH FOR **ME?**
FOR **YOU?** ARE YOU CRAZY, LULU? MAKE YOUR **OWN** WISH!
PLEASE, TUB! **PLEASE!** IT'S **VERY** IMPORTANT!
WHAT DO YOU WANT ME TO WISH FOR YOU?

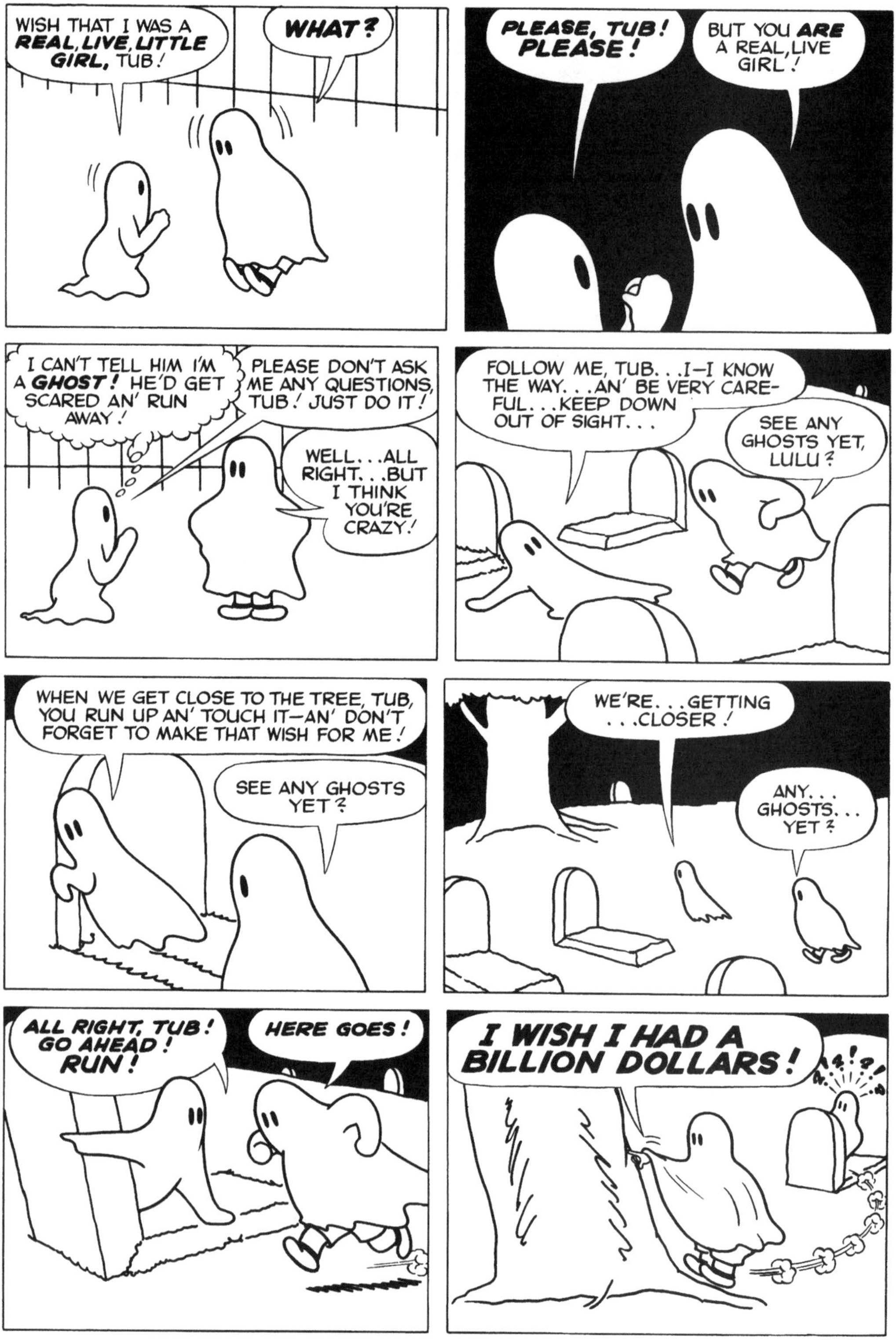
WISH THAT I WAS A REAL, LIVE, LITTLE GIRL, TUB!
WHAT?
PLEASE, TUB! PLEASE!
BUT YOU ARE A REAL, LIVE GIRL!
I CAN'T TELL HIM I'M A GHOST! HE'D GET SCARED AN' RUN AWAY!
PLEASE DON'T ASK ME ANY QUESTIONS, TUB! JUST DO IT!
WELL...ALL RIGHT...BUT I THINK YOU'RE CRAZY!
FOLLOW ME, TUB...I—I KNOW THE WAY...AN' BE VERY CARE-FUL...KEEP DOWN OUT OF SIGHT...
SEE ANY GHOSTS YET, LULU?
WHEN WE GET CLOSE TO THE TREE, TUB, YOU RUN UP AN' TOUCH IT—AN' DON'T FORGET TO MAKE THAT WISH FOR ME!
SEE ANY GHOSTS YET?
WE'RE...GETTING ...CLOSER!
ANY... GHOSTS... YET?
ALL RIGHT, TUB! GO AHEAD! RUN!
HERE GOES!
I WISH I HAD A BILLION DOLLARS!

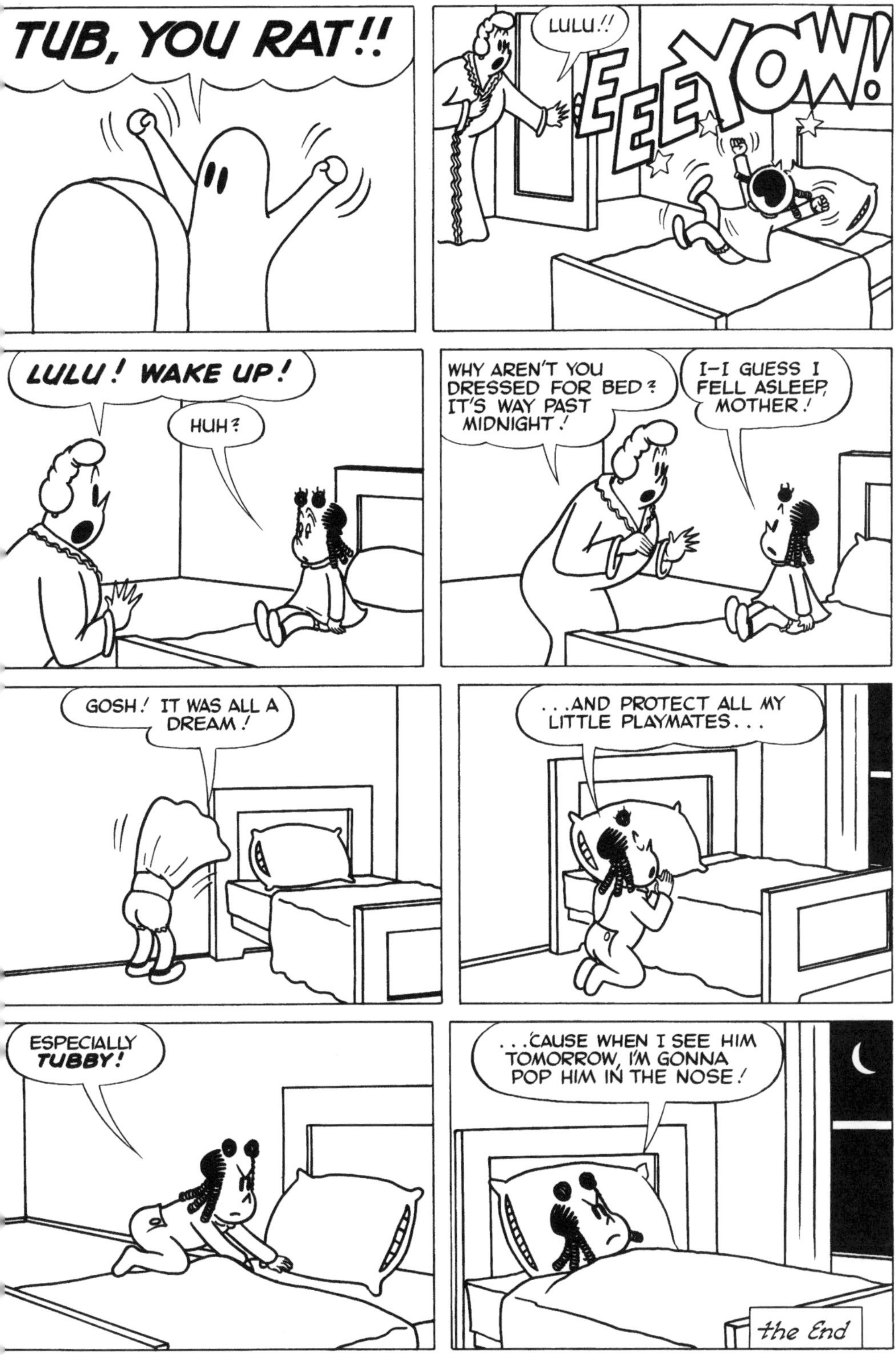
TUB, YOU RAT!!
LULU!!
EEEYOW!
LULU! WAKE UP!
HUH?
WHY AREN'T YOU DRESSED FOR BED? IT'S WAY PAST MIDNIGHT!
I-I GUESS I FELL ASLEEP, MOTHER!
GOSH! IT WAS ALL A DREAM!
...AND PROTECT ALL MY LITTLE PLAYMATES...
ESPECIALLY TUBBY!
...'CAUSE WHEN I SEE HIM TOMORROW, I'M GONNA POP HIM IN THE NOSE!
the End

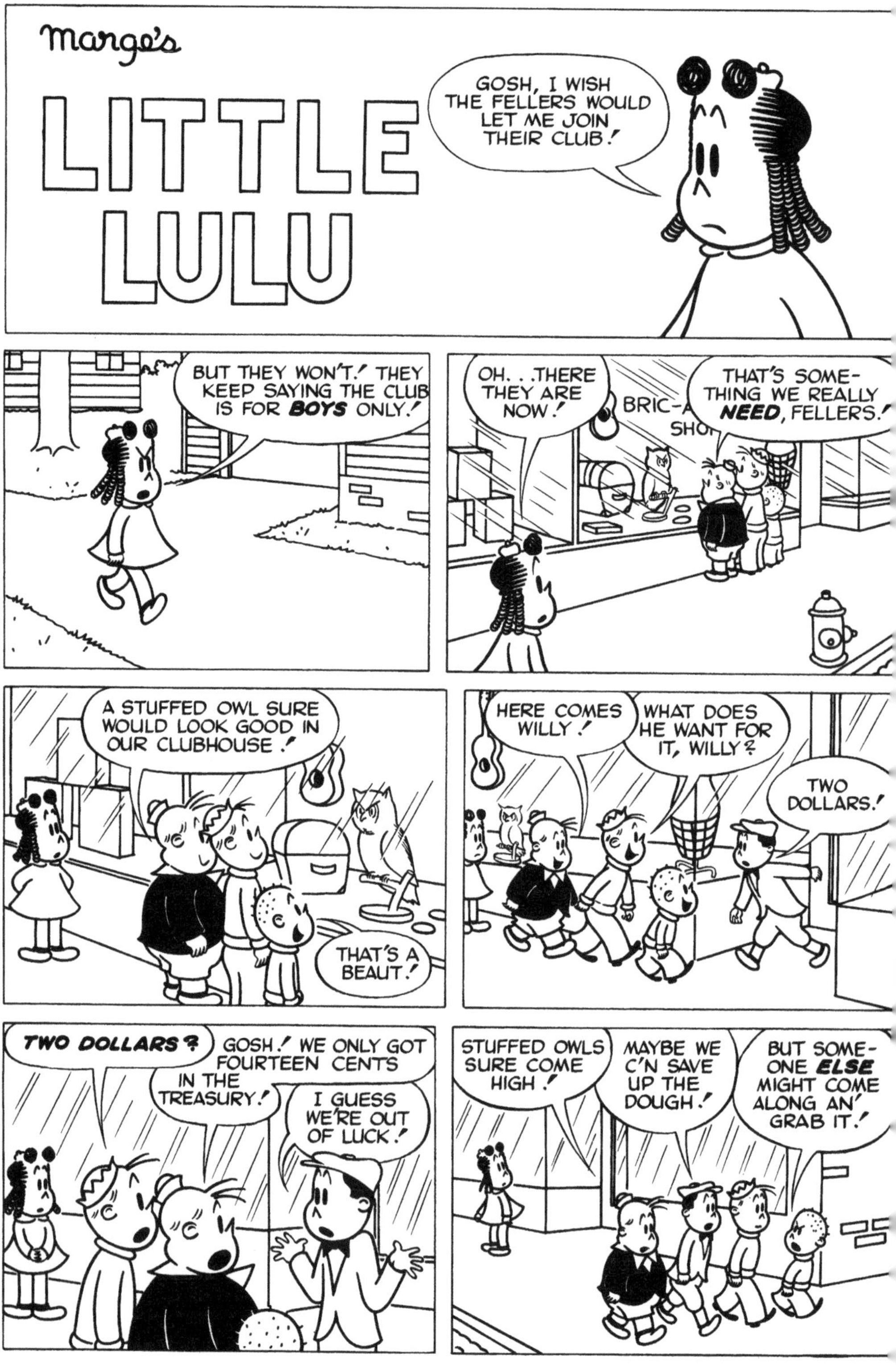

Marge's
LITTLE LULU
GOSH, I WISH THE FELLERS WOULD LET ME JOIN THEIR CLUB!
BUT THEY WON'T! THEY KEEP SAYING THE CLUB IS FOR BOYS ONLY!
OH. . .THERE THEY ARE NOW!
BRIC-A
SHO
THAT'S SOMETHING WE REALLY NEED, FELLERS!
A STUFFED OWL SURE WOULD LOOK GOOD IN OUR CLUBHOUSE!
THAT'S A BEAUT!
HERE COMES WILLY!
WHAT DOES HE WANT FOR IT, WILLY?
TWO DOLLARS!
TWO DOLLARS?
GOSH! WE ONLY GOT FOURTEEN CENTS IN THE TREASURY!
I GUESS WE'RE OUT OF LUCK!
STUFFED OWLS SURE COME HIGH!
MAYBE WE C'N SAVE UP THE DOUGH!
BUT SOMEONE ELSE MIGHT COME ALONG AN' GRAB IT!

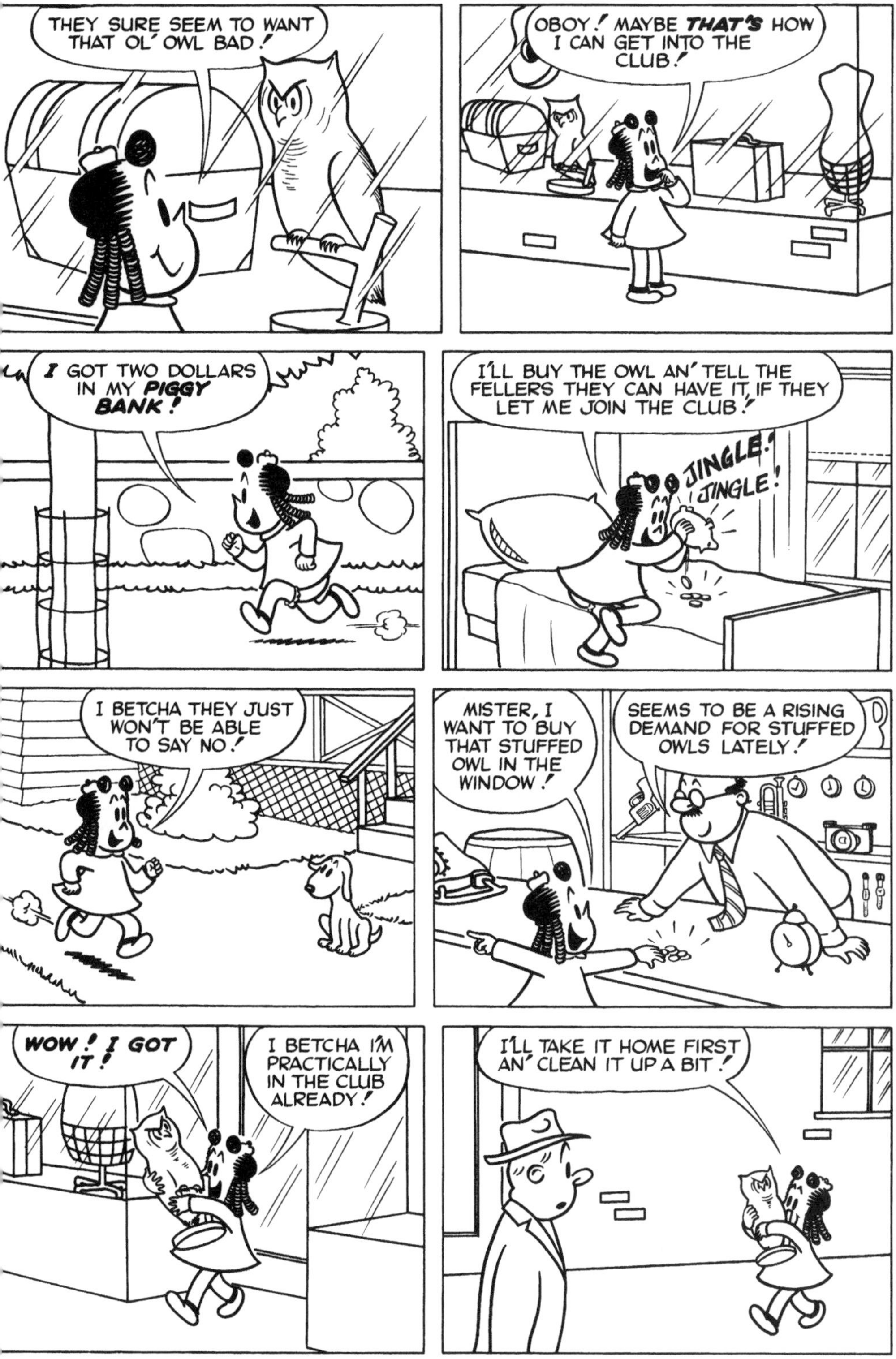
THEY SURE SEEM TO WANT THAT OL' OWL BAD!
OBOY! MAYBE THAT'S HOW I CAN GET INTO THE CLUB!
I GOT TWO DOLLARS IN MY PIGGY BANK!
I'LL BUY THE OWL AN' TELL THE FELLERS THEY CAN HAVE IT, IF THEY LET ME JOIN THE CLUB!
JINGLE! JINGLE!
I BETCHA THEY JUST WON'T BE ABLE TO SAY NO!
MISTER, I WANT TO BUY THAT STUFFED OWL IN THE WINDOW!
SEEMS TO BE A RISING DEMAND FOR STUFFED OWLS LATELY!
WOW! I GOT IT!
I BETCHA I'M PRACTICALLY IN THE CLUB ALREADY!
I'LL TAKE IT HOME FIRST AN' CLEAN IT UP A BIT!

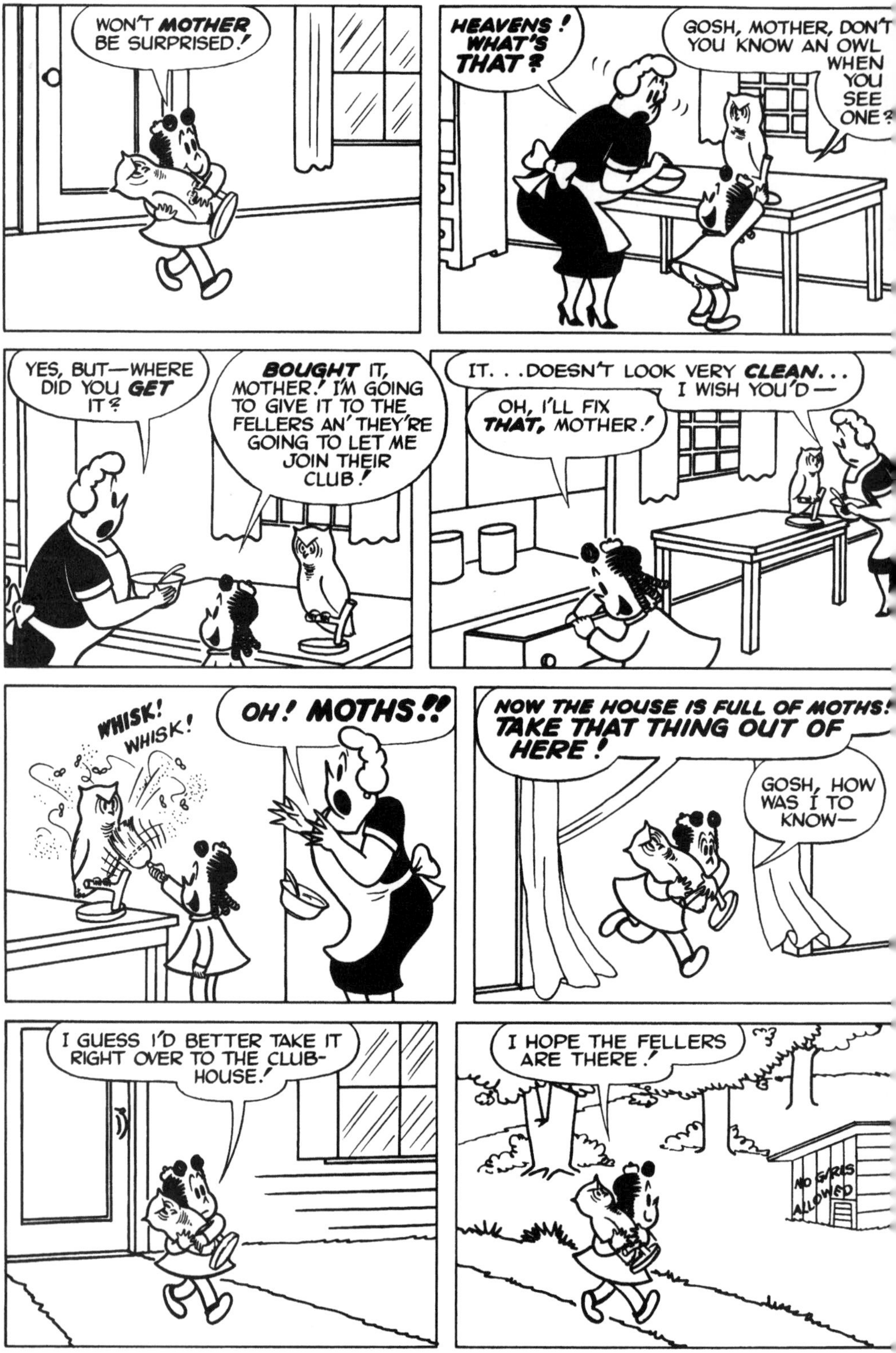

WON'T MOTHER BE SURPRISED!
HEAVENS! WHAT'S THAT?
GOSH, MOTHER, DON'T YOU KNOW AN OWL WHEN YOU SEE ONE?
YES, BUT—WHERE DID YOU GET IT?
BOUGHT IT, MOTHER! I'M GOING TO GIVE IT TO THE FELLERS AN' THEY'RE GOING TO LET ME JOIN THEIR CLUB!
IT. . .DOESN'T LOOK VERY CLEAN. . . I WISH YOU'D—
OH, I'LL FIX THAT, MOTHER!
WHISK! WHISK!
OH! MOTHS!!
NOW THE HOUSE IS FULL OF MOTHS! TAKE THAT THING OUT OF HERE!
GOSH, HOW WAS I TO KNOW—
I GUESS I'D BETTER TAKE IT RIGHT OVER TO THE CLUB-HOUSE!
I HOPE THE FELLERS ARE THERE!
NO GIRLS ALLOWED

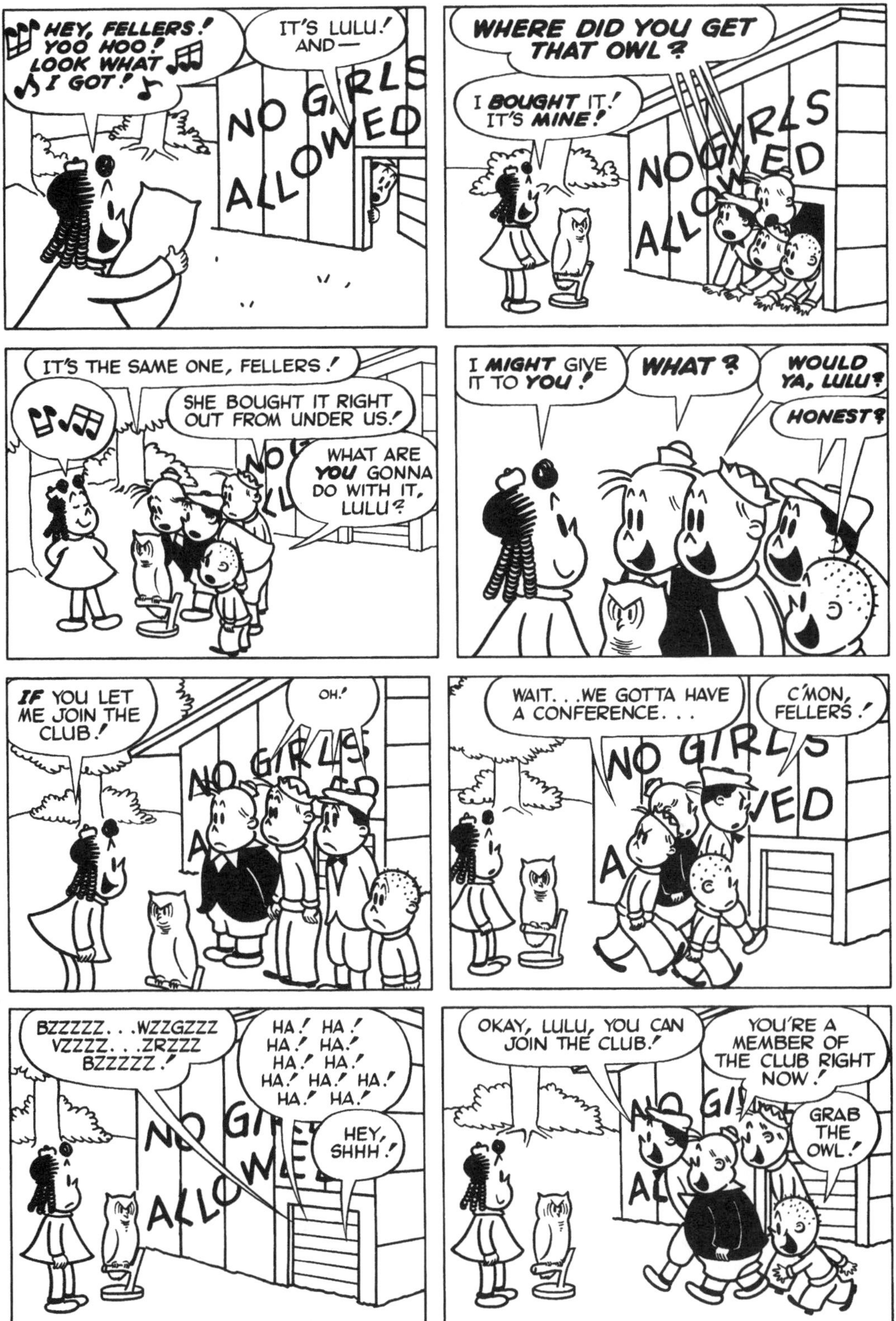
HEY, FELLERS! YOO HOO! LOOK WHAT I GOT!
IT'S LULU! AND—
NO GIRLS ALLOWED
WHERE DID YOU GET THAT OWL?
I BOUGHT IT! IT'S MINE!
NO GIRLS ALLOWED
IT'S THE SAME ONE, FELLERS!
SHE BOUGHT IT RIGHT OUT FROM UNDER US!
WHAT ARE YOU GONNA DO WITH IT, LULU?
I MIGHT GIVE IT TO YOU!
WHAT?
WOULD YA, LULU?
HONEST?
IF YOU LET ME JOIN THE CLUB!
OH!
NO GIRLS
WAIT. . .WE GOTTA HAVE A CONFERENCE. . .
C'MON, FELLERS!
NO GIRLS
BZZZZZ. . .WZZGZZZ VZZZZ. . .ZRZZZ BZZZZZ!
HA! HA! HA! HA! HA! HA! HA! HA! HA! HA! HA!
HEY, SHHH!
OKAY, LULU, YOU CAN JOIN THE CLUB!
YOU'RE A MEMBER OF THE CLUB RIGHT NOW!
GRAB THE OWL!

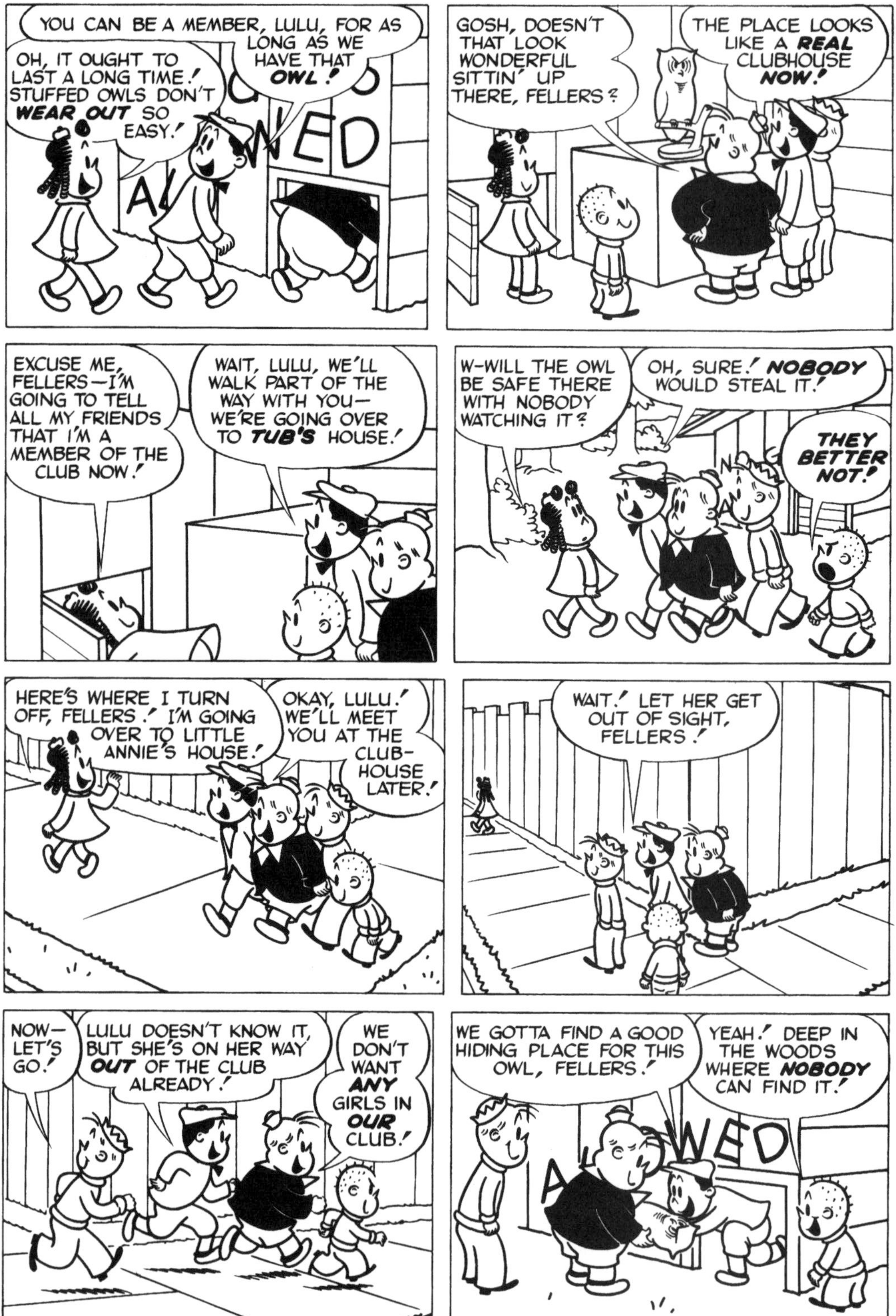
YOU CAN BE A MEMBER, LULU, FOR AS LONG AS WE HAVE THAT OWL!
OH, IT OUGHT TO LAST A LONG TIME! STUFFED OWLS DON'T WEAR OUT SO EASY!
GOSH, DOESN'T THAT LOOK WONDERFUL SITTIN' UP THERE, FELLERS?
THE PLACE LOOKS LIKE A REAL CLUBHOUSE NOW!
EXCUSE ME, FELLERS—I'M GOING TO TELL ALL MY FRIENDS THAT I'M A MEMBER OF THE CLUB NOW!
WAIT, LULU, WE'LL WALK PART OF THE WAY WITH YOU—WE'RE GOING OVER TO TUB'S HOUSE!
W-WILL THE OWL BE SAFE THERE WITH NOBODY WATCHING IT?
OH, SURE! NOBODY WOULD STEAL IT!
THEY BETTER NOT!
HERE'S WHERE I TURN OFF, FELLERS! I'M GOING OVER TO LITTLE ANNIE'S HOUSE!
OKAY, LULU! WE'LL MEET YOU AT THE CLUB-HOUSE LATER!
WAIT! LET HER GET OUT OF SIGHT, FELLERS!
NOW—LET'S GO!
LULU DOESN'T KNOW IT, BUT SHE'S ON HER WAY OUT OF THE CLUB ALREADY!
WE DON'T WANT ANY GIRLS IN OUR CLUB!
WE GOTTA FIND A GOOD HIDING PLACE FOR THIS OWL, FELLERS!
YEAH! DEEP IN THE WOODS WHERE NOBODY CAN FIND IT!

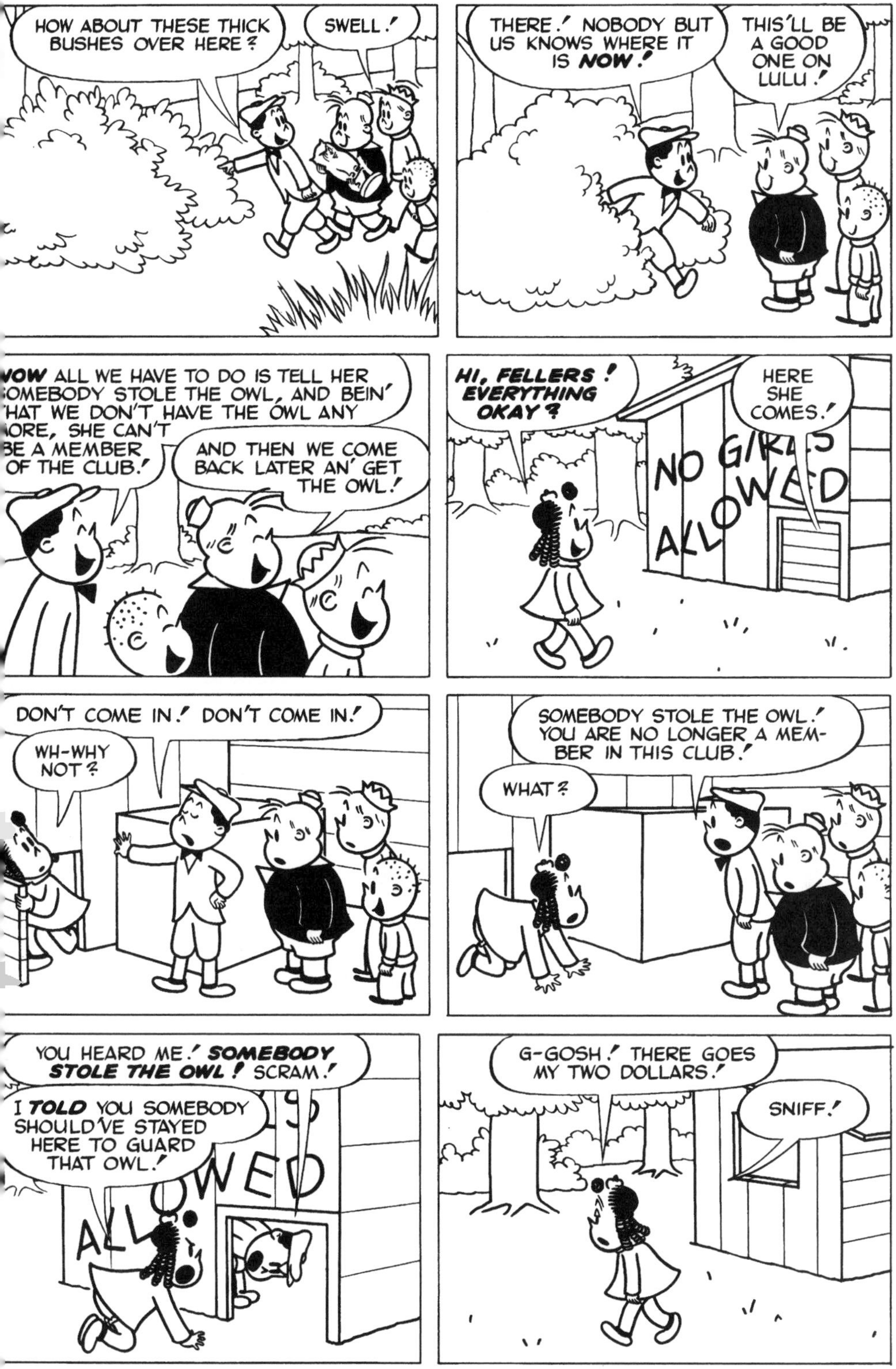

HOW ABOUT THESE THICK BUSHES OVER HERE?
SWELL!
THERE! NOBODY BUT US KNOWS WHERE IT IS **NOW**!
THIS'LL BE A GOOD ONE ON LULU!
NOW ALL WE HAVE TO DO IS TELL HER SOMEBODY STOLE THE OWL, AND BEIN' THAT WE DON'T HAVE THE OWL ANY MORE, SHE CAN'T BE A MEMBER OF THE CLUB!
AND THEN WE COME BACK LATER AN' GET THE OWL!
HI, FELLERS! EVERYTHING OKAY?
HERE SHE COMES!
NO GIRLS ALLOWED
DON'T COME IN! DON'T COME IN!
WH-WHY NOT?
SOMEBODY STOLE THE OWL! YOU ARE NO LONGER A MEMBER IN THIS CLUB!
WHAT?
YOU HEARD ME! **SOMEBODY STOLE THE OWL!** SCRAM!
I **TOLD** YOU SOMEBODY SHOULD'VE STAYED HERE TO GUARD THAT OWL!
G-GOSH! THERE GOES MY TWO DOLLARS!
SNIFF!

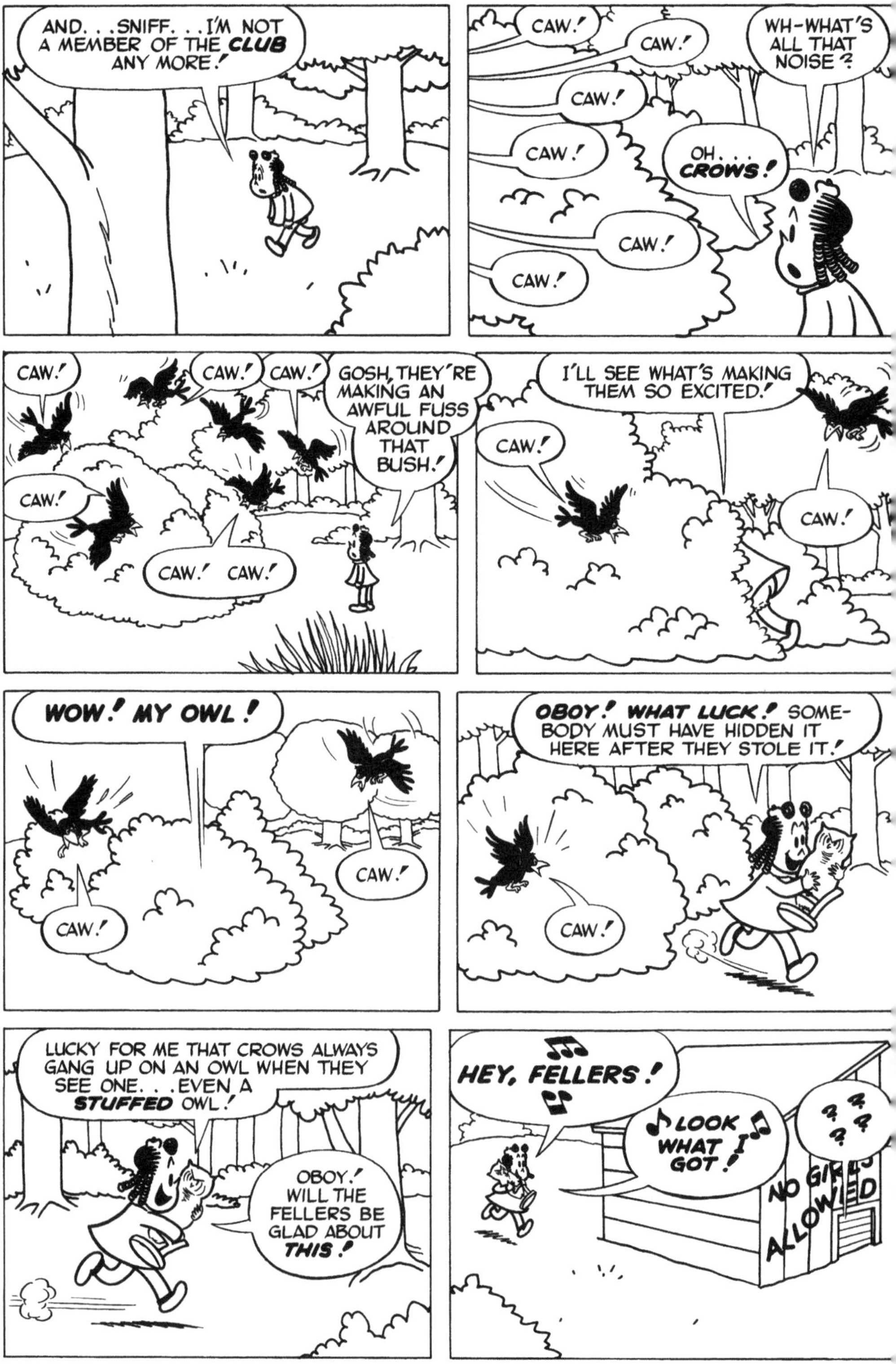
AND. . .SNIFF. . .I'M NOT A MEMBER OF THE CLUB ANY MORE!
CAW!
CAW!
WH-WHAT'S ALL THAT NOISE?
CAW!
CAW!
OH. . . CROWS!
CAW!
CAW!
CAW!
CAW!
CAW!
GOSH, THEY'RE MAKING AN AWFUL FUSS AROUND THAT BUSH!
CAW!
CAW! CAW!
I'LL SEE WHAT'S MAKING THEM SO EXCITED!
CAW!
CAW!
WOW! MY OWL!
CAW!
CAW!
OBOY! WHAT LUCK! SOMEBODY MUST HAVE HIDDEN IT HERE AFTER THEY STOLE IT!
CAW!
LUCKY FOR ME THAT CROWS ALWAYS GANG UP ON AN OWL WHEN THEY SEE ONE. . .EVEN A STUFFED OWL!
OBOY! WILL THE FELLERS BE GLAD ABOUT THIS!
HEY, FELLERS!
LOOK WHAT I GOT!
? ? ? ?

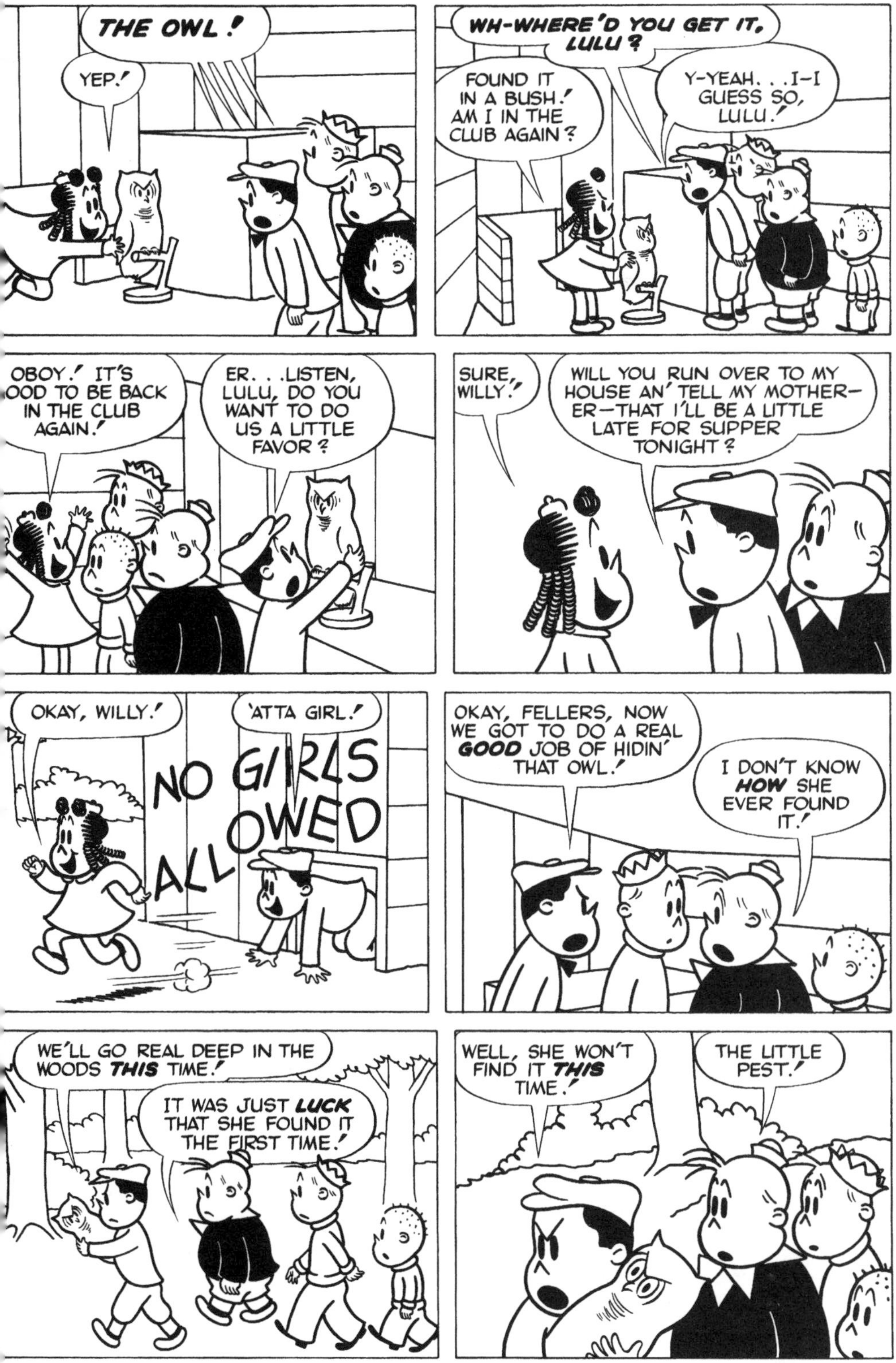
THE OWL!
YEP!
WH-WHERE'D YOU GET IT, LULU?
FOUND IT IN A BUSH! AM I IN THE CLUB AGAIN?
Y-YEAH. . .I-I GUESS SO, LULU!
OBOY! IT'S OOD TO BE BACK IN THE CLUB AGAIN!
ER. . .LISTEN, LULU, DO YOU WANT TO DO US A LITTLE FAVOR?
SURE, WILLY!
WILL YOU RUN OVER TO MY HOUSE AN' TELL MY MOTHER— ER—THAT I'LL BE A LITTLE LATE FOR SUPPER TONIGHT?
OKAY, WILLY!
'ATTA GIRL!
NO GIRLS ALLOWED
OKAY, FELLERS, NOW WE GOT TO DO A REAL GOOD JOB OF HIDIN' THAT OWL!
I DON'T KNOW HOW SHE EVER FOUND IT!
WE'LL GO REAL DEEP IN THE WOODS THIS TIME!
IT WAS JUST LUCK THAT SHE FOUND IT THE FIRST TIME!
WELL, SHE WON'T FIND IT THIS TIME!
THE LITTLE PEST!

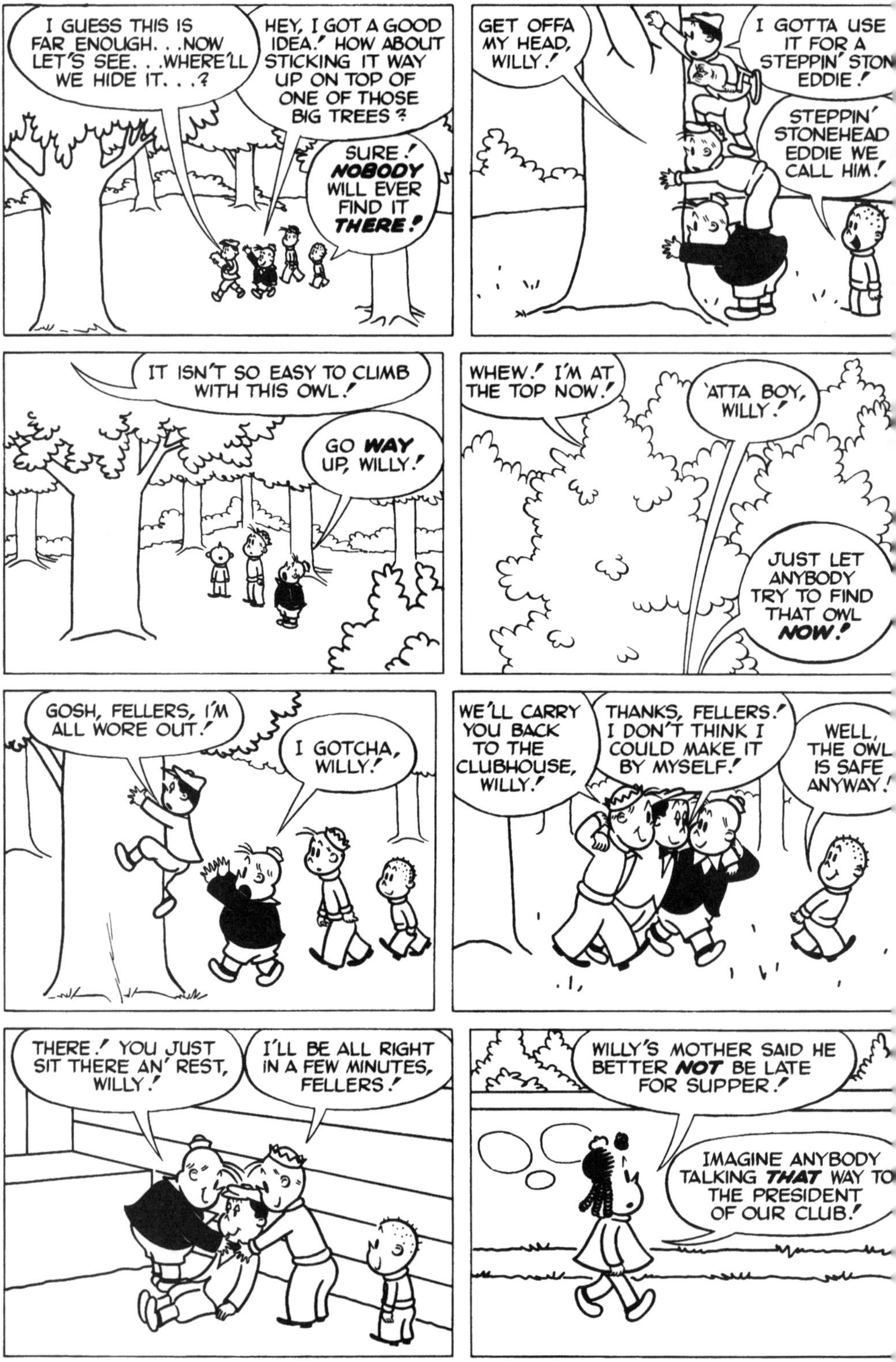
I GUESS THIS IS FAR ENOUGH. . .NOW LET'S SEE. . .WHERE'LL WE HIDE IT. . .?
HEY, I GOT A GOOD IDEA! HOW ABOUT STICKING IT WAY UP ON TOP OF ONE OF THOSE BIG TREES?
SURE! NOBODY WILL EVER FIND IT THERE!
GET OFFA MY HEAD, WILLY!
I GOTTA USE IT FOR A STEPPIN' STON EDDIE!
STEPPIN' STONEHEAD EDDIE WE CALL HIM!
IT ISN'T SO EASY TO CLIMB WITH THIS OWL!
GO WAY UP, WILLY!
WHEW! I'M AT THE TOP NOW!
'ATTA BOY, WILLY!
JUST LET ANYBODY TRY TO FIND THAT OWL NOW!
GOSH, FELLERS, I'M ALL WORE OUT!
I GOTCHA, WILLY!
WE'LL CARRY YOU BACK TO THE CLUBHOUSE, WILLY!
THANKS, FELLERS! I DON'T THINK I COULD MAKE IT BY MYSELF!
WELL, THE OWL IS SAFE ANYWAY!
THERE! YOU JUST SIT THERE AN' REST, WILLY!
I'LL BE ALL RIGHT IN A FEW MINUTES, FELLERS!
WILLY'S MOTHER SAID HE BETTER NOT BE LATE FOR SUPPER!
IMAGINE ANYBODY TALKING THAT WAY TO THE PRESIDENT OF OUR CLUB!

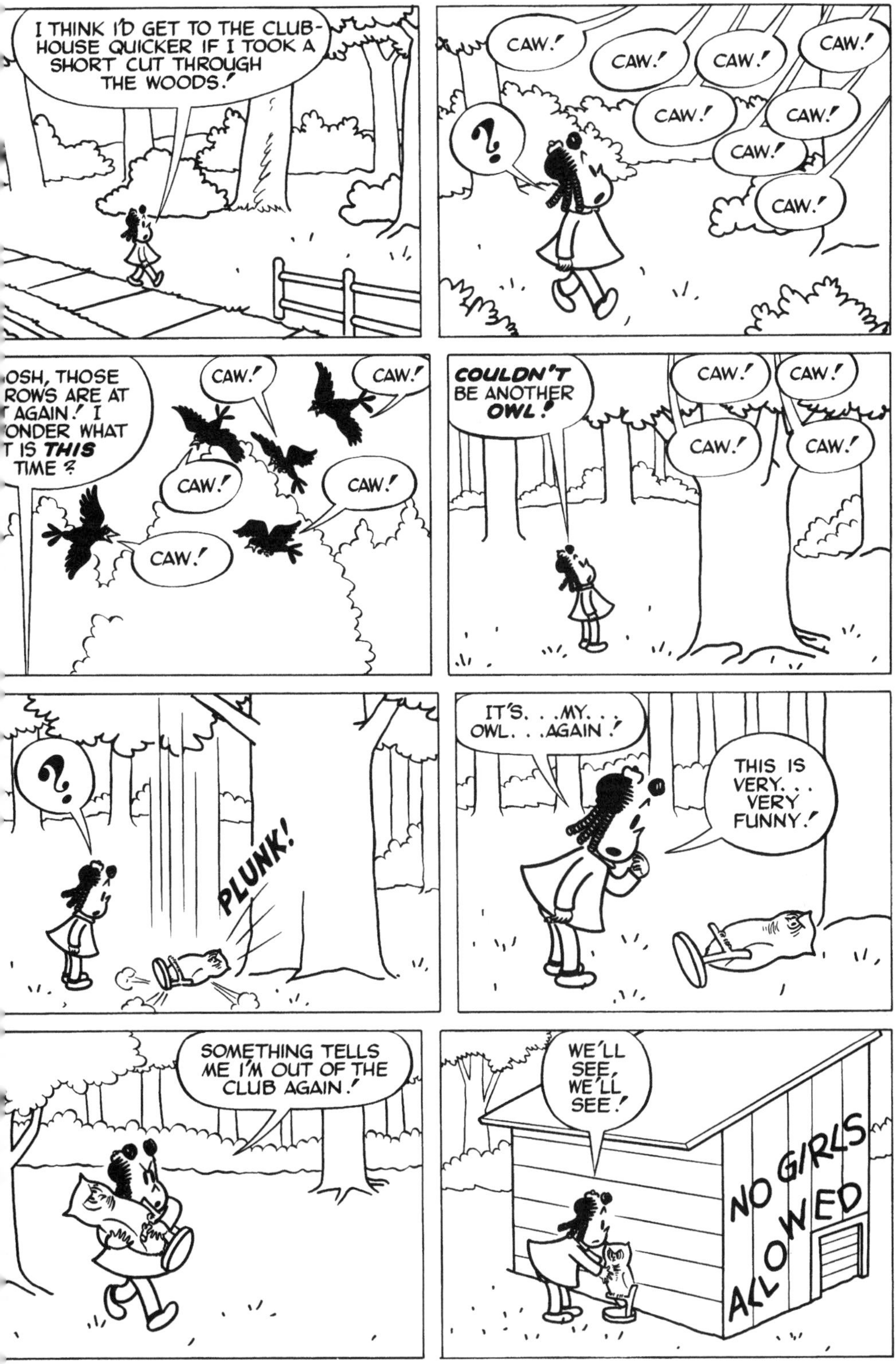
I THINK I'D GET TO THE CLUB-HOUSE QUICKER IF I TOOK A SHORT CUT THROUGH THE WOODS!
CAW!
CAW!
CAW!
CAW!
CAW!
CAW!
CAW!
CAW!
?
OSH, THOSE ROWS ARE AT AGAIN! I ONDER WHAT T IS THIS TIME ?
CAW!
CAW!
CAW!
CAW!
CAW!
COULDN'T BE ANOTHER OWL!
CAW!
CAW!
CAW!
CAW!
?
PLUNK!
IT'S. . .MY. . . OWL. . .AGAIN!
THIS IS VERY. . . VERY FUNNY!
SOMETHING TELLS ME I'M OUT OF THE CLUB AGAIN!
WE'LL SEE, WE'LL SEE!
NO GIRLS ALLOWED

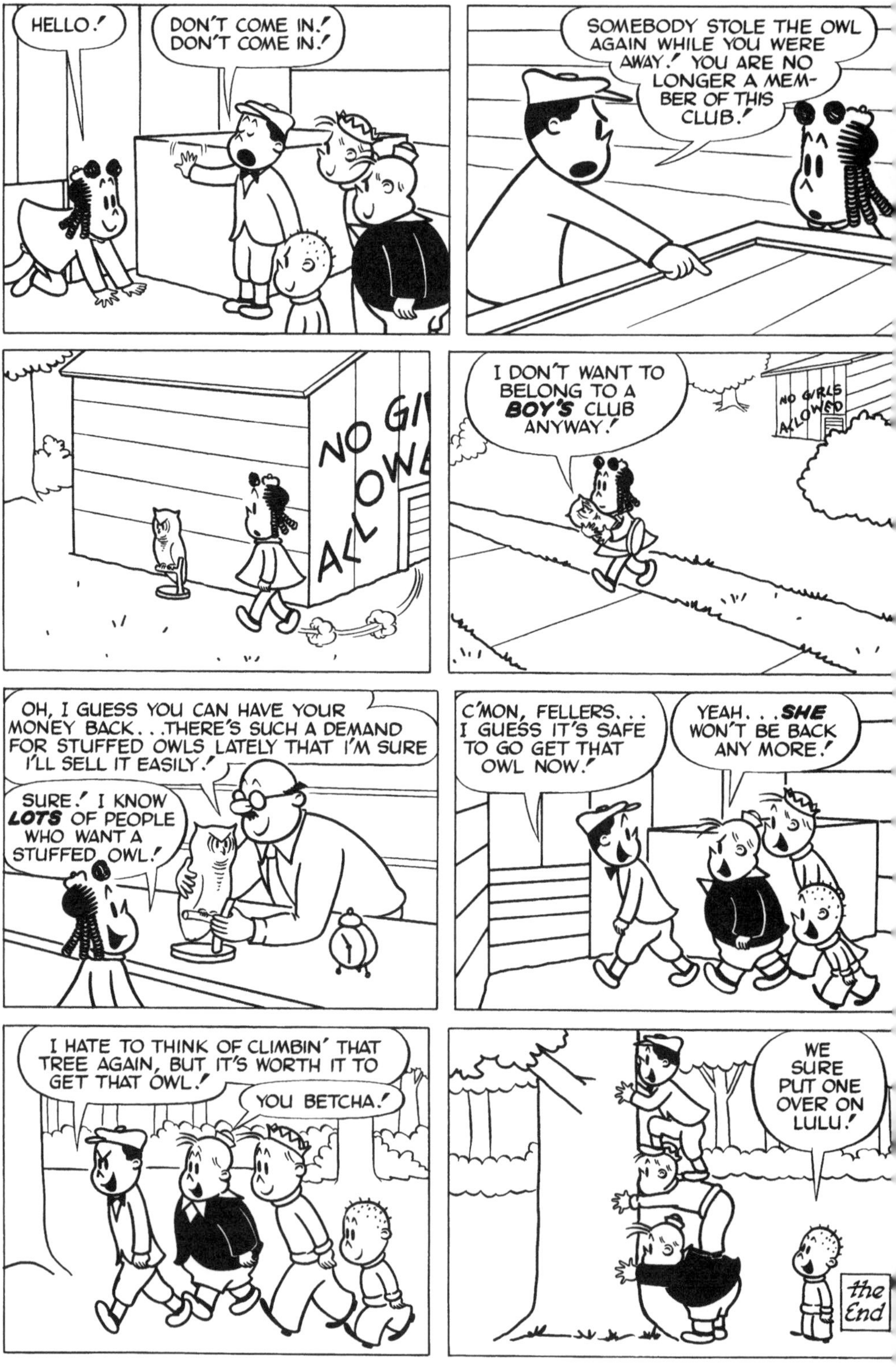
HELLO.!
DON'T COME IN.! DON'T COME IN.!
SOMEBODY STOLE THE OWL AGAIN WHILE YOU WERE AWAY.! YOU ARE NO LONGER A MEMBER OF THIS CLUB.!
NO GI
ALLOWE
I DON'T WANT TO BELONG TO A **BOY'S** CLUB ANYWAY.!
NO GIRLS ALLOWED
OH, I GUESS YOU CAN HAVE YOUR MONEY BACK...THERE'S SUCH A DEMAND FOR STUFFED OWLS LATELY THAT I'M SURE I'LL SELL IT EASILY.!
SURE.! I KNOW **LOTS** OF PEOPLE WHO WANT A STUFFED OWL.!
C'MON, FELLERS... I GUESS IT'S SAFE TO GO GET THAT OWL NOW.!
YEAH...**SHE** WON'T BE BACK ANY MORE.!
I HATE TO THINK OF CLIMBIN' THAT TREE AGAIN, BUT IT'S WORTH IT TO GET THAT OWL.!
YOU BETCHA.!
WE SURE PUT ONE OVER ON LULU.!
the End

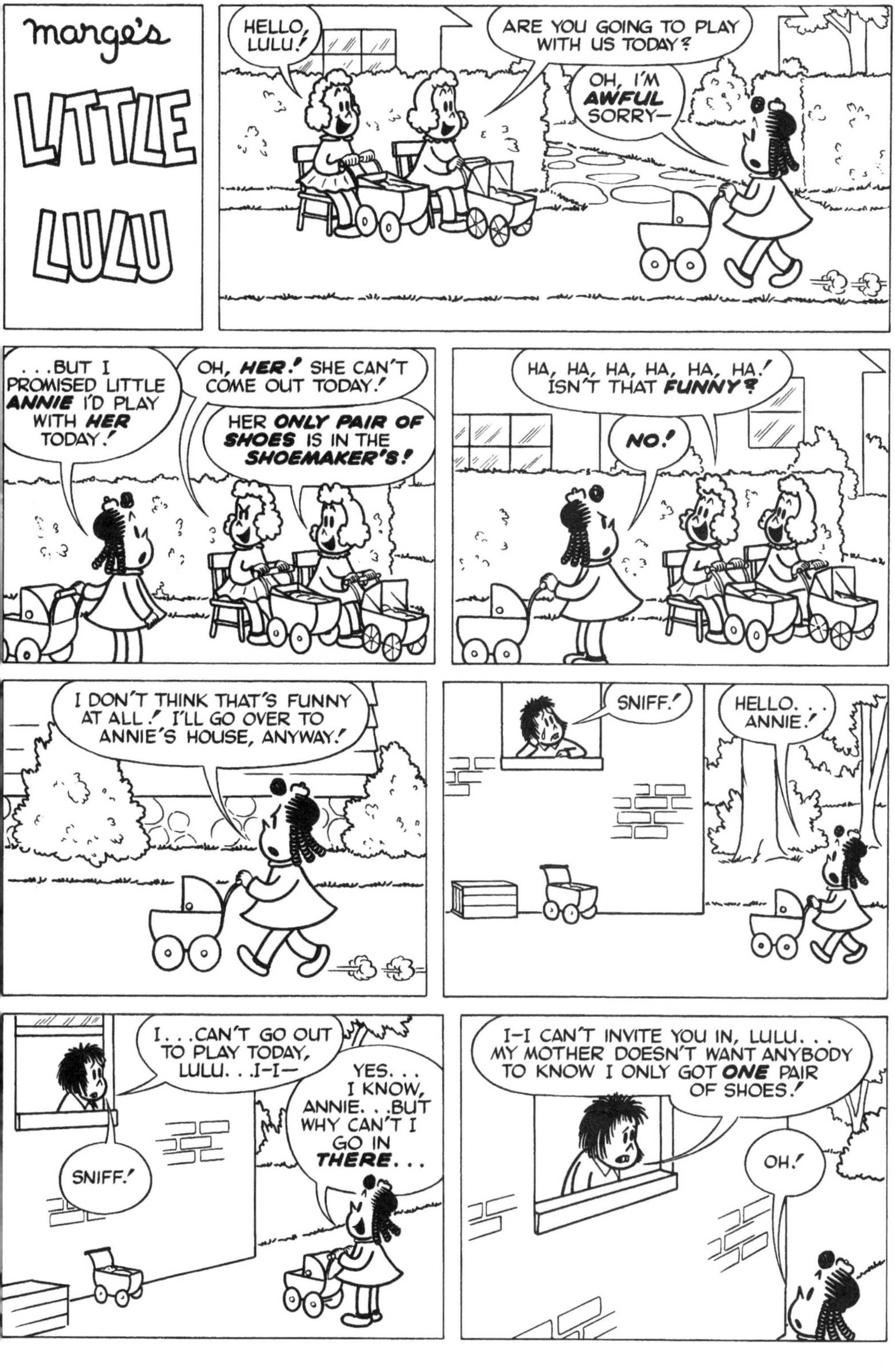
marge's
LITTLE LULU
HELLO, LULU!
ARE YOU GOING TO PLAY WITH US TODAY?
OH, I'M AWFUL SORRY—
...BUT I PROMISED LITTLE ANNIE I'D PLAY WITH HER TODAY!
OH, HER! SHE CAN'T COME OUT TODAY!
HER ONLY PAIR OF SHOES IS IN THE SHOEMAKER'S!
HA, HA, HA, HA, HA, HA! ISN'T THAT FUNNY?
NO!
I DON'T THINK THAT'S FUNNY AT ALL! I'LL GO OVER TO ANNIE'S HOUSE, ANYWAY!
SNIFF!
HELLO... ANNIE!
I...CAN'T GO OUT TO PLAY TODAY, LULU...I-I—
SNIFF!
YES... I KNOW, ANNIE...BUT WHY CAN'T I GO IN THERE...
I-I CAN'T INVITE YOU IN, LULU... MY MOTHER DOESN'T WANT ANYBODY TO KNOW I ONLY GOT ONE PAIR OF SHOES!
OH!

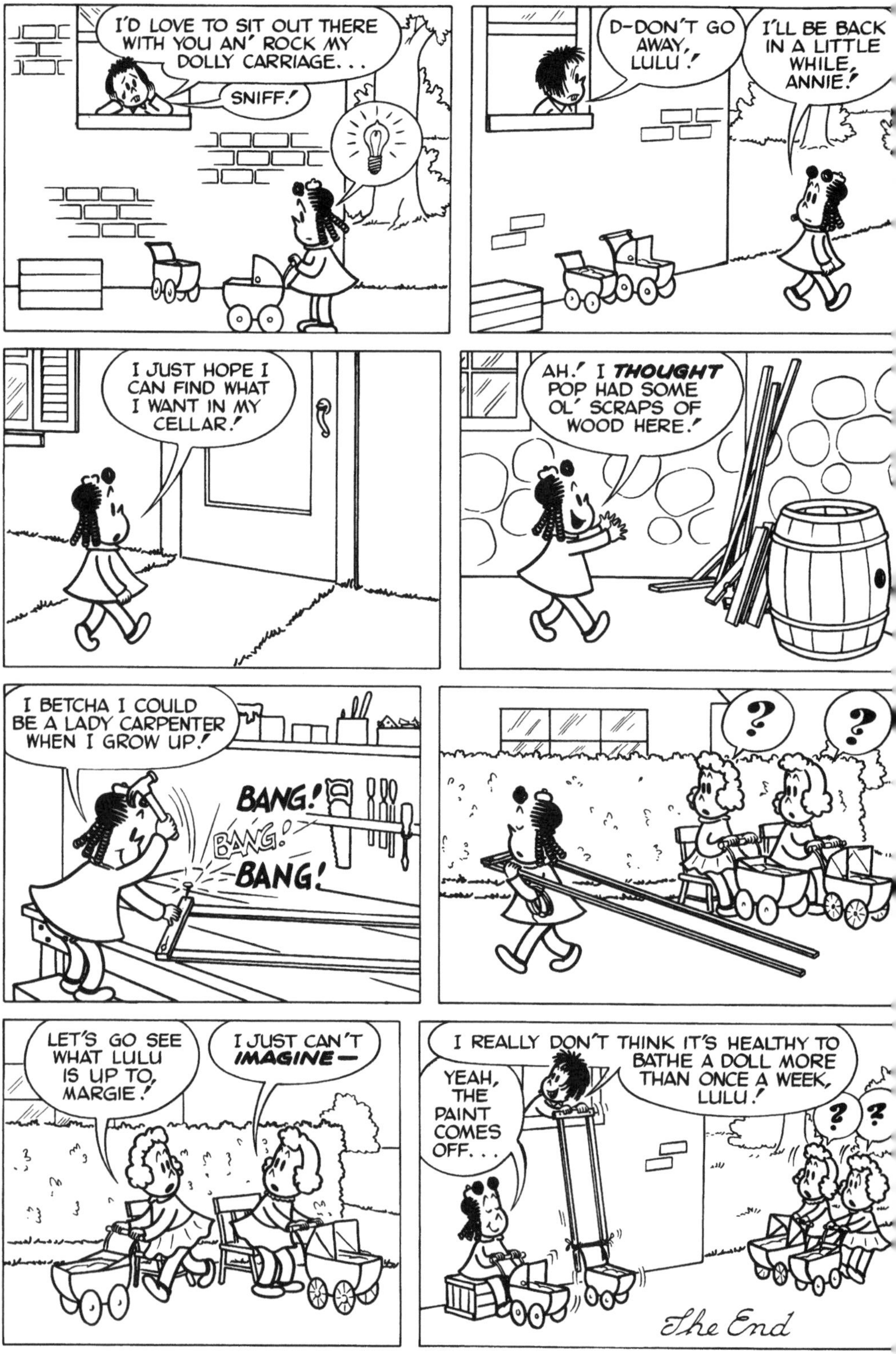

I'D LOVE TO SIT OUT THERE WITH YOU AN' ROCK MY DOLLY CARRIAGE...
SNIFF!
D-DON'T GO AWAY, LULU!
I'LL BE BACK IN A LITTLE WHILE, ANNIE!
I JUST HOPE I CAN FIND WHAT I WANT IN MY CELLAR!
AH! I **THOUGHT** POP HAD SOME OL' SCRAPS OF WOOD HERE!
I BETCHA I COULD BE A LADY CARPENTER WHEN I GROW UP!
BANG!
BANG!
BANG!
?
?
LET'S GO SEE WHAT LULU IS UP TO, MARGIE!
I JUST CAN'T ***IMAGINE***—
I REALLY DON'T THINK IT'S HEALTHY TO BATHE A DOLL MORE THAN ONCE A WEEK, LULU!
YEAH, THE PAINT COMES OFF...
?
?
The End

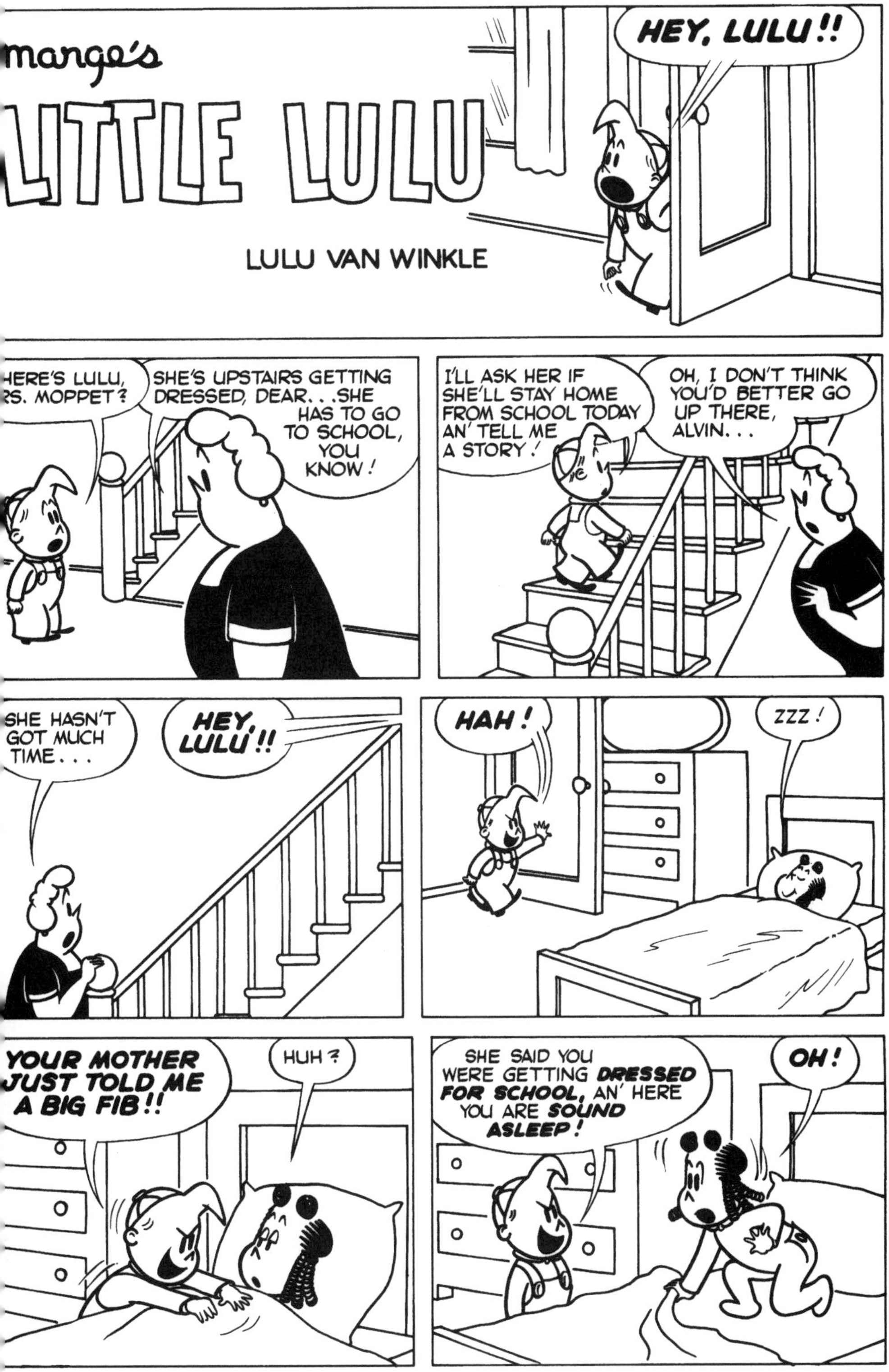

marge's
LITTLE LULU
LULU VAN WINKLE
HEY, LULU!!
HERE'S LULU, RS. MOPPET?
SHE'S UPSTAIRS GETTING DRESSED, DEAR...SHE HAS TO GO TO SCHOOL, YOU KNOW!
I'LL ASK HER IF SHE'LL STAY HOME FROM SCHOOL TODAY AN' TELL ME A STORY!
OH, I DON'T THINK YOU'D BETTER GO UP THERE, ALVIN...
SHE HASN'T GOT MUCH TIME...
HEY, LULU!!
HAH!
ZZZ!
YOUR MOTHER JUST TOLD ME A BIG FIB!!
HUH?
SHE SAID YOU WERE GETTING DRESSED FOR SCHOOL, AN' HERE YOU ARE SOUND ASLEEP!
OH!

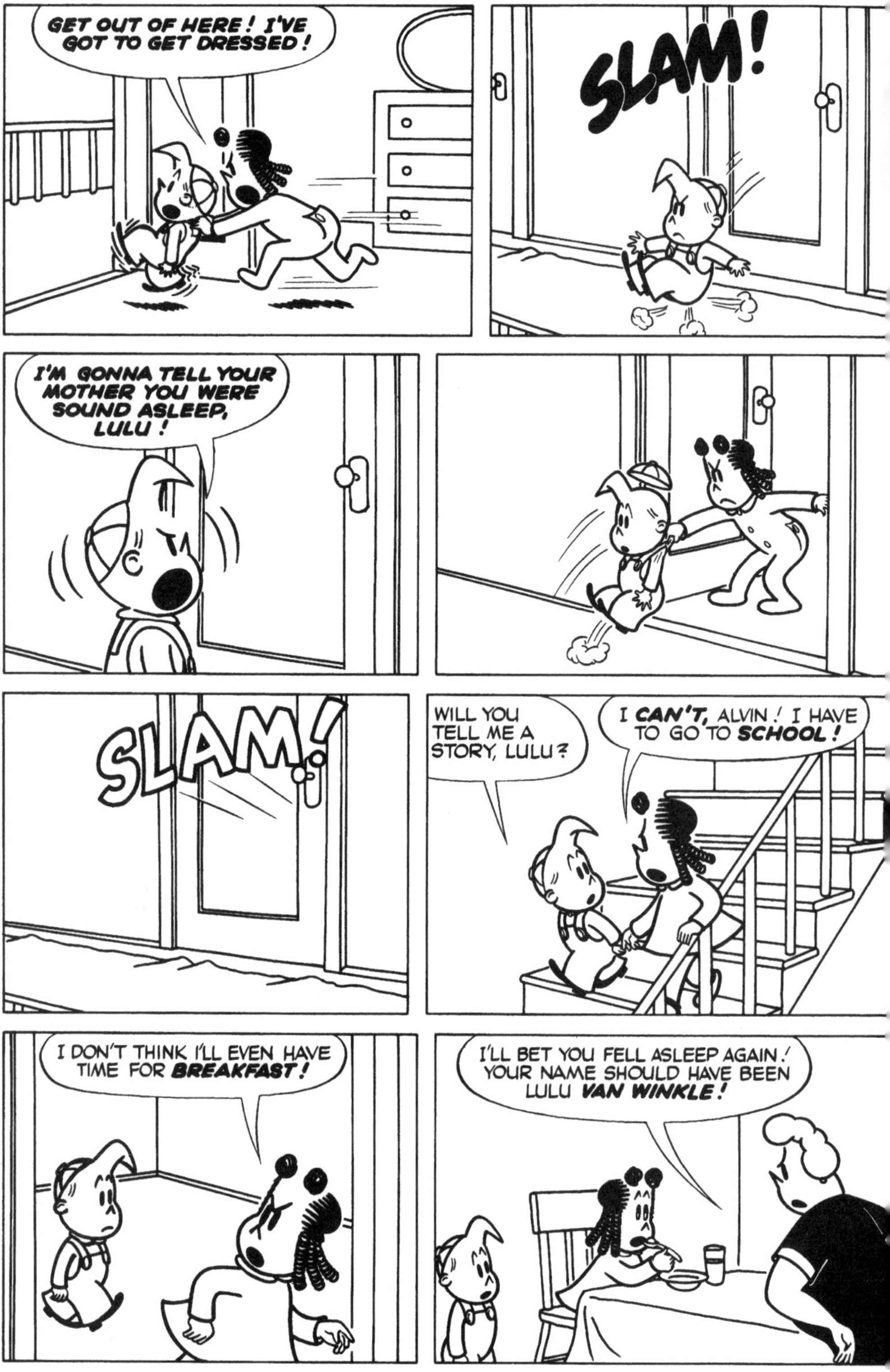
GET OUT OF HERE! I'VE GOT TO GET DRESSED!
SLAM!
I'M GONNA TELL YOUR MOTHER YOU WERE SOUND ASLEEP, LULU!
SLAM!
WILL YOU TELL ME A STORY, LULU?
I CAN'T, ALVIN! I HAVE TO GO TO SCHOOL!
I DON'T THINK I'LL EVEN HAVE TIME FOR BREAKFAST!
I'LL BET YOU FELL ASLEEP AGAIN! YOUR NAME SHOULD HAVE BEEN LULU VAN WINKLE!

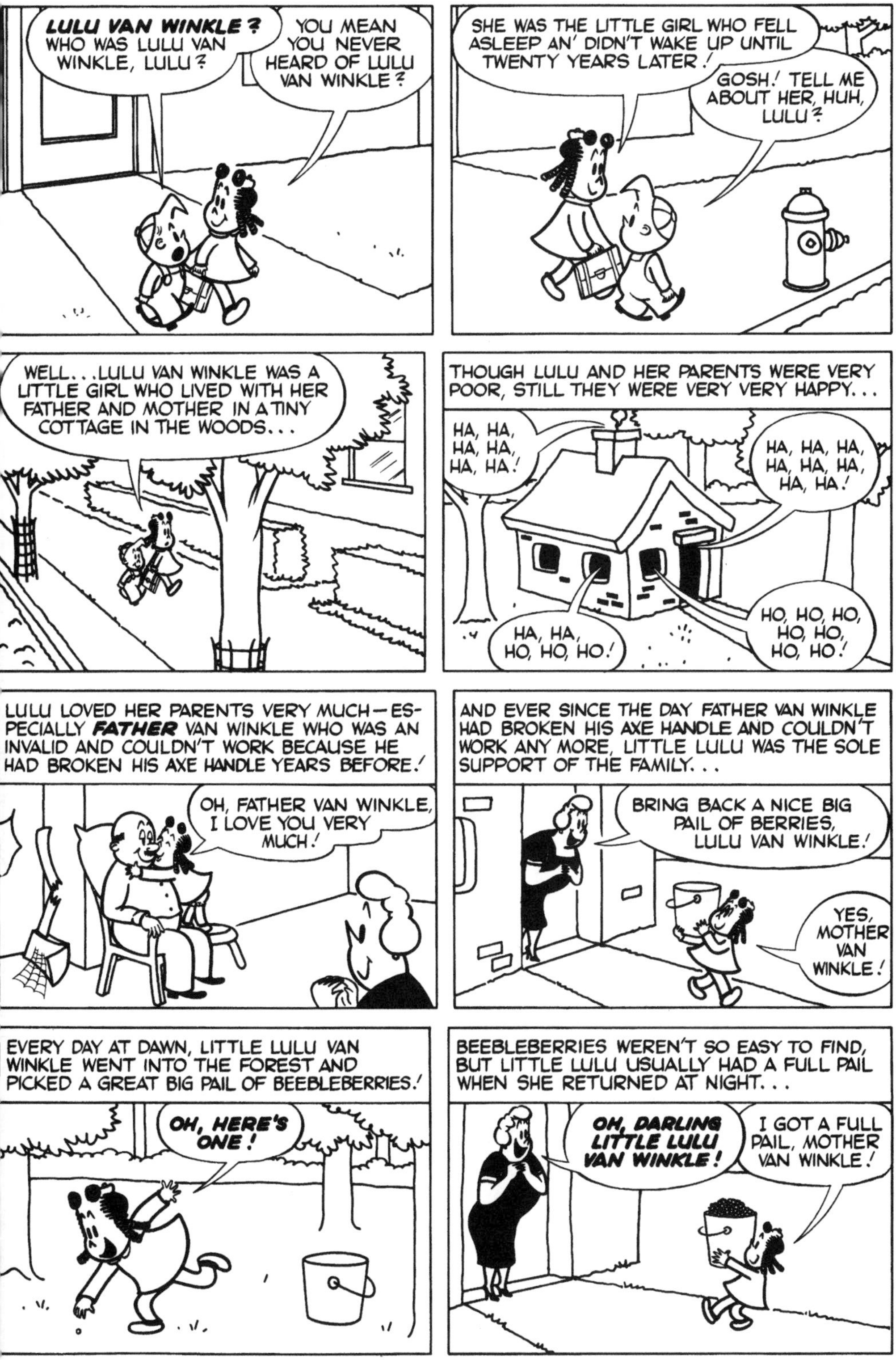
LULU VAN WINKLE? WHO WAS LULU VAN WINKLE, LULU?
YOU MEAN YOU NEVER HEARD OF LULU VAN WINKLE?
SHE WAS THE LITTLE GIRL WHO FELL ASLEEP AN' DIDN'T WAKE UP UNTIL TWENTY YEARS LATER!
GOSH! TELL ME ABOUT HER, HUH, LULU?
WELL...LULU VAN WINKLE WAS A LITTLE GIRL WHO LIVED WITH HER FATHER AND MOTHER IN A TINY COTTAGE IN THE WOODS...
THOUGH LULU AND HER PARENTS WERE VERY POOR, STILL THEY WERE VERY VERY HAPPY...
HA, HA, HA, HA, HA, HA!
HA, HA, HA, HA, HA, HA, HA, HA!
HA, HA, HO, HO, HO!
HO, HO, HO, HO, HO, HO, HO!
LULU LOVED HER PARENTS VERY MUCH—ESPECIALLY FATHER VAN WINKLE WHO WAS AN INVALID AND COULDN'T WORK BECAUSE HE HAD BROKEN HIS AXE HANDLE YEARS BEFORE!
OH, FATHER VAN WINKLE, I LOVE YOU VERY MUCH!
AND EVER SINCE THE DAY FATHER VAN WINKLE HAD BROKEN HIS AXE HANDLE AND COULDN'T WORK ANY MORE, LITTLE LULU WAS THE SOLE SUPPORT OF THE FAMILY...
BRING BACK A NICE BIG PAIL OF BERRIES, LULU VAN WINKLE!
YES, MOTHER VAN WINKLE!
EVERY DAY AT DAWN, LITTLE LULU VAN WINKLE WENT INTO THE FOREST AND PICKED A GREAT BIG PAIL OF BEEBLEBERRIES!
OH, HERE'S ONE!
BEEBLEBERRIES WEREN'T SO EASY TO FIND, BUT LITTLE LULU USUALLY HAD A FULL PAIL WHEN SHE RETURNED AT NIGHT...
OH, DARLING LITTLE LULU VAN WINKLE!
I GOT A FULL PAIL, MOTHER VAN WINKLE!

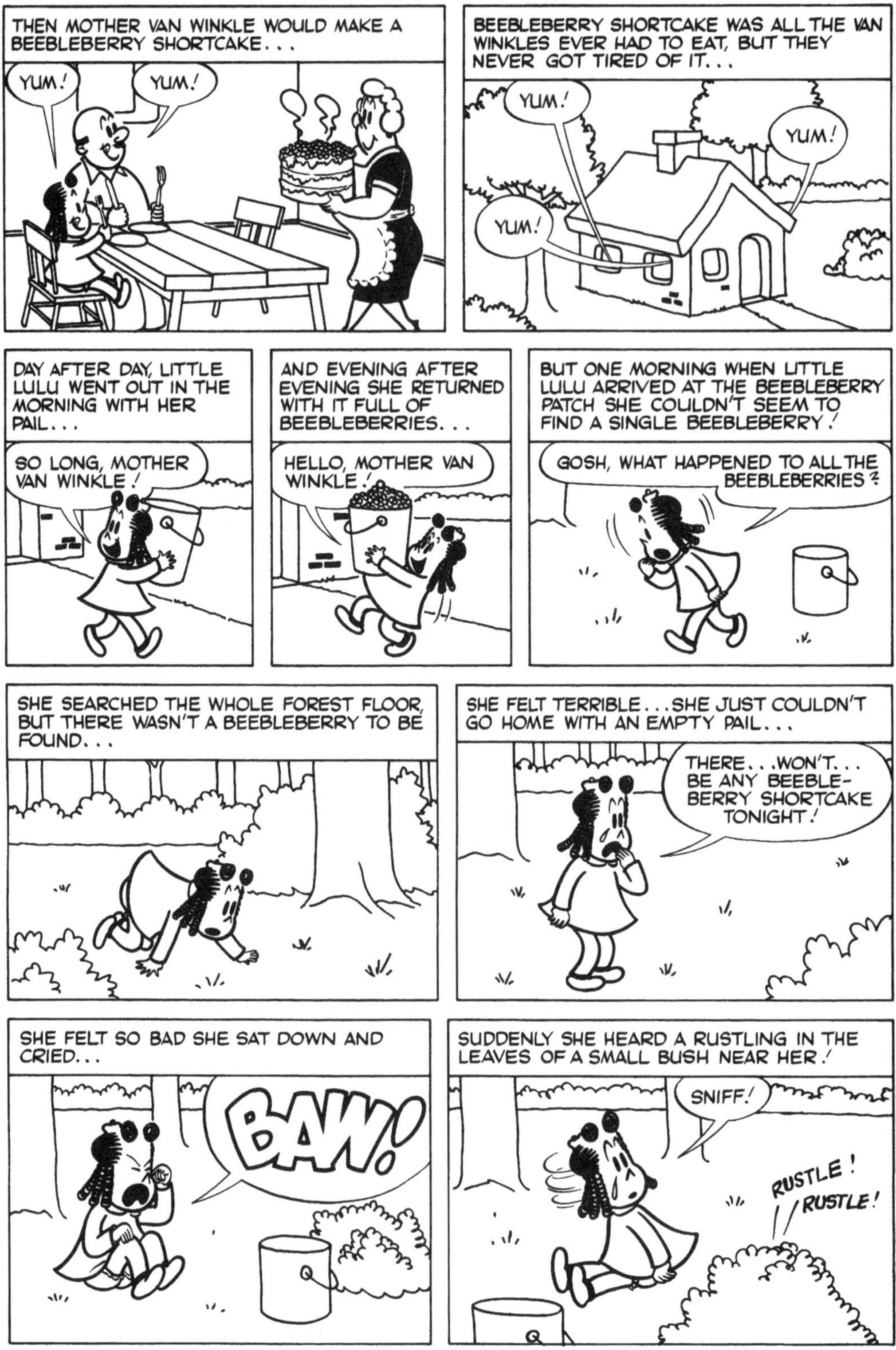
THEN MOTHER VAN WINKLE WOULD MAKE A BEEBLEBERRY SHORTCAKE...
YUM!
YUM!
BEEBLEBERRY SHORTCAKE WAS ALL THE VAN WINKLES EVER HAD TO EAT, BUT THEY NEVER GOT TIRED OF IT...
YUM!
YUM!
YUM!
DAY AFTER DAY, LITTLE LULU WENT OUT IN THE MORNING WITH HER PAIL...
SO LONG, MOTHER VAN WINKLE!
AND EVENING AFTER EVENING SHE RETURNED WITH IT FULL OF BEEBLEBERRIES...
HELLO, MOTHER VAN WINKLE!
BUT ONE MORNING WHEN LITTLE LULU ARRIVED AT THE BEEBLEBERRY PATCH SHE COULDN'T SEEM TO FIND A SINGLE BEEBLEBERRY!
GOSH, WHAT HAPPENED TO ALL THE BEEBLEBERRIES?
SHE SEARCHED THE WHOLE FOREST FLOOR, BUT THERE WASN'T A BEEBLEBERRY TO BE FOUND...
SHE FELT TERRIBLE...SHE JUST COULDN'T GO HOME WITH AN EMPTY PAIL...
THERE...WON'T... BE ANY BEEBLE-BERRY SHORTCAKE TONIGHT!
SHE FELT SO BAD SHE SAT DOWN AND CRIED...
BAW!
SUDDENLY SHE HEARD A RUSTLING IN THE LEAVES OF A SMALL BUSH NEAR HER!
SNIFF!
RUSTLE!
RUSTLE!

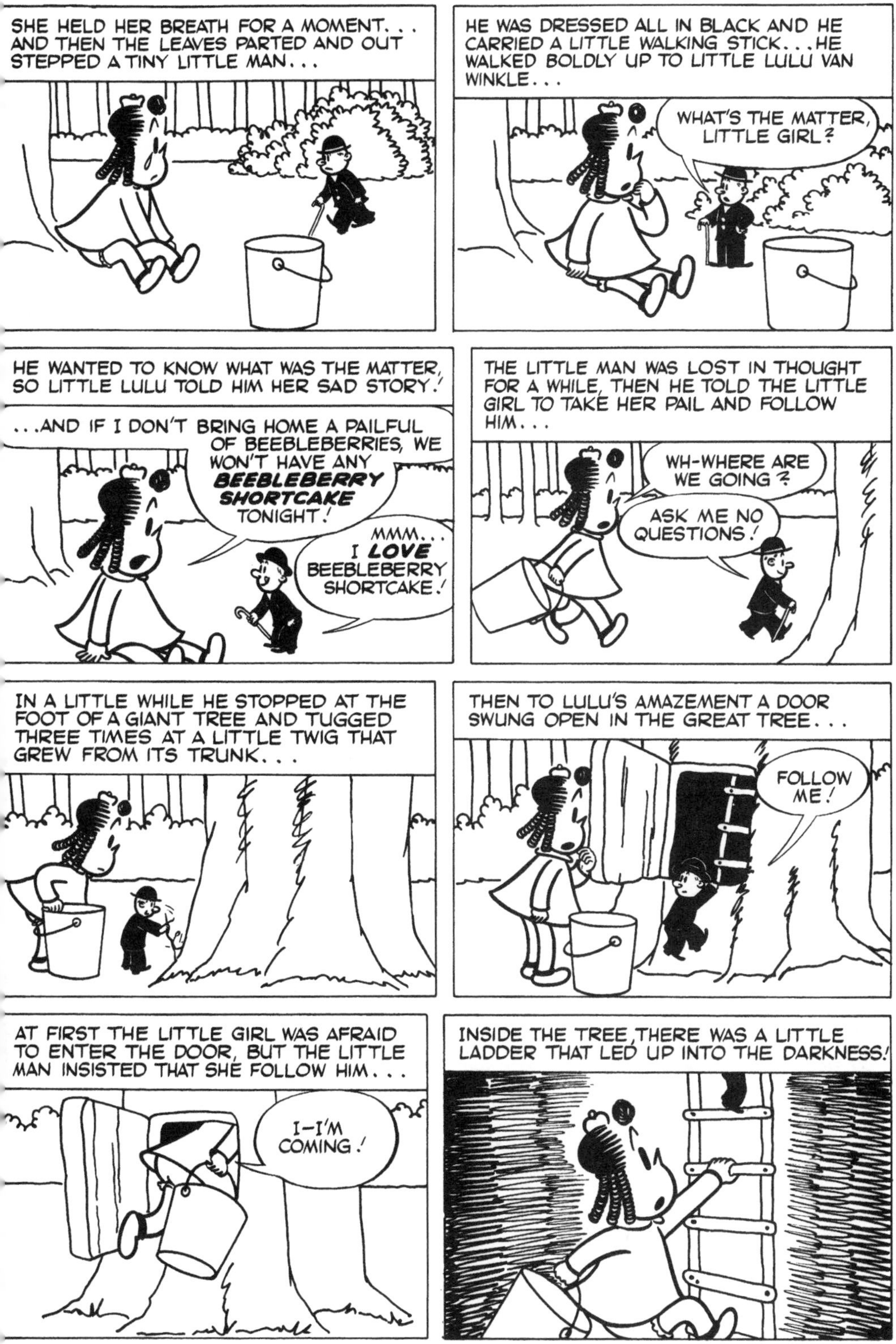
SHE HELD HER BREATH FOR A MOMENT. . . AND THEN THE LEAVES PARTED AND OUT STEPPED A TINY LITTLE MAN. . .
HE WAS DRESSED ALL IN BLACK AND HE CARRIED A LITTLE WALKING STICK. . . HE WALKED BOLDLY UP TO LITTLE LULU VAN WINKLE. . .
WHAT'S THE MATTER, LITTLE GIRL?
HE WANTED TO KNOW WHAT WAS THE MATTER, SO LITTLE LULU TOLD HIM HER SAD STORY!
. . .AND IF I DON'T BRING HOME A PAILFUL OF BEEBLEBERRIES, WE WON'T HAVE ANY BEEBLEBERRY SHORTCAKE TONIGHT!
MMM. . . I LOVE BEEBLEBERRY SHORTCAKE!
THE LITTLE MAN WAS LOST IN THOUGHT FOR A WHILE, THEN HE TOLD THE LITTLE GIRL TO TAKE HER PAIL AND FOLLOW HIM. . .
WH-WHERE ARE WE GOING?
ASK ME NO QUESTIONS!
IN A LITTLE WHILE HE STOPPED AT THE FOOT OF A GIANT TREE AND TUGGED THREE TIMES AT A LITTLE TWIG THAT GREW FROM ITS TRUNK. . .
THEN TO LULU'S AMAZEMENT A DOOR SWUNG OPEN IN THE GREAT TREE. . .
FOLLOW ME!
AT FIRST THE LITTLE GIRL WAS AFRAID TO ENTER THE DOOR, BUT THE LITTLE MAN INSISTED THAT SHE FOLLOW HIM. . .
I-I'M COMING!
INSIDE THE TREE, THERE WAS A LITTLE LADDER THAT LED UP INTO THE DARKNESS!

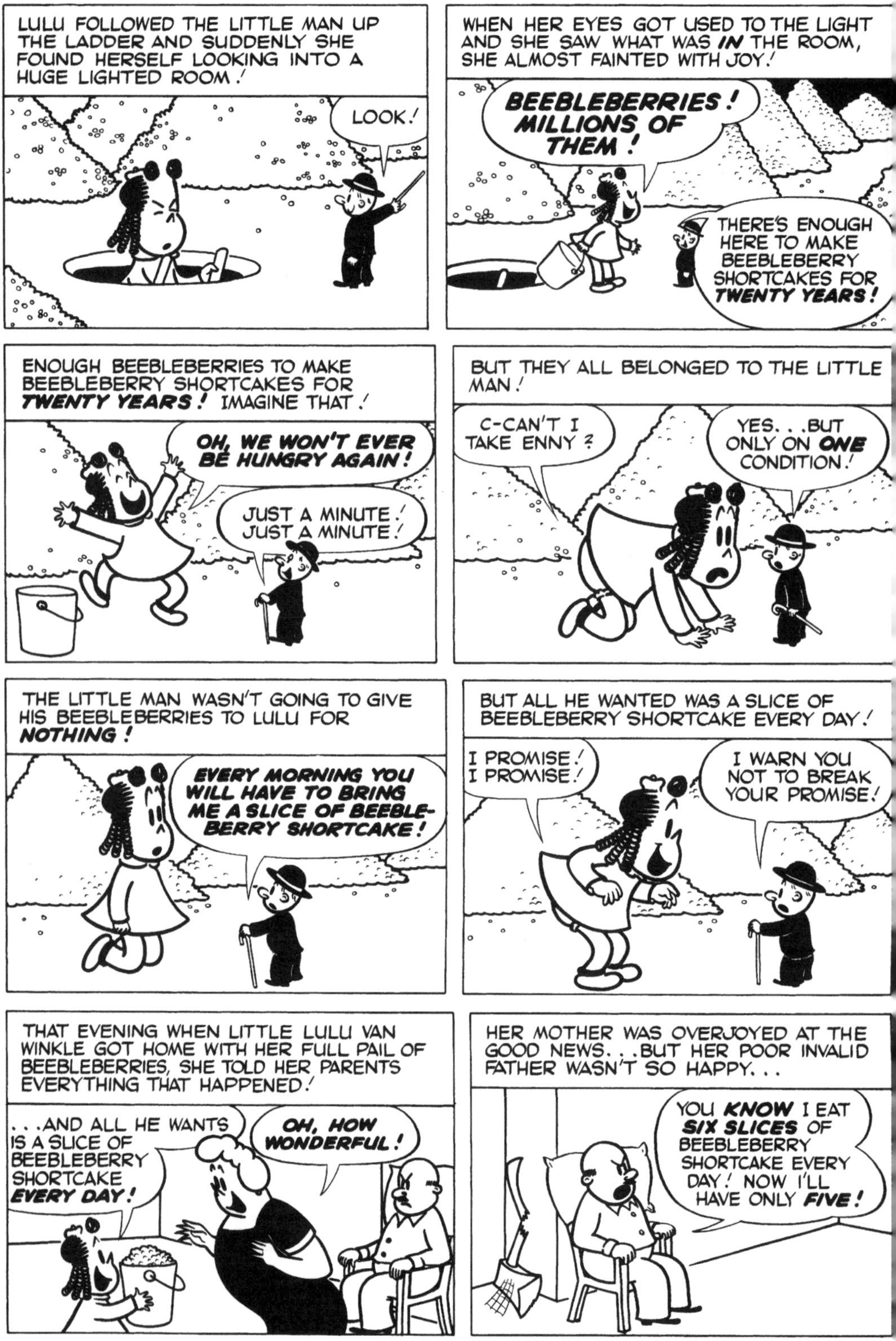

LULU FOLLOWED THE LITTLE MAN UP THE LADDER AND SUDDENLY SHE FOUND HERSELF LOOKING INTO A HUGE LIGHTED ROOM!
LOOK!
WHEN HER EYES GOT USED TO THE LIGHT AND SHE SAW WHAT WAS IN THE ROOM, SHE ALMOST FAINTED WITH JOY!
BEEBLEBERRIES! MILLIONS OF THEM!
THERE'S ENOUGH HERE TO MAKE BEEBLEBERRY SHORTCAKES FOR TWENTY YEARS!
ENOUGH BEEBLEBERRIES TO MAKE BEEBLEBERRY SHORTCAKES FOR TWENTY YEARS! IMAGINE THAT!
OH, WE WON'T EVER BE HUNGRY AGAIN!
JUST A MINUTE! JUST A MINUTE!
BUT THEY ALL BELONGED TO THE LITTLE MAN!
C-CAN'T I TAKE ENNY?
YES. . .BUT ONLY ON ONE CONDITION!
THE LITTLE MAN WASN'T GOING TO GIVE HIS BEEBLEBERRIES TO LULU FOR NOTHING!
EVERY MORNING YOU WILL HAVE TO BRING ME A SLICE OF BEEBLEBERRY SHORTCAKE!
BUT ALL HE WANTED WAS A SLICE OF BEEBLEBERRY SHORTCAKE EVERY DAY!
I PROMISE! I PROMISE!
I WARN YOU NOT TO BREAK YOUR PROMISE!
THAT EVENING WHEN LITTLE LULU VAN WINKLE GOT HOME WITH HER FULL PAIL OF BEEBLEBERRIES, SHE TOLD HER PARENTS EVERYTHING THAT HAPPENED!
. . .AND ALL HE WANTS IS A SLICE OF BEEBLEBERRY SHORTCAKE EVERY DAY!
OH, HOW WONDERFUL!
HER MOTHER WAS OVERJOYED AT THE GOOD NEWS. . .BUT HER POOR INVALID FATHER WASN'T SO HAPPY. . .
YOU KNOW I EAT SIX SLICES OF BEEBLEBERRY SHORTCAKE EVERY DAY! NOW I'LL HAVE ONLY FIVE!

EVERY MORNING LITTLE LULU LEFT HER HOUSE WITH A SLICE OF BEEBLEBERRY SHORTCAKE IN HER PAIL...

AND EVERY MORNING SHE ALWAYS FOUND THE LITTLE MAN EAGERLY WAITING FOR HER!

HERE IS YOUR BEEBLEBERRY SHORTCAKE!

GIMME!

THEN LITTLE LULU WOULD GO TO THE BIG TREE AND PULL THE TWIG THREE TIMES!

ONE... TWO... THREE...

MUNCH! MUNCH! MUNCH!

IN A LITTLE WHILE SHE WOULD BE BACK HOME WITH A BIG PAIL OF BEEBLEBERRIES!

HERE I AM!

THIS WENT ON UNTIL ONE EVENING MOTHER VAN WINKLE MADE AN ESPECIALLY DELICIOUS CAKE...

BOY! THAT SURE LOOKS GOOD!

UM, UM!

WE MUSN'T FORGET TO LEAVE ONE PIECE FOR THE LITTLE MAN!

IN LESS TIME THAN IT TAKES TO TELL, ALL THAT WAS LEFT WAS THE ONE SLICE FOR THE LITTLE MAN...

I FEEL STUFFED!

ME TOO!

OH, I FEEL SO SLEEPY!

THE FAMILY SAT THERE AT THE TABLE AND DOZED...AND ONE BY ONE THEY FELL ASLEEP...

ZZZ!

ZZZ! ZZZ!

IN A LITTLE WHILE ONE OF FATHER VAN WINKLE'S EYES OPENED...THEN THE OTHER...AND THEY WERE BOTH LOOKING AT THE SLICE OF CAKE ON THE TABLE...

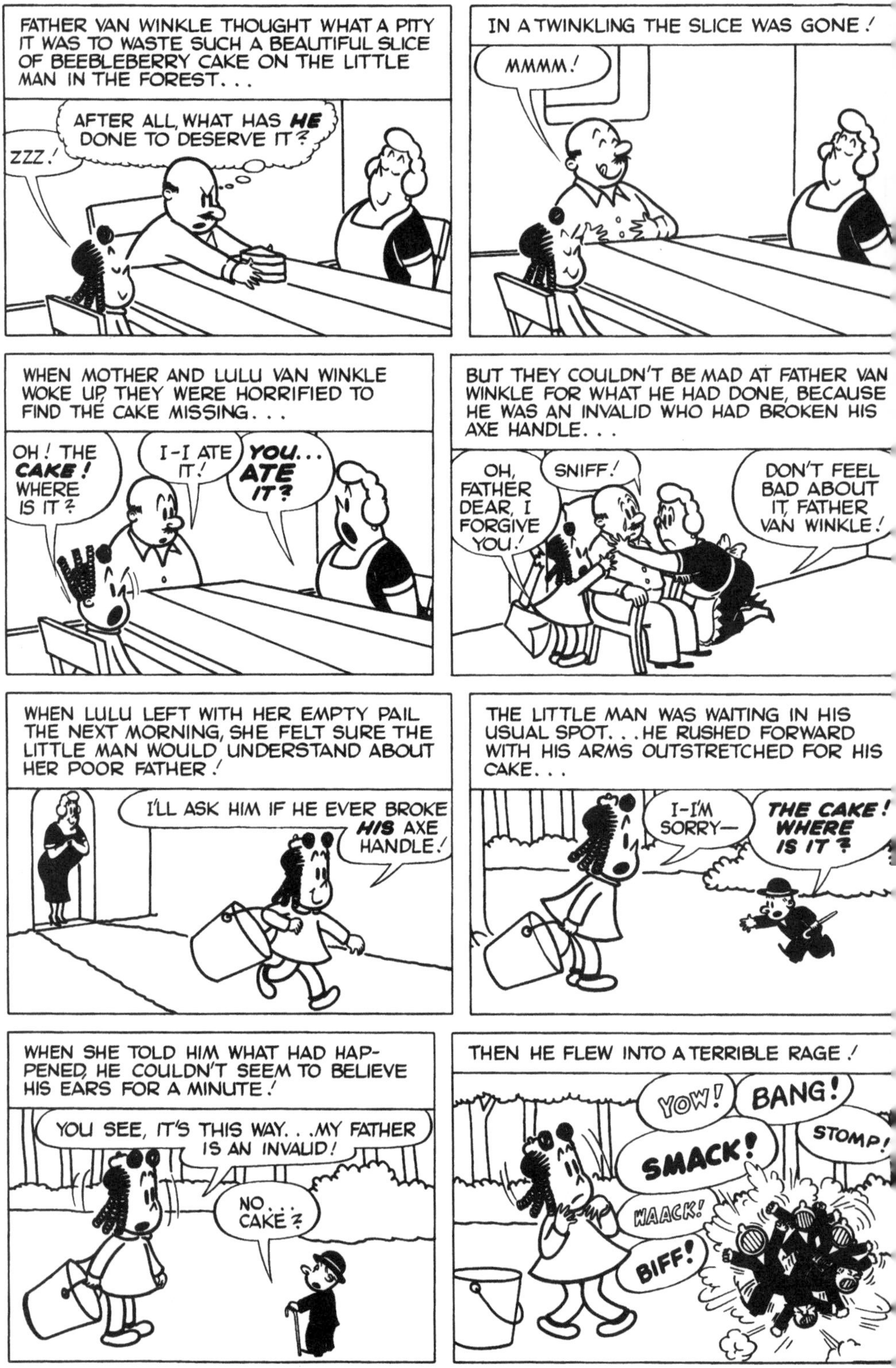
FATHER VAN WINKLE THOUGHT WHAT A PITY IT WAS TO WASTE SUCH A BEAUTIFUL SLICE OF BEEBLEBERRY CAKE ON THE LITTLE MAN IN THE FOREST. . .
ZZZ!
AFTER ALL, WHAT HAS HE DONE TO DESERVE IT?
IN A TWINKLING THE SLICE WAS GONE!
MMMM!
WHEN MOTHER AND LULU VAN WINKLE WOKE UP, THEY WERE HORRIFIED TO FIND THE CAKE MISSING. . .
OH! THE CAKE! WHERE IS IT?
I-I ATE IT!
YOU... ATE IT?
BUT THEY COULDN'T BE MAD AT FATHER VAN WINKLE FOR WHAT HE HAD DONE, BECAUSE HE WAS AN INVALID WHO HAD BROKEN HIS AXE HANDLE. . .
OH, FATHER DEAR, I FORGIVE YOU!
SNIFF!
DON'T FEEL BAD ABOUT IT, FATHER VAN WINKLE!
WHEN LULU LEFT WITH HER EMPTY PAIL THE NEXT MORNING, SHE FELT SURE THE LITTLE MAN WOULD UNDERSTAND ABOUT HER POOR FATHER!
I'LL ASK HIM IF HE EVER BROKE HIS AXE HANDLE!
THE LITTLE MAN WAS WAITING IN HIS USUAL SPOT. . .HE RUSHED FORWARD WITH HIS ARMS OUTSTRETCHED FOR HIS CAKE. . .
I-I'M SORRY—
THE CAKE! WHERE IS IT?
WHEN SHE TOLD HIM WHAT HAD HAPPENED, HE COULDN'T SEEM TO BELIEVE HIS EARS FOR A MINUTE!
YOU SEE, IT'S THIS WAY. . .MY FATHER IS AN INVALID!
NO. . . CAKE?
THEN HE FLEW INTO A TERRIBLE RAGE!
YOW!
BANG!
STOMP!
SMACK!
WAACK!
BIFF!

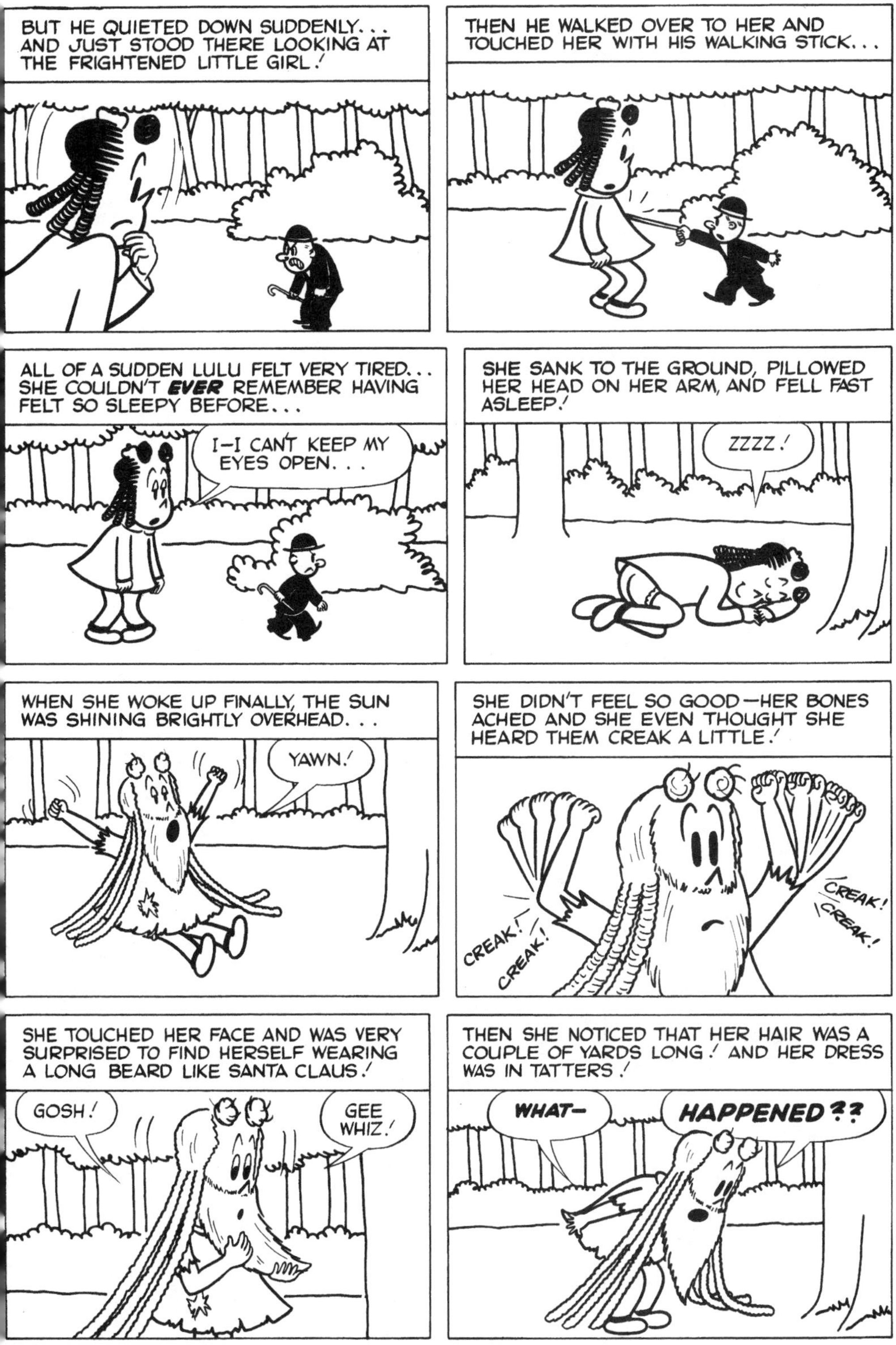
BUT HE QUIETED DOWN SUDDENLY. . . AND JUST STOOD THERE LOOKING AT THE FRIGHTENED LITTLE GIRL!
THEN HE WALKED OVER TO HER AND TOUCHED HER WITH HIS WALKING STICK. . .
ALL OF A SUDDEN LULU FELT VERY TIRED. . . SHE COULDN'T EVER REMEMBER HAVING FELT SO SLEEPY BEFORE. . .
I-I CAN'T KEEP MY EYES OPEN. . .
SHE SANK TO THE GROUND, PILLOWED HER HEAD ON HER ARM, AND FELL FAST ASLEEP!
ZZZZ!
WHEN SHE WOKE UP FINALLY, THE SUN WAS SHINING BRIGHTLY OVERHEAD. . .
YAWN!
SHE DIDN'T FEEL SO GOOD—HER BONES ACHED AND SHE EVEN THOUGHT SHE HEARD THEM CREAK A LITTLE!
CREAK! CREAK!
CREAK! CREAK!
SHE TOUCHED HER FACE AND WAS VERY SURPRISED TO FIND HERSELF WEARING A LONG BEARD LIKE SANTA CLAUS!
GOSH!
GEE WHIZ!
THEN SHE NOTICED THAT HER HAIR WAS A COUPLE OF YARDS LONG! AND HER DRESS WAS IN TATTERS!
WHAT—
HAPPENED??

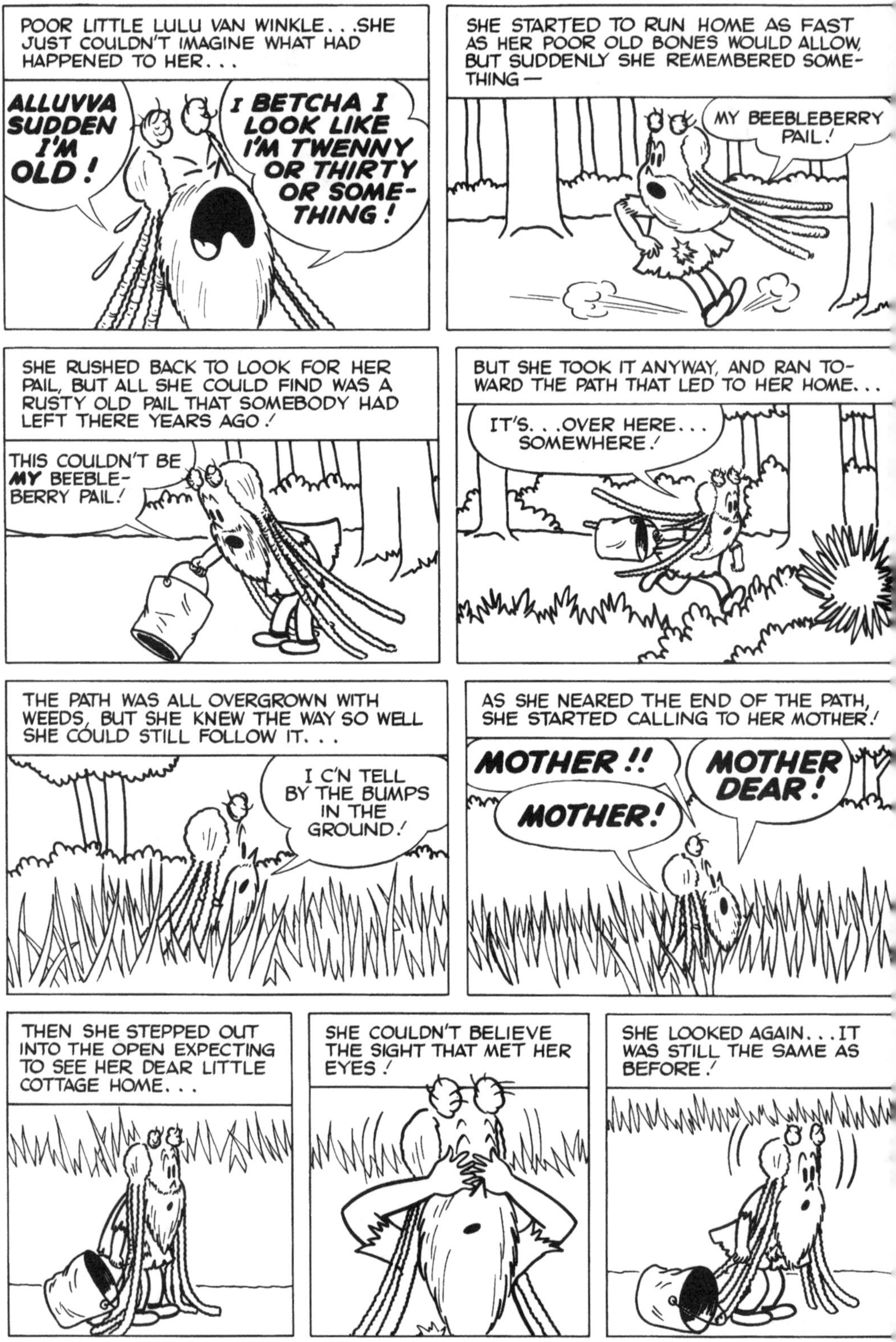
POOR LITTLE LULU VAN WINKLE. . .SHE JUST COULDN'T IMAGINE WHAT HAD HAPPENED TO HER. . .
ALLUVVA SUDDEN I'M OLD!
I BETCHA I LOOK LIKE I'M TWENNY OR THIRTY OR SOME-THING!
SHE STARTED TO RUN HOME AS FAST AS HER POOR OLD BONES WOULD ALLOW, BUT SUDDENLY SHE REMEMBERED SOME-THING—
MY BEEBLEBERRY PAIL!
SHE RUSHED BACK TO LOOK FOR HER PAIL, BUT ALL SHE COULD FIND WAS A RUSTY OLD PAIL THAT SOMEBODY HAD LEFT THERE YEARS AGO!
THIS COULDN'T BE MY BEEBLE-BERRY PAIL!
BUT SHE TOOK IT ANYWAY, AND RAN TO-WARD THE PATH THAT LED TO HER HOME. . .
IT'S. . .OVER HERE. . . SOMEWHERE!
THE PATH WAS ALL OVERGROWN WITH WEEDS, BUT SHE KNEW THE WAY SO WELL SHE COULD STILL FOLLOW IT. . .
I C'N TELL BY THE BUMPS IN THE GROUND!
AS SHE NEARED THE END OF THE PATH, SHE STARTED CALLING TO HER MOTHER!
MOTHER!!
MOTHER!
MOTHER DEAR!
THEN SHE STEPPED OUT INTO THE OPEN EXPECTING TO SEE HER DEAR LITTLE COTTAGE HOME. . .
SHE COULDN'T BELIEVE THE SIGHT THAT MET HER EYES!
SHE LOOKED AGAIN. . .IT WAS STILL THE SAME AS BEFORE!

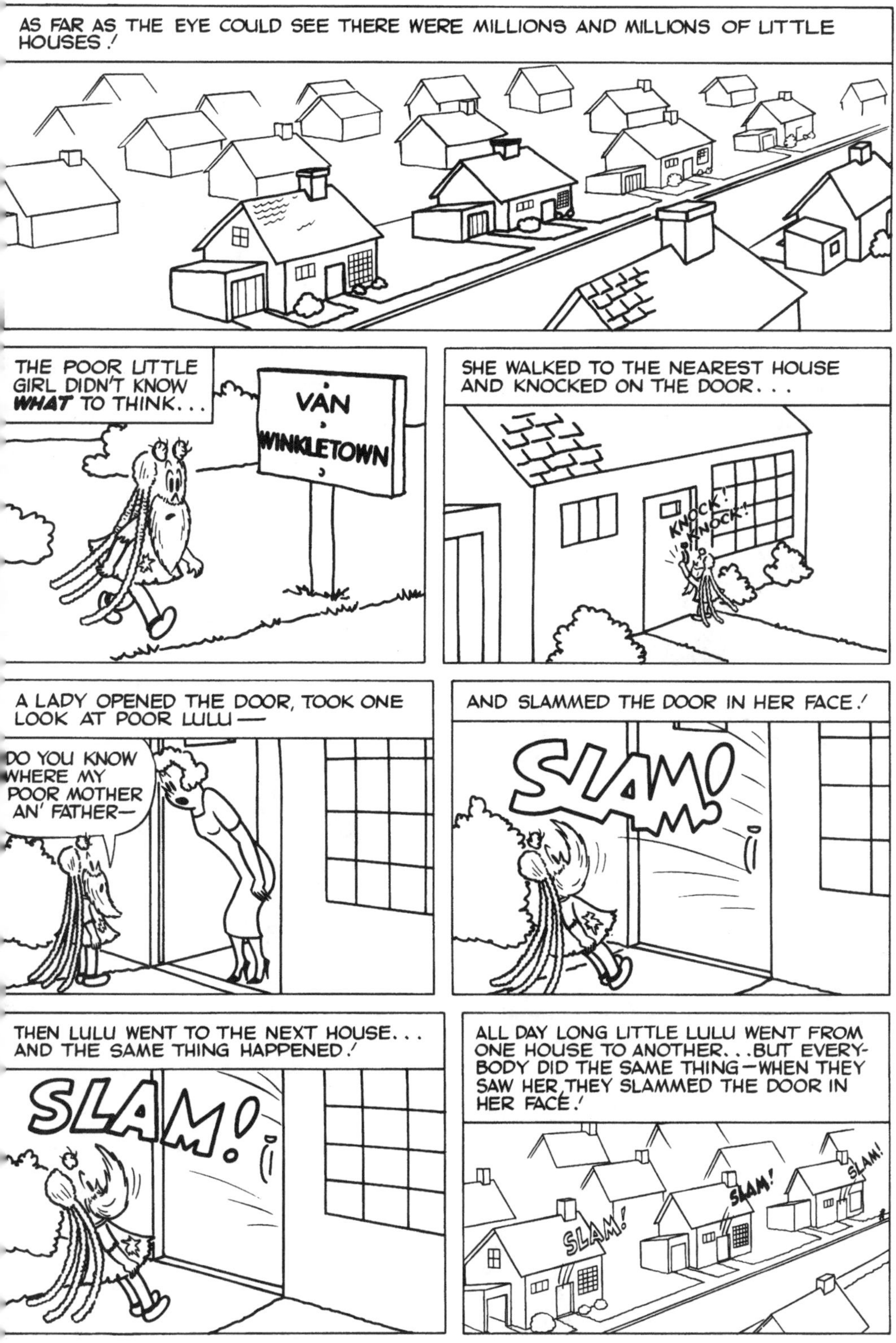
AS FAR AS THE EYE COULD SEE THERE WERE MILLIONS AND MILLIONS OF LITTLE HOUSES!
THE POOR LITTLE GIRL DIDN'T KNOW WHAT TO THINK...
VAN WINKLETOWN
SHE WALKED TO THE NEAREST HOUSE AND KNOCKED ON THE DOOR...
KNOCK! KNOCK!
A LADY OPENED THE DOOR, TOOK ONE LOOK AT POOR LULU—
DO YOU KNOW WHERE MY POOR MOTHER AN' FATHER—
AND SLAMMED THE DOOR IN HER FACE!
SLAM!
THEN LULU WENT TO THE NEXT HOUSE... AND THE SAME THING HAPPENED!
SLAM!
ALL DAY LONG LITTLE LULU WENT FROM ONE HOUSE TO ANOTHER...BUT EVERYBODY DID THE SAME THING—WHEN THEY SAW HER THEY SLAMMED THE DOOR IN HER FACE!
SLAM!
SLAM!
SLAM!

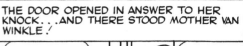

FINALLY SHE DECIDED TO TRY JUST ONE MORE HOME BEFORE GIVING UP...

RENTING AGENT

KNOCK! KNOCK!

THE DOOR OPENED IN ANSWER TO HER KNOCK...AND THERE STOOD MOTHER VAN WINKLE!

MOTHER!!

LULU!

MOTHER VAN WINKLE HAD RECOGNIZED HER DEAR DAUGHTER EVEN IN A BEARD...

OH, DARLING, WHERE HAVE YOU BEEN THESE LAST TWENTY YEARS?

A KID LIKE YOU SHOULDN'T STAY OUT SO LATE!

WELL...IT TURNED OUT THAT LITTLE LULU VAN WINKLE HAD SLEPT IN THE FOREST FOR *TWENTY YEARS!* AND DURING THAT TIME HER MOTHER AND FATHER BUILT A LOT OF HOUSES AN' GOT VERY RICH!

DID LULU LIVE HAPPILY EVER AFTER?

OH, SURE! SHE GOT A SHAVE AND WASHED UP AND —

DID SHE HAFTA GO TO *SCHOOL?*

SCHOOL? SCHOOL?

YEAH... SCHOOL!

OH!

I'M LATE!

IF LULU THINKS FOR ONE MINUTE I BELIEVE ANY OF THOSE SILLY STORIES—

the End

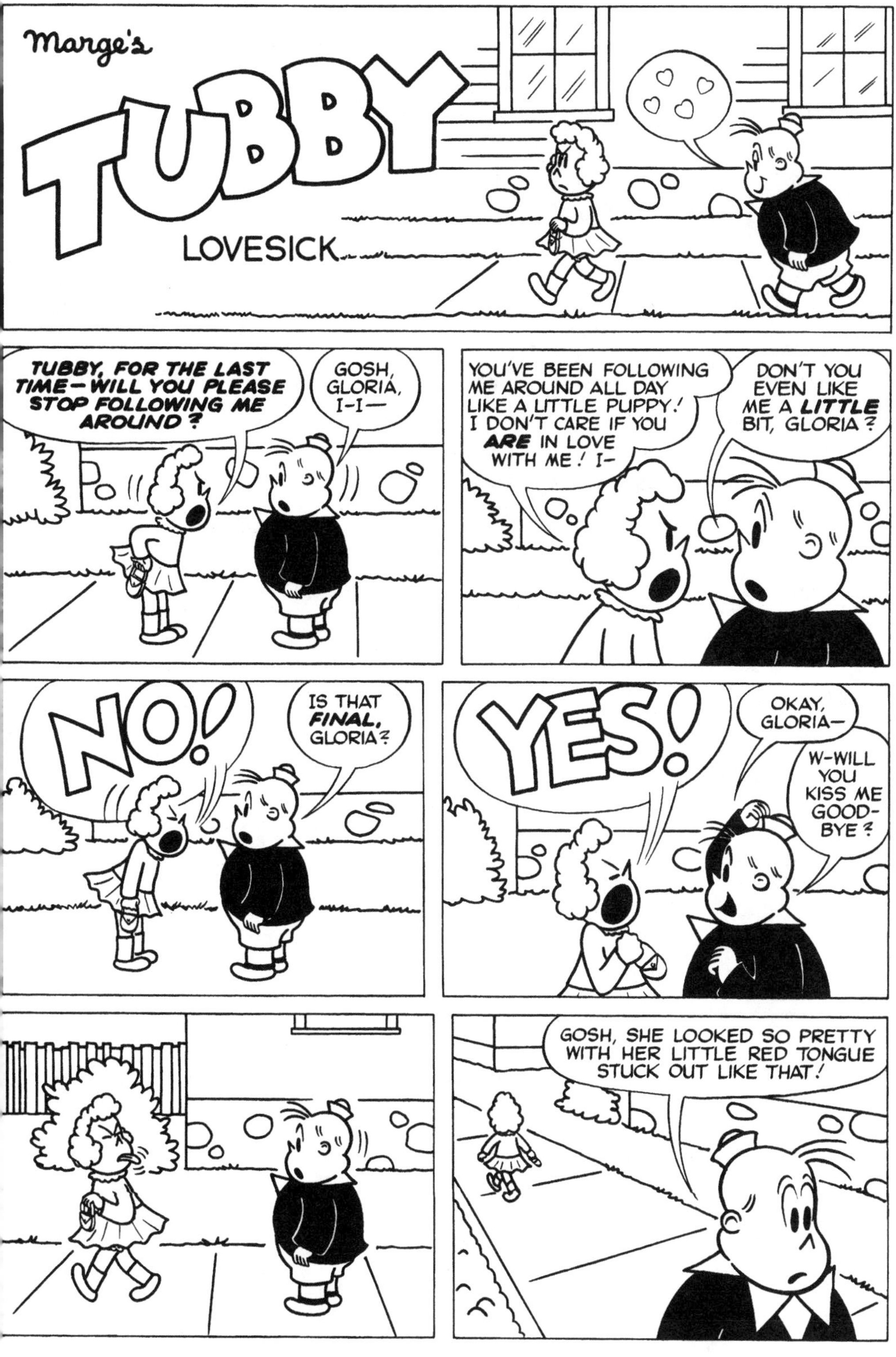
Marge's
TUBBY
LOVESICK
TUBBY, FOR THE LAST TIME—WILL YOU PLEASE STOP FOLLOWING ME AROUND?
GOSH, GLORIA, I-I—
YOU'VE BEEN FOLLOWING ME AROUND ALL DAY LIKE A LITTLE PUPPY! I DON'T CARE IF YOU ARE IN LOVE WITH ME! I-
DON'T YOU EVEN LIKE ME A LITTLE BIT, GLORIA?
NO!
IS THAT FINAL, GLORIA?
YES!
OKAY, GLORIA—
W-WILL YOU KISS ME GOOD-BYE?
GOSH, SHE LOOKED SO PRETTY WITH HER LITTLE RED TONGUE STUCK OUT LIKE THAT!

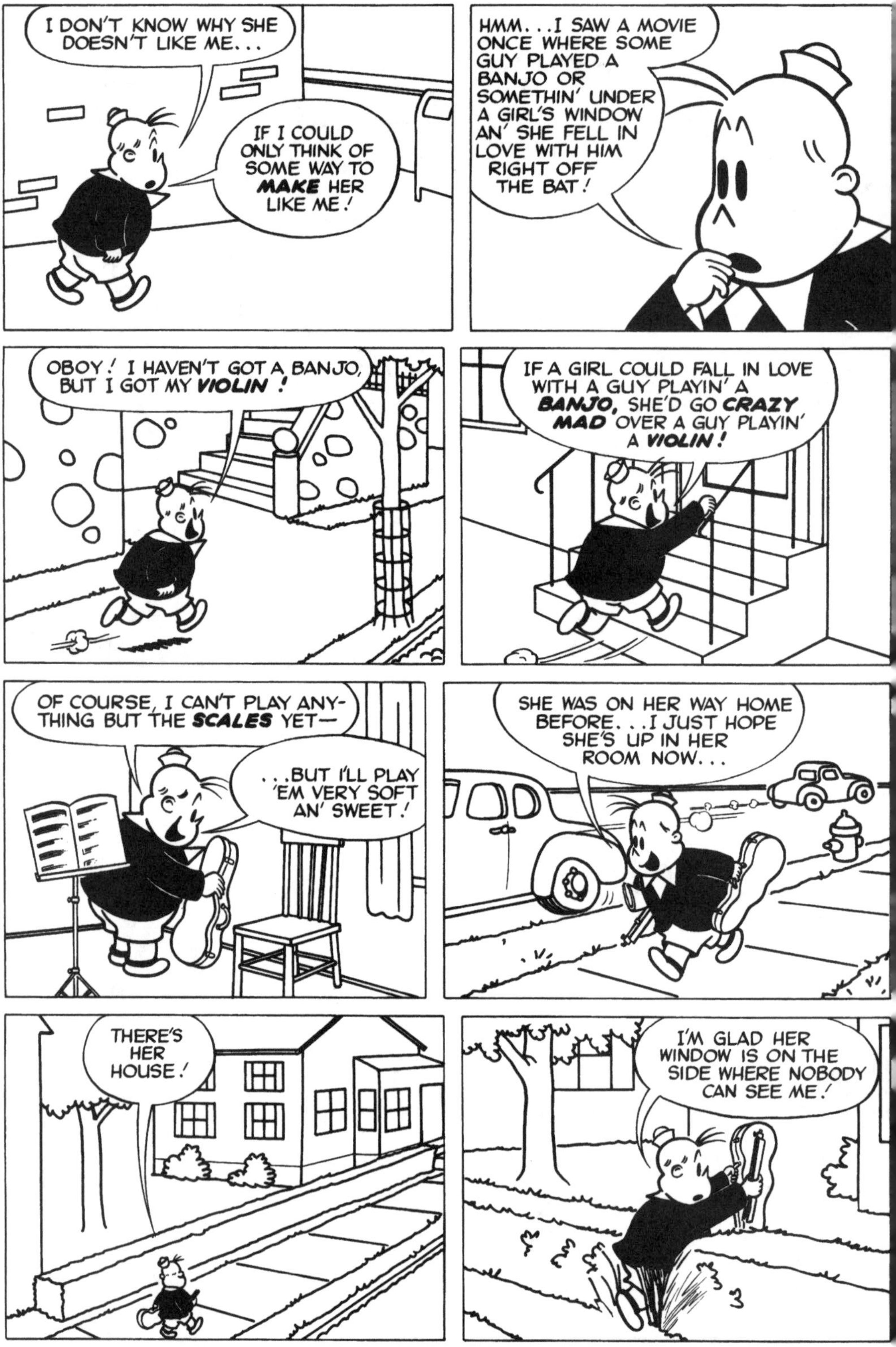
I DON'T KNOW WHY SHE DOESN'T LIKE ME...
IF I COULD ONLY THINK OF SOME WAY TO MAKE HER LIKE ME!
HMM...I SAW A MOVIE ONCE WHERE SOME GUY PLAYED A BANJO OR SOMETHIN' UNDER A GIRL'S WINDOW AN' SHE FELL IN LOVE WITH HIM RIGHT OFF THE BAT!
OBOY! I HAVEN'T GOT A BANJO, BUT I GOT MY VIOLIN!
IF A GIRL COULD FALL IN LOVE WITH A GUY PLAYIN' A BANJO, SHE'D GO CRAZY MAD OVER A GUY PLAYIN' A VIOLIN!
OF COURSE, I CAN'T PLAY ANYTHING BUT THE SCALES YET—
...BUT I'LL PLAY 'EM VERY SOFT AN' SWEET!
SHE WAS ON HER WAY HOME BEFORE...I JUST HOPE SHE'S UP IN HER ROOM NOW...
THERE'S HER HOUSE!
I'M GLAD HER WINDOW IS ON THE SIDE WHERE NOBODY CAN SEE ME!

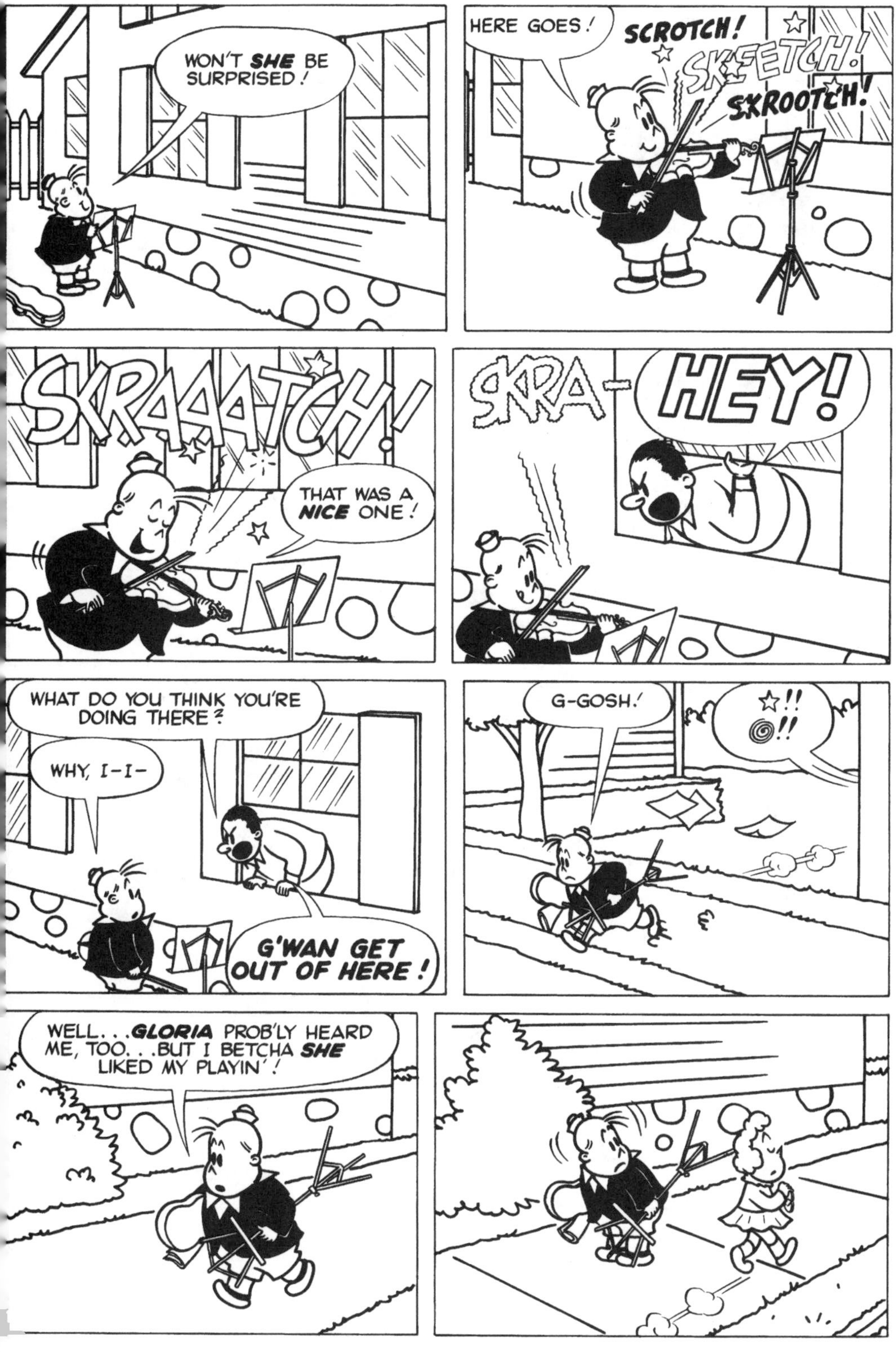
WON'T SHE BE SURPRISED!
HERE GOES!
SCROTCH!
SKEETCH!
SKROOTCH!
SKRAAATCH!
THAT WAS A NICE ONE!
SKRA-
HEY!
WHAT DO YOU THINK YOU'RE DOING THERE?
WHY, I-I-
G'WAN GET OUT OF HERE!
G-GOSH!
WELL...GLORIA PROB'LY HEARD ME, TOO...BUT I BETCHA SHE LIKED MY PLAYIN'!

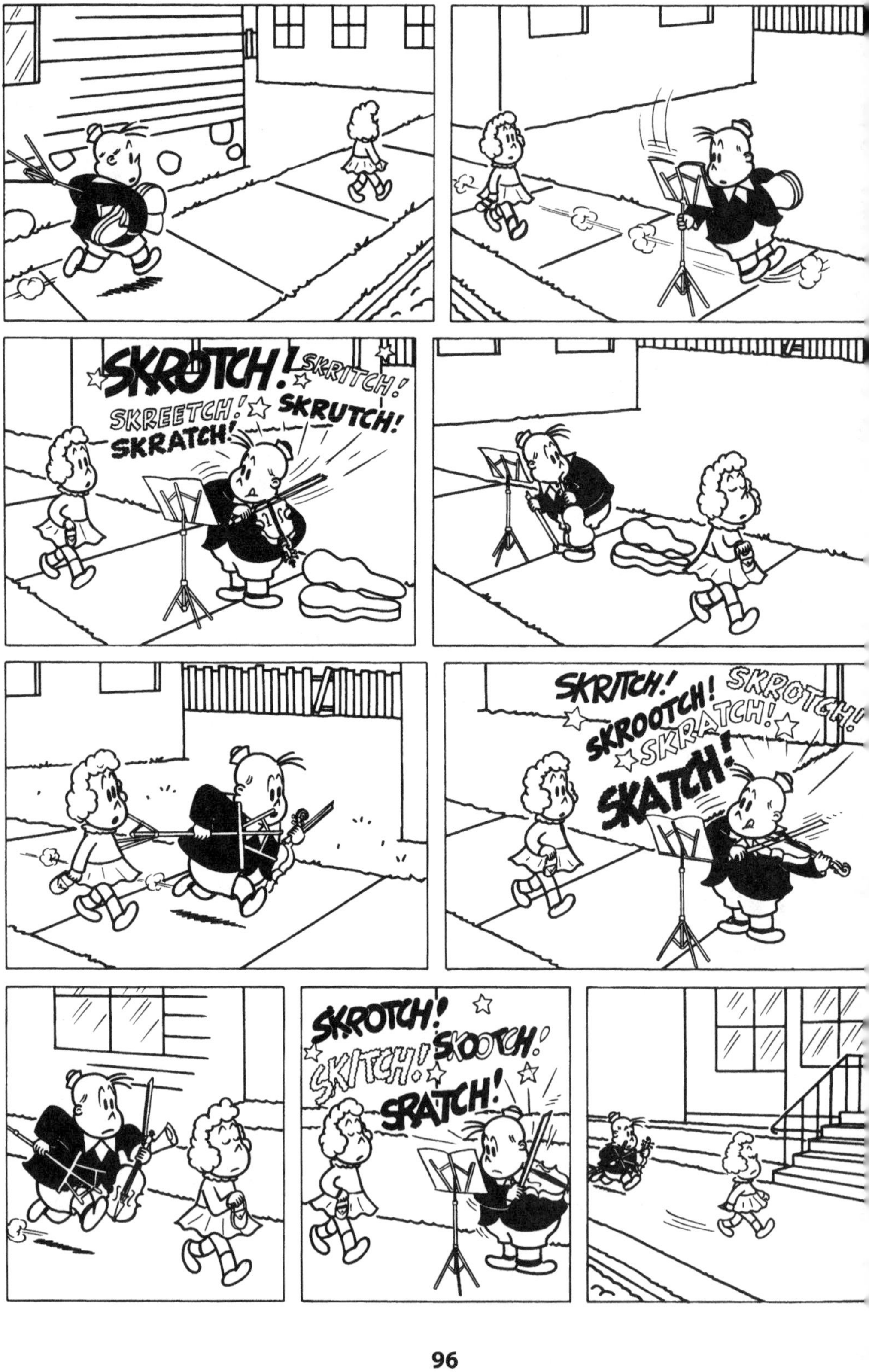
SKROTCH!
SKRITCH!
SKREETCH!
SKRUTCH!
SKRATCH!
SKRITCH!
SKROOTCH!
SKROTCH!
SKRATCH!
SKATCH!
SKROTCH!
SKITCH!
SKOOTCH!
SRATCH!

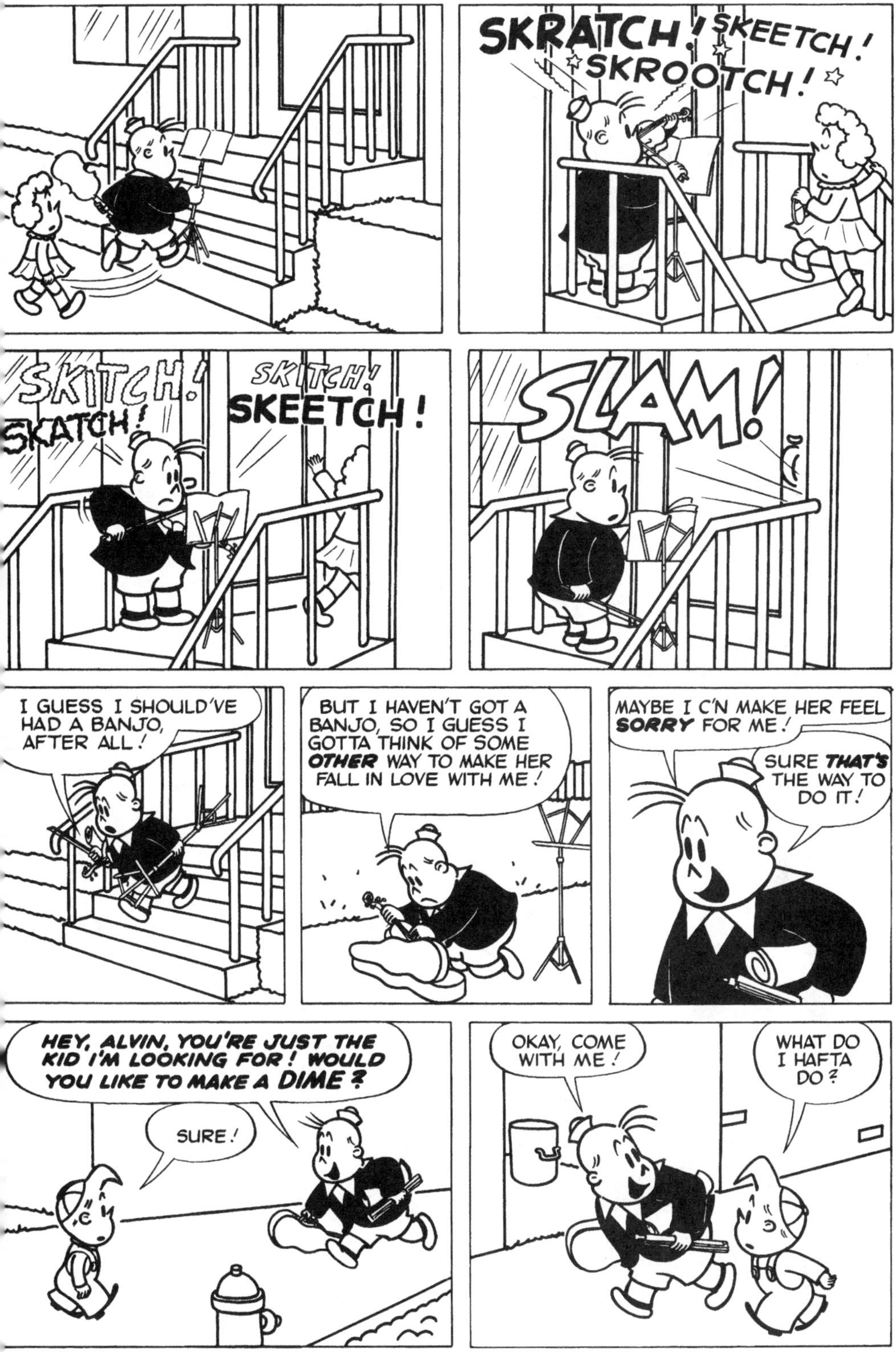
SKRATCH! SKEETCH!
SKROOTCH!
SKITCH!
SKATCH!
SKITCH!
SKEETCH!
SLAM!
I GUESS I SHOULD'VE HAD A BANJO, AFTER ALL!
BUT I HAVEN'T GOT A BANJO, SO I GUESS I GOTTA THINK OF SOME OTHER WAY TO MAKE HER FALL IN LOVE WITH ME!
MAYBE I C'N MAKE HER FEEL SORRY FOR ME!
SURE THAT'S THE WAY TO DO IT!
HEY, ALVIN, YOU'RE JUST THE KID I'M LOOKING FOR! WOULD YOU LIKE TO MAKE A DIME?
SURE!
OKAY, COME WITH ME!
WHAT DO I HAFTA DO?

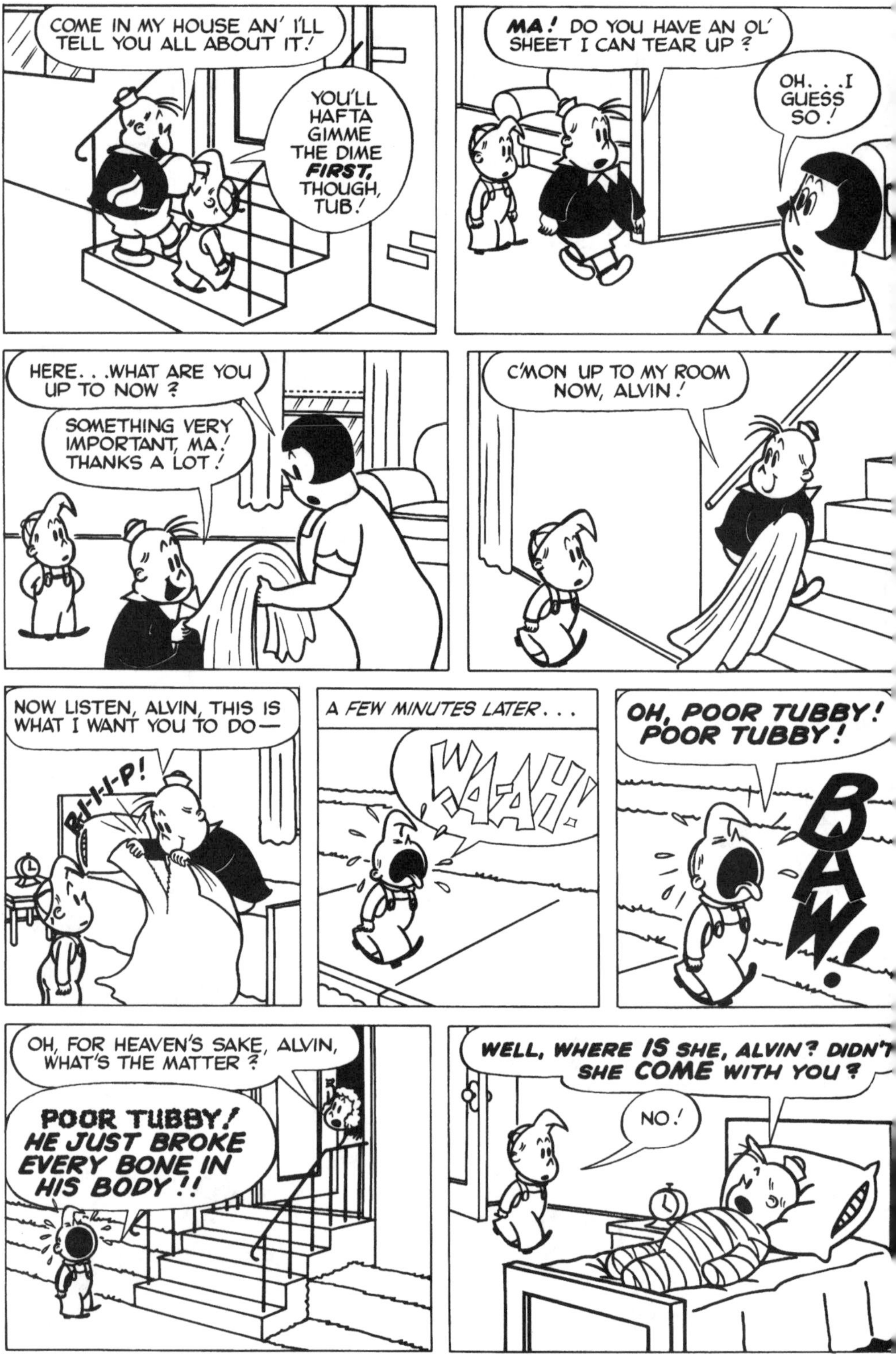

COME IN MY HOUSE AN' I'LL TELL YOU ALL ABOUT IT!
YOU'LL HAFTA GIMME THE DIME FIRST, THOUGH, TUB!
MA! DO YOU HAVE AN OL' SHEET I CAN TEAR UP?
OH. . .I GUESS SO!
HERE. . .WHAT ARE YOU UP TO NOW?
SOMETHING VERY IMPORTANT, MA! THANKS A LOT!
C'MON UP TO MY ROOM NOW, ALVIN!
NOW LISTEN, ALVIN, THIS IS WHAT I WANT YOU TO DO—
R-I-I-I-P!
A FEW MINUTES LATER. . .
WA-AH!
OH, POOR TUBBY! POOR TUBBY!
BAW!
OH, FOR HEAVEN'S SAKE, ALVIN, WHAT'S THE MATTER?
POOR TUBBY! HE JUST BROKE EVERY BONE IN HIS BODY!!
WELL, WHERE IS SHE, ALVIN? DIDN'T SHE COME WITH YOU?
NO!

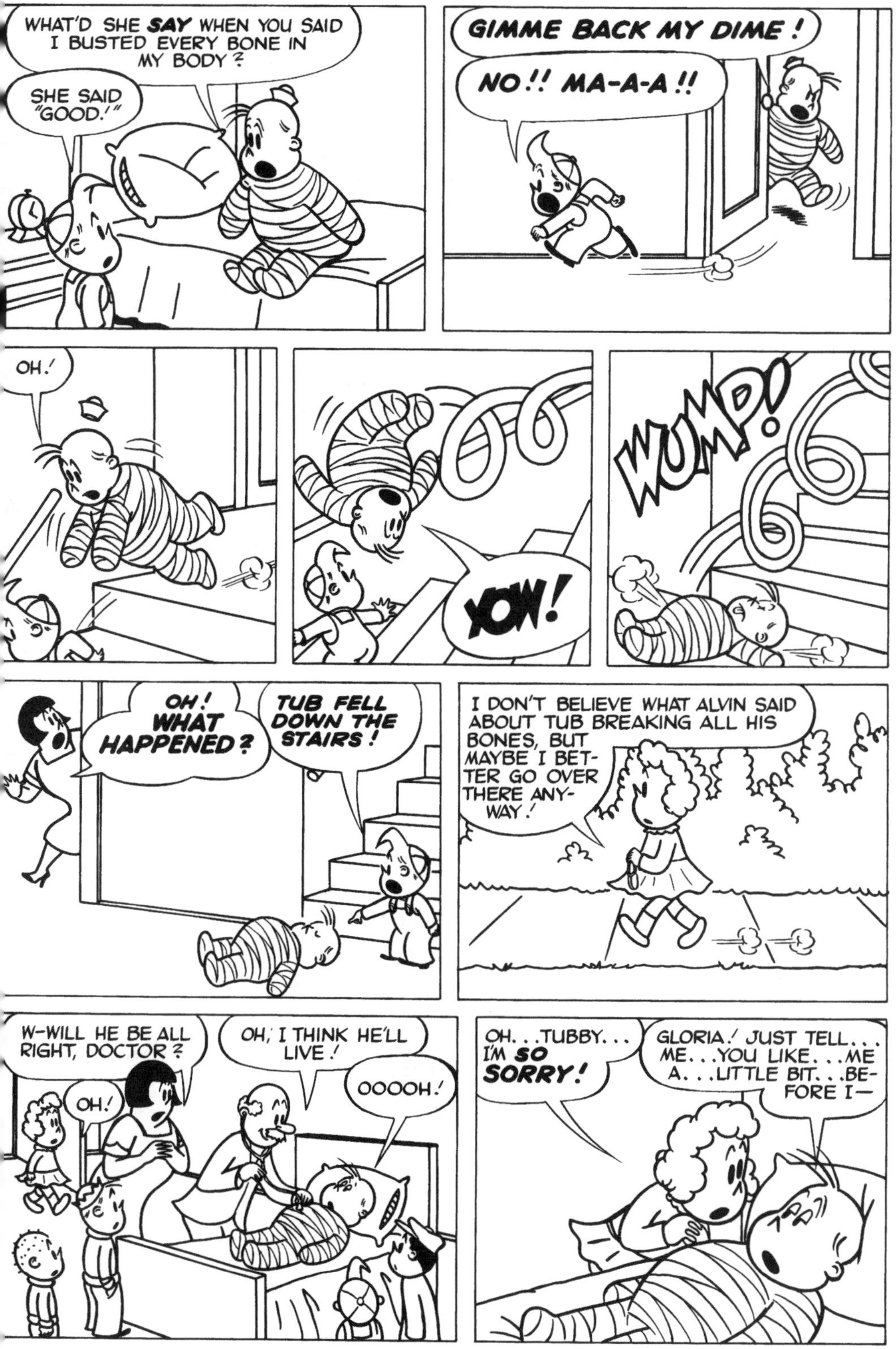
WHAT'D SHE SAY WHEN YOU SAID I BUSTED EVERY BONE IN MY BODY?
SHE SAID "GOOD!"
GIMME BACK MY DIME!
NO!! MA-A-A!!
OH!
YOW!
WUMP!
OH! WHAT HAPPENED?
TUB FELL DOWN THE STAIRS!
I DON'T BELIEVE WHAT ALVIN SAID ABOUT TUB BREAKING ALL HIS BONES, BUT MAYBE I BETTER GO OVER THERE ANYWAY!
W-WILL HE BE ALL RIGHT, DOCTOR?
OH, I THINK HE'LL LIVE!
OH!
OOOOH!
OH...TUBBY...I'M SO SORRY!
GLORIA! JUST TELL...ME...YOU LIKE...ME A...LITTLE BIT...BEFORE I—

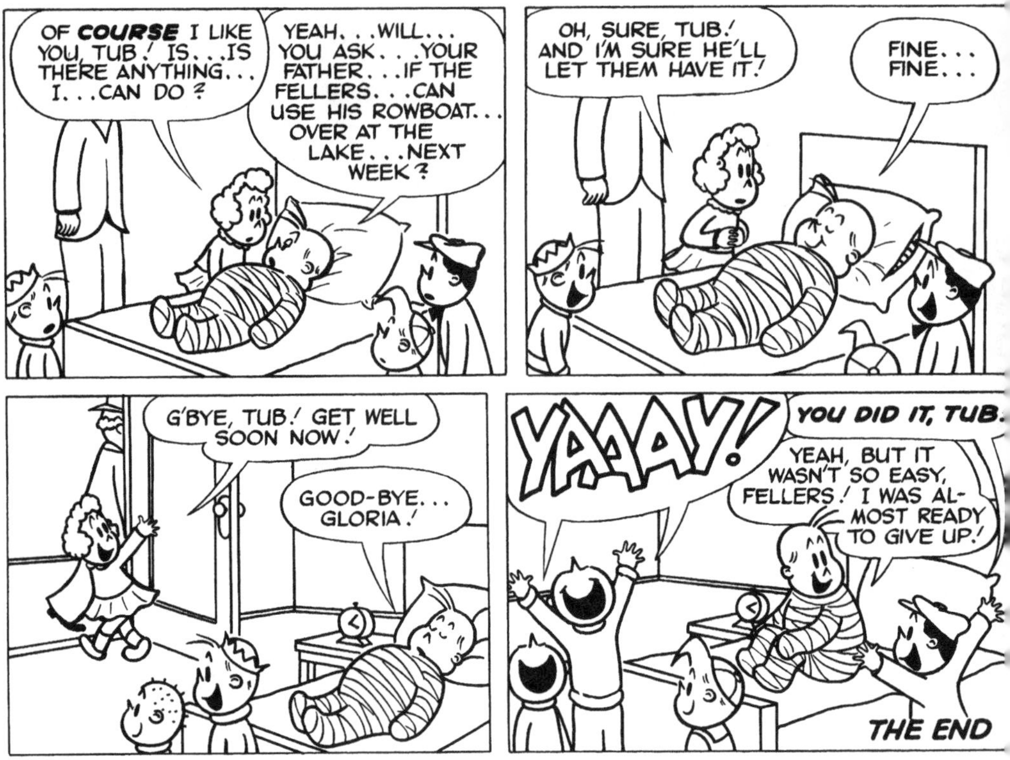
OF COURSE I LIKE YOU, TUB! IS...IS THERE ANYTHING... I...CAN DO?
YEAH...WILL... YOU ASK...YOUR FATHER...IF THE FELLERS...CAN USE HIS ROWBOAT... OVER AT THE LAKE...NEXT WEEK?
OH, SURE, TUB! AND I'M SURE HE'LL LET THEM HAVE IT!
FINE... FINE...
G'BYE, TUB! GET WELL SOON NOW!
GOOD-BYE... GLORIA!
YAAAY!
YOU DID IT, TUB!
YEAH, BUT IT WASN'T SO EASY, FELLERS! I WAS AL-MOST READY TO GIVE UP!
THE END

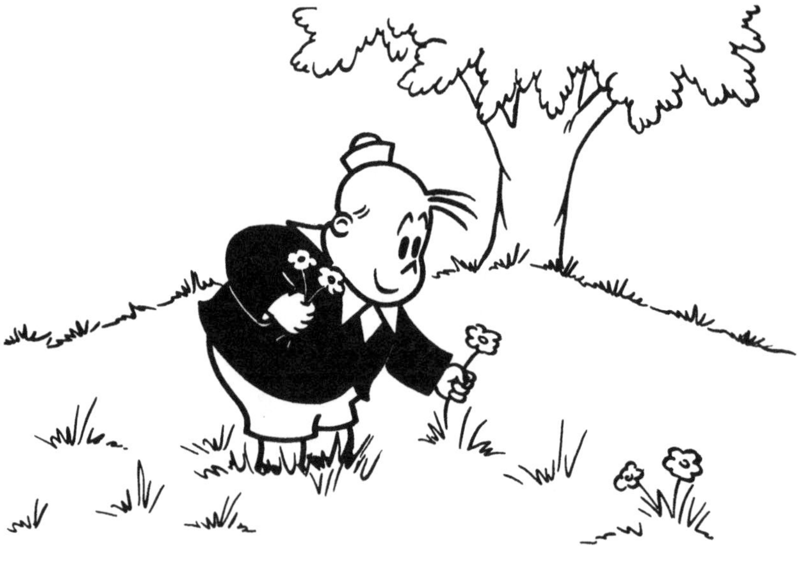

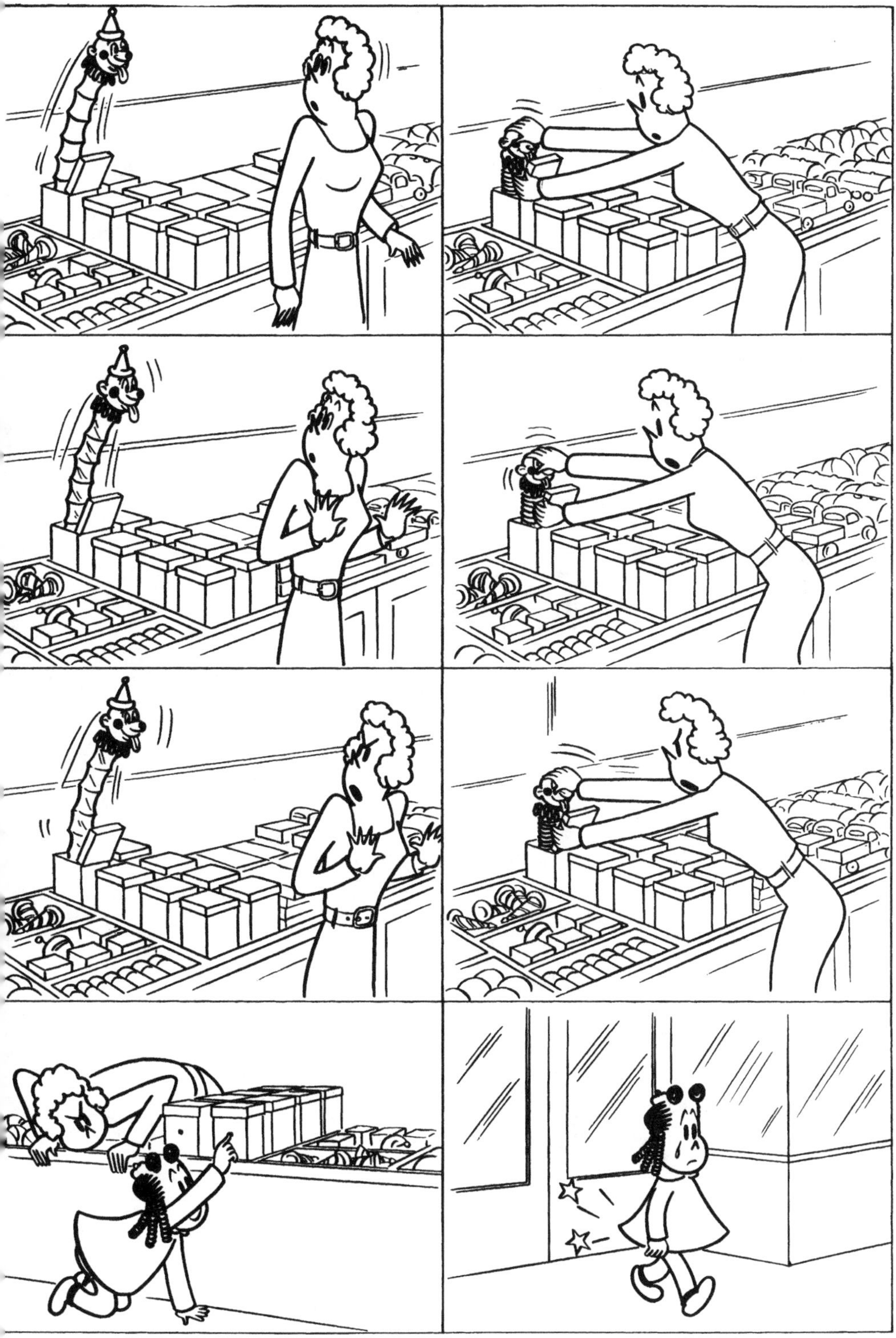

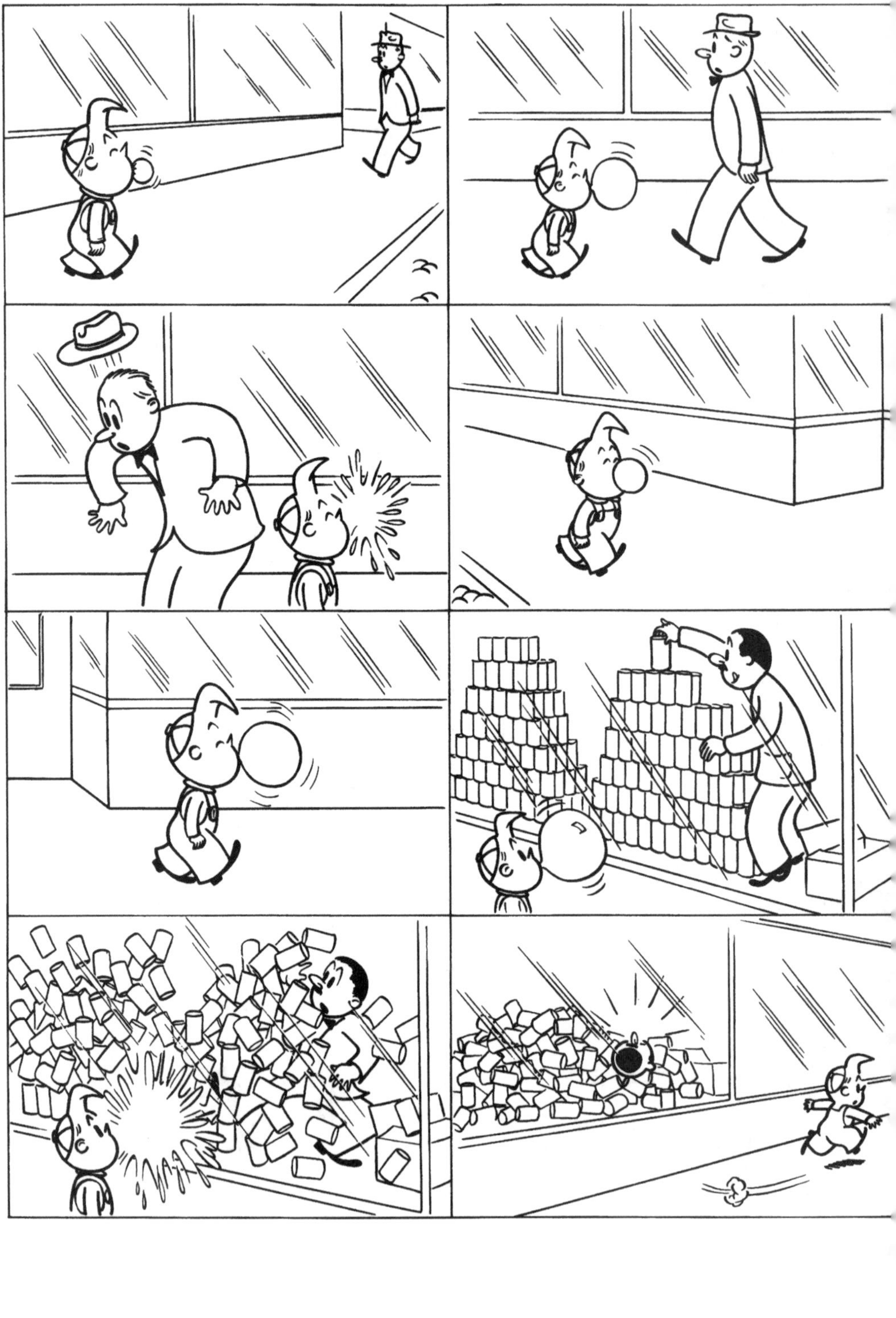

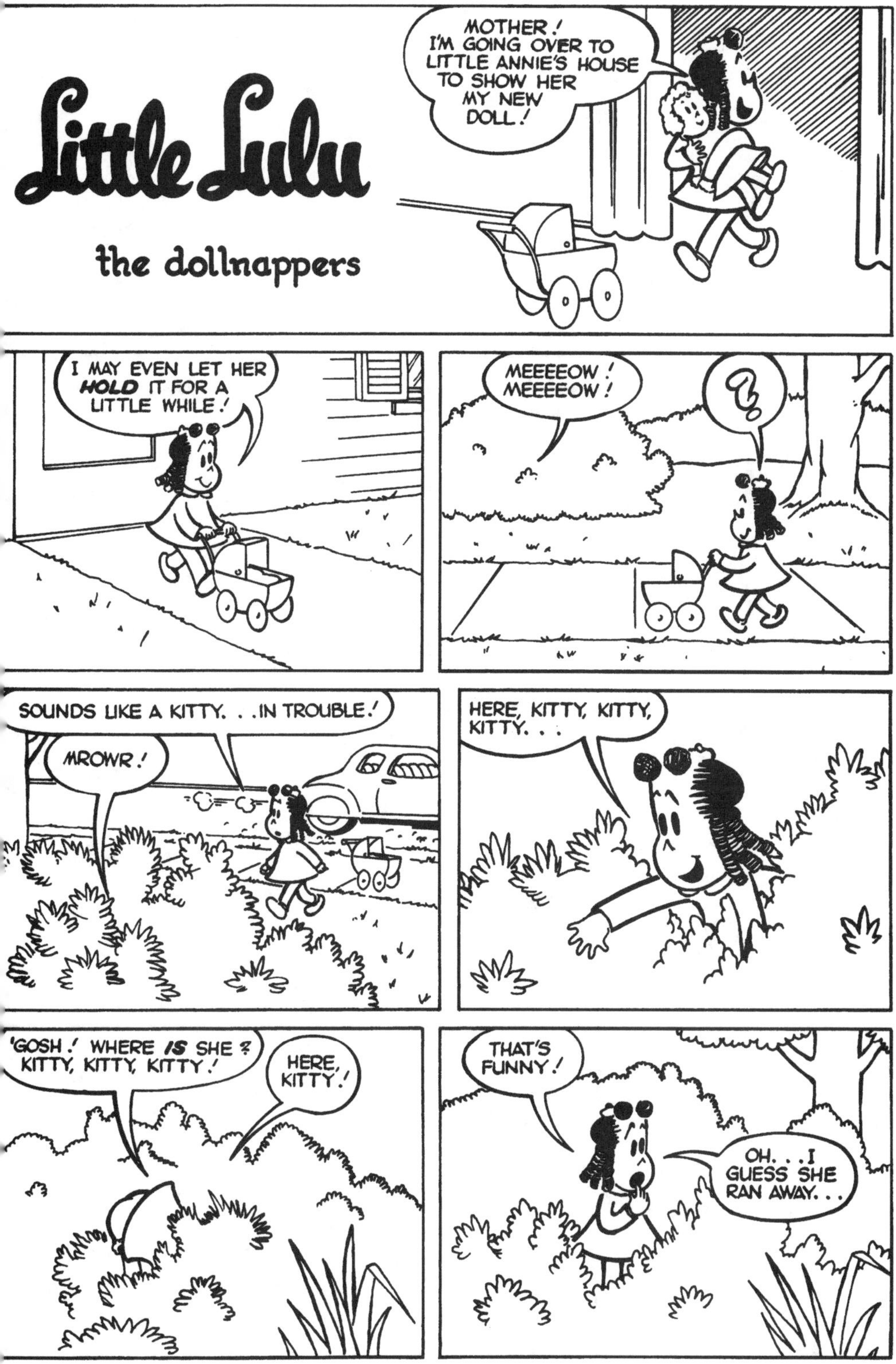
Little Lulu
the dollnappers
MOTHER! I'M GOING OVER TO LITTLE ANNIE'S HOUSE TO SHOW HER MY NEW DOLL!
I MAY EVEN LET HER HOLD IT FOR A LITTLE WHILE!
MEEEEOW! MEEEEOW!
?
SOUNDS LIKE A KITTY. . .IN TROUBLE!
MROWR!
HERE, KITTY, KITTY, KITTY. . .
'GOSH! WHERE IS SHE? KITTY, KITTY, KITTY!
HERE, KITTY!
THAT'S FUNNY!
OH. . .I GUESS SHE RAN AWAY. . .

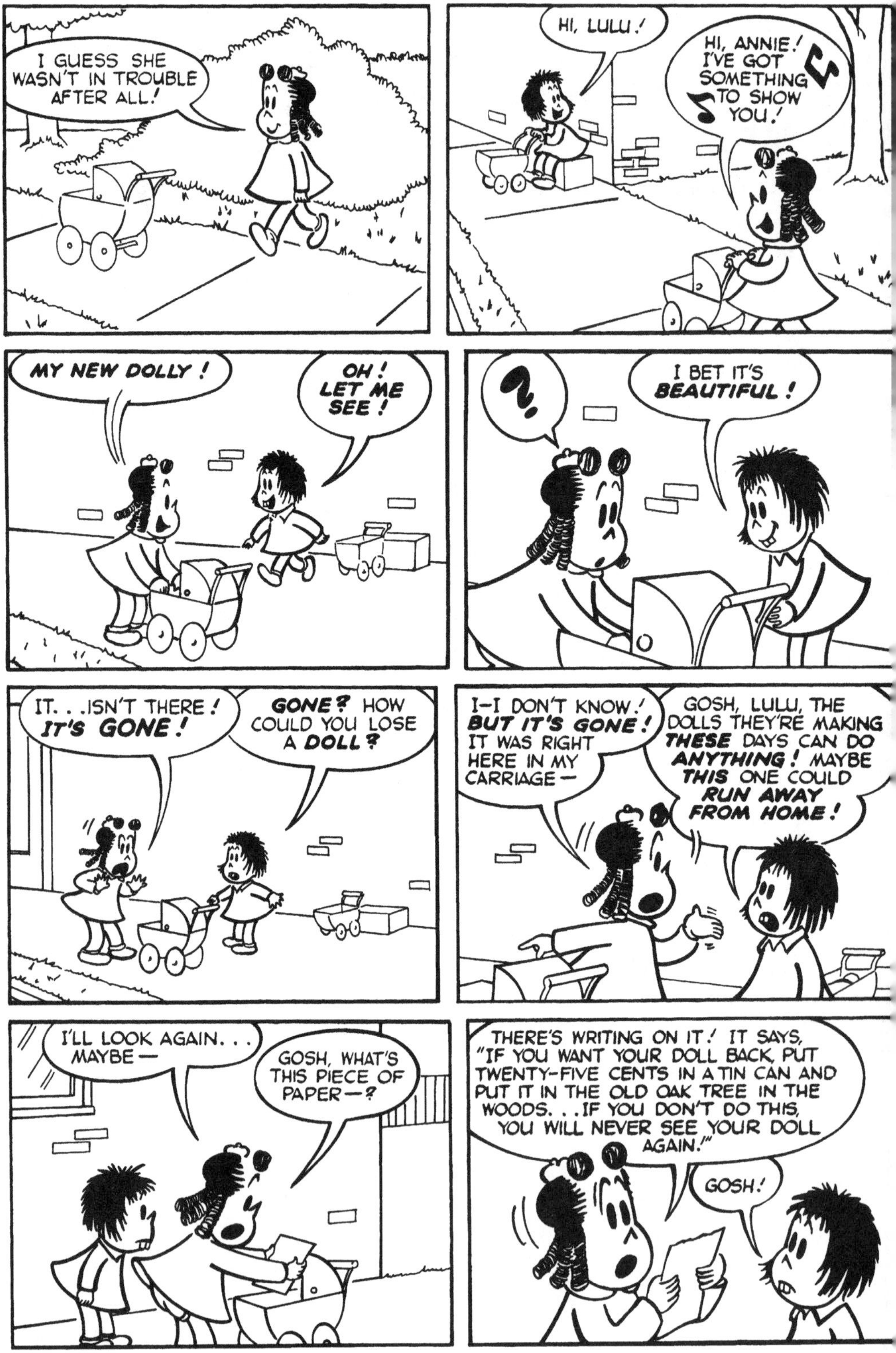
I GUESS SHE WASN'T IN TROUBLE AFTER ALL!
HI, LULU!
HI, ANNIE! I'VE GOT SOMETHING TO SHOW YOU!
MY NEW DOLLY!
OH! LET ME SEE!
I BET IT'S BEAUTIFUL!
IT. . .ISN'T THERE! IT'S GONE!
GONE? HOW COULD YOU LOSE A DOLL?
I-I DON'T KNOW! BUT IT'S GONE! IT WAS RIGHT HERE IN MY CARRIAGE—
GOSH, LULU, THE DOLLS THEY'RE MAKING THESE DAYS CAN DO ANYTHING! MAYBE THIS ONE COULD RUN AWAY FROM HOME!
I'LL LOOK AGAIN. . . MAYBE—
GOSH, WHAT'S THIS PIECE OF PAPER—?
THERE'S WRITING ON IT! IT SAYS, "IF YOU WANT YOUR DOLL BACK, PUT TWENTY-FIVE CENTS IN A TIN CAN AND PUT IT IN THE OLD OAK TREE IN THE WOODS. . .IF YOU DON'T DO THIS, YOU WILL NEVER SEE YOUR DOLL AGAIN!"
GOSH!

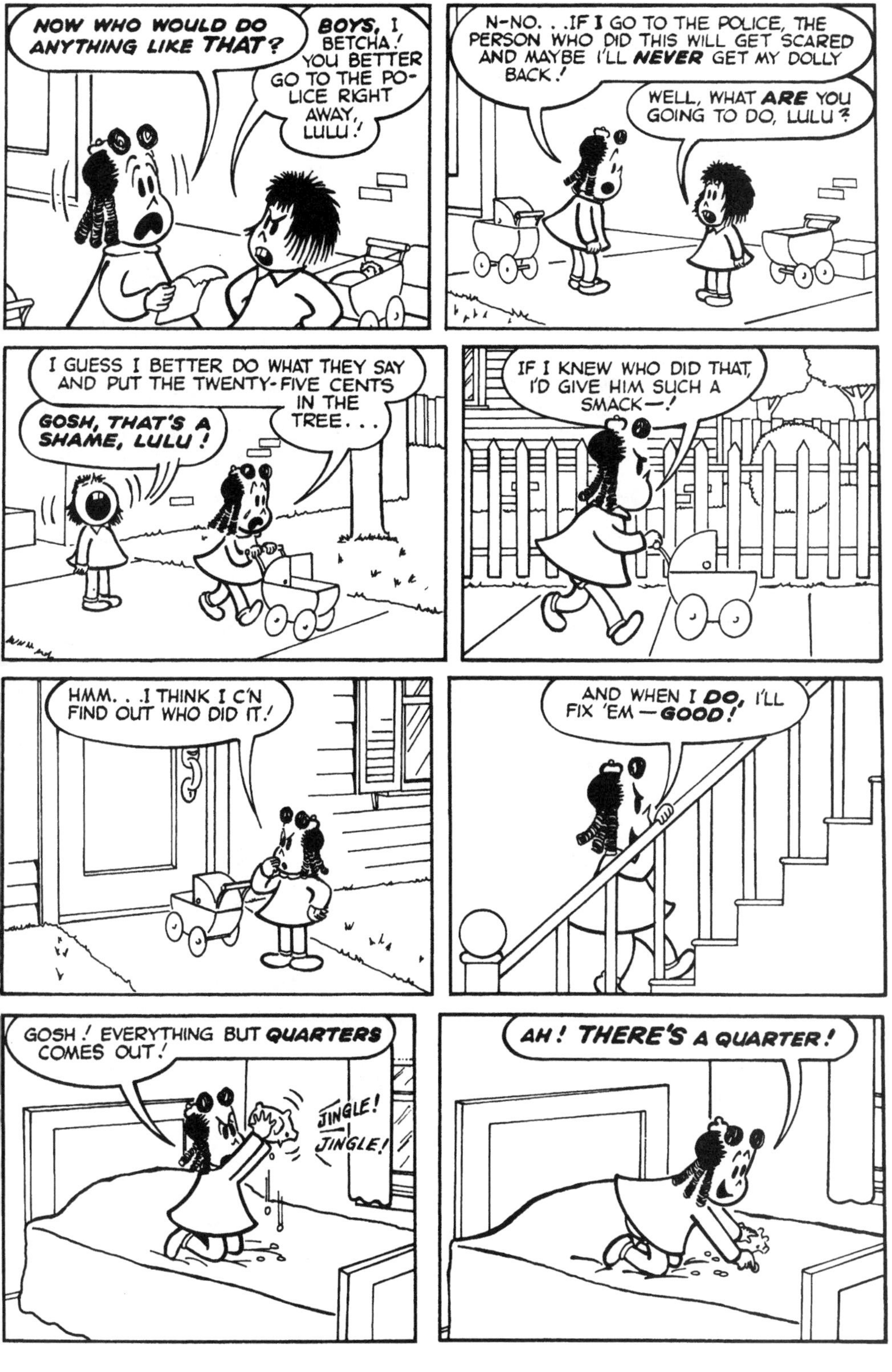
NOW WHO WOULD DO ANYTHING LIKE THAT?
BOYS, I BETCHA! YOU BETTER GO TO THE POLICE RIGHT AWAY, LULU!
N-NO. . .IF I GO TO THE POLICE, THE PERSON WHO DID THIS WILL GET SCARED AND MAYBE I'LL NEVER GET MY DOLLY BACK!
WELL, WHAT ARE YOU GOING TO DO, LULU?
I GUESS I BETTER DO WHAT THEY SAY AND PUT THE TWENTY-FIVE CENTS IN THE TREE. . .
GOSH, THAT'S A SHAME, LULU!
IF I KNEW WHO DID THAT, I'D GIVE HIM SUCH A SMACK—!
HMM. . .I THINK I C'N FIND OUT WHO DID IT!
AND WHEN I DO, I'LL FIX 'EM—GOOD!
GOSH! EVERYTHING BUT QUARTERS COMES OUT!
JINGLE! JINGLE!
AH! THERE'S A QUARTER!

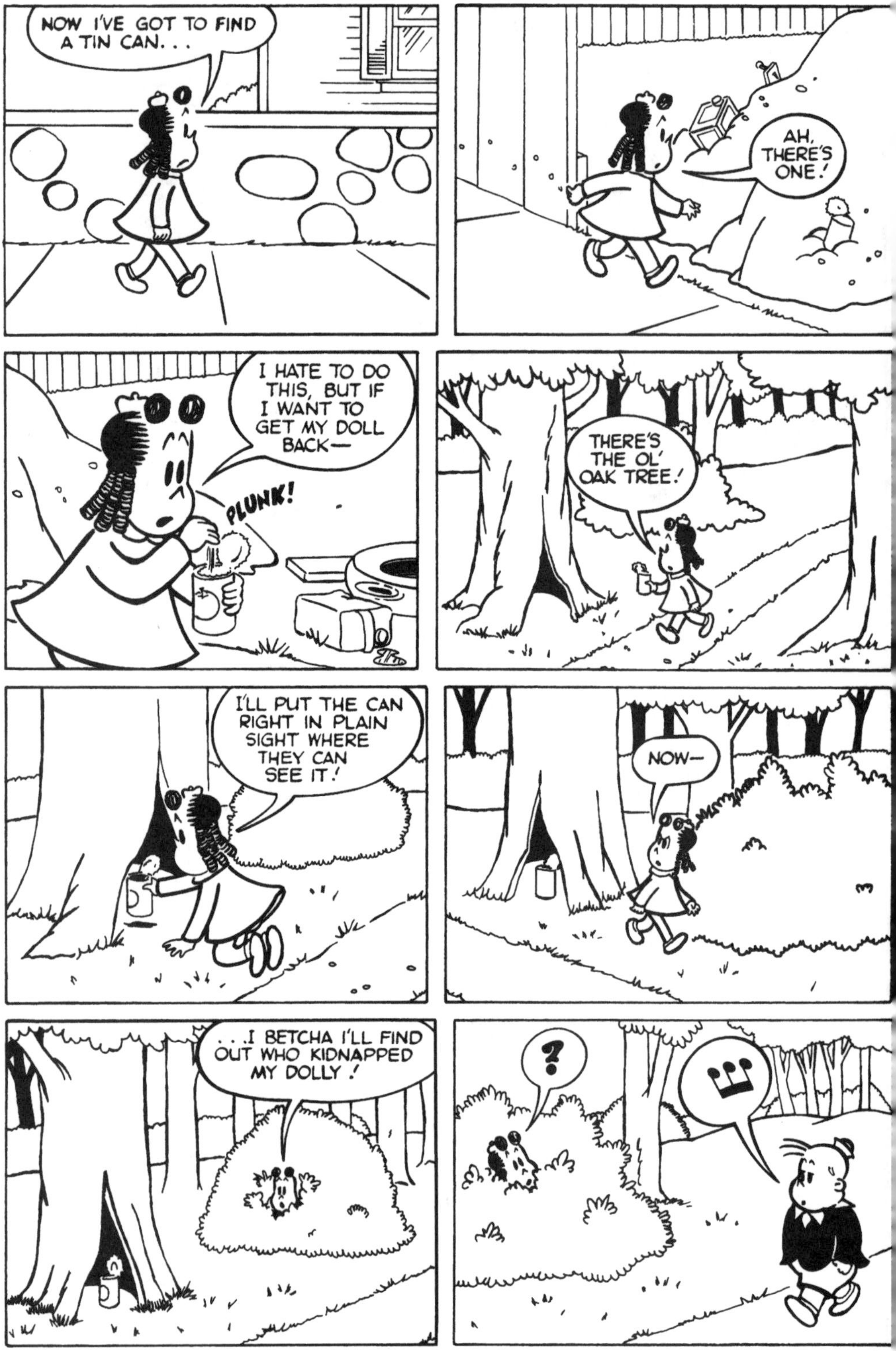
NOW I'VE GOT TO FIND A TIN CAN...
AH, THERE'S ONE!
I HATE TO DO THIS, BUT IF I WANT TO GET MY DOLL BACK—
PLUNK!
THERE'S THE OL' OAK TREE!
I'LL PUT THE CAN RIGHT IN PLAIN SIGHT WHERE THEY CAN SEE IT!
NOW—
...I BETCHA I'LL FIND OUT WHO KIDNAPPED MY DOLLY!
?

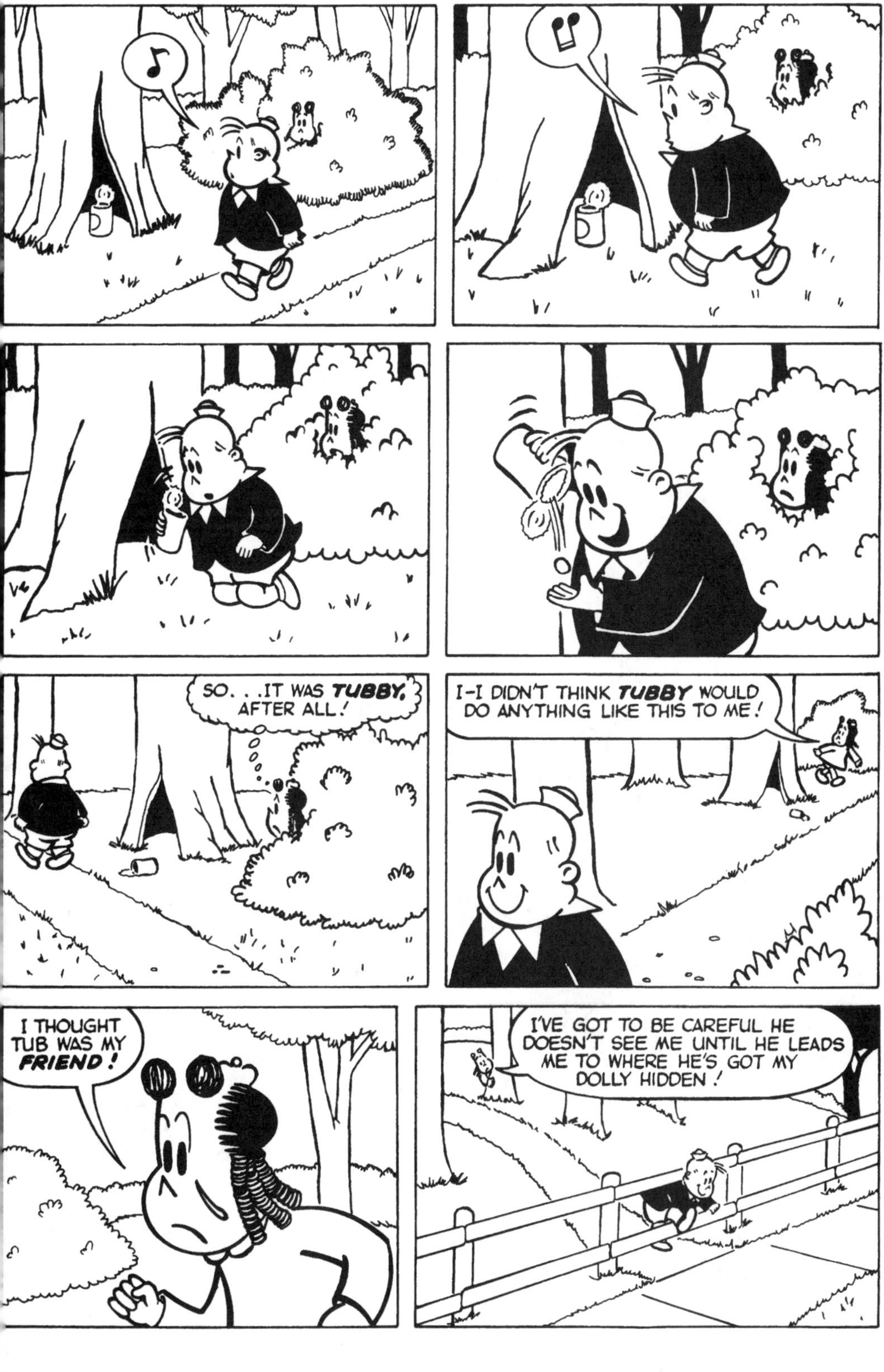
SO. . .IT WAS TUBBY, AFTER ALL!
I-I DIDN'T THINK TUBBY WOULD DO ANYTHING LIKE THIS TO ME!
I THOUGHT TUB WAS MY FRIEND!
I'VE GOT TO BE CAREFUL HE DOESN'T SEE ME UNTIL HE LEADS ME TO WHERE HE'S GOT MY DOLLY HIDDEN!

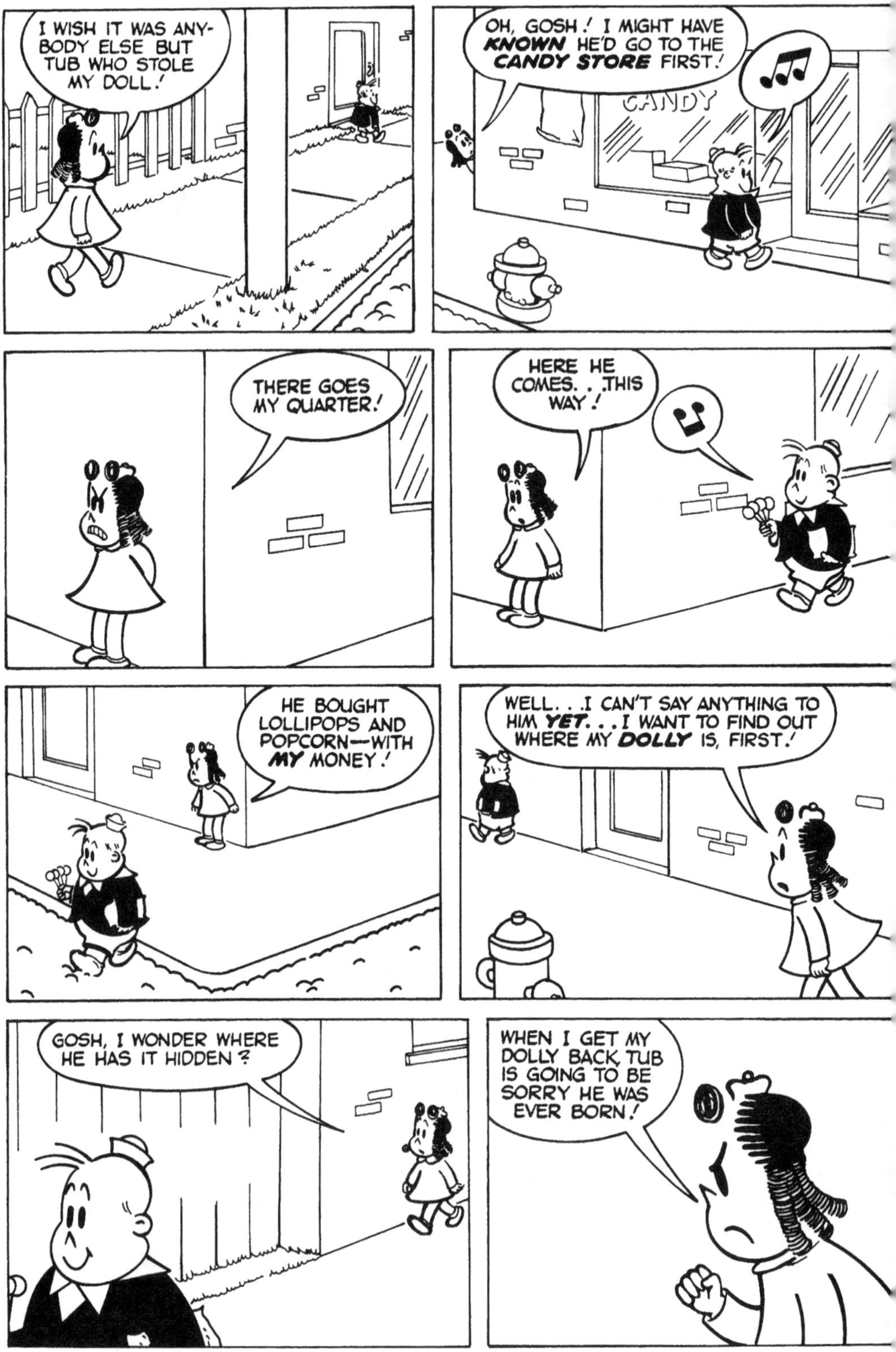

I WISH IT WAS ANYBODY ELSE BUT TUB WHO STOLE MY DOLL!
OH, GOSH! I MIGHT HAVE **KNOWN** HE'D GO TO THE **CANDY STORE** FIRST!
CANDY
THERE GOES MY QUARTER!
HERE HE COMES. . .THIS WAY!
HE BOUGHT LOLLIPOPS AND POPCORN—WITH **MY** MONEY!
WELL. . .I CAN'T SAY ANYTHING TO HIM **YET**. . .I WANT TO FIND OUT WHERE MY **DOLLY** IS, FIRST!
GOSH, I WONDER WHERE HE HAS IT HIDDEN?
WHEN I GET MY DOLLY BACK, TUB IS GOING TO BE SORRY HE WAS EVER BORN!

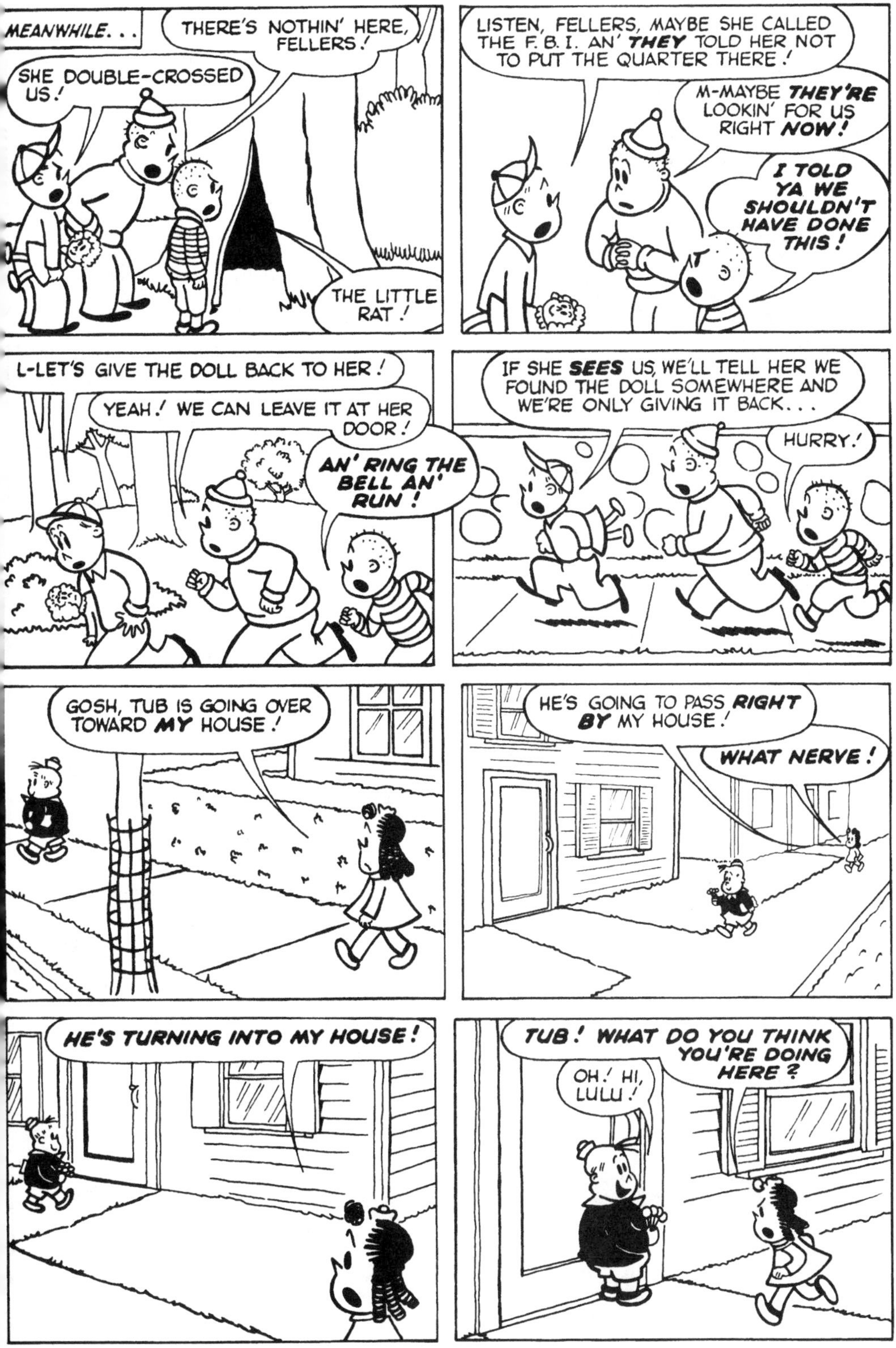

MEANWHILE . . .
THERE'S NOTHIN' HERE, FELLERS!
SHE DOUBLE-CROSSED US!
THE LITTLE RAT!
LISTEN, FELLERS, MAYBE SHE CALLED THE F. B. I. AN' **THEY** TOLD HER NOT TO PUT THE QUARTER THERE!
M-MAYBE **THEY'RE** LOOKIN' FOR US RIGHT **NOW!**
I TOLD YA WE SHOULDN'T HAVE DONE THIS!
L-LET'S GIVE THE DOLL BACK TO HER!
YEAH! WE CAN LEAVE IT AT HER DOOR!
AN' RING THE BELL AN' RUN!
IF SHE **SEES** US, WE'LL TELL HER WE FOUND THE DOLL SOMEWHERE AND WE'RE ONLY GIVING IT BACK . . .
HURRY!
GOSH, TUB IS GOING OVER TOWARD **MY** HOUSE!
HE'S GOING TO PASS **RIGHT BY** MY HOUSE!
WHAT NERVE!
HE'S TURNING INTO MY HOUSE!
TUB! WHAT DO YOU THINK YOU'RE DOING HERE?
OH! HI, LULU!

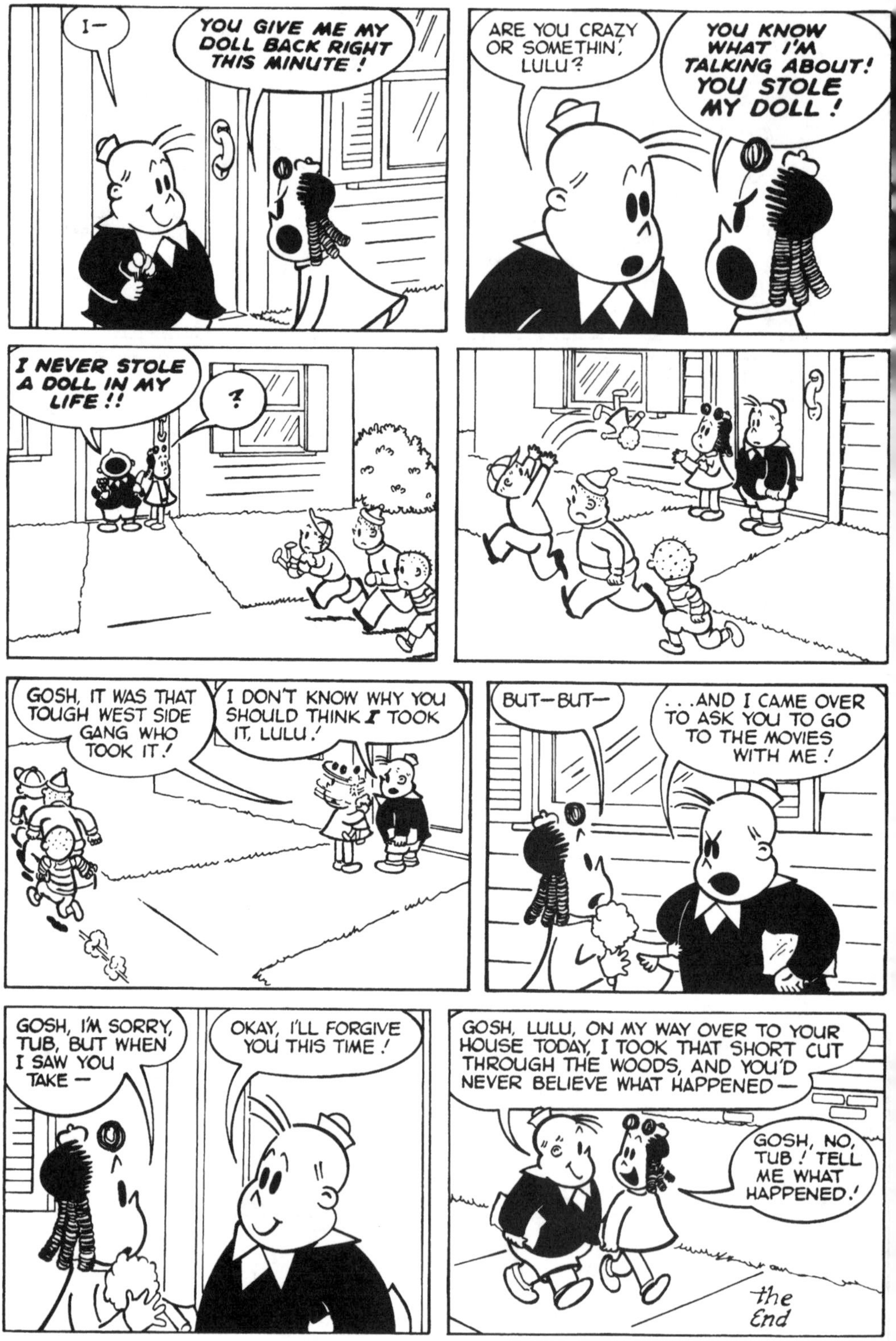
I—
YOU GIVE ME MY DOLL BACK RIGHT THIS MINUTE!
ARE YOU CRAZY OR SOMETHIN', LULU?
YOU KNOW WHAT I'M TALKING ABOUT! YOU STOLE MY DOLL!
I NEVER STOLE A DOLL IN MY LIFE!!
?
GOSH, IT WAS THAT TOUGH WEST SIDE GANG WHO TOOK IT!
I DON'T KNOW WHY YOU SHOULD THINK I TOOK IT, LULU!
BUT—BUT—
...AND I CAME OVER TO ASK YOU TO GO TO THE MOVIES WITH ME!
GOSH, I'M SORRY, TUB, BUT WHEN I SAW YOU TAKE—
OKAY, I'LL FORGIVE YOU THIS TIME!
GOSH, LULU, ON MY WAY OVER TO YOUR HOUSE TODAY, I TOOK THAT SHORT CUT THROUGH THE WOODS, AND YOU'D NEVER BELIEVE WHAT HAPPENED—
GOSH, NO, TUB! TELL ME WHAT HAPPENED!
the End

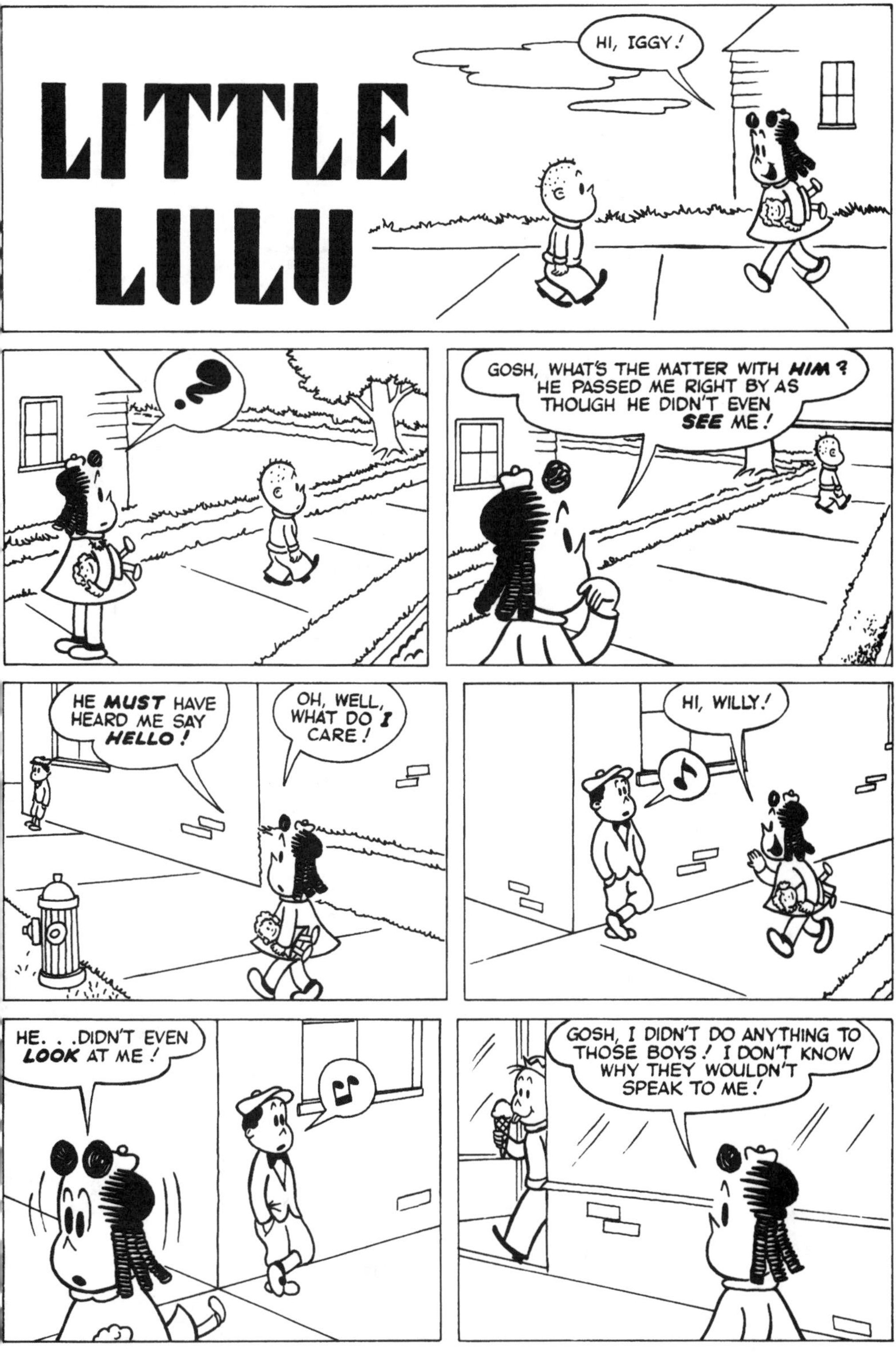
LITTLE LULU
HI, IGGY!
?
GOSH, WHAT'S THE MATTER WITH HIM? HE PASSED ME RIGHT BY AS THOUGH HE DIDN'T EVEN SEE ME!
HE MUST HAVE HEARD ME SAY HELLO!
OH, WELL, WHAT DO I CARE!
HI, WILLY!
HE. . .DIDN'T EVEN LOOK AT ME!
GOSH, I DIDN'T DO ANYTHING TO THOSE BOYS! I DON'T KNOW WHY THEY WOULDN'T SPEAK TO ME!

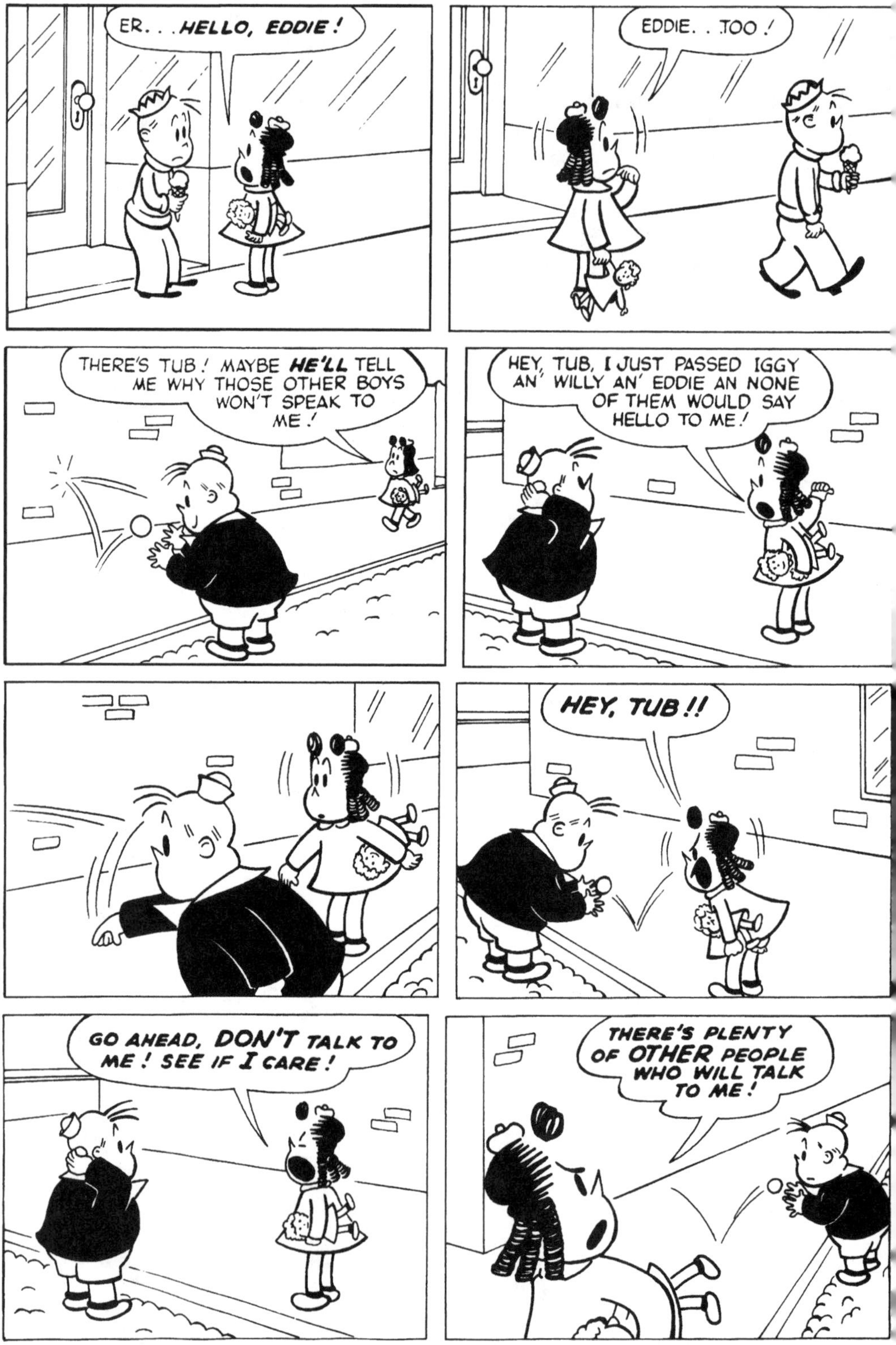
ER. . .HELLO, EDDIE!
EDDIE. . .TOO!
THERE'S TUB! MAYBE HE'LL TELL ME WHY THOSE OTHER BOYS WON'T SPEAK TO ME!
HEY, TUB, I JUST PASSED IGGY AN' WILLY AN' EDDIE AN NONE OF THEM WOULD SAY HELLO TO ME!
HEY, TUB!!
GO AHEAD, DON'T TALK TO ME! SEE IF I CARE!
THERE'S PLENTY OF OTHER PEOPLE WHO WILL TALK TO ME!

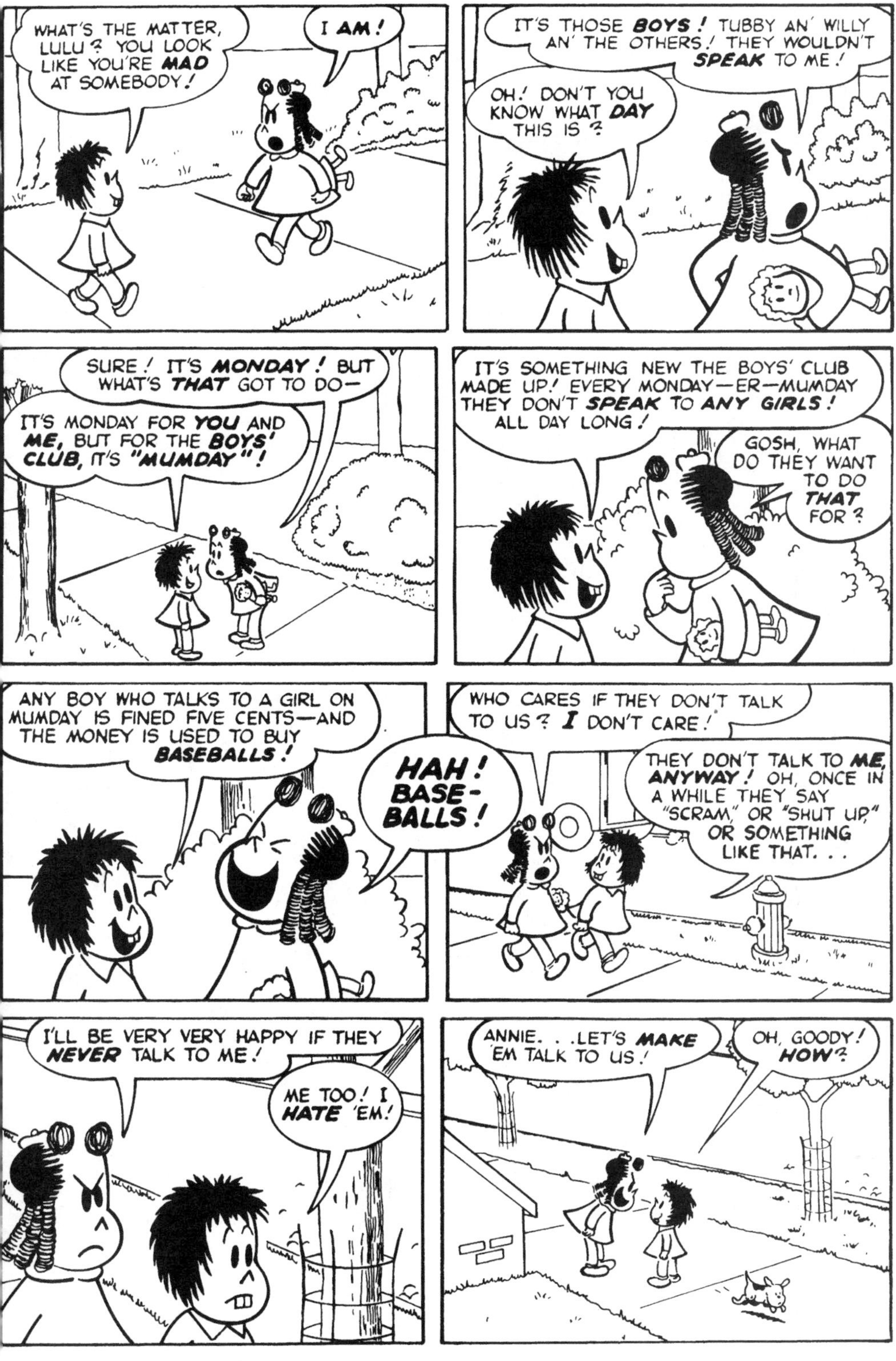
WHAT'S THE MATTER, LULU? YOU LOOK LIKE YOU'RE MAD AT SOMEBODY!
I AM!
IT'S THOSE BOYS! TUBBY AN' WILLY AN' THE OTHERS! THEY WOULDN'T SPEAK TO ME!
OH! DON'T YOU KNOW WHAT DAY THIS IS?
SURE! IT'S MONDAY! BUT WHAT'S THAT GOT TO DO—
IT'S MONDAY FOR YOU AND ME, BUT FOR THE BOYS' CLUB, IT'S "MUMDAY"!
IT'S SOMETHING NEW THE BOYS' CLUB MADE UP! EVERY MONDAY—ER—MUMDAY THEY DON'T SPEAK TO ANY GIRLS! ALL DAY LONG!
GOSH, WHAT DO THEY WANT TO DO THAT FOR?
ANY BOY WHO TALKS TO A GIRL ON MUMDAY IS FINED FIVE CENTS—AND THE MONEY IS USED TO BUY BASEBALLS!
HAH! BASE-BALLS!
WHO CARES IF THEY DON'T TALK TO US? I DON'T CARE!
THEY DON'T TALK TO ME, ANYWAY! OH, ONCE IN A WHILE THEY SAY "SCRAM," OR "SHUT UP," OR SOMETHING LIKE THAT. . .
I'LL BE VERY VERY HAPPY IF THEY NEVER TALK TO ME!
ME TOO! I HATE 'EM!
ANNIE. . .LET'S MAKE 'EM TALK TO US!
OH, GOODY! HOW?

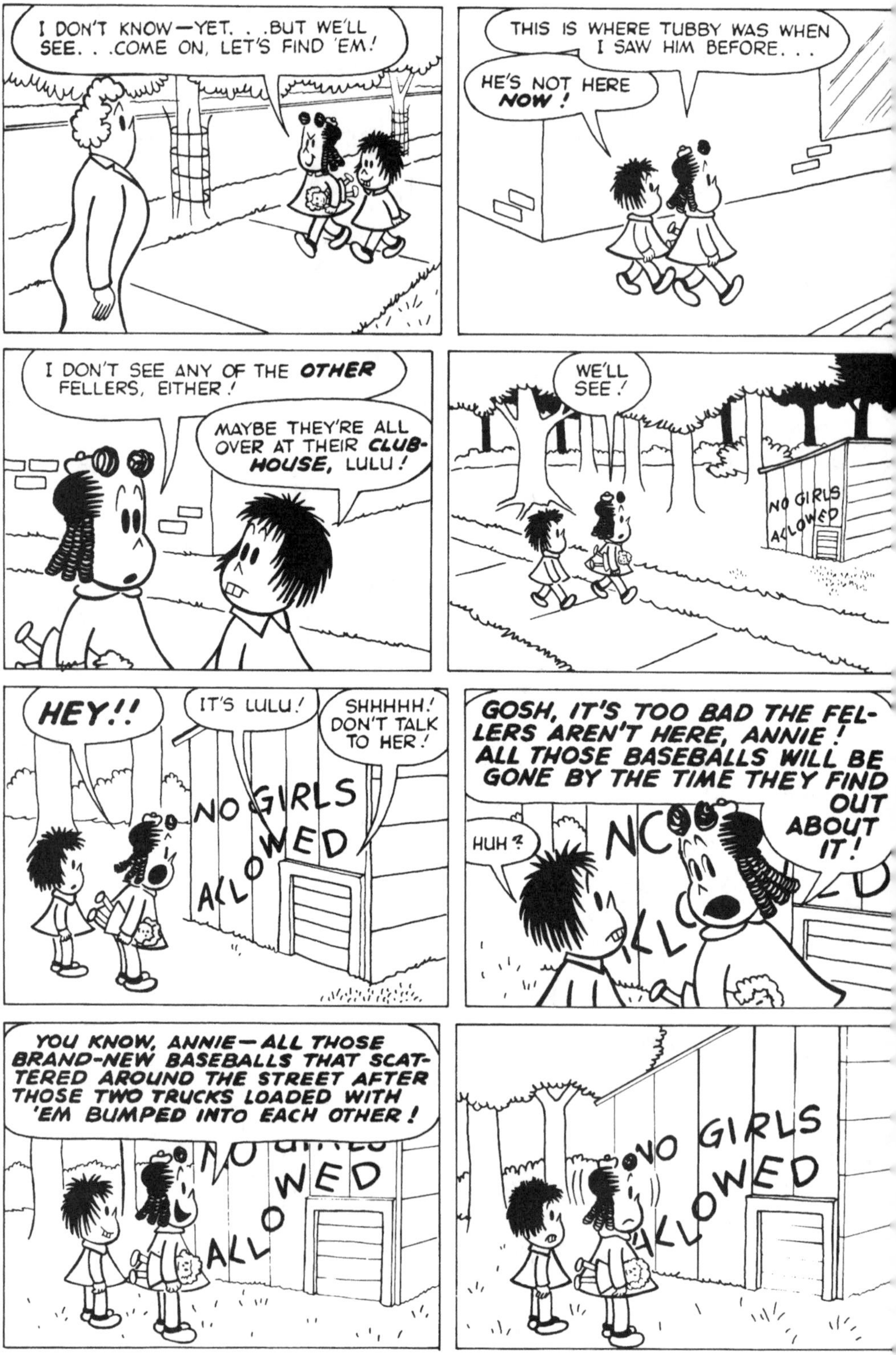
I DON'T KNOW—YET. . .BUT WE'LL SEE. . .COME ON, LET'S FIND 'EM!
THIS IS WHERE TUBBY WAS WHEN I SAW HIM BEFORE. . .
HE'S NOT HERE **NOW!**
I DON'T SEE ANY OF THE **OTHER** FELLERS, EITHER!
MAYBE THEY'RE ALL OVER AT THEIR **CLUB-HOUSE,** LULU!
WE'LL SEE!
NO GIRLS ALLOWED
HEY!!
IT'S LULU!
SHHHHH! DON'T TALK TO HER!
NO GIRLS ALLOWED
GOSH, IT'S TOO BAD THE FEL-LERS AREN'T HERE, ANNIE! ALL THOSE BASEBALLS WILL BE GONE BY THE TIME THEY FIND OUT ABOUT IT!
HUH?
YOU KNOW, ANNIE—ALL THOSE BRAND-NEW BASEBALLS THAT SCAT-TERED AROUND THE STREET AFTER THOSE TWO TRUCKS LOADED WITH 'EM BUMPED INTO EACH OTHER!
NO GIRLS ALLOWED

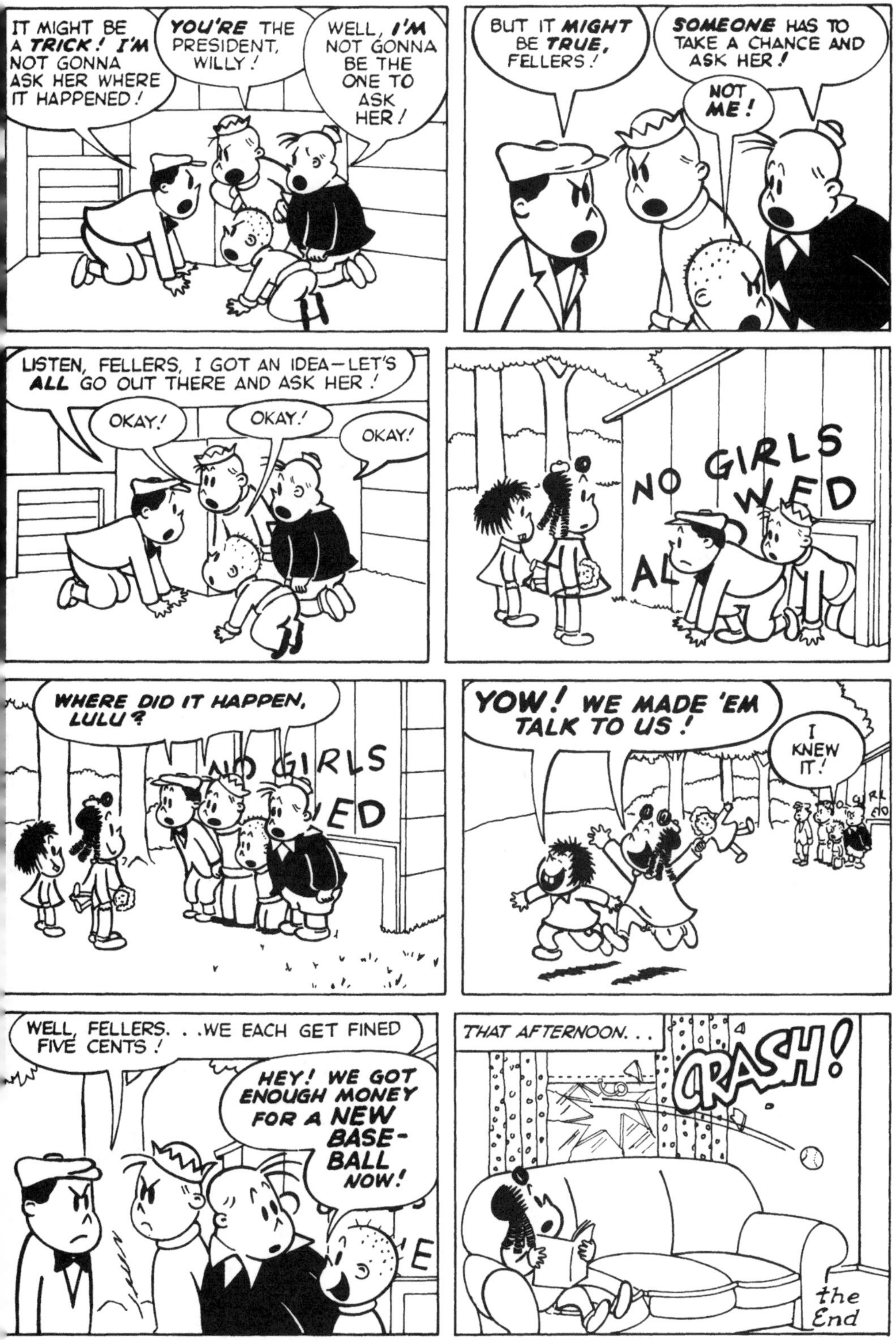
IT MIGHT BE A TRICK! I'M NOT GONNA ASK HER WHERE IT HAPPENED!
YOU'RE THE PRESIDENT, WILLY!
WELL, I'M NOT GONNA BE THE ONE TO ASK HER!
BUT IT MIGHT BE TRUE, FELLERS!
SOMEONE HAS TO TAKE A CHANCE AND ASK HER!
NOT ME!
LISTEN, FELLERS, I GOT AN IDEA—LET'S ALL GO OUT THERE AND ASK HER!
OKAY!
OKAY!
OKAY!
NO GIRLS AL WED
WHERE DID IT HAPPEN, LULU?
YOW! WE MADE 'EM TALK TO US!
I KNEW IT!
WELL, FELLERS. . .WE EACH GET FINED FIVE CENTS!
HEY! WE GOT ENOUGH MONEY FOR A NEW BASE-BALL NOW!
THAT AFTERNOON. . .
CRASH!
the End

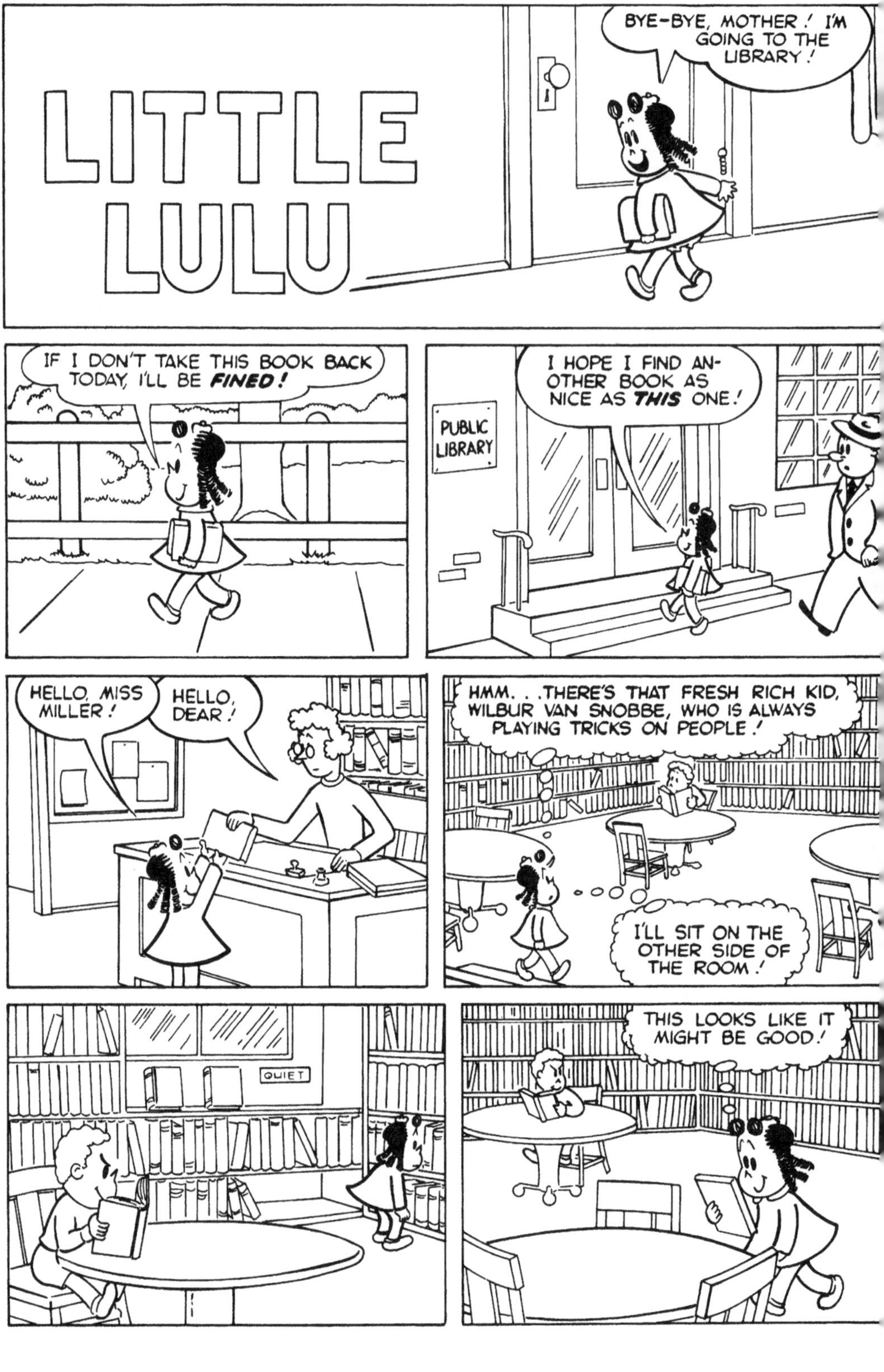
LITTLE LULU
BYE-BYE, MOTHER! I'M GOING TO THE LIBRARY!
IF I DON'T TAKE THIS BOOK BACK TODAY, I'LL BE *FINED!*
PUBLIC LIBRARY
I HOPE I FIND ANOTHER BOOK AS NICE AS *THIS* ONE!
HELLO, MISS MILLER!
HELLO, DEAR!
HMM. . .THERE'S THAT FRESH RICH KID, WILBUR VAN SNOBBE, WHO IS ALWAYS PLAYING TRICKS ON PEOPLE!
I'LL SIT ON THE OTHER SIDE OF THE ROOM!
QUIET
THIS LOOKS LIKE IT MIGHT BE GOOD!

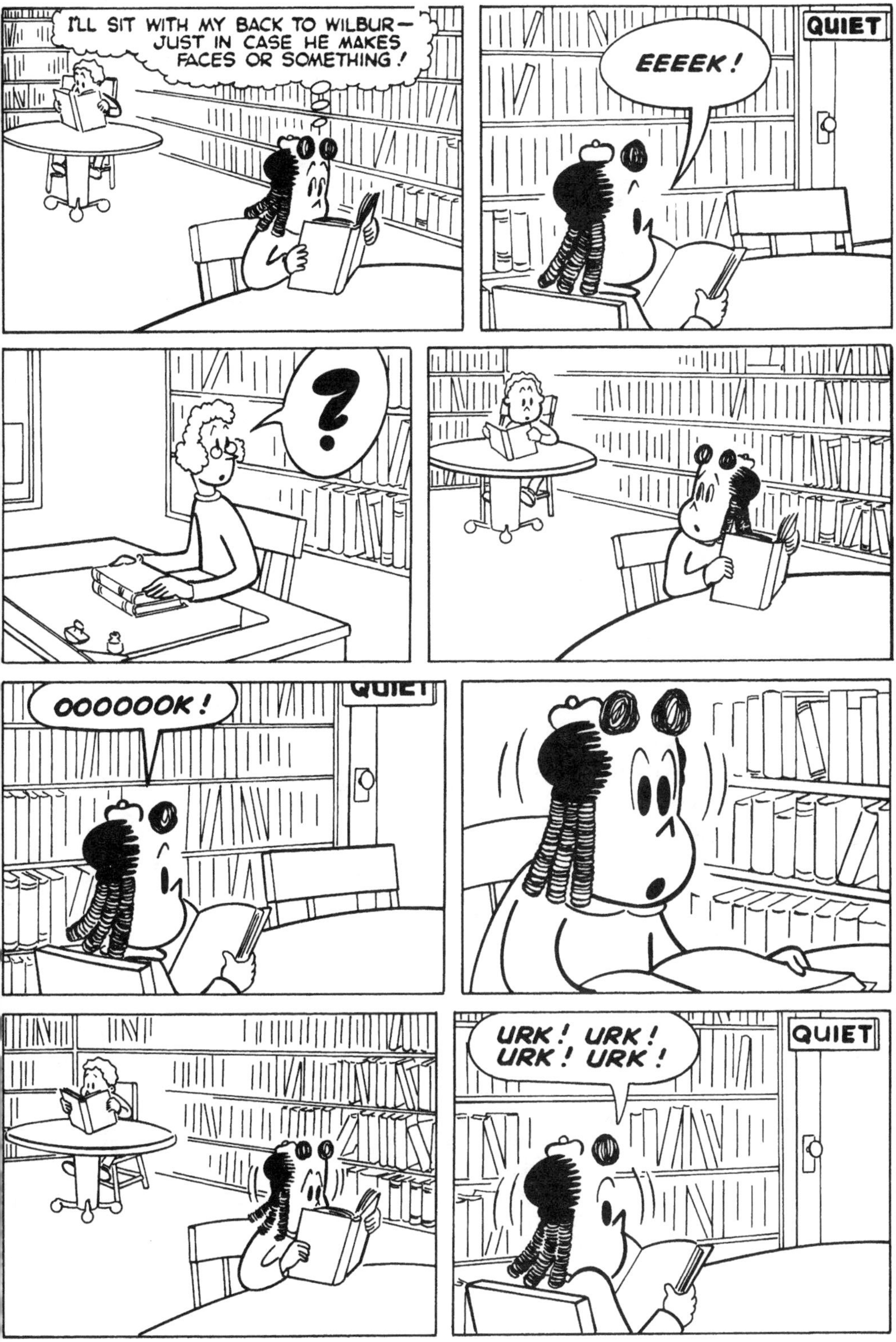
I'LL SIT WITH MY BACK TO WILBUR— JUST IN CASE HE MAKES FACES OR SOMETHING!
QUIET
EEEEK!
?
OOOOOOK!
QUIET
URK! URK! URK! URK!

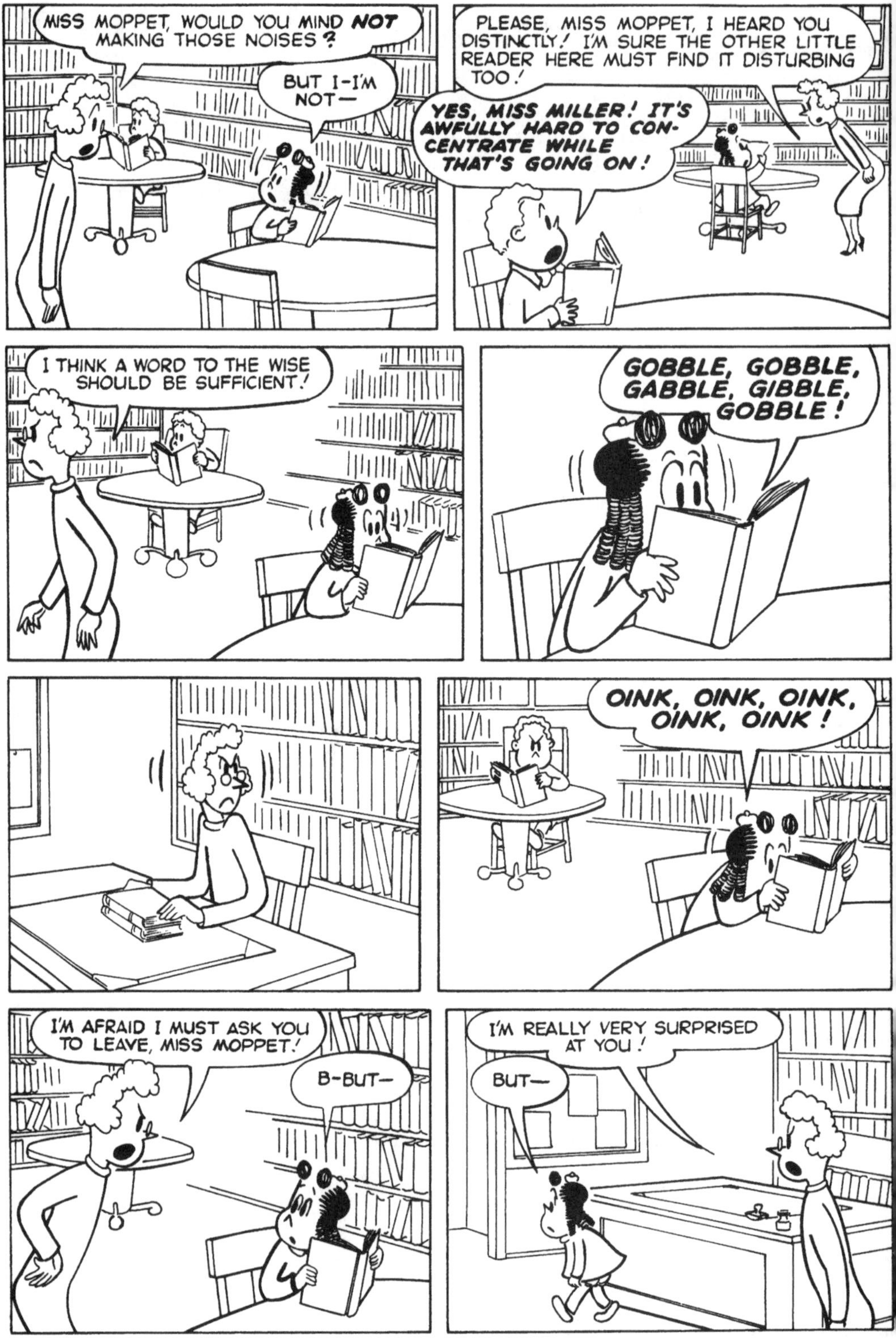
MISS MOPPET, WOULD YOU MIND NOT MAKING THOSE NOISES?
BUT I-I'M NOT—
PLEASE, MISS MOPPET, I HEARD YOU DISTINCTLY! I'M SURE THE OTHER LITTLE READER HERE MUST FIND IT DISTURBING TOO!
YES, MISS MILLER! IT'S AWFULLY HARD TO CONCENTRATE WHILE THAT'S GOING ON!
I THINK A WORD TO THE WISE SHOULD BE SUFFICIENT!
GOBBLE, GOBBLE, GABBLE, GIBBLE, GOBBLE!
OINK, OINK, OINK, OINK, OINK!
I'M AFRAID I MUST ASK YOU TO LEAVE, MISS MOPPET!
B-BUT—
I'M REALLY VERY SURPRISED AT YOU!
BUT—

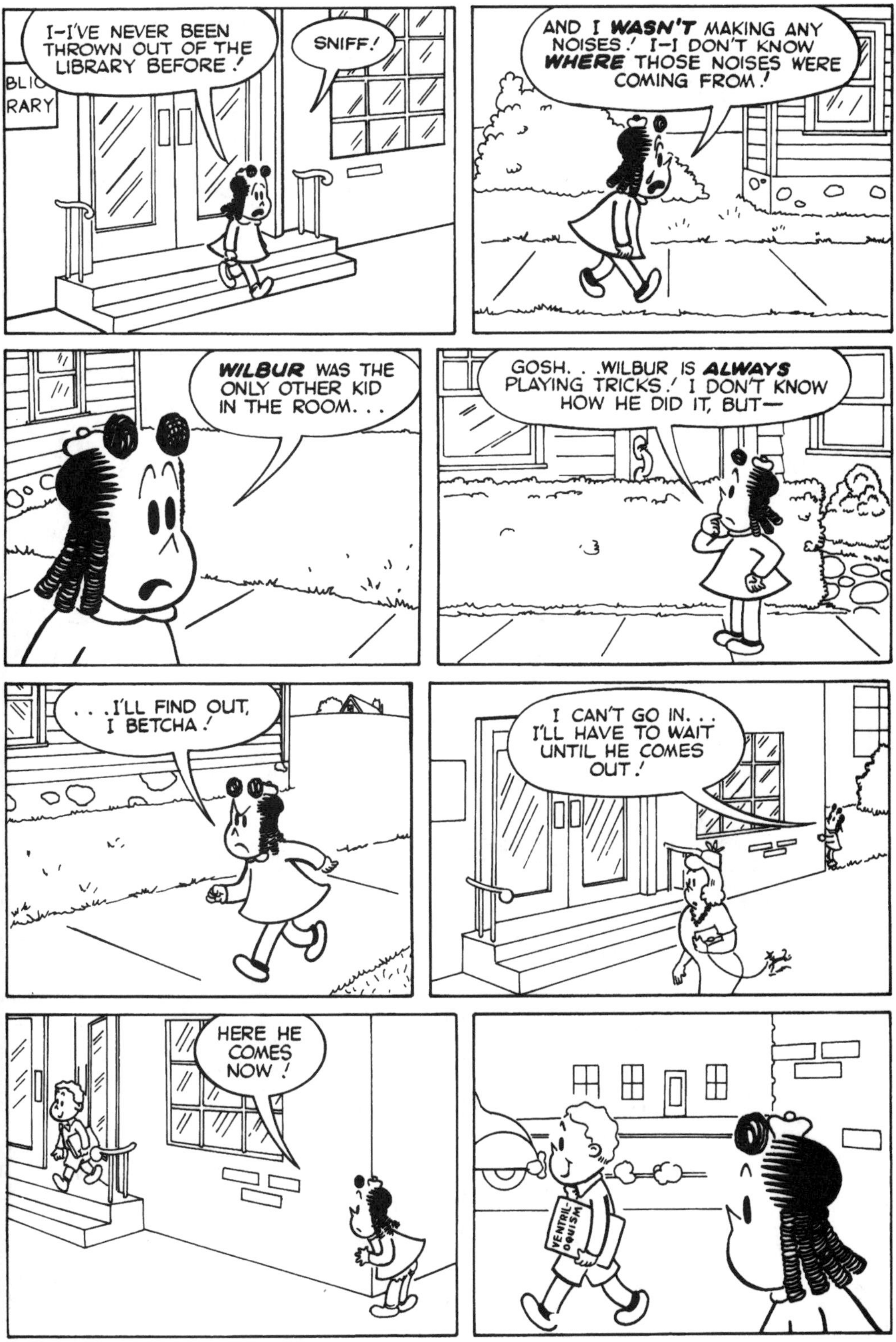
I-I'VE NEVER BEEN THROWN OUT OF THE LIBRARY BEFORE!
SNIFF!
BLIC
RARY
AND I WASN'T MAKING ANY NOISES! I-I DON'T KNOW WHERE THOSE NOISES WERE COMING FROM!
WILBUR WAS THE ONLY OTHER KID IN THE ROOM...
GOSH...WILBUR IS ALWAYS PLAYING TRICKS! I DON'T KNOW HOW HE DID IT, BUT—
...I'LL FIND OUT, I BETCHA!
I CAN'T GO IN... I'LL HAVE TO WAIT UNTIL HE COMES OUT!
HERE HE COMES NOW!
VENTRIL-OQUISM

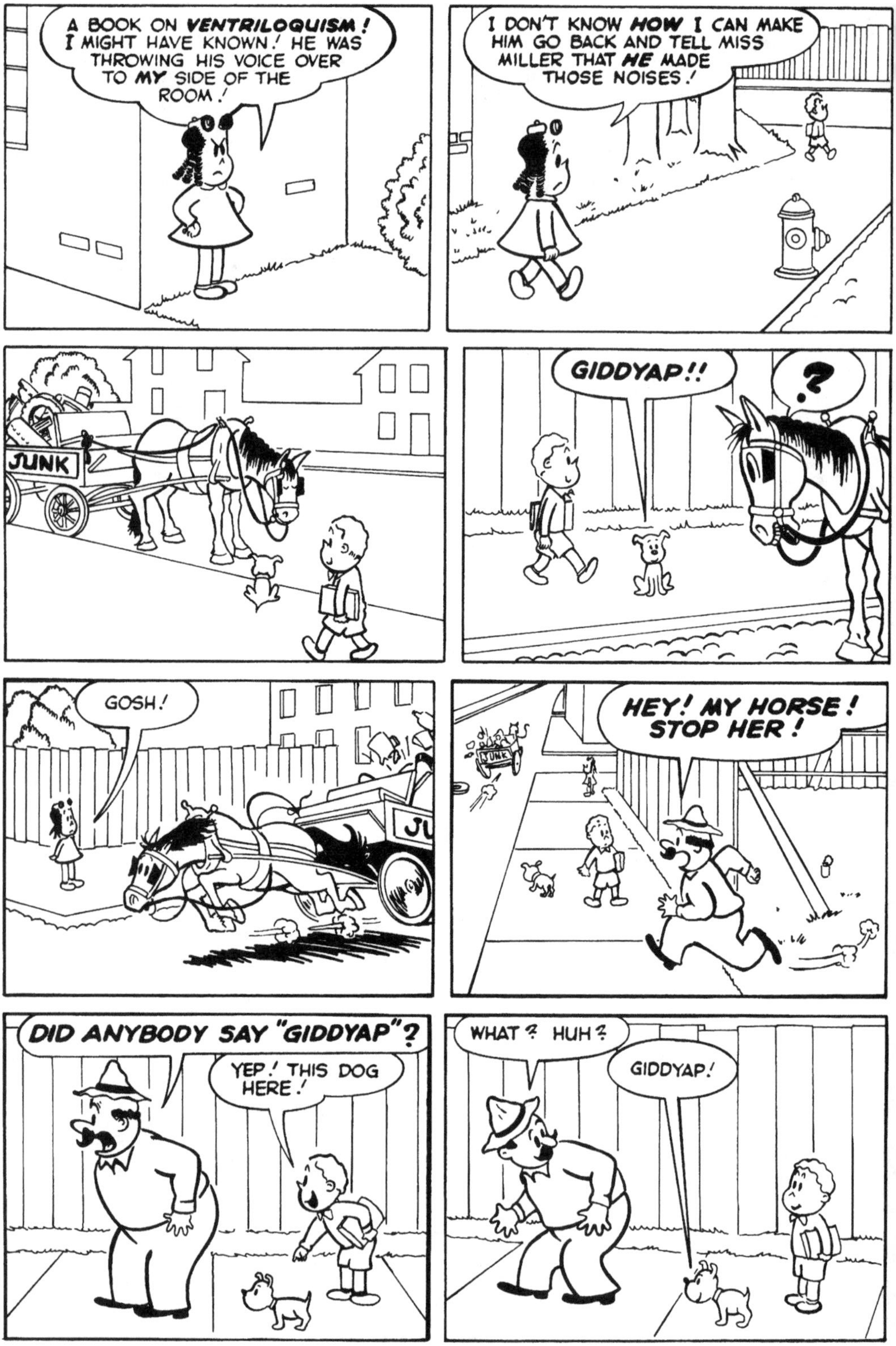
A BOOK ON **VENTRILOQUISM!** I MIGHT HAVE KNOWN! HE WAS THROWING HIS VOICE OVER TO **MY** SIDE OF THE ROOM!
I DON'T KNOW **HOW** I CAN MAKE HIM GO BACK AND TELL MISS MILLER THAT **HE** MADE THOSE NOISES!
JUNK
GIDDYAP!!
?
GOSH!
HEY! MY HORSE! STOP HER!
JUNK
DID ANYBODY SAY "GIDDYAP"?
YEP! THIS DOG HERE!
WHAT? HUH?
GIDDYAP!

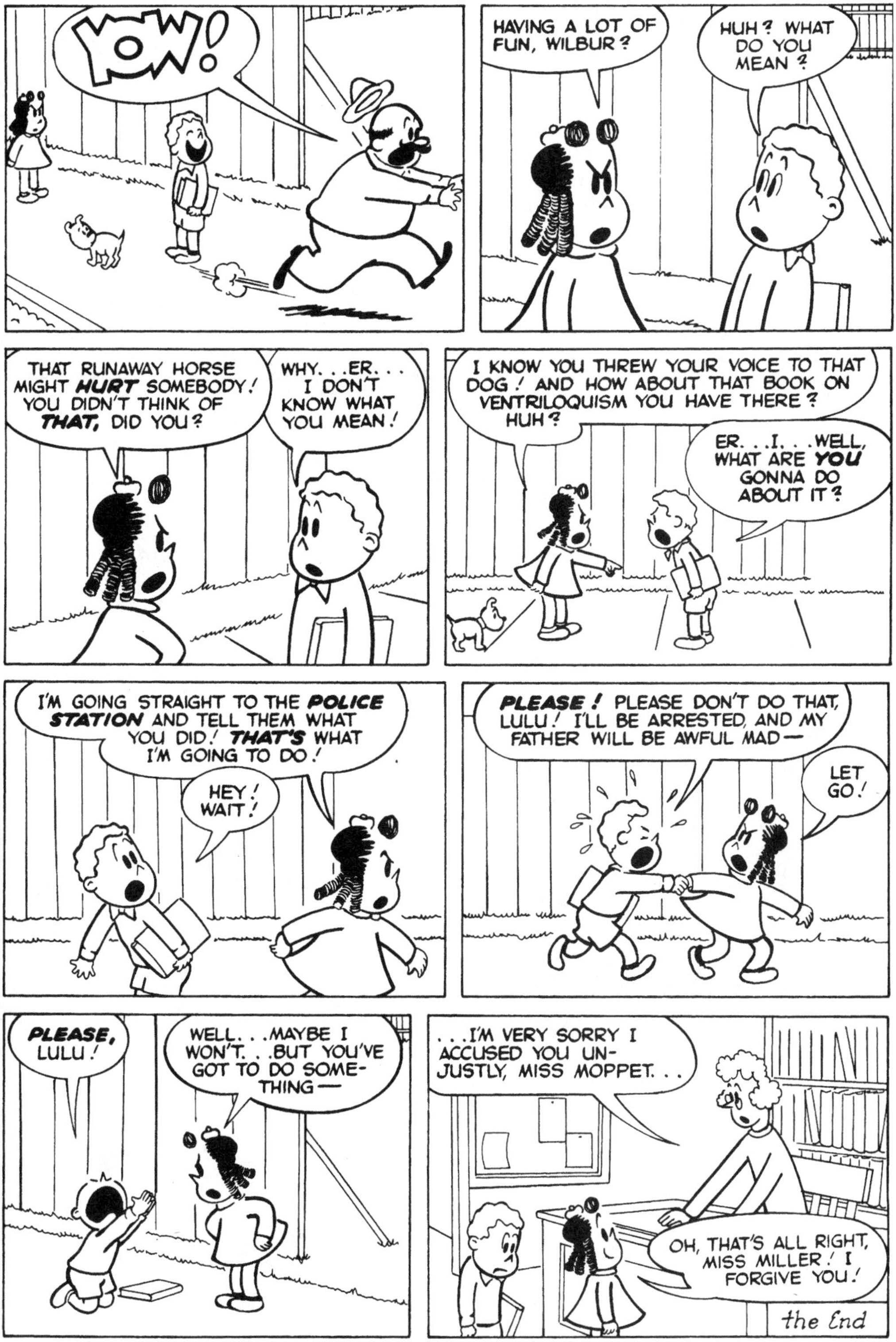

YOW!
HAVING A LOT OF FUN, WILBUR?
HUH? WHAT DO YOU MEAN?
THAT RUNAWAY HORSE MIGHT HURT SOMEBODY! YOU DIDN'T THINK OF THAT, DID YOU?
WHY. . .ER. . . I DON'T KNOW WHAT YOU MEAN!
I KNOW YOU THREW YOUR VOICE TO THAT DOG! AND HOW ABOUT THAT BOOK ON VENTRILOQUISM YOU HAVE THERE? HUH?
ER. . .I. . .WELL, WHAT ARE YOU GONNA DO ABOUT IT?
I'M GOING STRAIGHT TO THE POLICE STATION AND TELL THEM WHAT YOU DID! THAT'S WHAT I'M GOING TO DO!
HEY! WAIT!
PLEASE! PLEASE DON'T DO THAT, LULU! I'LL BE ARRESTED, AND MY FATHER WILL BE AWFUL MAD—
LET GO!
PLEASE, LULU!
WELL. . .MAYBE I WON'T. . .BUT YOU'VE GOT TO DO SOME-THING—
. . .I'M VERY SORRY I ACCUSED YOU UN-JUSTLY, MISS MOPPET. . .
OH, THAT'S ALL RIGHT, MISS MILLER! I FORGIVE YOU!
the End

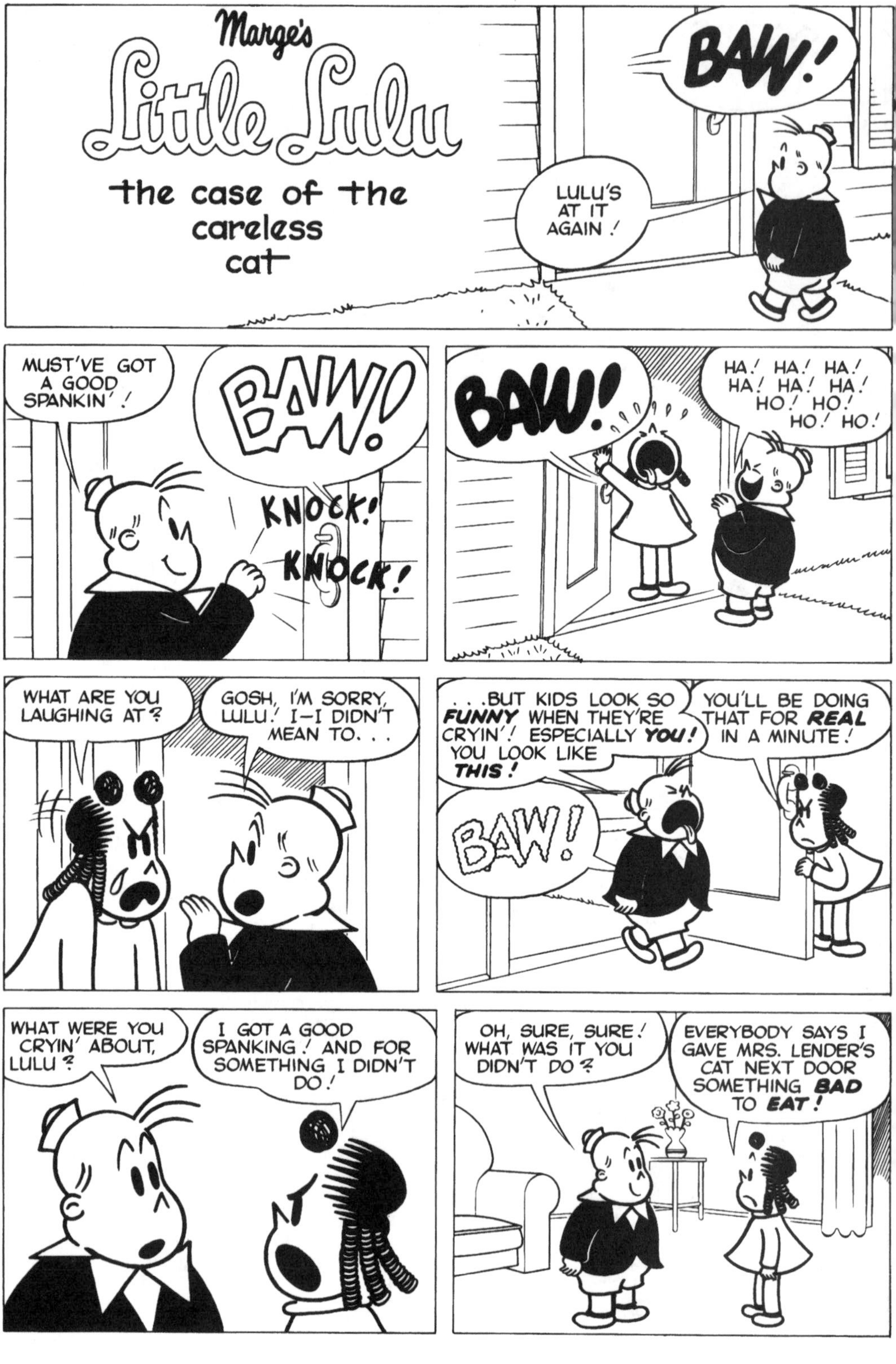
Marge's
Little Lulu
the case of the careless cat
BAW!
LULU'S AT IT AGAIN!
MUST'VE GOT A GOOD SPANKIN'!
BAW!
KNOCK! KNOCK!
BAW!
HA! HA! HA! HA! HA! HA! HO! HO! HO! HO!
WHAT ARE YOU LAUGHING AT?
GOSH, I'M SORRY, LULU! I—I DIDN'T MEAN TO. . .
. . .BUT KIDS LOOK SO FUNNY WHEN THEY'RE CRYIN'! ESPECIALLY YOU! YOU LOOK LIKE THIS!
BAW!
YOU'LL BE DOING THAT FOR REAL IN A MINUTE!
WHAT WERE YOU CRYIN' ABOUT, LULU?
I GOT A GOOD SPANKING! AND FOR SOMETHING I DIDN'T DO!
OH, SURE, SURE! WHAT WAS IT YOU DIDN'T DO?
EVERYBODY SAYS I GAVE MRS. LENDER'S CAT NEXT DOOR SOMETHING BAD TO EAT!

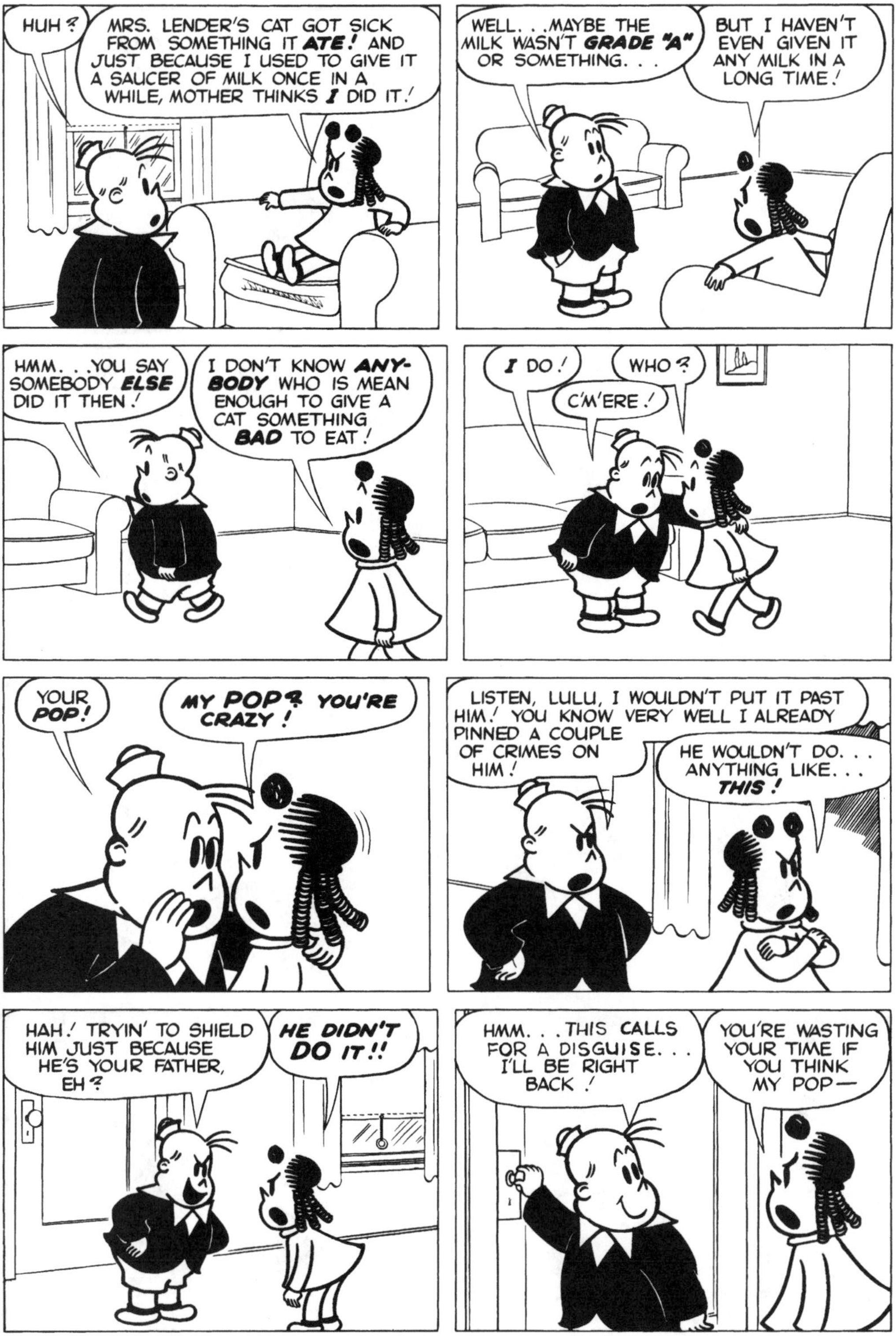
HUH?
MRS. LENDER'S CAT GOT SICK FROM SOMETHING IT ATE! AND JUST BECAUSE I USED TO GIVE IT A SAUCER OF MILK ONCE IN A WHILE, MOTHER THINKS I DID IT!
WELL. . .MAYBE THE MILK WASN'T GRADE "A" OR SOMETHING. . .
BUT I HAVEN'T EVEN GIVEN IT ANY MILK IN A LONG TIME!
HMM. . .YOU SAY SOMEBODY ELSE DID IT THEN!
I DON'T KNOW ANYBODY WHO IS MEAN ENOUGH TO GIVE A CAT SOMETHING BAD TO EAT!
I DO!
WHO?
C'M'ERE!
YOUR POP!
MY POP? YOU'RE CRAZY!
LISTEN, LULU, I WOULDN'T PUT IT PAST HIM! YOU KNOW VERY WELL I ALREADY PINNED A COUPLE OF CRIMES ON HIM!
HE WOULDN'T DO. . . ANYTHING LIKE. . . THIS!
HAH! TRYIN' TO SHIELD HIM JUST BECAUSE HE'S YOUR FATHER, EH?
HE DIDN'T DO IT!!
HMM. . .THIS CALLS FOR A DISGUISE. . . I'LL BE RIGHT BACK!
YOU'RE WASTING YOUR TIME IF YOU THINK MY POP—

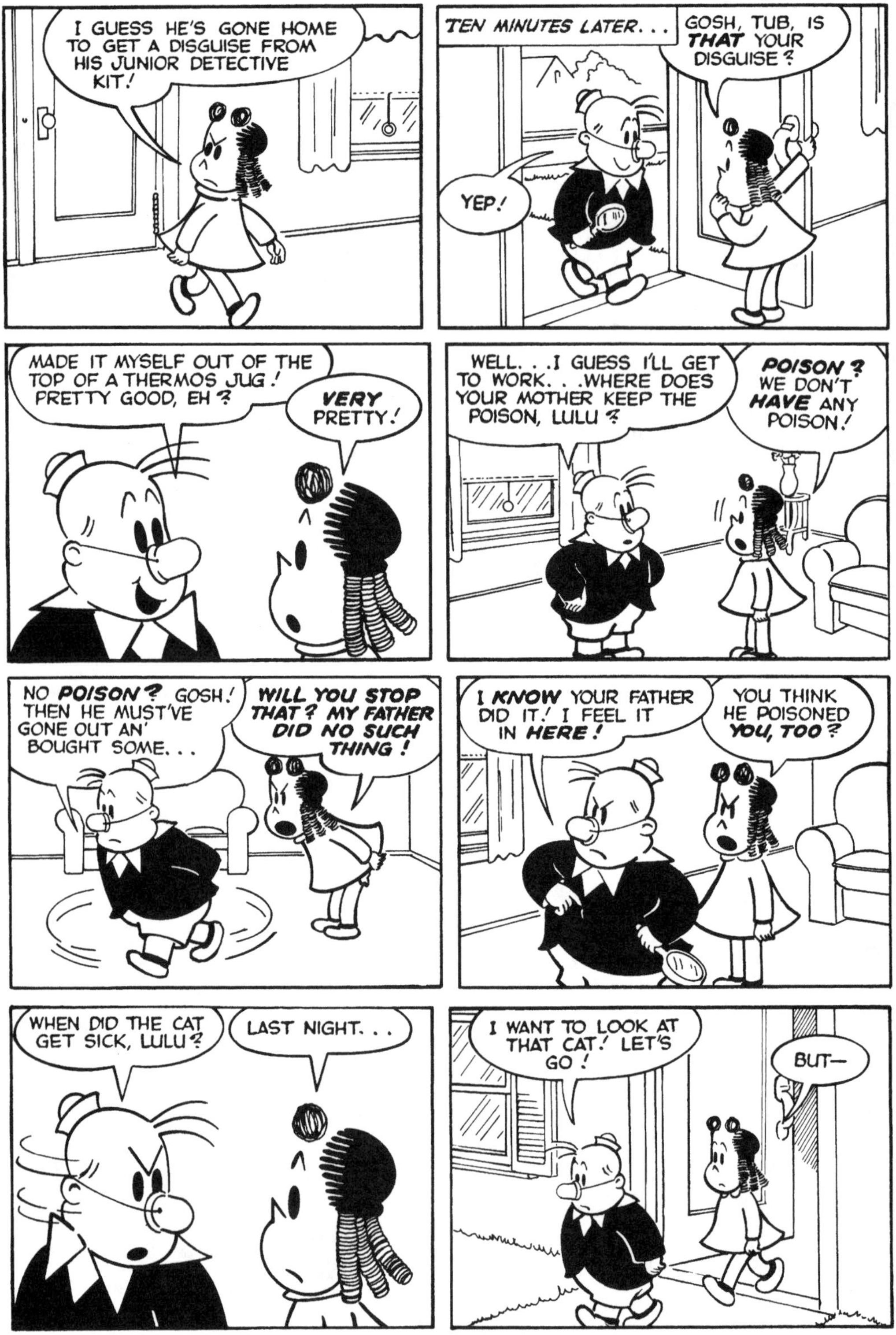
I GUESS HE'S GONE HOME TO GET A DISGUISE FROM HIS JUNIOR DETECTIVE KIT!
TEN MINUTES LATER...
GOSH, TUB, IS THAT YOUR DISGUISE?
YEP!
MADE IT MYSELF OUT OF THE TOP OF A THERMOS JUG! PRETTY GOOD, EH?
VERY PRETTY!
WELL...I GUESS I'LL GET TO WORK...WHERE DOES YOUR MOTHER KEEP THE POISON, LULU?
POISON? WE DON'T HAVE ANY POISON!
NO POISON? GOSH! THEN HE MUST'VE GONE OUT AN' BOUGHT SOME...
WILL YOU STOP THAT? MY FATHER DID NO SUCH THING!
I KNOW YOUR FATHER DID IT! I FEEL IT IN HERE!
YOU THINK HE POISONED YOU, TOO?
WHEN DID THE CAT GET SICK, LULU?
LAST NIGHT...
I WANT TO LOOK AT THAT CAT! LET'S GO!
BUT—

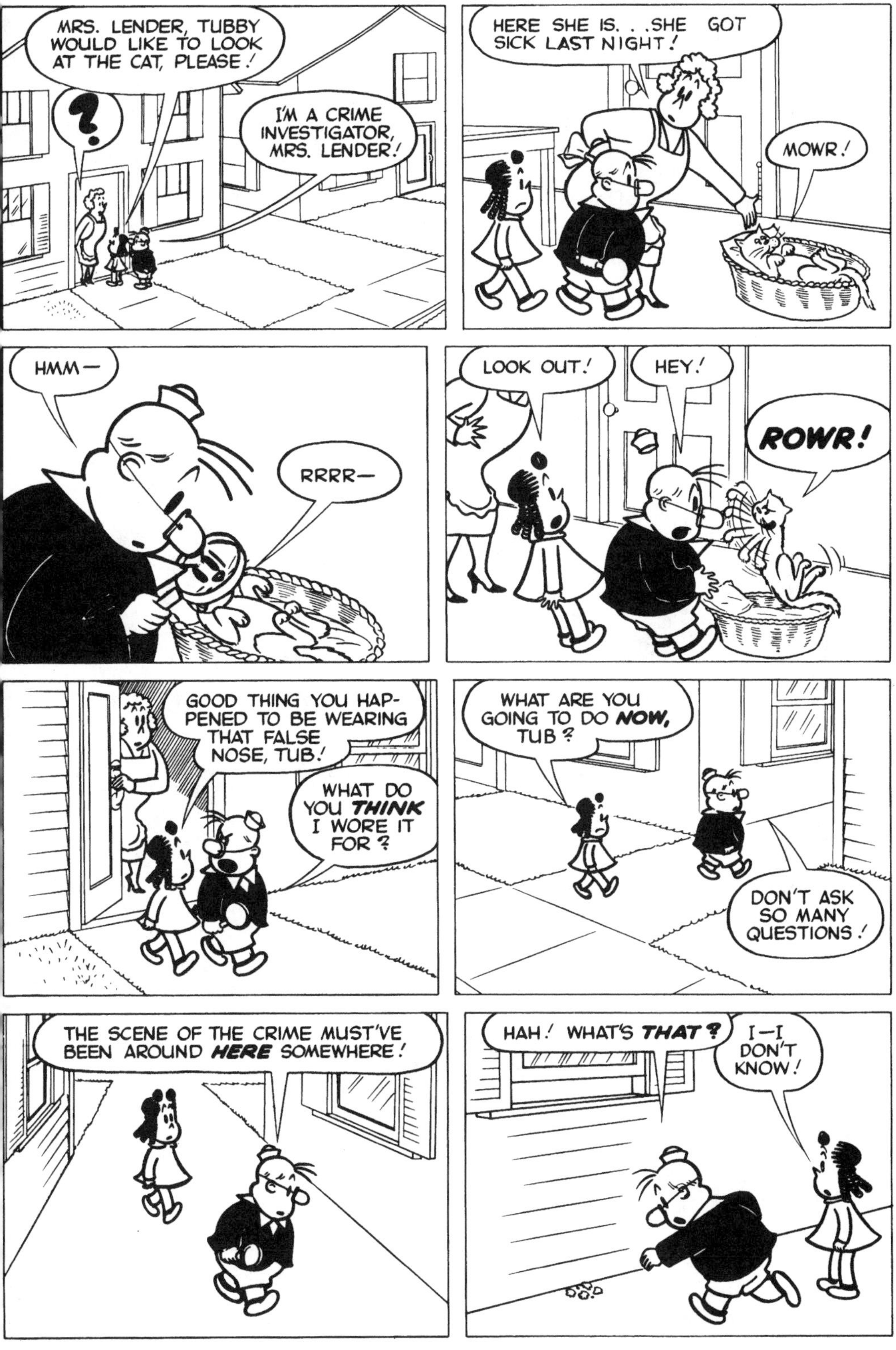
MRS. LENDER, TUBBY WOULD LIKE TO LOOK AT THE CAT, PLEASE!
?
I'M A CRIME INVESTIGATOR, MRS. LENDER!
HERE SHE IS. . .SHE GOT SICK LAST NIGHT!
MOWR!
HMM—
RRRR—
LOOK OUT!
HEY!
ROWR!
GOOD THING YOU HAPPENED TO BE WEARING THAT FALSE NOSE, TUB!
WHAT DO YOU THINK I WORE IT FOR?
WHAT ARE YOU GOING TO DO NOW, TUB?
DON'T ASK SO MANY QUESTIONS!
THE SCENE OF THE CRIME MUST'VE BEEN AROUND HERE SOMEWHERE!
HAH! WHAT'S THAT?
I—I DON'T KNOW!

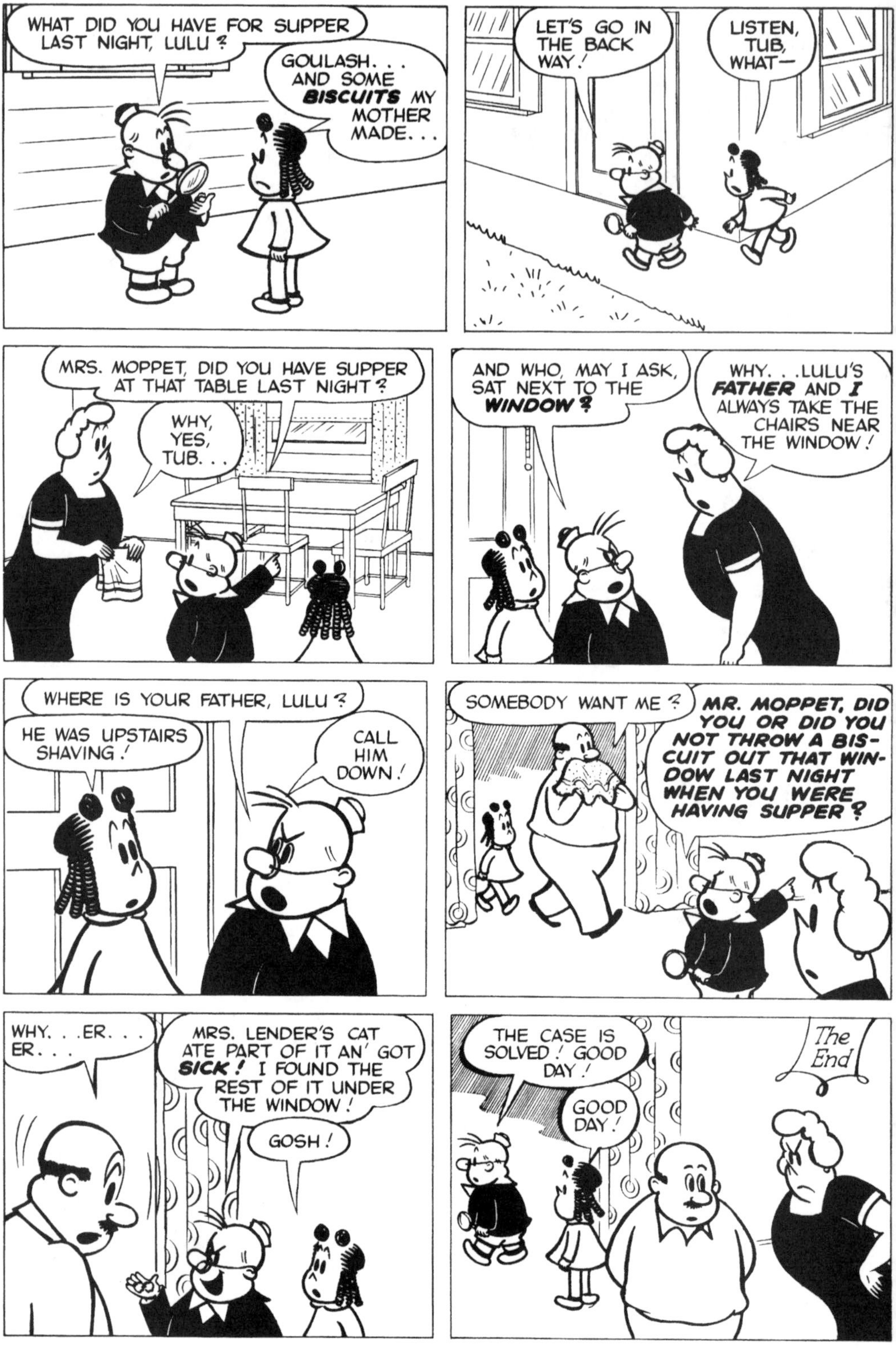

WHAT DID YOU HAVE FOR SUPPER LAST NIGHT, LULU?
GOULASH. . . AND SOME **BISCUITS** MY MOTHER MADE. . .
LET'S GO IN THE BACK WAY!
LISTEN, TUB, WHAT—
MRS. MOPPET, DID YOU HAVE SUPPER AT THAT TABLE LAST NIGHT?
WHY, YES, TUB. . .
AND WHO, MAY I ASK, SAT NEXT TO THE **WINDOW?**
WHY. . .LULU'S **FATHER** AND **I** ALWAYS TAKE THE CHAIRS NEAR THE WINDOW!
WHERE IS YOUR FATHER, LULU?
HE WAS UPSTAIRS SHAVING!
CALL HIM DOWN!
SOMEBODY WANT ME?
MR. MOPPET, DID YOU OR DID YOU NOT THROW A BISCUIT OUT THAT WINDOW LAST NIGHT WHEN YOU WERE HAVING SUPPER?
WHY. . .ER. . . ER. . .
MRS. LENDER'S CAT ATE PART OF IT AN' GOT **SICK!** I FOUND THE REST OF IT UNDER THE WINDOW!
GOSH!
THE CASE IS SOLVED! GOOD DAY!
GOOD DAY!
The End

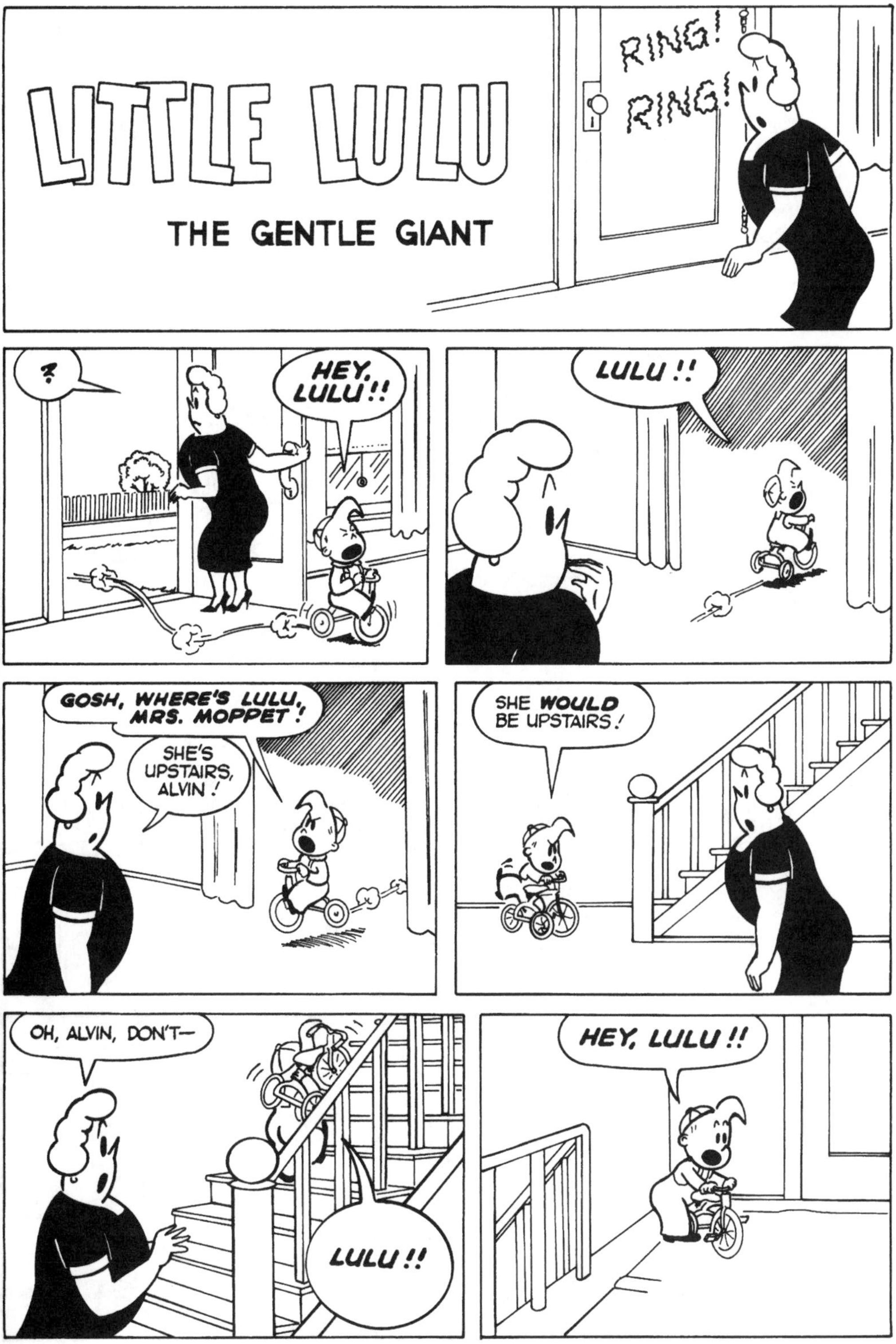
LITTLE LULU
THE GENTLE GIANT
RING! RING!
?
HEY, LULU!!
LULU!!
GOSH, WHERE'S LULU, MRS. MOPPET!
SHE'S UPSTAIRS, ALVIN!
SHE WOULD BE UPSTAIRS!
OH, ALVIN, DON'T—
LULU!!
HEY, LULU!!

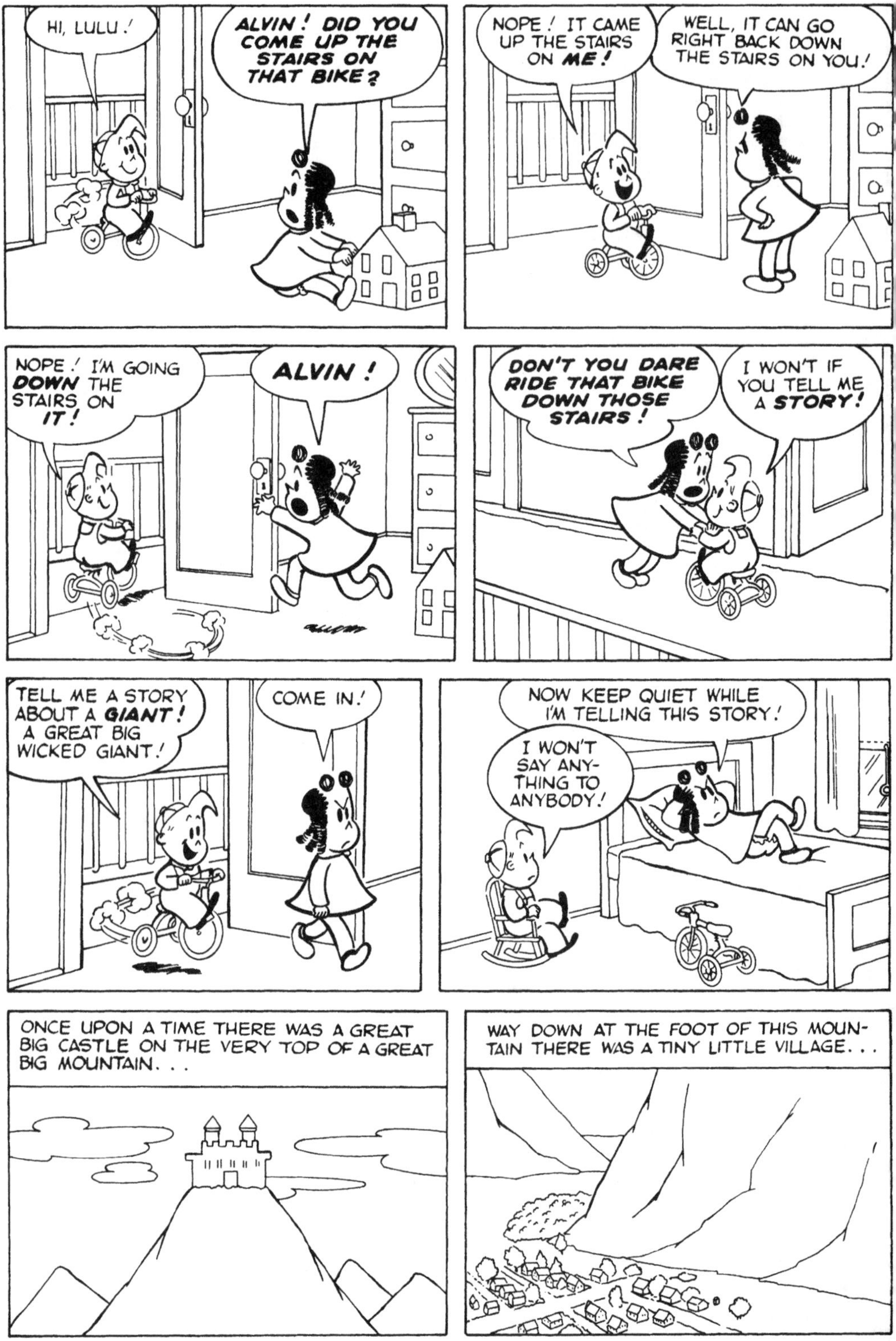
HI, LULU!
ALVIN! DID YOU COME UP THE STAIRS ON THAT BIKE?
NOPE! IT CAME UP THE STAIRS ON **ME**!
WELL, IT CAN GO RIGHT BACK DOWN THE STAIRS ON YOU!
NOPE! I'M GOING **DOWN** THE STAIRS ON **IT**!
ALVIN!
DON'T YOU DARE RIDE THAT BIKE DOWN THOSE STAIRS!
I WON'T IF YOU TELL ME A **STORY**!
TELL ME A STORY ABOUT A **GIANT**! A GREAT BIG WICKED GIANT!
COME IN!
NOW KEEP QUIET WHILE I'M TELLING THIS STORY!
I WON'T SAY ANY-THING TO ANYBODY!
ONCE UPON A TIME THERE WAS A GREAT BIG CASTLE ON THE VERY TOP OF A GREAT BIG MOUNTAIN. . .
WAY DOWN AT THE FOOT OF THIS MOUN-TAIN THERE WAS A TINY LITTLE VILLAGE. . .

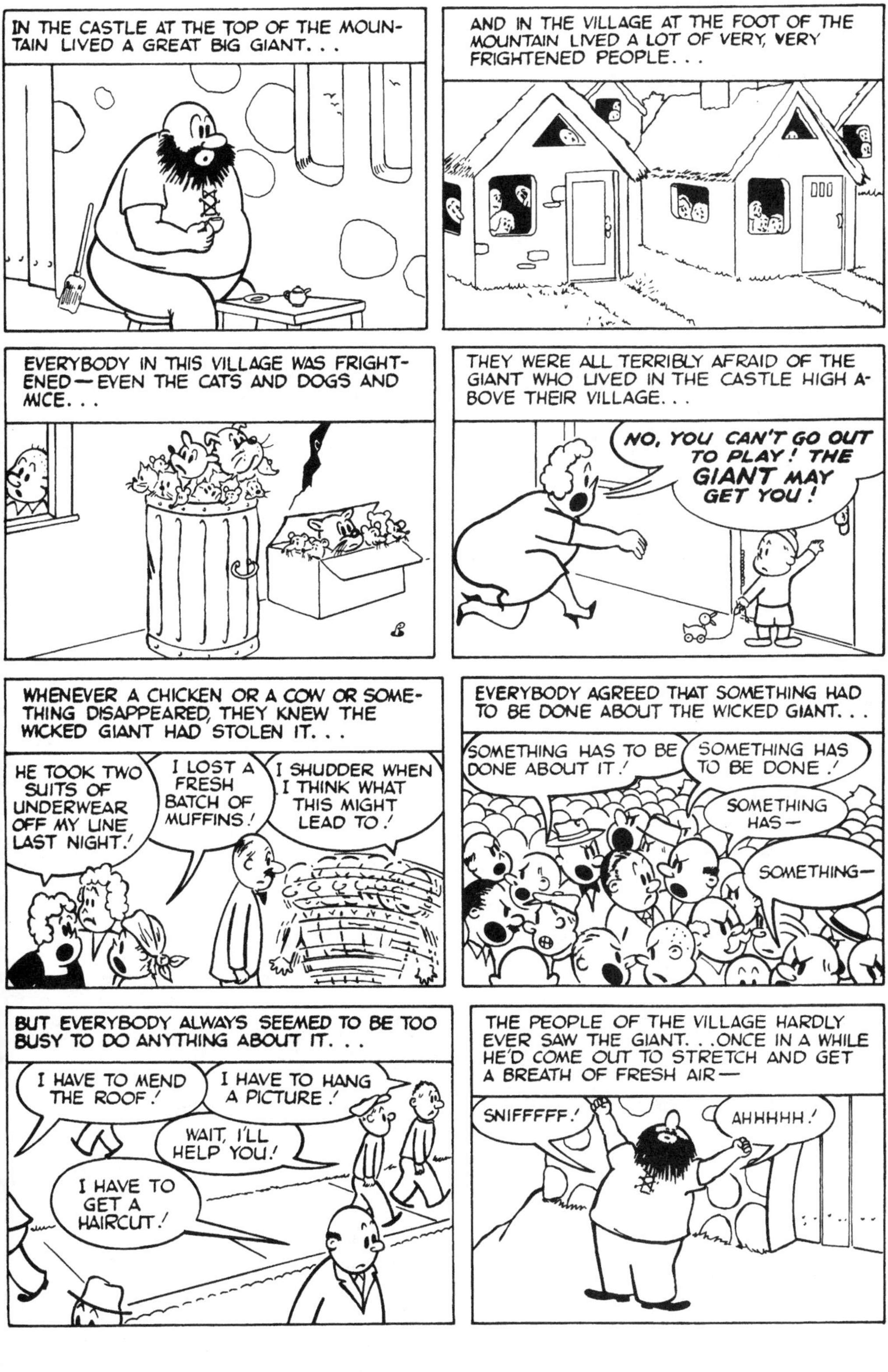
IN THE CASTLE AT THE TOP OF THE MOUNTAIN LIVED A GREAT BIG GIANT. . .
AND IN THE VILLAGE AT THE FOOT OF THE MOUNTAIN LIVED A LOT OF VERY, VERY FRIGHTENED PEOPLE. . .
EVERYBODY IN THIS VILLAGE WAS FRIGHTENED—EVEN THE CATS AND DOGS AND MICE. . .
THEY WERE ALL TERRIBLY AFRAID OF THE GIANT WHO LIVED IN THE CASTLE HIGH ABOVE THEIR VILLAGE. . .
NO, YOU CAN'T GO OUT TO PLAY! THE GIANT MAY GET YOU!
WHENEVER A CHICKEN OR A COW OR SOMETHING DISAPPEARED, THEY KNEW THE WICKED GIANT HAD STOLEN IT. . .
HE TOOK TWO SUITS OF UNDERWEAR OFF MY LINE LAST NIGHT!
I LOST A FRESH BATCH OF MUFFINS!
I SHUDDER WHEN I THINK WHAT THIS MIGHT LEAD TO!
EVERYBODY AGREED THAT SOMETHING HAD TO BE DONE ABOUT THE WICKED GIANT. . .
SOMETHING HAS TO BE DONE ABOUT IT!
SOMETHING HAS TO BE DONE!
SOMETHING HAS—
SOMETHING—
BUT EVERYBODY ALWAYS SEEMED TO BE TOO BUSY TO DO ANYTHING ABOUT IT. . .
I HAVE TO MEND THE ROOF!
I HAVE TO HANG A PICTURE!
WAIT, I'LL HELP YOU!
I HAVE TO GET A HAIRCUT!
THE PEOPLE OF THE VILLAGE HARDLY EVER SAW THE GIANT. . .ONCE IN A WHILE HE'D COME OUT TO STRETCH AND GET A BREATH OF FRESH AIR—
SNIFFFFF!
AHHHHH!

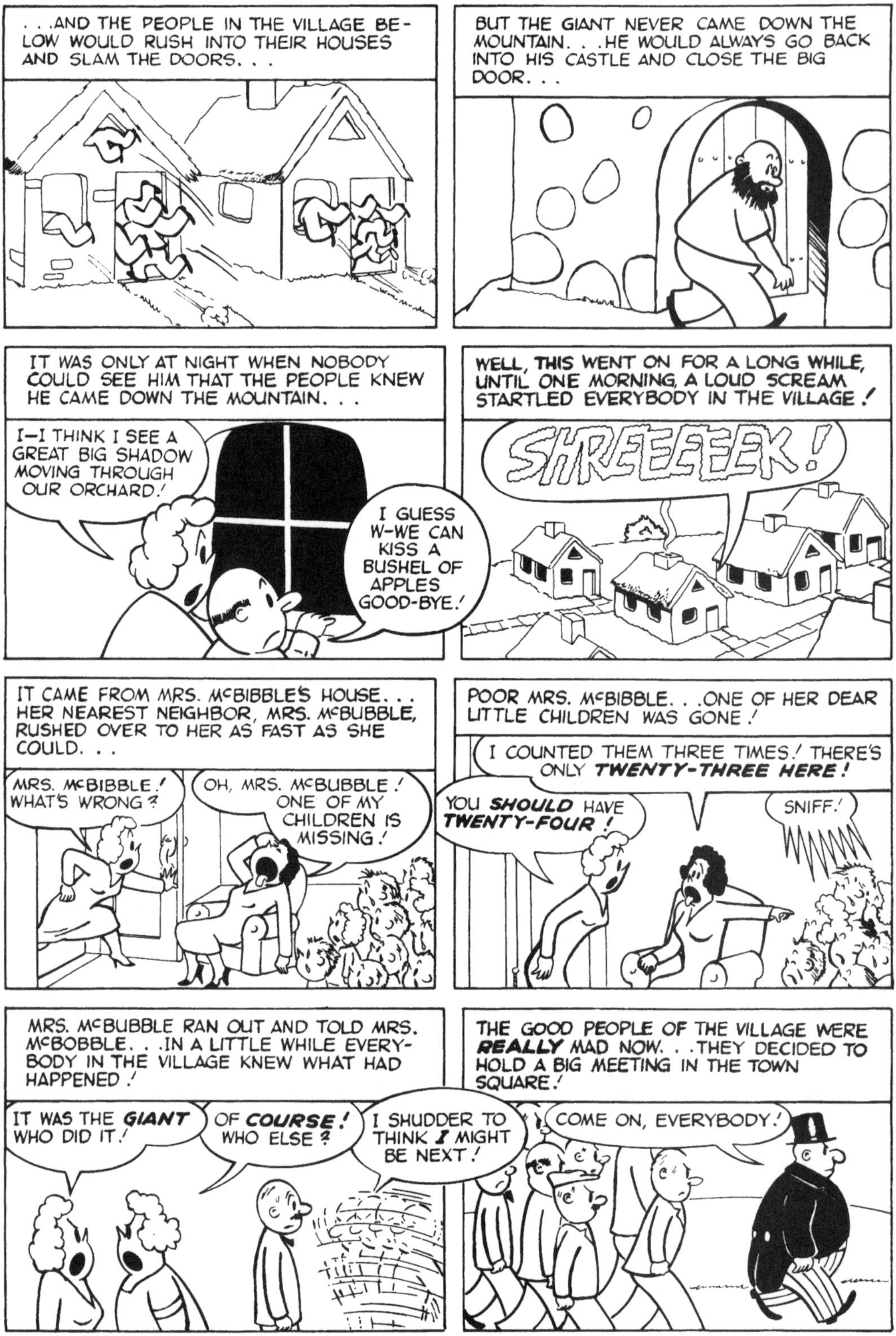
. . .AND THE PEOPLE IN THE VILLAGE BELOW WOULD RUSH INTO THEIR HOUSES AND SLAM THE DOORS. . .
BUT THE GIANT NEVER CAME DOWN THE MOUNTAIN. . .HE WOULD ALWAYS GO BACK INTO HIS CASTLE AND CLOSE THE BIG DOOR. . .
IT WAS ONLY AT NIGHT WHEN NOBODY COULD SEE HIM THAT THE PEOPLE KNEW HE CAME DOWN THE MOUNTAIN. . .
I—I THINK I SEE A GREAT BIG SHADOW MOVING THROUGH OUR ORCHARD!
I GUESS W-WE CAN KISS A BUSHEL OF APPLES GOOD-BYE!
WELL, THIS WENT ON FOR A LONG WHILE, UNTIL ONE MORNING, A LOUD SCREAM STARTLED EVERYBODY IN THE VILLAGE!
SHREEEEEK!
IT CAME FROM MRS. McBIBBLE'S HOUSE. . . HER NEAREST NEIGHBOR, MRS. McBUBBLE, RUSHED OVER TO HER AS FAST AS SHE COULD. . .
MRS. McBIBBLE! WHAT'S WRONG?
OH, MRS. McBUBBLE! ONE OF MY CHILDREN IS MISSING!
POOR MRS. McBIBBLE. . .ONE OF HER DEAR LITTLE CHILDREN WAS GONE!
I COUNTED THEM THREE TIMES! THERE'S ONLY TWENTY-THREE HERE!
YOU SHOULD HAVE TWENTY-FOUR!
SNIFF!
MRS. McBUBBLE RAN OUT AND TOLD MRS. McBOBBLE. . .IN A LITTLE WHILE EVERYBODY IN THE VILLAGE KNEW WHAT HAD HAPPENED!
IT WAS THE GIANT WHO DID IT!
OF COURSE! WHO ELSE?
I SHUDDER TO THINK I MIGHT BE NEXT!
THE GOOD PEOPLE OF THE VILLAGE WERE REALLY MAD NOW. . .THEY DECIDED TO HOLD A BIG MEETING IN THE TOWN SQUARE!
COME ON, EVERYBODY!

THE MAYOR, WHO WAS A VERY BRAVE MAN, SAID THAT AT LAST THE GIANT HAD GONE TOO FAR!

AT LAST THE GIANT HAS GONE TOO FAR!

HURRAY!

HURRAY!

HURRAY!

THEN HE SAID THAT THE TOWN WOULD PAY TWENTY-TWO DOLLARS REWARD TO ANYBODY WHO KILLED THE GIANT GOOD AND DEAD!

NONE OF THIS STUFF ABOUT BRINGING HIM BACK ALIVE!

HOORAY!

HOORAY!

THEN EVERYBODY WENT HOME BECAUSE THEY HAD THINGS TO DO!

I HAVE TO PLUG UP A MOUSEHOLE!

I HAVE TO TAKE MY SUNDAY PANTS TO THE TAILOR!

I'LL HELP YOU!

I'LL HAVE TO GET SOME REWARD POSTERS MADE!

WELL...THREE WEEKS PASSED, AND ONE DAY ON THE OUTSKIRTS OF TOWN, A RAGGED LITTLE GIRL WAS SEEN STROLLING ALONG...

HMPH!

SNIFF!

SHE WAS A POOR HOMELESS LITTLE GIRL WHO HAD JUST WANDERED INTO TOWN TO MAKE HER FORTUNE...

ZZZ!

REWARD! $22 WILL BE PAID TO ANYONE WHO BRINGS THE GIANT BACK DEAD!

GOSH, I'M HUNGRY!

BUT SHE DIDN'T GET VERY FAR BEFORE A POLICEMAN STOPPED HER...

YOU LOOK LIKE A LITTLE **BEGGAR!** WE DON'T ALLOW ANY LITTLE BEGGARS IN THIS TOWN!

REWARD! $22 WILL BE PAID TO ANYONE WHO BRINGS GIANT DEAD!

BUT— IF YOU LET ME STAY HERE **LONG** ENOUGH, I'LL BE A **BIG** BEGGAR!

HE WASN'T A VERY NICE POLICEMAN—HE WANTED THE POOR LITTLE GIRL TO GET OUT OF TOWN...

WE ONLY ALLOW PEOPLE WHO **WORK** TO COME INTO THIS TOWN!

REWARD! $22 WILL BE PAID TO ANYONE WHO BRINGS THE GIANT BACK DEAD!

JUST THEN THE LITTLE GIRL NOTICED A POSTER ON A WALL OFFERING A LOT OF MONEY TO ANYONE WHO KILLED A GIANT...

I **AM** GOING TO WORK! I'M GOING TO KILL THE **GIANT!**

YARD! D E RINGS THE GIANT BACK DEAD!

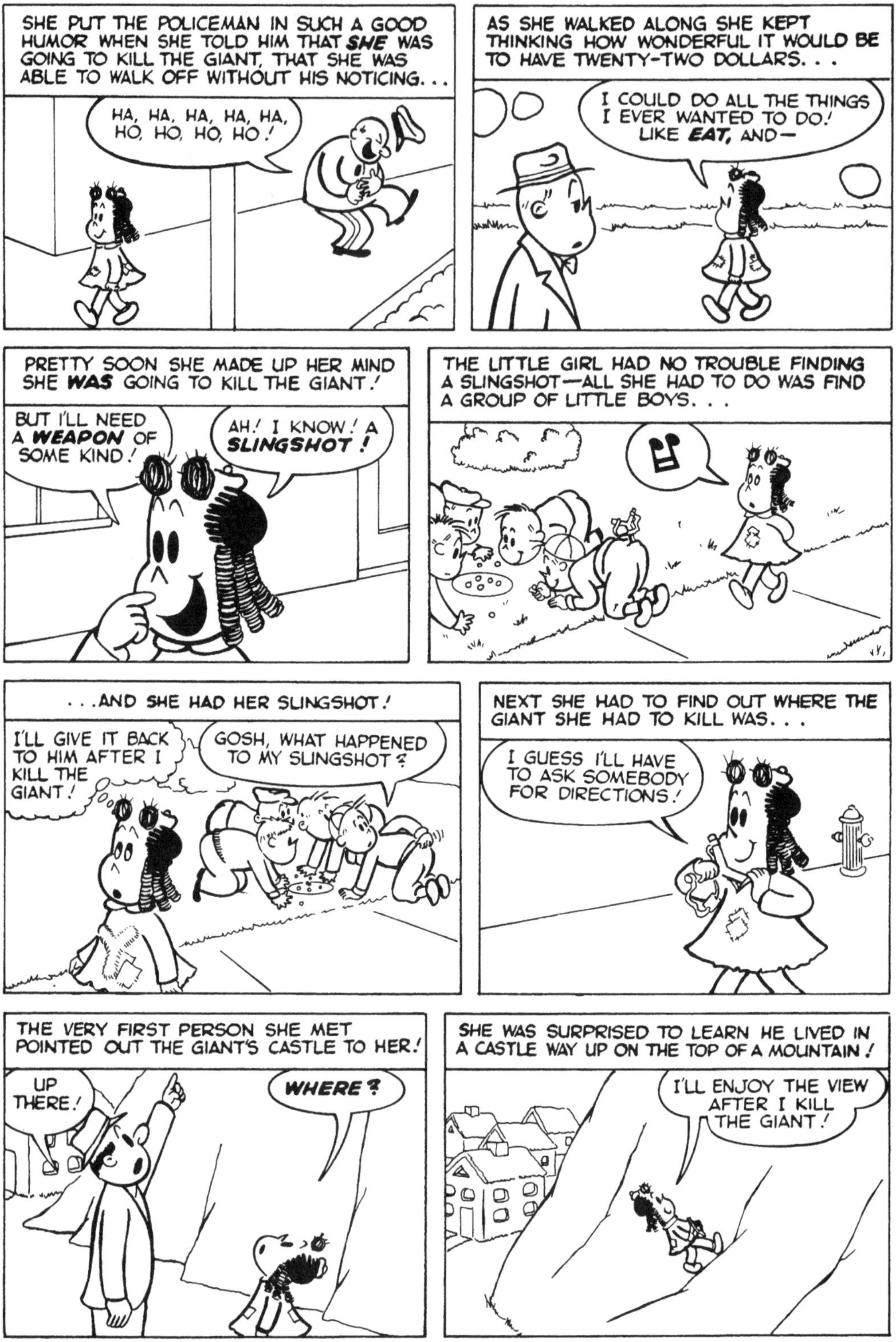
SHE PUT THE POLICEMAN IN SUCH A GOOD HUMOR WHEN SHE TOLD HIM THAT SHE WAS GOING TO KILL THE GIANT, THAT SHE WAS ABLE TO WALK OFF WITHOUT HIS NOTICING. . .
HA, HA, HA, HA, HA, HO, HO, HO, HO!
AS SHE WALKED ALONG SHE KEPT THINKING HOW WONDERFUL IT WOULD BE TO HAVE TWENTY-TWO DOLLARS. . .
I COULD DO ALL THE THINGS I EVER WANTED TO DO! LIKE EAT, AND—
PRETTY SOON SHE MADE UP HER MIND SHE WAS GOING TO KILL THE GIANT!
BUT I'LL NEED A WEAPON OF SOME KIND!
AH! I KNOW! A SLINGSHOT!
THE LITTLE GIRL HAD NO TROUBLE FINDING A SLINGSHOT—ALL SHE HAD TO DO WAS FIND A GROUP OF LITTLE BOYS. . .
. . .AND SHE HAD HER SLINGSHOT!
I'LL GIVE IT BACK TO HIM AFTER I KILL THE GIANT!
GOSH, WHAT HAPPENED TO MY SLINGSHOT?
NEXT SHE HAD TO FIND OUT WHERE THE GIANT SHE HAD TO KILL WAS. . .
I GUESS I'LL HAVE TO ASK SOMEBODY FOR DIRECTIONS!
THE VERY FIRST PERSON SHE MET POINTED OUT THE GIANT'S CASTLE TO HER!
UP THERE!
WHERE?
SHE WAS SURPRISED TO LEARN HE LIVED IN A CASTLE WAY UP ON THE TOP OF A MOUNTAIN!
I'LL ENJOY THE VIEW AFTER I KILL THE GIANT!

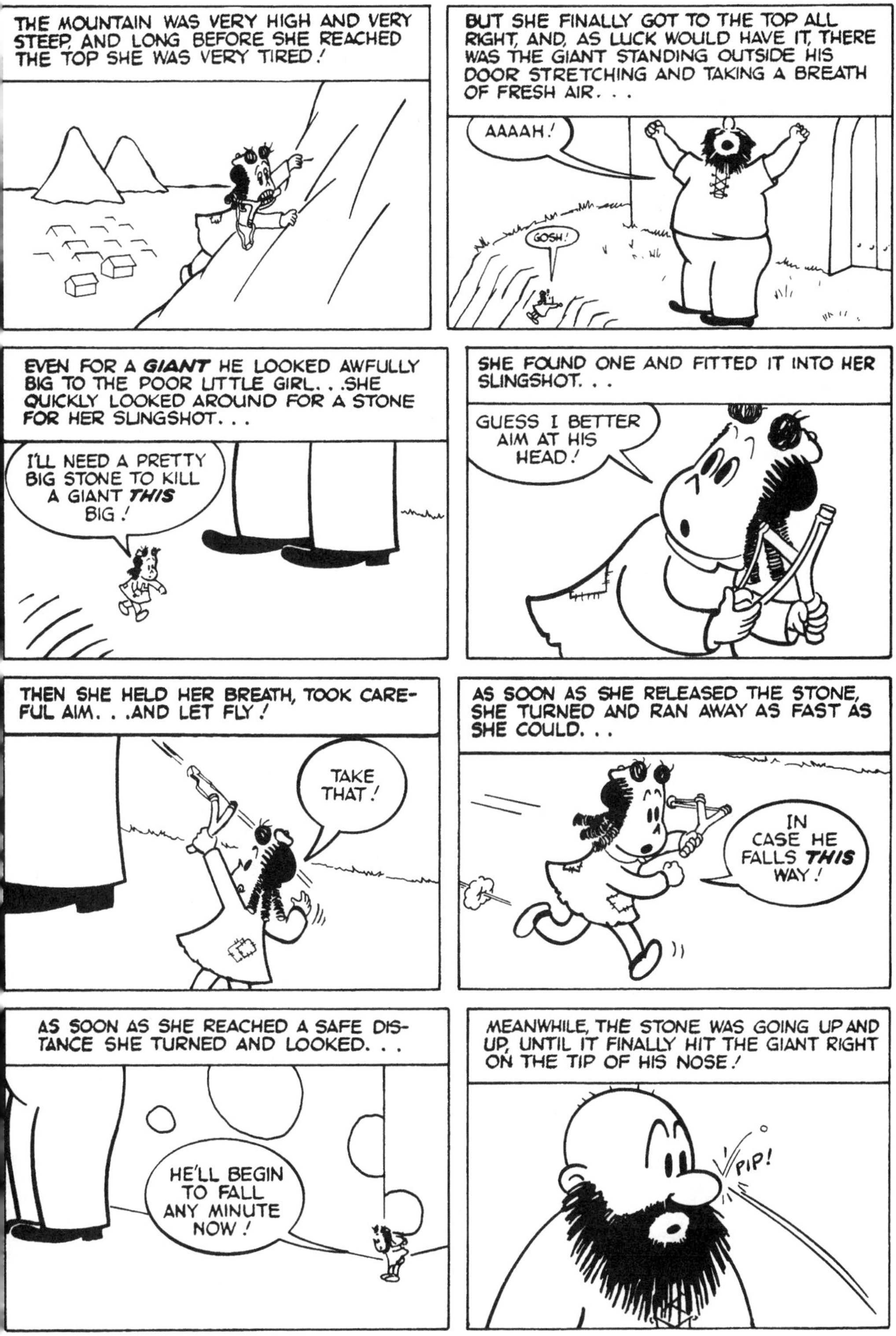

THE MOUNTAIN WAS VERY HIGH AND VERY STEEP, AND LONG BEFORE SHE REACHED THE TOP SHE WAS VERY TIRED!
BUT SHE FINALLY GOT TO THE TOP ALL RIGHT, AND, AS LUCK WOULD HAVE IT, THERE WAS THE GIANT STANDING OUTSIDE HIS DOOR STRETCHING AND TAKING A BREATH OF FRESH AIR. . .
AAAAH!
GOSH!
EVEN FOR A GIANT HE LOOKED AWFULLY BIG TO THE POOR LITTLE GIRL. . .SHE QUICKLY LOOKED AROUND FOR A STONE FOR HER SLINGSHOT. . .
I'LL NEED A PRETTY BIG STONE TO KILL A GIANT THIS BIG!
SHE FOUND ONE AND FITTED IT INTO HER SLINGSHOT. . .
GUESS I BETTER AIM AT HIS HEAD!
THEN SHE HELD HER BREATH, TOOK CAREFUL AIM. . .AND LET FLY!
TAKE THAT!
AS SOON AS SHE RELEASED THE STONE, SHE TURNED AND RAN AWAY AS FAST AS SHE COULD. . .
IN CASE HE FALLS THIS WAY!
AS SOON AS SHE REACHED A SAFE DISTANCE SHE TURNED AND LOOKED. . .
HE'LL BEGIN TO FALL ANY MINUTE NOW!
MEANWHILE, THE STONE WAS GOING UP AND UP, UNTIL IT FINALLY HIT THE GIANT RIGHT ON THE TIP OF HIS NOSE!
PIP!

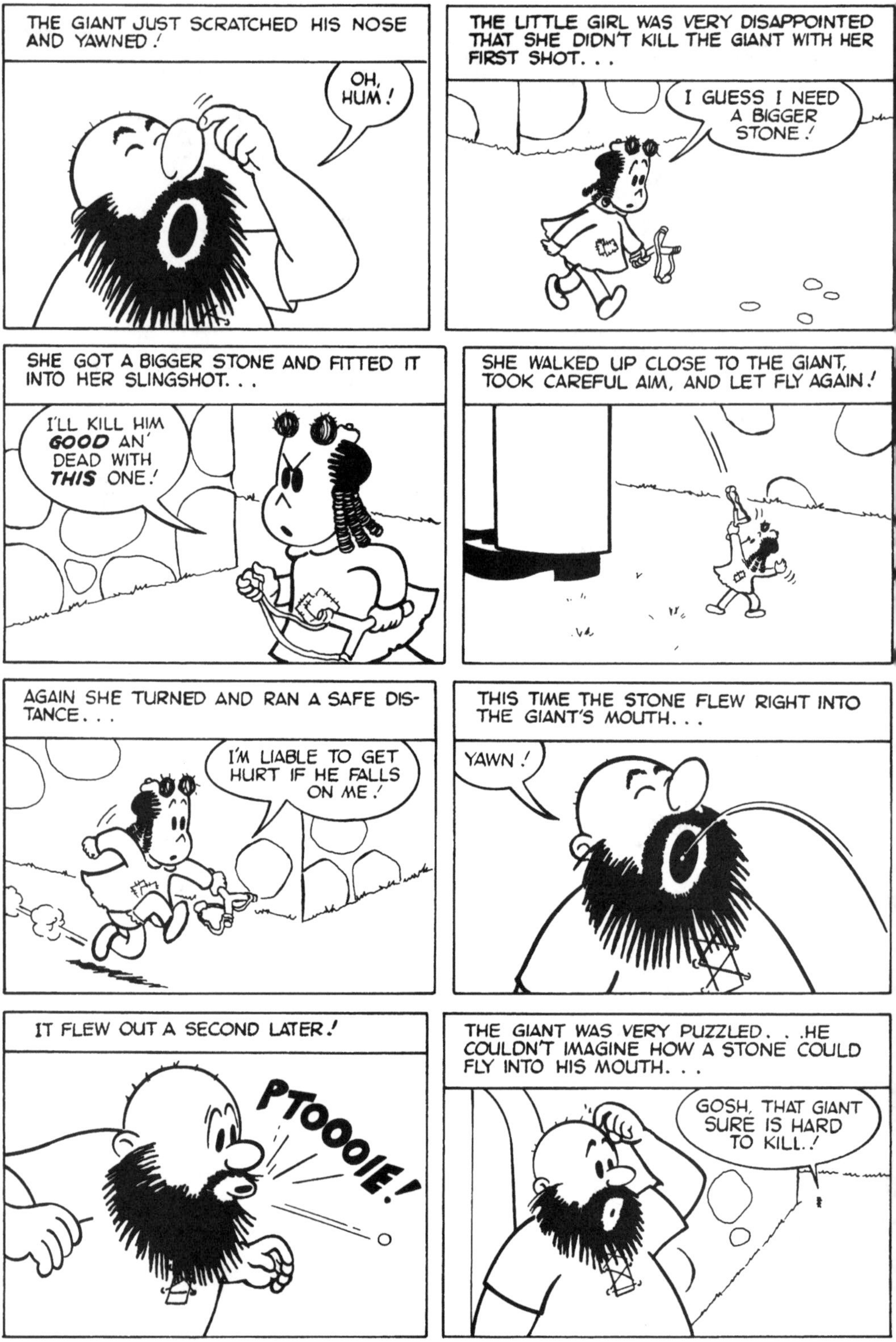
THE GIANT JUST SCRATCHED HIS NOSE AND YAWNED!
OH, HUM!
THE LITTLE GIRL WAS VERY DISAPPOINTED THAT SHE DIDN'T KILL THE GIANT WITH HER FIRST SHOT. . .
I GUESS I NEED A BIGGER STONE!
SHE GOT A BIGGER STONE AND FITTED IT INTO HER SLINGSHOT. . .
I'LL KILL HIM GOOD AN' DEAD WITH THIS ONE!
SHE WALKED UP CLOSE TO THE GIANT, TOOK CAREFUL AIM, AND LET FLY AGAIN!
AGAIN SHE TURNED AND RAN A SAFE DISTANCE. . .
I'M LIABLE TO GET HURT IF HE FALLS ON ME!
THIS TIME THE STONE FLEW RIGHT INTO THE GIANT'S MOUTH. . .
YAWN!
IT FLEW OUT A SECOND LATER!
PTOOOIE!
THE GIANT WAS VERY PUZZLED. . .HE COULDN'T IMAGINE HOW A STONE COULD FLY INTO HIS MOUTH. . .
GOSH, THAT GIANT SURE IS HARD TO KILL.!

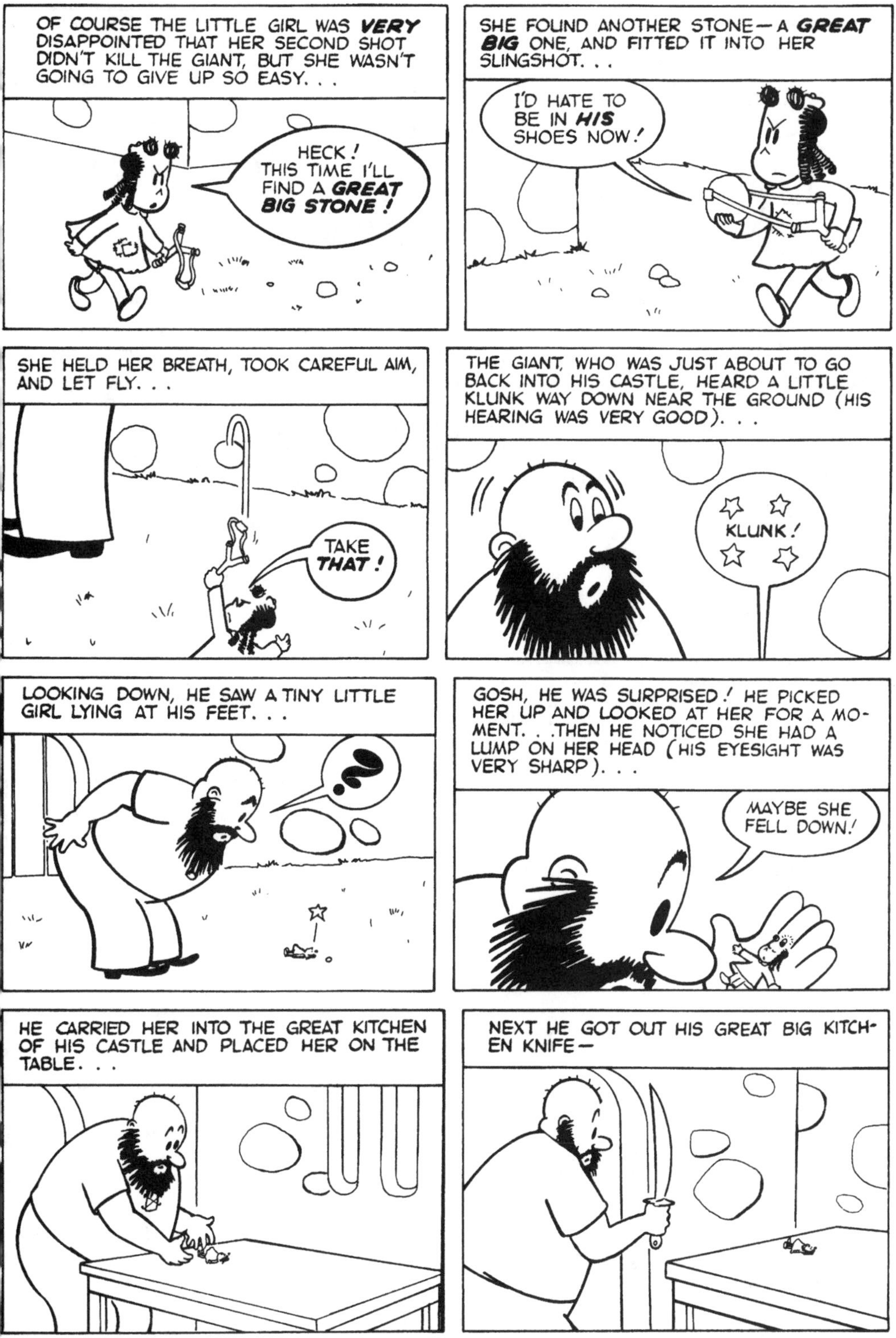
OF COURSE THE LITTLE GIRL WAS VERY DISAPPOINTED THAT HER SECOND SHOT DIDN'T KILL THE GIANT, BUT SHE WASN'T GOING TO GIVE UP SO EASY. . .
HECK! THIS TIME I'LL FIND A GREAT BIG STONE!
SHE FOUND ANOTHER STONE—A GREAT BIG ONE, AND FITTED IT INTO HER SLINGSHOT. . .
I'D HATE TO BE IN HIS SHOES NOW!
SHE HELD HER BREATH, TOOK CAREFUL AIM, AND LET FLY. . .
TAKE THAT!
THE GIANT, WHO WAS JUST ABOUT TO GO BACK INTO HIS CASTLE, HEARD A LITTLE KLUNK WAY DOWN NEAR THE GROUND (HIS HEARING WAS VERY GOOD). . .
KLUNK!
LOOKING DOWN, HE SAW A TINY LITTLE GIRL LYING AT HIS FEET. . .
?
GOSH, HE WAS SURPRISED! HE PICKED HER UP AND LOOKED AT HER FOR A MOMENT. . .THEN HE NOTICED SHE HAD A LUMP ON HER HEAD (HIS EYESIGHT WAS VERY SHARP). . .
MAYBE SHE FELL DOWN!
HE CARRIED HER INTO THE GREAT KITCHEN OF HIS CASTLE AND PLACED HER ON THE TABLE. . .
NEXT HE GOT OUT HIS GREAT BIG KITCHEN KNIFE—

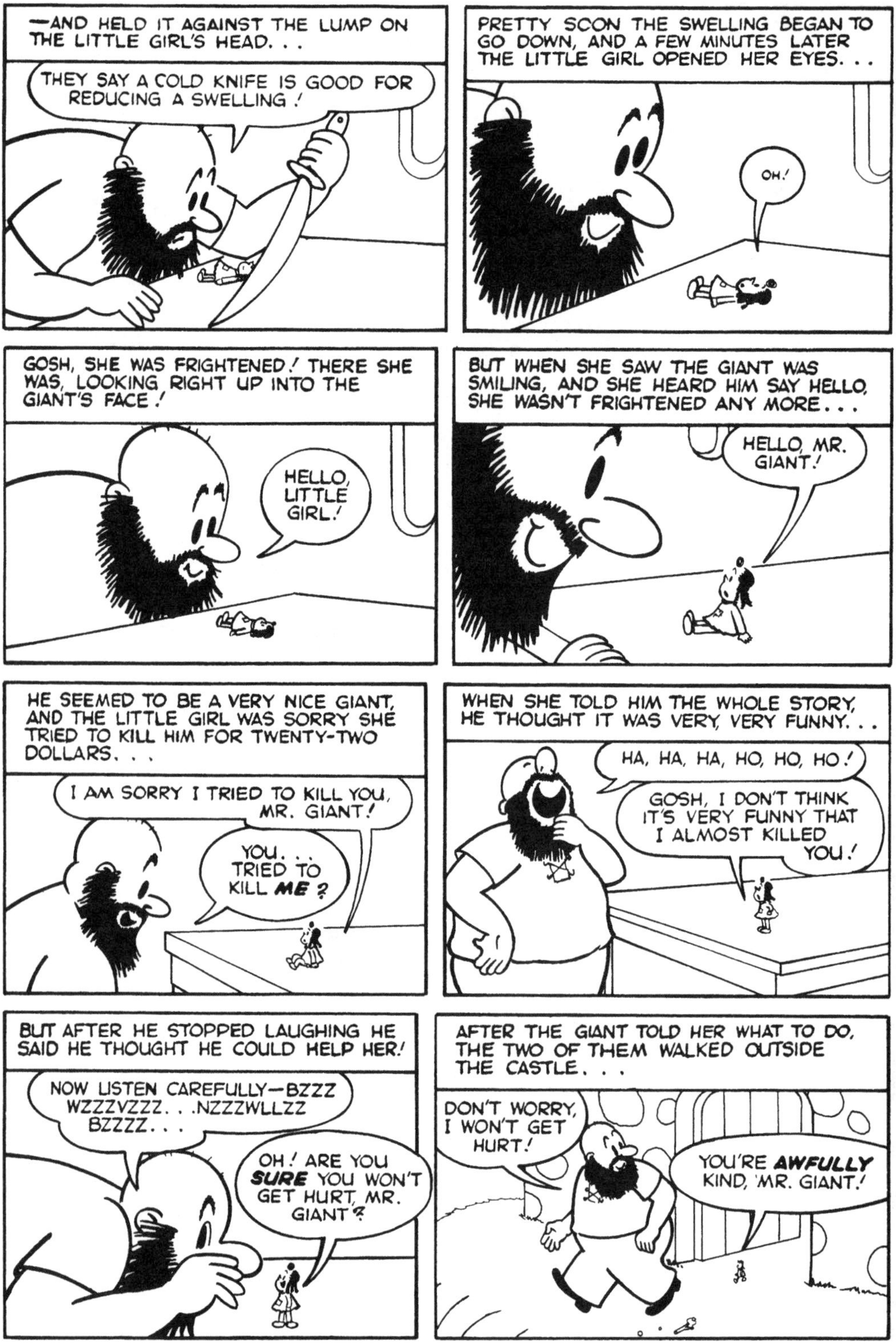
—AND HELD IT AGAINST THE LUMP ON THE LITTLE GIRL'S HEAD. . .
THEY SAY A COLD KNIFE IS GOOD FOR REDUCING A SWELLING!
PRETTY SOON THE SWELLING BEGAN TO GO DOWN, AND A FEW MINUTES LATER THE LITTLE GIRL OPENED HER EYES. . .
OH!
GOSH, SHE WAS FRIGHTENED! THERE SHE WAS, LOOKING RIGHT UP INTO THE GIANT'S FACE!
HELLO, LITTLE GIRL!
BUT WHEN SHE SAW THE GIANT WAS SMILING, AND SHE HEARD HIM SAY HELLO, SHE WASN'T FRIGHTENED ANY MORE. . .
HELLO, MR. GIANT!
HE SEEMED TO BE A VERY NICE GIANT, AND THE LITTLE GIRL WAS SORRY SHE TRIED TO KILL HIM FOR TWENTY-TWO DOLLARS. . .
I AM SORRY I TRIED TO KILL YOU, MR. GIANT!
YOU. . . TRIED TO KILL ***ME***?
WHEN SHE TOLD HIM THE WHOLE STORY, HE THOUGHT IT WAS VERY, VERY FUNNY. . .
HA, HA, HA, HO, HO, HO!
GOSH, I DON'T THINK IT'S VERY FUNNY THAT I ALMOST KILLED YOU!
BUT AFTER HE STOPPED LAUGHING HE SAID HE THOUGHT HE COULD HELP HER!
NOW LISTEN CAREFULLY—BZZZ WZZZVZZZ. . .NZZZWLLZZ BZZZZ. . .
OH! ARE YOU ***SURE*** YOU WON'T GET HURT, MR. GIANT?
AFTER THE GIANT TOLD HER WHAT TO DO, THE TWO OF THEM WALKED OUTSIDE THE CASTLE. . .
DON'T WORRY, I WON'T GET HURT!
YOU'RE ***AWFULLY*** KIND, MR. GIANT!

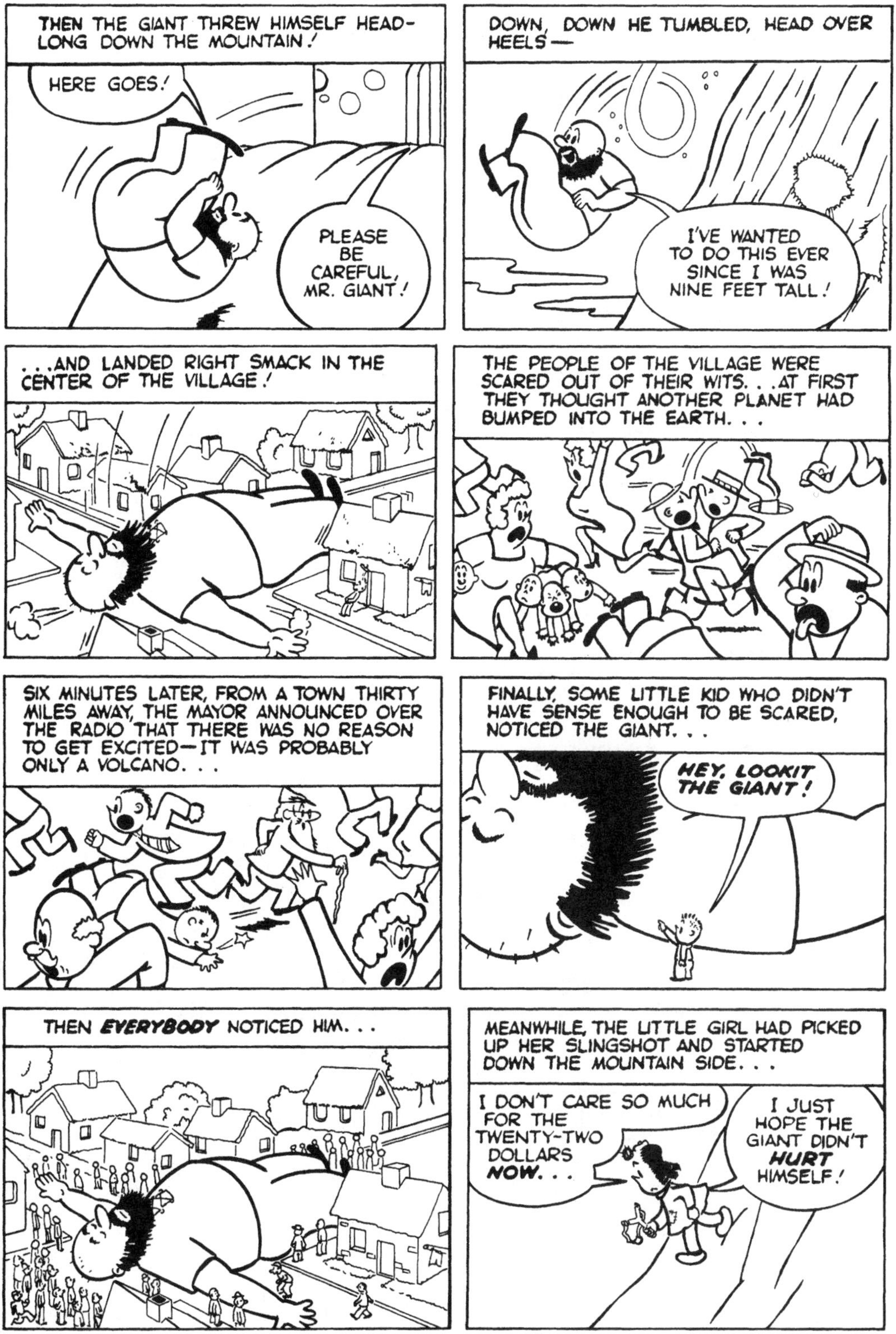
THEN THE GIANT THREW HIMSELF HEADLONG DOWN THE MOUNTAIN!
HERE GOES!
PLEASE BE CAREFUL, MR. GIANT!
DOWN, DOWN HE TUMBLED, HEAD OVER HEELS—
I'VE WANTED TO DO THIS EVER SINCE I WAS NINE FEET TALL!
...AND LANDED RIGHT SMACK IN THE CENTER OF THE VILLAGE!
THE PEOPLE OF THE VILLAGE WERE SCARED OUT OF THEIR WITS...AT FIRST THEY THOUGHT ANOTHER PLANET HAD BUMPED INTO THE EARTH...
SIX MINUTES LATER, FROM A TOWN THIRTY MILES AWAY, THE MAYOR ANNOUNCED OVER THE RADIO THAT THERE WAS NO REASON TO GET EXCITED—IT WAS PROBABLY ONLY A VOLCANO...
FINALLY, SOME LITTLE KID WHO DIDN'T HAVE SENSE ENOUGH TO BE SCARED, NOTICED THE GIANT...
HEY, LOOKIT THE GIANT!
THEN EVERYBODY NOTICED HIM...
MEANWHILE, THE LITTLE GIRL HAD PICKED UP HER SLINGSHOT AND STARTED DOWN THE MOUNTAIN SIDE...
I DON'T CARE SO MUCH FOR THE TWENTY-TWO DOLLARS NOW...
I JUST HOPE THE GIANT DIDN'T HURT HIMSELF!

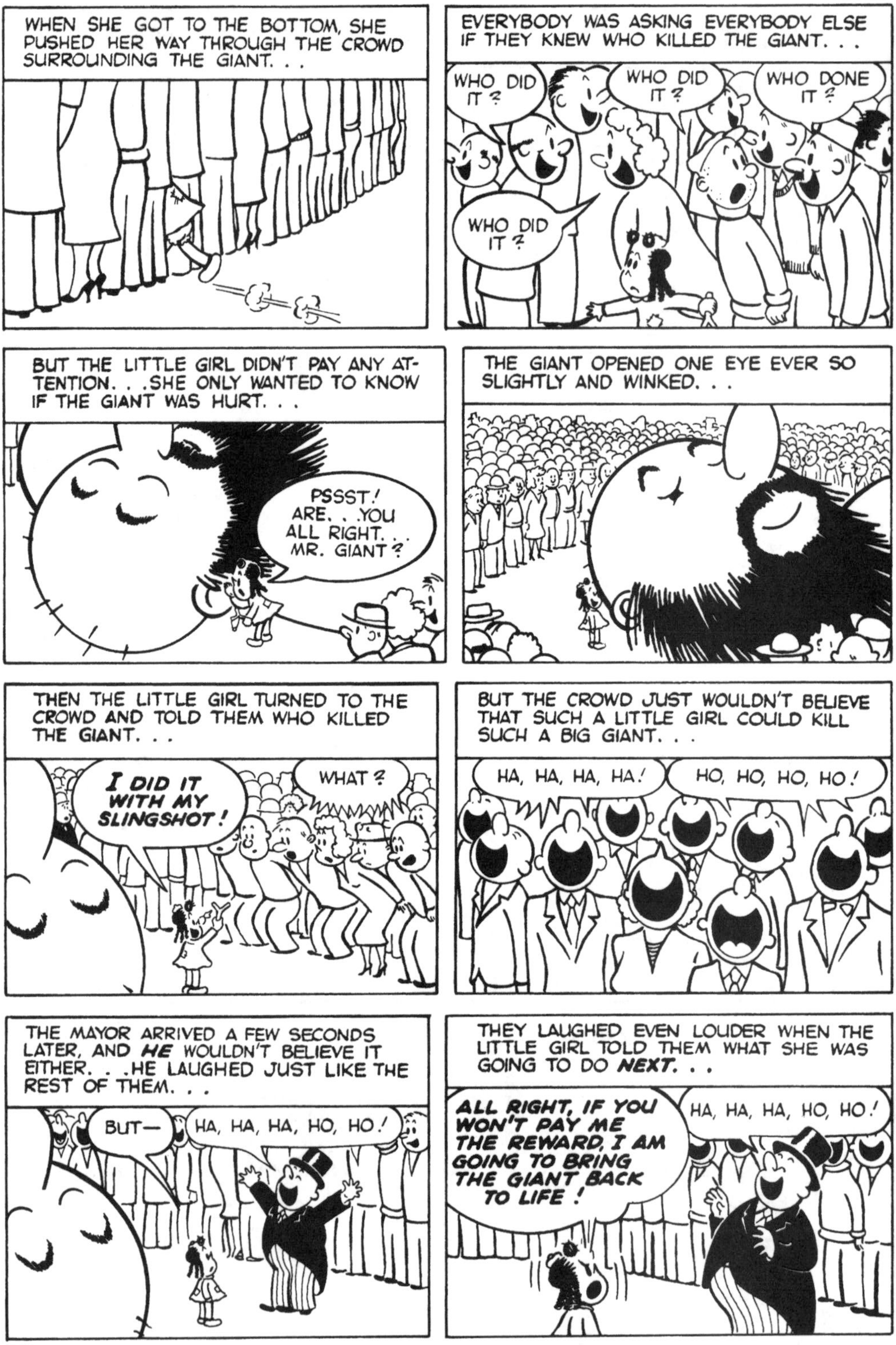
WHEN SHE GOT TO THE BOTTOM, SHE PUSHED HER WAY THROUGH THE CROWD SURROUNDING THE GIANT. . .
EVERYBODY WAS ASKING EVERYBODY ELSE IF THEY KNEW WHO KILLED THE GIANT. . .
WHO DID IT ?
WHO DID IT ?
WHO DONE IT ?
WHO DID IT ?
BUT THE LITTLE GIRL DIDN'T PAY ANY ATTENTION. . .SHE ONLY WANTED TO KNOW IF THE GIANT WAS HURT. . .
PSSST! ARE. . .YOU ALL RIGHT. . . MR. GIANT ?
THE GIANT OPENED ONE EYE EVER SO SLIGHTLY AND WINKED. . .
THEN THE LITTLE GIRL TURNED TO THE CROWD AND TOLD THEM WHO KILLED THE GIANT. . .
I DID IT WITH MY SLINGSHOT!
WHAT ?
BUT THE CROWD JUST WOULDN'T BELIEVE THAT SUCH A LITTLE GIRL COULD KILL SUCH A BIG GIANT. . .
HA, HA, HA, HA!
HO, HO, HO, HO!
THE MAYOR ARRIVED A FEW SECONDS LATER, AND HE WOULDN'T BELIEVE IT EITHER. . .HE LAUGHED JUST LIKE THE REST OF THEM. . .
BUT—
HA, HA, HA, HO, HO!
THEY LAUGHED EVEN LOUDER WHEN THE LITTLE GIRL TOLD THEM WHAT SHE WAS GOING TO DO NEXT. . .
ALL RIGHT, IF YOU WON'T PAY ME THE REWARD, I AM GOING TO BRING THE GIANT BACK TO LIFE!
HA, HA, HA, HO, HO!

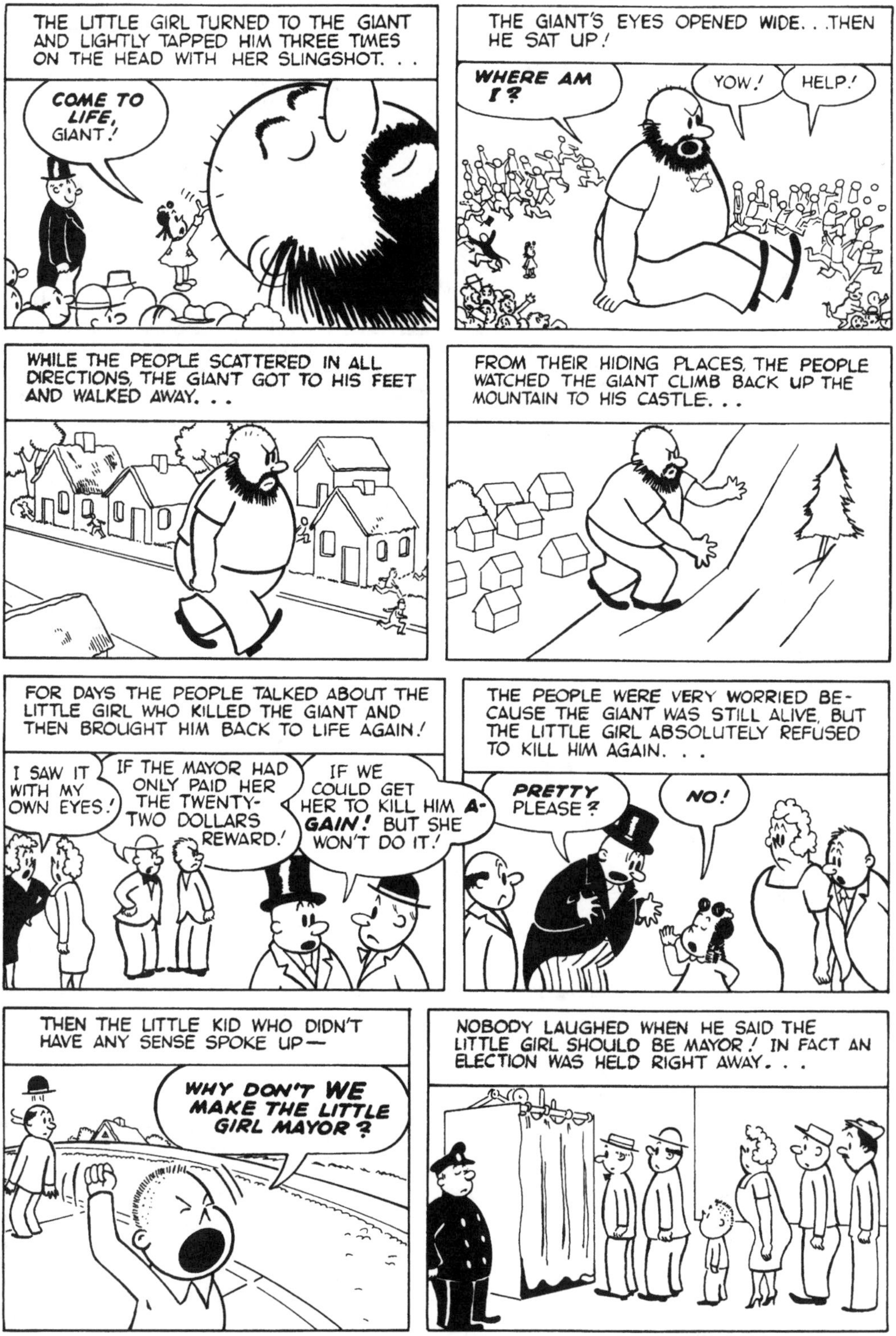

THE LITTLE GIRL TURNED TO THE GIANT AND LIGHTLY TAPPED HIM THREE TIMES ON THE HEAD WITH HER SLINGSHOT. . .
COME TO LIFE, GIANT!
THE GIANT'S EYES OPENED WIDE. . .THEN HE SAT UP!
WHERE AM I?
YOW!
HELP!
WHILE THE PEOPLE SCATTERED IN ALL DIRECTIONS, THE GIANT GOT TO HIS FEET AND WALKED AWAY. . .
FROM THEIR HIDING PLACES, THE PEOPLE WATCHED THE GIANT CLIMB BACK UP THE MOUNTAIN TO HIS CASTLE. . .
FOR DAYS THE PEOPLE TALKED ABOUT THE LITTLE GIRL WHO KILLED THE GIANT AND THEN BROUGHT HIM BACK TO LIFE AGAIN!
I SAW IT WITH MY OWN EYES!
IF THE MAYOR HAD ONLY PAID HER THE TWENTY-TWO DOLLARS REWARD!
IF WE COULD GET HER TO KILL HIM AGAIN! BUT SHE WON'T DO IT!
THE PEOPLE WERE VERY WORRIED BECAUSE THE GIANT WAS STILL ALIVE, BUT THE LITTLE GIRL ABSOLUTELY REFUSED TO KILL HIM AGAIN. . .
PRETTY PLEASE?
NO!
THEN THE LITTLE KID WHO DIDN'T HAVE ANY SENSE SPOKE UP—
WHY DON'T WE MAKE THE LITTLE GIRL MAYOR?
NOBODY LAUGHED WHEN HE SAID THE LITTLE GIRL SHOULD BE MAYOR! IN FACT AN ELECTION WAS HELD RIGHT AWAY. . .

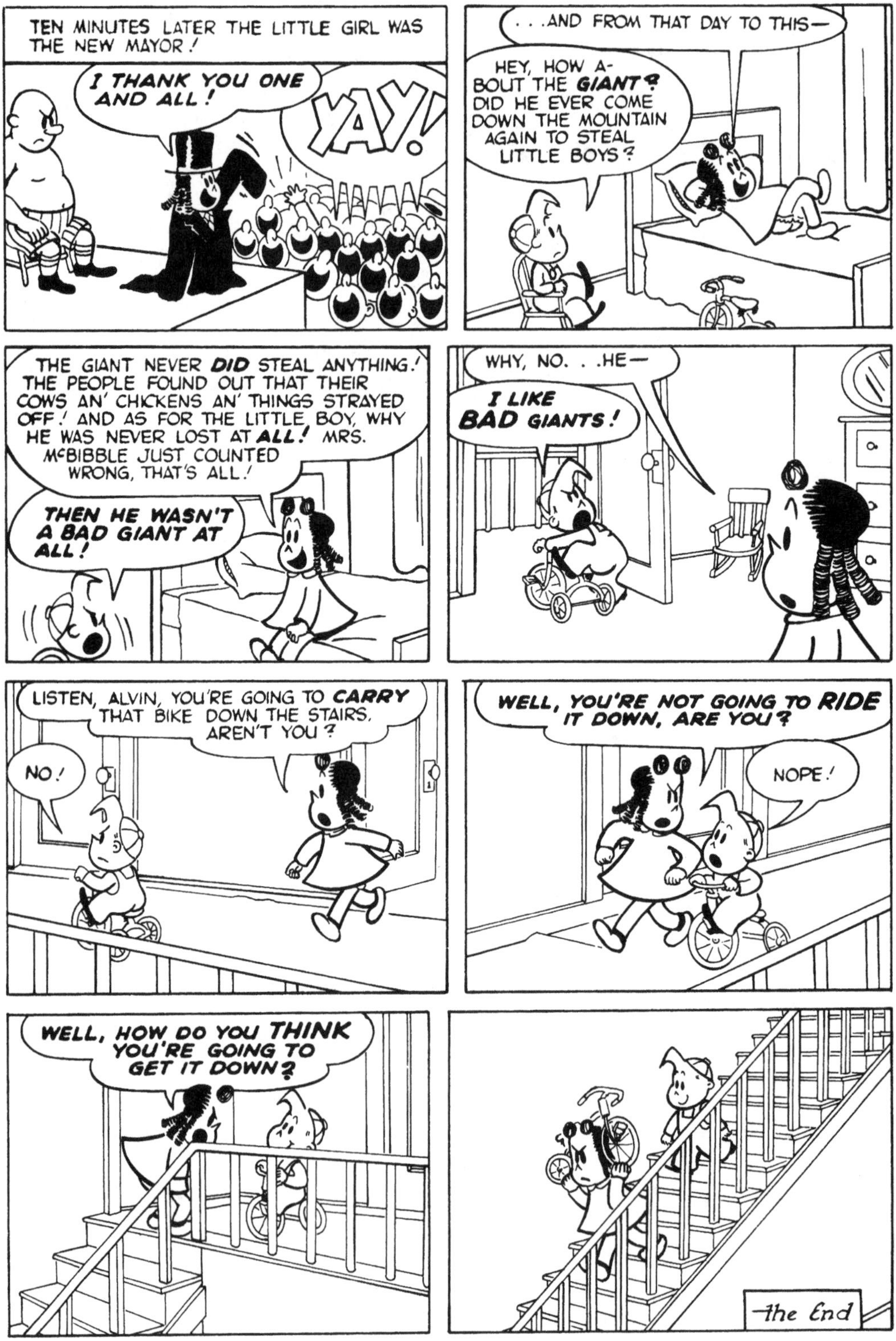

TEN MINUTES LATER THE LITTLE GIRL WAS THE NEW MAYOR!
I THANK YOU ONE AND ALL!
YAY!
. . .AND FROM THAT DAY TO THIS—
HEY, HOW A-BOUT THE GIANT? DID HE EVER COME DOWN THE MOUNTAIN AGAIN TO STEAL LITTLE BOYS?
THE GIANT NEVER DID STEAL ANYTHING! THE PEOPLE FOUND OUT THAT THEIR COWS AN' CHICKENS AN' THINGS STRAYED OFF! AND AS FOR THE LITTLE BOY, WHY HE WAS NEVER LOST AT ALL! MRS. McBIBBLE JUST COUNTED WRONG, THAT'S ALL!
THEN HE WASN'T A BAD GIANT AT ALL!
WHY, NO. . .HE—
I LIKE BAD GIANTS!
LISTEN, ALVIN, YOU'RE GOING TO CARRY THAT BIKE DOWN THE STAIRS, AREN'T YOU?
NO!
WELL, YOU'RE NOT GOING TO RIDE IT DOWN, ARE YOU?
NOPE!
WELL, HOW DO YOU THINK YOU'RE GOING TO GET IT DOWN?
The End

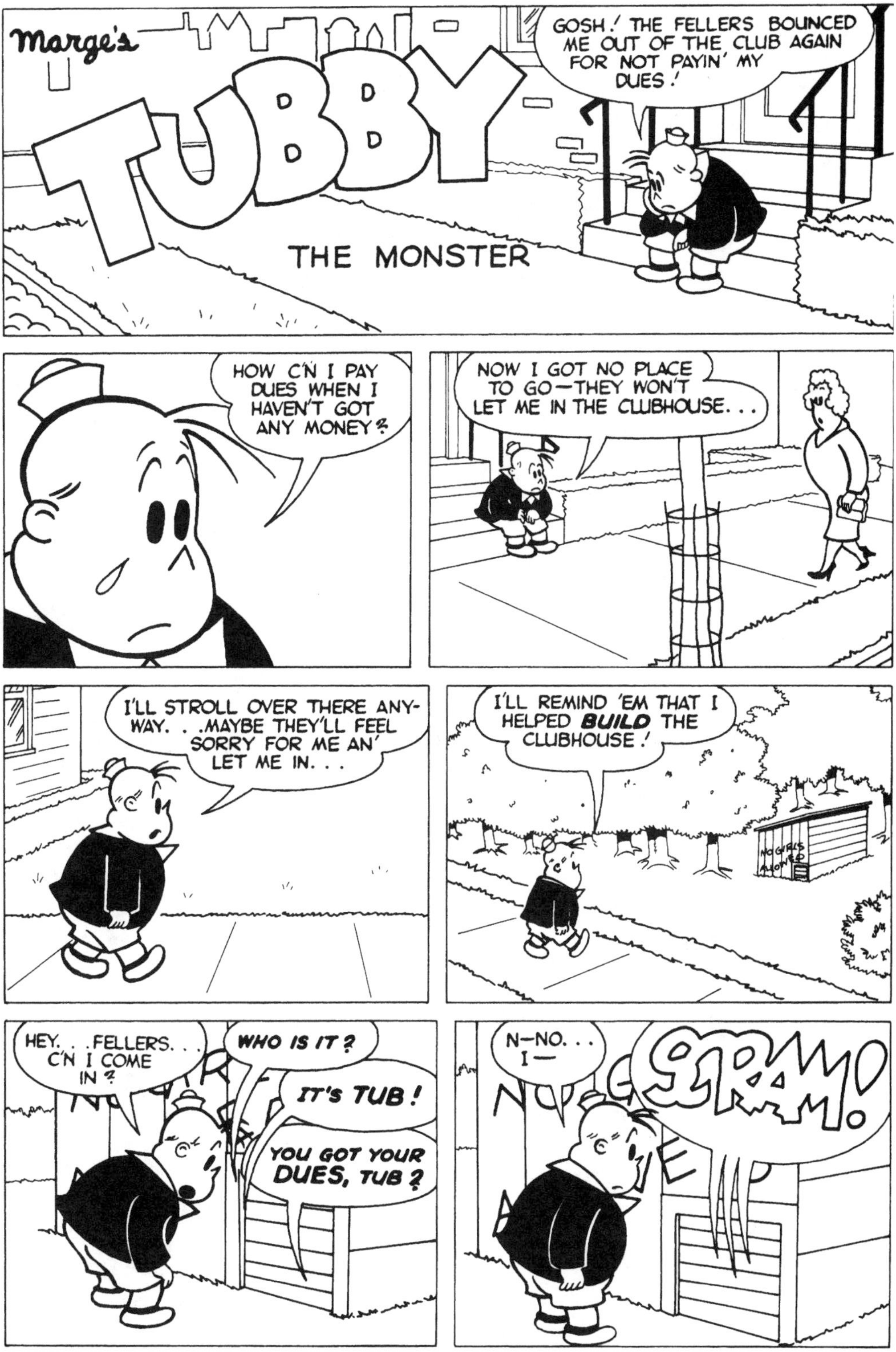
Marge's
TUBBY
THE MONSTER
GOSH! THE FELLERS BOUNCED ME OUT OF THE CLUB AGAIN FOR NOT PAYIN' MY DUES!
HOW C'N I PAY DUES WHEN I HAVEN'T GOT ANY MONEY?
NOW I GOT NO PLACE TO GO—THEY WON'T LET ME IN THE CLUBHOUSE...
I'LL STROLL OVER THERE ANYWAY. . .MAYBE THEY'LL FEEL SORRY FOR ME AN' LET ME IN...
I'LL REMIND 'EM THAT I HELPED BUILD THE CLUBHOUSE!
NO GIRLS ALLOWED
HEY. . .FELLERS. . . C'N I COME IN?
WHO IS IT?
IT'S TUB!
YOU GOT YOUR DUES, TUB?
N-NO. . . I—
SCRAM!

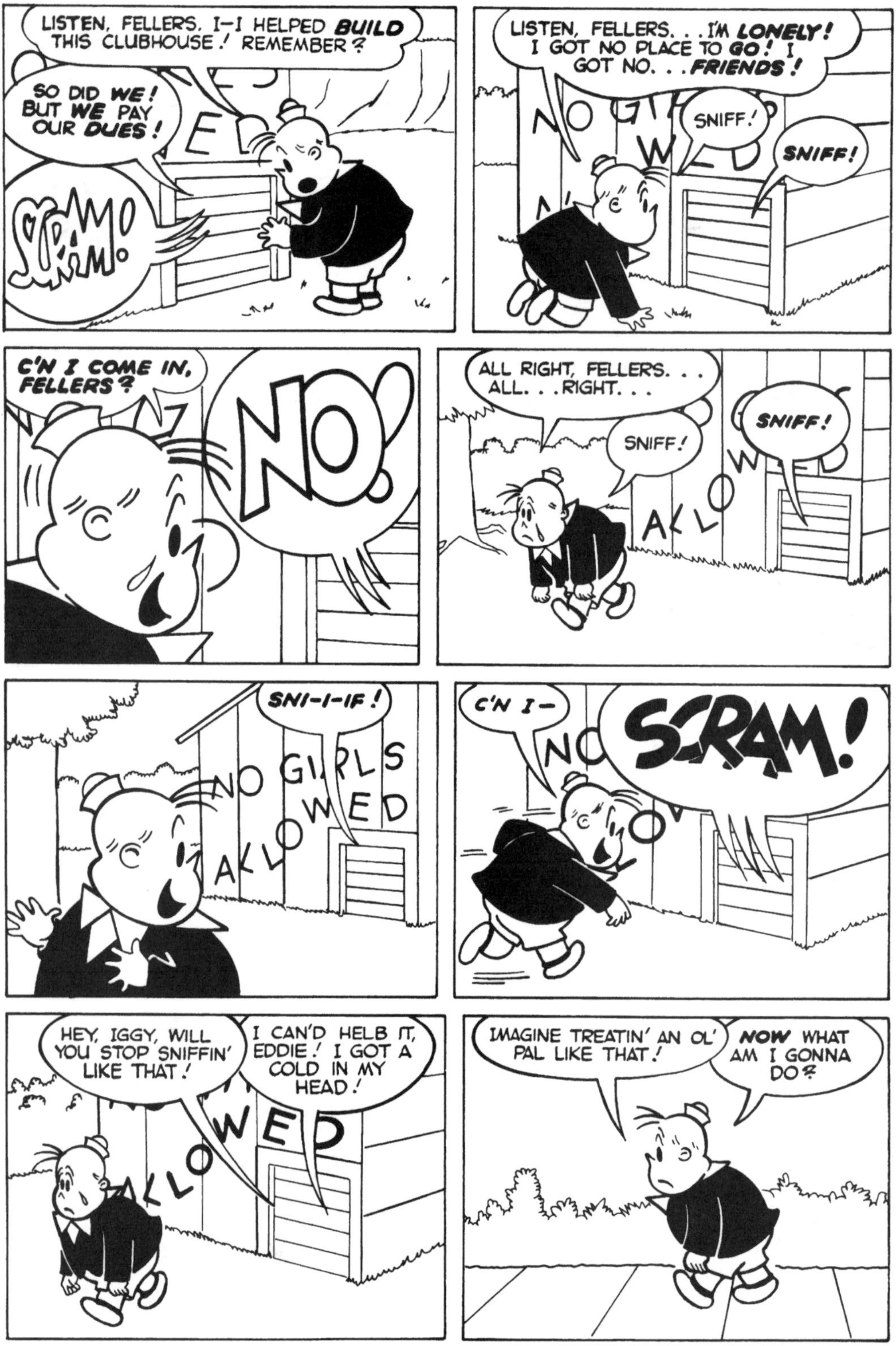
LISTEN, FELLERS, I—I HELPED BUILD THIS CLUBHOUSE! REMEMBER?
SO DID WE! BUT WE PAY OUR DUES!
SCRAM! SCRAM!
LISTEN, FELLERS. . . I'M LONELY! I GOT NO PLACE TO GO! I GOT NO. . . FRIENDS!
SNIFF!
SNIFF!
C'N I COME IN, FELLERS?
NO!
ALL RIGHT, FELLERS. . . ALL. . . RIGHT. . .
SNIFF!
SNIFF!
SNI-I-IF!
NO GIRLS ALLOWED
C'N I—
SCRAM!
HEY, IGGY, WILL YOU STOP SNIFFIN' LIKE THAT!
I CAN'D HELB IT, EDDIE! I GOT A COLD IN MY HEAD!
IMAGINE TREATIN' AN OL' PAL LIKE THAT!
NOW WHAT AM I GONNA DO?

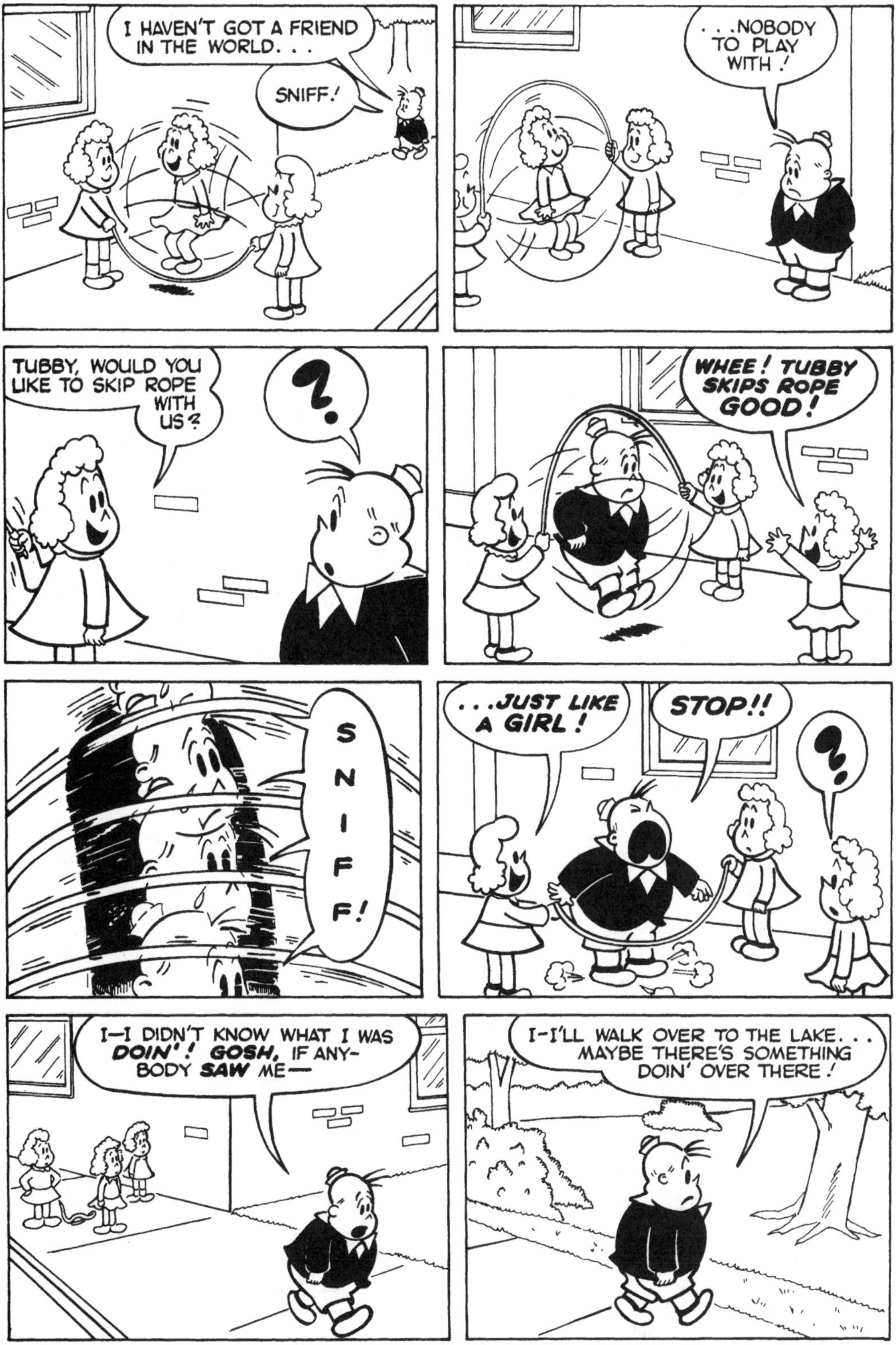
I HAVEN'T GOT A FRIEND IN THE WORLD. . .
SNIFF!
. . .NOBODY TO PLAY WITH!
TUBBY, WOULD YOU LIKE TO SKIP ROPE WITH US?
?
WHEE! TUBBY SKIPS ROPE GOOD!
SNIFF!
. . .JUST LIKE A GIRL!
STOP!!
?
I—I DIDN'T KNOW WHAT I WAS DOIN'! GOSH, IF ANY-BODY SAW ME—
I-I'LL WALK OVER TO THE LAKE. . . MAYBE THERE'S SOMETHING DOIN' OVER THERE!

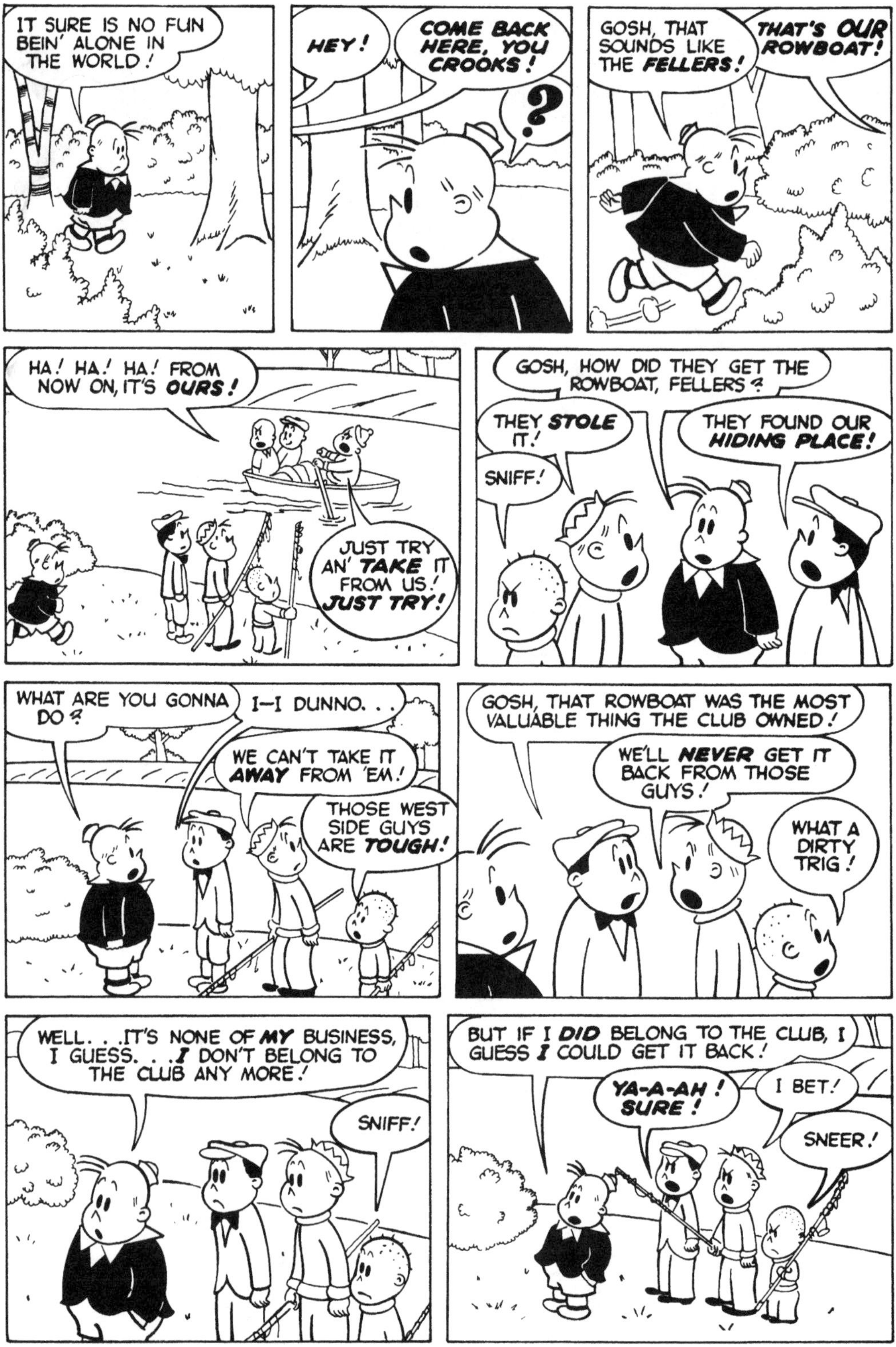
IT SURE IS NO FUN BEIN' ALONE IN THE WORLD!
HEY!
COME BACK HERE, YOU CROOKS!
?
GOSH, THAT SOUNDS LIKE THE FELLERS!
THAT'S OUR ROWBOAT!
HA! HA! HA! FROM NOW ON, IT'S OURS!
JUST TRY AN' TAKE IT FROM US! JUST TRY!
GOSH, HOW DID THEY GET THE ROWBOAT, FELLERS?
THEY STOLE IT!
THEY FOUND OUR HIDING PLACE!
SNIFF!
WHAT ARE YOU GONNA DO?
I—I DUNNO. . .
WE CAN'T TAKE IT AWAY FROM 'EM!
THOSE WEST SIDE GUYS ARE TOUGH!
GOSH, THAT ROWBOAT WAS THE MOST VALUABLE THING THE CLUB OWNED!
WE'LL NEVER GET IT BACK FROM THOSE GUYS!
WHAT A DIRTY TRIG!
WELL. . .IT'S NONE OF MY BUSINESS, I GUESS. . .I DON'T BELONG TO THE CLUB ANY MORE!
SNIFF!
BUT IF I DID BELONG TO THE CLUB, I GUESS I COULD GET IT BACK!
YA-A-AH! SURE!
I BET!
SNEER!

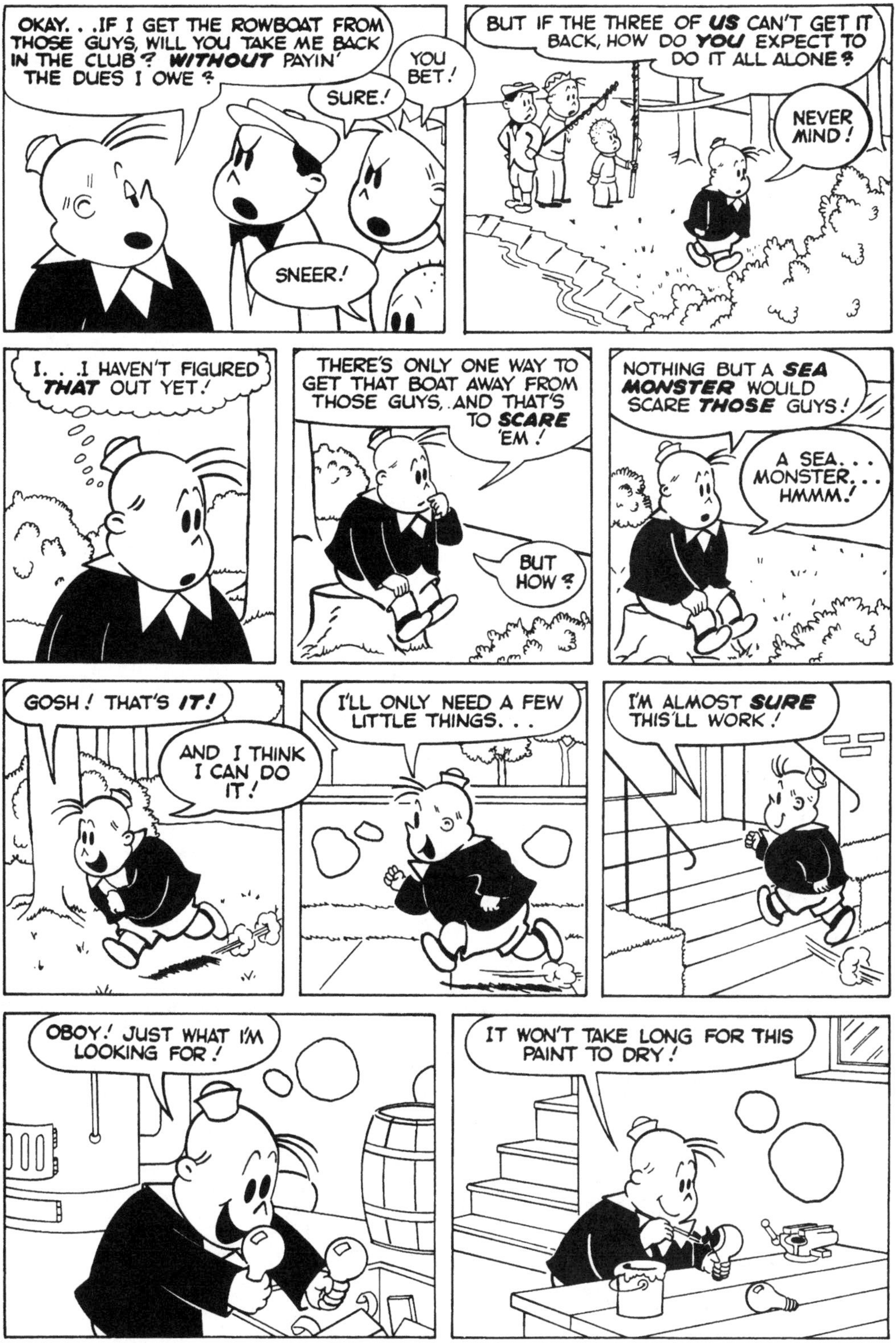
OKAY. . .IF I GET THE ROWBOAT FROM THOSE GUYS, WILL YOU TAKE ME BACK IN THE CLUB? WITHOUT PAYIN' THE DUES I OWE?
SURE!
YOU BET!
SNEER!
BUT IF THE THREE OF US CAN'T GET IT BACK, HOW DO YOU EXPECT TO DO IT ALL ALONE?
NEVER MIND!
I. . .I HAVEN'T FIGURED THAT OUT YET!
THERE'S ONLY ONE WAY TO GET THAT BOAT AWAY FROM THOSE GUYS, AND THAT'S TO SCARE 'EM!
BUT HOW?
NOTHING BUT A SEA MONSTER WOULD SCARE THOSE GUYS!
A SEA. . . MONSTER. . . HMMM!
GOSH! THAT'S IT!
AND I THINK I CAN DO IT!
I'LL ONLY NEED A FEW LITTLE THINGS. . .
I'M ALMOST SURE THIS'LL WORK!
OBOY! JUST WHAT I'M LOOKING FOR!
IT WON'T TAKE LONG FOR THIS PAINT TO DRY!

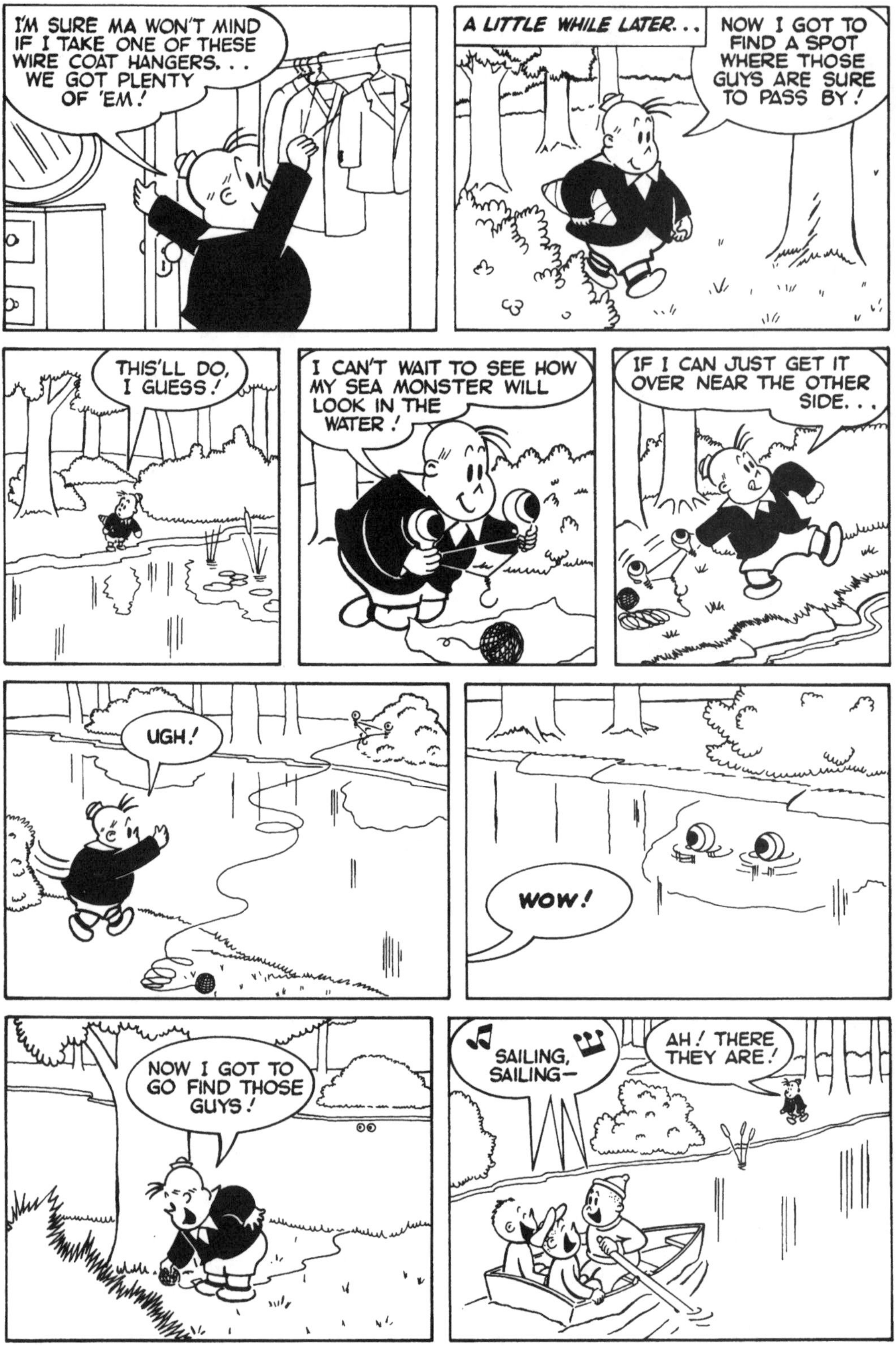
I'M SURE MA WON'T MIND IF I TAKE ONE OF THESE WIRE COAT HANGERS. . . WE GOT PLENTY OF 'EM!
A LITTLE WHILE LATER. . .
NOW I GOT TO FIND A SPOT WHERE THOSE GUYS ARE SURE TO PASS BY!
THIS'LL DO, I GUESS!
I CAN'T WAIT TO SEE HOW MY SEA MONSTER WILL LOOK IN THE WATER!
IF I CAN JUST GET IT OVER NEAR THE OTHER SIDE. . .
UGH!
WOW!
NOW I GOT TO GO FIND THOSE GUYS!
SAILING, SAILING—
AH! THERE THEY ARE!

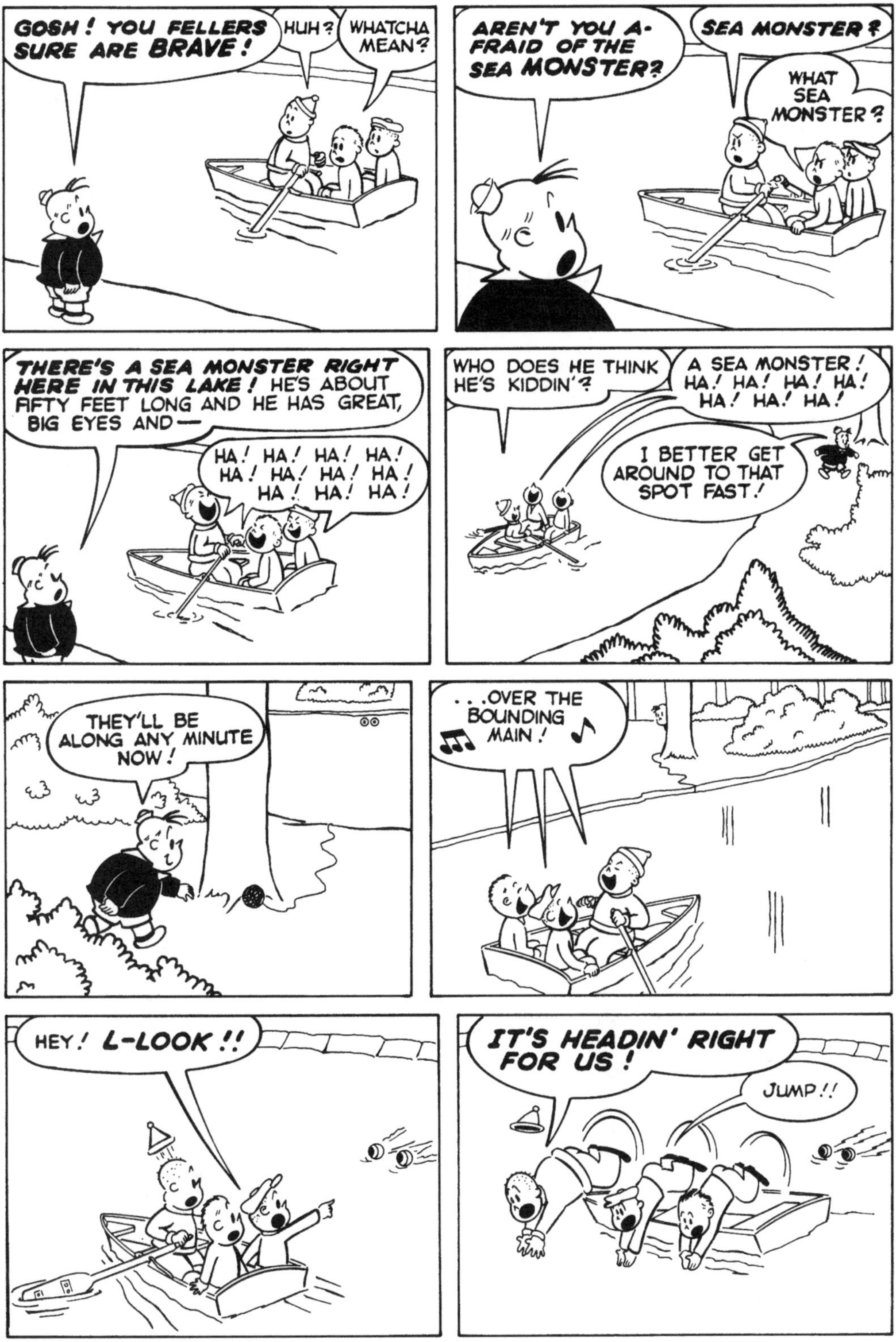
GOSH! YOU FELLERS SURE ARE BRAVE!
HUH?
WHATCHA MEAN?
AREN'T YOU A-FRAID OF THE SEA MONSTER?
SEA MONSTER?
WHAT SEA MONSTER?
THERE'S A SEA MONSTER RIGHT HERE IN THIS LAKE! HE'S ABOUT FIFTY FEET LONG AND HE HAS GREAT, BIG EYES AND—
HA! HA! HA! HA! HA! HA! HA! HA! HA! HA! HA!
WHO DOES HE THINK HE'S KIDDIN'?
A SEA MONSTER! HA! HA! HA! HA! HA! HA! HA!
I BETTER GET AROUND TO THAT SPOT FAST!
THEY'LL BE ALONG ANY MINUTE NOW!
. . .OVER THE BOUNDING MAIN!
HEY! L-LOOK!!
IT'S HEADIN' RIGHT FOR US!
JUMP!!

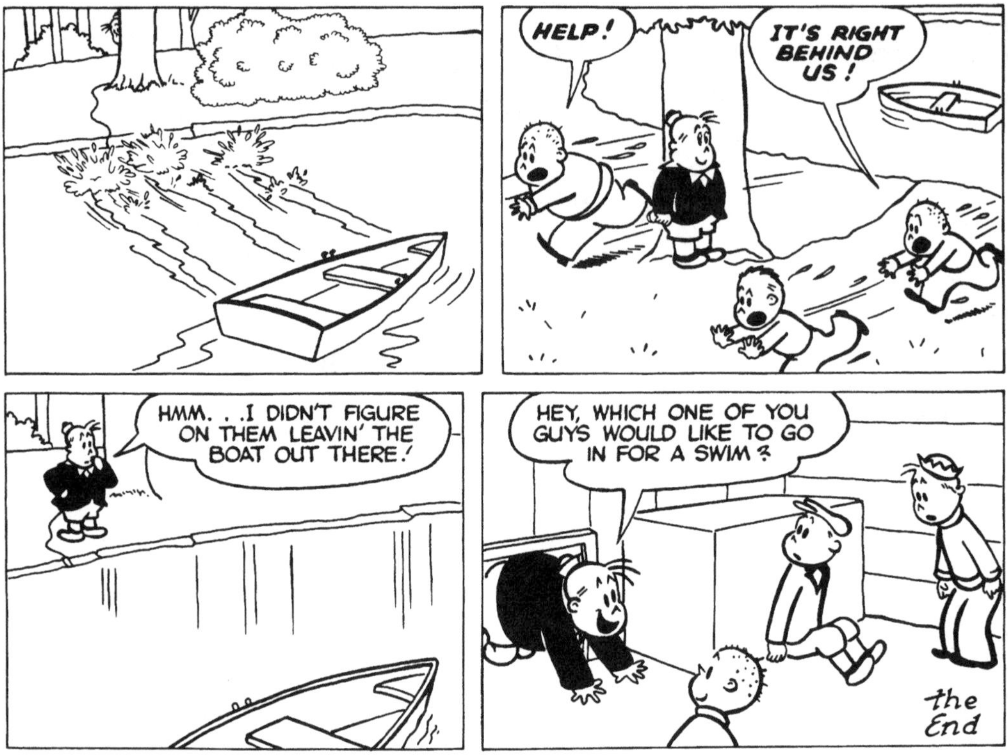
HELP!
IT'S RIGHT BEHIND US!
HMM. . .I DIDN'T FIGURE ON THEM LEAVIN' THE BOAT OUT THERE!
HEY, WHICH ONE OF YOU GUYS WOULD LIKE TO GO IN FOR A SWIM?
the End

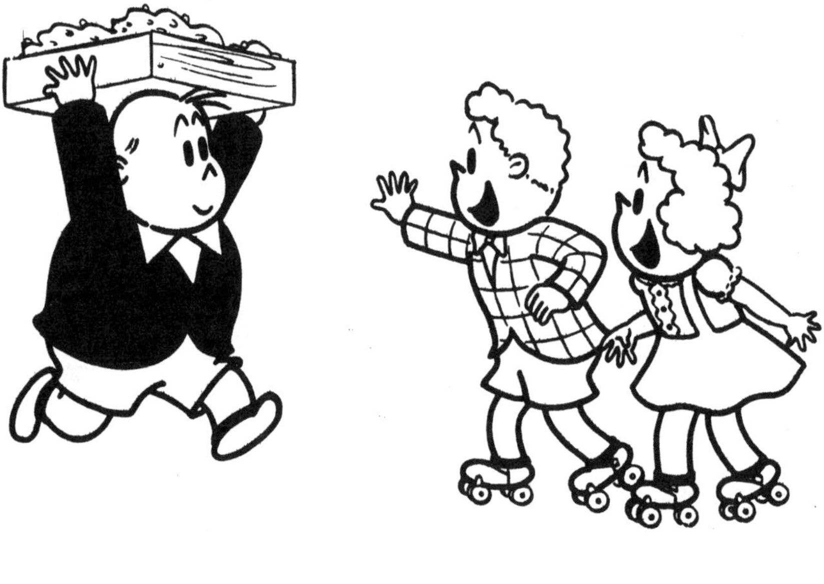

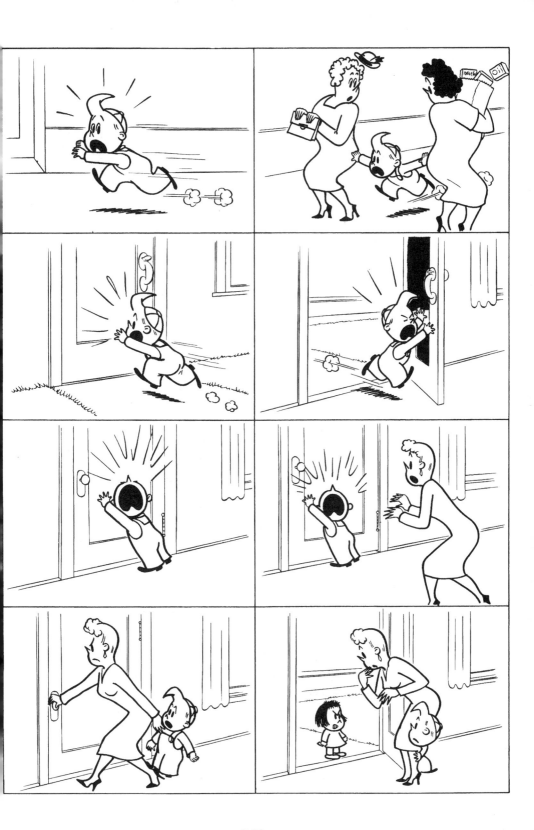

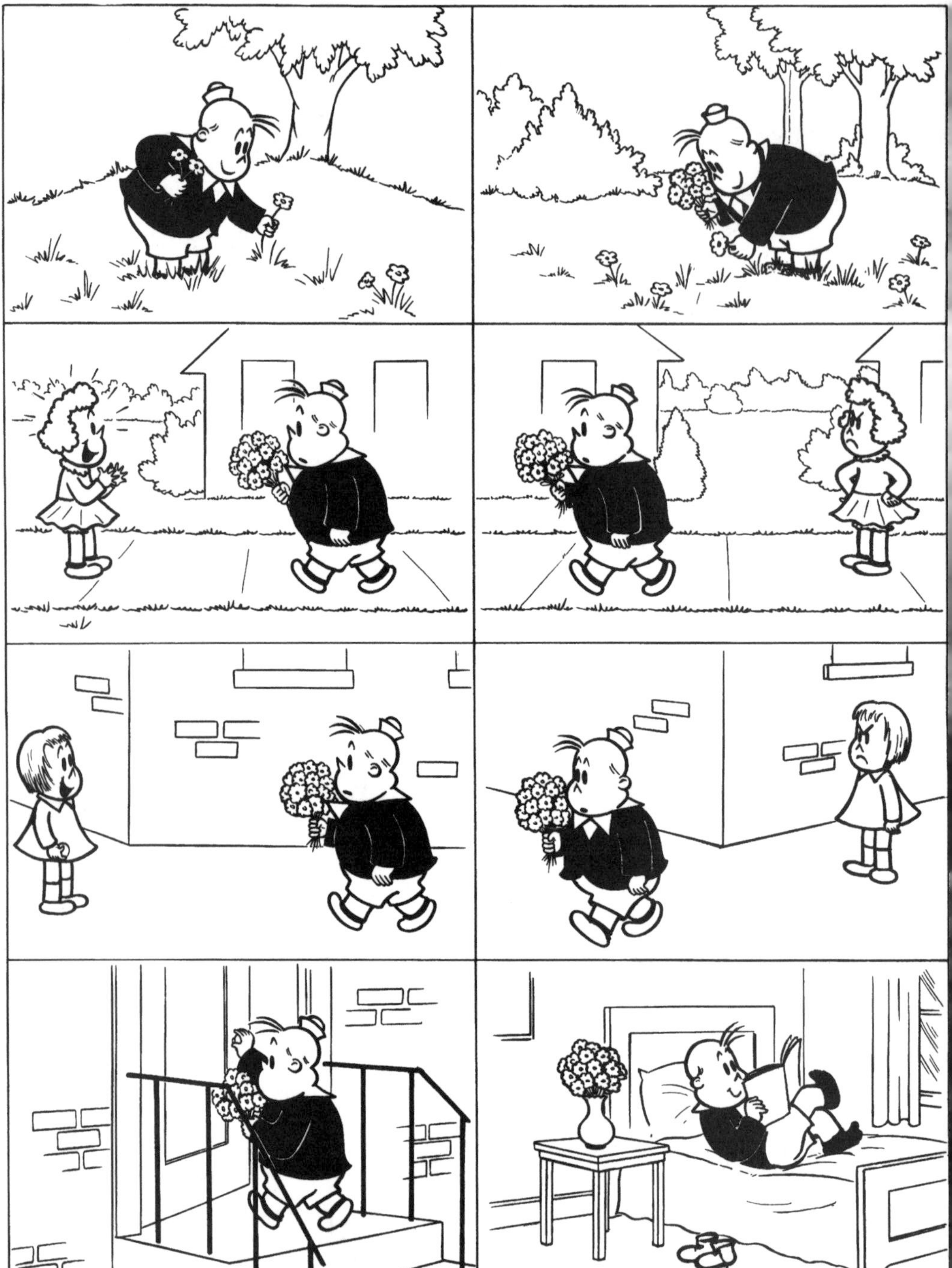

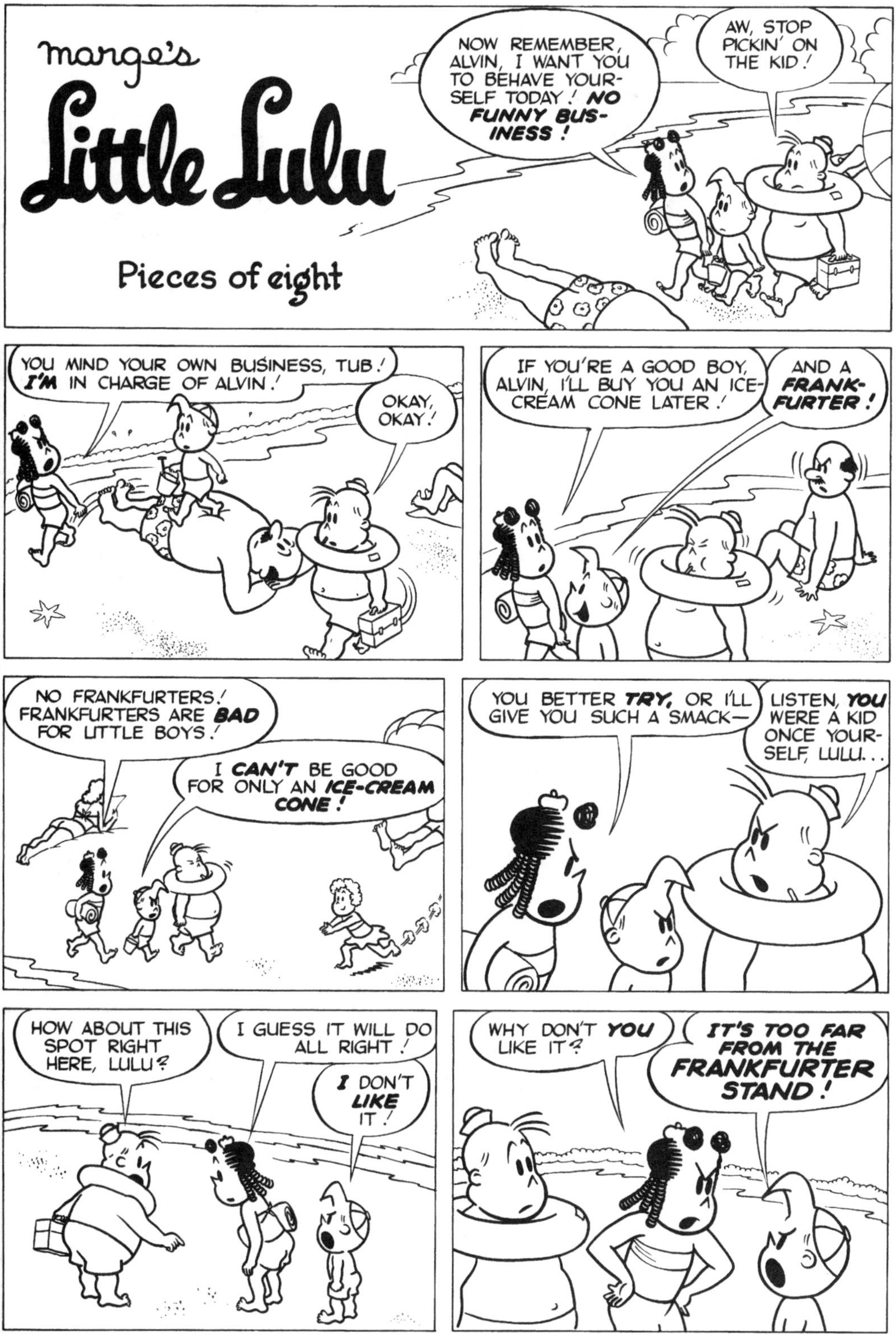
marge's
Little Lulu
Pieces of eight
NOW REMEMBER, ALVIN, I WANT YOU TO BEHAVE YOURSELF TODAY! NO FUNNY BUSINESS!
AW, STOP PICKIN' ON THE KID!
YOU MIND YOUR OWN BUSINESS, TUB! I'M IN CHARGE OF ALVIN!
OKAY, OKAY!
IF YOU'RE A GOOD BOY, ALVIN, I'LL BUY YOU AN ICE-CREAM CONE LATER!
AND A FRANKFURTER!
NO FRANKFURTERS! FRANKFURTERS ARE BAD FOR LITTLE BOYS!
I CAN'T BE GOOD FOR ONLY AN ICE-CREAM CONE!
YOU BETTER TRY, OR I'LL GIVE YOU SUCH A SMACK—
LISTEN, YOU WERE A KID ONCE YOURSELF, LULU...
HOW ABOUT THIS SPOT RIGHT HERE, LULU?
I GUESS IT WILL DO ALL RIGHT!
I DON'T LIKE IT!
WHY DON'T YOU LIKE IT?
IT'S TOO FAR FROM THE FRANKFURTER STAND!

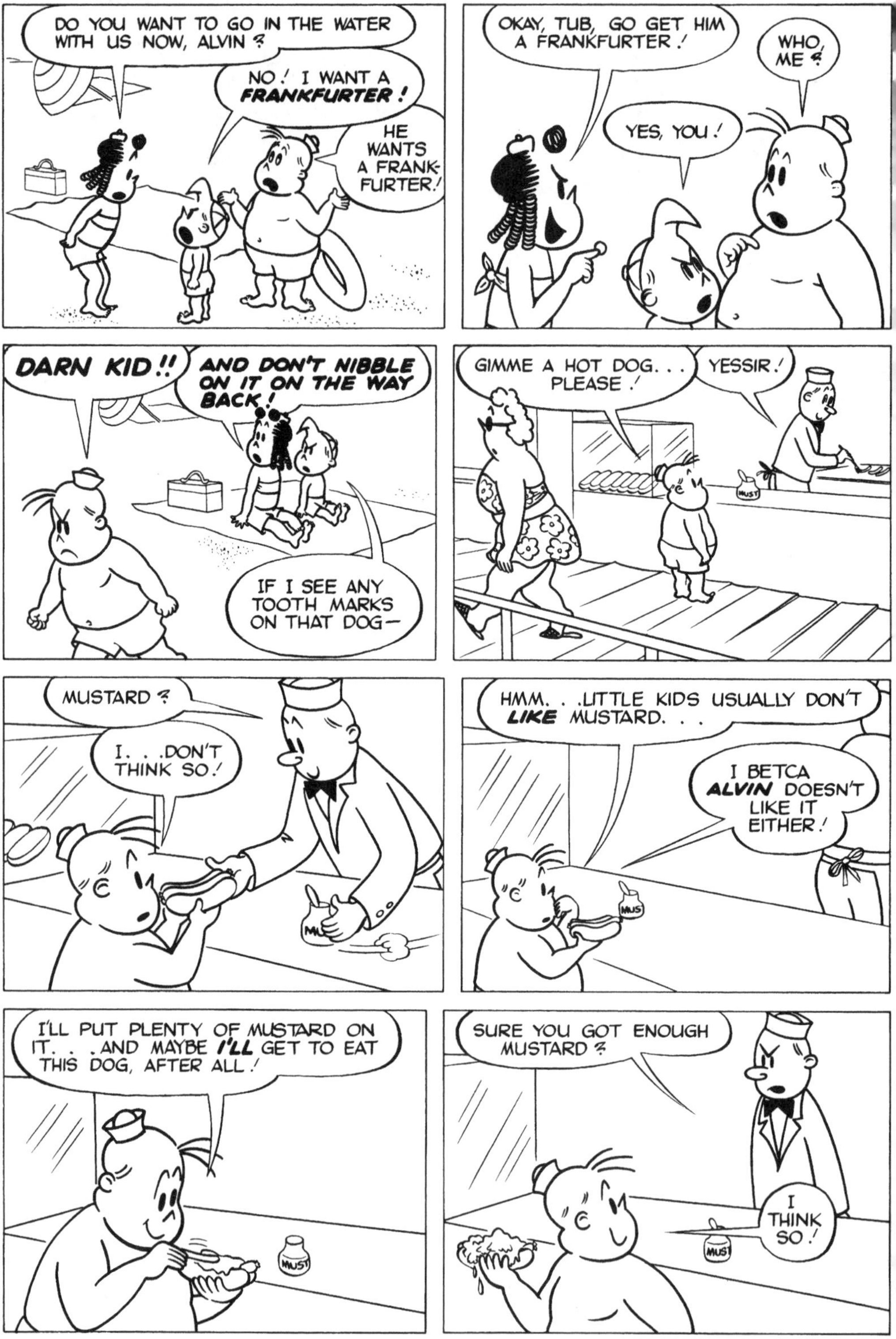
DO YOU WANT TO GO IN THE WATER WITH US NOW, ALVIN ?
NO! I WANT A FRANKFURTER!
HE WANTS A FRANKFURTER!
OKAY, TUB, GO GET HIM A FRANKFURTER!
WHO, ME ?
YES, YOU!
DARN KID!!
AND DON'T NIBBLE ON IT ON THE WAY BACK!
IF I SEE ANY TOOTH MARKS ON THAT DOG—
GIMME A HOT DOG... PLEASE!
YESSIR!
MUST
MUSTARD ?
I...DON'T THINK SO!
HMM...LITTLE KIDS USUALLY DON'T LIKE MUSTARD...
I BETCA ALVIN DOESN'T LIKE IT EITHER!
I'LL PUT PLENTY OF MUSTARD ON IT...AND MAYBE I'LL GET TO EAT THIS DOG, AFTER ALL!
MUST
SURE YOU GOT ENOUGH MUSTARD ?
I THINK SO!
MUST

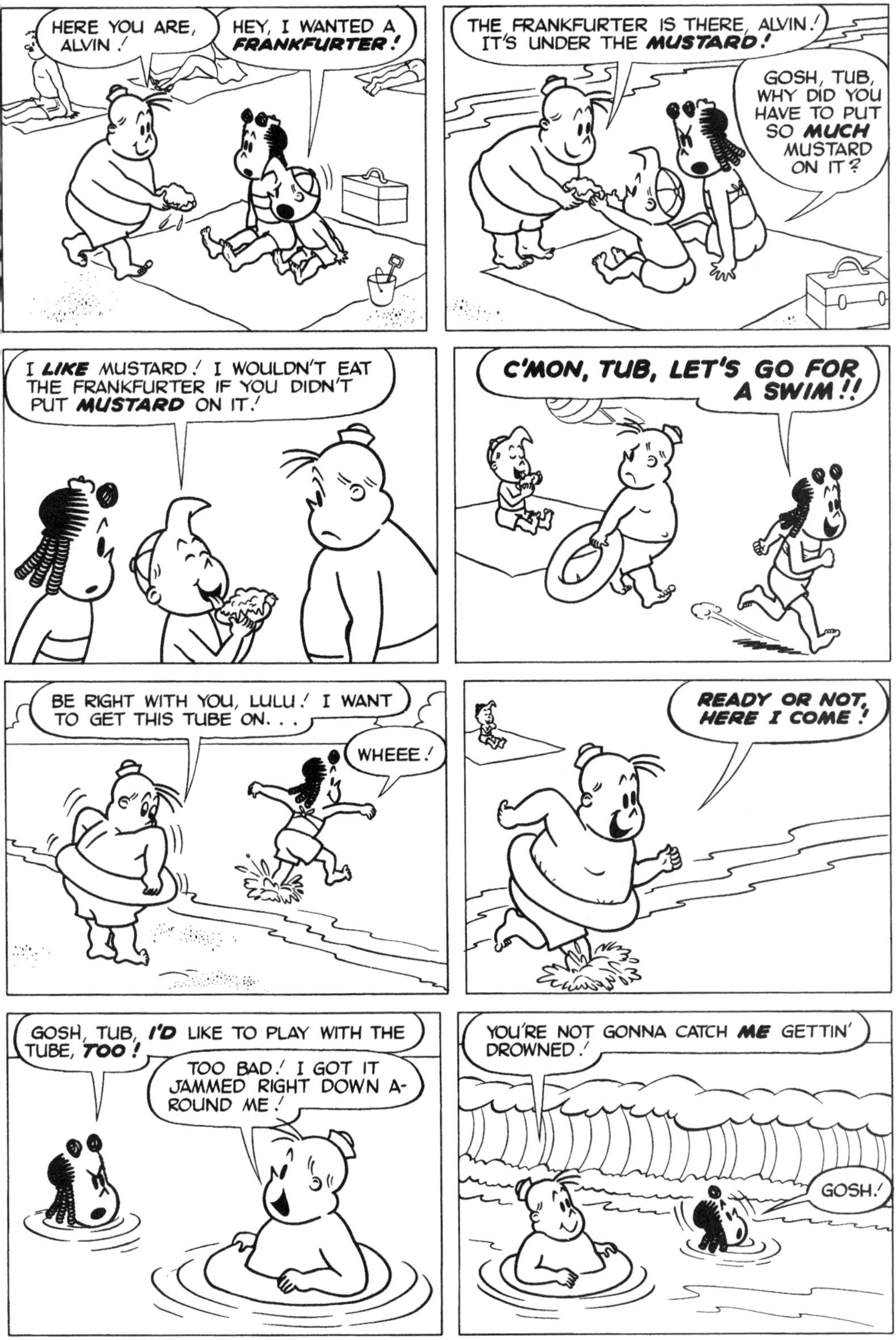
HERE YOU ARE, ALVIN!
HEY, I WANTED A **FRANKFURTER**!
THE FRANKFURTER IS THERE, ALVIN! IT'S UNDER THE **MUSTARD**!
GOSH, TUB, WHY DID YOU HAVE TO PUT SO **MUCH** MUSTARD ON IT?
I **LIKE** MUSTARD! I WOULDN'T EAT THE FRANKFURTER IF YOU DIDN'T PUT **MUSTARD** ON IT!
C'MON, TUB, LET'S GO FOR A SWIM!!
BE RIGHT WITH YOU, LULU! I WANT TO GET THIS TUBE ON. . .
WHEEE!
READY OR NOT, HERE I COME!
GOSH, TUB, **I'D** LIKE TO PLAY WITH THE TUBE, **TOO**!
TOO BAD! I GOT IT JAMMED RIGHT DOWN A-ROUND ME!
YOU'RE NOT GONNA CATCH **ME** GETTIN' DROWNED!
GOSH!

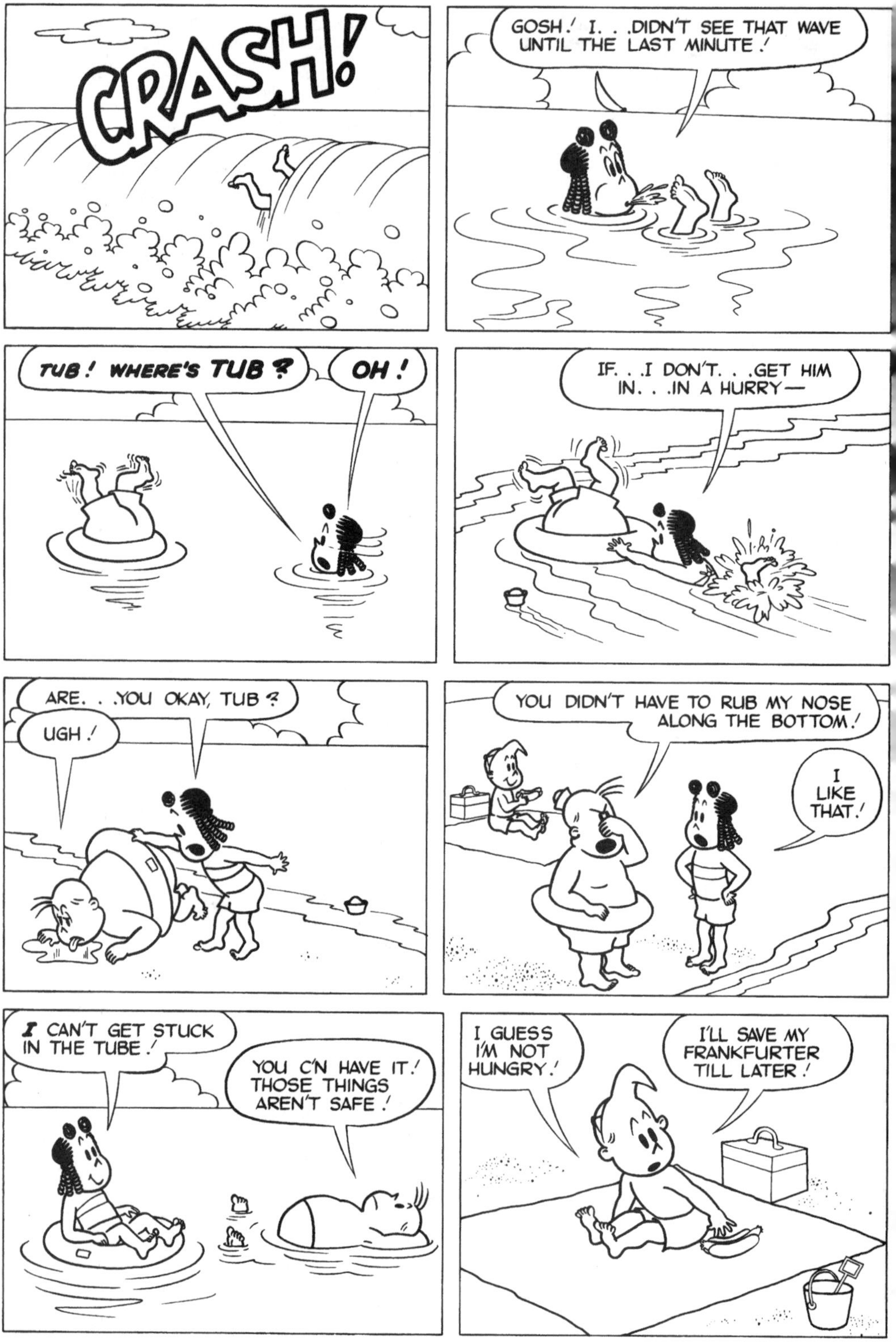
CRASH!
GOSH! I. . .DIDN'T SEE THAT WAVE UNTIL THE LAST MINUTE!
TUB! WHERE'S TUB?
OH!
IF. . .I DON'T. . .GET HIM IN. . .IN A HURRY—
ARE. . .YOU OKAY, TUB?
UGH!
YOU DIDN'T HAVE TO RUB MY NOSE ALONG THE BOTTOM!
I LIKE THAT!
I CAN'T GET STUCK IN THE TUBE!
YOU C'N HAVE IT! THOSE THINGS AREN'T SAFE!
I GUESS I'M NOT HUNGRY!
I'LL SAVE MY FRANKFURTER TILL LATER!

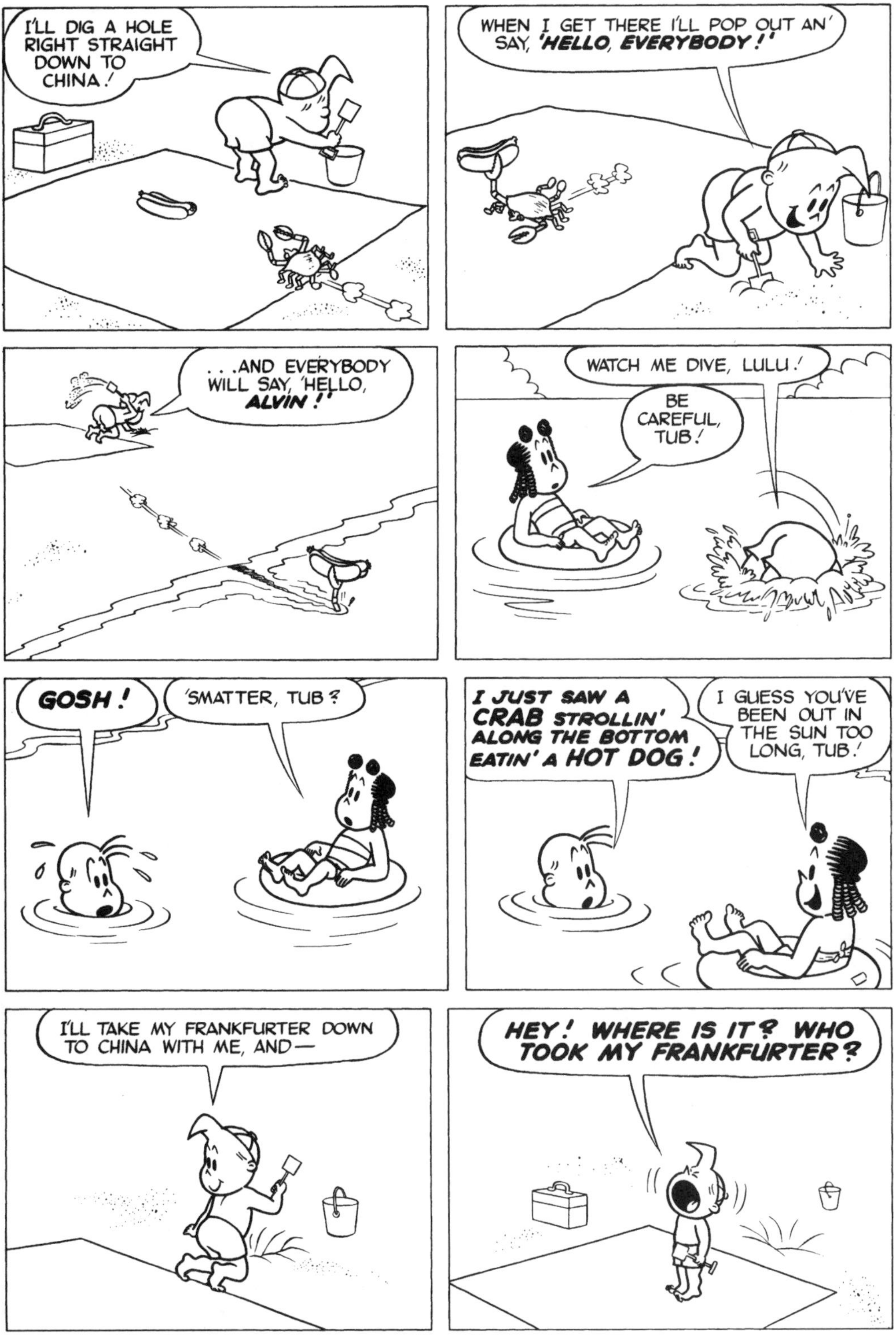
I'LL DIG A HOLE RIGHT STRAIGHT DOWN TO CHINA!
WHEN I GET THERE I'LL POP OUT AN' SAY, 'HELLO, EVERYBODY!'
...AND EVERYBODY WILL SAY, 'HELLO, ALVIN!'
WATCH ME DIVE, LULU!
BE CAREFUL, TUB!
GOSH!
'SMATTER, TUB?
I JUST SAW A CRAB STROLLIN' ALONG THE BOTTOM EATIN' A HOT DOG!
I GUESS YOU'VE BEEN OUT IN THE SUN TOO LONG, TUB!
I'LL TAKE MY FRANKFURTER DOWN TO CHINA WITH ME, AND—
HEY! WHERE IS IT? WHO TOOK MY FRANKFURTER?

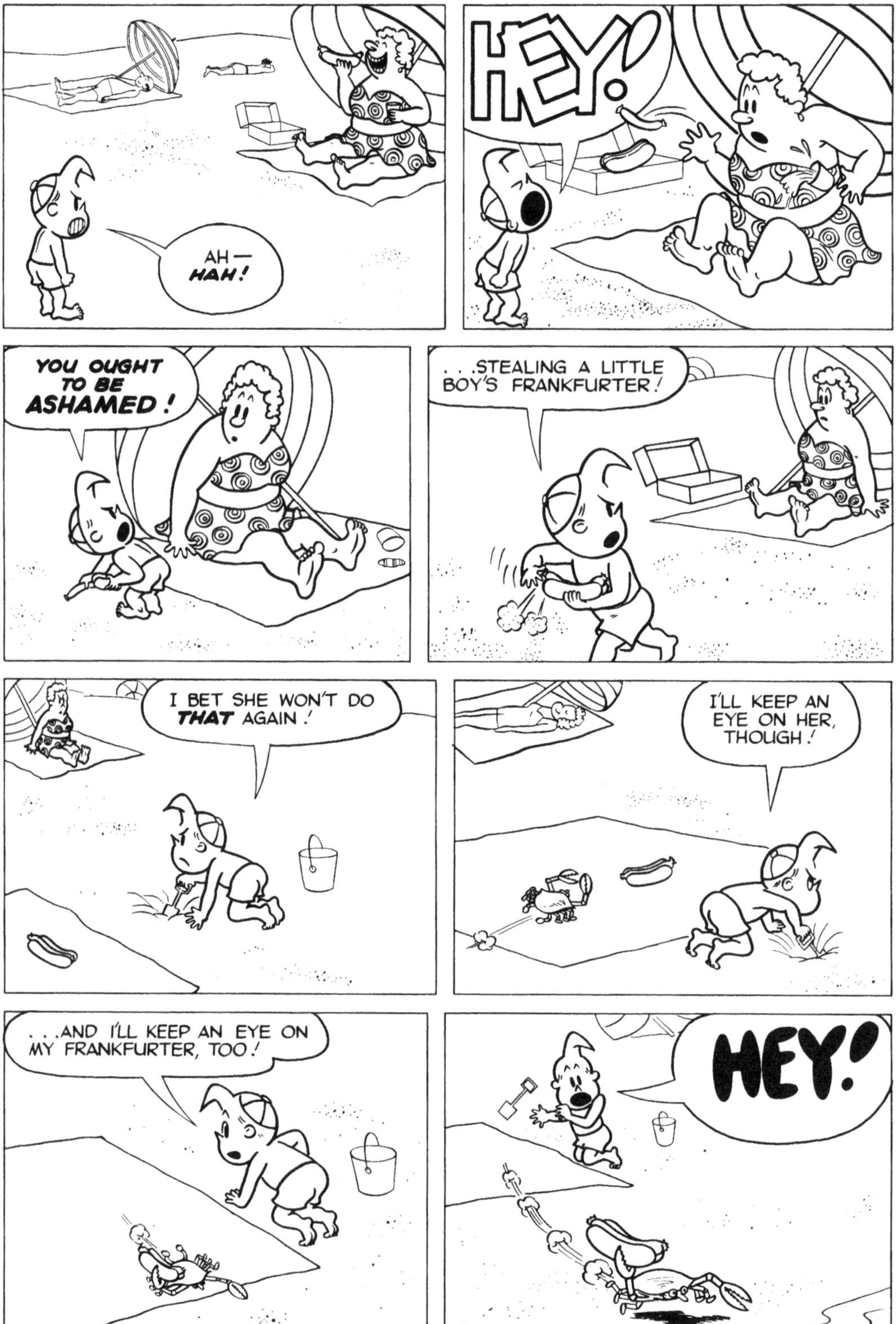
AH— HAH!
HEY!
YOU OUGHT TO BE ASHAMED!
. . .STEALING A LITTLE BOY'S FRANKFURTER!
I BET SHE WON'T DO THAT AGAIN!
I'LL KEEP AN EYE ON HER, THOUGH!
. . .AND I'LL KEEP AN EYE ON MY FRANKFURTER, TOO!
HEY!

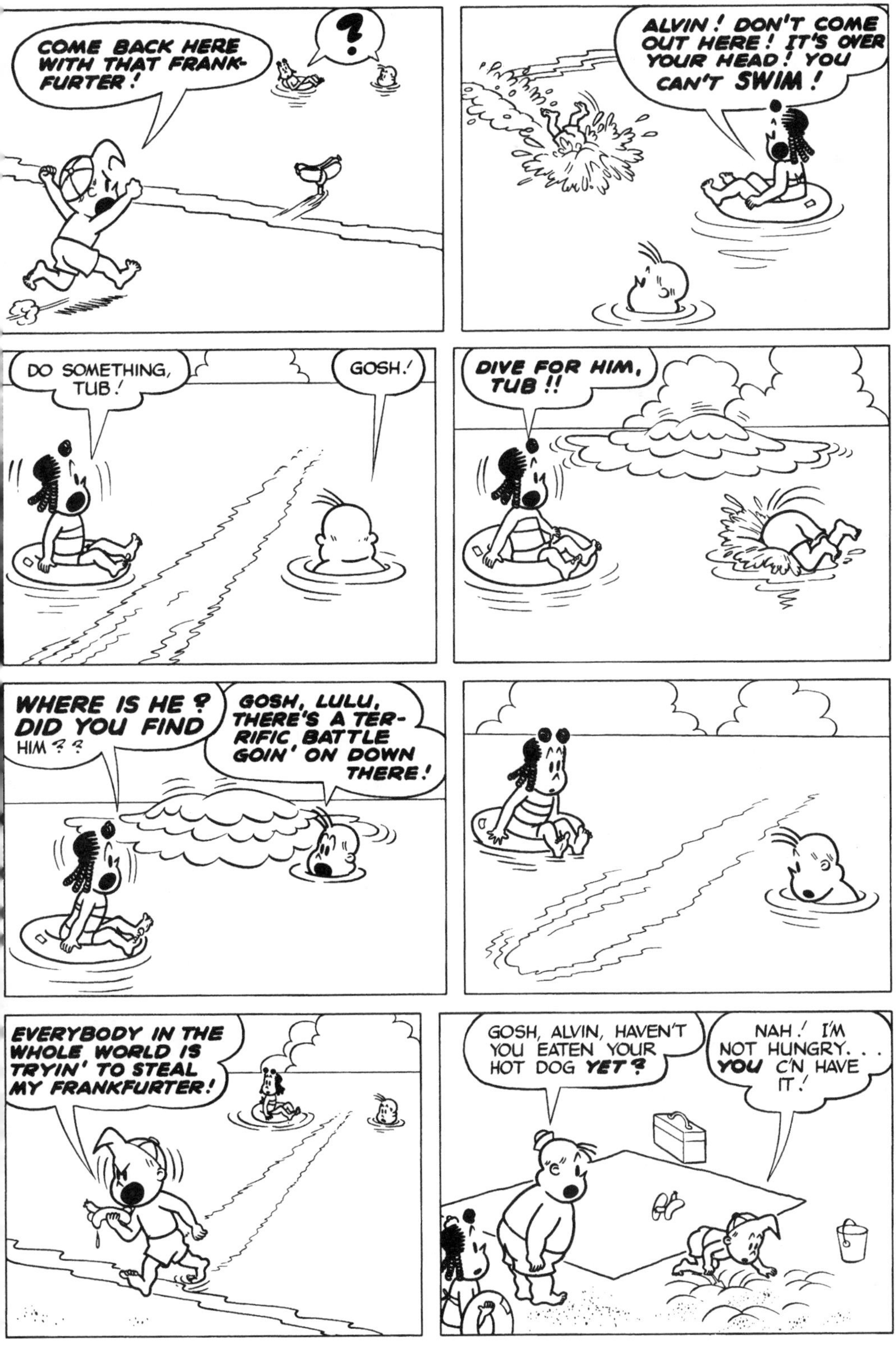
COME BACK HERE WITH THAT FRANK-FURTER!
?
ALVIN! DON'T COME OUT HERE! IT'S OVER YOUR HEAD! YOU CAN'T SWIM!
DO SOMETHING, TUB!
GOSH!
DIVE FOR HIM, TUB!!
WHERE IS HE? DID YOU FIND HIM??
GOSH, LULU, THERE'S A TER-RIFIC BATTLE GOIN' ON DOWN THERE!
EVERYBODY IN THE WHOLE WORLD IS TRYIN' TO STEAL MY FRANKFURTER!
GOSH, ALVIN, HAVEN'T YOU EATEN YOUR HOT DOG YET?
NAH! I'M NOT HUNGRY. . . YOU C'N HAVE IT!

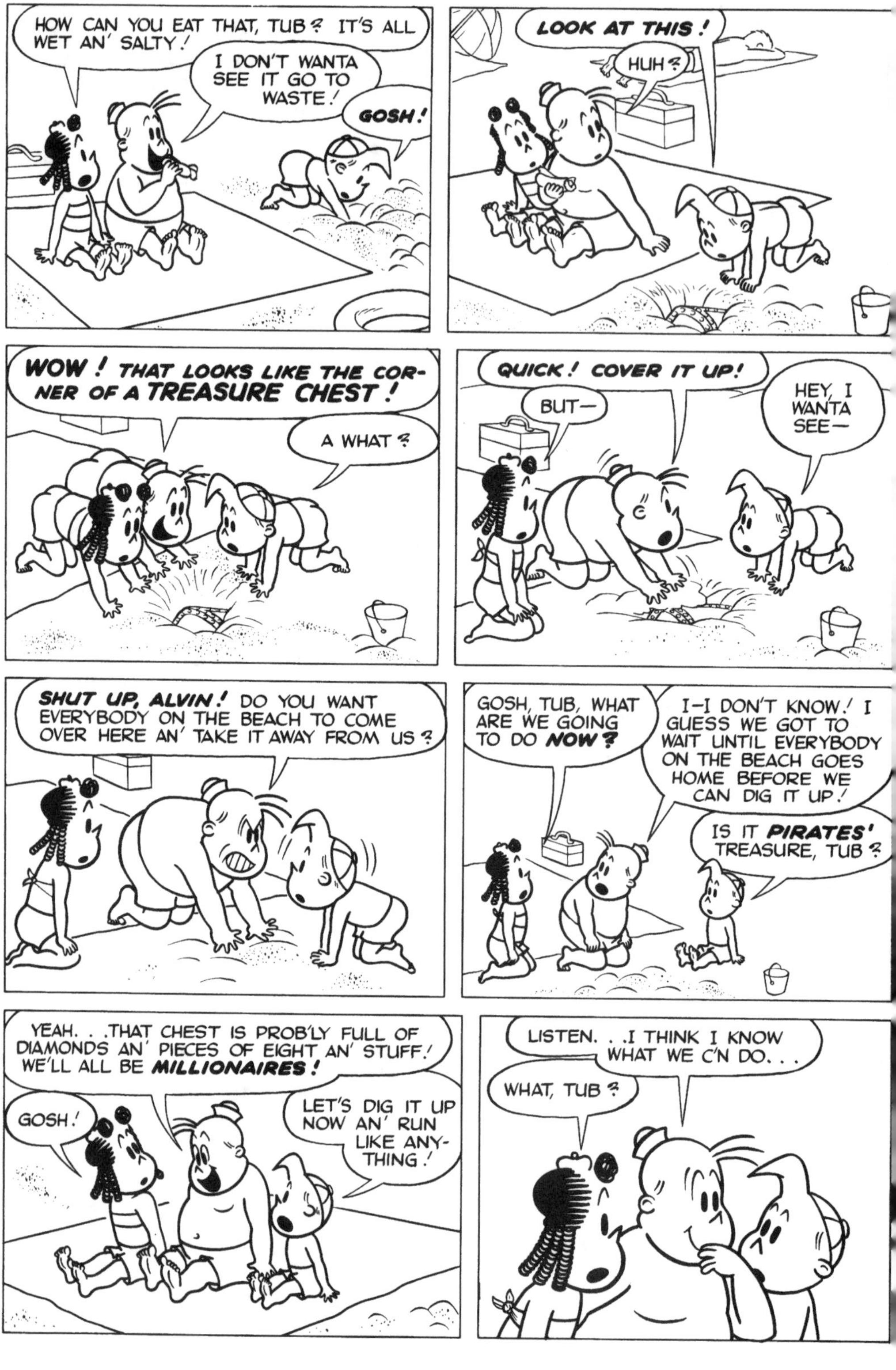
HOW CAN YOU EAT THAT, TUB? IT'S ALL WET AN' SALTY!
I DON'T WANTA SEE IT GO TO WASTE!
GOSH!
LOOK AT THIS!
HUH?
WOW! THAT LOOKS LIKE THE CORNER OF A TREASURE CHEST!
A WHAT?
QUICK! COVER IT UP!
BUT—
HEY, I WANTA SEE—
SHUT UP, ALVIN! DO YOU WANT EVERYBODY ON THE BEACH TO COME OVER HERE AN' TAKE IT AWAY FROM US?
GOSH, TUB, WHAT ARE WE GOING TO DO NOW?
I—I DON'T KNOW! I GUESS WE GOT TO WAIT UNTIL EVERYBODY ON THE BEACH GOES HOME BEFORE WE CAN DIG IT UP!
IS IT PIRATES' TREASURE, TUB?
YEAH. . .THAT CHEST IS PROB'LY FULL OF DIAMONDS AN' PIECES OF EIGHT AN' STUFF! WE'LL ALL BE MILLIONAIRES!
GOSH!
LET'S DIG IT UP NOW AN' RUN LIKE ANYTHING!
LISTEN. . .I THINK I KNOW WHAT WE C'N DO. . .
WHAT, TUB?

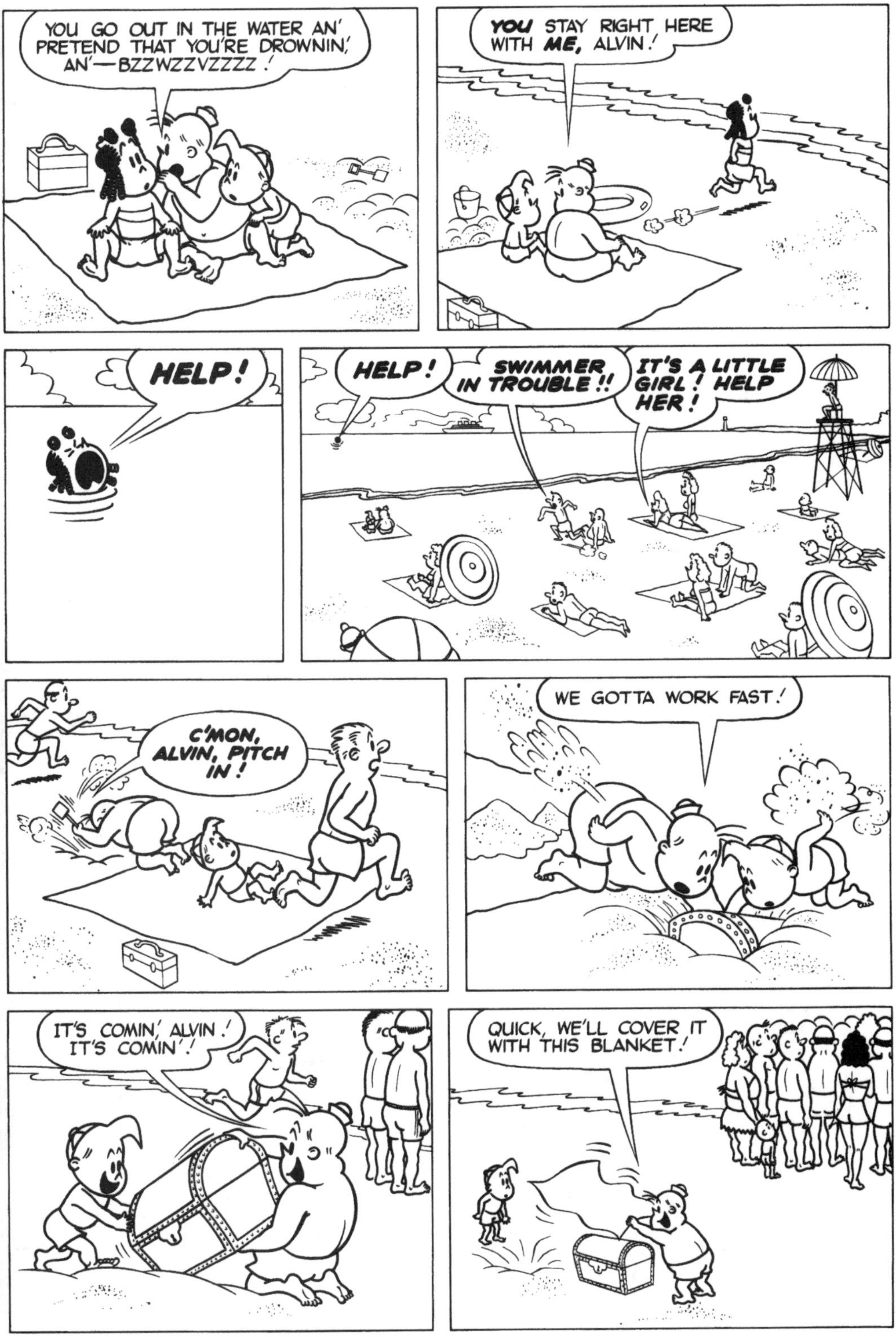
YOU GO OUT IN THE WATER AN' PRETEND THAT YOU'RE DROWNIN,' AN'—BZZWZZVZZZZ!
YOU STAY RIGHT HERE WITH ME, ALVIN!
HELP!
HELP!
SWIMMER IN TROUBLE!!
IT'S A LITTLE GIRL! HELP HER!
C'MON, ALVIN, PITCH IN!
WE GOTTA WORK FAST!
IT'S COMIN,' ALVIN! IT'S COMIN'!
QUICK, WE'LL COVER IT WITH THIS BLANKET!

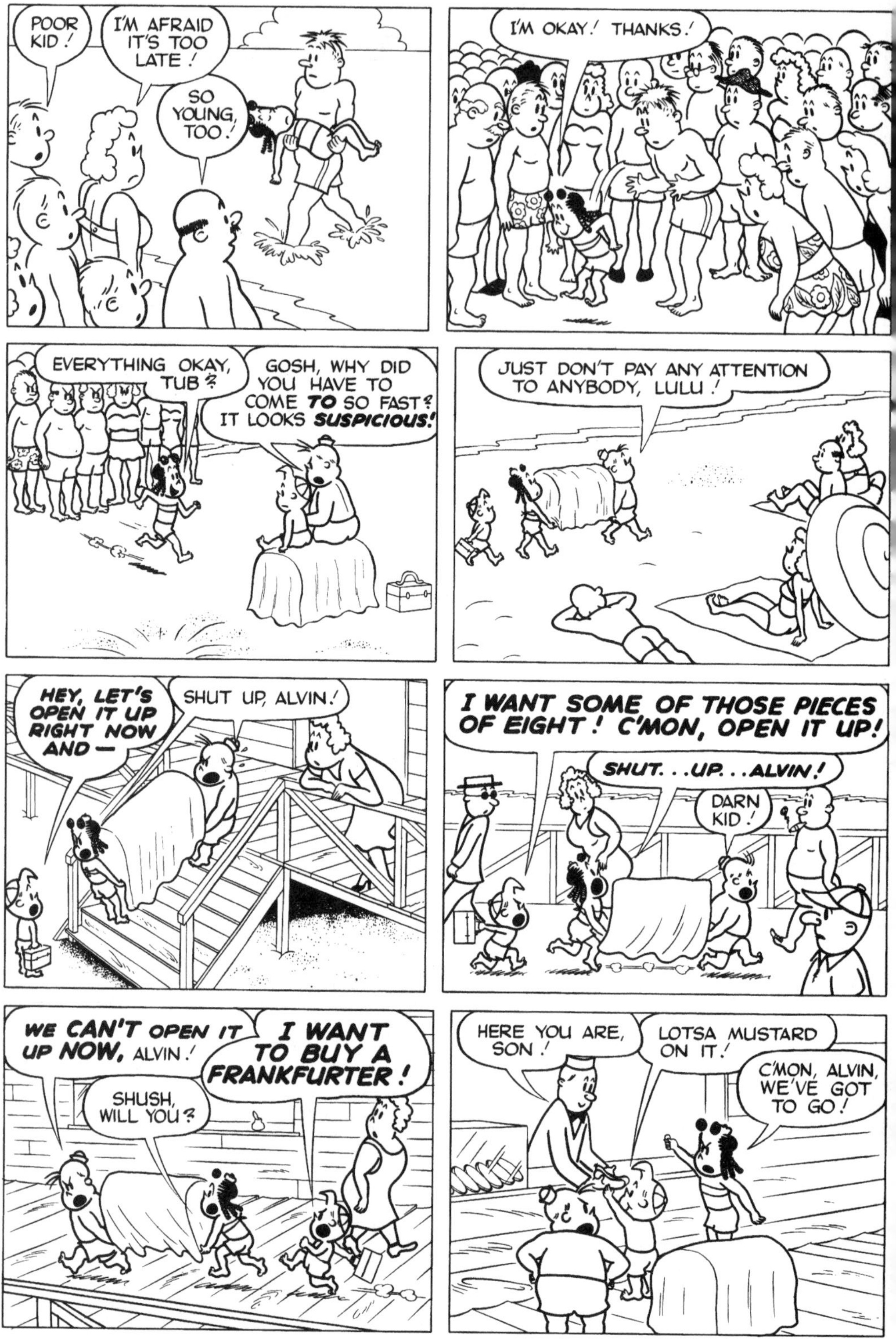
POOR KID!
I'M AFRAID IT'S TOO LATE!
SO YOUNG, TOO!
I'M OKAY! THANKS!
EVERYTHING OKAY, TUB?
GOSH, WHY DID YOU HAVE TO COME TO SO FAST? IT LOOKS SUSPICIOUS!
JUST DON'T PAY ANY ATTENTION TO ANYBODY, LULU!
HEY, LET'S OPEN IT UP RIGHT NOW AND—
SHUT UP, ALVIN!
I WANT SOME OF THOSE PIECES OF EIGHT! C'MON, OPEN IT UP!
SHUT...UP...ALVIN!
DARN KID!
WE CAN'T OPEN IT UP NOW, ALVIN!
I WANT TO BUY A FRANKFURTER!
SHUSH, WILL YOU?
HERE YOU ARE, SON!
LOTSA MUSTARD ON IT!
C'MON, ALVIN, WE'VE GOT TO GO!

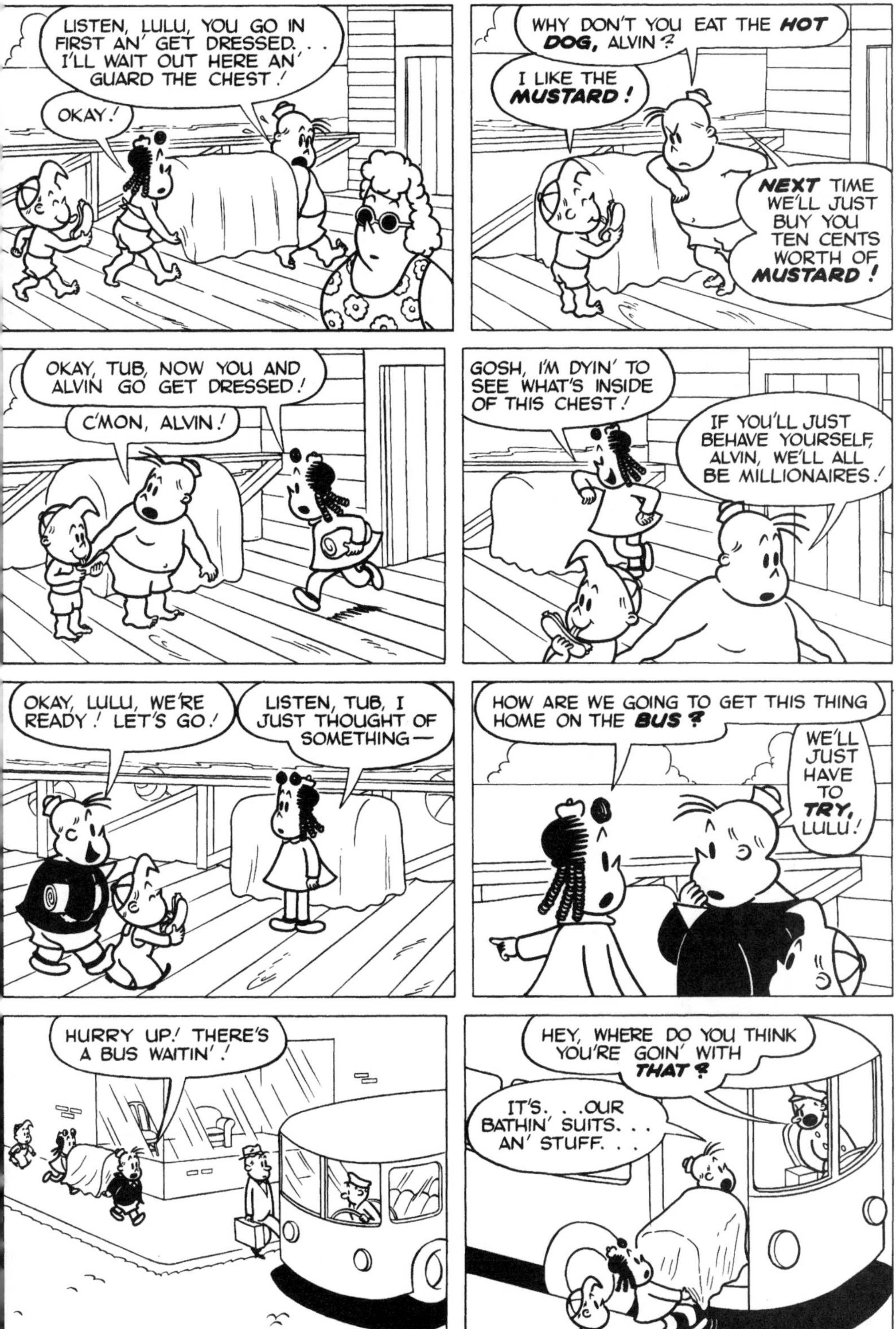
LISTEN, LULU, YOU GO IN FIRST AN' GET DRESSED. . . I'LL WAIT OUT HERE AN' GUARD THE CHEST!
OKAY!
WHY DON'T YOU EAT THE HOT DOG, ALVIN?
I LIKE THE MUSTARD!
NEXT TIME WE'LL JUST BUY YOU TEN CENTS WORTH OF MUSTARD!
OKAY, TUB, NOW YOU AND ALVIN GO GET DRESSED!
C'MON, ALVIN!
GOSH, I'M DYIN' TO SEE WHAT'S INSIDE OF THIS CHEST!
IF YOU'LL JUST BEHAVE YOURSELF, ALVIN, WE'LL ALL BE MILLIONAIRES!
OKAY, LULU, WE'RE READY! LET'S GO!
LISTEN, TUB, I JUST THOUGHT OF SOMETHING—
HOW ARE WE GOING TO GET THIS THING HOME ON THE BUS?
WE'LL JUST HAVE TO TRY, LULU!
HURRY UP! THERE'S A BUS WAITIN'!
HEY, WHERE DO YOU THINK YOU'RE GOIN' WITH THAT?
IT'S. . .OUR BATHIN' SUITS. . . AN' STUFF. . .

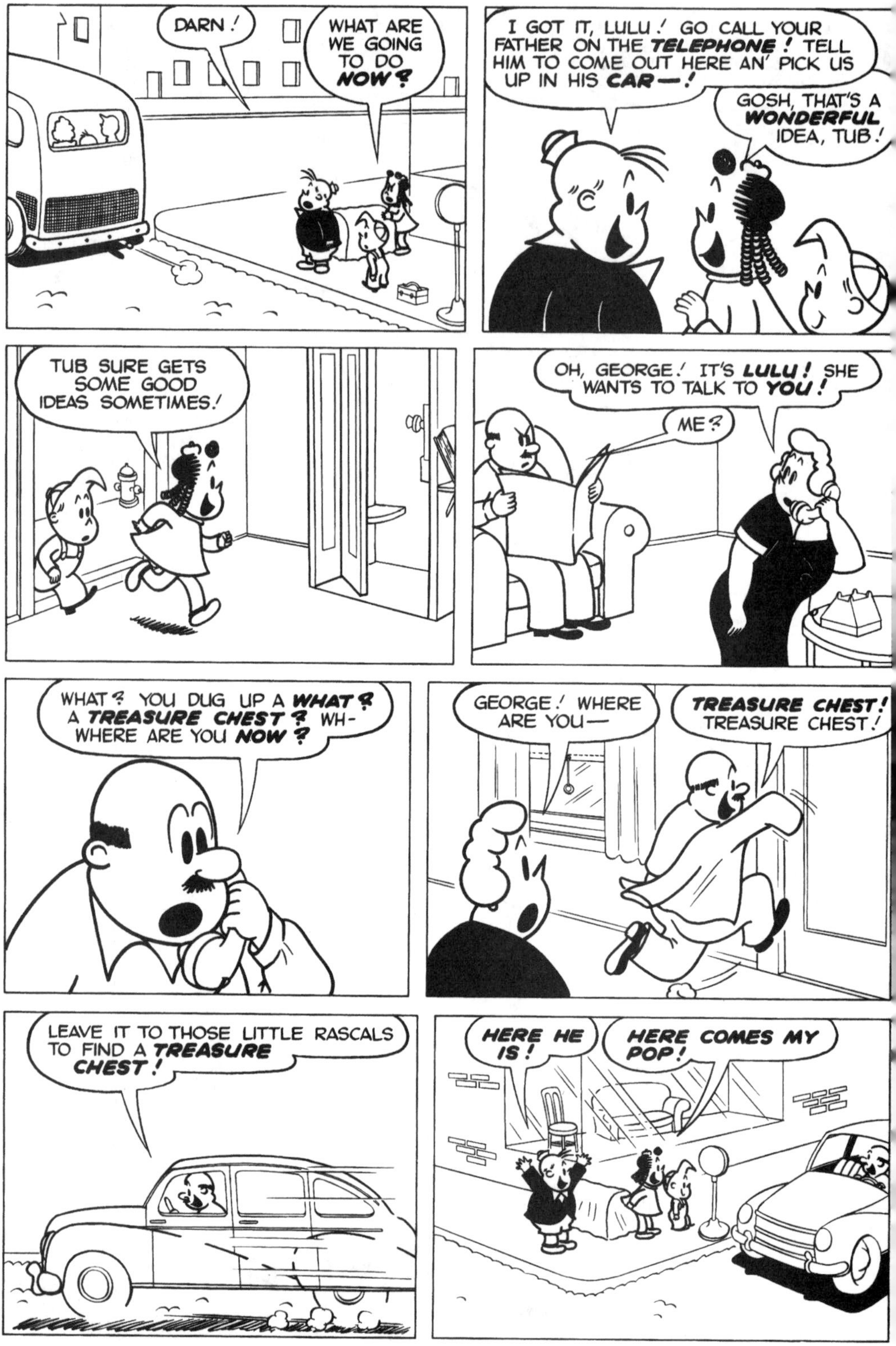
DARN!
WHAT ARE WE GOING TO DO NOW?
I GOT IT, LULU! GO CALL YOUR FATHER ON THE TELEPHONE! TELL HIM TO COME OUT HERE AN' PICK US UP IN HIS CAR—!
GOSH, THAT'S A WONDERFUL IDEA, TUB!
TUB SURE GETS SOME GOOD IDEAS SOMETIMES!
OH, GEORGE! IT'S LULU! SHE WANTS TO TALK TO YOU!
ME?
WHAT? YOU DUG UP A WHAT? A TREASURE CHEST? WH-WHERE ARE YOU NOW?
GEORGE! WHERE ARE YOU—
TREASURE CHEST! TREASURE CHEST!
LEAVE IT TO THOSE LITTLE RASCALS TO FIND A TREASURE CHEST!
HERE HE IS!
HERE COMES MY POP!

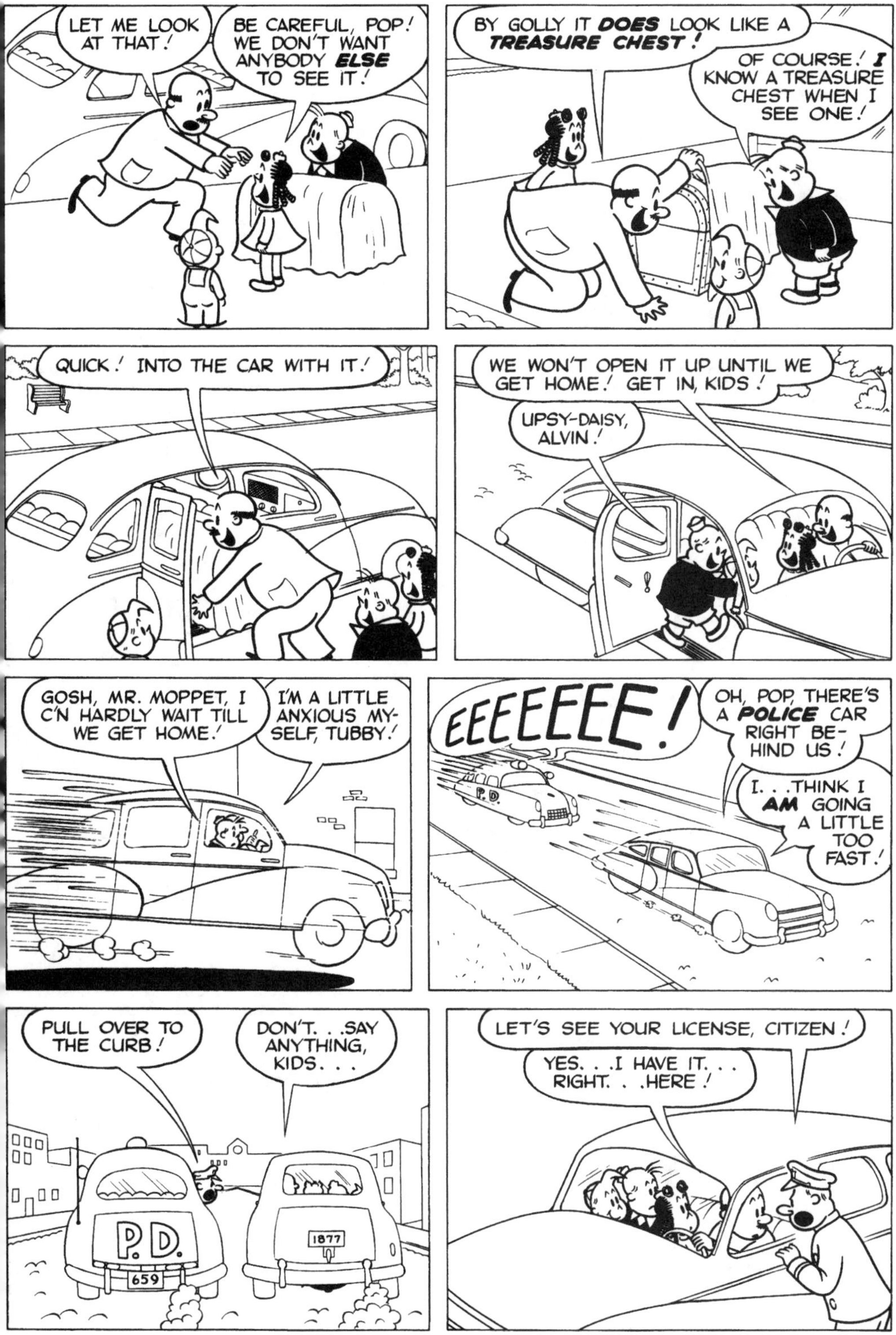

LET ME LOOK AT THAT!
BE CAREFUL, POP! WE DON'T WANT ANYBODY ELSE TO SEE IT!
BY GOLLY IT DOES LOOK LIKE A TREASURE CHEST!
OF COURSE! I KNOW A TREASURE CHEST WHEN I SEE ONE!
QUICK! INTO THE CAR WITH IT!
WE WON'T OPEN IT UP UNTIL WE GET HOME! GET IN, KIDS!
UPSY-DAISY, ALVIN!
GOSH, MR. MOPPET, I C'N HARDLY WAIT TILL WE GET HOME!
I'M A LITTLE ANXIOUS MY-SELF, TUBBY!
EEEEEEE!
OH, POP, THERE'S A POLICE CAR RIGHT BE-HIND US!
I. . .THINK I AM GOING A LITTLE TOO FAST!
P.D.
PULL OVER TO THE CURB!
DON'T. . .SAY ANYTHING, KIDS. . .
P.D.
659
1877
LET'S SEE YOUR LICENSE, CITIZEN!
YES. . .I HAVE IT. . . RIGHT. . .HERE!

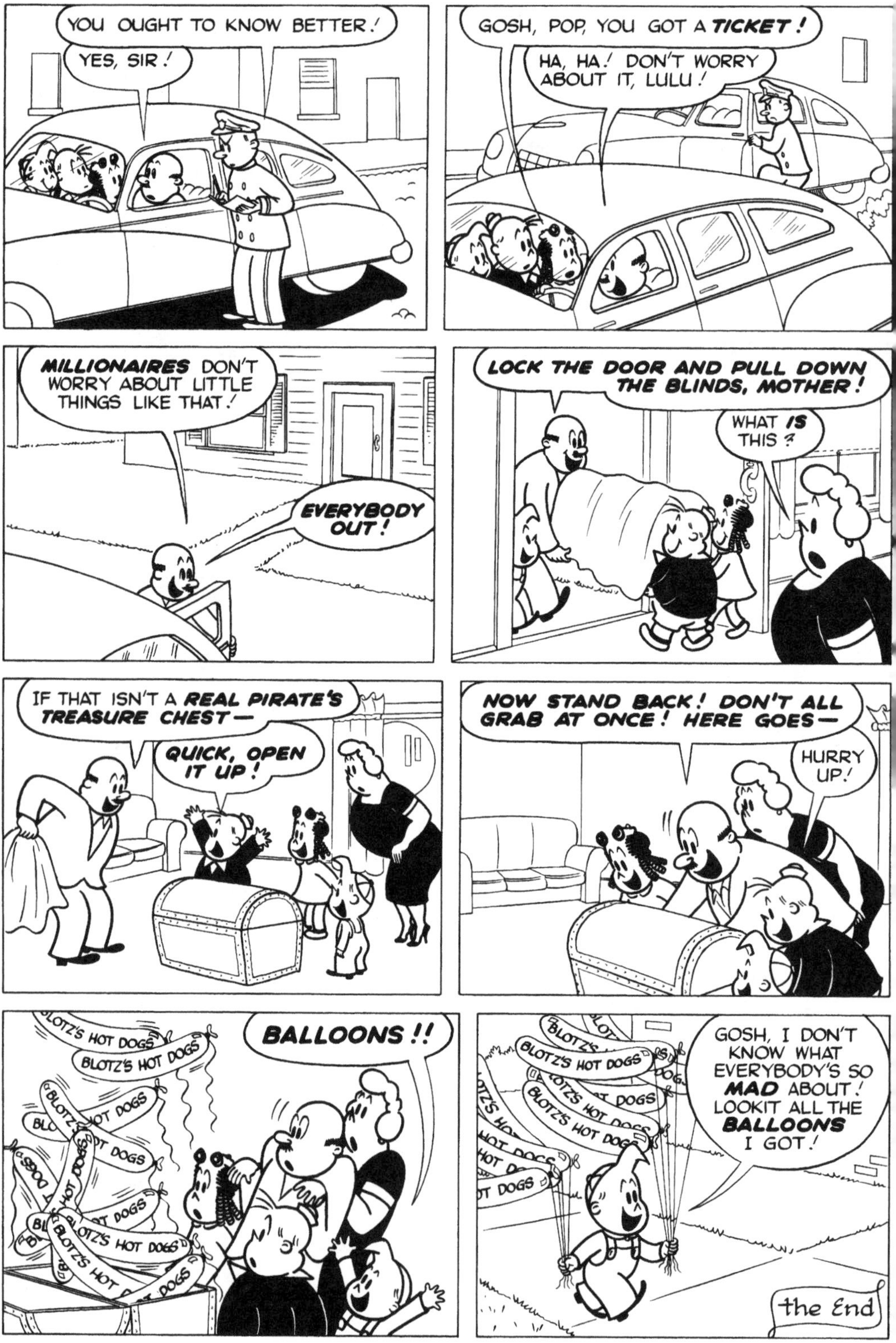
YOU OUGHT TO KNOW BETTER!
YES, SIR!
GOSH, POP, YOU GOT A TICKET!
HA, HA! DON'T WORRY ABOUT IT, LULU!
MILLIONAIRES DON'T WORRY ABOUT LITTLE THINGS LIKE THAT!
EVERYBODY OUT!
LOCK THE DOOR AND PULL DOWN THE BLINDS, MOTHER!
WHAT IS THIS?
IF THAT ISN'T A REAL PIRATE'S TREASURE CHEST—
QUICK, OPEN IT UP!
NOW STAND BACK! DON'T ALL GRAB AT ONCE! HERE GOES—
HURRY UP!
BALLOONS!!
BLOTZ'S HOT DOGS
GOSH, I DON'T KNOW WHAT EVERYBODY'S SO MAD ABOUT! LOOKIT ALL THE BALLOONS I GOT!
the End

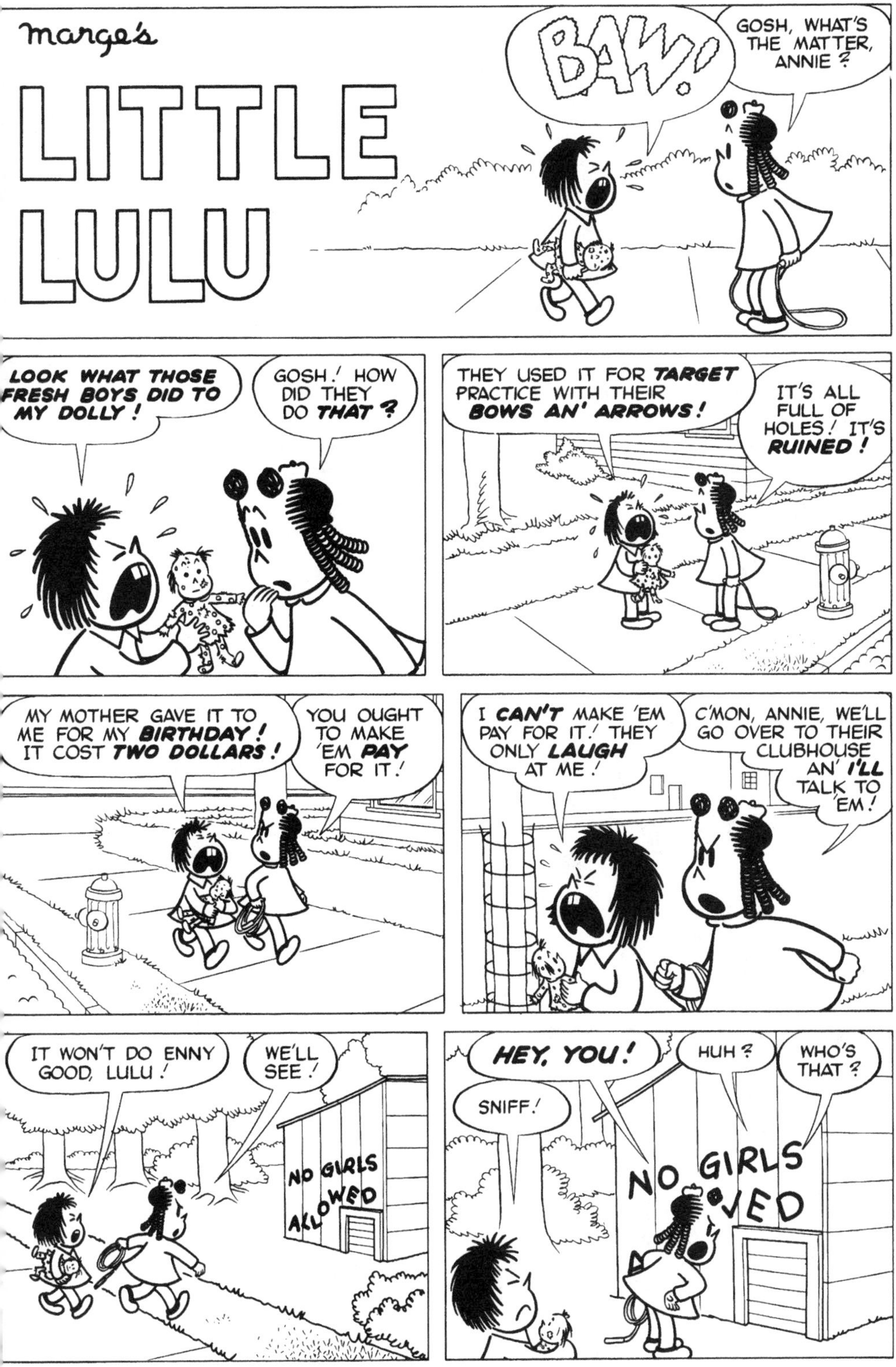
marge's
LITTLE LULU
BAW!
GOSH, WHAT'S THE MATTER, ANNIE?
LOOK WHAT THOSE FRESH BOYS DID TO MY DOLLY!
GOSH! HOW DID THEY DO THAT?
THEY USED IT FOR TARGET PRACTICE WITH THEIR BOWS AN' ARROWS!
IT'S ALL FULL OF HOLES! IT'S RUINED!
MY MOTHER GAVE IT TO ME FOR MY BIRTHDAY! IT COST TWO DOLLARS!
YOU OUGHT TO MAKE 'EM PAY FOR IT!
I CAN'T MAKE 'EM PAY FOR IT! THEY ONLY LAUGH AT ME!
C'MON, ANNIE, WE'LL GO OVER TO THEIR CLUBHOUSE AN' I'LL TALK TO 'EM!
IT WON'T DO ENNY GOOD, LULU!
WE'LL SEE!
NO GIRLS ALLOWED
HEY, YOU!
HUH?
WHO'S THAT?
SNIFF!
NO GIRLS ●VED

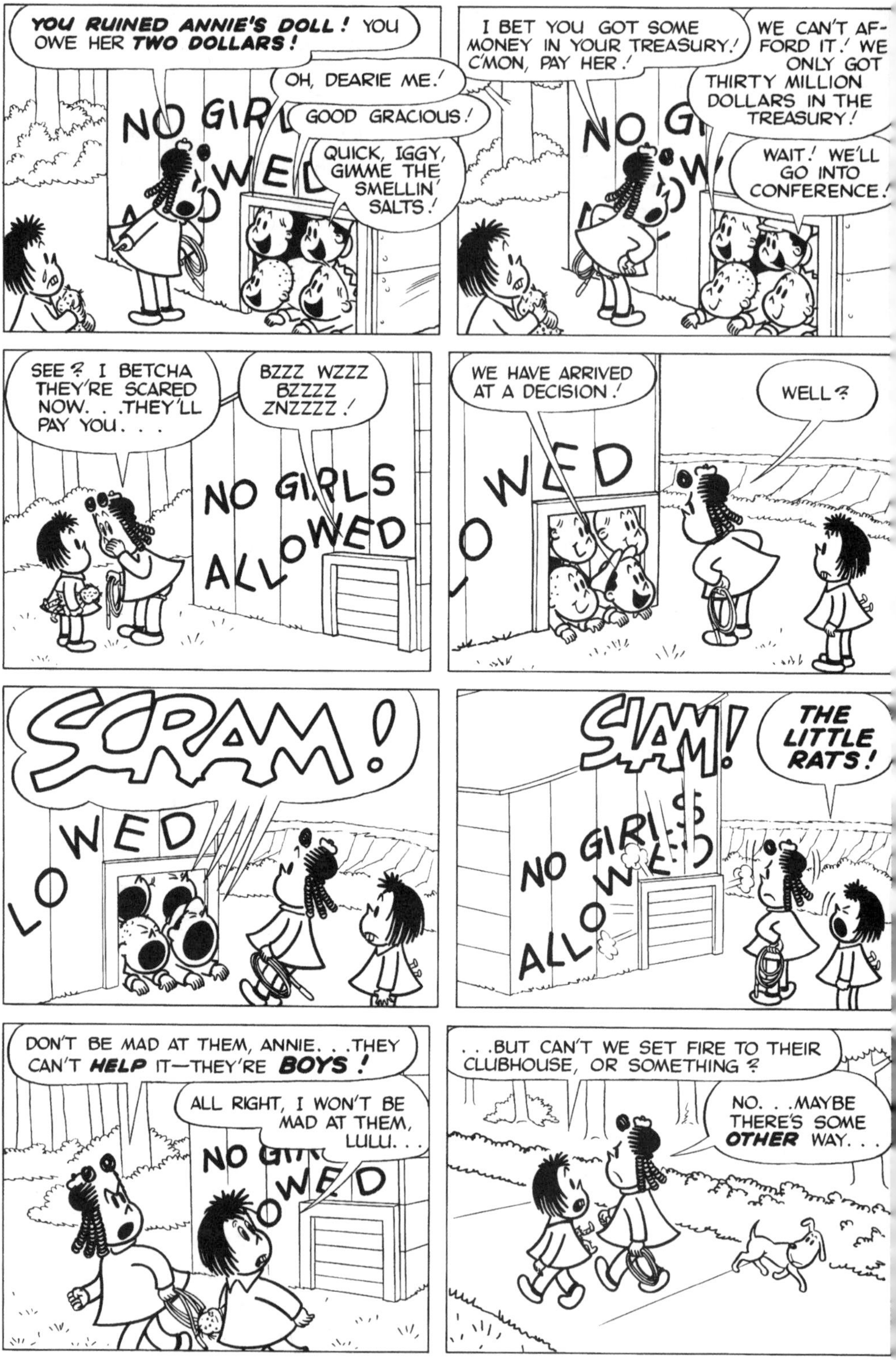
YOU RUINED ANNIE'S DOLL! YOU OWE HER TWO DOLLARS!
OH, DEARIE ME.!
GOOD GRACIOUS!
QUICK, IGGY, GIMME THE SMELLIN' SALTS!
NO GIRLS ALLOWED
I BET YOU GOT SOME MONEY IN YOUR TREASURY! C'MON, PAY HER!
WE CAN'T AFFORD IT! WE ONLY GOT THIRTY MILLION DOLLARS IN THE TREASURY!
WAIT! WE'LL GO INTO CONFERENCE!
SEE? I BETCHA THEY'RE SCARED NOW. . .THEY'LL PAY YOU. . .
BZZZ WZZZ BZZZZ ZNZZZZ!
WE HAVE ARRIVED AT A DECISION!
WELL?
SCRAM!
SLAM!
THE LITTLE RATS!
DON'T BE MAD AT THEM, ANNIE. . .THEY CAN'T HELP IT—THEY'RE BOYS!
ALL RIGHT, I WON'T BE MAD AT THEM, LULU. . .
. . .BUT CAN'T WE SET FIRE TO THEIR CLUBHOUSE, OR SOMETHING?
NO. . .MAYBE THERE'S SOME OTHER WAY. . .

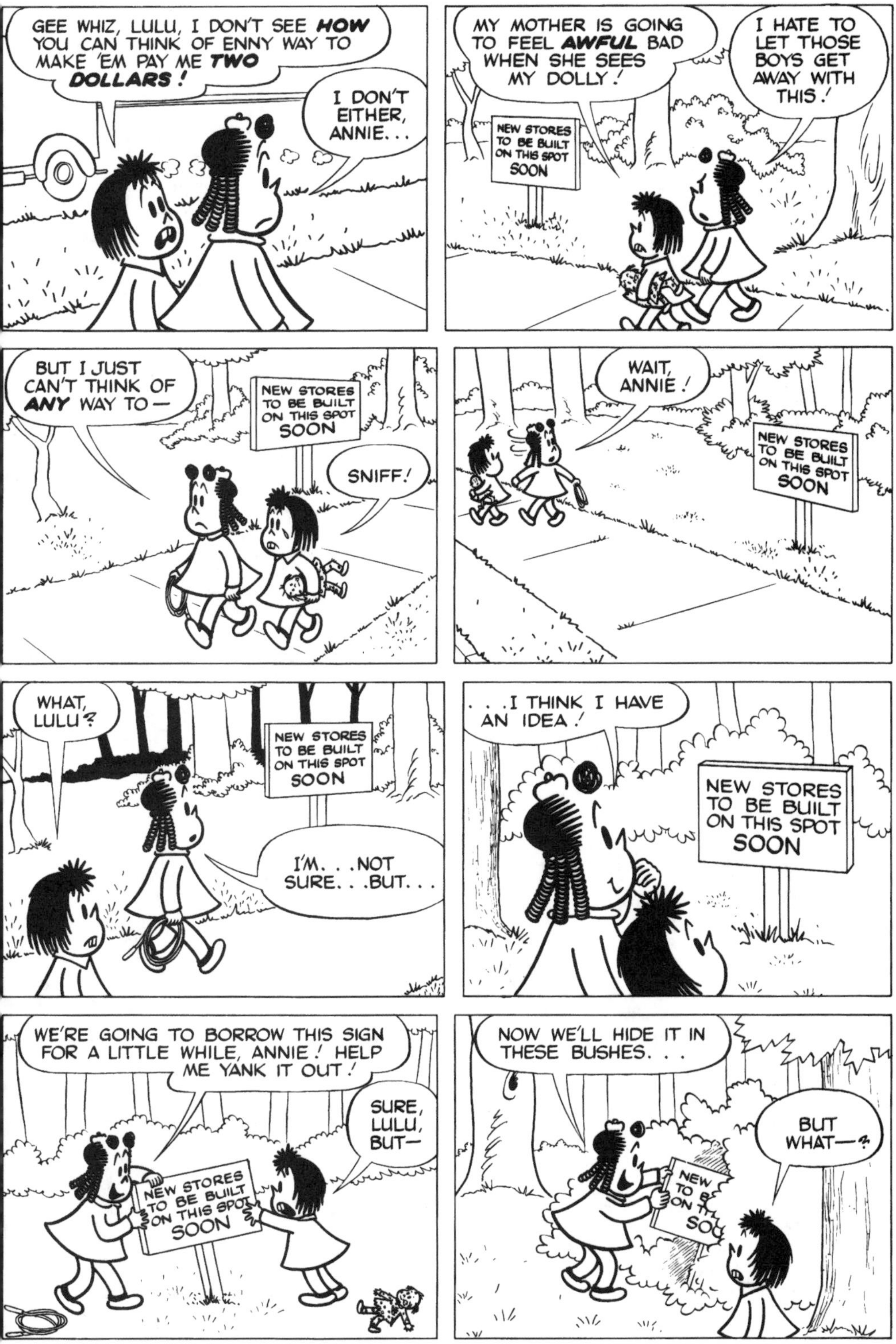

GEE WHIZ, LULU, I DON'T SEE **HOW** YOU CAN THINK OF ENNY WAY TO MAKE 'EM PAY ME **TWO DOLLARS**!
I DON'T EITHER, ANNIE. . .
MY MOTHER IS GOING TO FEEL **AWFUL** BAD WHEN SHE SEES MY DOLLY!
I HATE TO LET THOSE BOYS GET AWAY WITH THIS!
NEW STORES TO BE BUILT ON THIS SPOT SOON
BUT I JUST CAN'T THINK OF **ANY** WAY TO—
SNIFF!
WAIT, ANNIE!
WHAT, LULU?
I'M. . .NOT SURE. . .BUT. . .
. . .I THINK I HAVE AN IDEA!
WE'RE GOING TO BORROW THIS SIGN FOR A LITTLE WHILE, ANNIE! HELP ME YANK IT OUT!
SURE, LULU, BUT—
NOW WE'LL HIDE IT IN THESE BUSHES. . .
BUT WHAT—?

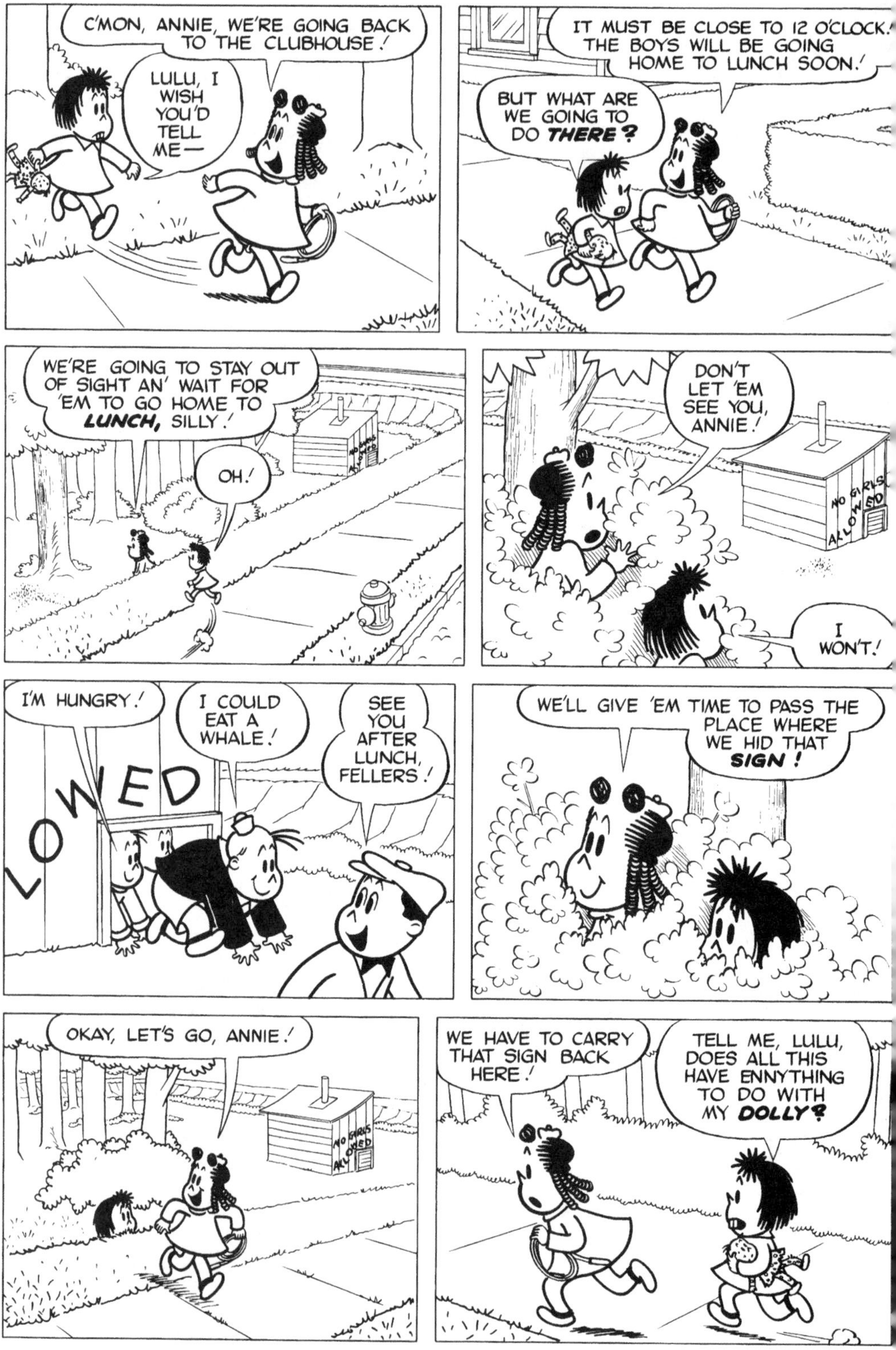
C'MON, ANNIE, WE'RE GOING BACK TO THE CLUBHOUSE!
LULU, I WISH YOU'D TELL ME—
IT MUST BE CLOSE TO 12 O'CLOCK! THE BOYS WILL BE GOING HOME TO LUNCH SOON!
BUT WHAT ARE WE GOING TO DO THERE?
WE'RE GOING TO STAY OUT OF SIGHT AN' WAIT FOR 'EM TO GO HOME TO LUNCH, SILLY!
OH!
NO GIRLS ALLOWED
DON'T LET 'EM SEE YOU, ANNIE!
NO GIRLS ALLOWED
I WON'T!
I'M HUNGRY!
I COULD EAT A WHALE!
SEE YOU AFTER LUNCH, FELLERS!
LOWED
WE'LL GIVE 'EM TIME TO PASS THE PLACE WHERE WE HID THAT SIGN!
OKAY, LET'S GO, ANNIE!
NO GIRLS ALLOWED
WE HAVE TO CARRY THAT SIGN BACK HERE!
TELL ME, LULU, DOES ALL THIS HAVE ENNYTHING TO DO WITH MY DOLLY?

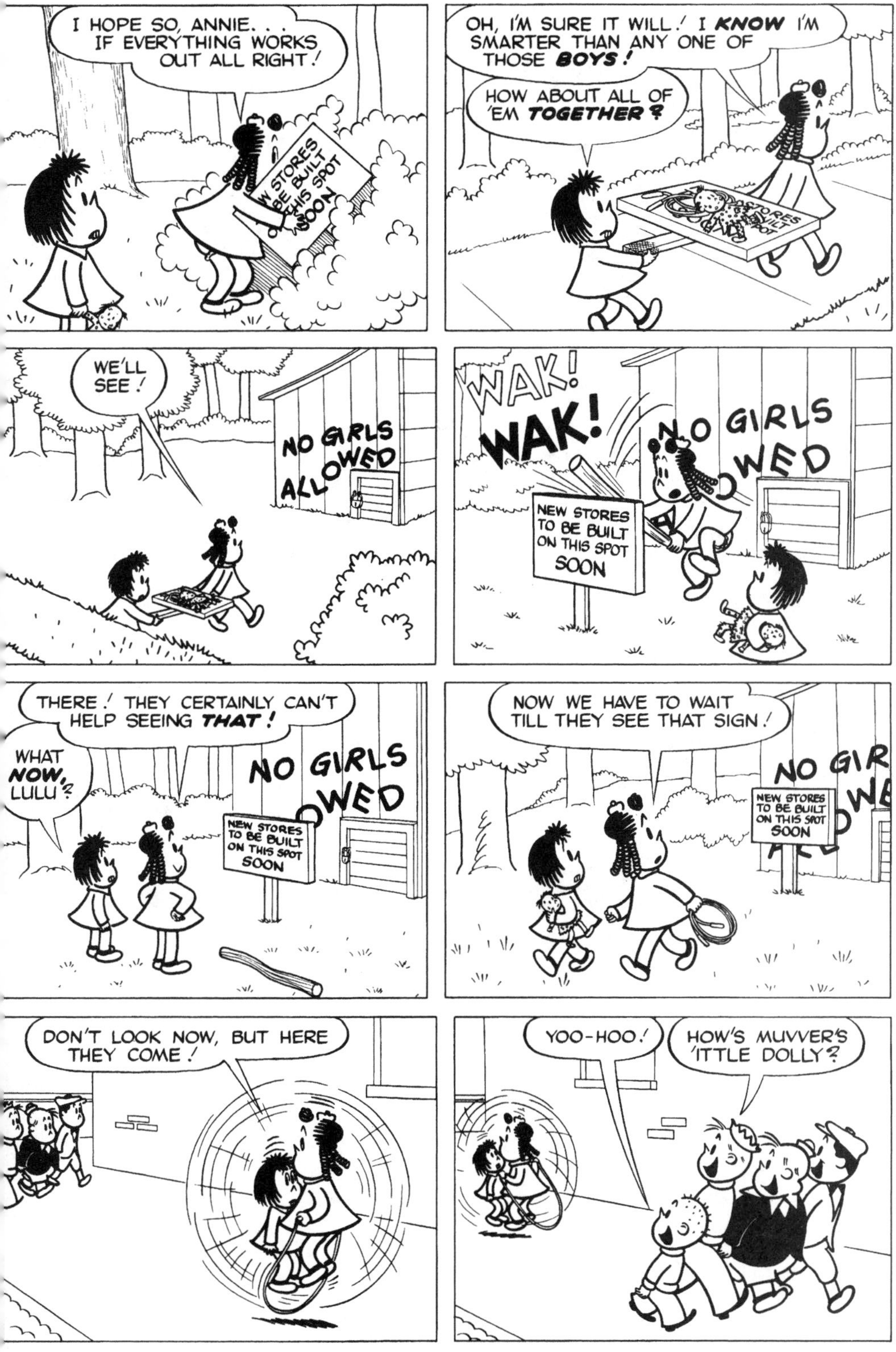
I HOPE SO, ANNIE. . . IF EVERYTHING WORKS OUT ALL RIGHT!
OH, I'M SURE IT WILL! I KNOW I'M SMARTER THAN ANY ONE OF THOSE BOYS!
HOW ABOUT ALL OF 'EM TOGETHER?
WE'LL SEE!
NO GIRLS ALLOWED
WAK!
WAK!
NEW STORES TO BE BUILT ON THIS SPOT SOON
THERE! THEY CERTAINLY CAN'T HELP SEEING THAT!
WHAT NOW, LULU?
NOW WE HAVE TO WAIT TILL THEY SEE THAT SIGN!
DON'T LOOK NOW, BUT HERE THEY COME!
YOO-HOO!
HOW'S MUVVER'S 'ITTLE DOLLY?

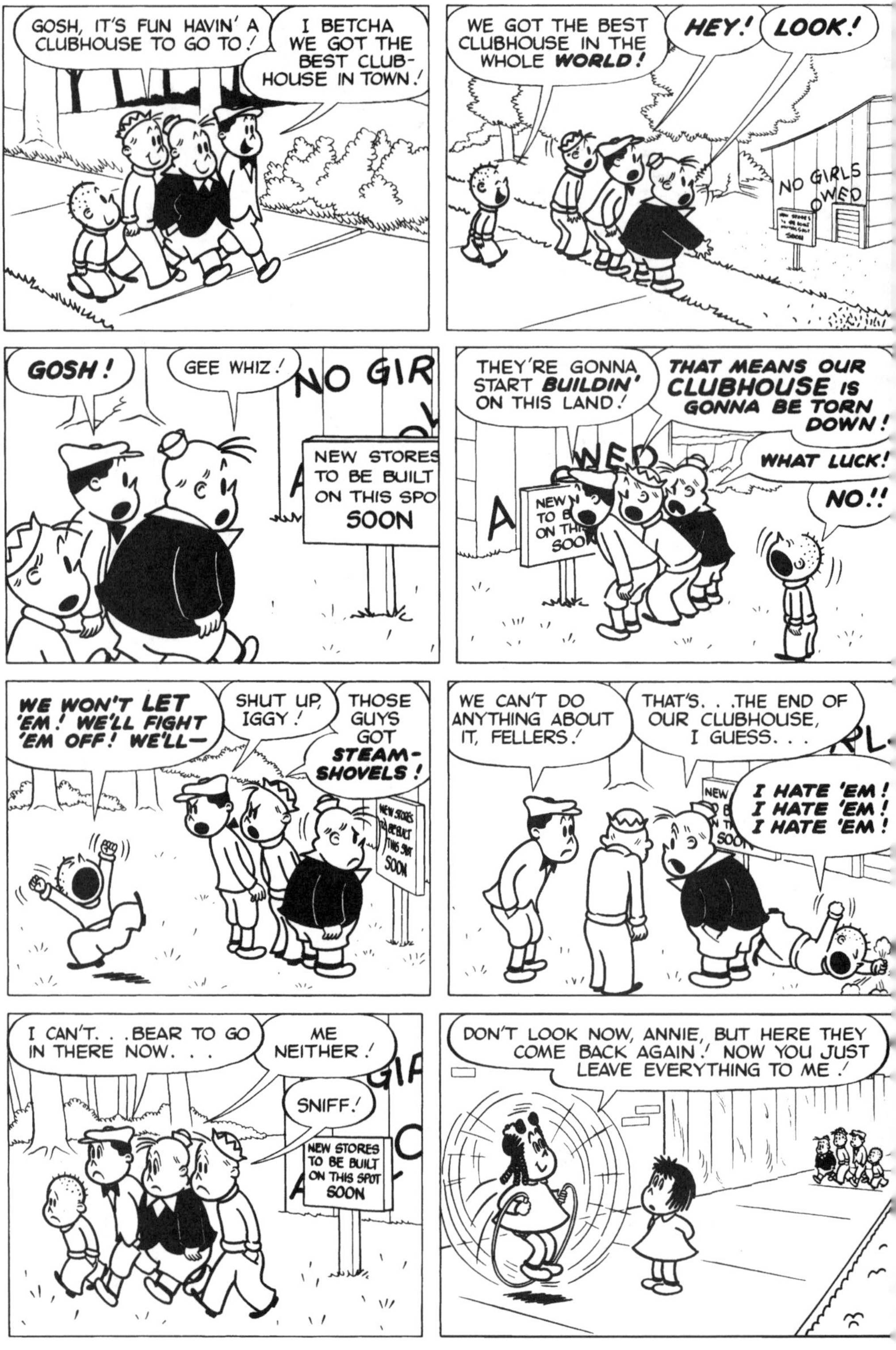
GOSH, IT'S FUN HAVIN' A CLUBHOUSE TO GO TO!
I BETCHA WE GOT THE BEST CLUB-HOUSE IN TOWN!
WE GOT THE BEST CLUBHOUSE IN THE WHOLE WORLD!
HEY!
LOOK!
NO GIRLS OWED
GOSH!
GEE WHIZ!
NEW STORES TO BE BUILT ON THIS SPOT SOON
THEY'RE GONNA START BUILDIN' ON THIS LAND!
THAT MEANS OUR CLUBHOUSE IS GONNA BE TORN DOWN!
WHAT LUCK!
NO!!
WE WON'T LET 'EM! WE'LL FIGHT 'EM OFF! WE'LL—
SHUT UP, IGGY!
THOSE GUYS GOT STEAM-SHOVELS!
NEW STORES TO BE BUILT THIS SPOT SOON
WE CAN'T DO ANYTHING ABOUT IT, FELLERS!
THAT'S. . .THE END OF OUR CLUBHOUSE, I GUESS. . .
I HATE 'EM! I HATE 'EM! I HATE 'EM!
I CAN'T. . .BEAR TO GO IN THERE NOW. . .
ME NEITHER!
SNIFF!
NEW STORES TO BE BUILT ON THIS SPOT SOON
DON'T LOOK NOW, ANNIE, BUT HERE THEY COME BACK AGAIN! NOW YOU JUST LEAVE EVERYTHING TO ME!

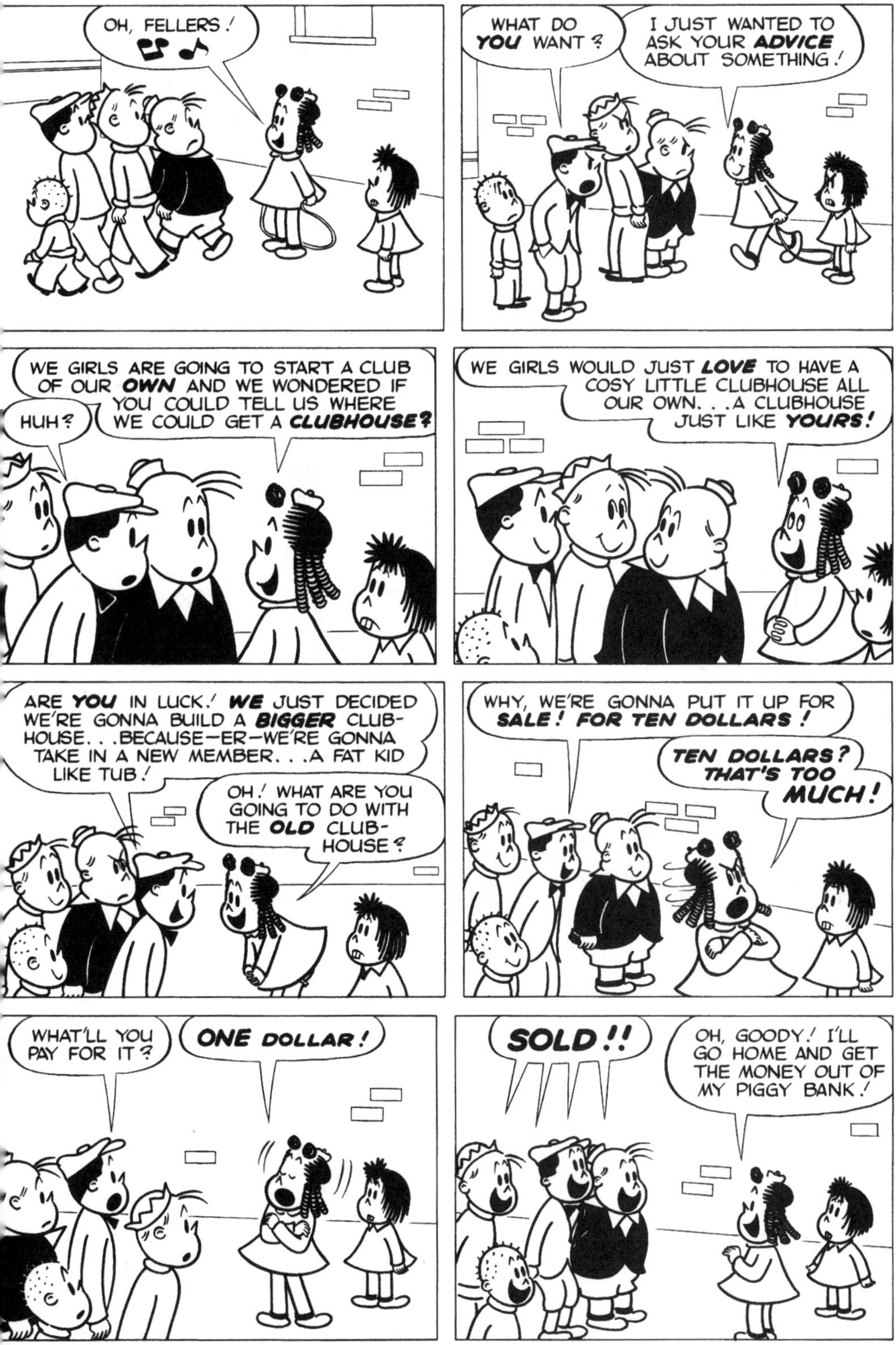
OH, FELLERS!
WHAT DO YOU WANT?
I JUST WANTED TO ASK YOUR ADVICE ABOUT SOMETHING!
WE GIRLS ARE GOING TO START A CLUB OF OUR OWN AND WE WONDERED IF YOU COULD TELL US WHERE WE COULD GET A CLUBHOUSE?
HUH?
WE GIRLS WOULD JUST LOVE TO HAVE A COSY LITTLE CLUBHOUSE ALL OUR OWN. . .A CLUBHOUSE JUST LIKE YOURS!
ARE YOU IN LUCK! WE JUST DECIDED WE'RE GONNA BUILD A BIGGER CLUB-HOUSE. . .BECAUSE—ER—WE'RE GONNA TAKE IN A NEW MEMBER. . .A FAT KID LIKE TUB!
OH! WHAT ARE YOU GOING TO DO WITH THE OLD CLUB-HOUSE?
WHY, WE'RE GONNA PUT IT UP FOR SALE! FOR TEN DOLLARS!
TEN DOLLARS? THAT'S TOO MUCH!
WHAT'LL YOU PAY FOR IT?
ONE DOLLAR!
SOLD!!
OH, GOODY! I'LL GO HOME AND GET THE MONEY OUT OF MY PIGGY BANK!

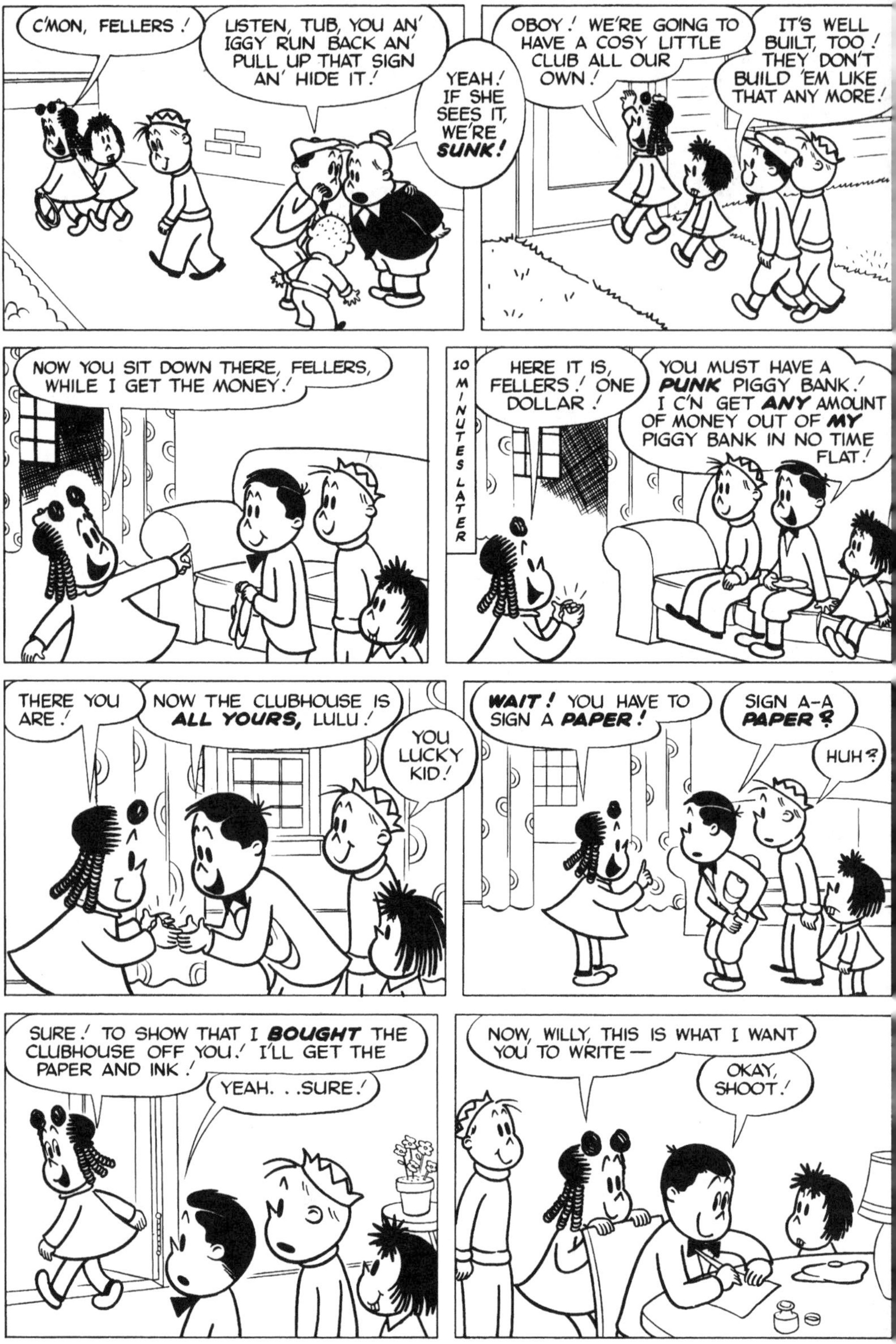
C'MON, FELLERS!
LISTEN, TUB, YOU AN' IGGY RUN BACK AN' PULL UP THAT SIGN AN' HIDE IT!
YEAH! IF SHE SEES IT, WE'RE SUNK!
OBOY! WE'RE GOING TO HAVE A COSY LITTLE CLUB ALL OUR OWN!
IT'S WELL BUILT, TOO! THEY DON'T BUILD 'EM LIKE THAT ANY MORE!
NOW YOU SIT DOWN THERE, FELLERS, WHILE I GET THE MONEY!
10 MINUTES LATER
HERE IT IS, FELLERS! ONE DOLLAR!
YOU MUST HAVE A PUNK PIGGY BANK! I C'N GET ANY AMOUNT OF MONEY OUT OF MY PIGGY BANK IN NO TIME FLAT!
THERE YOU ARE!
NOW THE CLUBHOUSE IS ALL YOURS, LULU!
YOU LUCKY KID!
WAIT! YOU HAVE TO SIGN A PAPER!
SIGN A-A PAPER?
HUH?
SURE! TO SHOW THAT I BOUGHT THE CLUBHOUSE OFF YOU! I'LL GET THE PAPER AND INK!
YEAH. . .SURE!
NOW, WILLY, THIS IS WHAT I WANT YOU TO WRITE—
OKAY, SHOOT!

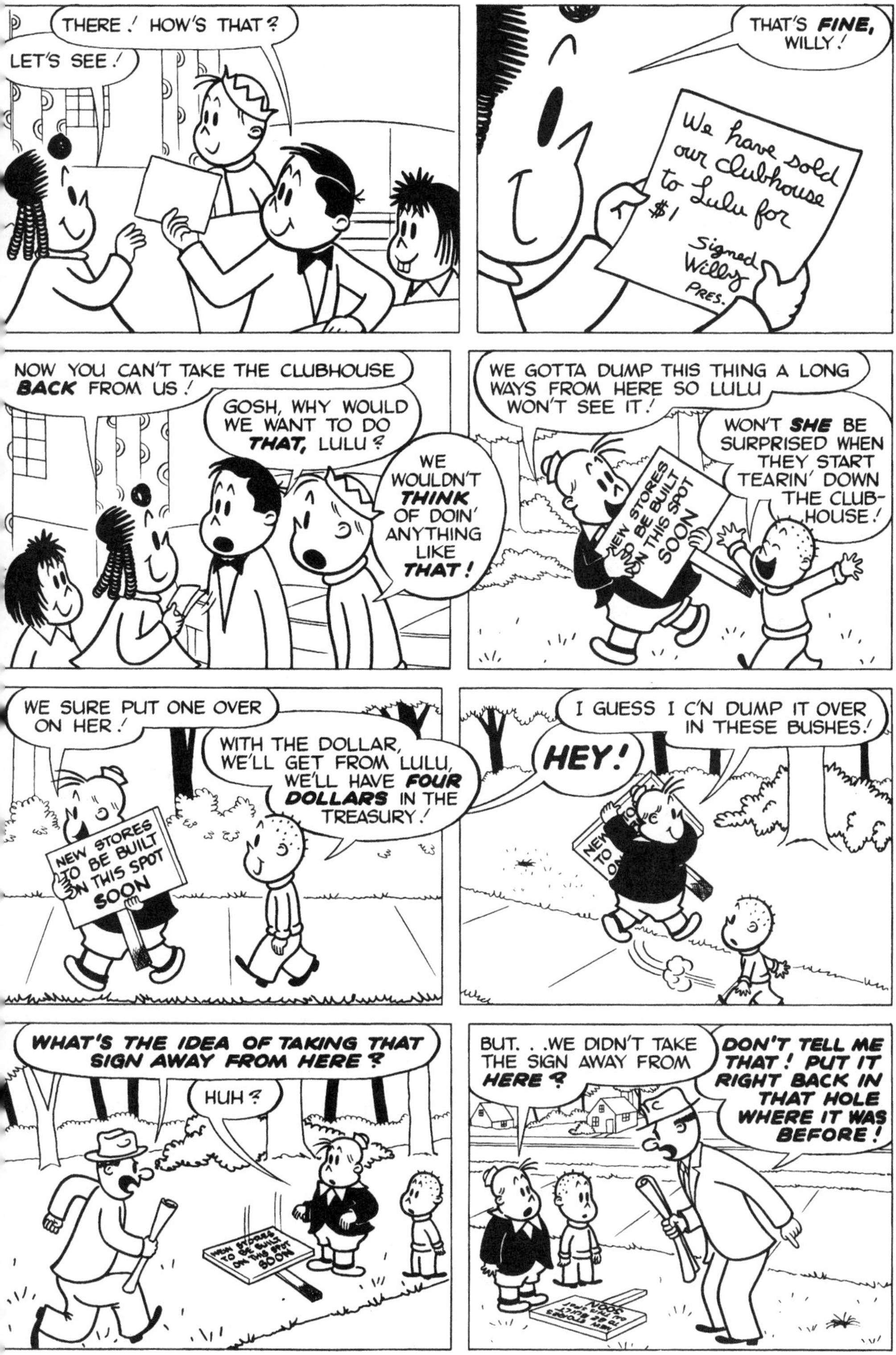
THERE! HOW'S THAT?
LET'S SEE!
THAT'S FINE, WILLY!
We have sold our clubhouse to Lulu for $1
Signed Willy Pres.
NOW YOU CAN'T TAKE THE CLUBHOUSE BACK FROM US!
GOSH, WHY WOULD WE WANT TO DO THAT, LULU?
WE WOULDN'T THINK OF DOIN' ANYTHING LIKE THAT!
WE GOTTA DUMP THIS THING A LONG WAYS FROM HERE SO LULU WON'T SEE IT!
WON'T SHE BE SURPRISED WHEN THEY START TEARIN' DOWN THE CLUB-HOUSE!
NEW STORES TO BE BUILT ON THIS SPOT SOON
WE SURE PUT ONE OVER ON HER!
WITH THE DOLLAR, WE'LL GET FROM LULU, WE'LL HAVE FOUR DOLLARS IN THE TREASURY!
NEW STORES TO BE BUILT ON THIS SPOT SOON
I GUESS I C'N DUMP IT OVER IN THESE BUSHES!
HEY!
WHAT'S THE IDEA OF TAKING THAT SIGN AWAY FROM HERE?
HUH?
NEW STORES TO BE BUILT ON THIS SPOT SOON
BUT. . .WE DIDN'T TAKE THE SIGN AWAY FROM HERE?
DON'T TELL ME THAT! PUT IT RIGHT BACK IN THAT HOLE WHERE IT WAS BEFORE!

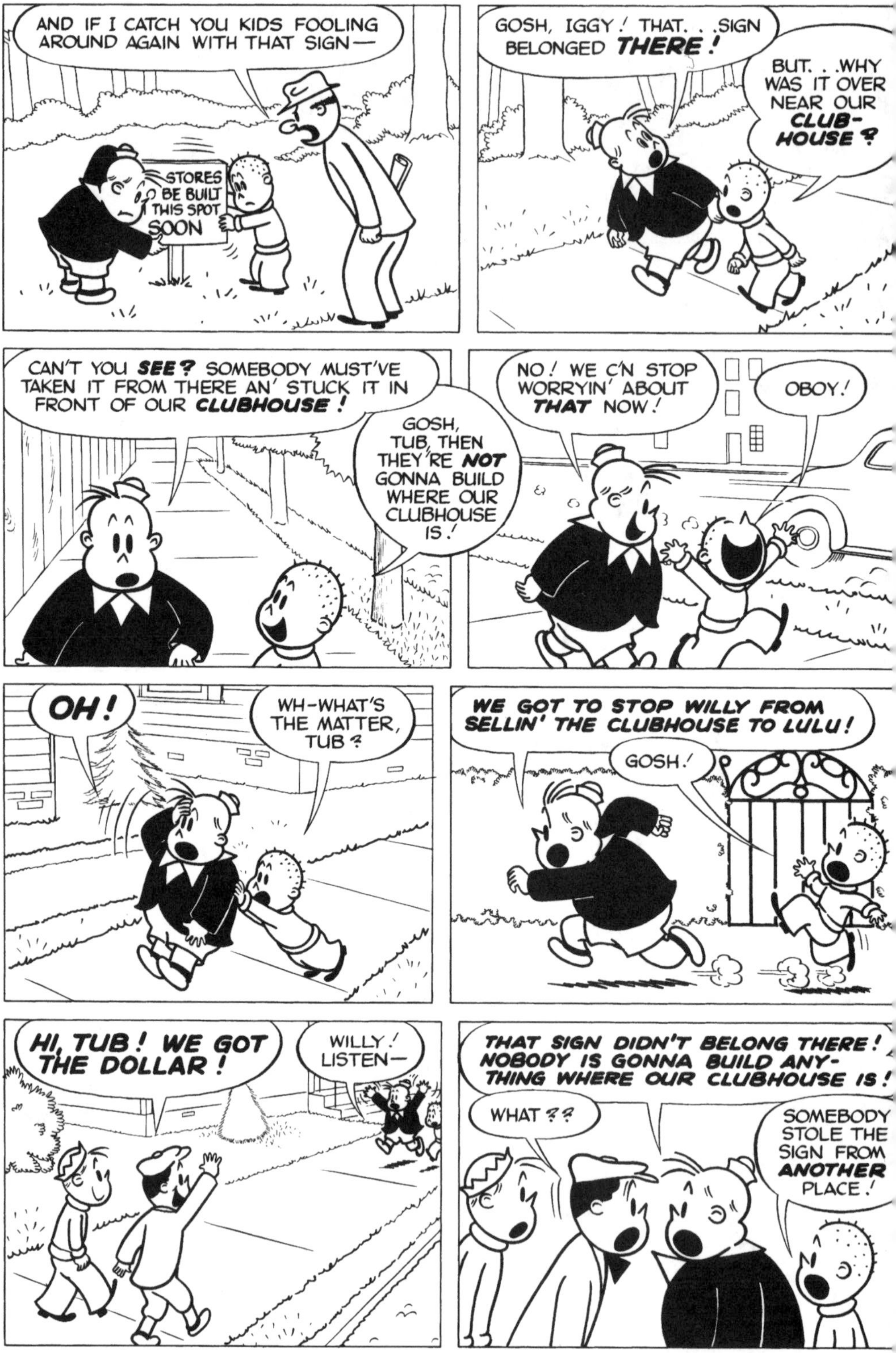
AND IF I CATCH YOU KIDS FOOLING AROUND AGAIN WITH THAT SIGN—
STORES BE BUILT THIS SPOT SOON
GOSH, IGGY! THAT. . .SIGN BELONGED THERE!
BUT. . .WHY WAS IT OVER NEAR OUR CLUB-HOUSE?
CAN'T YOU SEE? SOMEBODY MUST'VE TAKEN IT FROM THERE AN' STUCK IT IN FRONT OF OUR CLUBHOUSE!
GOSH, TUB, THEN THEY'RE NOT GONNA BUILD WHERE OUR CLUBHOUSE IS!
NO! WE C'N STOP WORRYIN' ABOUT THAT NOW!
OBOY!
OH!
WH-WHAT'S THE MATTER, TUB?
WE GOT TO STOP WILLY FROM SELLIN' THE CLUBHOUSE TO LULU!
GOSH!
HI, TUB! WE GOT THE DOLLAR!
WILLY! LISTEN—
THAT SIGN DIDN'T BELONG THERE! NOBODY IS GONNA BUILD ANY-THING WHERE OUR CLUBHOUSE IS!
WHAT??
SOMEBODY STOLE THE SIGN FROM ANOTHER PLACE!

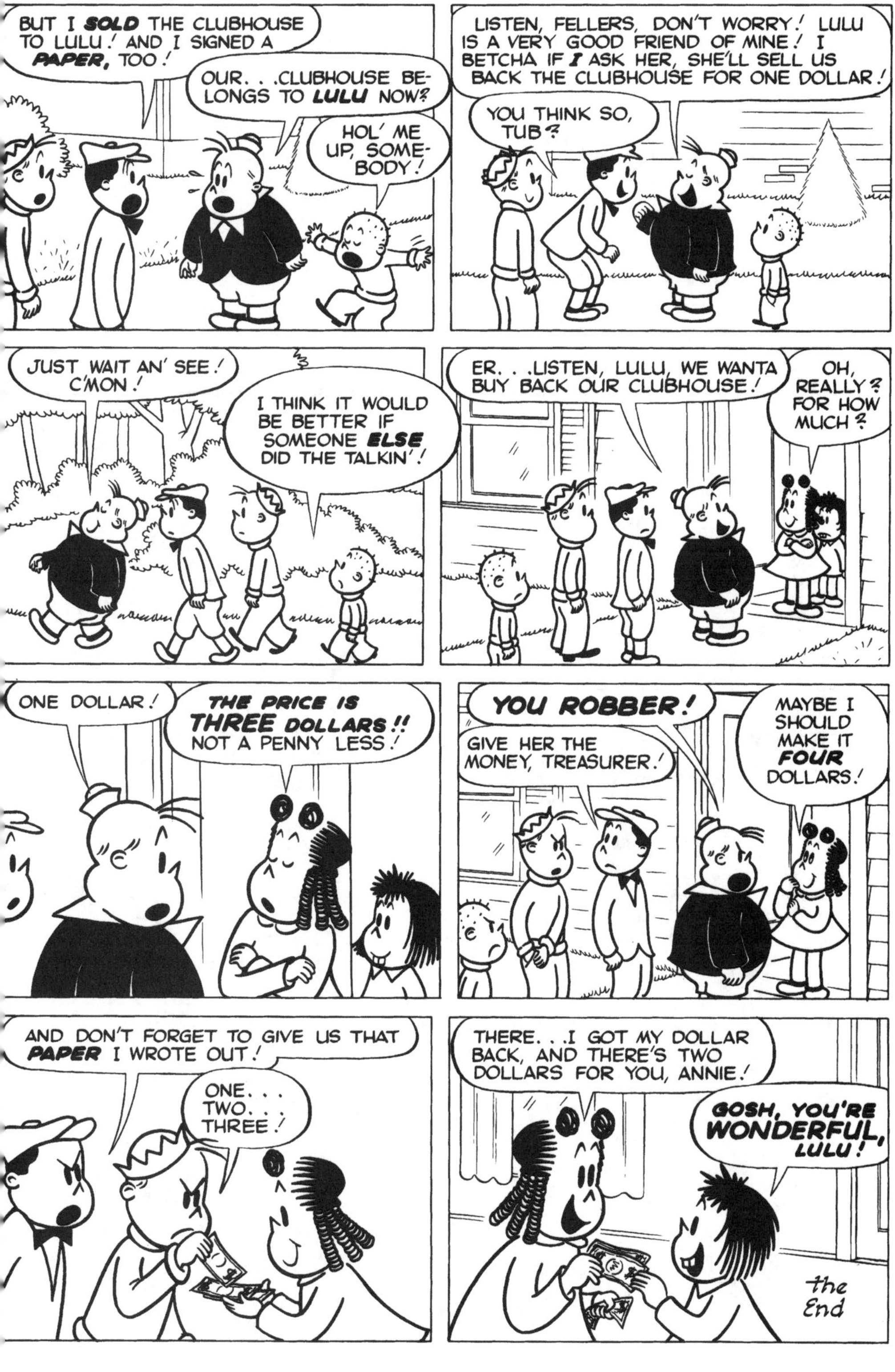
BUT I SOLD THE CLUBHOUSE TO LULU! AND I SIGNED A PAPER, TOO!
OUR. . .CLUBHOUSE BELONGS TO LULU NOW?
HOL' ME UP, SOMEBODY!
LISTEN, FELLERS, DON'T WORRY! LULU IS A VERY GOOD FRIEND OF MINE! I BETCHA IF I ASK HER, SHE'LL SELL US BACK THE CLUBHOUSE FOR ONE DOLLAR!
YOU THINK SO, TUB?
JUST WAIT AN' SEE! C'MON!
I THINK IT WOULD BE BETTER IF SOMEONE ELSE DID THE TALKIN'!
ER. . .LISTEN, LULU, WE WANTA BUY BACK OUR CLUBHOUSE!
OH, REALLY? FOR HOW MUCH?
ONE DOLLAR!
THE PRICE IS THREE DOLLARS!! NOT A PENNY LESS!
YOU ROBBER!
GIVE HER THE MONEY, TREASURER!
MAYBE I SHOULD MAKE IT FOUR DOLLARS!
AND DON'T FORGET TO GIVE US THAT PAPER I WROTE OUT!
ONE. . . TWO. . . THREE. . .!
THERE. . .I GOT MY DOLLAR BACK, AND THERE'S TWO DOLLARS FOR YOU, ANNIE!
GOSH, YOU'RE WONDERFUL, LULU!
the End

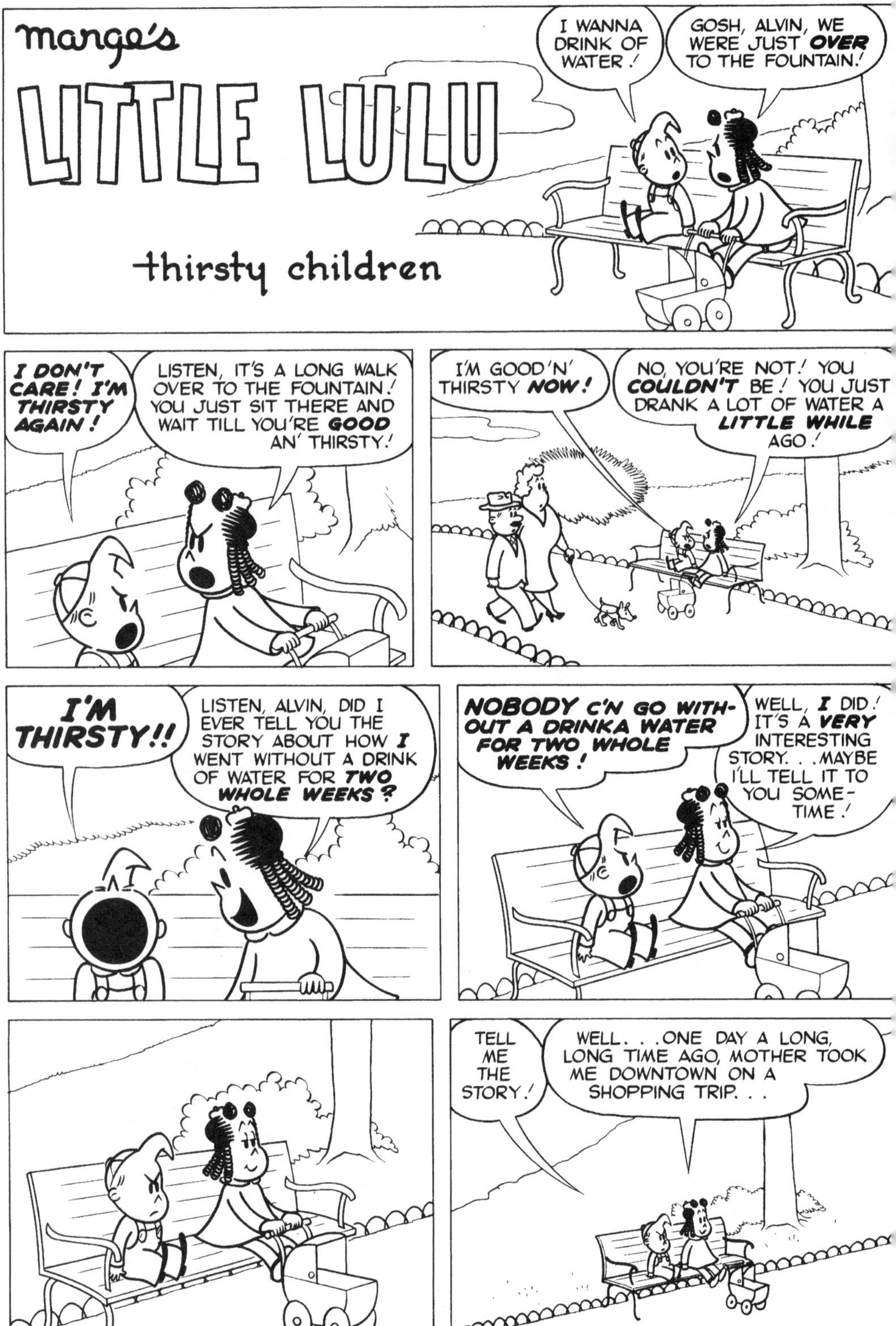
marge's
LITTLE LULU
thirsty children
I WANNA DRINK OF WATER!
GOSH, ALVIN, WE WERE JUST OVER TO THE FOUNTAIN!
I DON'T CARE! I'M THIRSTY AGAIN!
LISTEN, IT'S A LONG WALK OVER TO THE FOUNTAIN! YOU JUST SIT THERE AND WAIT TILL YOU'RE GOOD AN' THIRSTY!
I'M GOOD'N' THIRSTY NOW!
NO, YOU'RE NOT! YOU COULDN'T BE! YOU JUST DRANK A LOT OF WATER A LITTLE WHILE AGO!
I'M THIRSTY!!
LISTEN, ALVIN, DID I EVER TELL YOU THE STORY ABOUT HOW I WENT WITHOUT A DRINK OF WATER FOR TWO WHOLE WEEKS?
NOBODY C'N GO WITH-OUT A DRINKA WATER FOR TWO WHOLE WEEKS!
WELL, I DID! IT'S A VERY INTERESTING STORY. . .MAYBE I'LL TELL IT TO YOU SOME-TIME!
TELL ME THE STORY!
WELL. . .ONE DAY A LONG, LONG TIME AGO, MOTHER TOOK ME DOWNTOWN ON A SHOPPING TRIP. . .

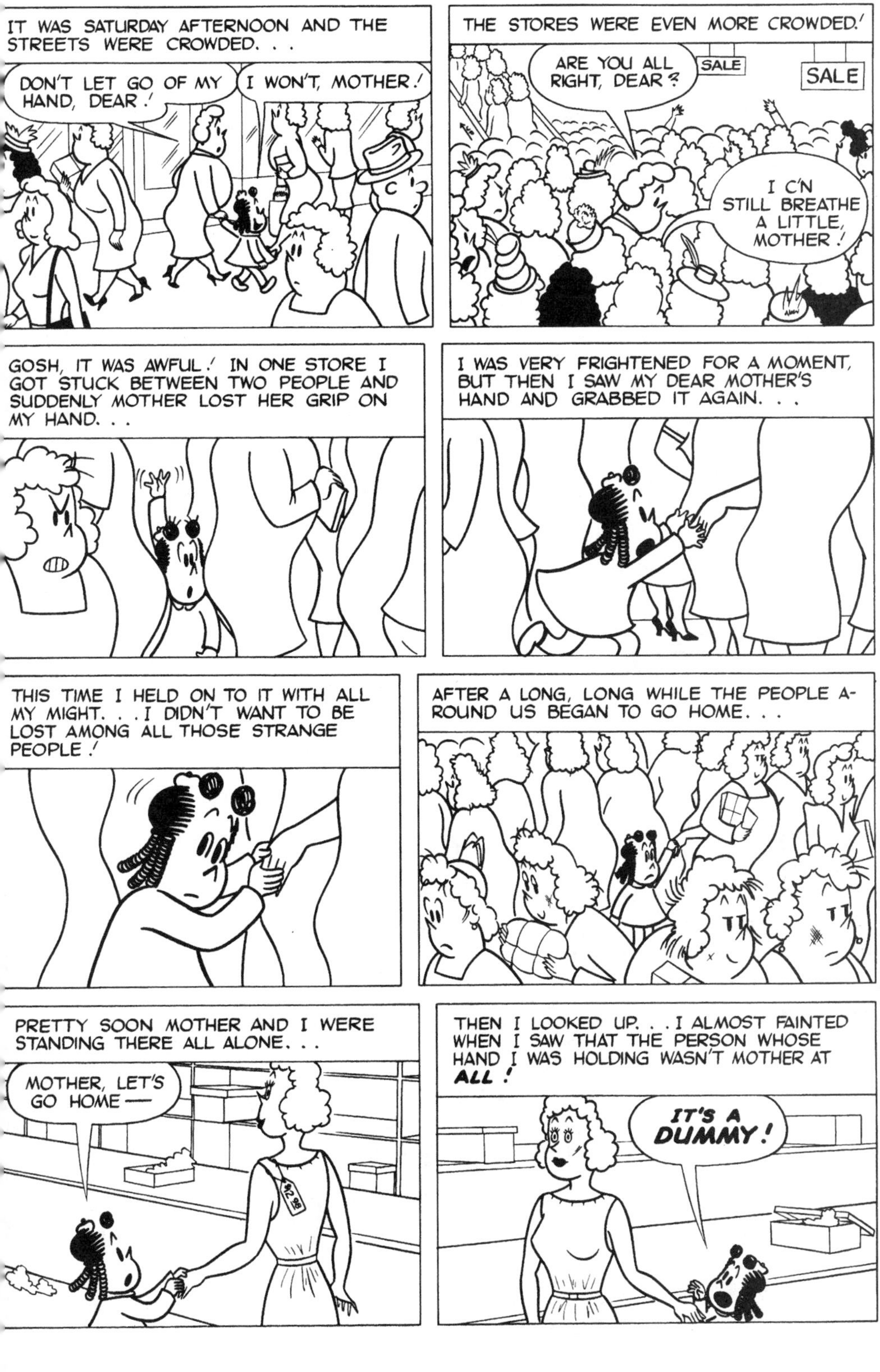
IT WAS SATURDAY AFTERNOON AND THE STREETS WERE CROWDED. . .
DON'T LET GO OF MY HAND, DEAR.!
I WON'T, MOTHER.!
THE STORES WERE EVEN MORE CROWDED.!
ARE YOU ALL RIGHT, DEAR?
SALE
SALE
I C'N STILL BREATHE A LITTLE, MOTHER.!
GOSH, IT WAS AWFUL.! IN ONE STORE I GOT STUCK BETWEEN TWO PEOPLE AND SUDDENLY MOTHER LOST HER GRIP ON MY HAND. . .
I WAS VERY FRIGHTENED FOR A MOMENT, BUT THEN I SAW MY DEAR MOTHER'S HAND AND GRABBED IT AGAIN. . .
THIS TIME I HELD ON TO IT WITH ALL MY MIGHT. . . I DIDN'T WANT TO BE LOST AMONG ALL THOSE STRANGE PEOPLE.!
AFTER A LONG, LONG WHILE THE PEOPLE A-ROUND US BEGAN TO GO HOME. . .
PRETTY SOON MOTHER AND I WERE STANDING THERE ALL ALONE. . .
MOTHER, LET'S GO HOME—
THEN I LOOKED UP. . . I ALMOST FAINTED WHEN I SAW THAT THE PERSON WHOSE HAND I WAS HOLDING WASN'T MOTHER AT ALL!
IT'S A DUMMY!

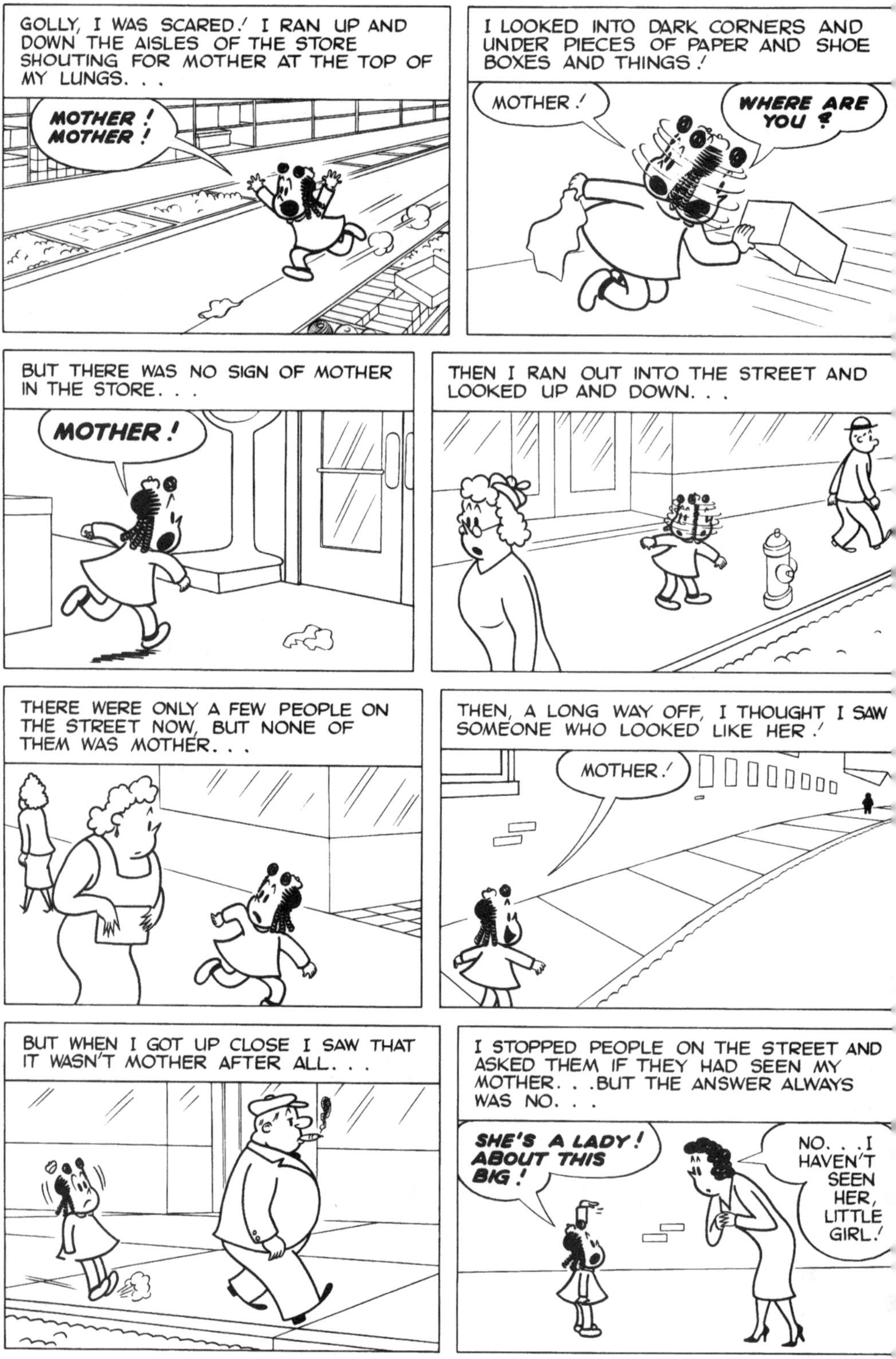
GOLLY, I WAS SCARED! I RAN UP AND DOWN THE AISLES OF THE STORE SHOUTING FOR MOTHER AT THE TOP OF MY LUNGS. . .
MOTHER! MOTHER!
I LOOKED INTO DARK CORNERS AND UNDER PIECES OF PAPER AND SHOE BOXES AND THINGS!
MOTHER!
WHERE ARE YOU?
BUT THERE WAS NO SIGN OF MOTHER IN THE STORE. . .
MOTHER!
THEN I RAN OUT INTO THE STREET AND LOOKED UP AND DOWN. . .
THERE WERE ONLY A FEW PEOPLE ON THE STREET NOW, BUT NONE OF THEM WAS MOTHER. . .
THEN, A LONG WAY OFF, I THOUGHT I SAW SOMEONE WHO LOOKED LIKE HER!
MOTHER!
BUT WHEN I GOT UP CLOSE I SAW THAT IT WASN'T MOTHER AFTER ALL. . .
I STOPPED PEOPLE ON THE STREET AND ASKED THEM IF THEY HAD SEEN MY MOTHER. . .BUT THE ANSWER ALWAYS WAS NO. . .
SHE'S A LADY! ABOUT THIS BIG!
NO. . .I HAVEN'T SEEN HER, LITTLE GIRL!

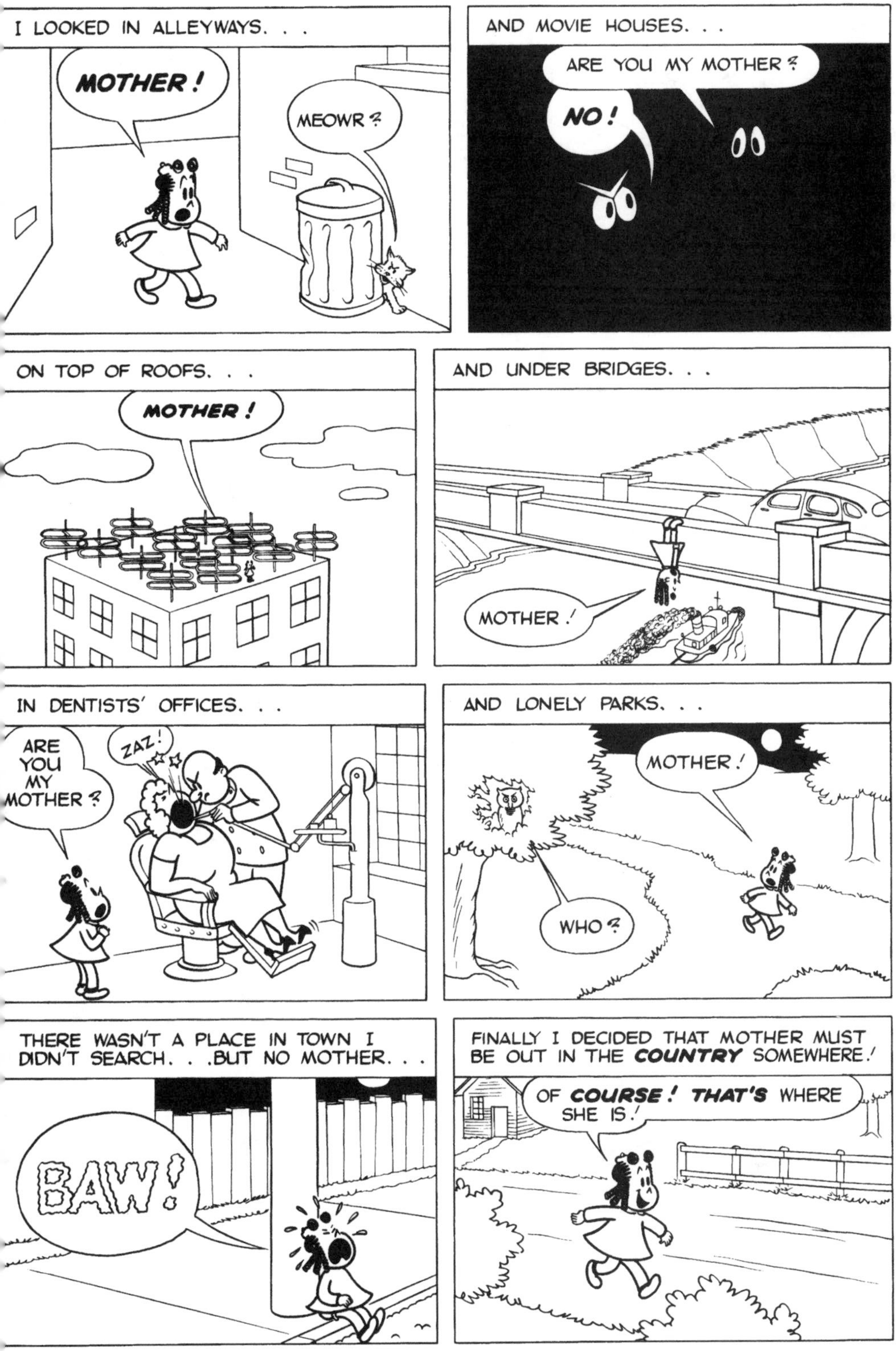
I LOOKED IN ALLEYWAYS. . .
MOTHER!
MEOWR?
AND MOVIE HOUSES. . .
ARE YOU MY MOTHER?
NO!
ON TOP OF ROOFS. . .
MOTHER!
AND UNDER BRIDGES. . .
MOTHER!
IN DENTISTS' OFFICES. . .
ARE YOU MY MOTHER?
ZAZ!
AND LONELY PARKS. . .
MOTHER!
WHO?
THERE WASN'T A PLACE IN TOWN I DIDN'T SEARCH. . .BUT NO MOTHER. . .
BAW!
FINALLY I DECIDED THAT MOTHER MUST BE OUT IN THE COUNTRY SOMEWHERE!
OF COURSE! THAT'S WHERE SHE IS!

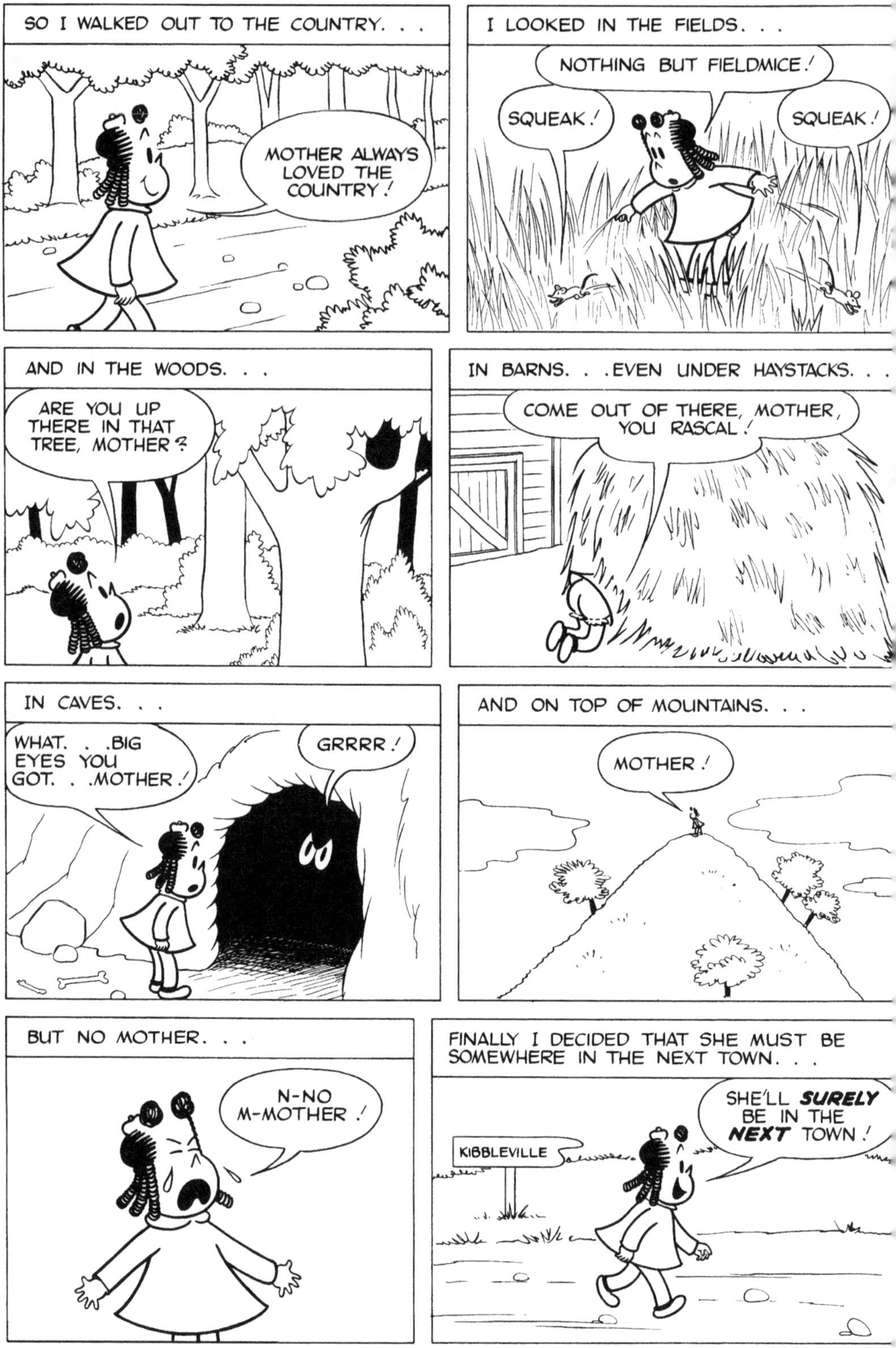
SO I WALKED OUT TO THE COUNTRY. . .
MOTHER ALWAYS LOVED THE COUNTRY!
I LOOKED IN THE FIELDS. . .
NOTHING BUT FIELDMICE!
SQUEAK!
SQUEAK!
AND IN THE WOODS. . .
ARE YOU UP THERE IN THAT TREE, MOTHER?
IN BARNS. . .EVEN UNDER HAYSTACKS. . .
COME OUT OF THERE, MOTHER, YOU RASCAL!
IN CAVES. . .
WHAT. . .BIG EYES YOU GOT. . .MOTHER!
GRRRR!
AND ON TOP OF MOUNTAINS. . .
MOTHER!
BUT NO MOTHER. . .
N-NO M-MOTHER!
FINALLY I DECIDED THAT SHE MUST BE SOMEWHERE IN THE NEXT TOWN. . .
KIBBLEVILLE
SHE'LL SURELY BE IN THE NEXT TOWN!

I SEARCHED THE NEXT TOWN, AND THE NEXT TOWN, AND THE NEXT TOWN. . .
YOU ARE LEAVING GLORIOUS SPINDLEVILLE
I SEARCHED EVERY TOWN IN THE UNITED STATES. . .BUT STILL NO SIGN OF MY MOTHER. . .
GOSH, THERE AREN'T ANY MORE TOWNS LEFT!
PUBLIC LIBRARY
SHUSH
THEN ONE DAY WHILE I WAS DOWN BY THE WATERFRONT WATCHING THE BIG SHIPS GO OUT, IT SUDDENLY DAWNED ON ME THAT MY POOR MOTHER MUST BE IN SOME OTHER COUNTRY!
WHEN NO ONE WAS LOOKING I CLIMBED UP A BIG ROPE ONTO A SHIP. . .
IT WASN'T SO EASY FINDING A GOOD SAFE HIDING PLACE, BUT I FOUND ONE ALL RIGHT. . .
IN A LITTLE WHILE THE SHIP STEAMED OUT TO SEA, AND I WAS ON MY WAY TO EUROPE AND MY POOR, DEAR MOTHER. . .
A COUPLE OF WEEKS WENT BY, AND I WAS JUST BEGINNING TO GET A LITTLE TIRED OF MY HIDING PLACE, WHEN I HEARD A LOT OF SHOUTING BELOW. . .
LAND AHEAD!
ENGLAND!
GOSH!
WE WERE GOING TO LAND IN ENGLAND! GOSH, I WAS EXCITED! I COULD HARDLY WAIT TO SEE MY MOTHER!
OBOY, OBOY, OBOY!

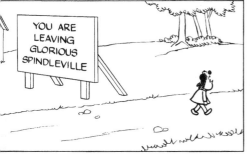

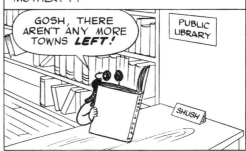

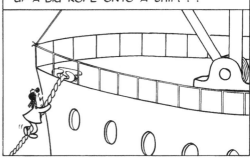

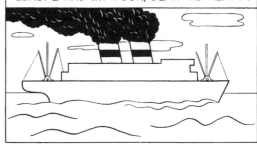

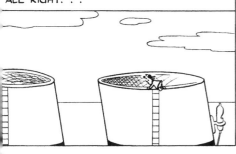

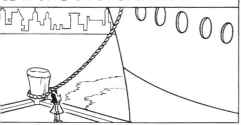

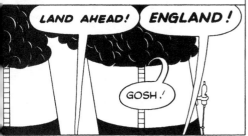

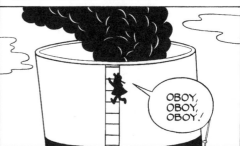

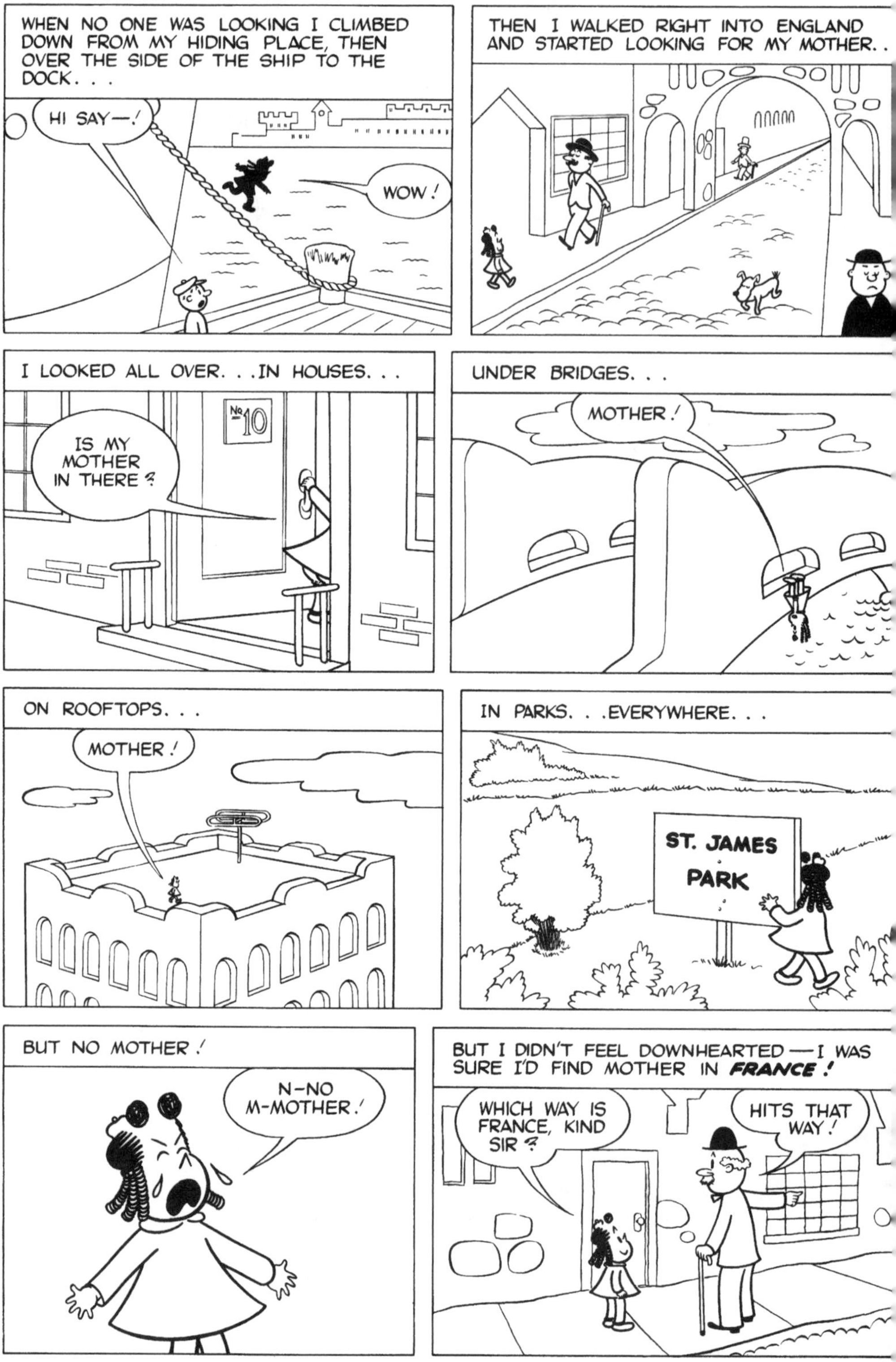
WHEN NO ONE WAS LOOKING I CLIMBED DOWN FROM MY HIDING PLACE, THEN OVER THE SIDE OF THE SHIP TO THE DOCK. . .
HI SAY—!
WOW!
THEN I WALKED RIGHT INTO ENGLAND AND STARTED LOOKING FOR MY MOTHER. .
I LOOKED ALL OVER. . .IN HOUSES. . .
No 10
IS MY MOTHER IN THERE?
UNDER BRIDGES. . .
MOTHER!
ON ROOFTOPS. . .
MOTHER!
IN PARKS. . .EVERYWHERE. . .
ST. JAMES PARK
BUT NO MOTHER!
N-NO M-MOTHER!
BUT I DIDN'T FEEL DOWNHEARTED—I WAS SURE I'D FIND MOTHER IN FRANCE!
WHICH WAY IS FRANCE, KIND SIR?
HITS THAT WAY!

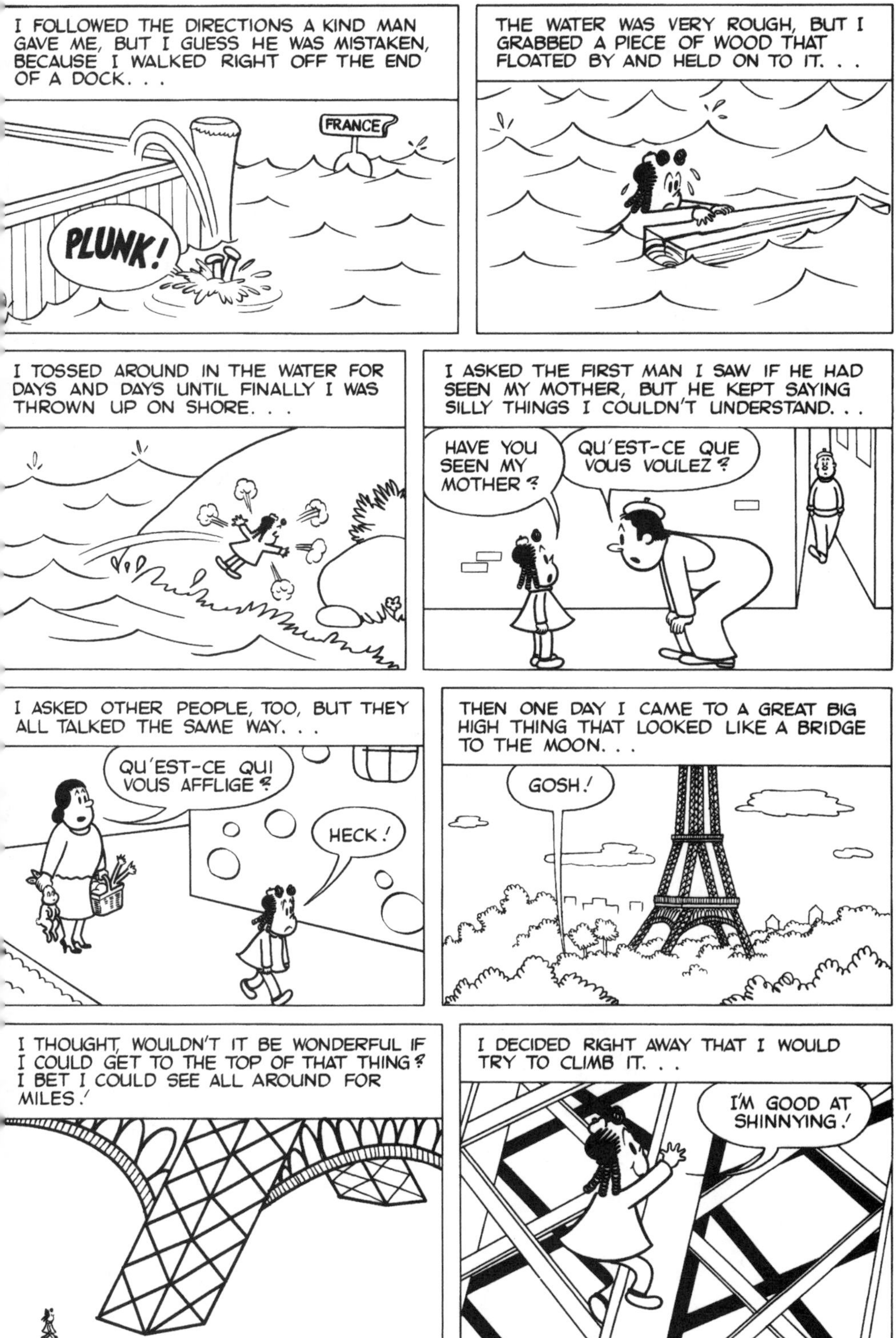
I FOLLOWED THE DIRECTIONS A KIND MAN GAVE ME, BUT I GUESS HE WAS MISTAKEN, BECAUSE I WALKED RIGHT OFF THE END OF A DOCK. . .
FRANCE
PLUNK!
THE WATER WAS VERY ROUGH, BUT I GRABBED A PIECE OF WOOD THAT FLOATED BY AND HELD ON TO IT. . .
I TOSSED AROUND IN THE WATER FOR DAYS AND DAYS UNTIL FINALLY I WAS THROWN UP ON SHORE. . .
I ASKED THE FIRST MAN I SAW IF HE HAD SEEN MY MOTHER, BUT HE KEPT SAYING SILLY THINGS I COULDN'T UNDERSTAND. . .
HAVE YOU SEEN MY MOTHER?
QU'EST-CE QUE VOUS VOULEZ?
I ASKED OTHER PEOPLE, TOO, BUT THEY ALL TALKED THE SAME WAY. . .
QU'EST-CE QUI VOUS AFFLIGE?
HECK!
THEN ONE DAY I CAME TO A GREAT BIG HIGH THING THAT LOOKED LIKE A BRIDGE TO THE MOON. . .
GOSH!
I THOUGHT, WOULDN'T IT BE WONDERFUL IF I COULD GET TO THE TOP OF THAT THING? I BET I COULD SEE ALL AROUND FOR MILES!
I DECIDED RIGHT AWAY THAT I WOULD TRY TO CLIMB IT. . .
I'M GOOD AT SHINNYING!

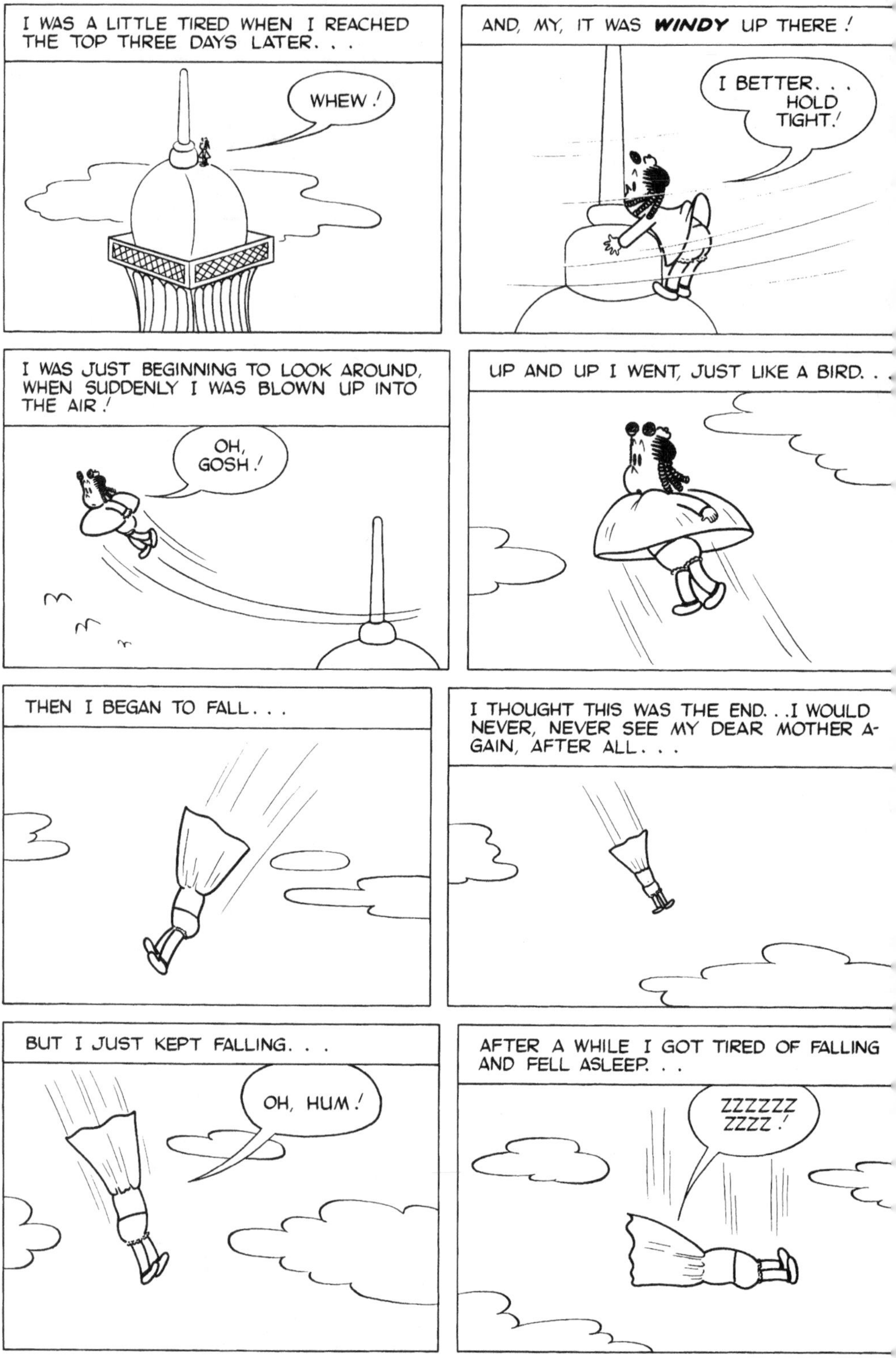
I WAS A LITTLE TIRED WHEN I REACHED THE TOP THREE DAYS LATER. . .
WHEW!
AND, MY, IT WAS **WINDY** UP THERE!
I BETTER. . . HOLD TIGHT!
I WAS JUST BEGINNING TO LOOK AROUND, WHEN SUDDENLY I WAS BLOWN UP INTO THE AIR!
OH, GOSH!
UP AND UP I WENT, JUST LIKE A BIRD. . .
THEN I BEGAN TO FALL. . .
I THOUGHT THIS WAS THE END. . .I WOULD NEVER, NEVER SEE MY DEAR MOTHER A-GAIN, AFTER ALL. . .
BUT I JUST KEPT FALLING. . .
OH, HUM!
AFTER A WHILE I GOT TIRED OF FALLING AND FELL ASLEEP. . .
ZZZZZZ ZZZZ!

I WOKE UP FOR A MOMENT WHEN I FELT MYSELF HITTING SOMETHING...

THEN I GUESS I WENT RIGHT BACK TO SLEEP AGAIN...

WHEN I WOKE UP AGAIN I SMELLED SOMETHING WONDERFUL COOKING...

MMMM...WHAT IS THAT *DELICIOUS* SMELL?

THEN I SAW THAT I WAS IN A GREAT BIG POT, AND THERE WAS A BUNCH OF CANNIBALS ALL AROUND ME!

YEEEEEEEOW!

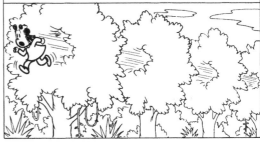

I HOLLERED AND JUMPED STRAIGHT UP OUT OF THE POT AND GRABBED THE BRANCH OF A TREE OVERHEAD!

THEN I RACED OFF THROUGH THE TREES JUST LIKE A MONKEY—ONLY BETTER, BECAUSE *I* DID IT "NO HANDS"!

BUT THE TREES CAME TO AN END SUDDENLY AND I FELL OFF INTO SOME SOFT SAND...

I GOT UP AND KEPT RUNNING...

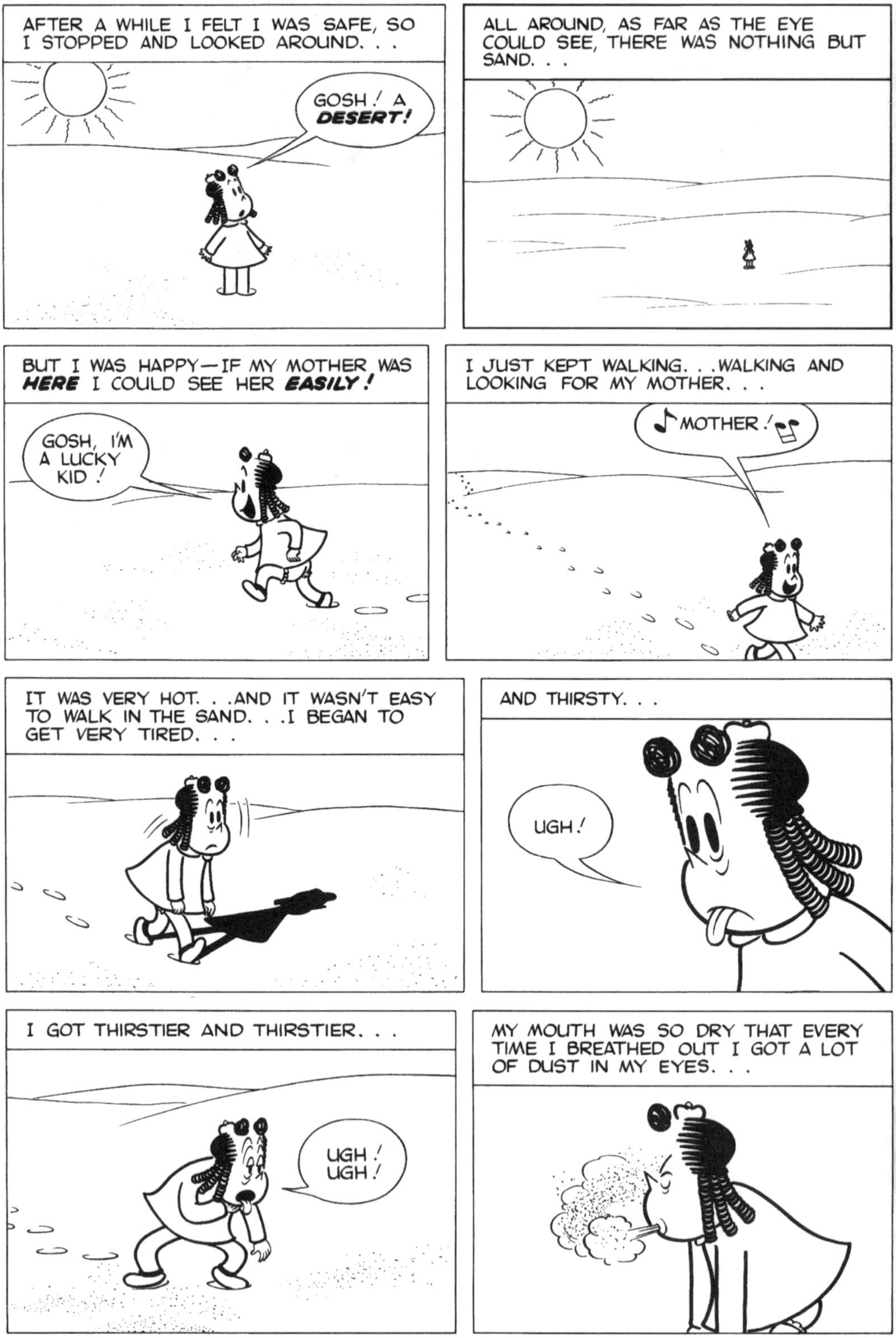
AFTER A WHILE I FELT I WAS SAFE, SO I STOPPED AND LOOKED AROUND. . .
GOSH! A DESERT!
ALL AROUND, AS FAR AS THE EYE COULD SEE, THERE WAS NOTHING BUT SAND. . .
BUT I WAS HAPPY—IF MY MOTHER WAS HERE I COULD SEE HER EASILY!
GOSH, I'M A LUCKY KID!
I JUST KEPT WALKING. . .WALKING AND LOOKING FOR MY MOTHER. . .
MOTHER!
IT WAS VERY HOT. . .AND IT WASN'T EASY TO WALK IN THE SAND. . .I BEGAN TO GET VERY TIRED. . .
AND THIRSTY. . .
UGH!
I GOT THIRSTIER AND THIRSTIER. . .
UGH! UGH!
MY MOUTH WAS SO DRY THAT EVERY TIME I BREATHED OUT I GOT A LOT OF DUST IN MY EYES. . .

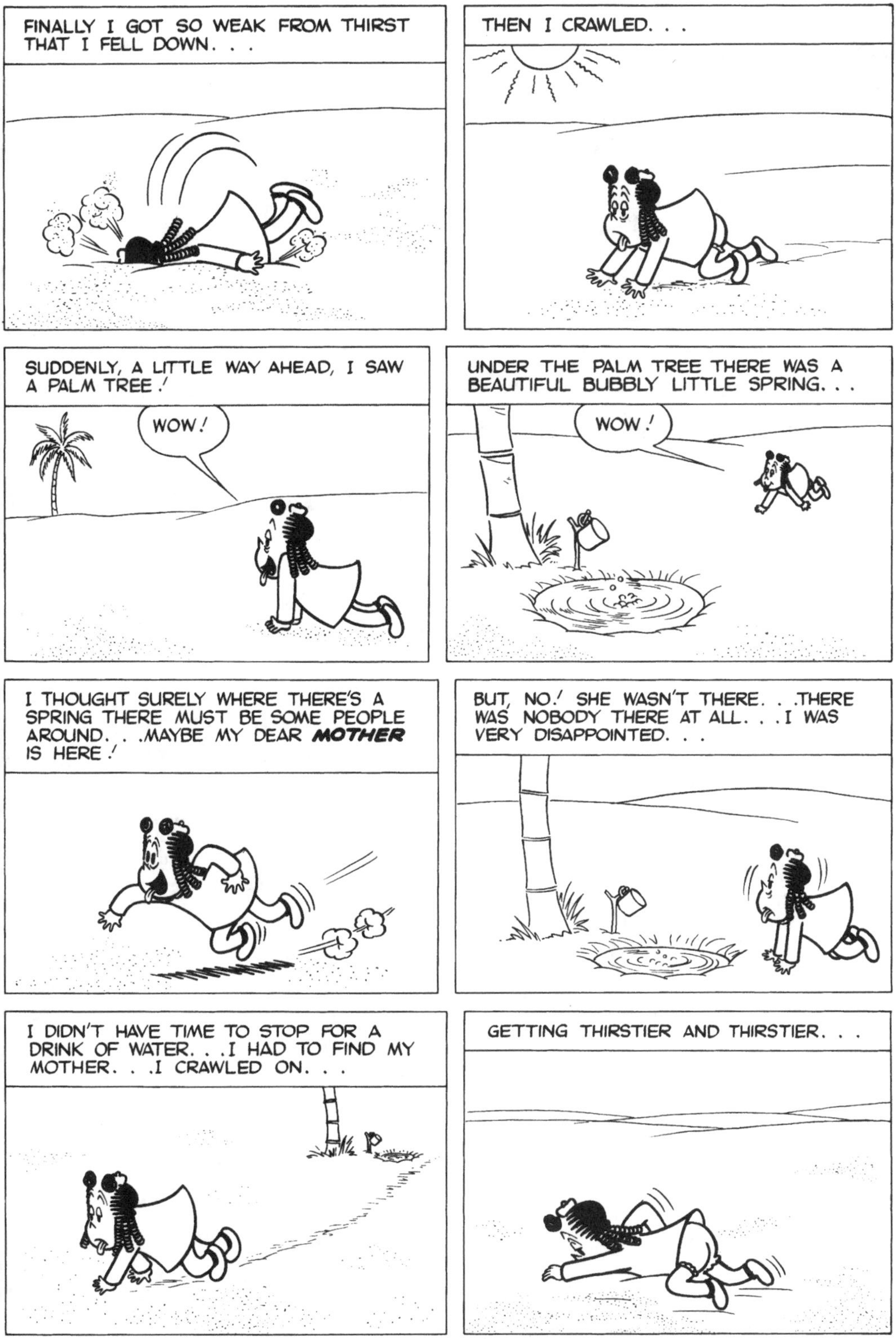
FINALLY I GOT SO WEAK FROM THIRST THAT I FELL DOWN. . .
THEN I CRAWLED. . .
SUDDENLY, A LITTLE WAY AHEAD, I SAW A PALM TREE!
WOW!
UNDER THE PALM TREE THERE WAS A BEAUTIFUL BUBBLY LITTLE SPRING. . .
WOW!
I THOUGHT SURELY WHERE THERE'S A SPRING THERE MUST BE SOME PEOPLE AROUND. . .MAYBE MY DEAR **MOTHER** IS HERE!
BUT, NO! SHE WASN'T THERE. . .THERE WAS NOBODY THERE AT ALL. . .I WAS VERY DISAPPOINTED. . .
I DIDN'T HAVE TIME TO STOP FOR A DRINK OF WATER. . .I HAD TO FIND MY MOTHER. . .I CRAWLED ON. . .
GETTING THIRSTIER AND THIRSTIER. . .

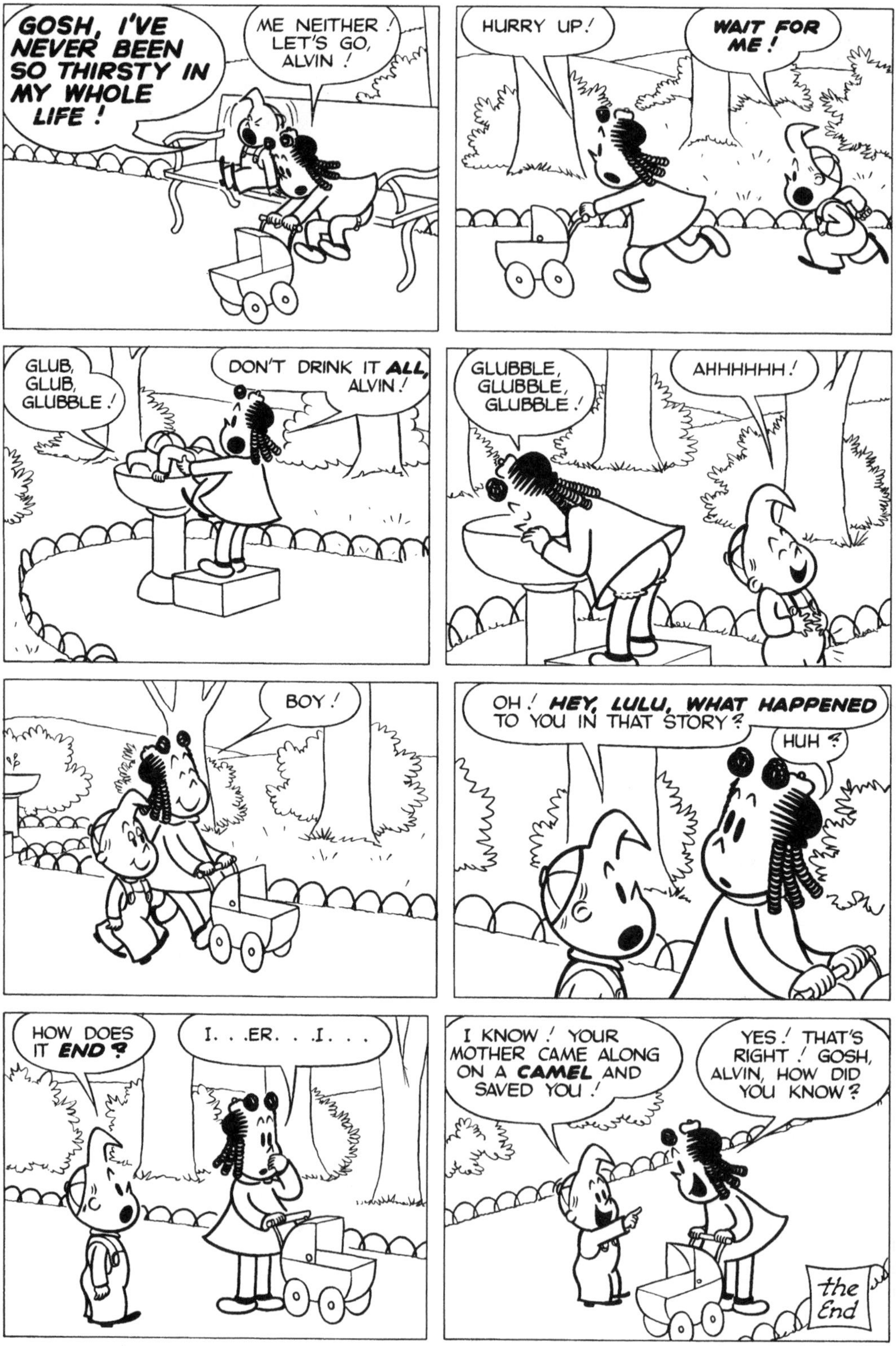
GOSH, I'VE NEVER BEEN SO THIRSTY IN MY WHOLE LIFE!
ME NEITHER! LET'S GO, ALVIN!
HURRY UP!
WAIT FOR ME!
GLUB, GLUB, GLUBBLE!
DON'T DRINK IT ALL, ALVIN!
GLUBBLE, GLUBBLE, GLUBBLE!
AHHHHHH!
BOY!
OH! HEY, LULU, WHAT HAPPENED TO YOU IN THAT STORY?
HUH?
HOW DOES IT END?
I. . .ER. . .I. . .
I KNOW! YOUR MOTHER CAME ALONG ON A CAMEL AND SAVED YOU!
YES! THAT'S RIGHT! GOSH, ALVIN, HOW DID YOU KNOW?
the End

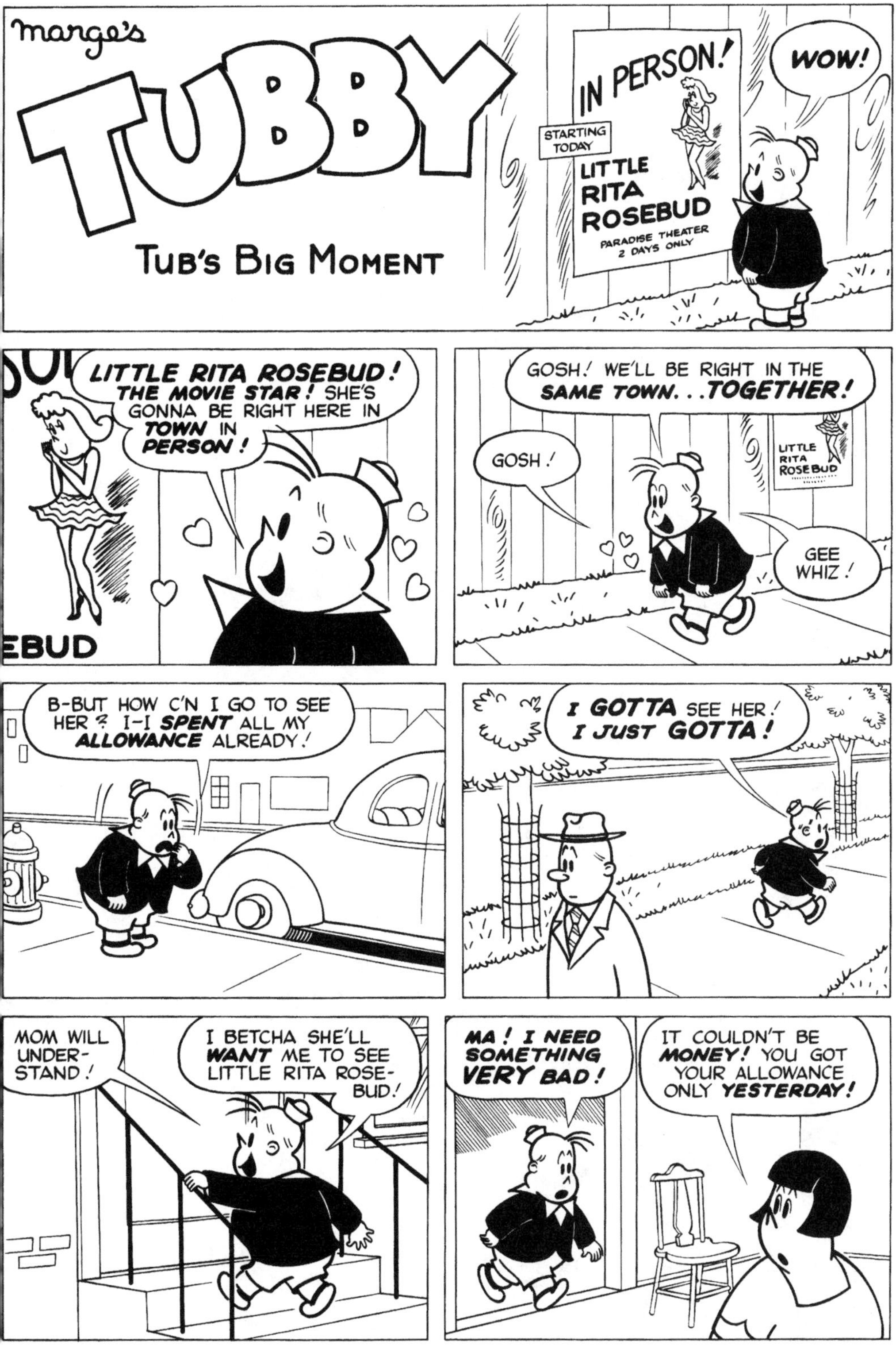
marge's
TUBBY
TUB'S BIG MOMENT
IN PERSON!
STARTING TODAY
LITTLE RITA ROSEBUD
PARADISE THEATER 2 DAYS ONLY
WOW!
LITTLE RITA ROSEBUD! THE MOVIE STAR! SHE'S GONNA BE RIGHT HERE IN TOWN IN PERSON!
GOSH! WE'LL BE RIGHT IN THE SAME TOWN. . .TOGETHER!
GOSH!
LITTLE RITA ROSEBUD
GEE WHIZ!
B-BUT HOW C'N I GO TO SEE HER? I-I SPENT ALL MY ALLOWANCE ALREADY!
I GOTTA SEE HER! I JUST GOTTA!
MOM WILL UNDER-STAND!
I BETCHA SHE'LL WANT ME TO SEE LITTLE RITA ROSE-BUD!
MA! I NEED SOMETHING VERY BAD!
IT COULDN'T BE MONEY! YOU GOT YOUR ALLOWANCE ONLY YESTERDAY!

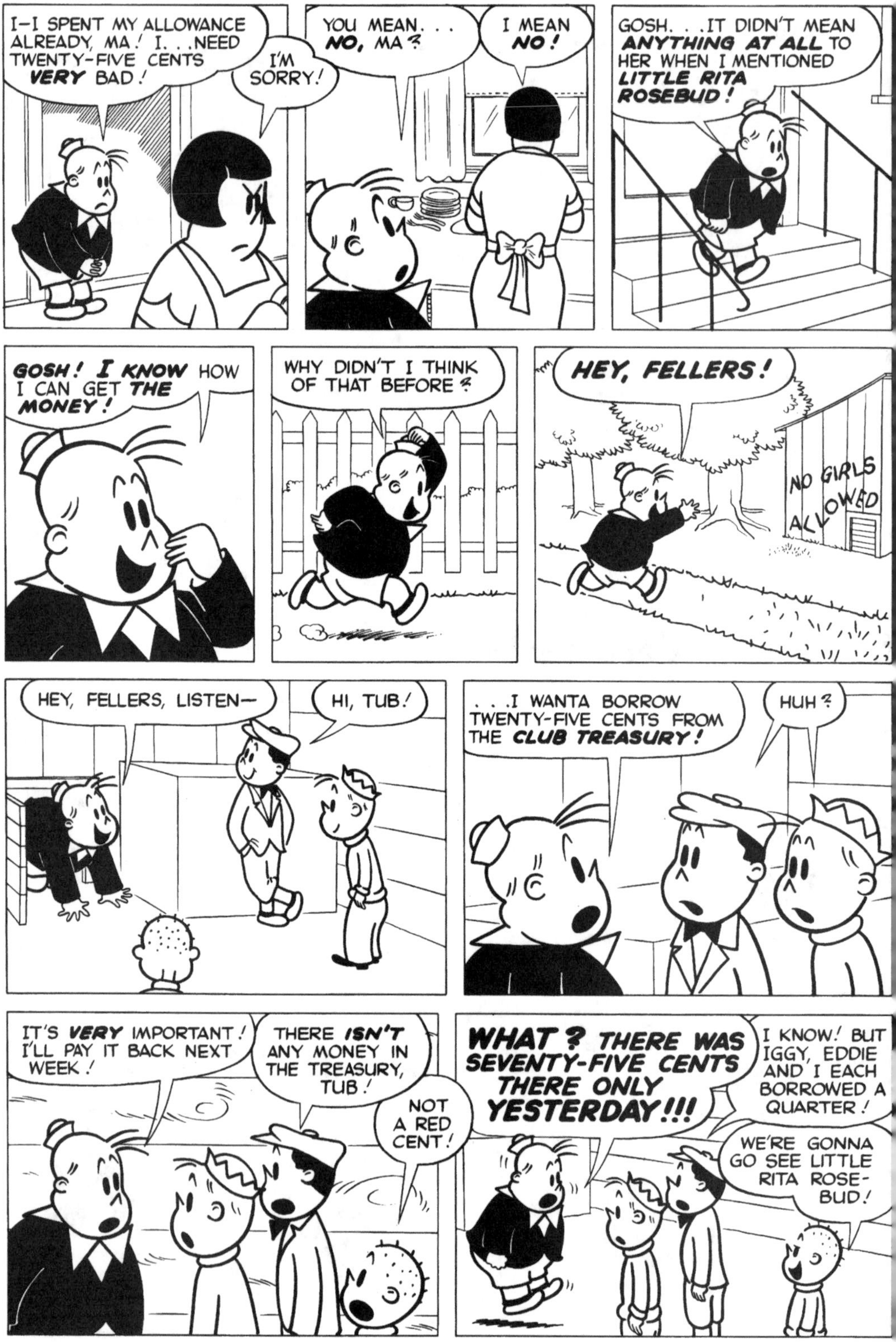

I–I SPENT MY ALLOWANCE ALREADY, MA! I. . .NEED TWENTY-FIVE CENTS **VERY** BAD!
I'M SORRY!
YOU MEAN. . . **NO,** MA?
I MEAN **NO!**
GOSH. . .IT DIDN'T MEAN **ANYTHING AT ALL** TO HER WHEN I MENTIONED **LITTLE RITA ROSEBUD!**
GOSH! I KNOW HOW I CAN GET **THE MONEY!**
WHY DIDN'T I THINK OF THAT BEFORE?
HEY, FELLERS!
NO GIRLS ALLOWED
HEY, FELLERS, LISTEN—
HI, TUB!
. . .I WANTA BORROW TWENTY-FIVE CENTS FROM THE **CLUB TREASURY!**
HUH?
IT'S **VERY** IMPORTANT! I'LL PAY IT BACK NEXT WEEK!
THERE **ISN'T** ANY MONEY IN THE TREASURY, TUB!
NOT A RED CENT!
WHAT? THERE WAS SEVENTY-FIVE CENTS THERE ONLY YESTERDAY!!!
I KNOW! BUT IGGY, EDDIE AND I EACH BORROWED A QUARTER!
WE'RE GONNA GO SEE LITTLE RITA ROSE-BUD!

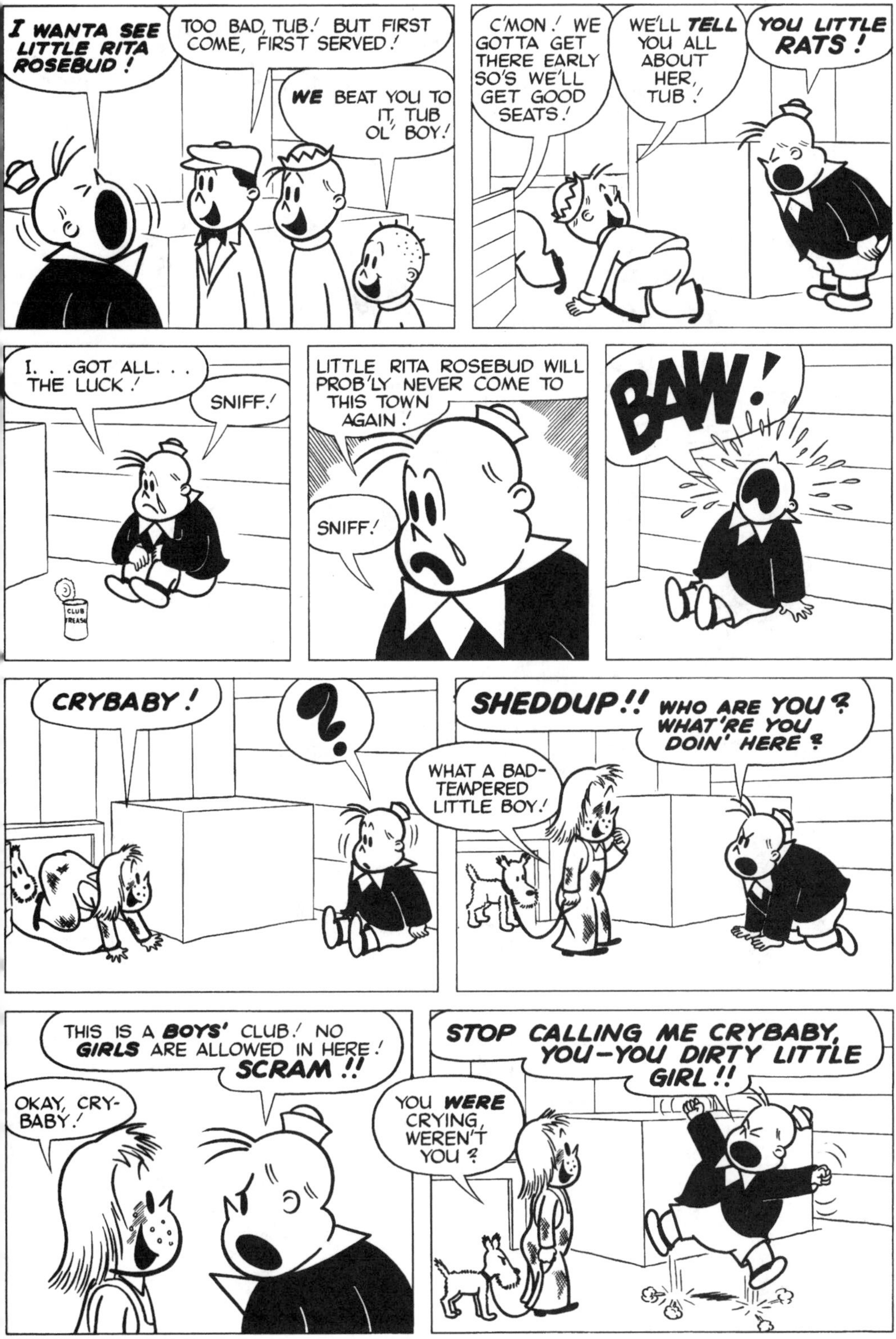
I WANTA SEE LITTLE RITA ROSEBUD!
TOO BAD, TUB! BUT FIRST COME, FIRST SERVED!
WE BEAT YOU TO IT, TUB OL' BOY!
C'MON! WE GOTTA GET THERE EARLY SO'S WE'LL GET GOOD SEATS!
WE'LL TELL YOU ALL ABOUT HER, TUB!
YOU LITTLE RATS!
I. . .GOT ALL. . . THE LUCK!
SNIFF!
CLUB TREASU
LITTLE RITA ROSEBUD WILL PROB'LY NEVER COME TO THIS TOWN AGAIN!
SNIFF!
BAW!
CRYBABY!
?
SHEDDUP!! WHO ARE YOU? WHAT'RE YOU DOIN' HERE?
WHAT A BAD-TEMPERED LITTLE BOY!
THIS IS A BOYS' CLUB! NO GIRLS ARE ALLOWED IN HERE! SCRAM!!
OKAY, CRY-BABY!
STOP CALLING ME CRYBABY, YOU—YOU DIRTY LITTLE GIRL!!
YOU WERE CRYING, WEREN'T YOU?

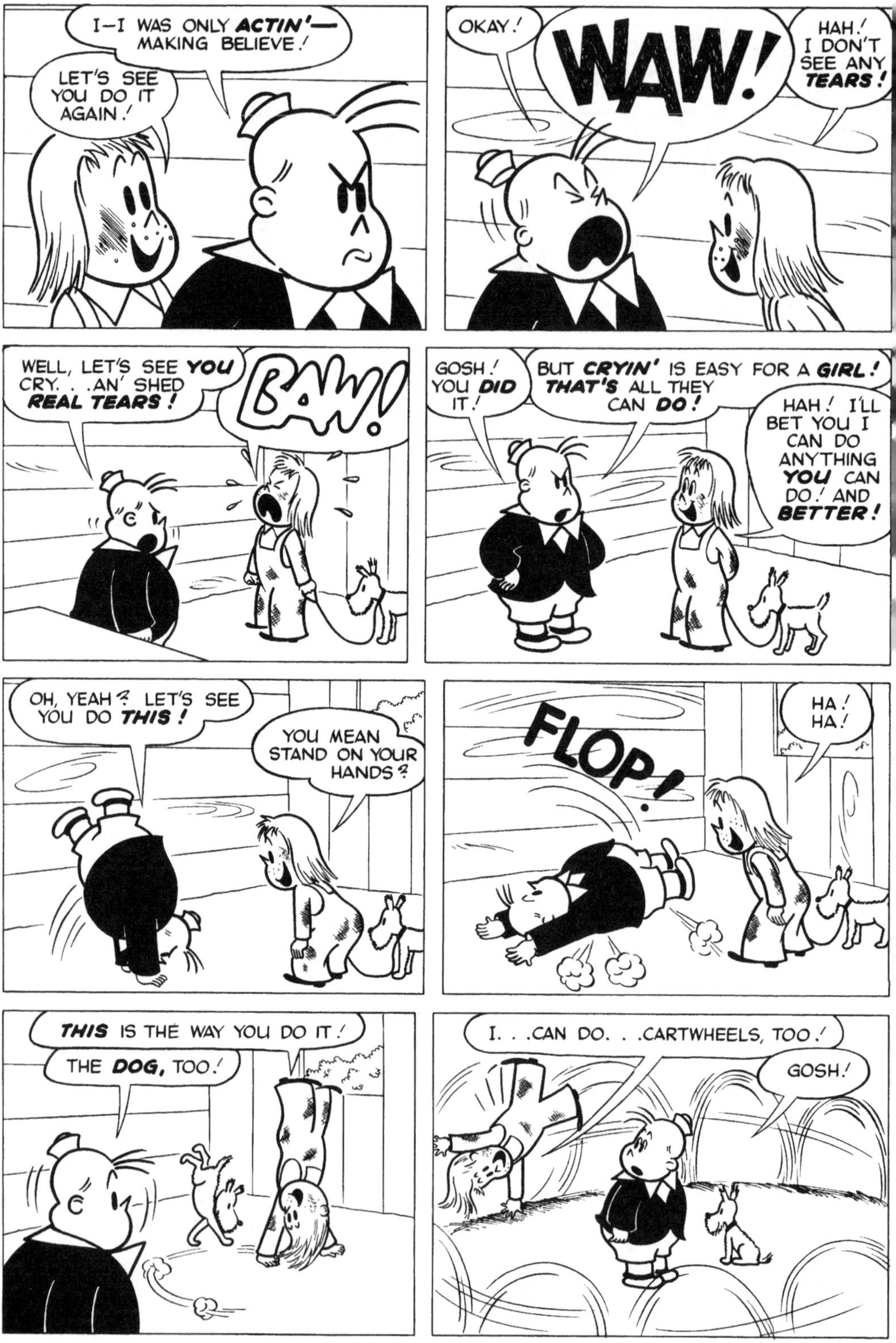
I—I WAS ONLY ACTIN'— MAKING BELIEVE!
LET'S SEE YOU DO IT AGAIN!
OKAY!
WAW!
HAH! I DON'T SEE ANY TEARS!
WELL, LET'S SEE YOU CRY. . .AN' SHED REAL TEARS!
BAW!
GOSH! YOU DID IT!
BUT CRYIN' IS EASY FOR A GIRL! THAT'S ALL THEY CAN DO!
HAH! I'LL BET YOU I CAN DO ANYTHING YOU CAN DO! AND BETTER!
OH, YEAH? LET'S SEE YOU DO THIS!
YOU MEAN STAND ON YOUR HANDS?
FLOP!
HA! HA!
THIS IS THE WAY YOU DO IT!
THE DOG, TOO!
I. . .CAN DO. . .CARTWHEELS, TOO!
GOSH!

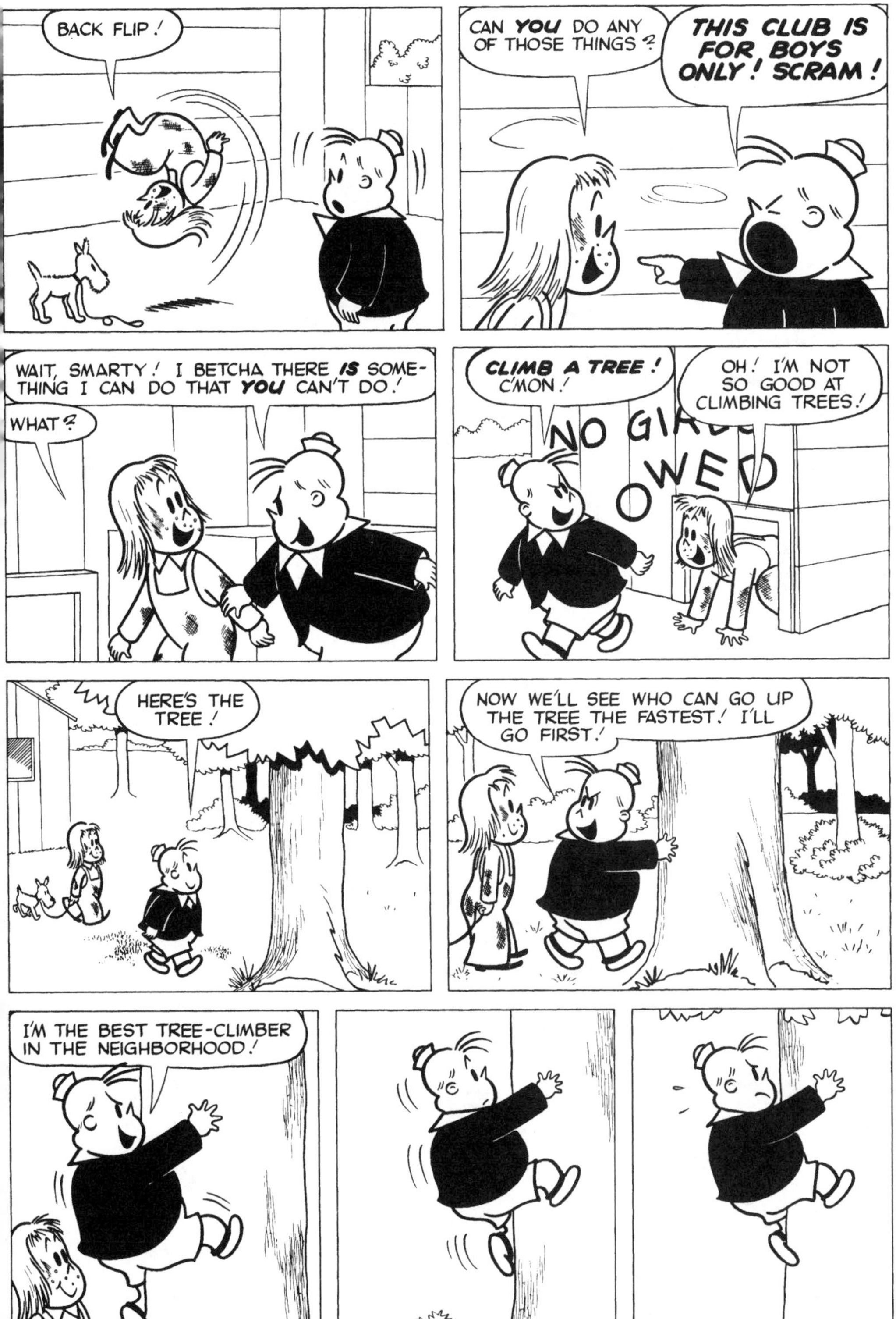
BACK FLIP!
CAN YOU DO ANY OF THOSE THINGS?
THIS CLUB IS FOR BOYS ONLY! SCRAM!
WAIT, SMARTY! I BETCHA THERE IS SOME-THING I CAN DO THAT YOU CAN'T DO!
WHAT?
CLIMB A TREE! C'MON!
NO GI
OWED
OH! I'M NOT SO GOOD AT CLIMBING TREES!
HERE'S THE TREE!
NOW WE'LL SEE WHO CAN GO UP THE TREE THE FASTEST! I'LL GO FIRST!
I'M THE BEST TREE-CLIMBER IN THE NEIGHBORHOOD!

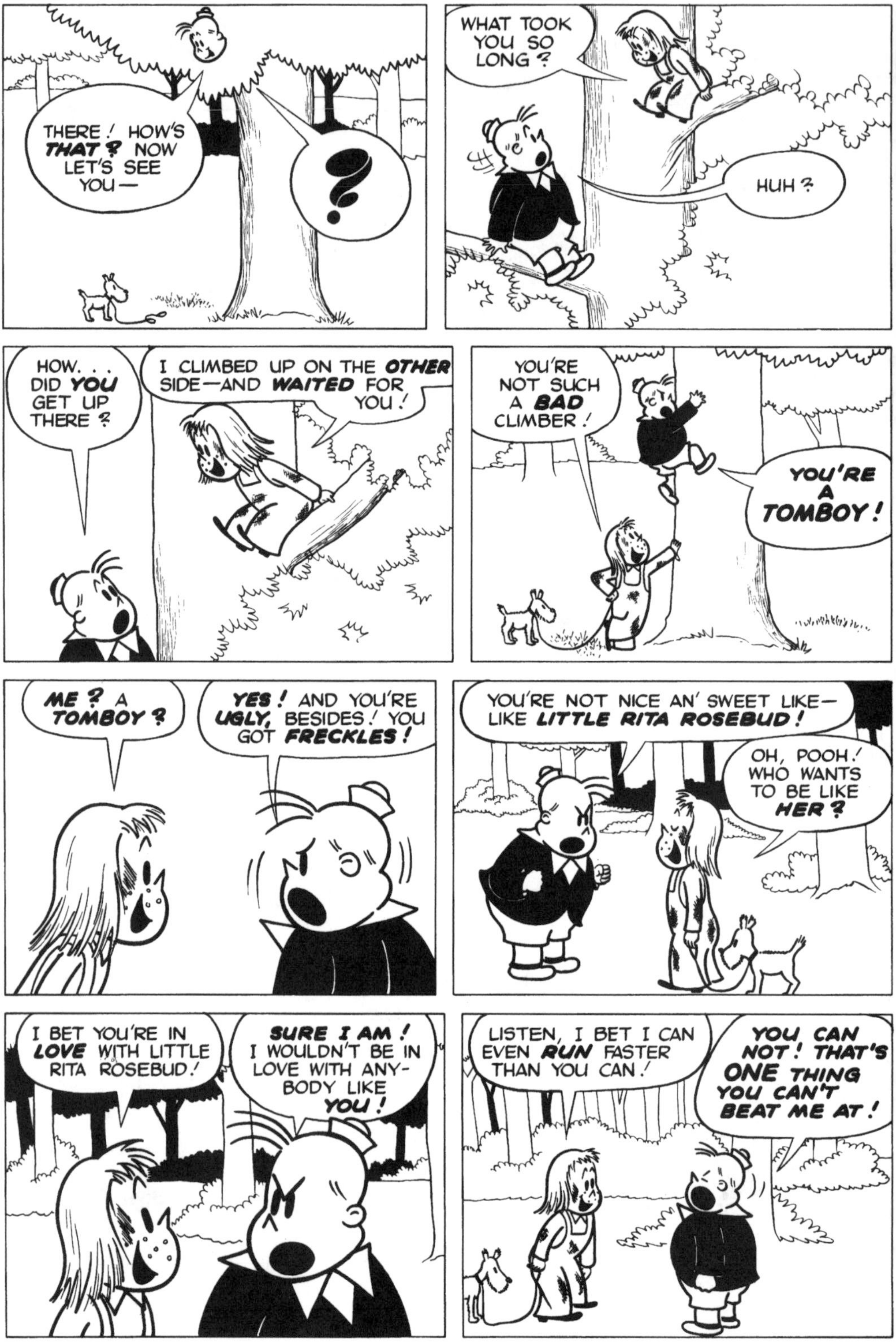
THERE! HOW'S THAT? NOW LET'S SEE YOU—
?
WHAT TOOK YOU SO LONG?
HUH?
HOW. . . DID YOU GET UP THERE?
I CLIMBED UP ON THE OTHER SIDE—AND WAITED FOR YOU!
YOU'RE NOT SUCH A BAD CLIMBER!
YOU'RE A TOMBOY!
ME? A TOMBOY?
YES! AND YOU'RE UGLY, BESIDES! YOU GOT FRECKLES!
YOU'RE NOT NICE AN' SWEET LIKE— LIKE LITTLE RITA ROSEBUD!
OH, POOH! WHO WANTS TO BE LIKE HER?
I BET YOU'RE IN LOVE WITH LITTLE RITA ROSEBUD!
SURE I AM! I WOULDN'T BE IN LOVE WITH ANY-BODY LIKE YOU!
LISTEN, I BET I CAN EVEN RUN FASTER THAN YOU CAN!
YOU CAN NOT! THAT'S ONE THING YOU CAN'T BEAT ME AT!

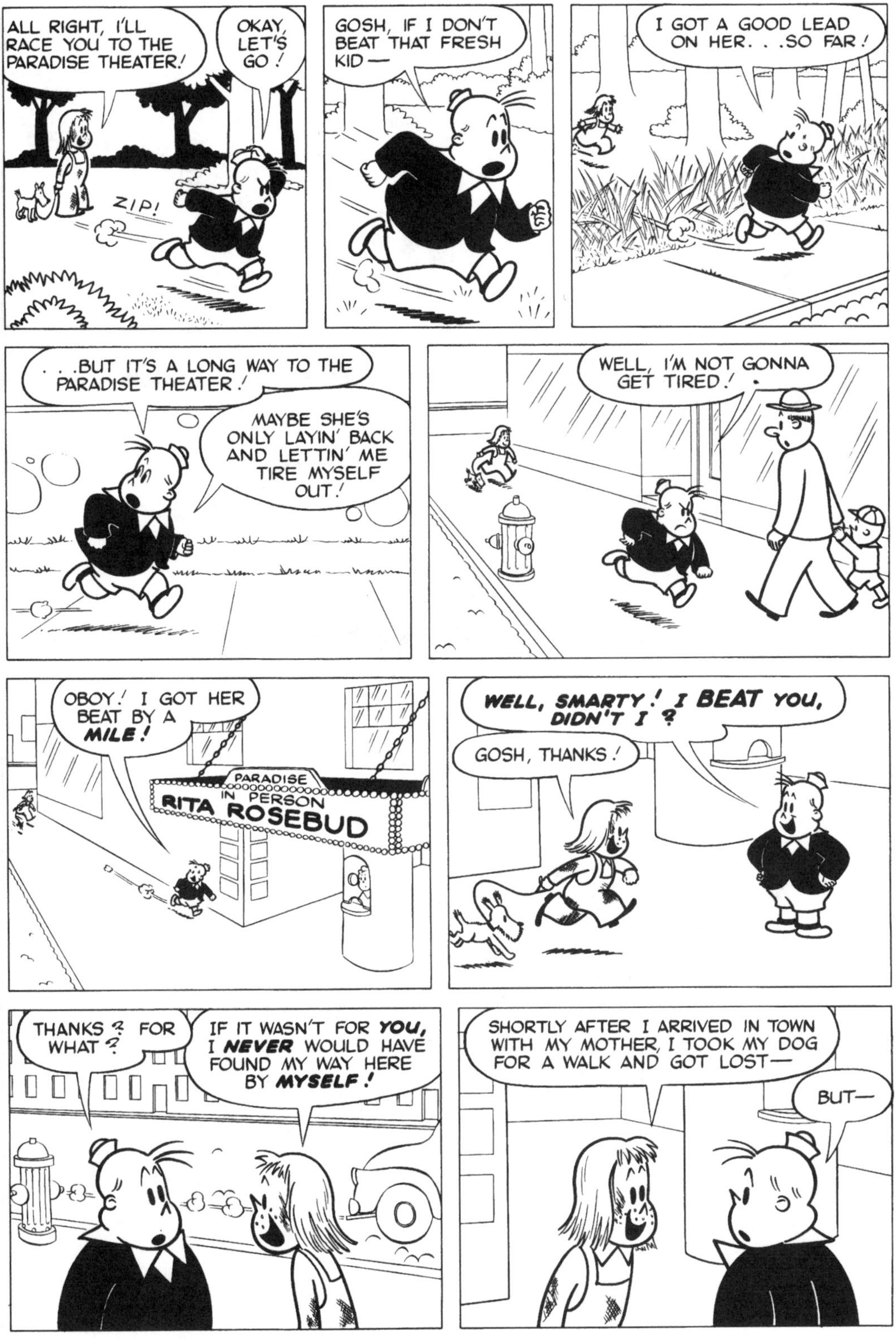
ALL RIGHT, I'LL RACE YOU TO THE PARADISE THEATER!
OKAY, LET'S GO!
ZIP!
GOSH, IF I DON'T BEAT THAT FRESH KID—
I GOT A GOOD LEAD ON HER. . .SO FAR!
. . .BUT IT'S A LONG WAY TO THE PARADISE THEATER!
MAYBE SHE'S ONLY LAYIN' BACK AND LETTIN' ME TIRE MYSELF OUT!
WELL, I'M NOT GONNA GET TIRED!
OBOY! I GOT HER BEAT BY A MILE!
PARADISE
IN PERSON
RITA ROSEBUD
WELL, SMARTY! I BEAT YOU, DIDN'T I?
GOSH, THANKS!
THANKS? FOR WHAT?
IF IT WASN'T FOR YOU, I NEVER WOULD HAVE FOUND MY WAY HERE BY MYSELF!
SHORTLY AFTER I ARRIVED IN TOWN WITH MY MOTHER, I TOOK MY DOG FOR A WALK AND GOT LOST—
BUT—

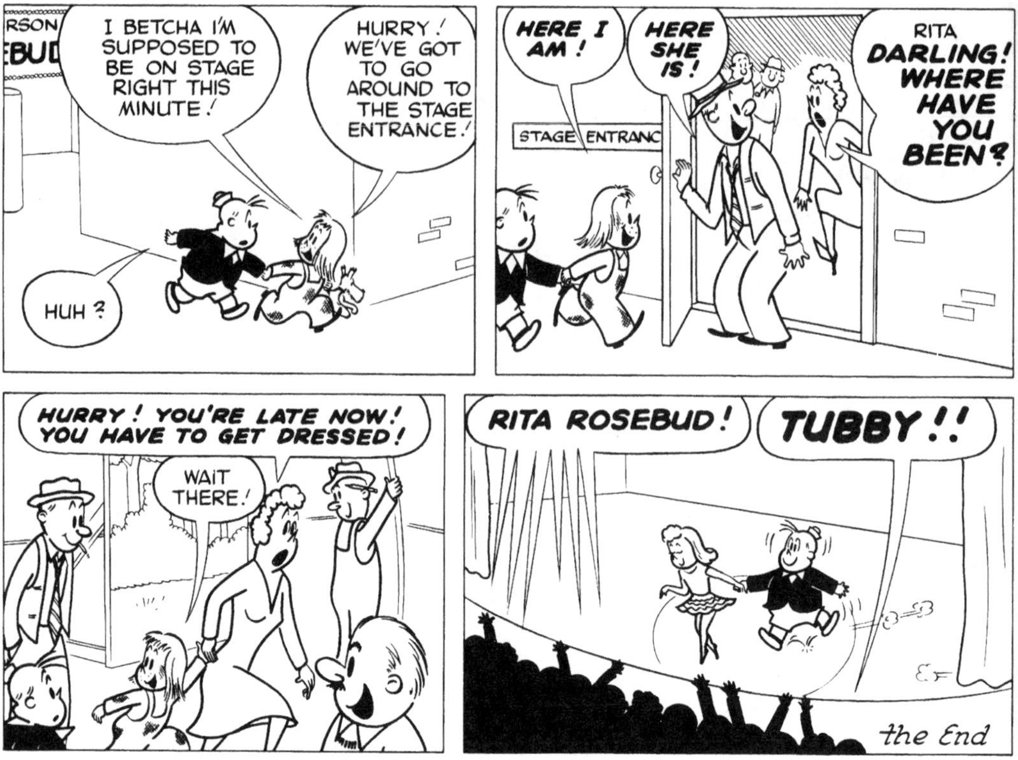
RSON
BUD
I BETCHA I'M SUPPOSED TO BE ON STAGE RIGHT THIS MINUTE!
HURRY! WE'VE GOT TO GO AROUND TO THE STAGE ENTRANCE!
HUH?
HERE I AM!
HERE SHE IS!
RITA DARLING! WHERE HAVE YOU BEEN?
STAGE ENTRANC
HURRY! YOU'RE LATE NOW! YOU HAVE TO GET DRESSED!
WAIT THERE!
RITA ROSEBUD!
TUBBY!!
the End

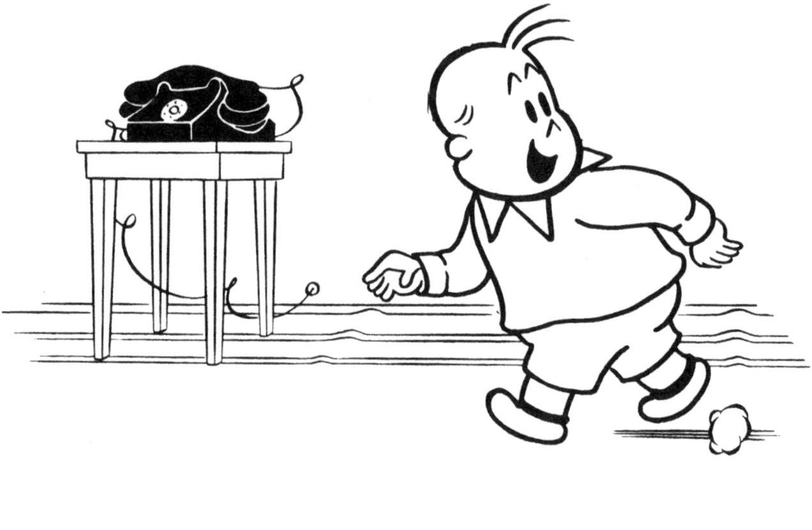

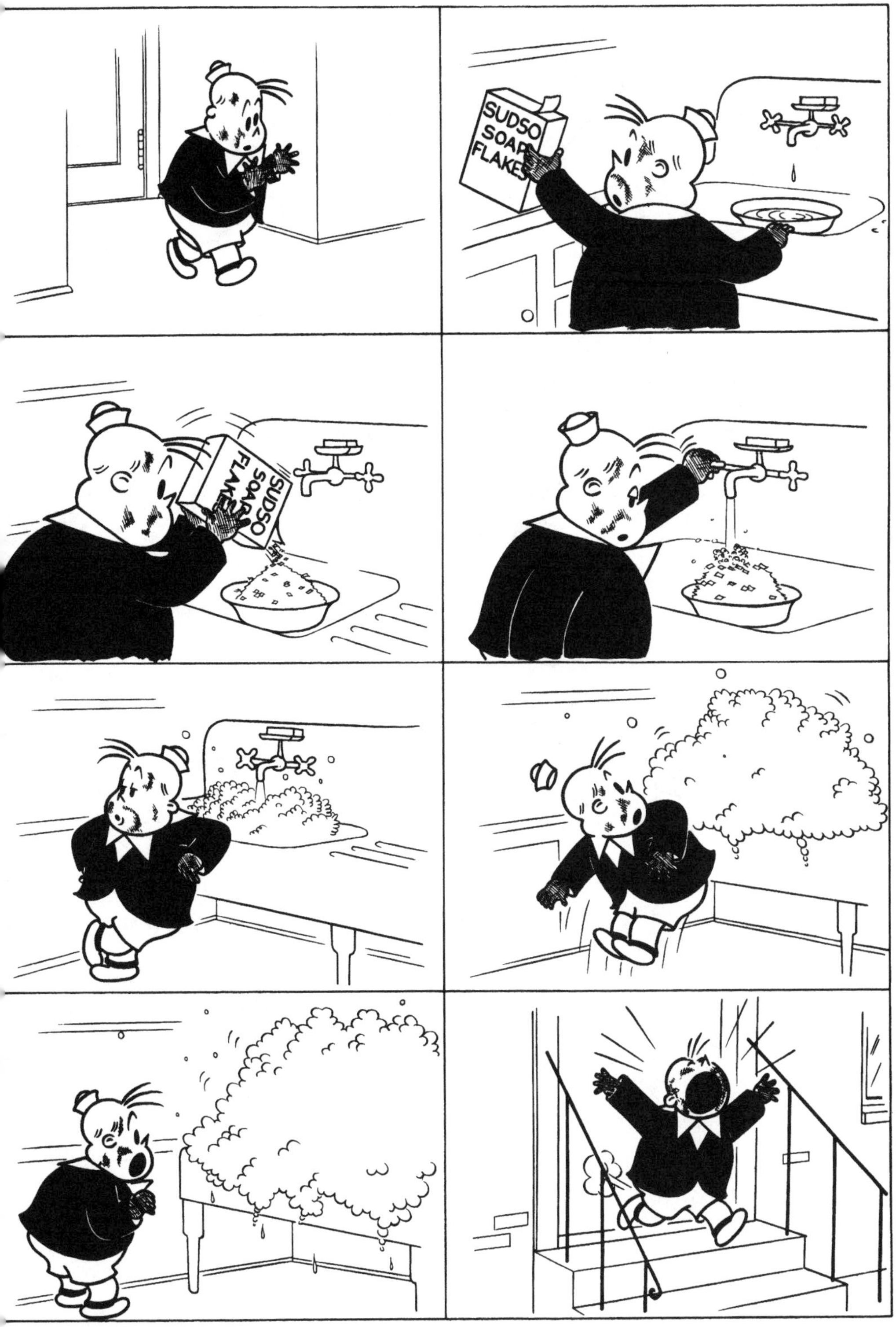
SUDSO SOAP FLAKES

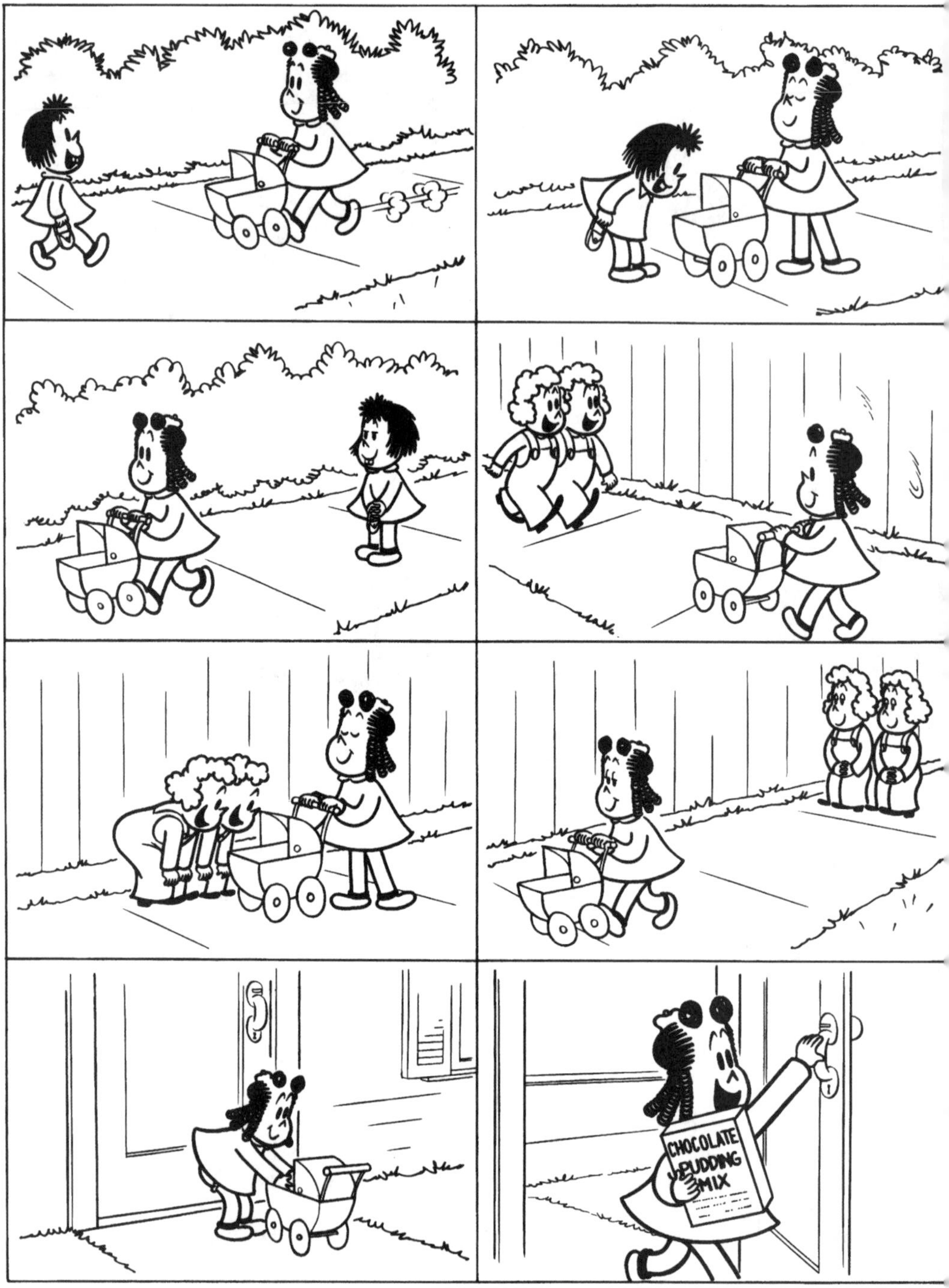
CHOCOLATE
PUDDING
MIX

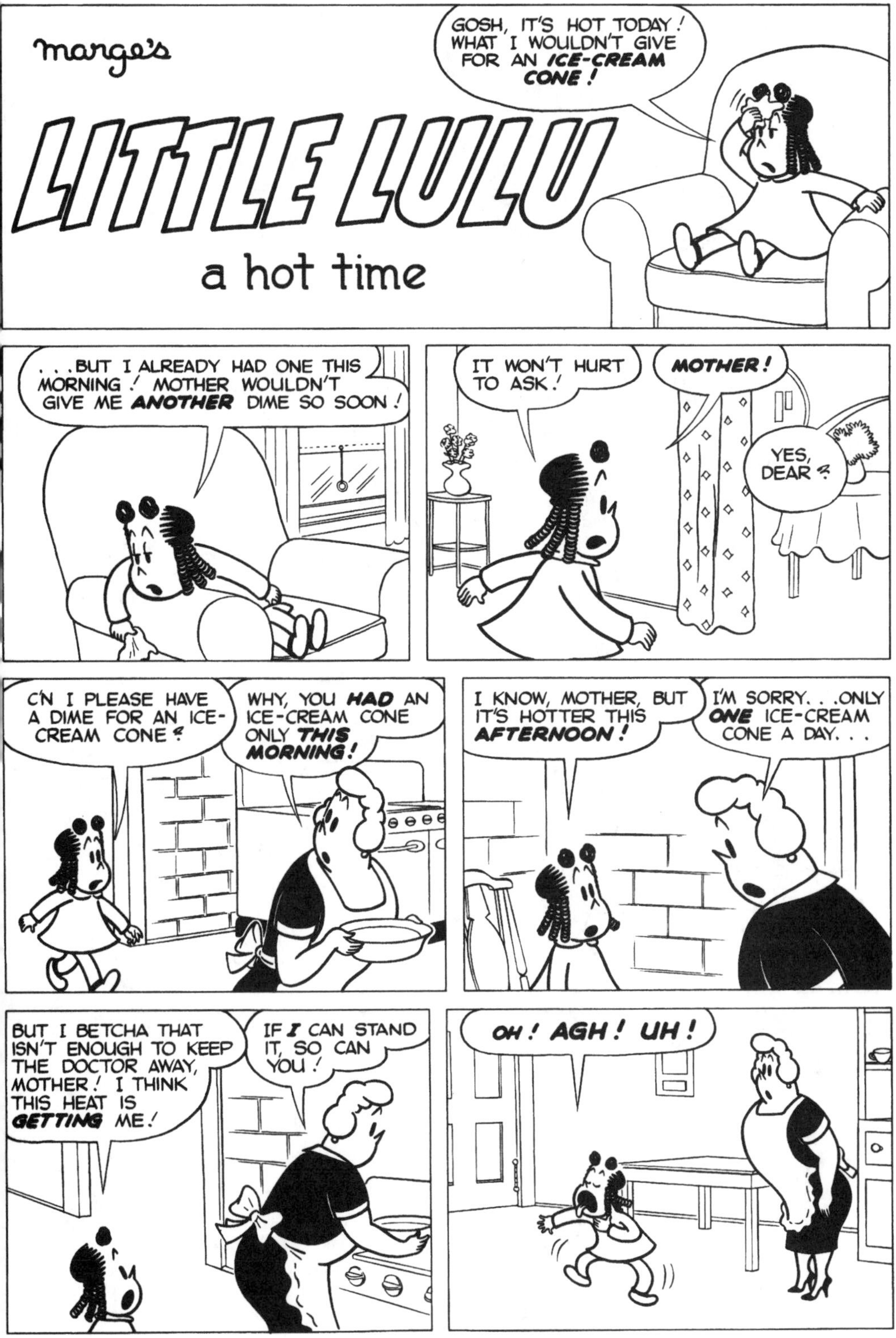
marge's
LITTLE LULU
a hot time
GOSH, IT'S HOT TODAY! WHAT I WOULDN'T GIVE FOR AN ICE-CREAM CONE!
. . .BUT I ALREADY HAD ONE THIS MORNING! MOTHER WOULDN'T GIVE ME ANOTHER DIME SO SOON!
IT WON'T HURT TO ASK!
MOTHER!
YES, DEAR?
C'N I PLEASE HAVE A DIME FOR AN ICE-CREAM CONE?
WHY, YOU HAD AN ICE-CREAM CONE ONLY THIS MORNING!
I KNOW, MOTHER, BUT IT'S HOTTER THIS AFTERNOON!
I'M SORRY. . .ONLY ONE ICE-CREAM CONE A DAY. . .
BUT I BETCHA THAT ISN'T ENOUGH TO KEEP THE DOCTOR AWAY, MOTHER! I THINK THIS HEAT IS GETTING ME!
IF I CAN STAND IT, SO CAN YOU!
OH! AGH! UH!

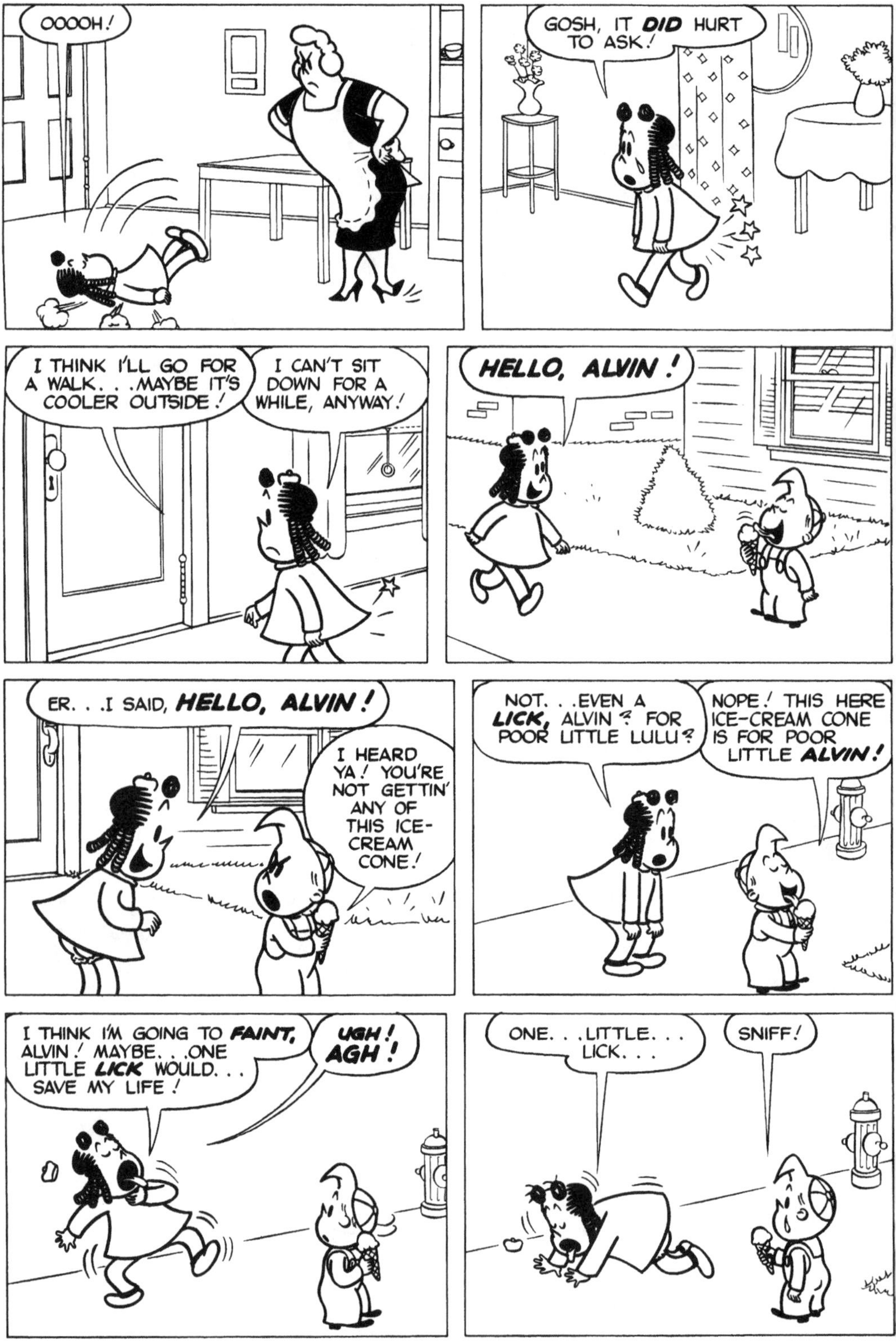
OOOOH!
GOSH, IT DID HURT TO ASK!
I THINK I'LL GO FOR A WALK. . .MAYBE IT'S COOLER OUTSIDE!
I CAN'T SIT DOWN FOR A WHILE, ANYWAY!
HELLO, ALVIN!
ER. . .I SAID, HELLO, ALVIN!
I HEARD YA! YOU'RE NOT GETTIN' ANY OF THIS ICE-CREAM CONE!
NOT. . .EVEN A LICK, ALVIN? FOR POOR LITTLE LULU?
NOPE! THIS HERE ICE-CREAM CONE IS FOR POOR LITTLE ALVIN!
I THINK I'M GOING TO FAINT, ALVIN! MAYBE. . .ONE LITTLE LICK WOULD. . . SAVE MY LIFE!
UGH! AGH!
ONE. . .LITTLE. . . LICK. . .
SNIFF!

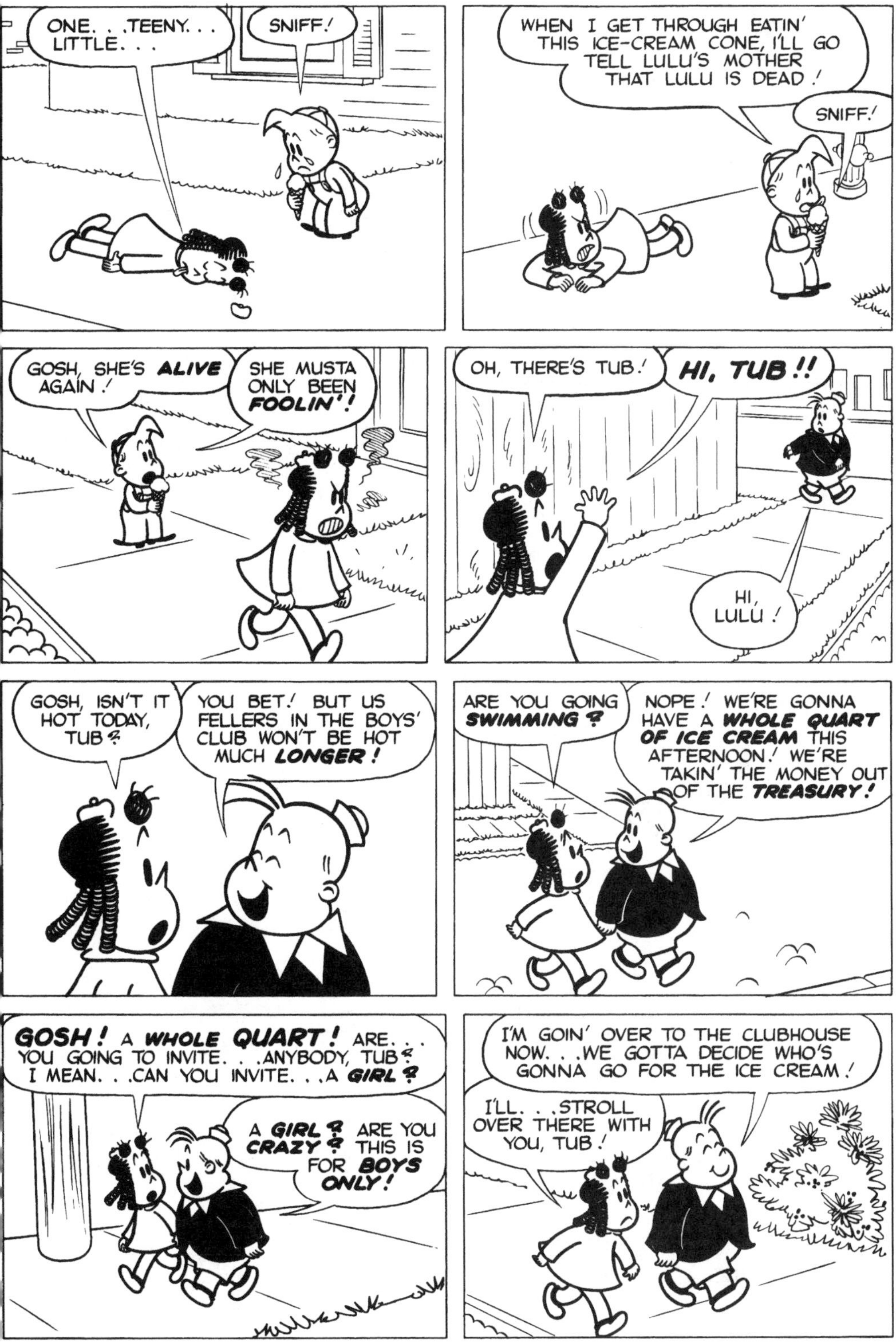
ONE. . .TEENY. . . LITTLE. . .
SNIFF!
WHEN I GET THROUGH EATIN' THIS ICE-CREAM CONE, I'LL GO TELL LULU'S MOTHER THAT LULU IS DEAD!
SNIFF!
GOSH, SHE'S ALIVE AGAIN!
SHE MUSTA ONLY BEEN FOOLIN'!
OH, THERE'S TUB!
HI, TUB!!
HI, LULU!
GOSH, ISN'T IT HOT TODAY, TUB?
YOU BET! BUT US FELLERS IN THE BOYS' CLUB WON'T BE HOT MUCH LONGER!
ARE YOU GOING SWIMMING?
NOPE! WE'RE GONNA HAVE A WHOLE QUART OF ICE CREAM THIS AFTERNOON! WE'RE TAKIN' THE MONEY OUT OF THE TREASURY!
GOSH! A WHOLE QUART! ARE. . . YOU GOING TO INVITE. . .ANYBODY, TUB? I MEAN. . .CAN YOU INVITE. . .A GIRL?
A GIRL? ARE YOU CRAZY? THIS IS FOR BOYS ONLY!
I'M GOIN' OVER TO THE CLUBHOUSE NOW. . .WE GOTTA DECIDE WHO'S GONNA GO FOR THE ICE CREAM!
I'LL. . .STROLL OVER THERE WITH YOU, TUB!

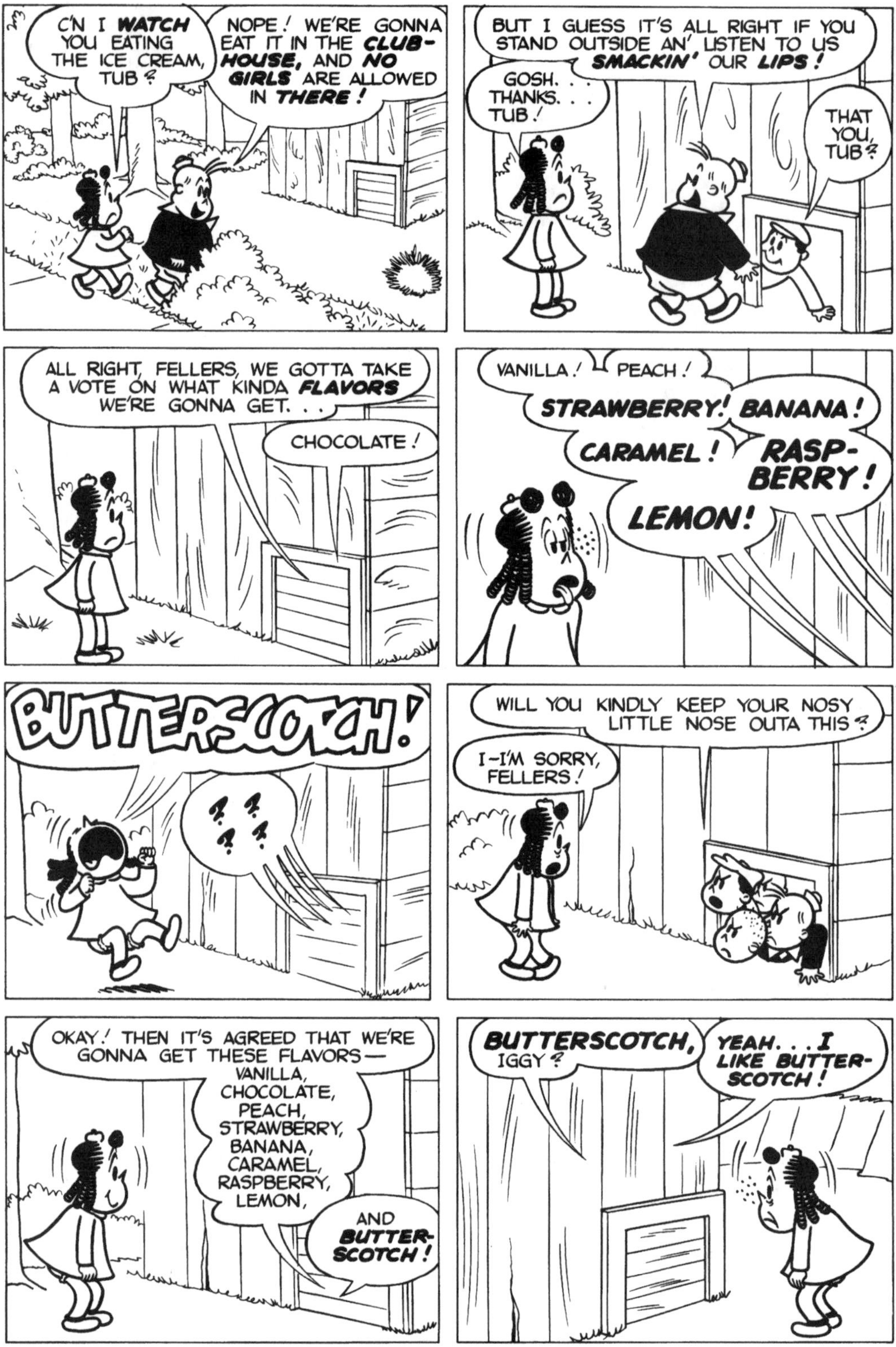
C'N I WATCH YOU EATING THE ICE CREAM, TUB?
NOPE! WE'RE GONNA EAT IT IN THE CLUB-HOUSE, AND NO GIRLS ARE ALLOWED IN THERE!
BUT I GUESS IT'S ALL RIGHT IF YOU STAND OUTSIDE AN' LISTEN TO US SMACKIN' OUR LIPS!
GOSH. . . THANKS. . . TUB!
THAT YOU, TUB?
ALL RIGHT, FELLERS, WE GOTTA TAKE A VOTE ON WHAT KINDA FLAVORS WE'RE GONNA GET. . .
CHOCOLATE!
VANILLA!
PEACH!
STRAWBERRY!
BANANA!
CARAMEL!
RASP-BERRY!
LEMON!
BUTTERSCOTCH!
WILL YOU KINDLY KEEP YOUR NOSY LITTLE NOSE OUTA THIS?
I-I'M SORRY, FELLERS!
OKAY! THEN IT'S AGREED THAT WE'RE GONNA GET THESE FLAVORS— VANILLA, CHOCOLATE, PEACH, STRAWBERRY, BANANA, CARAMEL, RASPBERRY, LEMON,
AND BUTTER-SCOTCH!
BUTTERSCOTCH, IGGY?
YEAH. . . I LIKE BUTTER-SCOTCH!

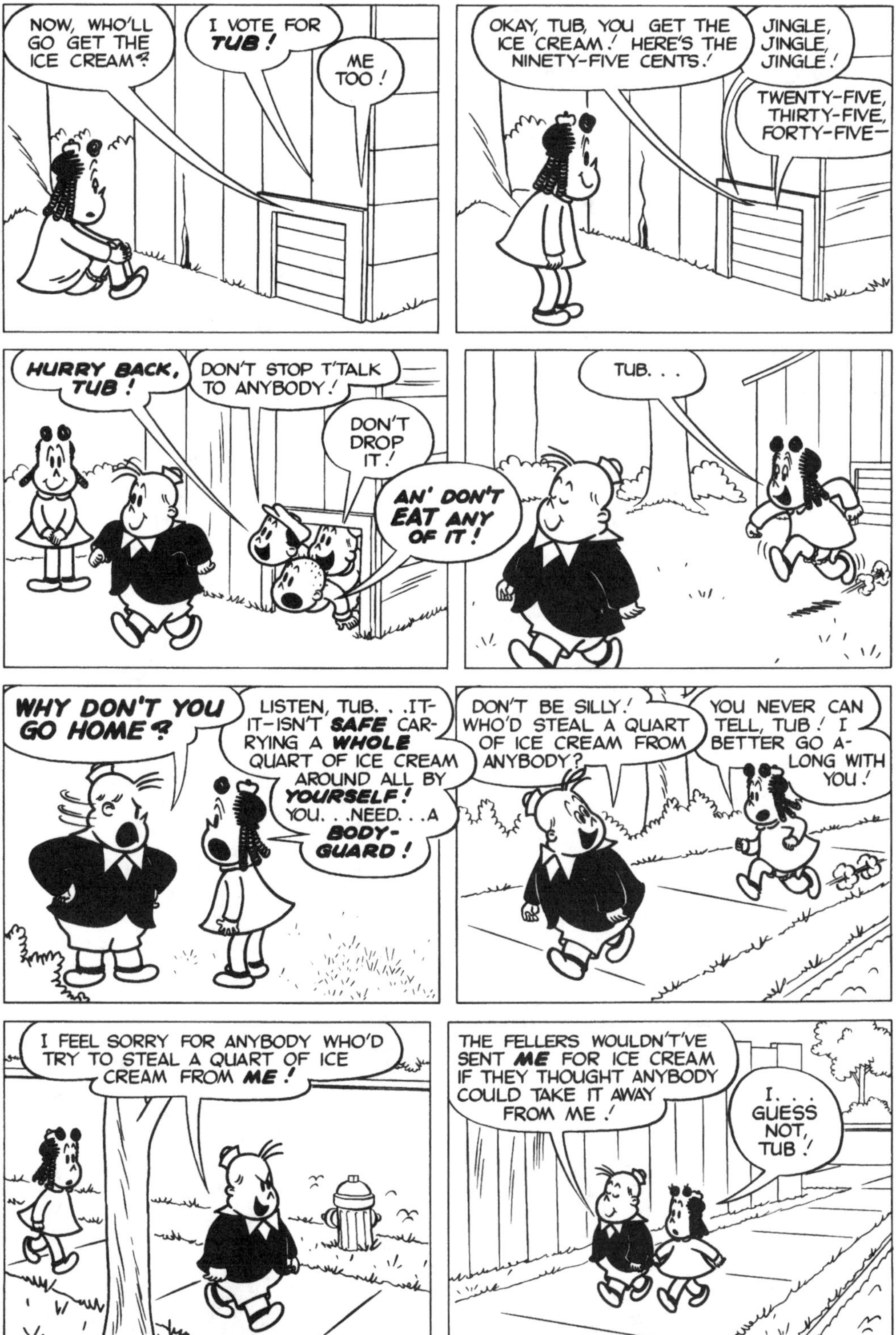
NOW, WHO'LL GO GET THE ICE CREAM?
I VOTE FOR TUB!
ME TOO!
OKAY, TUB, YOU GET THE ICE CREAM! HERE'S THE NINETY-FIVE CENTS!
JINGLE, JINGLE, JINGLE!
TWENTY-FIVE, THIRTY-FIVE, FORTY-FIVE—
HURRY BACK, TUB!
DON'T STOP T'TALK TO ANYBODY!
DON'T DROP IT!
AN' DON'T EAT ANY OF IT!
TUB. . .
WHY DON'T YOU GO HOME?
LISTEN, TUB. . .IT-IT-ISN'T SAFE CARRYING A WHOLE QUART OF ICE CREAM AROUND ALL BY YOURSELF! YOU. . .NEED. . .A BODY-GUARD!
DON'T BE SILLY! WHO'D STEAL A QUART OF ICE CREAM FROM ANYBODY?
YOU NEVER CAN TELL, TUB! I BETTER GO A-LONG WITH YOU!
I FEEL SORRY FOR ANYBODY WHO'D TRY TO STEAL A QUART OF ICE CREAM FROM ME!
THE FELLERS WOULDN'T'VE SENT ME FOR ICE CREAM IF THEY THOUGHT ANYBODY COULD TAKE IT AWAY FROM ME!
I. . . GUESS NOT, TUB!

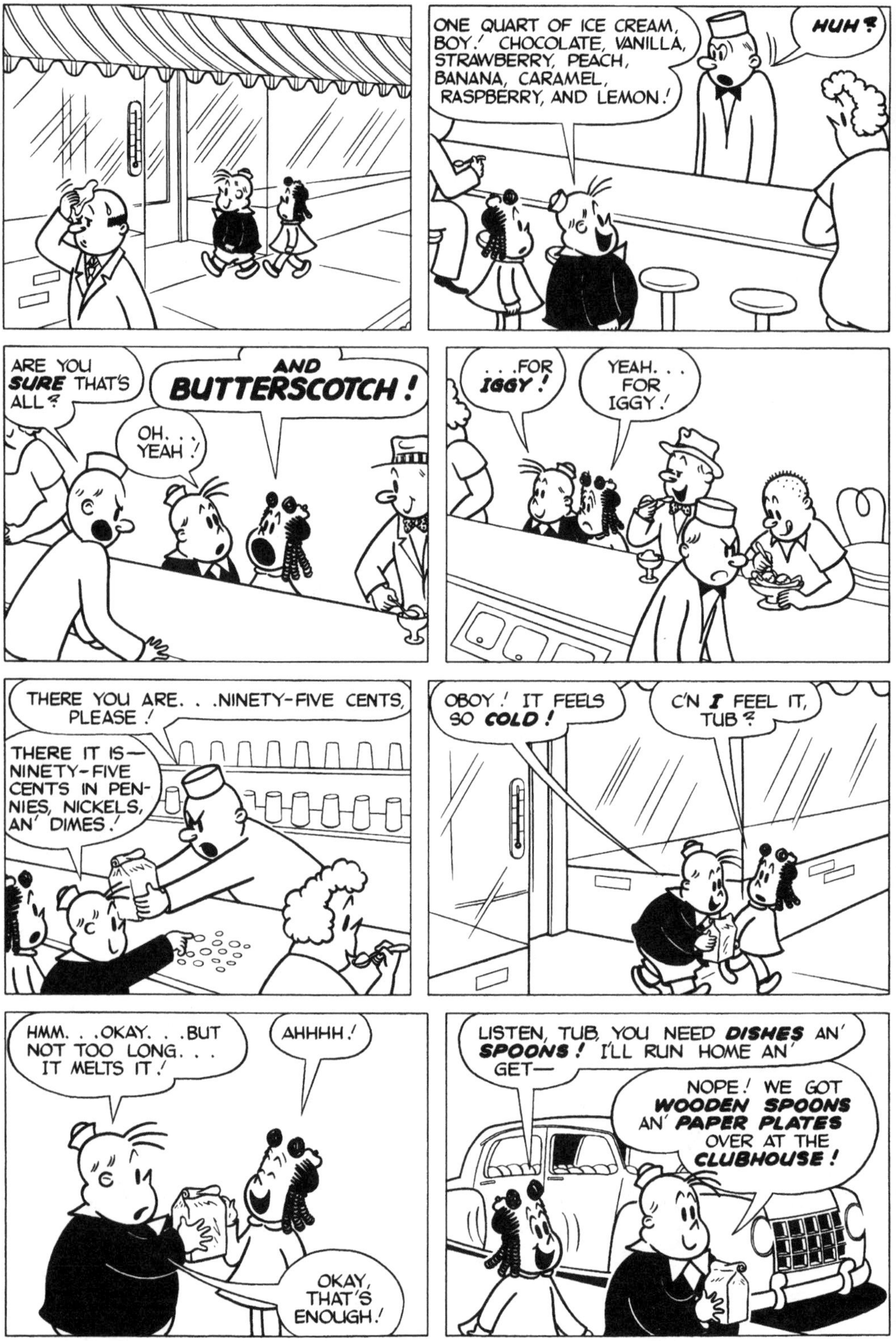
ONE QUART OF ICE CREAM, BOY.! CHOCOLATE, VANILLA, STRAWBERRY, PEACH, BANANA, CARAMEL, RASPBERRY, AND LEMON.!
HUH?
ARE YOU SURE THAT'S ALL?
AND BUTTERSCOTCH!
OH. . . YEAH.!
. . .FOR IGGY!
YEAH. . . FOR IGGY.!
THERE YOU ARE. . .NINETY-FIVE CENTS, PLEASE!
THERE IT IS—NINETY-FIVE CENTS IN PENNIES, NICKELS, AN' DIMES.!
OBOY! IT FEELS SO COLD!
C'N I FEEL IT, TUB?
HMM. . .OKAY. . .BUT NOT TOO LONG. . . IT MELTS IT.!
AHHHH.!
OKAY, THAT'S ENOUGH.!
LISTEN, TUB, YOU NEED DISHES AN' SPOONS! I'LL RUN HOME AN' GET—
NOPE! WE GOT WOODEN SPOONS AN' PAPER PLATES OVER AT THE CLUBHOUSE!

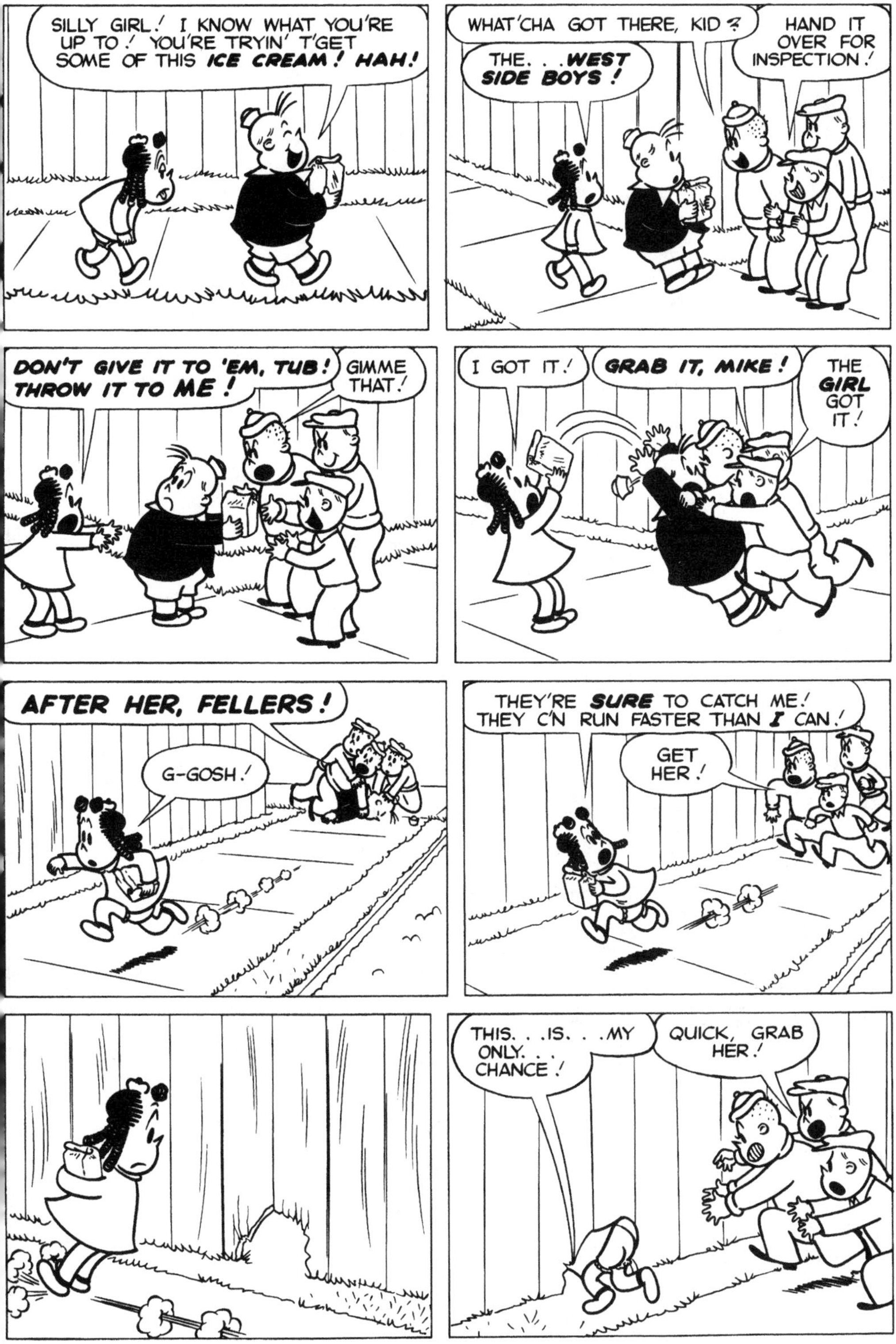
SILLY GIRL! I KNOW WHAT YOU'RE UP TO! YOU'RE TRYIN' T'GET SOME OF THIS ICE CREAM! HAH!
WHAT'CHA GOT THERE, KID?
THE. . .WEST SIDE BOYS!
HAND IT OVER FOR INSPECTION!
DON'T GIVE IT TO 'EM, TUB! THROW IT TO ME!
GIMME THAT!
I GOT IT!
GRAB IT, MIKE!
THE GIRL GOT IT!
AFTER HER, FELLERS!
G-GOSH!
THEY'RE SURE TO CATCH ME! THEY C'N RUN FASTER THAN I CAN!
GET HER!
THIS. . .IS. . .MY ONLY. . . CHANCE!
QUICK, GRAB HER!

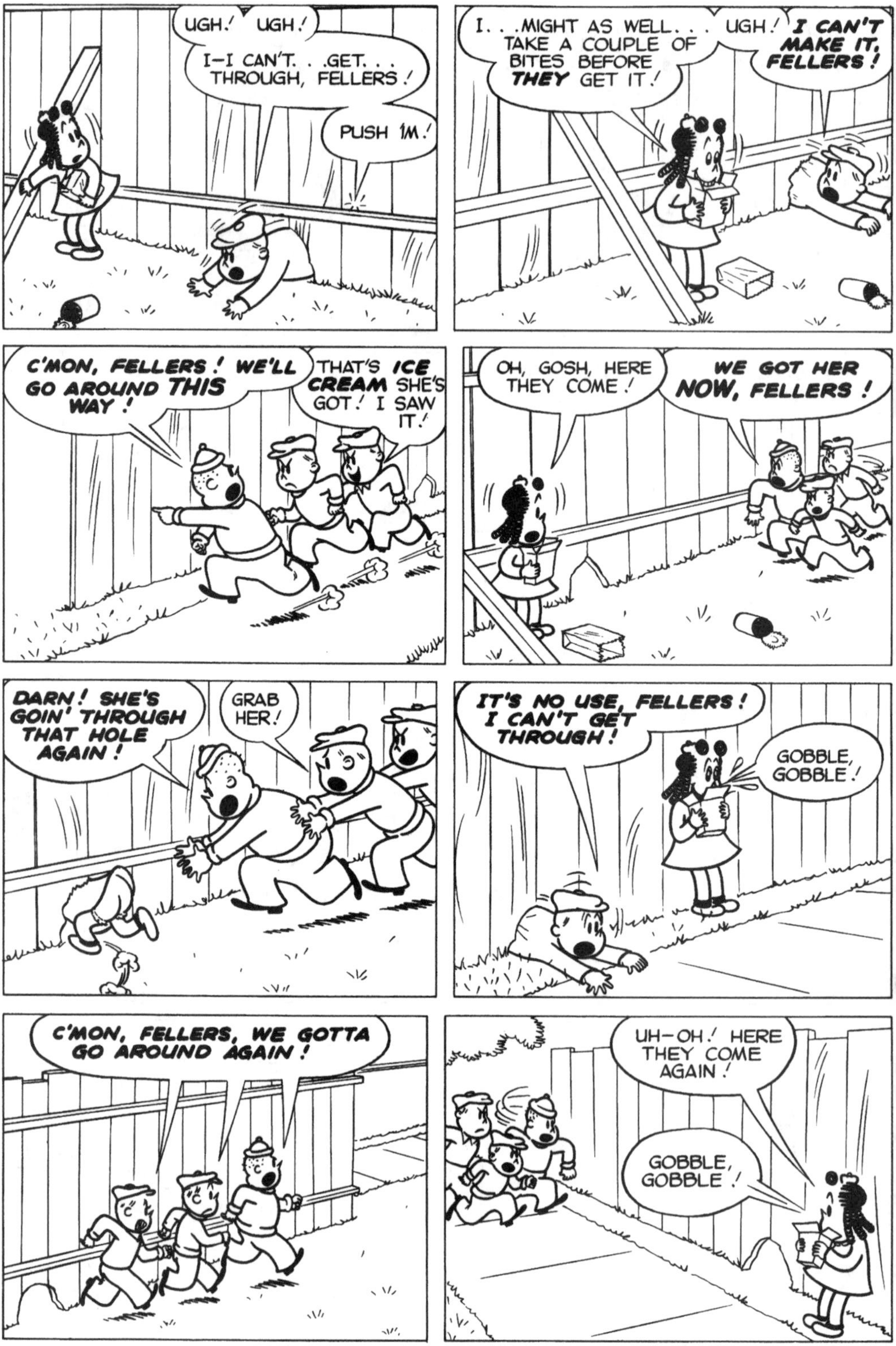
UGH.! UGH.!
I—I CAN'T. . .GET. . . THROUGH, FELLERS.!
PUSH 'IM.!
I. . .MIGHT AS WELL. . . TAKE A COUPLE OF BITES BEFORE THEY GET IT.!
UGH.! I CAN'T MAKE IT, FELLERS!
C'MON, FELLERS! WE'LL GO AROUND THIS WAY!
THAT'S ICE CREAM SHE'S GOT! I SAW IT!
OH, GOSH, HERE THEY COME!
WE GOT HER NOW, FELLERS!
DARN! SHE'S GOIN' THROUGH THAT HOLE AGAIN!
GRAB HER!
IT'S NO USE, FELLERS! I CAN'T GET THROUGH!
GOBBLE, GOBBLE!
C'MON, FELLERS, WE GOTTA GO AROUND AGAIN!
UH-OH! HERE THEY COME AGAIN!
GOBBLE, GOBBLE!

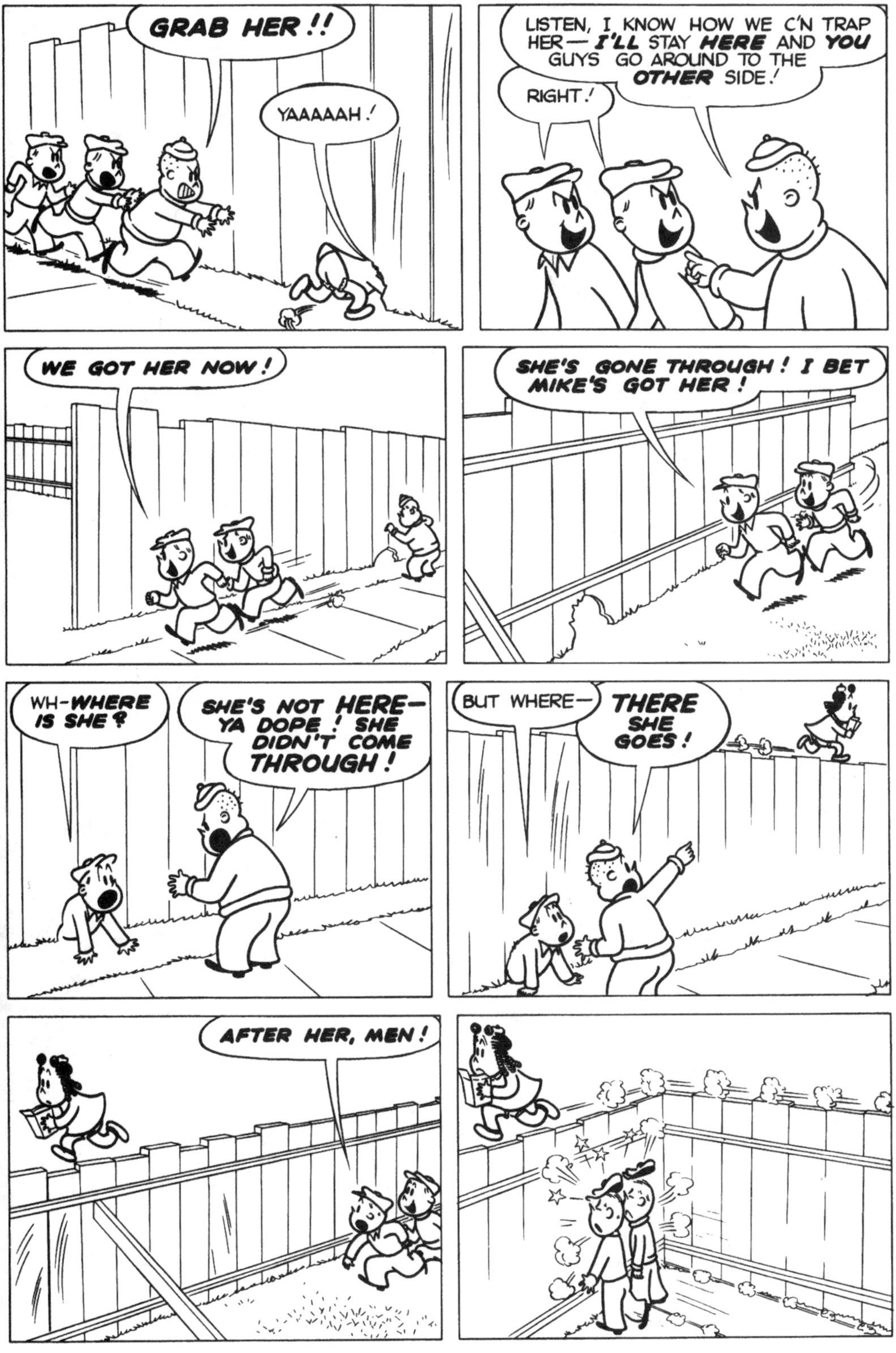
GRAB HER !!
YAAAAAH !
LISTEN, I KNOW HOW WE C'N TRAP HER— I'LL STAY HERE AND YOU GUYS GO AROUND TO THE OTHER SIDE !
RIGHT !
WE GOT HER NOW !
SHE'S GONE THROUGH ! I BET MIKE'S GOT HER !
WH-WHERE IS SHE ?
SHE'S NOT HERE— YA DOPE ! SHE DIDN'T COME THROUGH !
BUT WHERE—
THERE SHE GOES !
AFTER HER, MEN !

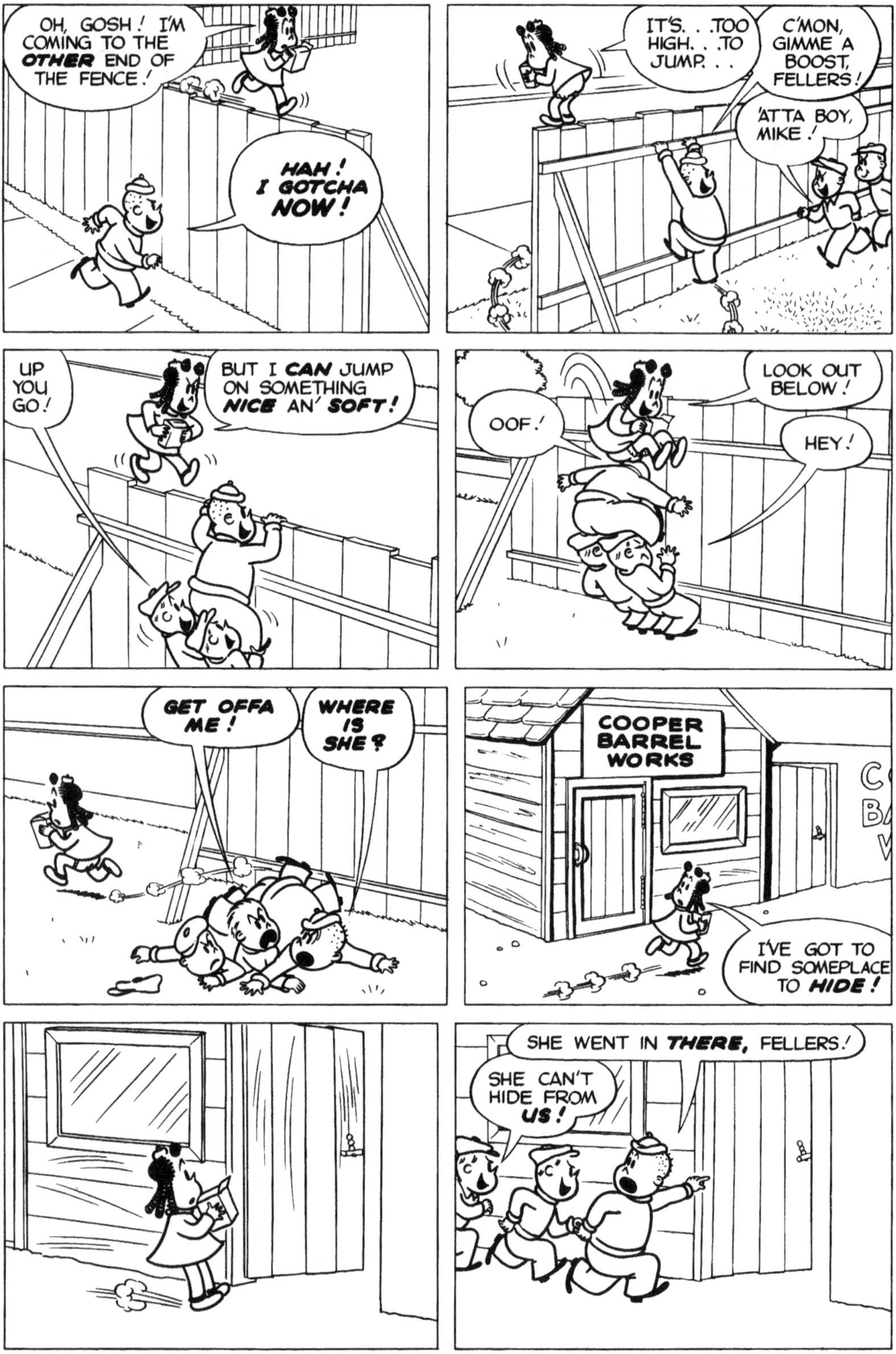
OH, GOSH! I'M COMING TO THE OTHER END OF THE FENCE!
HAH! I GOTCHA NOW!
IT'S. . .TOO HIGH. . .TO JUMP. . .
C'MON, GIMME A BOOST, FELLERS!
'ATTA BOY, MIKE!
UP YOU GO!
BUT I CAN JUMP ON SOMETHING NICE AN' SOFT!
LOOK OUT BELOW!
OOF!
HEY!
GET OFFA ME!
WHERE IS SHE?
COOPER BARREL WORKS
I'VE GOT TO FIND SOMEPLACE TO HIDE!
SHE WENT IN THERE, FELLERS!
SHE CAN'T HIDE FROM US!

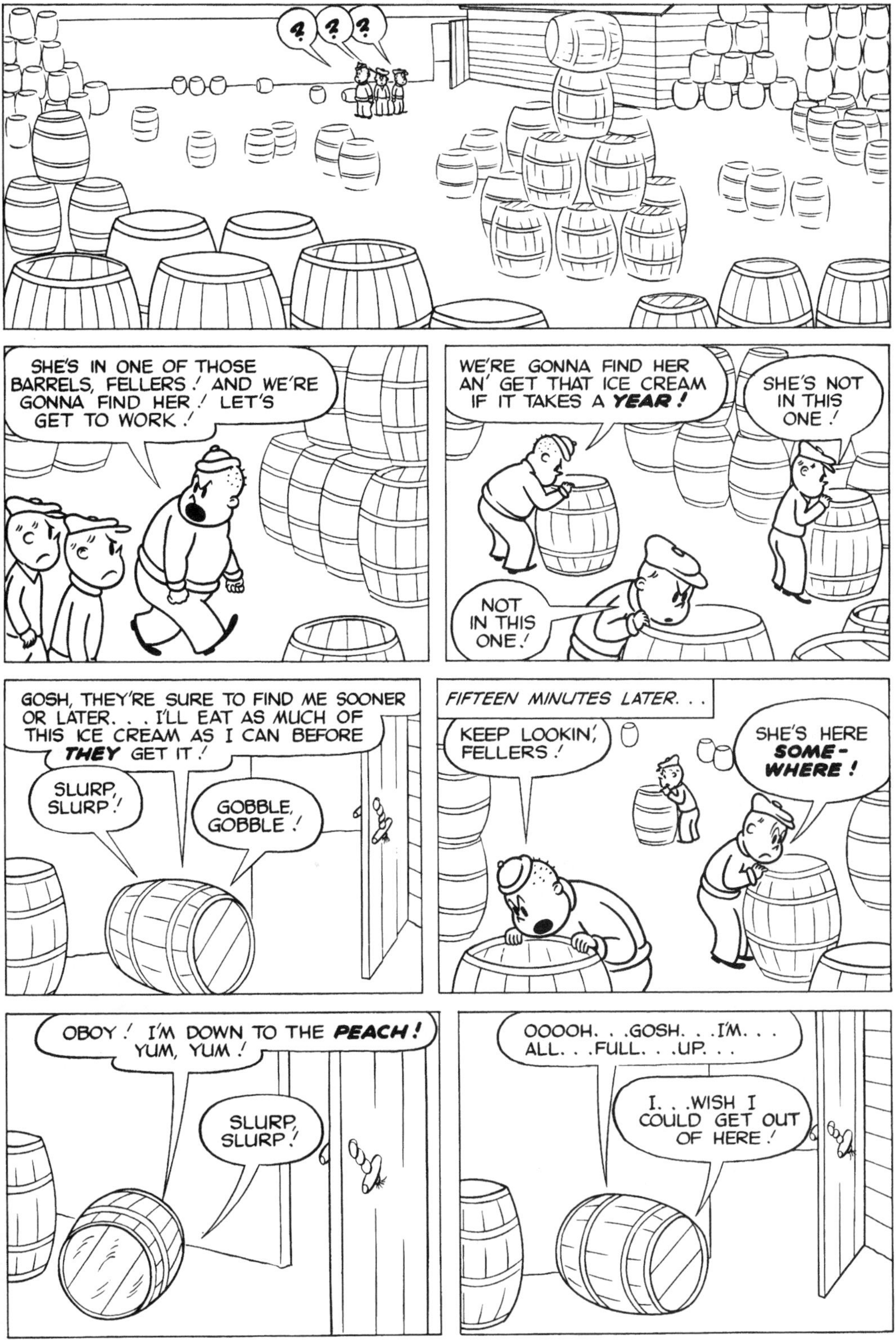

?
?
?
SHE'S IN ONE OF THOSE BARRELS, FELLERS! AND WE'RE GONNA FIND HER! LET'S GET TO WORK!
WE'RE GONNA FIND HER AN' GET THAT ICE CREAM IF IT TAKES A **YEAR!**
SHE'S NOT IN THIS ONE!
NOT IN THIS ONE!
GOSH, THEY'RE SURE TO FIND ME SOONER OR LATER. . . I'LL EAT AS MUCH OF THIS ICE CREAM AS I CAN BEFORE **THEY** GET IT!
SLURP, SLURP!
GOBBLE, GOBBLE!
FIFTEEN MINUTES LATER. . .
KEEP LOOKIN', FELLERS!
SHE'S HERE **SOME-WHERE!**
OBOY! I'M DOWN TO THE **PEACH!** YUM, YUM!
SLURP, SLURP!
OOOOH. . .GOSH. . .I'M. . . ALL. . .FULL. . .UP. . .
I. . .WISH I COULD GET OUT OF HERE!

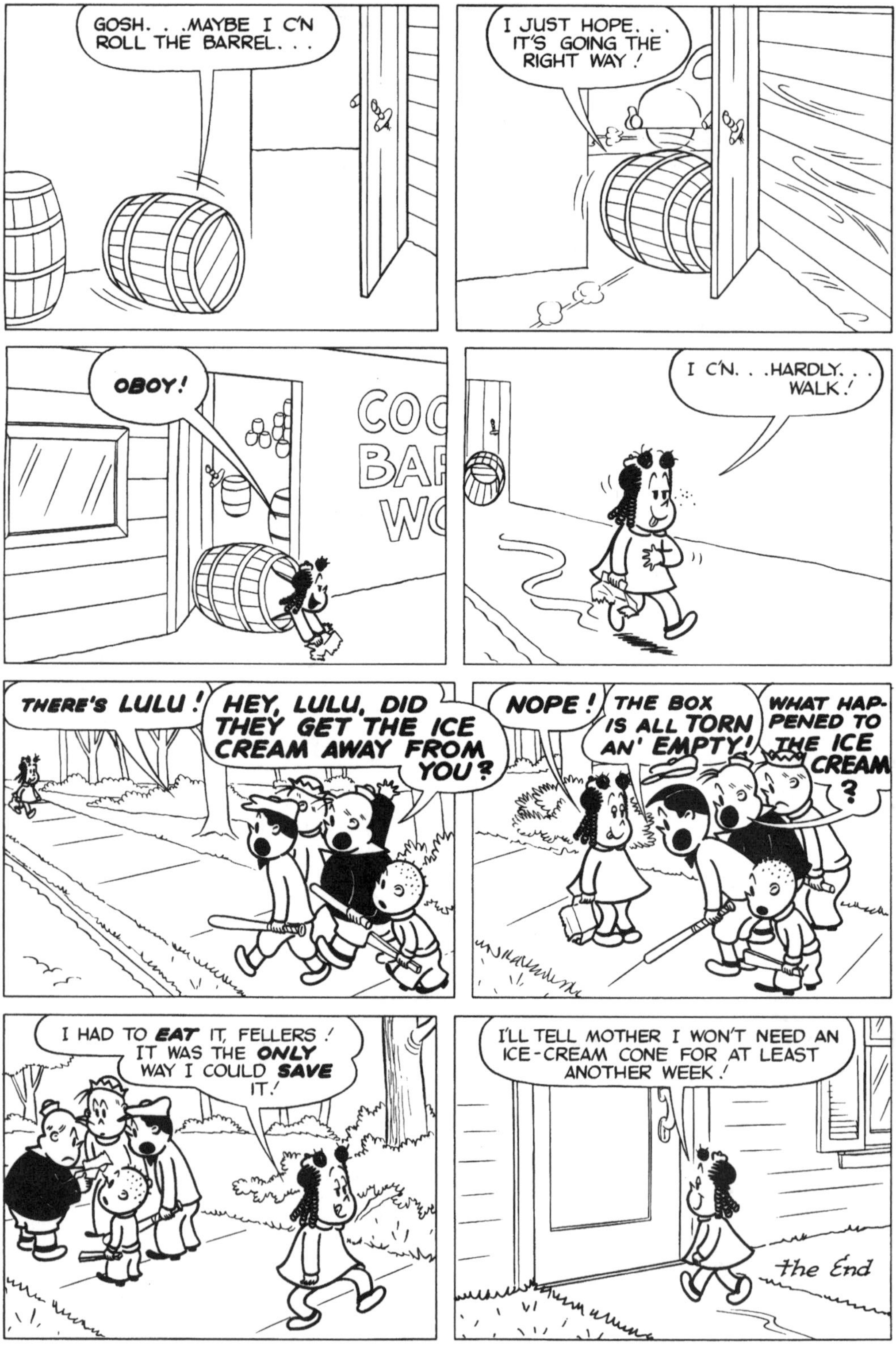
GOSH. . .MAYBE I C'N ROLL THE BARREL. . .
I JUST HOPE. . . IT'S GOING THE RIGHT WAY !
OBOY!
COO
BAR
WO
I C'N. . .HARDLY. . . WALK.!
THERE'S LULU !
HEY, LULU, DID THEY GET THE ICE CREAM AWAY FROM YOU?
NOPE !
THE BOX IS ALL TORN AN' EMPTY!
WHAT HAPPENED TO THE ICE CREAM ?
I HAD TO EAT IT, FELLERS ! IT WAS THE ONLY WAY I COULD SAVE IT.!
I'LL TELL MOTHER I WON'T NEED AN ICE-CREAM CONE FOR AT LEAST ANOTHER WEEK.!
the End

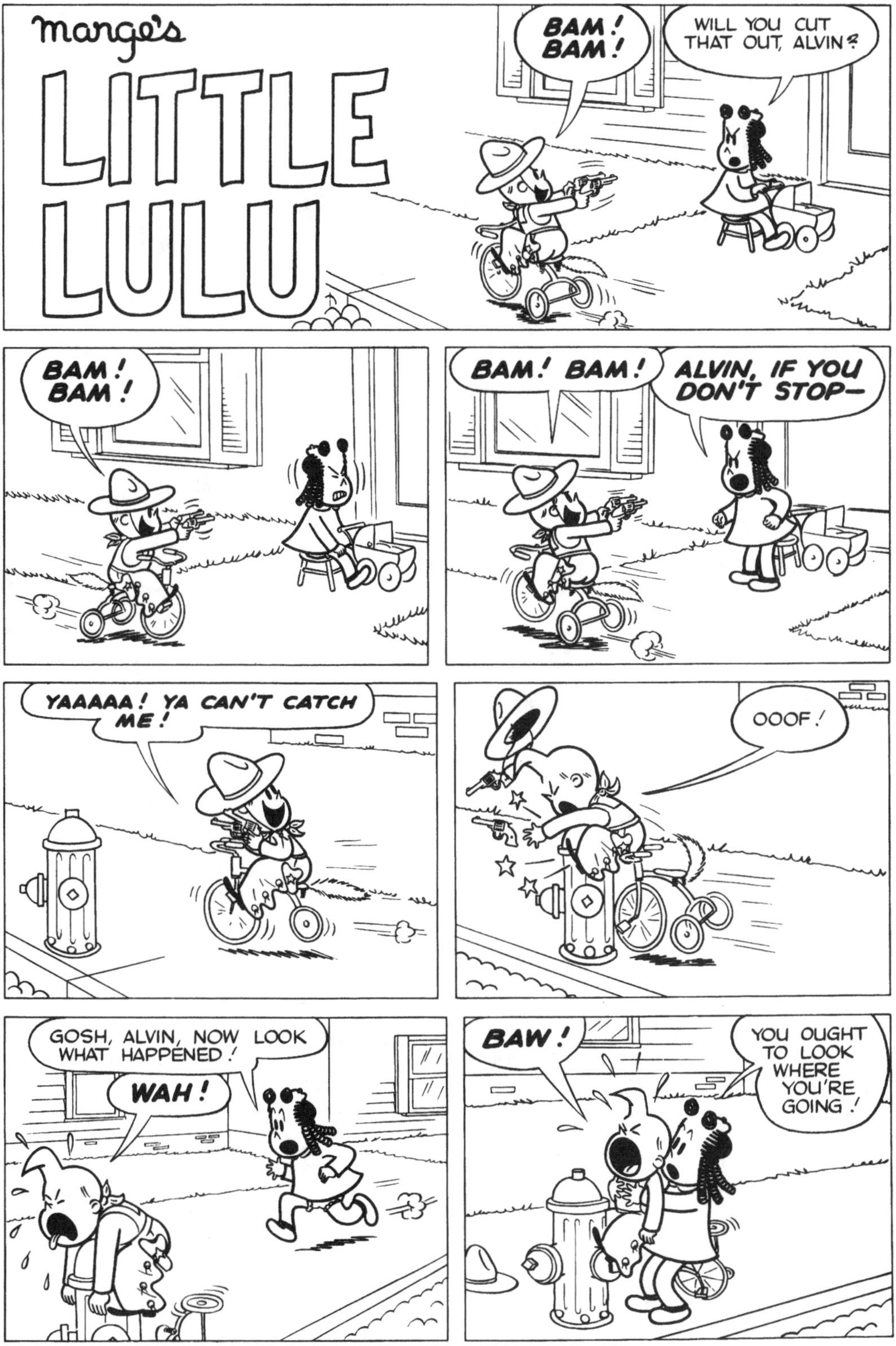
Marge's
LITTLE LULU
BAM! BAM!
WILL YOU CUT THAT OUT, ALVIN?
BAM! BAM!
BAM! BAM!
ALVIN, IF YOU DON'T STOP—
YAAAAA! YA CAN'T CATCH ME!
OOOF!
GOSH, ALVIN, NOW LOOK WHAT HAPPENED!
WAH!
BAW!
YOU OUGHT TO LOOK WHERE YOU'RE GOING!

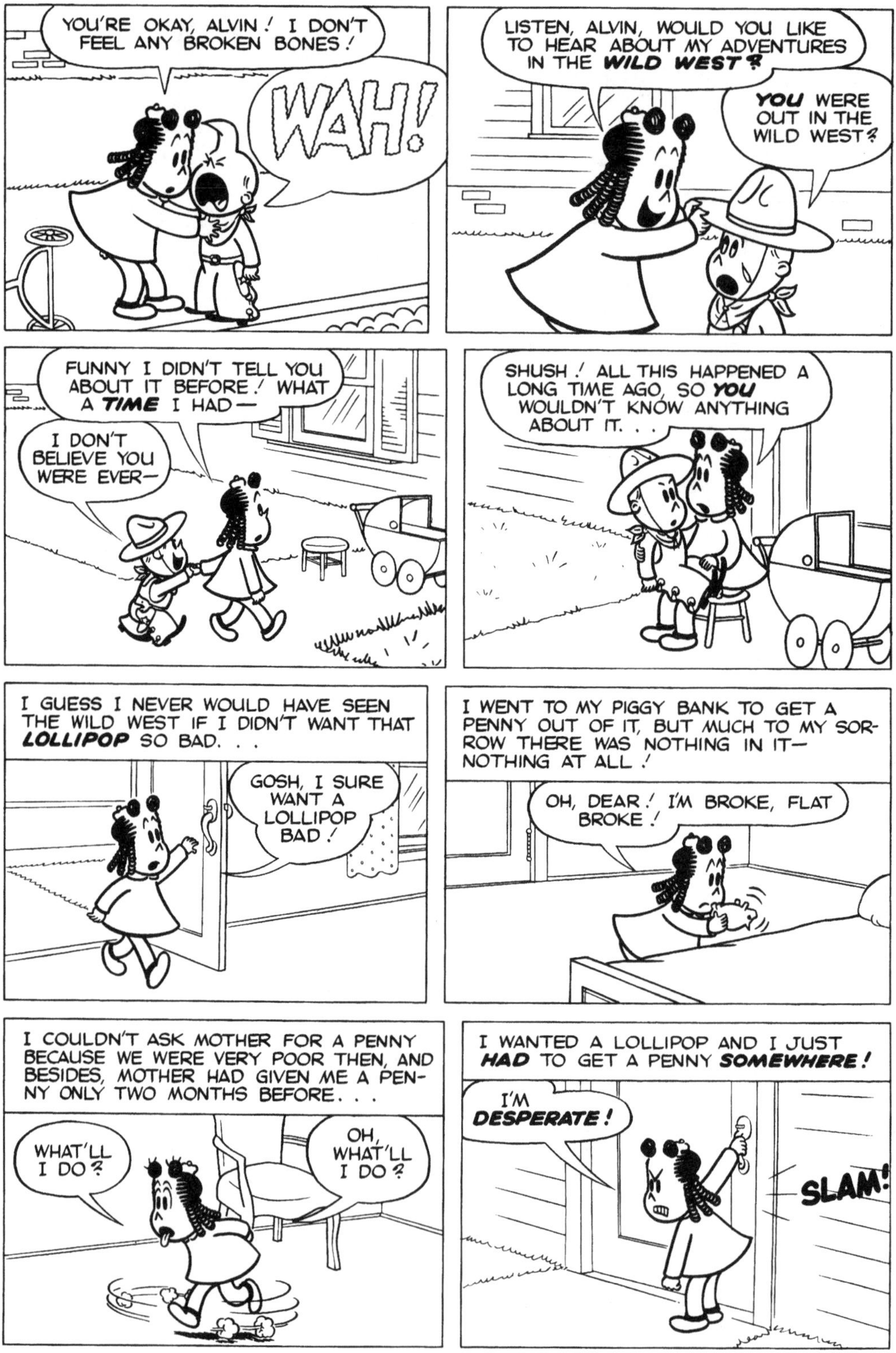
YOU'RE OKAY, ALVIN! I DON'T FEEL ANY BROKEN BONES!
WAH!
LISTEN, ALVIN, WOULD YOU LIKE TO HEAR ABOUT MY ADVENTURES IN THE WILD WEST?
YOU WERE OUT IN THE WILD WEST?
FUNNY I DIDN'T TELL YOU ABOUT IT BEFORE! WHAT A TIME I HAD—
I DON'T BELIEVE YOU WERE EVER—
SHUSH! ALL THIS HAPPENED A LONG TIME AGO, SO YOU WOULDN'T KNOW ANYTHING ABOUT IT. . .
I GUESS I NEVER WOULD HAVE SEEN THE WILD WEST IF I DIDN'T WANT THAT LOLLIPOP SO BAD. . .
GOSH, I SURE WANT A LOLLIPOP BAD!
I WENT TO MY PIGGY BANK TO GET A PENNY OUT OF IT, BUT MUCH TO MY SORROW THERE WAS NOTHING IN IT— NOTHING AT ALL!
OH, DEAR! I'M BROKE, FLAT BROKE!
I COULDN'T ASK MOTHER FOR A PENNY BECAUSE WE WERE VERY POOR THEN, AND BESIDES, MOTHER HAD GIVEN ME A PENNY ONLY TWO MONTHS BEFORE. . .
WHAT'LL I DO?
OH, WHAT'LL I DO?
I WANTED A LOLLIPOP AND I JUST HAD TO GET A PENNY SOMEWHERE!
I'M DESPERATE!
SLAM!

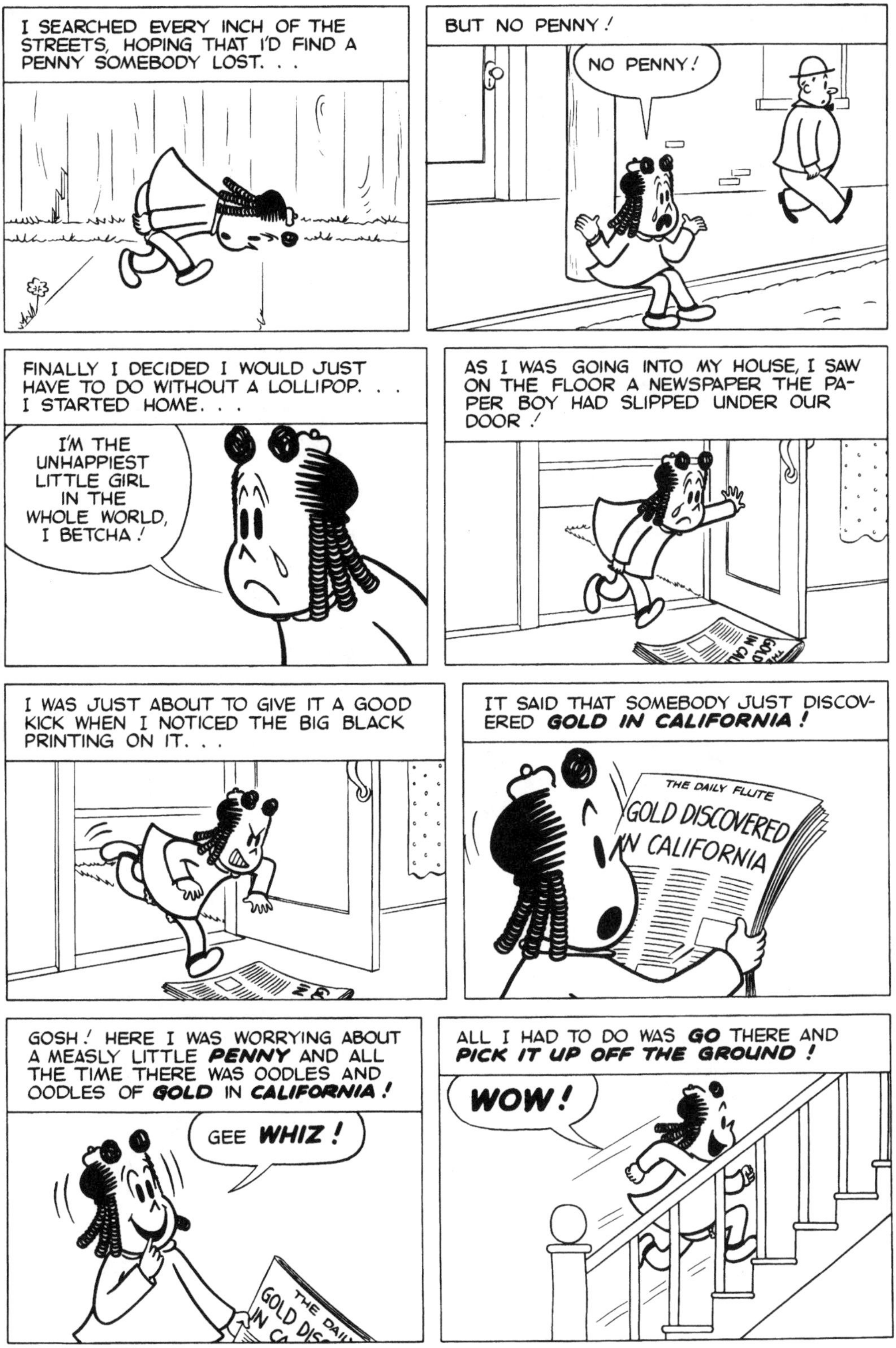
I SEARCHED EVERY INCH OF THE STREETS, HOPING THAT I'D FIND A PENNY SOMEBODY LOST. . .
BUT NO PENNY!
NO PENNY!
FINALLY I DECIDED I WOULD JUST HAVE TO DO WITHOUT A LOLLIPOP. . . I STARTED HOME. . .
I'M THE UNHAPPIEST LITTLE GIRL IN THE WHOLE WORLD, I BETCHA!
AS I WAS GOING INTO MY HOUSE, I SAW ON THE FLOOR A NEWSPAPER THE PAPER BOY HAD SLIPPED UNDER OUR DOOR!
I WAS JUST ABOUT TO GIVE IT A GOOD KICK WHEN I NOTICED THE BIG BLACK PRINTING ON IT. . .
IT SAID THAT SOMEBODY JUST DISCOVERED GOLD IN CALIFORNIA!
THE DAILY FLUTE
GOLD DISCOVERED IN CALIFORNIA
GOSH! HERE I WAS WORRYING ABOUT A MEASLY LITTLE PENNY AND ALL THE TIME THERE WAS OODLES AND OODLES OF GOLD IN CALIFORNIA!
GEE WHIZ!
ALL I HAD TO DO WAS GO THERE AND PICK IT UP OFF THE GROUND!
WOW!

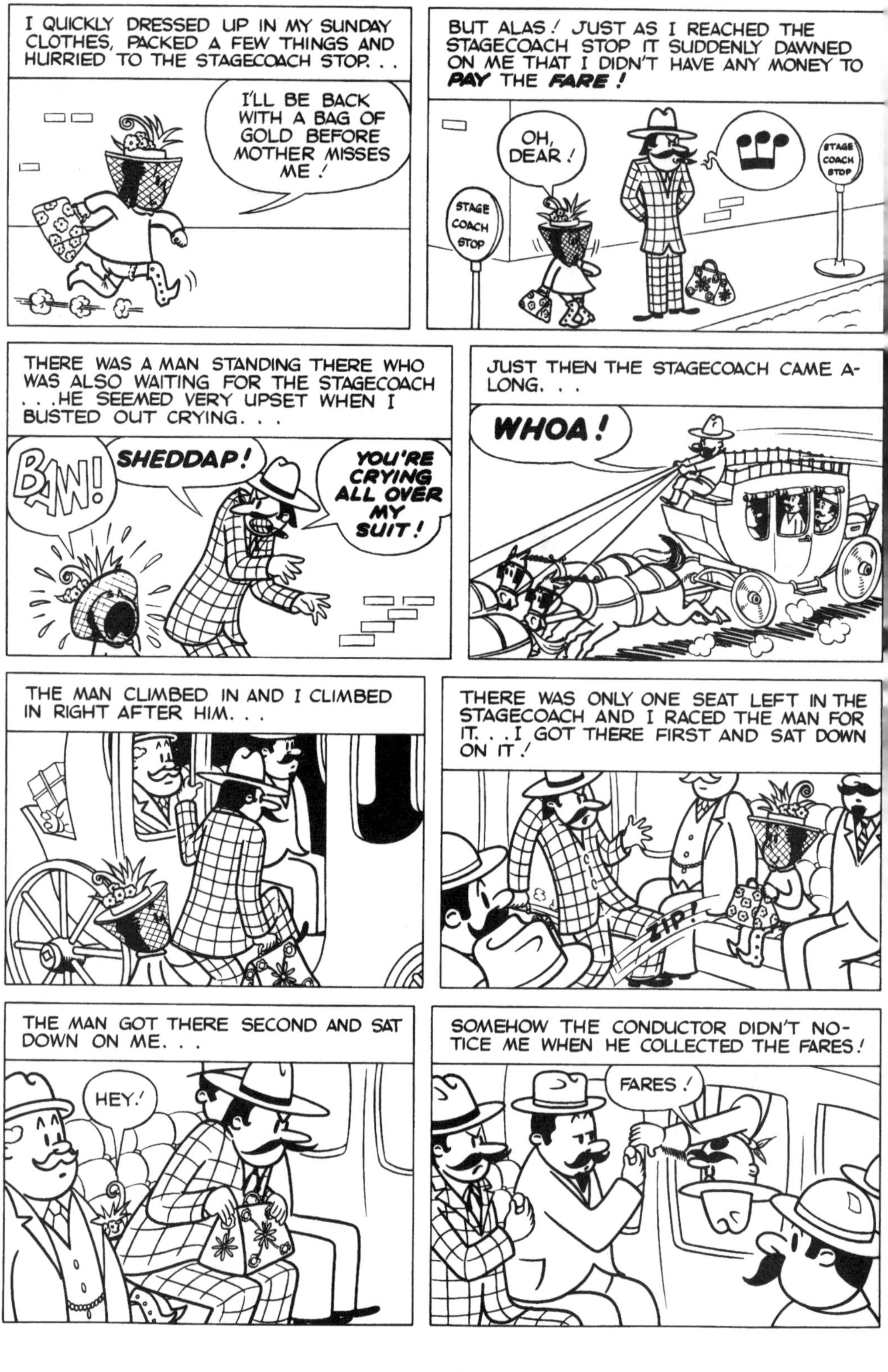
I QUICKLY DRESSED UP IN MY SUNDAY CLOTHES, PACKED A FEW THINGS AND HURRIED TO THE STAGECOACH STOP. . .
I'LL BE BACK WITH A BAG OF GOLD BEFORE MOTHER MISSES ME!
BUT ALAS! JUST AS I REACHED THE STAGECOACH STOP IT SUDDENLY DAWNED ON ME THAT I DIDN'T HAVE ANY MONEY TO PAY THE FARE!
OH, DEAR!
STAGE COACH STOP
STAGE COACH STOP
THERE WAS A MAN STANDING THERE WHO WAS ALSO WAITING FOR THE STAGECOACH . . .HE SEEMED VERY UPSET WHEN I BUSTED OUT CRYING. . .
BAW!
SHEDDAP!
YOU'RE CRYING ALL OVER MY SUIT!
JUST THEN THE STAGECOACH CAME A-LONG. . .
WHOA!
THE MAN CLIMBED IN AND I CLIMBED IN RIGHT AFTER HIM. . .
THERE WAS ONLY ONE SEAT LEFT IN THE STAGECOACH AND I RACED THE MAN FOR IT. . .I GOT THERE FIRST AND SAT DOWN ON IT!
ZIP!
THE MAN GOT THERE SECOND AND SAT DOWN ON ME. . .
HEY!
SOMEHOW THE CONDUCTOR DIDN'T NO-TICE ME WHEN HE COLLECTED THE FARES!
FARES!

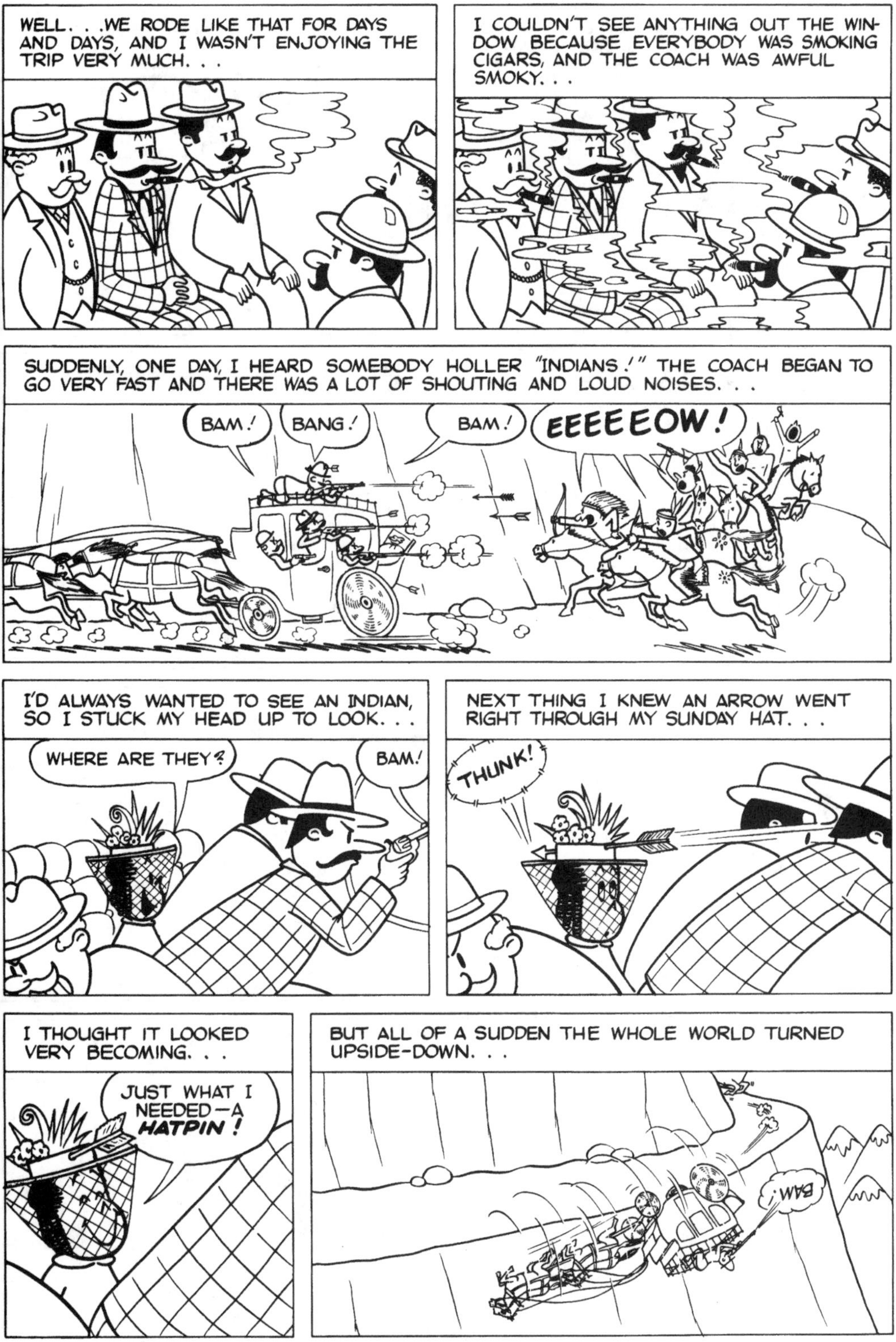

WELL. . .WE RODE LIKE THAT FOR DAYS AND DAYS, AND I WASN'T ENJOYING THE TRIP VERY MUCH. . .
I COULDN'T SEE ANYTHING OUT THE WIN-DOW BECAUSE EVERYBODY WAS SMOKING CIGARS, AND THE COACH WAS AWFUL SMOKY. . .
SUDDENLY, ONE DAY, I HEARD SOMEBODY HOLLER "INDIANS!" THE COACH BEGAN TO GO VERY FAST AND THERE WAS A LOT OF SHOUTING AND LOUD NOISES. . .
BAM!
BANG!
BAM!
EEEEEOW!
I'D ALWAYS WANTED TO SEE AN INDIAN, SO I STUCK MY HEAD UP TO LOOK. . .
WHERE ARE THEY?
BAM!
NEXT THING I KNEW AN ARROW WENT RIGHT THROUGH MY SUNDAY HAT. . .
THUNK!
I THOUGHT IT LOOKED VERY BECOMING. . .
JUST WHAT I NEEDED—A HATPIN!
BUT ALL OF A SUDDEN THE WHOLE WORLD TURNED UPSIDE-DOWN. . .
BAM!

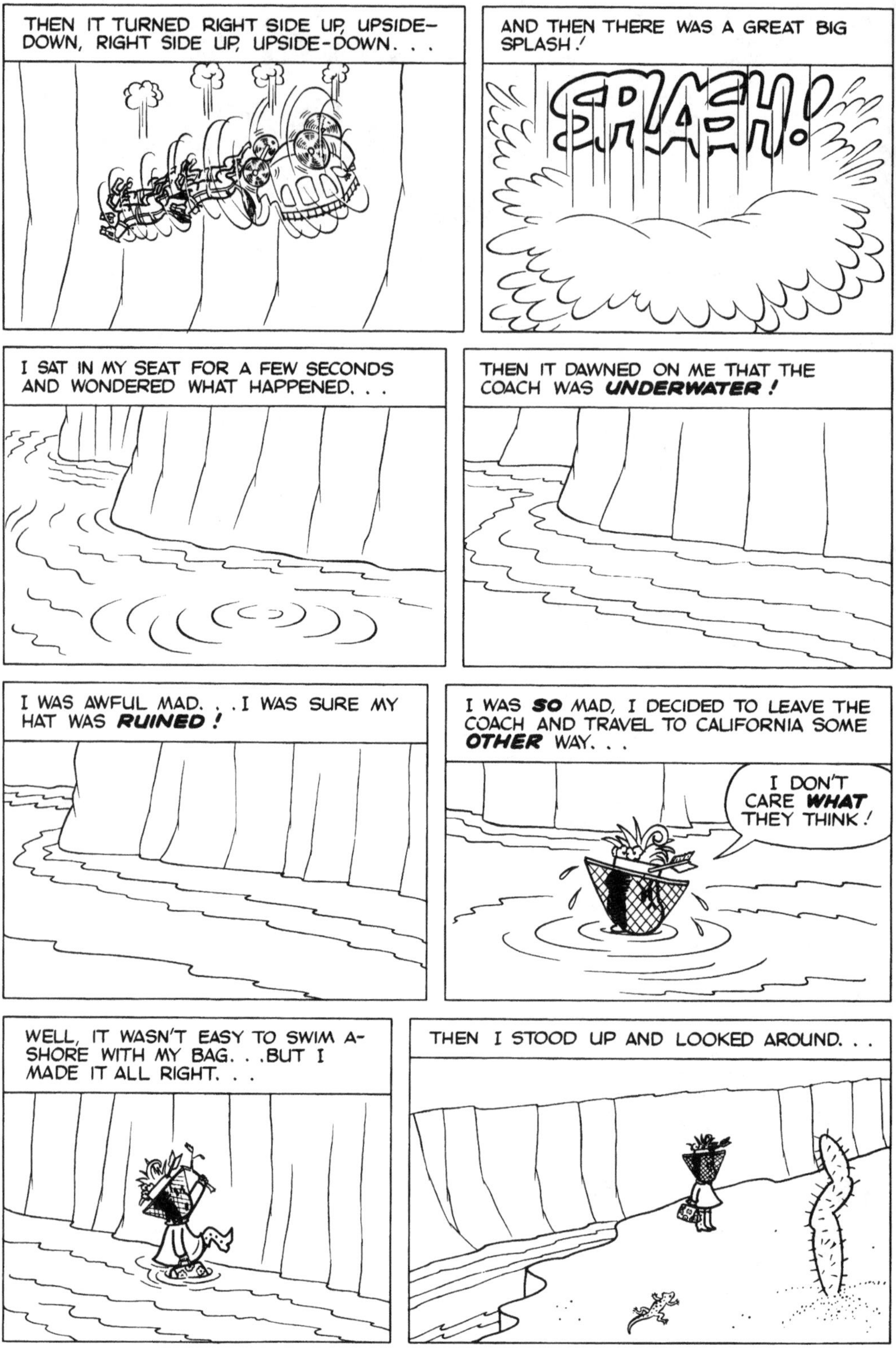
THEN IT TURNED RIGHT SIDE UP, UPSIDE-DOWN, RIGHT SIDE UP, UPSIDE-DOWN. . .
AND THEN THERE WAS A GREAT BIG SPLASH!
SPLASH!
I SAT IN MY SEAT FOR A FEW SECONDS AND WONDERED WHAT HAPPENED. . .
THEN IT DAWNED ON ME THAT THE COACH WAS UNDERWATER!
I WAS AWFUL MAD. . .I WAS SURE MY HAT WAS RUINED!
I WAS SO MAD, I DECIDED TO LEAVE THE COACH AND TRAVEL TO CALIFORNIA SOME OTHER WAY. . .
I DON'T CARE WHAT THEY THINK!
WELL, IT WASN'T EASY TO SWIM A-SHORE WITH MY BAG. . .BUT I MADE IT ALL RIGHT. . .
THEN I STOOD UP AND LOOKED AROUND. . .

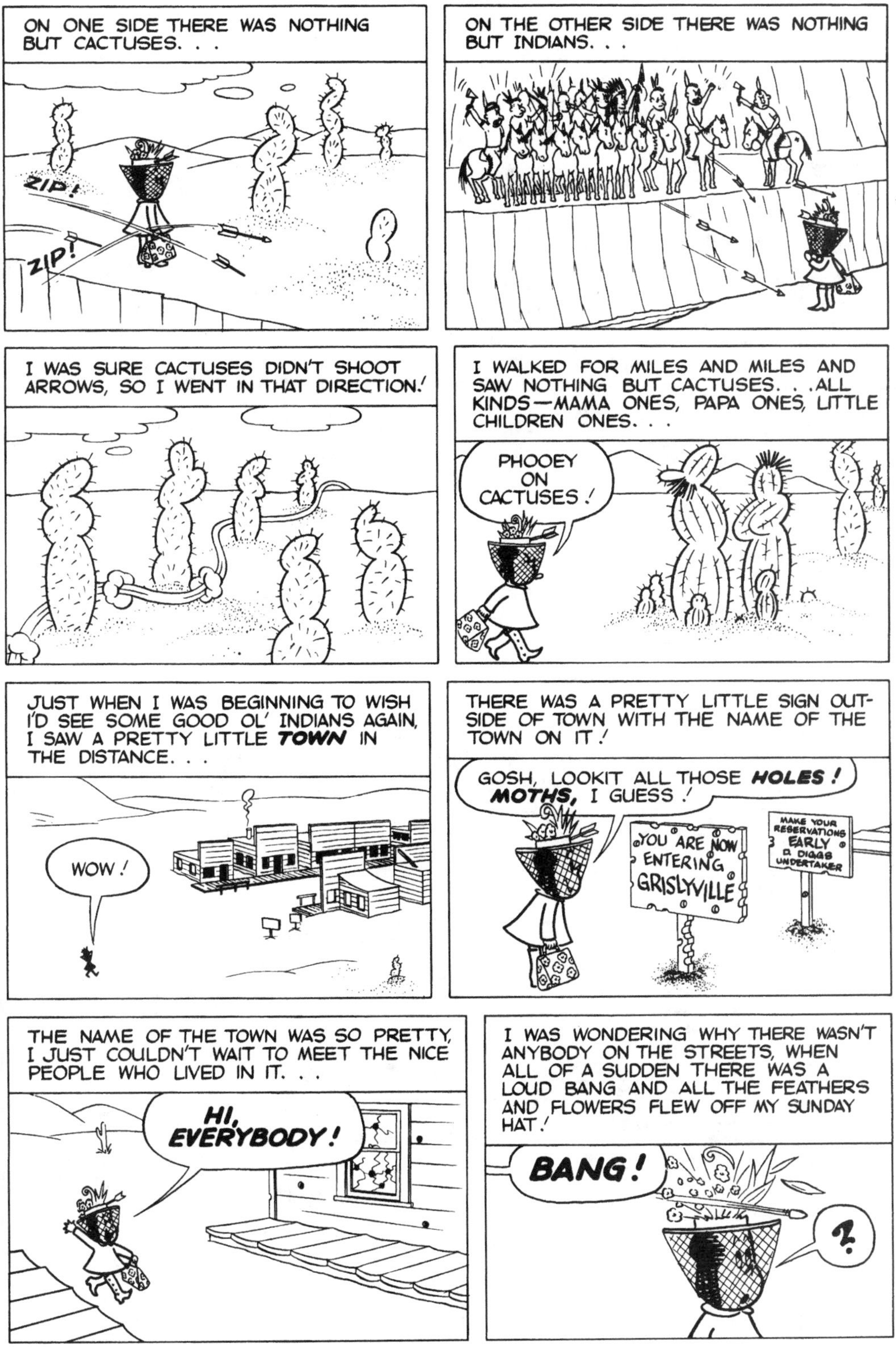
ON ONE SIDE THERE WAS NOTHING BUT CACTUSES. . .
ZIP!
ZIP!
ON THE OTHER SIDE THERE WAS NOTHING BUT INDIANS. . .
I WAS SURE CACTUSES DIDN'T SHOOT ARROWS, SO I WENT IN THAT DIRECTION!
I WALKED FOR MILES AND MILES AND SAW NOTHING BUT CACTUSES. . .ALL KINDS—MAMA ONES, PAPA ONES, LITTLE CHILDREN ONES. . .
PHOOEY ON CACTUSES!
JUST WHEN I WAS BEGINNING TO WISH I'D SEE SOME GOOD OL' INDIANS AGAIN, I SAW A PRETTY LITTLE TOWN IN THE DISTANCE. . .
WOW!
THERE WAS A PRETTY LITTLE SIGN OUTSIDE OF TOWN WITH THE NAME OF THE TOWN ON IT!
GOSH, LOOKIT ALL THOSE HOLES! MOTHS, I GUESS!
YOU ARE NOW ENTERING GRISLYVILLE
MAKE YOUR RESERVATIONS EARLY D. DIGGS UNDERTAKER
THE NAME OF THE TOWN WAS SO PRETTY, I JUST COULDN'T WAIT TO MEET THE NICE PEOPLE WHO LIVED IN IT. . .
HI, EVERYBODY!
I WAS WONDERING WHY THERE WASN'T ANYBODY ON THE STREETS, WHEN ALL OF A SUDDEN THERE WAS A LOUD BANG AND ALL THE FEATHERS AND FLOWERS FLEW OFF MY SUNDAY HAT!
BANG!
?

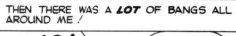
THEN THERE WAS A *LOT* OF BANGS ALL AROUND ME!

BANG! BANG! BAM! BAM! BANG!

WONDER WHAT'S GOING ON AROUND HERE?

I WAS PUZZLED FOR A LITTLE WHILE— THEN I FIGURED IT OUT—SOMEBODY WAS SHOOTING *GUNS* AT ME!

BANG! BAM!

HEY!

I RACED FOR THE NEAREST DOORWAY. . .

HOTEL

YOW!

WHEN I GOT INSIDE I SAW A MAN HIDING BEHIND A BIG DESK!

C-CLOSE THE DOOR!

I ASKED HIM IF I COULD STAY THERE A WHILE BECAUSE SOMEBODY WAS SHOOTING GUNS AT ME. . .

COULD I STAY HERE, MISTER? HUH? PLEASE?

SURE! THIS IS A *HOTEL*!

BUT THE MAN TOLD ME I WOULD HAVE TO PAY MONEY TO STAY THERE—AND I DIDN'T HAVE ANY MONEY. . .

GOSH, I *CAN'T* PAY *FIFTY CENTS* A WEEK!

HMM. . .I'LL SEE IF I CAN FIGURE SOMETHING OUT. . .

BUT HE WAS A KIND MAN—HE SAID HE WAS MAYOR OF THE TOWN AND WOULD GIVE ME A JOB SO THAT I COULD EARN ENOUGH MONEY TO STAY IN HIS HOUSE WHERE I WOULD BE SAFE!

THE *SHERIFF'S* JOB IS OPEN!

OH, GOODIE!

THEN HE PINNED A BIG SHINY STAR ON MY DRESS AND GAVE ME TWO GREAT BIG SHINY GUNS TO MATCH. . .

OH, BOY!

WE TOOK 'EM OFF THE OLD SHERIFF WHEN HE—ER—

THEN HE TOLD ME WHAT I WAS SUP- POSED TO DO IN MY NEW JOB... GOSH, IT SOUNDED LIKE FUN!

FIND THESE MEN AND TAKE 'EM TO JAIL...

DANNY DIMPLES CHARLIE CHUCKLE JOLLY JERRY

ALL I HAD TO DO WAS GO FIND SOME PEOPLE AND TAKE THEM TO JAIL...

THE NAMES SOUND SO *CUTE!*

THE FIRST PERSON I HAD TO FIND WAS DANNY DIMPLES!

I'LL TRY THIS BARBER- SHOP!

HEY, MISTER, DO YOU KNOW WHERE DANNY DIMPLES IS?

D-DANNY DIMPLES?

I ASKED A BARBER IF HE KNEW WHERE I COULD FIND DANNY DIMPLES, BUT HE DIDN'T SEEM TO KNOW...

GOSH!

STERILIZER

THEN I ASKED A MAN ON THE STREET...

MISTER, DO YOU KNOW WHERE DANNY DIMPLES IS?

HE DIDN'T SEEM TO KNOW EITHER...

FINALLY I CAME TO A FUNNY-LOOKING MAN WHO WAS SITTING ON A BOX AND EATING AN ICE-CREAM CONE!

MISTER, DO YOU KNOW WHERE DANNY DIMPLES IS?

I WAS VERY SURPRISED AND HAPPY WHEN HE SAID *HE* WAS DANNY DIMPLES!

YAH!

YAH! WHAT ABOUT IT?

OH, MR. DIMPLES, YOU HAVE TO COME TO JAIL WITH ME!

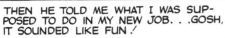

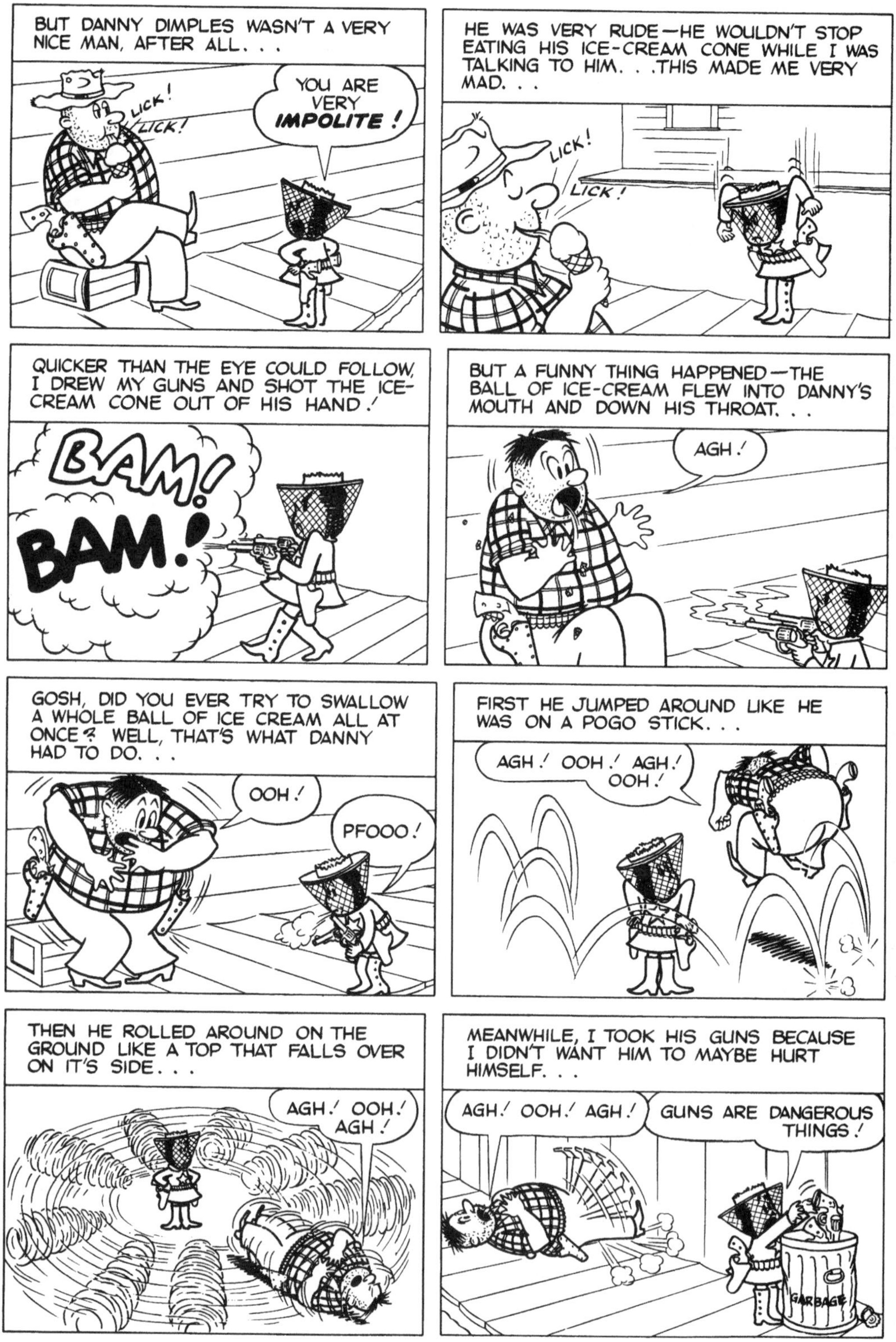
BUT DANNY DIMPLES WASN'T A VERY NICE MAN, AFTER ALL. . .
LICK! LICK!
YOU ARE VERY IMPOLITE!
HE WAS VERY RUDE—HE WOULDN'T STOP EATING HIS ICE-CREAM CONE WHILE I WAS TALKING TO HIM. . .THIS MADE ME VERY MAD. . .
LICK! LICK!
QUICKER THAN THE EYE COULD FOLLOW, I DREW MY GUNS AND SHOT THE ICE-CREAM CONE OUT OF HIS HAND!
BAM! BAM!
BUT A FUNNY THING HAPPENED—THE BALL OF ICE-CREAM FLEW INTO DANNY'S MOUTH AND DOWN HIS THROAT. . .
AGH!
GOSH, DID YOU EVER TRY TO SWALLOW A WHOLE BALL OF ICE CREAM ALL AT ONCE? WELL, THAT'S WHAT DANNY HAD TO DO. . .
OOH!
PFOOO!
FIRST HE JUMPED AROUND LIKE HE WAS ON A POGO STICK. . .
AGH! OOH! AGH! OOH!
THEN HE ROLLED AROUND ON THE GROUND LIKE A TOP THAT FALLS OVER ON IT'S SIDE. . .
AGH! OOH! AGH!
MEANWHILE, I TOOK HIS GUNS BECAUSE I DIDN'T WANT HIM TO MAYBE HURT HIMSELF. . .
AGH! OOH! AGH!
GUNS ARE DANGEROUS THINGS!
GARBAGE

WHEN HE QUIETED DOWN A LITTLE BIT, I GRABBED HIM BY THE FEET AND CARTED HIM OFF TO JAIL...

AGH! OOH!

THE NEXT ONE I HAD TO FIND WAS CHARLIE CHUCKLE...

CHARLIE CHUCKLE! I BET *HE'S* A MERRY PERSON!

AGH! OOH!

THE FIRST PERSON I MET ON THE STREET WAS AN INDIAN...

OH, MR. INDIAN, DO YOU KNOW CHARLIE CHUCKLE?

HUH?

WHEN I MENTIONED THE NAME CHARLIE CHUCKLE, HE TURNED AS PALE AS A SNOWMAN!

CH-CHARLIE CHUCKLE! UGH!

THEN HE RAN OFF AS FAST AS HE COULD...

GOSH!

NEXT I CAME TO A BUNCH OF MEN WHO WERE STANDING ON A STREET CORNER...

DOES ANYBODY HERE KNOW CHARLIE CHUCKLE?

WHEN I ASKED THEM IF THEY KNEW CHARLIE CHUCKLE EVERY ONE OF THEM FAINTED...

GOSH!

...EVEN A HORSE THAT WAS STANDING NEARBY FAINTED!

GOSH!

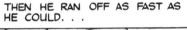

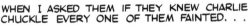

221

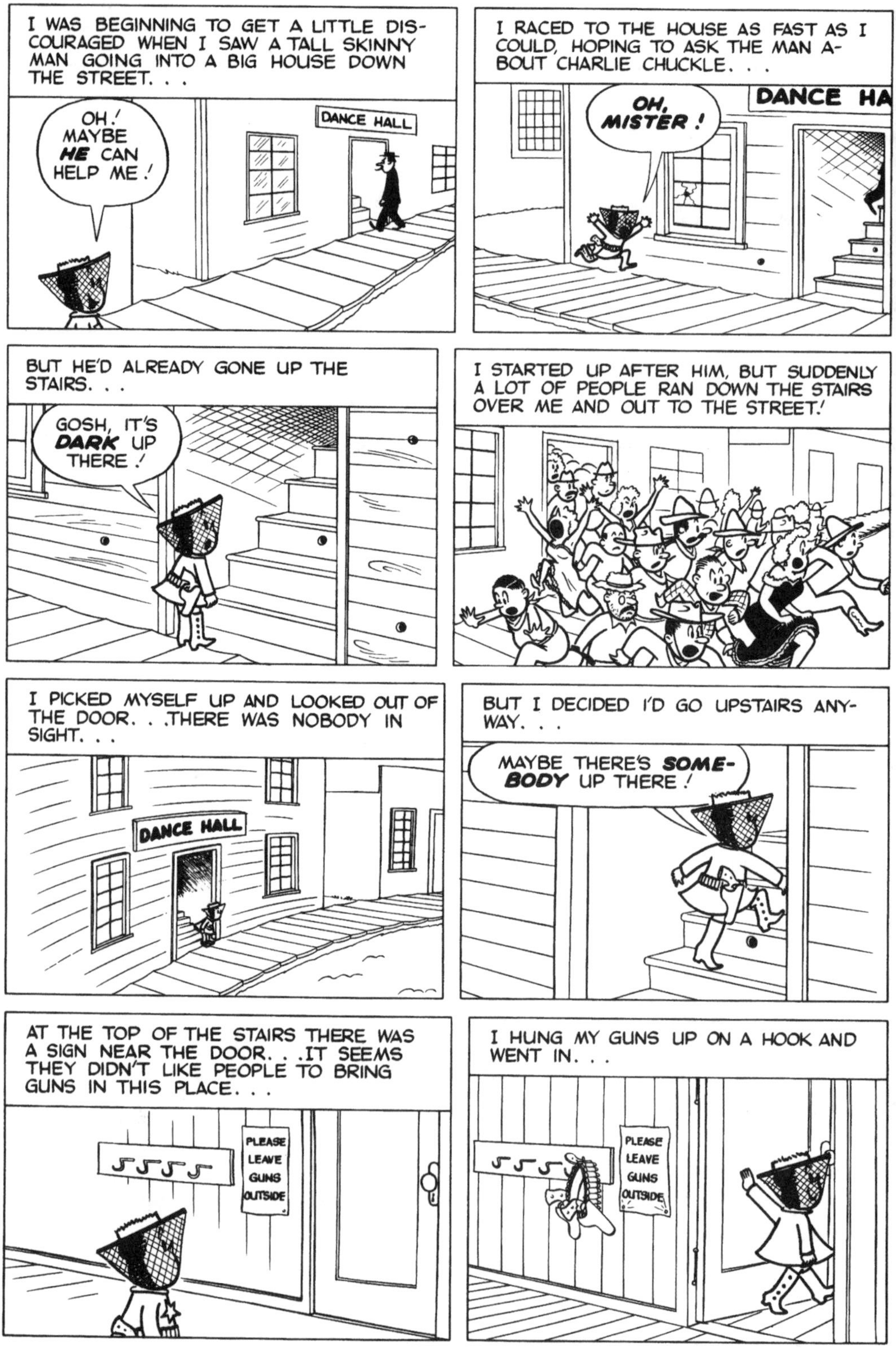
I WAS BEGINNING TO GET A LITTLE DISCOURAGED WHEN I SAW A TALL SKINNY MAN GOING INTO A BIG HOUSE DOWN THE STREET. . .
OH! MAYBE HE CAN HELP ME!
DANCE HALL
I RACED TO THE HOUSE AS FAST AS I COULD, HOPING TO ASK THE MAN ABOUT CHARLIE CHUCKLE. . .
OH, MISTER!
BUT HE'D ALREADY GONE UP THE STAIRS. . .
GOSH, IT'S DARK UP THERE!
I STARTED UP AFTER HIM, BUT SUDDENLY A LOT OF PEOPLE RAN DOWN THE STAIRS OVER ME AND OUT TO THE STREET!
I PICKED MYSELF UP AND LOOKED OUT OF THE DOOR. . .THERE WAS NOBODY IN SIGHT. . .
DANCE HALL
BUT I DECIDED I'D GO UPSTAIRS ANYWAY. . .
MAYBE THERE'S SOMEBODY UP THERE!
AT THE TOP OF THE STAIRS THERE WAS A SIGN NEAR THE DOOR. . .IT SEEMS THEY DIDN'T LIKE PEOPLE TO BRING GUNS IN THIS PLACE. . .
PLEASE LEAVE GUNS OUTSIDE
I HUNG MY GUNS UP ON A HOOK AND WENT IN. . .
PLEASE LEAVE GUNS OUTSIDE

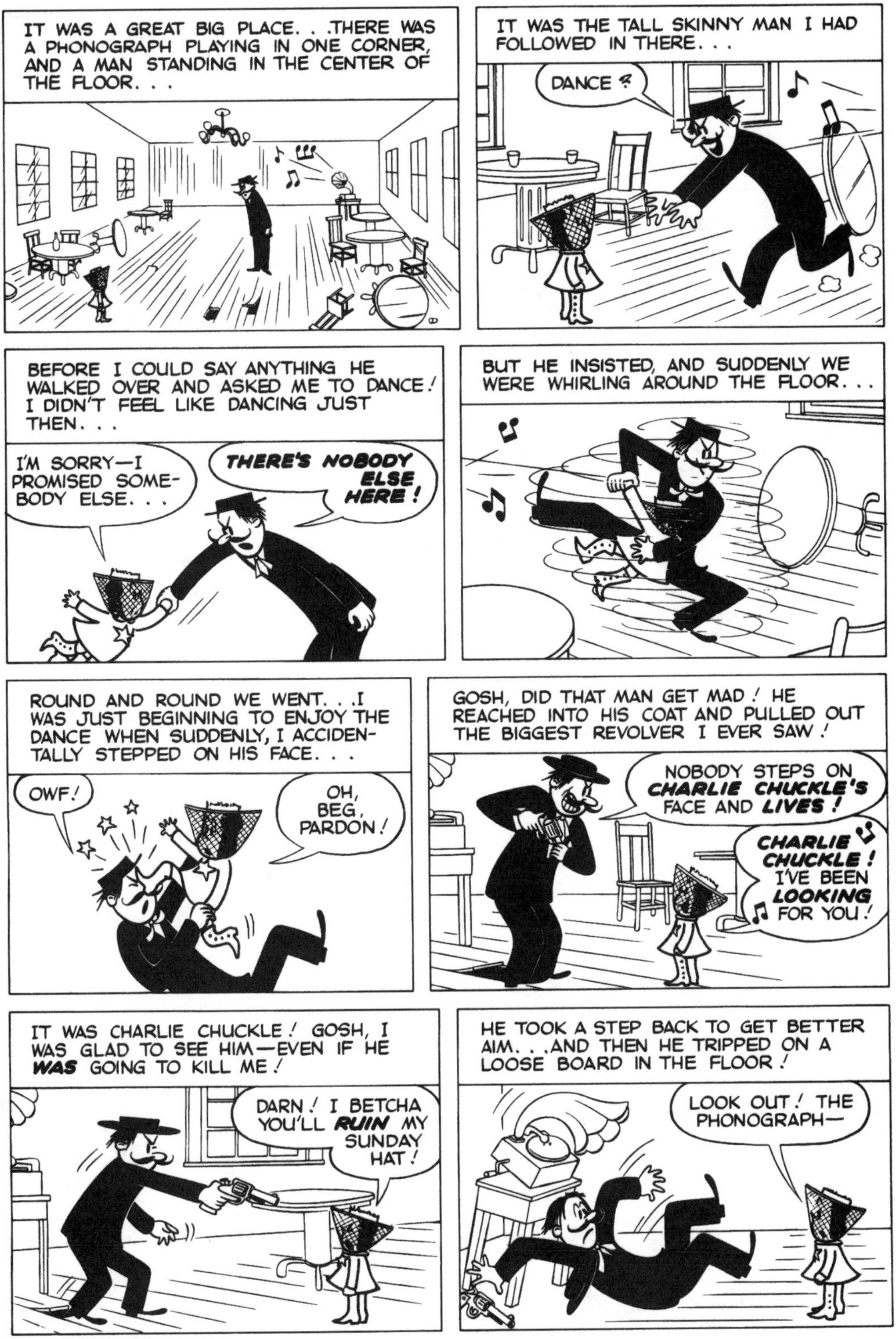

IT WAS A GREAT BIG PLACE. . .THERE WAS A PHONOGRAPH PLAYING IN ONE CORNER, AND A MAN STANDING IN THE CENTER OF THE FLOOR. . .
IT WAS THE TALL SKINNY MAN I HAD FOLLOWED IN THERE. . .
DANCE?
BEFORE I COULD SAY ANYTHING HE WALKED OVER AND ASKED ME TO DANCE! I DIDN'T FEEL LIKE DANCING JUST THEN. . .
I'M SORRY—I PROMISED SOMEBODY ELSE. . .
THERE'S NOBODY ELSE HERE!
BUT HE INSISTED, AND SUDDENLY WE WERE WHIRLING AROUND THE FLOOR. . .
ROUND AND ROUND WE WENT. . .I WAS JUST BEGINNING TO ENJOY THE DANCE WHEN SUDDENLY, I ACCIDENTALLY STEPPED ON HIS FACE. . .
OWF!
OH, BEG, PARDON!
GOSH, DID THAT MAN GET MAD! HE REACHED INTO HIS COAT AND PULLED OUT THE BIGGEST REVOLVER I EVER SAW!
NOBODY STEPS ON CHARLIE CHUCKLE'S FACE AND LIVES!
CHARLIE CHUCKLE! I'VE BEEN LOOKING FOR YOU!
IT WAS CHARLIE CHUCKLE! GOSH, I WAS GLAD TO SEE HIM—EVEN IF HE WAS GOING TO KILL ME!
DARN! I BETCHA YOU'LL RUIN MY SUNDAY HAT!
HE TOOK A STEP BACK TO GET BETTER AIM. . .AND THEN HE TRIPPED ON A LOOSE BOARD IN THE FLOOR!
LOOK OUT! THE PHONOGRAPH—

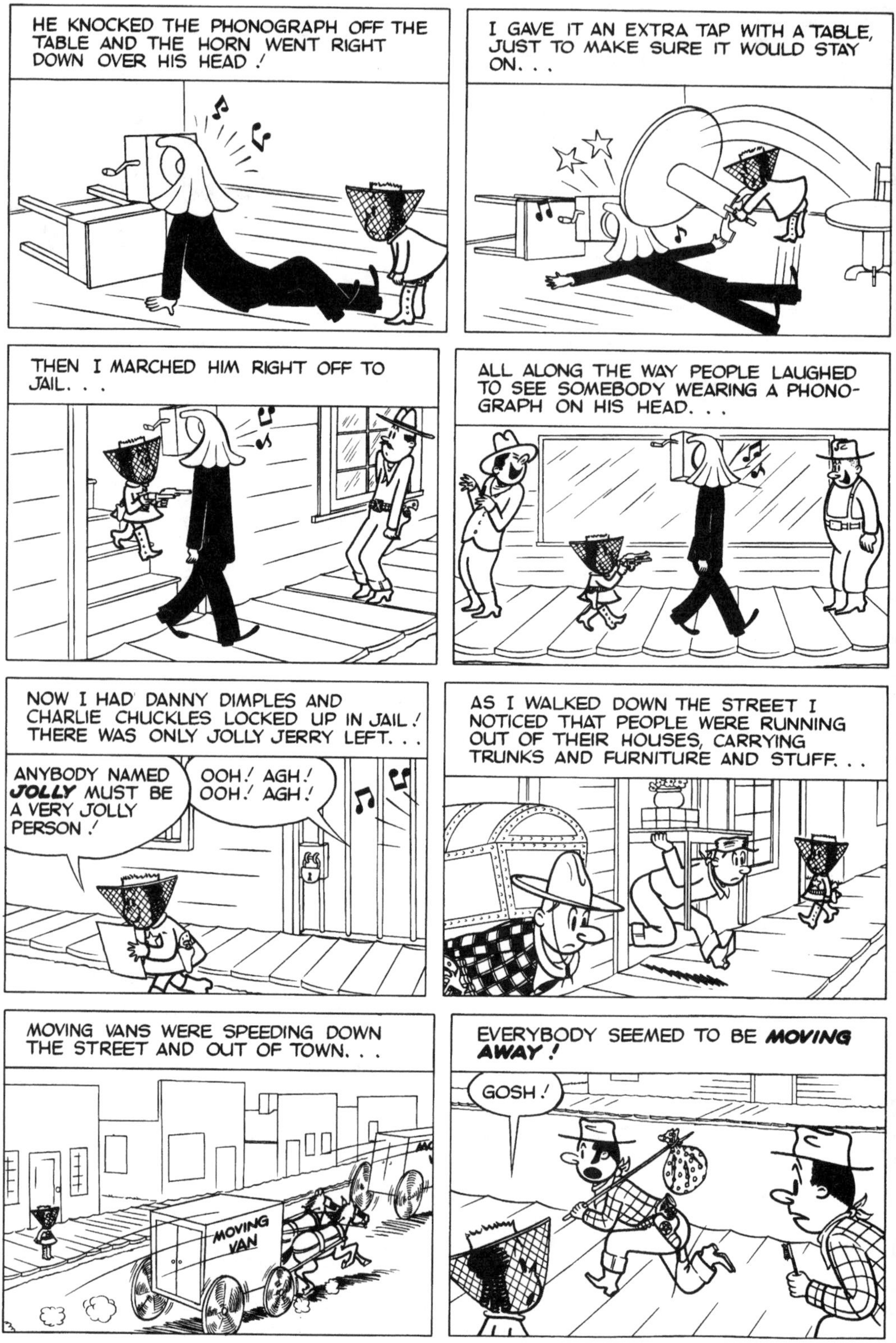

HE KNOCKED THE PHONOGRAPH OFF THE TABLE AND THE HORN WENT RIGHT DOWN OVER HIS HEAD!
I GAVE IT AN EXTRA TAP WITH A TABLE, JUST TO MAKE SURE IT WOULD STAY ON. . .
THEN I MARCHED HIM RIGHT OFF TO JAIL. . .
ALL ALONG THE WAY PEOPLE LAUGHED TO SEE SOMEBODY WEARING A PHONOGRAPH ON HIS HEAD. . .
NOW I HAD DANNY DIMPLES AND CHARLIE CHUCKLES LOCKED UP IN JAIL! THERE WAS ONLY JOLLY JERRY LEFT. . .
ANYBODY NAMED JOLLY MUST BE A VERY JOLLY PERSON!
OOH! AGH! OOH! AGH!
AS I WALKED DOWN THE STREET I NOTICED THAT PEOPLE WERE RUNNING OUT OF THEIR HOUSES, CARRYING TRUNKS AND FURNITURE AND STUFF. . .
MOVING VANS WERE SPEEDING DOWN THE STREET AND OUT OF TOWN. . .
MOVING VAN
EVERYBODY SEEMED TO BE MOVING AWAY!
GOSH!

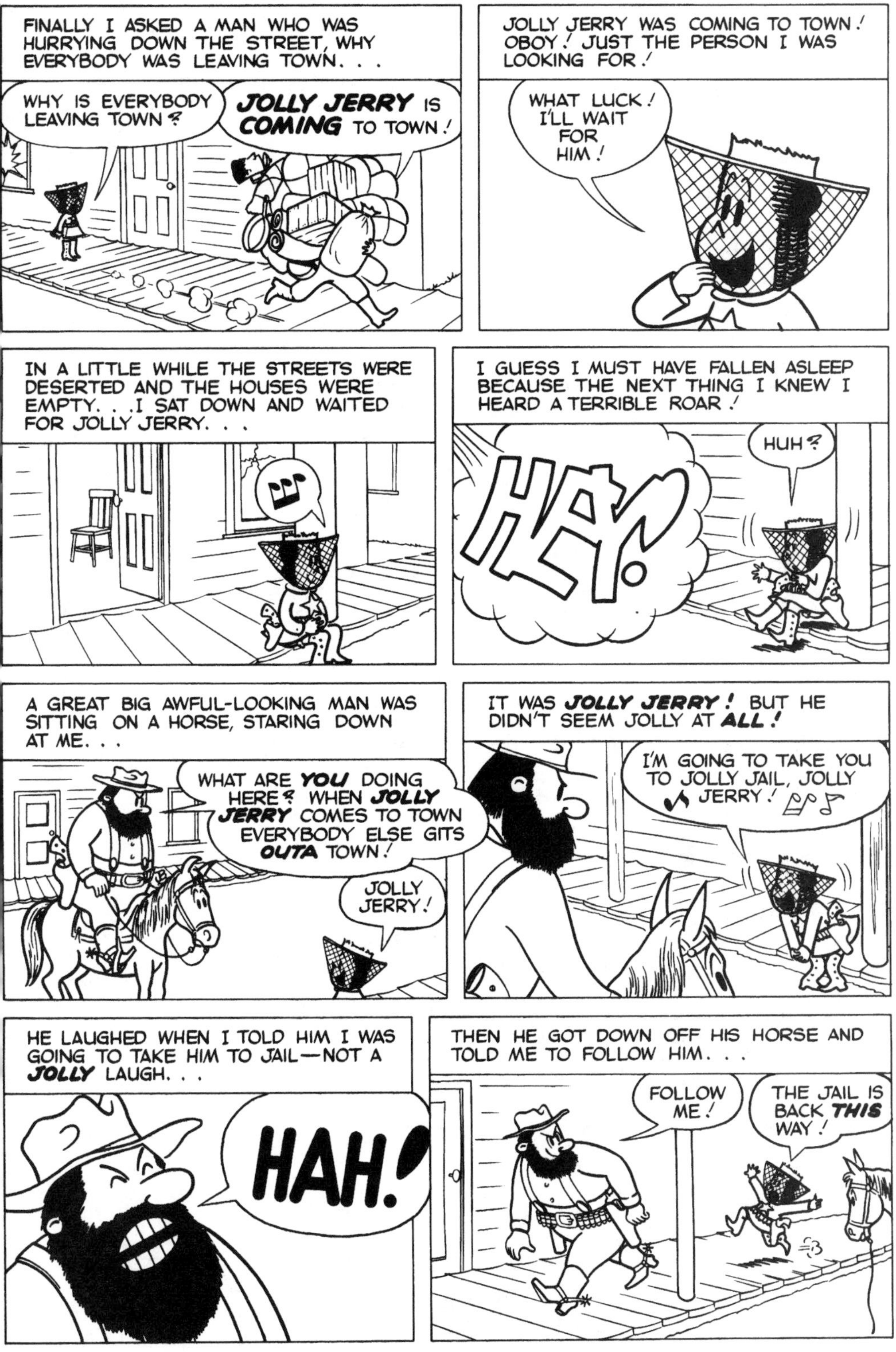
FINALLY I ASKED A MAN WHO WAS HURRYING DOWN THE STREET, WHY EVERYBODY WAS LEAVING TOWN. . .
WHY IS EVERYBODY LEAVING TOWN?
JOLLY JERRY IS COMING TO TOWN!
JOLLY JERRY WAS COMING TO TOWN! OBOY! JUST THE PERSON I WAS LOOKING FOR!
WHAT LUCK! I'LL WAIT FOR HIM!
IN A LITTLE WHILE THE STREETS WERE DESERTED AND THE HOUSES WERE EMPTY. . .I SAT DOWN AND WAITED FOR JOLLY JERRY. . .
I GUESS I MUST HAVE FALLEN ASLEEP BECAUSE THE NEXT THING I KNEW I HEARD A TERRIBLE ROAR!
HEY!
HUH?
A GREAT BIG AWFUL-LOOKING MAN WAS SITTING ON A HORSE, STARING DOWN AT ME. . .
WHAT ARE YOU DOING HERE? WHEN JOLLY JERRY COMES TO TOWN EVERYBODY ELSE GITS OUTA TOWN!
JOLLY JERRY!
IT WAS JOLLY JERRY! BUT HE DIDN'T SEEM JOLLY AT ALL!
I'M GOING TO TAKE YOU TO JOLLY JAIL, JOLLY JERRY!
HE LAUGHED WHEN I TOLD HIM I WAS GOING TO TAKE HIM TO JAIL—NOT A JOLLY LAUGH. . .
HAH!
THEN HE GOT DOWN OFF HIS HORSE AND TOLD ME TO FOLLOW HIM. . .
FOLLOW ME!
THE JAIL IS BACK THIS WAY!

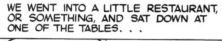

WE WENT INTO A LITTLE RESTAURANT, OR SOMETHING, AND SAT DOWN AT ONE OF THE TABLES. . .

YOU SIT DOWN OVER THERE!

SURE!

THEN JOLLY JERRY TOOK OUT A **PACK OF CARDS!**

NOW. . .WE'RE GONNA PLAY CARDS TO SEE IF I GO TO JAIL. . . .OR **YOU DIE!**

OH, GOODY! I **LOVE** TO PLAY CARDS!

GOSH, WE WERE GOING TO PLAY CARDS TO SEE WHETHER OR NOT JOLLY JERRY WOULD LET ME TAKE HIM TO JAIL!

WHAT GAME WOULD YOU LIKE T'PLAY?

LET'S PLAY "OLD MAID"!

I WAS SURE I'D WIN BECAUSE WE WERE GOING TO PLAY "OLD MAID" MY FAVORITE CARD GAME. . .

JUSTA MINUTE!

?

BUT BEFORE WE BEGAN, JOLLY JERRY TOOK OUT HIS GUNS AND PUT THEM ON THE TABLE. . .I PUT MY GUNS ON THE TABLE, TOO!

SLAM! SLAM!

THEN JOLLY JERRY DEALT OUT THE CARDS. . .

ONE FER YOU, ONE FER ME, ONE FER YOU—

DON'T **THROW** 'EM!

I LOOKED MY CARDS OVER AND—OH, GOODY! I DIDN'T HAVE THE "OLD MAID" CARD (THE QUEEN OF DIAMONDS)!

HAH! **YOU** GOT IT!

SHADDUP!

JOLLY JERRY HAD IT! NOW I WOULD HAVE TO BE CAREFUL I DIDN'T PICK THE OLD MAID CARD WHEN I DREW FROM JOLLY JERRY'S HAND. . .

DRAW!

DON'T RUSH ME!

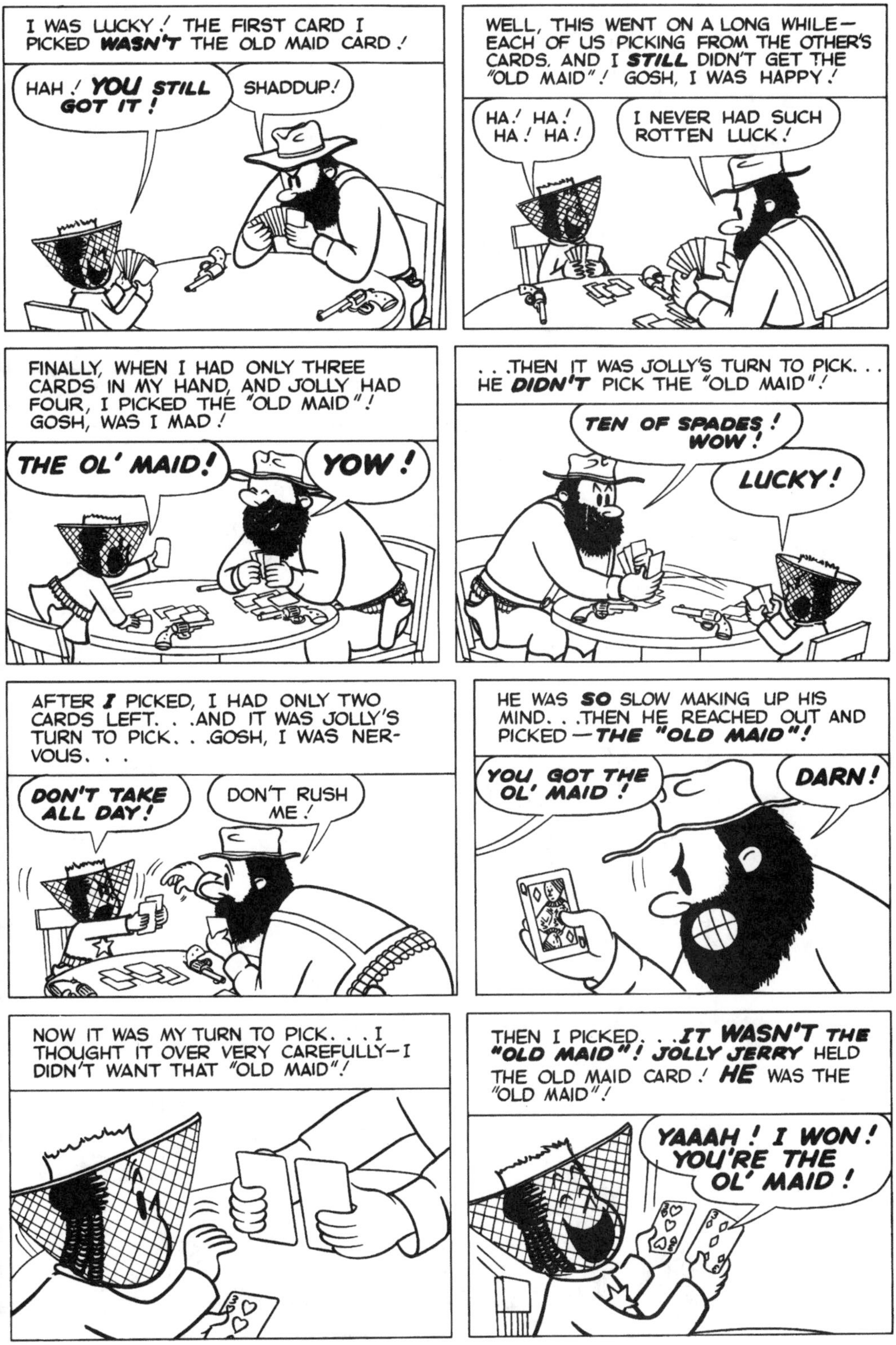
I WAS LUCKY! THE FIRST CARD I PICKED **WASN'T** THE OLD MAID CARD!
HAH! **YOU STILL GOT IT!**
SHADDUP!
WELL, THIS WENT ON A LONG WHILE— EACH OF US PICKING FROM THE OTHER'S CARDS, AND I **STILL** DIDN'T GET THE "OLD MAID"! GOSH, I WAS HAPPY!
HA! HA! HA! HA!
I NEVER HAD SUCH ROTTEN LUCK!
FINALLY, WHEN I HAD ONLY THREE CARDS IN MY HAND, AND JOLLY HAD FOUR, I PICKED THE "OLD MAID"! GOSH, WAS I MAD!
THE OL' MAID!
YOW!
...THEN IT WAS JOLLY'S TURN TO PICK... HE **DIDN'T** PICK THE "OLD MAID"!
TEN OF SPADES! WOW!
LUCKY!
AFTER **I** PICKED, I HAD ONLY TWO CARDS LEFT...AND IT WAS JOLLY'S TURN TO PICK...GOSH, I WAS NERVOUS...
DON'T TAKE ALL DAY!
DON'T RUSH ME!
HE WAS **SO** SLOW MAKING UP HIS MIND...THEN HE REACHED OUT AND PICKED—**THE "OLD MAID"!**
YOU GOT THE OL' MAID!
DARN!
NOW IT WAS MY TURN TO PICK...I THOUGHT IT OVER VERY CAREFULLY—I DIDN'T WANT THAT "OLD MAID"!
THEN I PICKED...**IT WASN'T THE "OLD MAID"! JOLLY JERRY** HELD THE OLD MAID CARD! **HE** WAS THE "OLD MAID"!
YAAAH! I WON! YOU'RE THE OL' MAID!

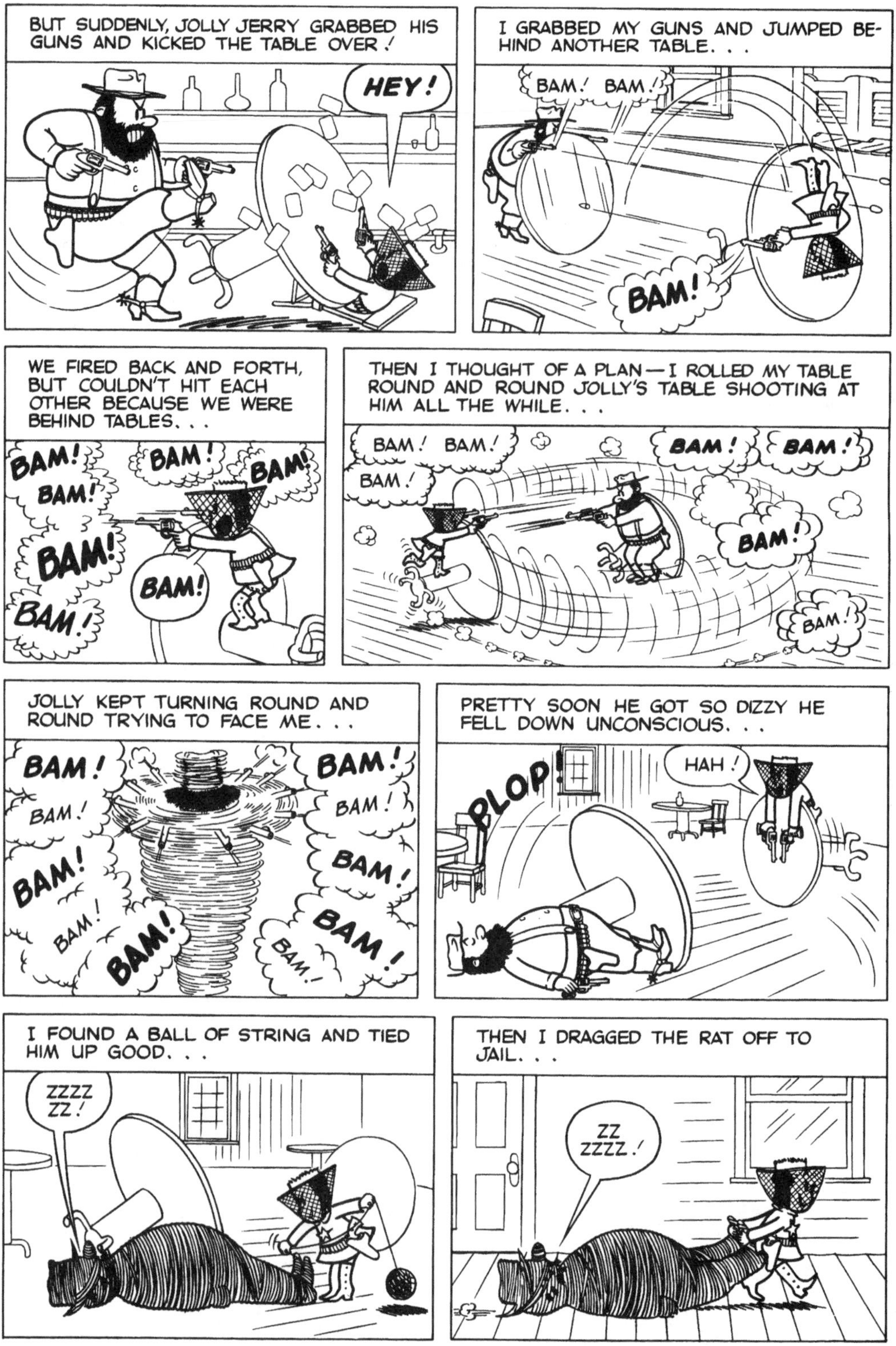
BUT SUDDENLY, JOLLY JERRY GRABBED HIS GUNS AND KICKED THE TABLE OVER!
HEY!
I GRABBED MY GUNS AND JUMPED BEHIND ANOTHER TABLE. . .
BAM! BAM!
BAM!
WE FIRED BACK AND FORTH, BUT COULDN'T HIT EACH OTHER BECAUSE WE WERE BEHIND TABLES. . .
BAM!
BAM!
BAM!
BAM!
BAM!
BAM!
BAM!
THEN I THOUGHT OF A PLAN—I ROLLED MY TABLE ROUND AND ROUND JOLLY'S TABLE SHOOTING AT HIM ALL THE WHILE. . .
BAM! BAM!
BAM!
BAM!
BAM!
BAM!
BAM!
JOLLY KEPT TURNING ROUND AND ROUND TRYING TO FACE ME. . .
BAM!
BAM!
BAM!
BAM!
BAM!
BAM!
BAM!
BAM!
BAM!
BAM!
PRETTY SOON HE GOT SO DIZZY HE FELL DOWN UNCONSCIOUS. . .
PLOP!
HAH!
I FOUND A BALL OF STRING AND TIED HIM UP GOOD. . .
ZZZZ ZZ!
THEN I DRAGGED THE RAT OFF TO JAIL. . .
ZZ ZZZZ!

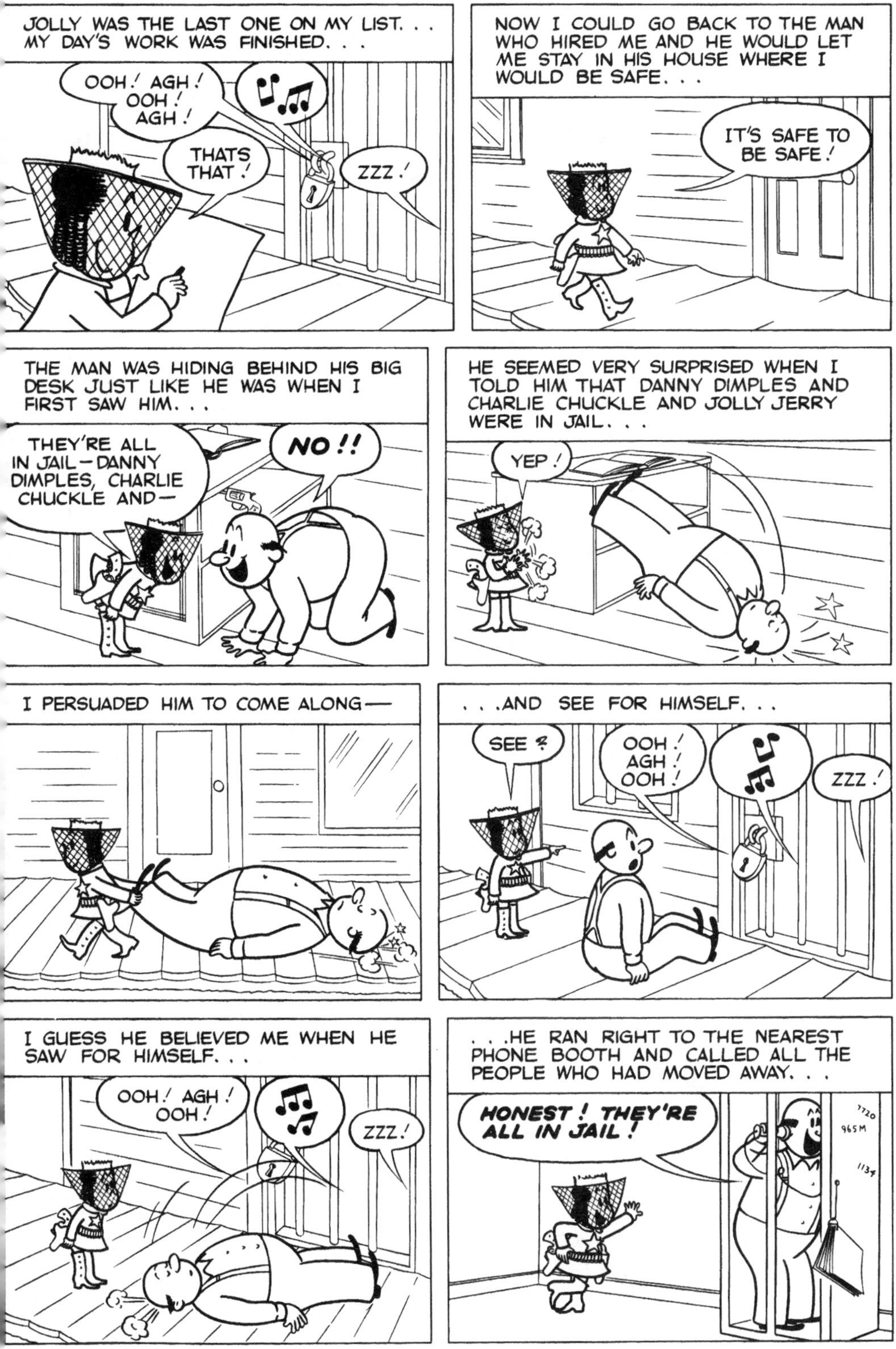

JOLLY WAS THE LAST ONE ON MY LIST. . . MY DAY'S WORK WAS FINISHED. . .
OOH! AGH! OOH! AGH!
THATS THAT!
ZZZ!
NOW I COULD GO BACK TO THE MAN WHO HIRED ME AND HE WOULD LET ME STAY IN HIS HOUSE WHERE I WOULD BE SAFE. . .
IT'S SAFE TO BE SAFE!
THE MAN WAS HIDING BEHIND HIS BIG DESK JUST LIKE HE WAS WHEN I FIRST SAW HIM. . .
THEY'RE ALL IN JAIL—DANNY DIMPLES, CHARLIE CHUCKLE AND—
NO!!
HE SEEMED VERY SURPRISED WHEN I TOLD HIM THAT DANNY DIMPLES AND CHARLIE CHUCKLE AND JOLLY JERRY WERE IN JAIL. . .
YEP!
I PERSUADED HIM TO COME ALONG—
. . .AND SEE FOR HIMSELF. . .
SEE?
OOH! AGH! OOH!
ZZZ!
I GUESS HE BELIEVED ME WHEN HE SAW FOR HIMSELF. . .
OOH! AGH! OOH!
ZZZ!
. . .HE RAN RIGHT TO THE NEAREST PHONE BOOTH AND CALLED ALL THE PEOPLE WHO HAD MOVED AWAY. . .
HONEST! THEY'RE ALL IN JAIL!

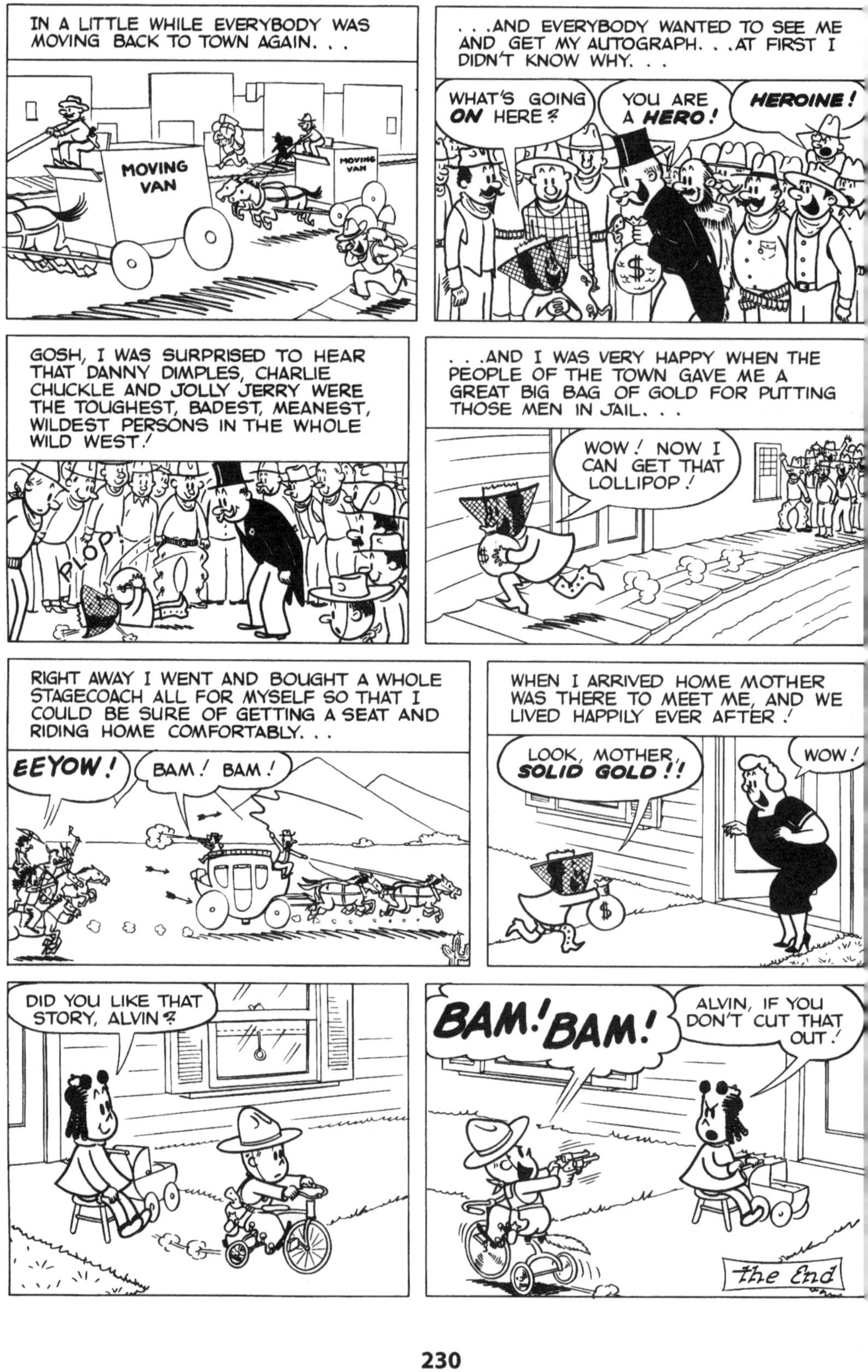
IN A LITTLE WHILE EVERYBODY WAS MOVING BACK TO TOWN AGAIN. . .
MOVING VAN
MOVING VAN
. . .AND EVERYBODY WANTED TO SEE ME AND GET MY AUTOGRAPH. . .AT FIRST I DIDN'T KNOW WHY. . .
WHAT'S GOING ON HERE?
YOU ARE A HERO!
HEROINE!
GOSH, I WAS SURPRISED TO HEAR THAT DANNY DIMPLES, CHARLIE CHUCKLE AND JOLLY JERRY WERE THE TOUGHEST, BADEST, MEANEST, WILDEST PERSONS IN THE WHOLE WILD WEST!
PLOP!
. . .AND I WAS VERY HAPPY WHEN THE PEOPLE OF THE TOWN GAVE ME A GREAT BIG BAG OF GOLD FOR PUTTING THOSE MEN IN JAIL. . .
WOW! NOW I CAN GET THAT LOLLIPOP!
RIGHT AWAY I WENT AND BOUGHT A WHOLE STAGECOACH ALL FOR MYSELF SO THAT I COULD BE SURE OF GETTING A SEAT AND RIDING HOME COMFORTABLY. . .
EEYOW!
BAM! BAM!
WHEN I ARRIVED HOME MOTHER WAS THERE TO MEET ME, AND WE LIVED HAPPILY EVER AFTER!
LOOK, MOTHER, SOLID GOLD!!
WOW!
DID YOU LIKE THAT STORY, ALVIN?
BAM! BAM!
ALVIN, IF YOU DON'T CUT THAT OUT!
the End

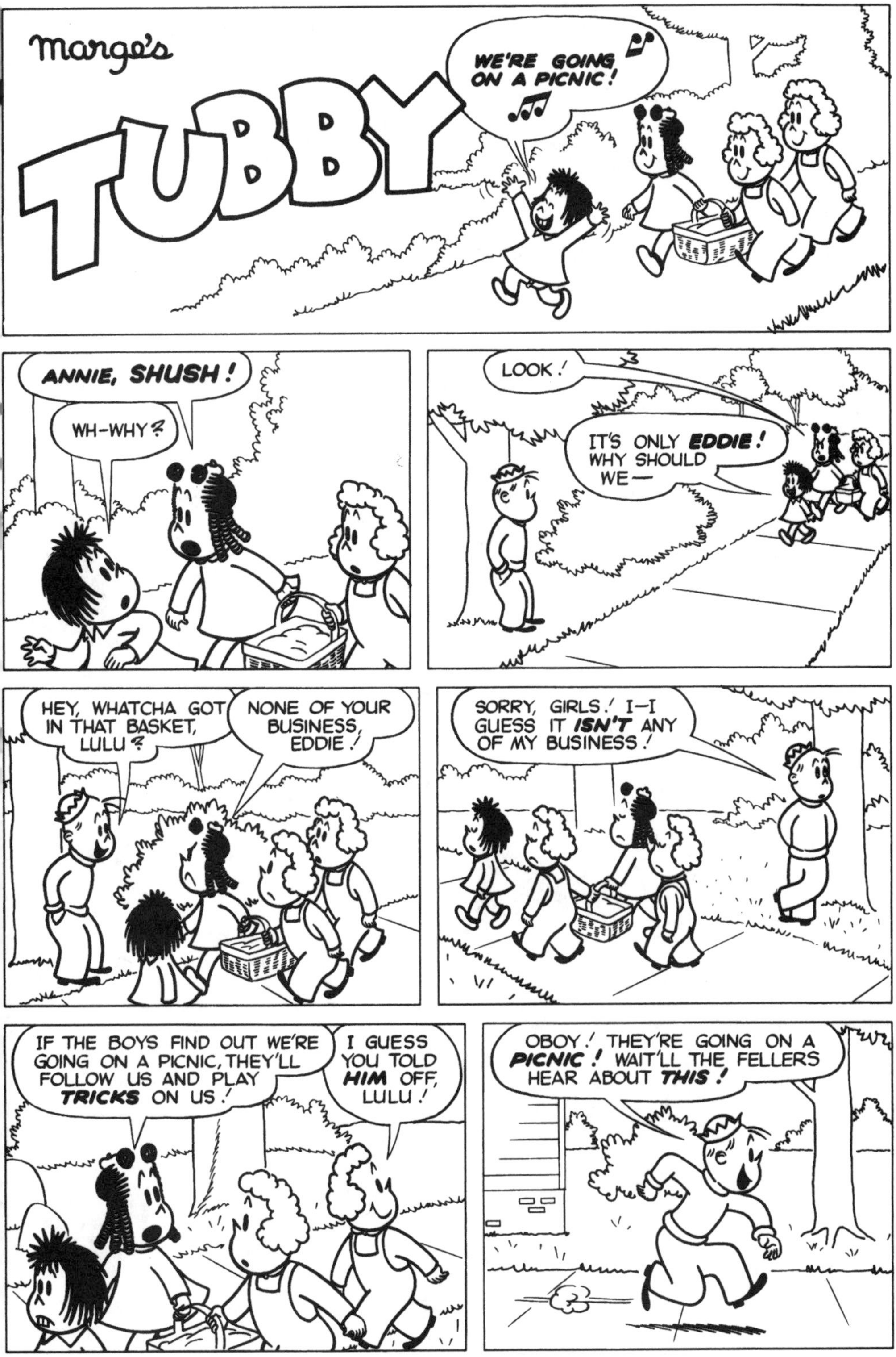
marge's
TUBBY
WE'RE GOING ON A PICNIC!
ANNIE, SHUSH!
WH-WHY?
LOOK!
IT'S ONLY EDDIE! WHY SHOULD WE—
HEY, WHATCHA GOT IN THAT BASKET, LULU?
NONE OF YOUR BUSINESS, EDDIE!
SORRY, GIRLS! I—I GUESS IT ISN'T ANY OF MY BUSINESS!
IF THE BOYS FIND OUT WE'RE GOING ON A PICNIC, THEY'LL FOLLOW US AND PLAY TRICKS ON US!
I GUESS YOU TOLD HIM OFF, LULU!
OBOY! THEY'RE GOING ON A PICNIC! WAIT'LL THE FELLERS HEAR ABOUT THIS!

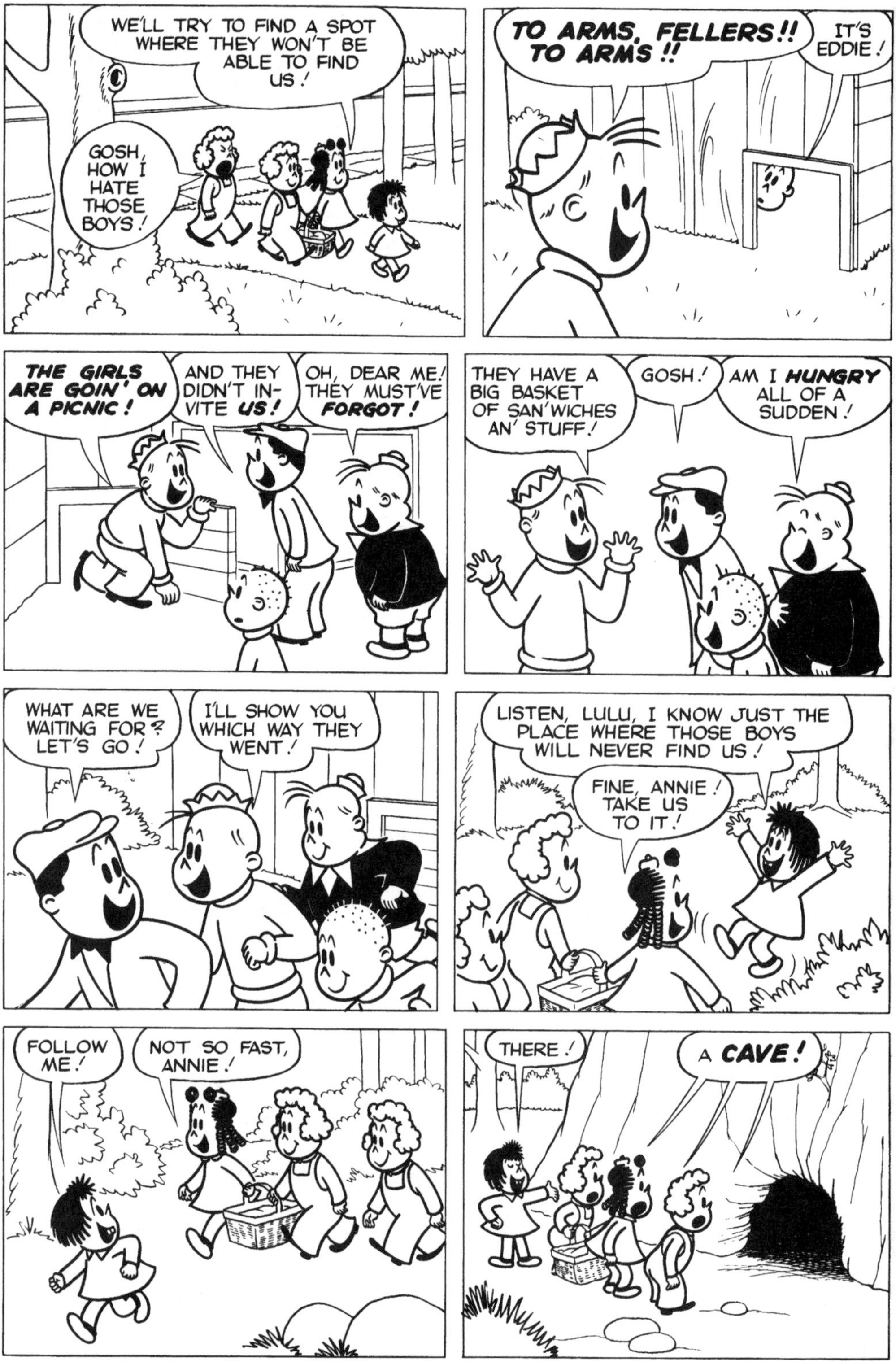

WE'LL TRY TO FIND A SPOT WHERE THEY WON'T BE ABLE TO FIND US!
GOSH, HOW I HATE THOSE BOYS!
TO ARMS, FELLERS!! TO ARMS!!
IT'S EDDIE!
THE GIRLS ARE GOIN' ON A PICNIC!
AND THEY DIDN'T IN-VITE US!
OH, DEAR ME! THEY MUST'VE FORGOT!
THEY HAVE A BIG BASKET OF SAN'WICHES AN' STUFF!
GOSH!
AM I HUNGRY ALL OF A SUDDEN!
WHAT ARE WE WAITING FOR? LET'S GO!
I'LL SHOW YOU WHICH WAY THEY WENT!
LISTEN, LULU, I KNOW JUST THE PLACE WHERE THOSE BOYS WILL NEVER FIND US!
FINE, ANNIE! TAKE US TO IT!
FOLLOW ME!
NOT SO FAST, ANNIE!
THERE!
A CAVE!

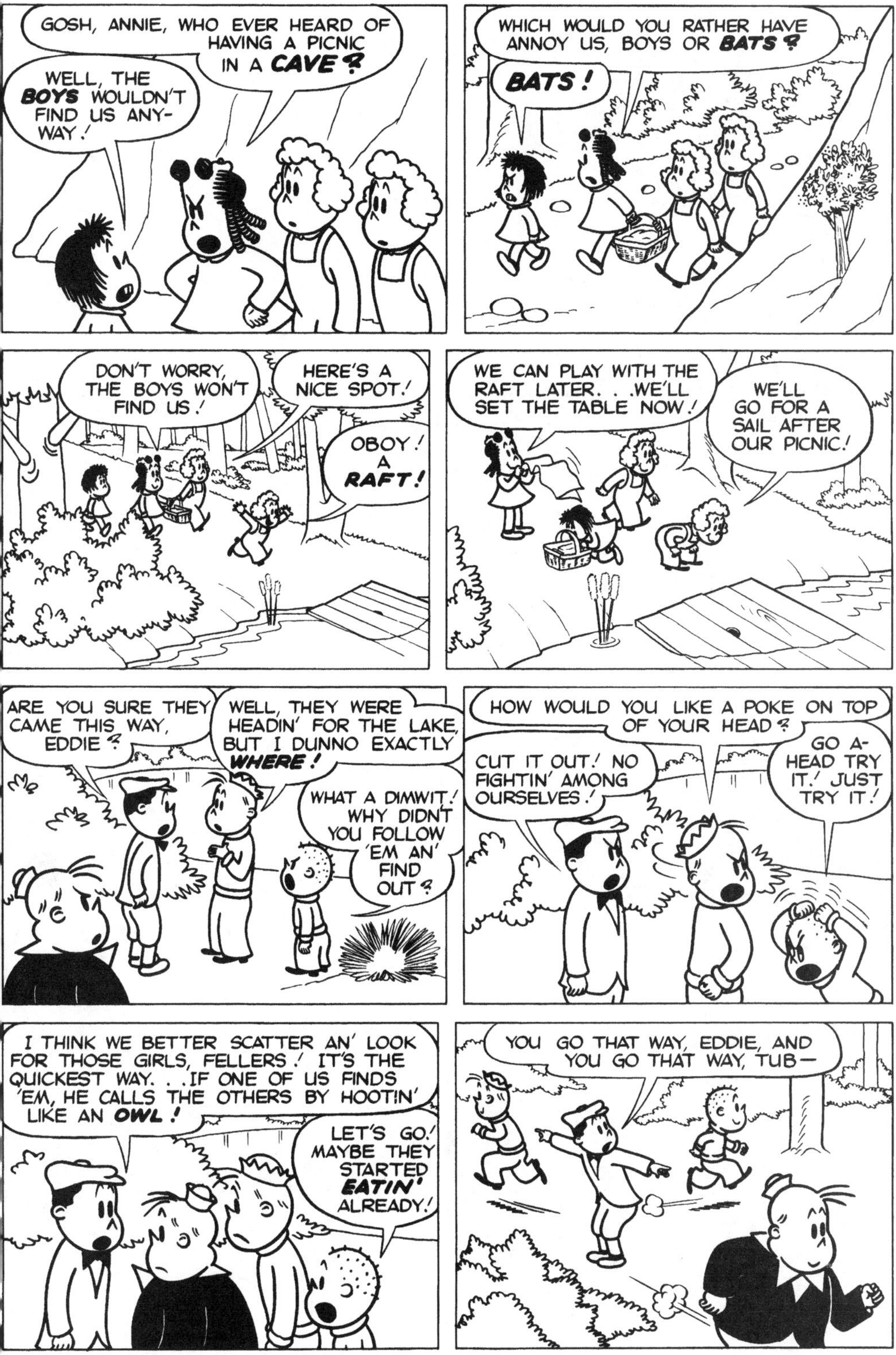

GOSH, ANNIE, WHO EVER HEARD OF HAVING A PICNIC IN A CAVE?
WELL, THE BOYS WOULDN'T FIND US ANYWAY!
WHICH WOULD YOU RATHER HAVE ANNOY US, BOYS OR BATS?
BATS!
DON'T WORRY, THE BOYS WON'T FIND US!
HERE'S A NICE SPOT!
OBOY! A RAFT!
WE CAN PLAY WITH THE RAFT LATER. . .WE'LL SET THE TABLE NOW!
WE'LL GO FOR A SAIL AFTER OUR PICNIC!
ARE YOU SURE THEY CAME THIS WAY, EDDIE?
WELL, THEY WERE HEADIN' FOR THE LAKE, BUT I DUNNO EXACTLY WHERE!
WHAT A DIMWIT! WHY DIDN'T YOU FOLLOW 'EM AN' FIND OUT?
HOW WOULD YOU LIKE A POKE ON TOP OF YOUR HEAD?
CUT IT OUT! NO FIGHTIN' AMONG OURSELVES!
GO AHEAD TRY IT! JUST TRY IT!
I THINK WE BETTER SCATTER AN' LOOK FOR THOSE GIRLS, FELLERS! IT'S THE QUICKEST WAY. . .IF ONE OF US FINDS 'EM, HE CALLS THE OTHERS BY HOOTIN' LIKE AN OWL!
LET'S GO! MAYBE THEY STARTED EATIN' ALREADY!
YOU GO THAT WAY, EDDIE, AND YOU GO THAT WAY, TUB—

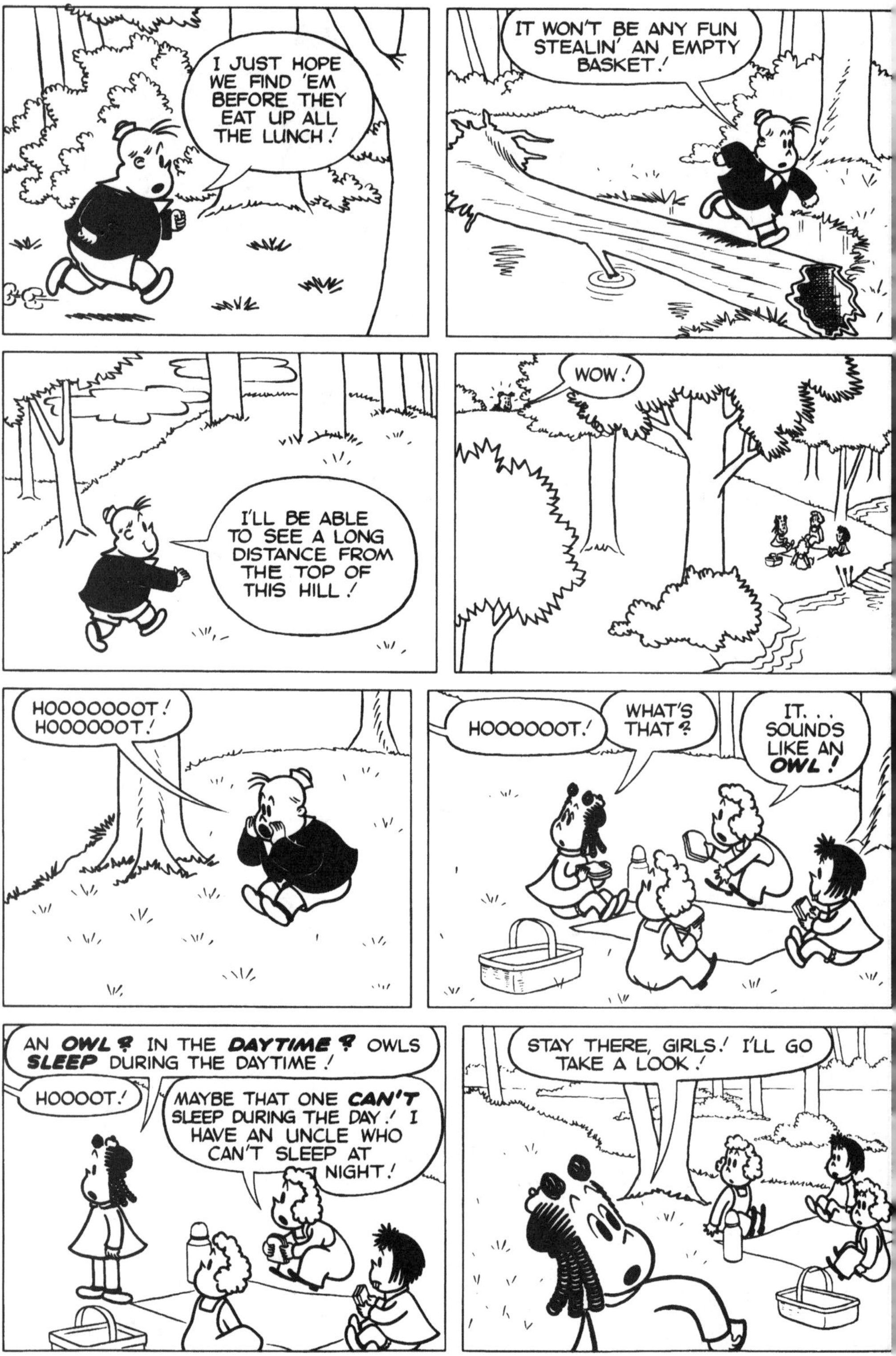
I JUST HOPE WE FIND 'EM BEFORE THEY EAT UP ALL THE LUNCH!
IT WON'T BE ANY FUN STEALIN' AN EMPTY BASKET!
I'LL BE ABLE TO SEE A LONG DISTANCE FROM THE TOP OF THIS HILL!
WOW!
HOOOOOOOT! HOOOOOOT!
HOOOOOOT!
WHAT'S THAT?
IT... SOUNDS LIKE AN OWL!
AN OWL? IN THE DAYTIME? OWLS SLEEP DURING THE DAYTIME!
HOOOOT!
MAYBE THAT ONE CAN'T SLEEP DURING THE DAY! I HAVE AN UNCLE WHO CAN'T SLEEP AT NIGHT!
STAY THERE, GIRLS! I'LL GO TAKE A LOOK!

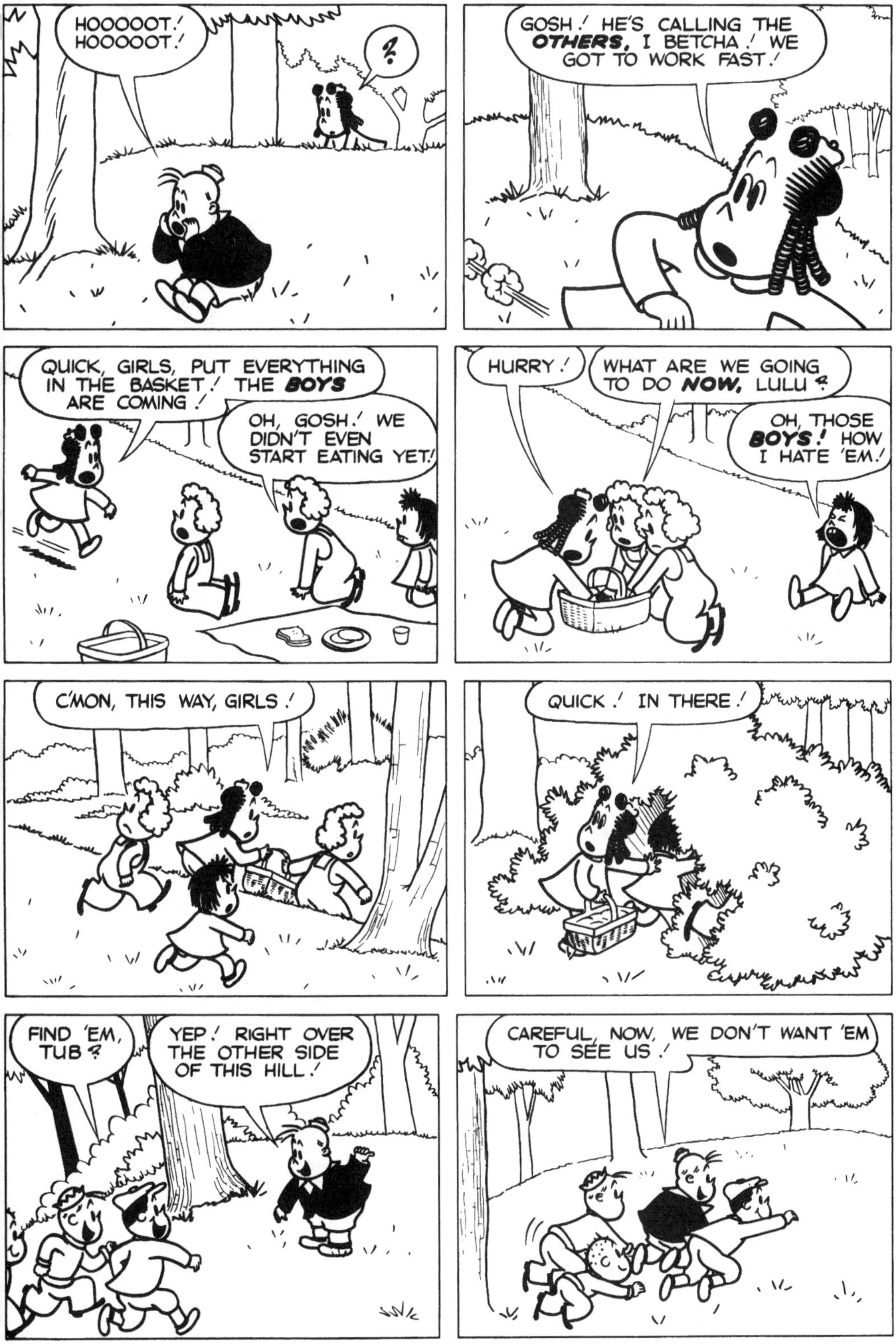
HOOOOOT! HOOOOOT!
?
GOSH! HE'S CALLING THE OTHERS, I BETCHA! WE GOT TO WORK FAST!
QUICK, GIRLS, PUT EVERYTHING IN THE BASKET! THE BOYS ARE COMING!
OH, GOSH! WE DIDN'T EVEN START EATING YET!
HURRY!
WHAT ARE WE GOING TO DO NOW, LULU?
OH, THOSE BOYS! HOW I HATE 'EM!
C'MON, THIS WAY, GIRLS!
QUICK! IN THERE!
FIND 'EM, TUB?
YEP! RIGHT OVER THE OTHER SIDE OF THIS HILL!
CAREFUL, NOW, WE DON'T WANT 'EM TO SEE US!

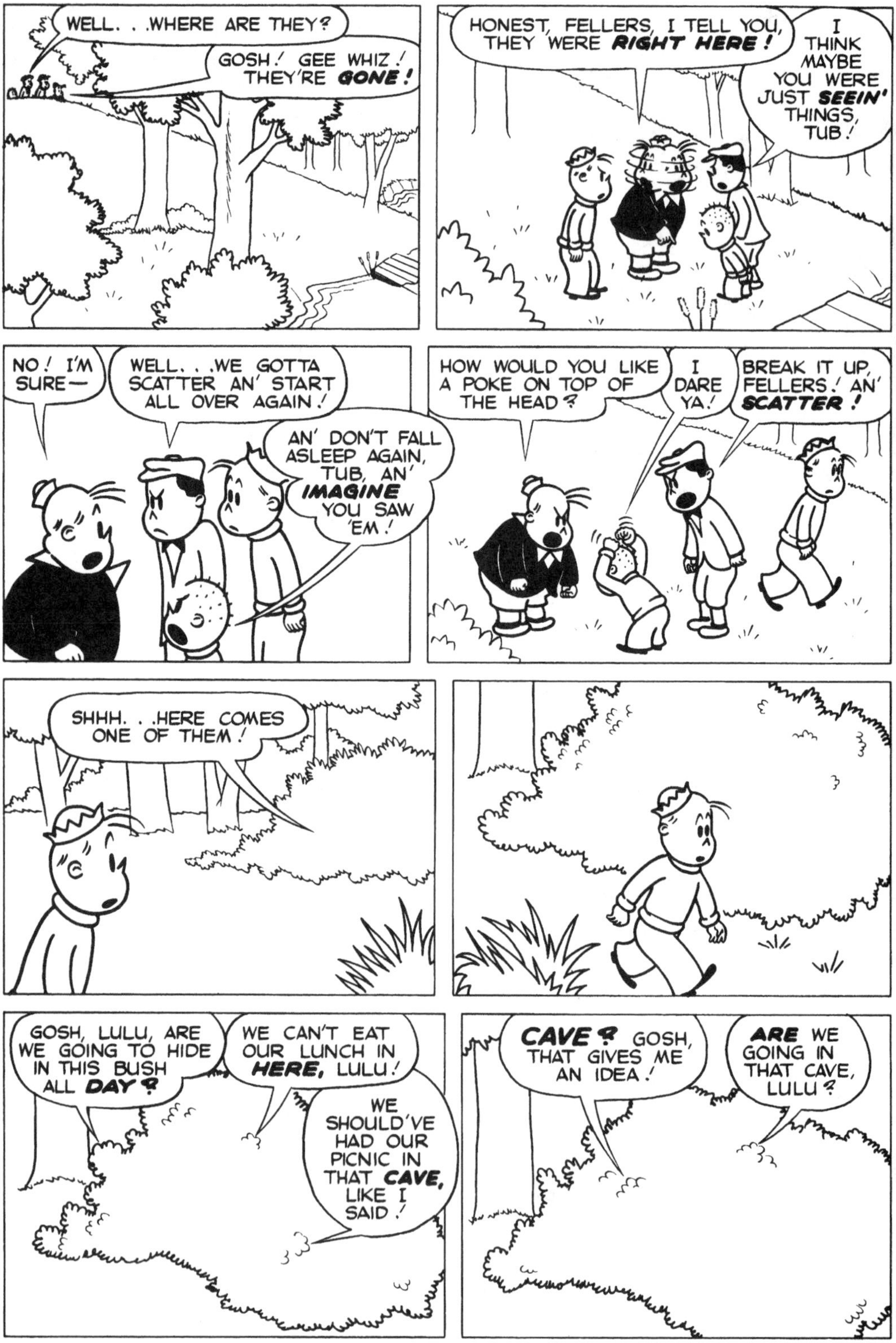

WELL. . .WHERE ARE THEY?
GOSH! GEE WHIZ! THEY'RE **GONE!**
HONEST, FELLERS, I TELL YOU, THEY WERE **RIGHT HERE!**
I THINK MAYBE YOU WERE JUST **SEEIN'** THINGS, TUB!
NO! I'M SURE—
WELL. . .WE GOTTA SCATTER AN' START ALL OVER AGAIN!
AN' DON'T FALL ASLEEP AGAIN, TUB, AN' **IMAGINE** YOU SAW 'EM!
HOW WOULD YOU LIKE A POKE ON TOP OF THE HEAD?
I DARE YA!
BREAK IT UP, FELLERS! AN' **SCATTER!**
SHHH. . .HERE COMES ONE OF THEM!
GOSH, LULU, ARE WE GOING TO HIDE IN THIS BUSH ALL **DAY?**
WE CAN'T EAT OUR LUNCH IN **HERE,** LULU!
WE SHOULD'VE HAD OUR PICNIC IN THAT **CAVE,** LIKE I SAID!
CAVE? GOSH, THAT GIVES ME AN IDEA!
ARE WE GOING IN THAT CAVE, LULU?

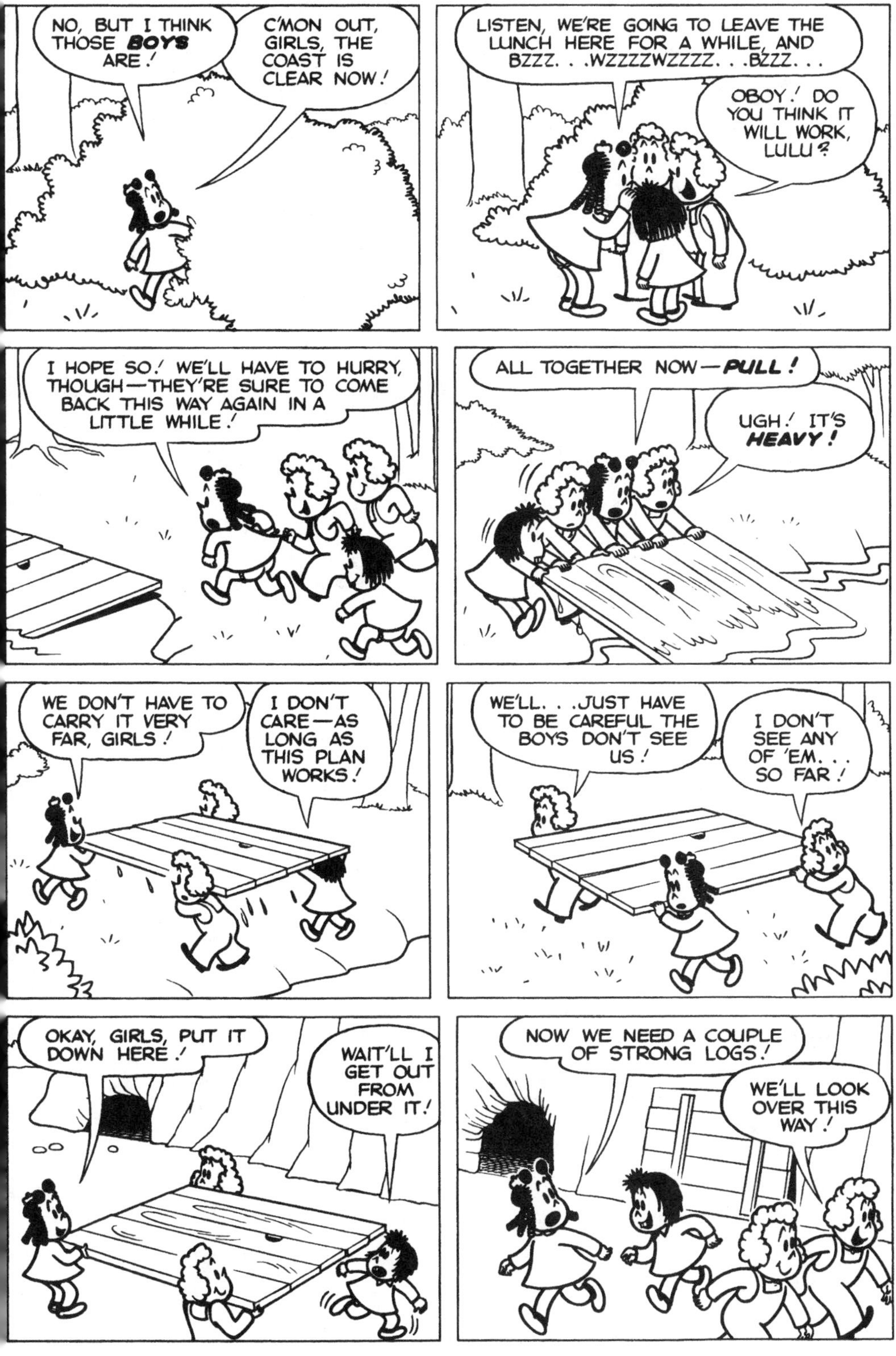

NO, BUT I THINK THOSE **BOYS** ARE!
C'MON OUT, GIRLS, THE COAST IS CLEAR NOW!
LISTEN, WE'RE GOING TO LEAVE THE LUNCH HERE FOR A WHILE, AND BZZZ. . .WZZZZWZZZZ. . .BZZZ. . .
OBOY! DO YOU THINK IT WILL WORK, LULU?
I HOPE SO! WE'LL HAVE TO HURRY, THOUGH—THEY'RE SURE TO COME BACK THIS WAY AGAIN IN A LITTLE WHILE!
ALL TOGETHER NOW—**PULL!**
UGH! IT'S **HEAVY!**
WE DON'T HAVE TO CARRY IT VERY FAR, GIRLS!
I DON'T CARE—AS LONG AS THIS PLAN WORKS!
WE'LL. . .JUST HAVE TO BE CAREFUL THE BOYS DON'T SEE US!
I DON'T SEE ANY OF 'EM. . . SO FAR!
OKAY, GIRLS, PUT IT DOWN HERE!
WAIT'LL I GET OUT FROM UNDER IT!
NOW WE NEED A COUPLE OF STRONG LOGS!
WE'LL LOOK OVER THIS WAY!

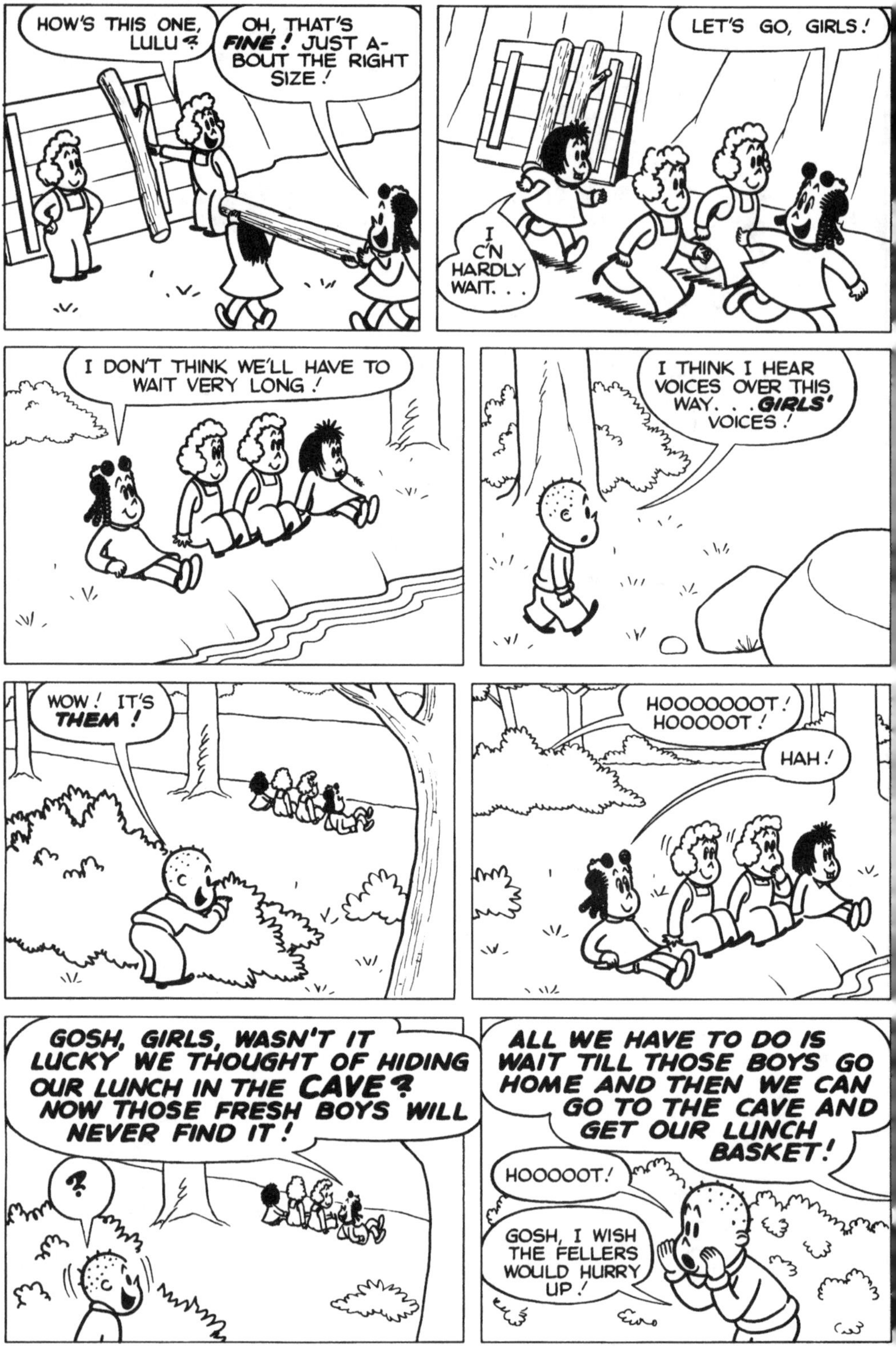
HOW'S THIS ONE, LULU?
OH, THAT'S FINE! JUST A-BOUT THE RIGHT SIZE!
LET'S GO, GIRLS!
I C'N HARDLY WAIT. . .
I DON'T THINK WE'LL HAVE TO WAIT VERY LONG!
I THINK I HEAR VOICES OVER THIS WAY. . .GIRLS' VOICES!
WOW! IT'S THEM!
HOOOOOOOT! HOOOOOT!
HAH!
GOSH, GIRLS, WASN'T IT LUCKY WE THOUGHT OF HIDING OUR LUNCH IN THE CAVE? NOW THOSE FRESH BOYS WILL NEVER FIND IT!
?
ALL WE HAVE TO DO IS WAIT TILL THOSE BOYS GO HOME AND THEN WE CAN GO TO THE CAVE AND GET OUR LUNCH BASKET!
HOOOOOT!
GOSH, I WISH THE FELLERS WOULD HURRY UP!

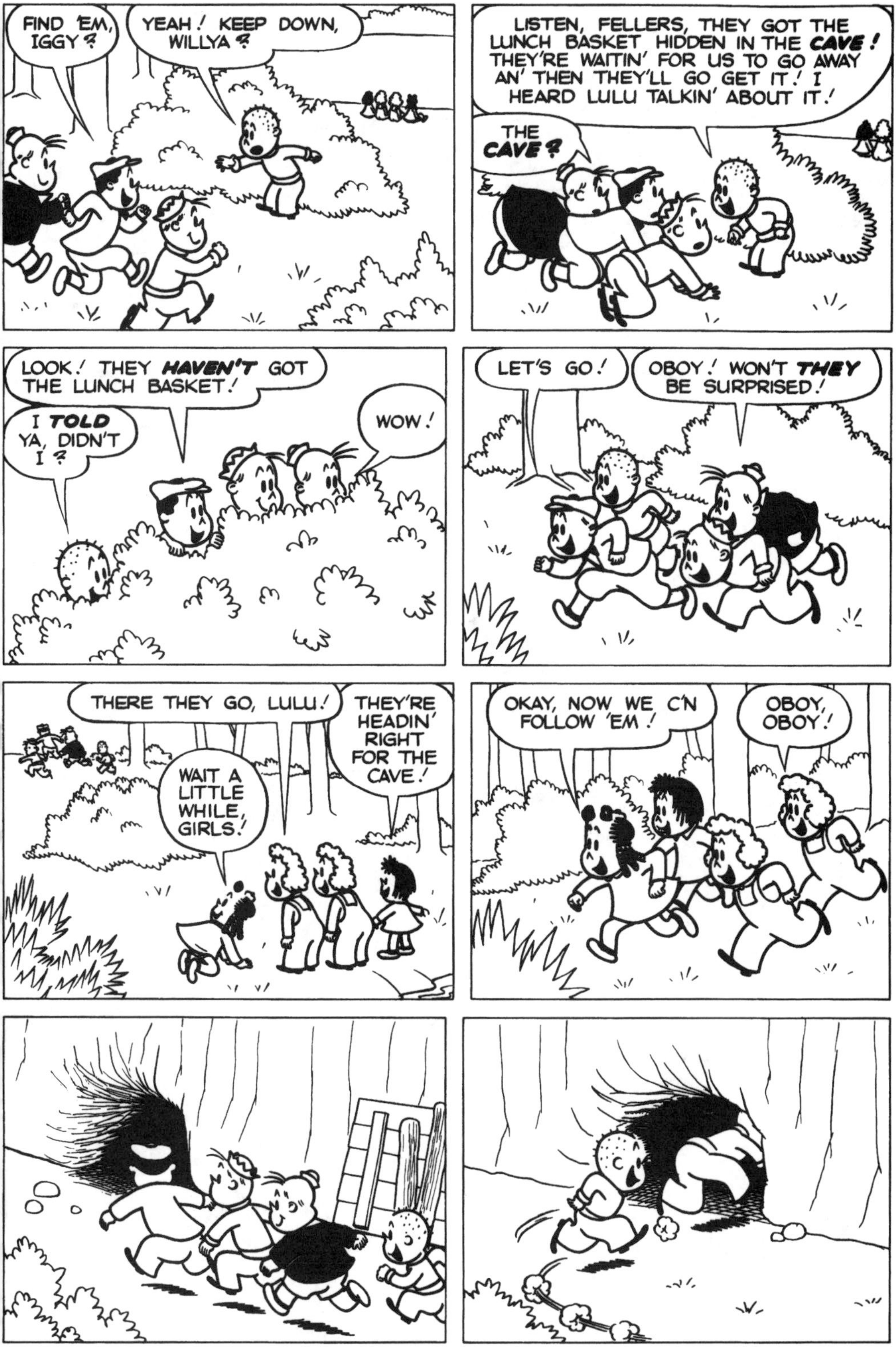
FIND 'EM, IGGY?
YEAH! KEEP DOWN, WILLYA?
LISTEN, FELLERS, THEY GOT THE LUNCH BASKET HIDDEN IN THE CAVE! THEY'RE WAITIN' FOR US TO GO AWAY AN' THEN THEY'LL GO GET IT! I HEARD LULU TALKIN' ABOUT IT!
THE CAVE?
LOOK! THEY HAVEN'T GOT THE LUNCH BASKET!
I TOLD YA, DIDN'T I?
WOW!
LET'S GO!
OBOY! WON'T THEY BE SURPRISED!
THERE THEY GO, LULU!
THEY'RE HEADIN' RIGHT FOR THE CAVE!
WAIT A LITTLE WHILE, GIRLS!
OKAY, NOW WE C'N FOLLOW 'EM!
OBOY, OBOY!

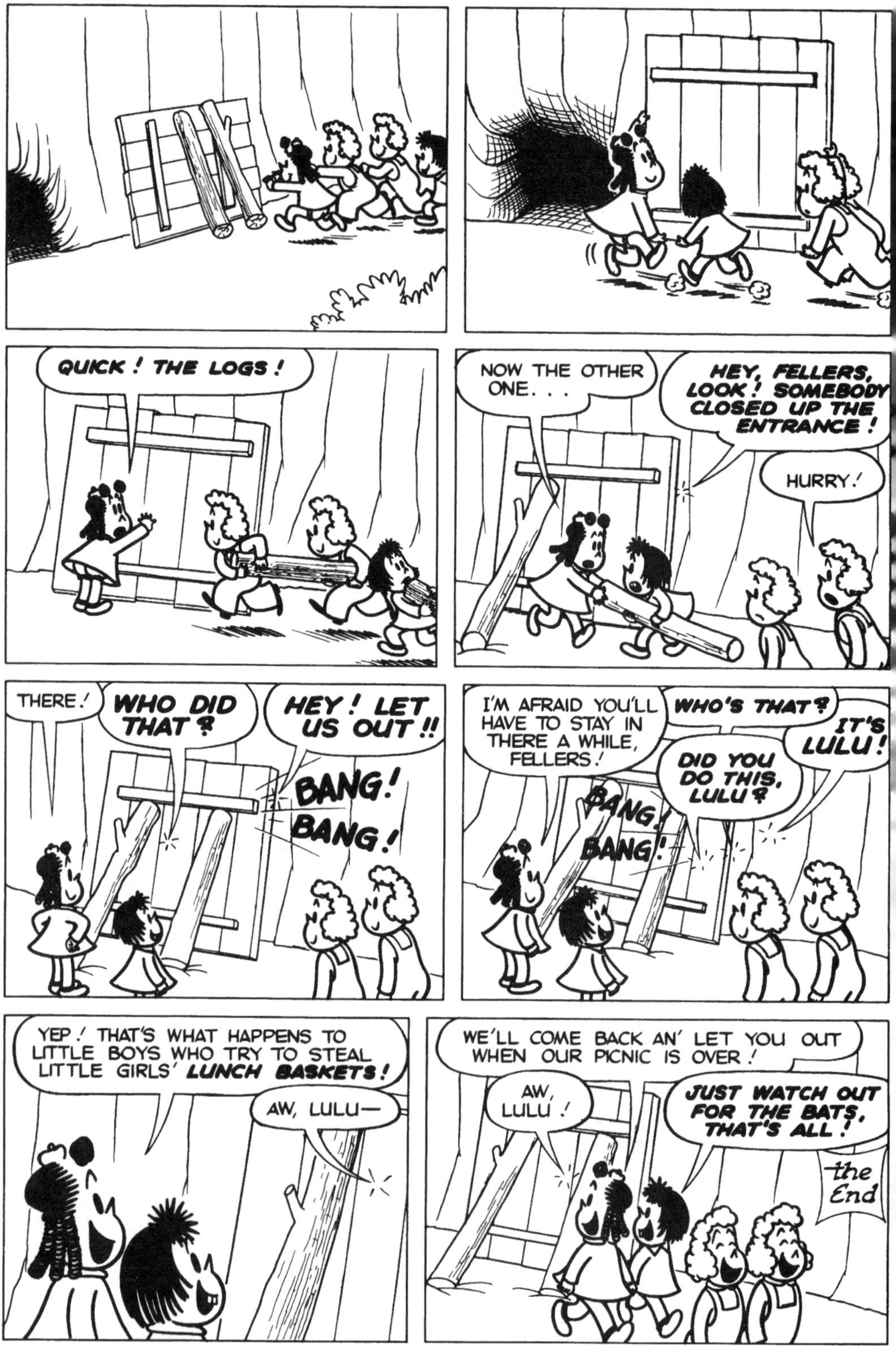
QUICK! THE LOGS!
NOW THE OTHER ONE. . .
HEY, FELLERS, LOOK! SOMEBODY CLOSED UP THE ENTRANCE!
HURRY!
THERE!
WHO DID THAT?
HEY! LET US OUT!!
BANG!
BANG!
I'M AFRAID YOU'LL HAVE TO STAY IN THERE A WHILE, FELLERS!
WHO'S THAT?
IT'S LULU!
DID YOU DO THIS, LULU?
BANG!
BANG!
YEP! THAT'S WHAT HAPPENS TO LITTLE BOYS WHO TRY TO STEAL LITTLE GIRLS' LUNCH BASKETS!
AW, LULU—
WE'LL COME BACK AN' LET YOU OUT WHEN OUR PICNIC IS OVER!
AW, LULU!
JUST WATCH OUT FOR THE BATS, THAT'S ALL!
the End

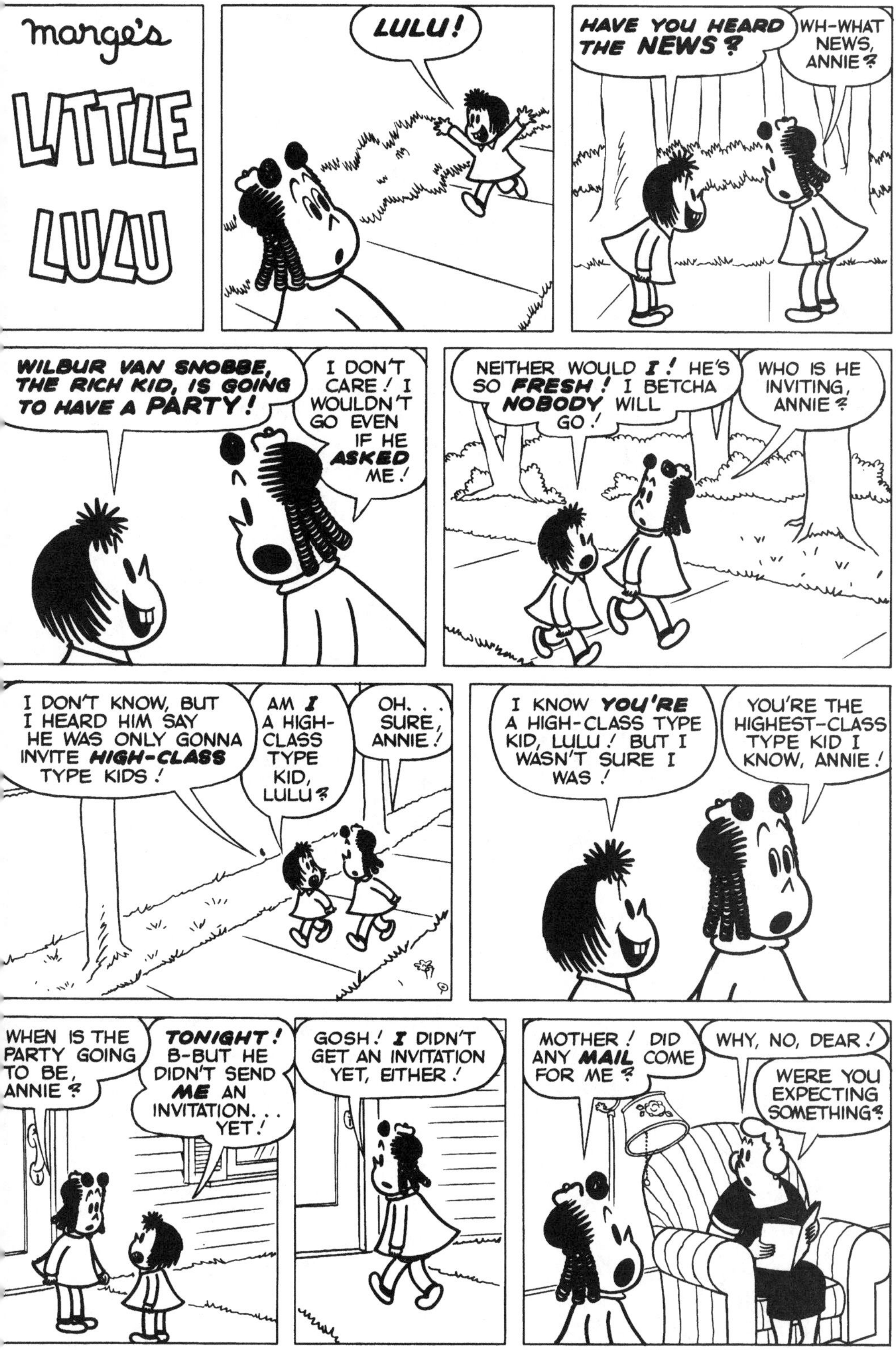
marge's
LITTLE LULU
LULU!
HAVE YOU HEARD THE NEWS?
WH-WHAT NEWS, ANNIE?
WILBUR VAN SNOBBE, THE RICH KID, IS GOING TO HAVE A PARTY!
I DON'T CARE! I WOULDN'T GO EVEN IF HE ASKED ME!
NEITHER WOULD I! HE'S SO FRESH! I BETCHA NOBODY WILL GO!
WHO IS HE INVITING, ANNIE?
I DON'T KNOW, BUT I HEARD HIM SAY HE WAS ONLY GONNA INVITE HIGH-CLASS TYPE KIDS!
AM I A HIGH-CLASS TYPE KID, LULU?
OH. . . SURE, ANNIE!
I KNOW YOU'RE A HIGH-CLASS TYPE KID, LULU! BUT I WASN'T SURE I WAS!
YOU'RE THE HIGHEST-CLASS TYPE KID I KNOW, ANNIE!
WHEN IS THE PARTY GOING TO BE, ANNIE?
TONIGHT! B-BUT HE DIDN'T SEND ME AN INVITATION. . . YET!
GOSH! I DIDN'T GET AN INVITATION YET, EITHER!
MOTHER! DID ANY MAIL COME FOR ME?
WHY, NO, DEAR!
WERE YOU EXPECTING SOMETHING?

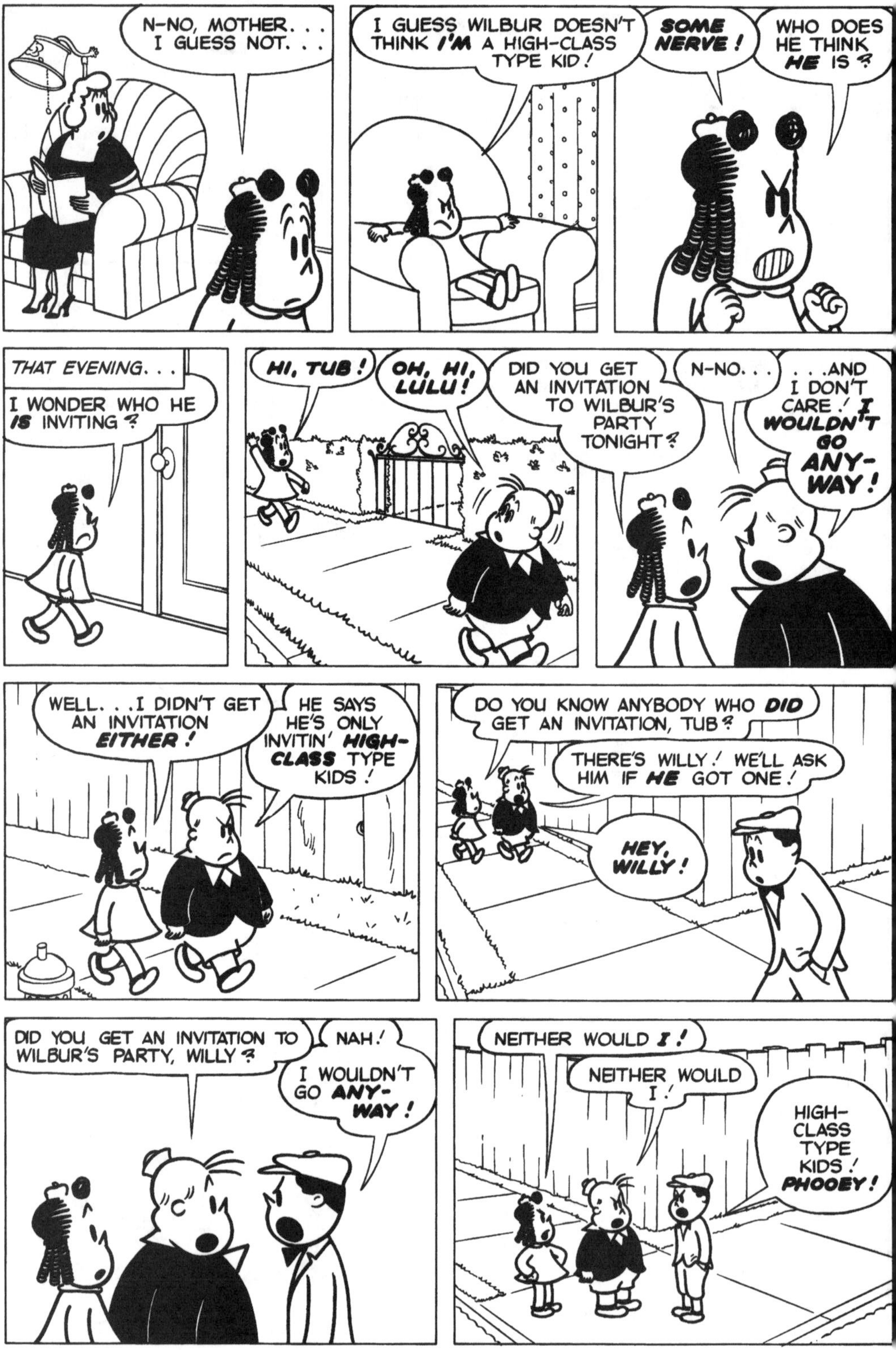
N-NO, MOTHER. . .
I GUESS NOT. . .
I GUESS WILBUR DOESN'T THINK I'M A HIGH-CLASS TYPE KID!
SOME NERVE!
WHO DOES HE THINK HE IS?
THAT EVENING. . .
I WONDER WHO HE IS INVITING?
HI, TUB!
OH, HI, LULU!
DID YOU GET AN INVITATION TO WILBUR'S PARTY TONIGHT?
N-NO. . .
. . .AND I DON'T CARE! I WOULDN'T GO ANY-WAY!
WELL. . .I DIDN'T GET AN INVITATION EITHER!
HE SAYS HE'S ONLY INVITIN' HIGH-CLASS TYPE KIDS!
DO YOU KNOW ANYBODY WHO DID GET AN INVITATION, TUB?
THERE'S WILLY! WE'LL ASK HIM IF HE GOT ONE!
HEY, WILLY!
DID YOU GET AN INVITATION TO WILBUR'S PARTY, WILLY?
NAH!
I WOULDN'T GO ANY-WAY!
NEITHER WOULD I!
NEITHER WOULD I!
HIGH-CLASS TYPE KIDS! PHOOEY!

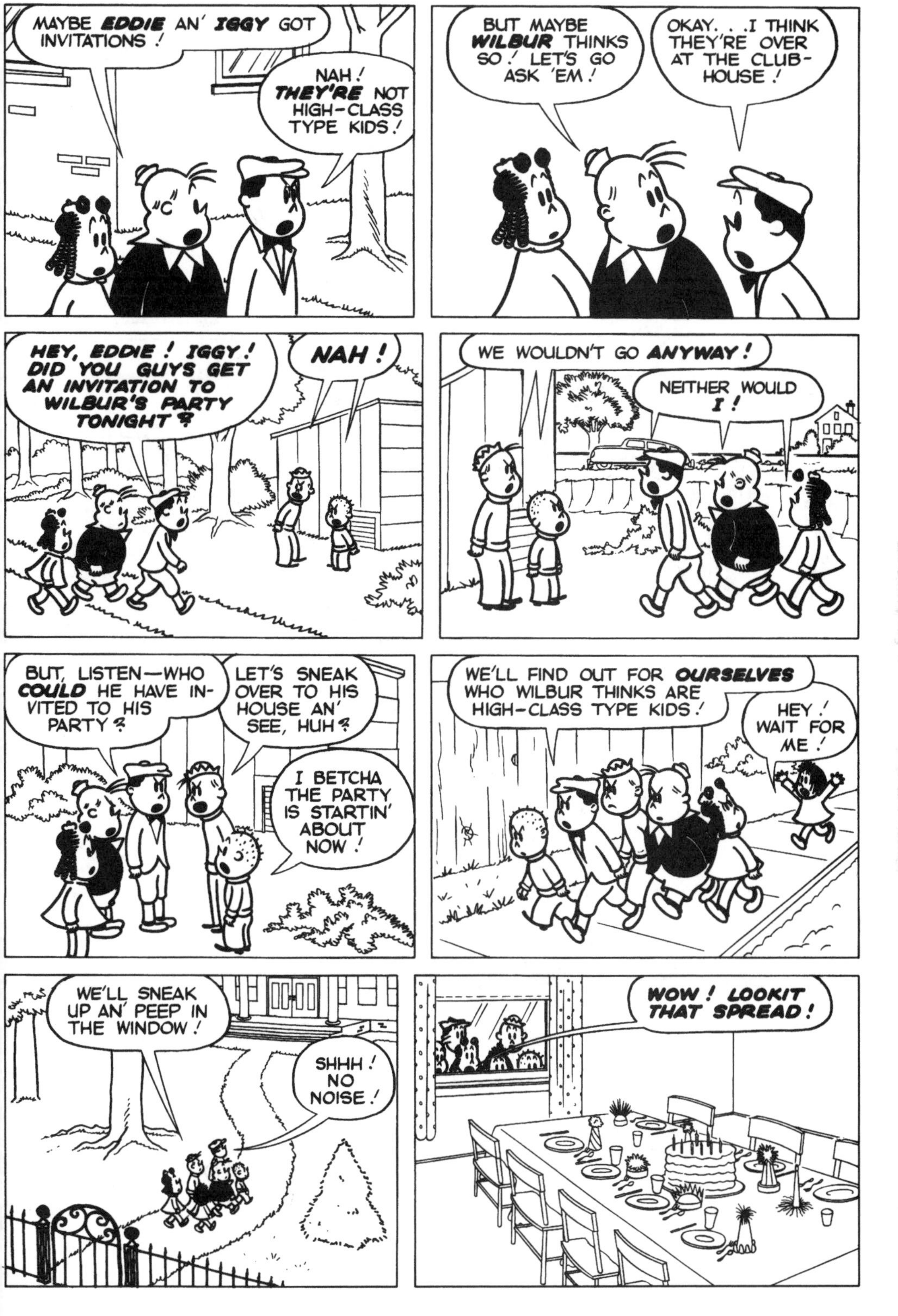
MAYBE EDDIE AN' IGGY GOT INVITATIONS!
NAH! THEY'RE NOT HIGH-CLASS TYPE KIDS!
BUT MAYBE WILBUR THINKS SO! LET'S GO ASK 'EM!
OKAY. . .I THINK THEY'RE OVER AT THE CLUB-HOUSE!
HEY, EDDIE! IGGY! DID YOU GUYS GET AN INVITATION TO WILBUR'S PARTY TONIGHT?
NAH!
WE WOULDN'T GO ANYWAY!
NEITHER WOULD I!
BUT, LISTEN—WHO COULD HE HAVE IN-VITED TO HIS PARTY?
LET'S SNEAK OVER TO HIS HOUSE AN' SEE, HUH?
I BETCHA THE PARTY IS STARTIN' ABOUT NOW!
WE'LL FIND OUT FOR OURSELVES WHO WILBUR THINKS ARE HIGH-CLASS TYPE KIDS!
HEY! WAIT FOR ME!
WE'LL SNEAK UP AN' PEEP IN THE WINDOW!
SHHH! NO NOISE!
WOW! LOOKIT THAT SPREAD!

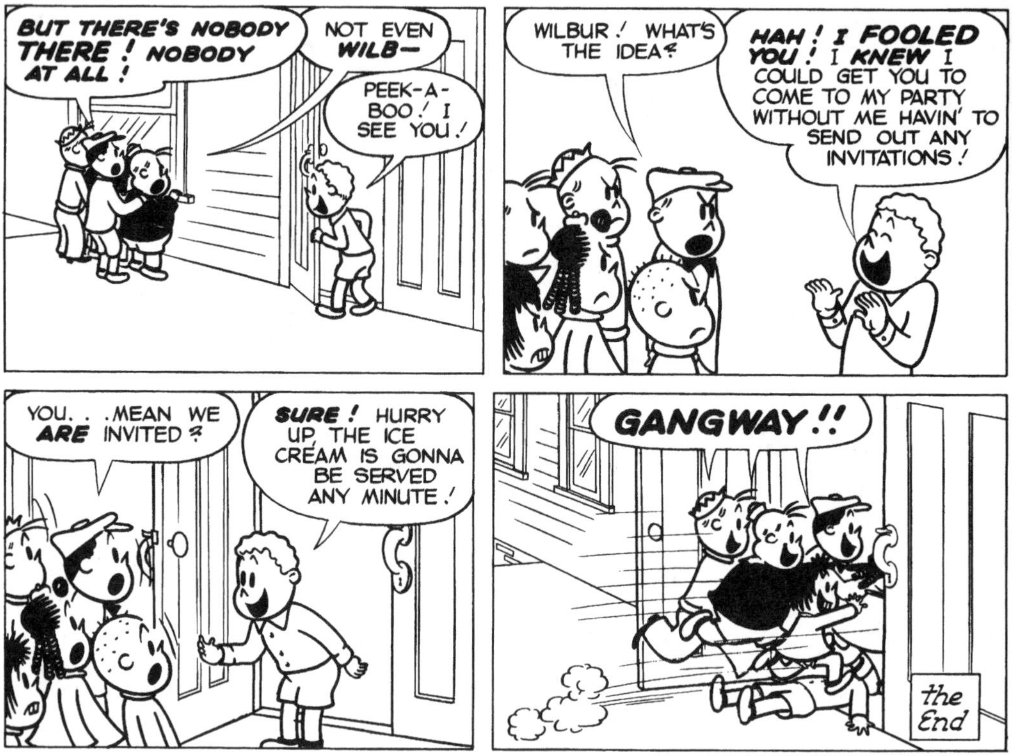
BUT THERE'S NOBODY THERE ! NOBODY AT ALL !
NOT EVEN WILB—
PEEK-A-BOO ! I SEE YOU !
WILBUR ! WHAT'S THE IDEA ?
HAH ! I FOOLED YOU ! I KNEW I COULD GET YOU TO COME TO MY PARTY WITHOUT ME HAVIN' TO SEND OUT ANY INVITATIONS !
YOU. . .MEAN WE ARE INVITED ?
SURE ! HURRY UP, THE ICE CREAM IS GONNA BE SERVED ANY MINUTE !
GANGWAY !!
the End

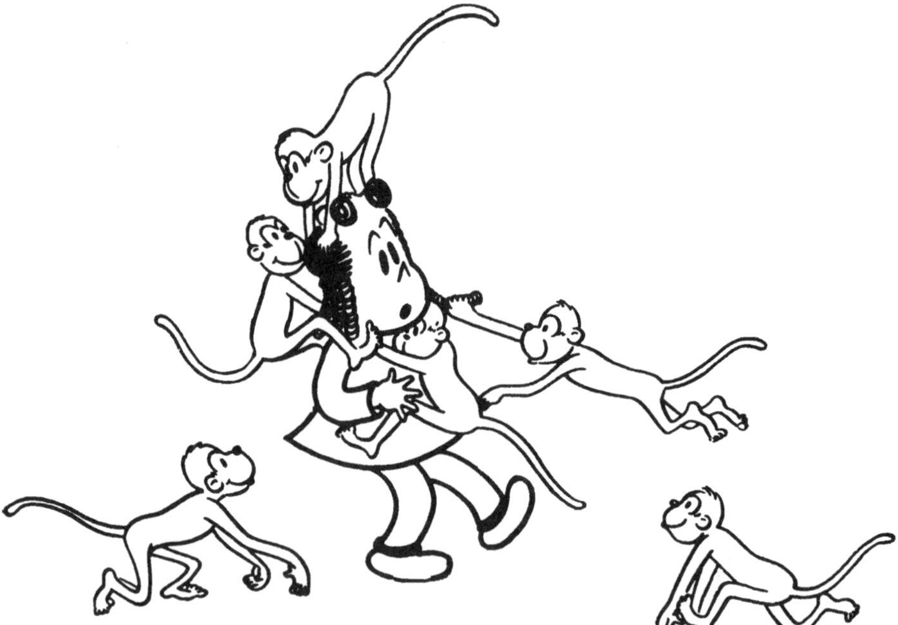

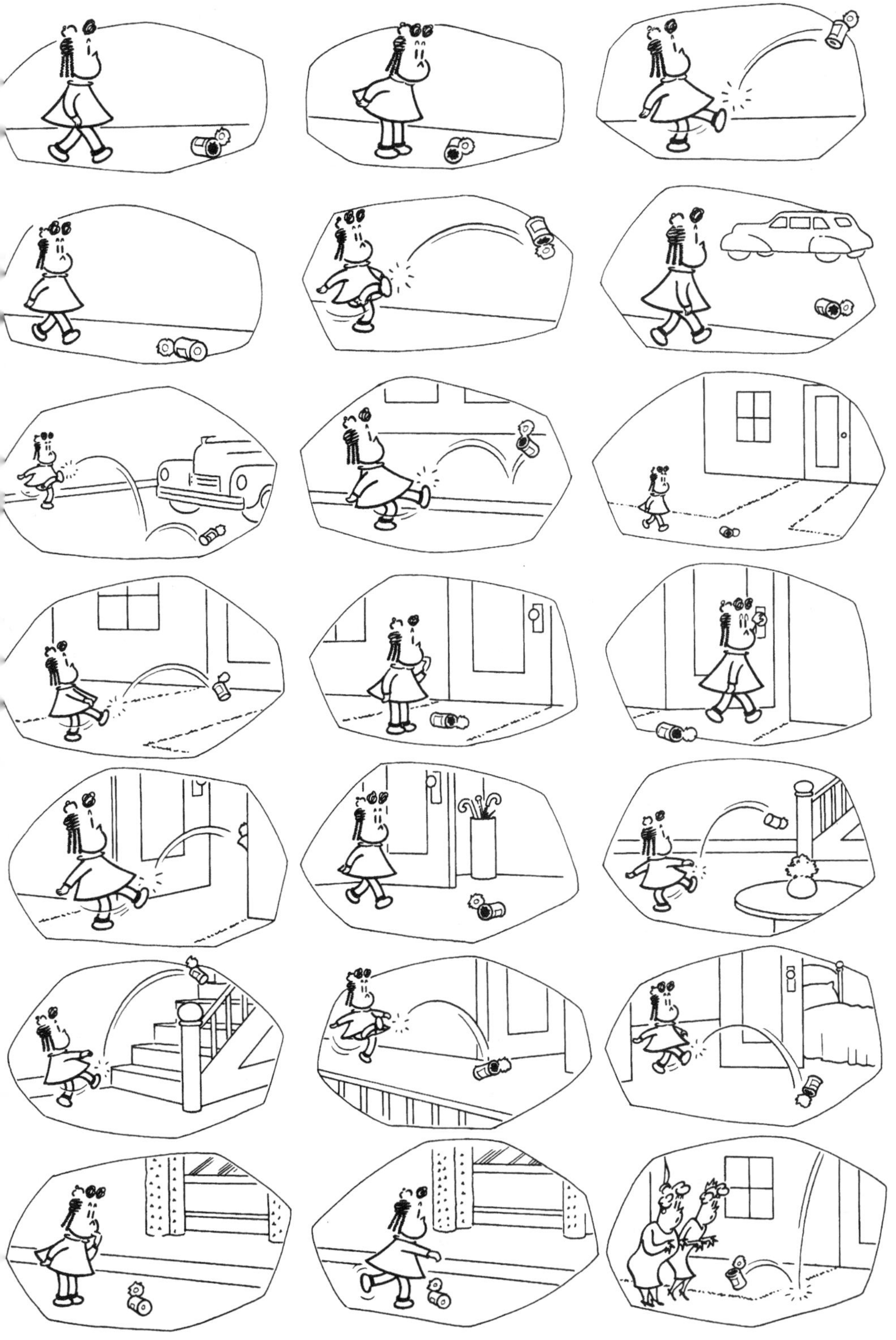

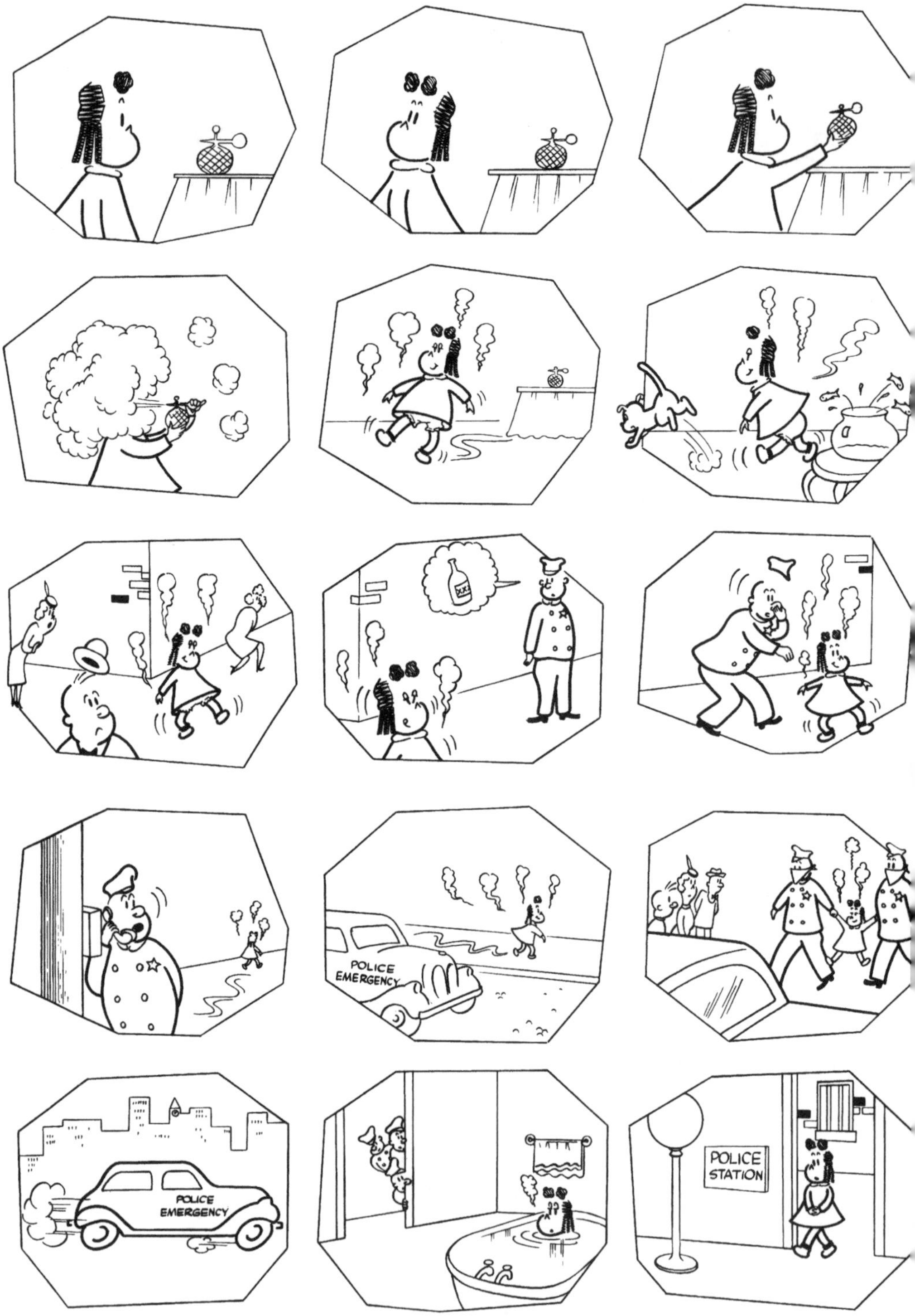

POLICE
EMERGENCY
POLICE
EMERGENCY
POLICE
STATION

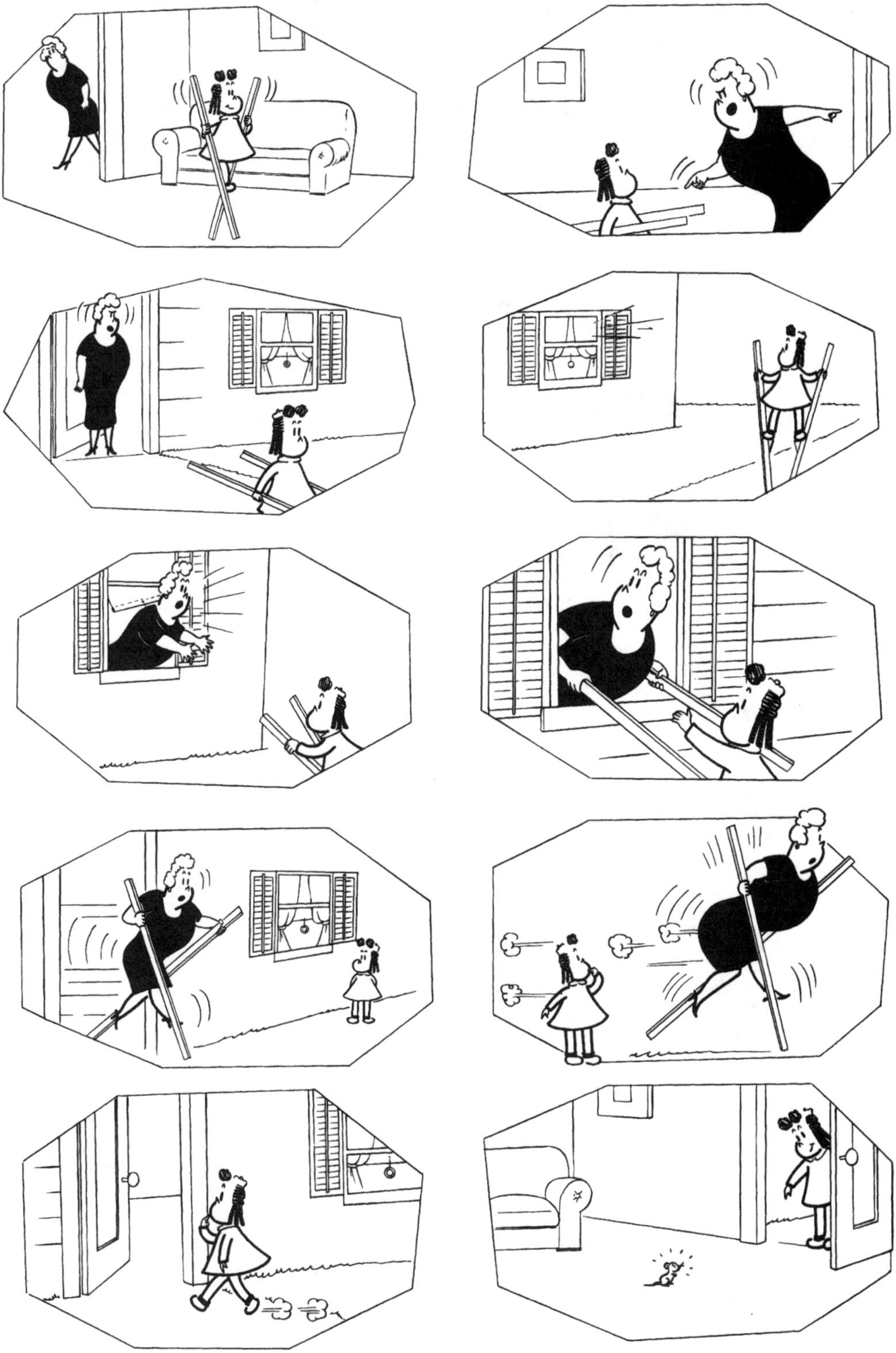

Little Lulu®